Contents

1   Introduction to Economics

Definition

1.1 The word 'Economics' is very much a part of present day vocabularies and is usually associated with some form of thrift or money saving behaviour. A more perceptive analysis would see economical behaviour as being an attempt to get the maximum satisfaction out of limited resources e.g. money, when a person has a choice. The word 'Economics' comes from the Greek 'oikon nomos' which translates literally as 'house rules' and in the present context means the principles on which a household orders its affairs. There are many definitions of economics all of which convey the same general meaning using different terms. The definition which I was taught as a student is "Economics is the study of the *influence of scarcity on human conduct* under circumstances in which man has *freedom of choice in allocating scarce resources between competing ends*". Lional Robbins defined it in the following words. "Economics is a science which studies *human behaviour* as a relationship between aims and *scarce resources* which have *alternative uses.*"

In both of the above definitions the key words have been written in italics and you can see the same idea being conveyed in both definitions. There are, of course, many other definitions but they are all basically the same.

Economics is a Social Science

1.2. The social sciences study different aspects of human behaviour, since economics studies an aspect of human conduct it is one of the social sciences. The early philosophers did not distinguish between the various social sciences, they considered them all to be part of Philosophy.

Need to Choose

1.3 We are all only too well aware of the fact that we cannot have everything that we desire i.e. that we must choose the manner in which we allocate our limited resources (income) among the almost infinite number of goods which we desire. Similarly producers must decide what goods they will manufacture from the limited resources which they have at their disposal. Thus economics implies the need to choose.

Scarcity

1.4. All of those goods and services with which economics is concerned are scarce, relative to the demand for them. The word scarcity as used in this context means that the supply is limited relative to demand. The test of whether or not a good is scarce is whether or not people are prepared to pay a price in order to obtain it. Goods for which people are prepared to pay a price are known as ECONOMIC GOODS. The characteristics of economic goods are set out and discussed in section 10.7.

1.5. Is economics a science?
A science is a classified body of knowledge. The subject matter of many

of the sciences is developed through relating cause and effect. In economics such a body of knowledge is developed through:

(a)   Observing events (effects) and analysing the forces which cause them (causes). This form of procedure is known as the *deductive method* of analysis.

(b)   From observing the constant outcome or reaction (effect) in response to the repetition of the same set of circumstances (cause) it may be possible to make generalised statements of tendency, e.g., that people buy more of a good when its price is reduced. This form of procedure is known as the *inductive method* of analysis.

1.6. In some of the sciences e.g. chemistry and physics, it is much easier to develop scientific knowledge because controlled experiments may be carried out in the laboratory and cause and effect may be established. It is

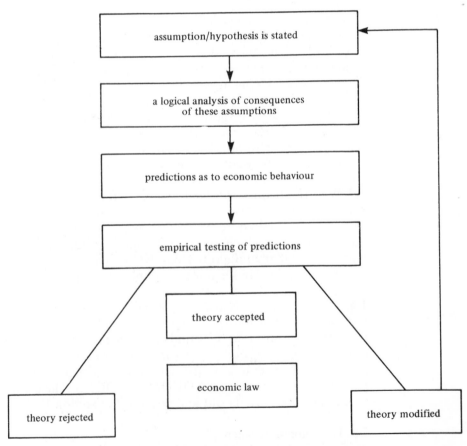

Fig. 1.6. Framework of an economic model.

not possible to conduct such controlled experiments in economics e.g. it is not possible to reduce by 10% the income of everyone in the economy so that the economist may observe and record the change in economic behaviour to which it would give rise. Economic knowledge is usually developed through the use of economic models.

Economic Laws

1.7. Economic models abstract from the real world the principal factors which influence and determine certain economic consequences. *Economic laws* are derived through an analysis of the interrelationships that exist within the model. *Economic laws are generalised statements as to human behaviour of an economic nature.* Because these economic laws are statements of a general tendency they will not apply in every case e.g., not everyone will buy more of a good when its price is reduced. However, through the statistical "law" of large numbers it is possible to predict what people in general will do, e.g., more of a good will be bought when its price is reduced.

Positive and Normative Statements

1.8. In scientific analysis it is usual to distinguish between positive statements and normative statements. Positive statements are statements of fact, they state what is, was, or will be; thus positive statements can be confirmed or denied by an analysis of facts. Normative statements, on the other hand, relate to how things ought to be ordered. Thus normative statements are value judgements and different people depending on their attitudes and beliefs, may disagree on normative statements.

These concepts can be related to economics. A positive economic statement could be on the following lines 'a 1% increase in food prices will increase the Consumer Price Index by 0.2%'. A normative statement would be 'an increase in the rate of inflation is preferable to an increase in the level of unemployment'.

Economics is a neutral science

1.9. Economics just like any other science is neutral. It analyses cause and effect on matters of an economic nature. It draws attention to the alternatives which are available, the cost of different courses of action and equilibrium situations under stated assumptions and given objectives. The fact that the alternatives chosen and the objectives being pursued will reflect the value judgements of the individual, the firm, the government or state does not detract from the inherent neutrality of economic science.

The margin

1.10. In economics we are all the time attempting to relate cause and effect i.e. the economic consequences of certain actions. Therefore, we are all the time focussing our attention on that area where change first takes place, e.g., if 100 people buy a good when its price is £130 and 98 people buy the same good when its price is increased to £131, we tend to say that 2 people less buy the good when its price was increased by £1 rather than say that 98 people continue to buy the good even when its price is increased by £1. The area where change first takes place is known as the *margin*. Thus we refer to the consumer who purchases an increased quantity when price is reduced or who buys a reduced quantity when price is increased as being the marginal consumer, i.e. the consumer who responds to a small change in price. Similarly, the additional goods which are bought when price is reduced or the goods which are not bought when price is increased are referred to as marginal goods. See also Section 10.2 to 10.6.

Micro-economics

1.11. The prefix micro as used in microeconomics comes from the Greek word 'mikros' meaning small. Thus microeconomics is the study of the economic behaviour or individual units e.g. individual households or individual firms. It is this micro aspect of economics which forms the subject matter of Chapters 2 to 22 of this book.

Macro-economics

1.12. Macroeconomics is the study of economic activities at the aggregate level, e.g., total employment, National Income, Balance of Payments etc.

QUESTIONS

Q1. Define Economics. Is it a science?

Q2. Distinguish between
(i) Micro and Macro Economics
(ii) Positive and Normative Economic Statements
(iii) Inductive and Deductive methods of analysis.

Q3. What is meant by "The Margin" as the term is used in Economics.

Q4. Set out the framework of an economic model.

Q5. Classify each of the following statements
(a) Lower rates of interest will lead to a higher level of investment
Normative/Postive

(b) The economic state of the nation would be improved if we bought more Irish made goods
Normative/Positive

(c) High rates of taxation are a disincentive to economic effort
Normative/Positive

2 Selling Price

2.1. Determination of selling price

In defining economics in Section 1.1. attention was drawn to the fact that the science of economics studies the effect of scarcity on human behaviour. You will recall that economic goods are scarce relative to the demand for them and therefore it is necessary to pay a sum of money (a price) in order to gain possession of them.

All of this implies that there is:

(a) a supply of the good or service
(b) a demand for the good or service
(c) a market through the working of which there is established a selling price for the good.

Definition of Market

2.2. A market is an economic relationship between all those who by their actions influence the supply of, or demand for, the good. Thus it includes not only buyers and sellers but also all those who could become either buyers or sellers if the selling price changes, together with the buyers and sellers of complementary and substitute goods who by their actions exert an influence on the market price of the good under discussion. Markets, in the economic sense, are not usually located in a single building or place, e.g., the second-hand car market is conducted to a large extent through advertisements in newspapers. Markets vary considerably in their size and in the extent of the area from which they draw their customers, varying from the local grocer whose catchment area is the immediate locality, to the market for Ford motor cars which embraces every country in the world.

Selling Price fluctuates to bring Supply and Demand into Balance

2.3. If the quantity of goods being offered for sale (i.e. the supply) is greater than the quantity which people wish to purchase (i.e. the demand) then the selling price of the good will be reduced. Conversely, if demand exceeds supply the selling price will be increased. Thus it can be seen that selling price fluctuates in order to strike a balance between the supply of, and demand for the good. The precise manner in which the selling price of the good will be determined is influenced by several factors including the characteristics of the good and the quantity on offer, e.g., an individual price may be negotiated in each case or the seller may offer the goods for sale at a stated selling price.

2.4. Individually negotiated prices

For this type of pricing to be possible there must be few buyers and/or sellers. The two most common examples of this system of pricing are:

(a)   Auctions
(b)   Haggling.

(a) Auctions

In an auction type sale there is one seller and a number of prospective buyers. The prospective buyers make offers or bids for the item, which is then sold to the person who offers the highest price. If the owner of the item refuses to sell to the highest bidder, the cost to him of retaining possession of the item is the price which he refused — he may be considered as paying or sacrificing that price in order to retain possession of the good. If a person refused an offer of £25 000 for a house, it is costing him £25 000 to retain possession of the house.

If all of the people seeking to purchase had the same amount of wealth, it could be considered that the item was sold to the person who felt the greatest need to possess it, since that is the person who is willing to pay the highest sum of money in order to acquire it. However, when the prospective buyers have not got equal wealth, this is not necessarily true because the payments of £15 000 by a person who is not very wealthy may constitute a much greater sacrifice than a payment of £25 000 by a very wealthy person.

(b) Haggling

This is the means by which prices are determined at animal fairs or in the sale of items such as second-hand motor cars. The prospective buyer has a range of prices, the upper limit being the highest amount which he is prepared to pay in order to gain possession of the good. Corresponding to this, the seller has a range of prices, and the minimum amount on the seller's range of prices is the lowest price which he is prepared to accept for the good. If the highest offer which he can get is below his minimum price, then he will not sell.

A person may be selling a house and the minimum price which he is prepared to accept is £25 000 but of course he will seek and accept the highest price above this which is obtainable. The prospective purchaser may have an upper price limit of £27 000 but of course he will endeavour to obtain the house for the lowest possible price below this figure. The situation may be perceived as set out in Fig. 2.4. Prices from £25 000 to £27 000 are common to both parties and this constitutes the bargaining range. The actual price which would be paid in this case would depend on the bargaining skill of the parties concerned.

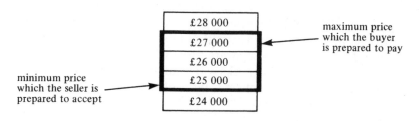

Fig. 2.4. The bargaining range.

2.5. Goods with fixed selling prices

The methods of determining price described in Section 2.4. may be adequate and suitable when sales are not frequent or when items being sold are to some extent different and individual. However, when goods are being sold in large quantities on a regular basis, e.g., the items which are sold in your local supermarket, the methods of setting prices described in section 2.4 would not be suitable. Can you imagine the situation at the supermarket check-out if each customer was haggling over the price of each item?.

Thus the vast majority of goods in which we are interested are offered for sale at a fixed selling price. The seller selects from a range of prices that selling price which he thinks will generate a level of sales which will give him (the seller) the greatest profit. The seller would like to charge each person the highest price which they are prepared to pay but this is not possible for the reasons described in the supermarket example in the previous paragraph. On the other hand, the lowest price at which the seller can afford to sell if he intends to remain in business is set by his costs of production plus some minimum profit which he must earn. If the price set by the seller is too high, the public will not buy the goods so that unsold stocks of the commodity will accumulate. It will be necessary to reduce the selling price of the item in order to clear the unsold stock and to create a demand which will justify continuing production. On the other hand, if the selling price is too low, in the sense that even though it covers the cost of production and provides some profit, it stimulates a level of demand which the producer cannot supply, then the seller will increase the selling price.

The Determination of Selling Price

2.6. There are three common elements in each of the three methods of determining selling price which have been described above, viz.,

(a)   a seller or supplier of the goods
(b)   a purchaser
(c)   a selling price which must be acceptable to both the seller and the purchaser. The selling price will bring into equilibrium the quantity supplied and the quantity demanded.

In the example of the auction there was only one item being offered for sale so that the price was continually increased until only one prospective purchaser remained. When goods are sold at fixed selling prices some people who purchase the goods would have been prepared to pay an even higher price rather than go without the good. However, because the seller couldn't negotiate a separate price with each purchaser he sets a fixed selling price which he thinks will result in a volume of sales which will give him (the seller) the highest total profits under the circumstances.

Consumer's Surplus

2.7. The fact that some people received the goods at a price lower than that which they would have been prepared to pay rather than do without the good gives rise to a concept known as *Consumer's Surplus. Consumer's Surplus is defined as the difference between the highest price which the purchaser would be prepared to pay rather than do without the good and what he actually paid.* This is discussed in greater detail in Chapter 10.

QUESTIONS

Q1. Write a short explanatory note on the concept of "markets".

Q2. Where prices are negotiated on an individual basis for each transaction the selling price will be
(a) the highest price which the buyer is prepared to pay
Yes/No

(b) the lowest price which the seller is prepared to accept
Yes/No

(c) not greater than the maximum price that the buyer is prepared to pay.
Yes/No

(d) not less than the minimum price which the seller is prepared to accept.
Yes/No

Q3. What are the common characteristics in each selling transaction?

Q4. What factors would a supplier take into account in deciding on the selling price of a good?

Q5. What is meant by Consumer's Surplus.

3 Demand

3.1. Demand is related to price

Demand must be distinguished from need or desire. There are people who have a desire and/or need for goods but they cannot acquire these goods because they have not got the money with which to buy them. This situation gives rise to a term *Effective Demand which is defined as desire supported by the necessary purchasing power*. Similarly there are people who, though they desire a commodity, prefer, i.e. have a stronger desire for, other commodities at existing selling prices.

Both the people who, though they need the commodity, cannot afford it and the people who, though they desire it, prefer to purchase some other commodity, might decide to purchase the commodity if its price was reduced. Also existing purchasers might buy larger quantities if the selling price were reduced. The larger quantities of new season's potatoes which are purchased as their price is reduced and the fact that shops reduce their selling prices and sell increased quantities at "sale time" are examples of increased demand at lower prices.

Thus the quantity demanded of a commodity can be meaningfully discussed only in the context of a given selling price. It isn't a case of 500 or 1000 being the quantity demanded but rather that 500 will be demanded when the price is £5 each and 1000 will be demanded when the price is £2 each.

3.2. An individual's demand for a commodity

Rather than discussing a number of different individuals purchasing a commodity, let us commence by considering one individual. To make our discussion more realistic we will take for our commodity an item which is purchased by a household on a regular basis, e.g., washing-up liquid. When the quantity which would be bought at each price is shown in the form of a table, this table is known as a *Demand Schedule*. Even if it is not explicitly stated, a demand schedule refers to a period of time.

Price per Container	Quantity Demanded
31p	1.
28p	2.
25p	3.
22p	4.

Table 3.2. Monthly Demand Schedule of Mrs. Jones for "Spotless" Washing-up Liquid

It is important to note that the only reason why Mrs. Jones has bought more is because of its change in price.

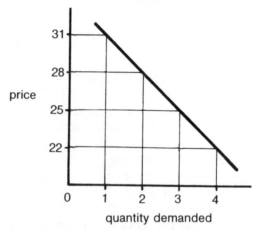

Fig. 3.2. An individual's demand curve drawn from data contained in Table 3.2

It should be noted that the point shown as 0 in Fig. 3.2 is known as the origin — it is the point from which the diagram starts, the co-ordinates are 0, 0, at this point — the price is zero and the quantity demanded is zero. Throughout the book reference will be made to the origin.

3.3. Demand curves

Demand curve is negatively sloped

If the demand schedule is expressed in the form of a diagram it is known as a demand curve. It is important to remember that demand curves are drawn with price on the vertical (or Y) axis and quantity on the horizontal (or X) axis.

The demand curve in fig. 3.2 is based on the information contained in the Demand Schedule — table 3.2. You will notice that the demand curve slopes downwards from left to right. This is the usual slope of a demand curve and signifies that the higher the price the lower the quantity that will be demanded and the lower the price the greater the quantity that will be demanded. Thus an increase in price (+) brings a decrease (-) in the quantity demanded while a decrease in price (-) brings an increase (+) in the quantity demanded. Since a change in price brings a change in the opposite direction in the quantity demand — a demand curve is said to be negatively sloped — it slopes downwards from left to right which signifies that high prices correspond to low levels of demand and low prices correspond to high levels of demand.

3.4. Market demand for a commodity

In Section 3.2. the demand of an individual — Mrs. Jones — for "Spotless" Washing-up Liquid was analysed. If we combine the demand at various prices of all individuals for this product we derive the market demand. Market demand is the aggregation of the individual demands.

Price per Container	Quantities Demanded by Individuals				Market Demand
	A	B	C	Others	
32	2200	1060	1600	4000	8860
31	2400	1270	1830	5320	10820
30	2750	1430	2400	6590	13170
29	2960	1600	2870	7860	15290
28	3120	1690	3140	9020	16970
27	3210	1770	3500	10980	19460
26	3300	1857	3820	13100	22077
25	3360	1940	4100	15400	24800
24	3395	2020	4410	17010	26835
23	3417	2080	4670	18600	28767
22	3423	2120	4790	20000	30333

Table 3.4 Market Demand Schedule for "Spotless" Washing-up liquid.

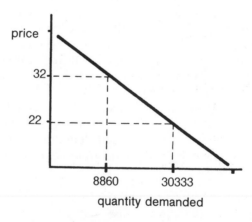

Fig. 3.4 Market demand curve drawn from Data contained in Table 3.4.

3.5. While demand curves are ofen drawn as straight lines this is usually done simply for convenience and obviously they may be curved as shown in fig 3.5. The exact shape of the curve depends on the relationship between price and quantity demanded — this relationship is discussed in greater detail in Chapter 9 where price elasticity of demand is explained.

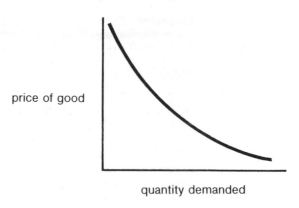

price of good

quantity demanded

Fig. 3.5. Downward Sloping demand curve.

3.6. Good with perverse demand characteristics

*Regressive/
Perverse
Demand
Curves
slope
depends*

Though demand curves may be of various shapes depending on the relationship between the price of the good and the quantity demanded, demand curves are *usually* negatively sloped as already illustrated because for most goods that you can think of a greater quantity of the good will be sold if its price is reduced. This idea may be expressed another way by saying that if a firm wants to sell more of a good it can usually do so by lowering its price. (Of course it may not suit the firm to lower its price even though it will sell more but that is an issue which we will come to later). However, there are certain goods, a greater quantity of which will *not* be purchased when their price is reduced. In fact there may be a reduction in demand when their price is reduced and an increase in demand when their price is increased. The demand for such goods is said to be perverse and their demand curve is said to be regressive i.e. *it slopes upwards from left to right, signifying that more will be bought at higher prices.*

price

quantity demanded

Fig. 3.6. Regressive/Perverse demand curve.

While it is interesting to discuss these goods it should be clearly understood that they are exceptional cases, few in number, and the phenomenon discussed will apply only over a certain price range and/or due to exceptional circumstances.

Goods with a regressive demand curve are usually known as Giffen Goods in recognition of the fact that Sir Robert Giffen, the Victorian economist, was first to draw attention to the phenomenon.

There are three well known categories of goods, the demand for which may be perverse.

(a)   *Necessities* which constitute a large part of the expenditure of poor people. These goods are necessities which are relatively cheap in price so that most people can afford to purchase the quantity of them which they require. Examples of such goods are white bread and potatoes. (In the rest of this discussion bread will be quoted as being representative of all such goods). In these circumstances a reduction in the price of bread is not likely to result in people buying more of it since even before its price was reduced people could afford to buy the quantity of it which they required. On the other hand if the price of bread is increased, since it is a necessity and originally its price was fairly low, then people would probably continue to purchase the quantity they require even after the price increase. They would get the extra money by cutting down on something else which is less of a necessity. This is one of the reasons why government keeps a close watch for price increases in goods such as bread lest bakeries take advantage of this situation. Conversely if the price of bread is reduced, it is not likely that there will be an increase in the demand for it. If people were able to buy that quantity of bread which they required at the higher price they will not need to buy extra quantities now that is price is reduced. They will use the money which they save through buying the same quantity of bread at a reduced price to buy other goods. In fact they may spend some of their extra purchasing power to buy some food other than bread and thus may eat less bread after its price has been reduced. The situation may be imagined to be on the following lines. A poor family of very limited means may be found to consume bread and/or potatoes at most meals in order to try to maintain their health and to keep hunger pains from their stomach. If the price of either or both of these goods falls then the family is a little better off provided their income is not reduced by a similar amount. They will then be in a position to substitute a more expensive foodstuff into their diet for at least one of the meals. However, if the price of potatoes or bread is increased, the poor family who spend a large proportion of their income on these goods, have their real income reduced. They are not able to afford any alternative more expensive foodstuff and will revert to a diet consisting almost exclusively of potatoes and bread. You will have noticed that the more well-to-do people tend to eat less white bread and potatoes than do the poorer sections of the community. It is for this reason that the demand for bread is not likely to fall significantly when its price is increased, so that governments keep a close watch on price increases on goods of this nature. Conversely you won't see bread being offered at "sale prices" because the price reduction is unlikely to result in a significant increase in the quantity sold and may conceivably result in a reduction of demand. Some American textbooks quote readymade suits and remould tyres as examples of Giffen Goods.

(b) *Status Symbols/Snob Items/Ostentatious Goods/Conspicuous Consumption.* All of these terms refer to the same concept which may be considered as follows. There are some commodities, e.g. expensive jewellery, furs, Rolls Royce Cars, where exclusiveness and expensiveness is an integral part of their attractiveness to purchasers. If the selling prices of items of this nature were reduced by a small amount, it is unlikely that many additional people would be able to afford them. On the other hand they would become less expensive, perhaps less exclusive, and therefore less desirable to those wealthy people who would be contemplating a purchase of this nature.

For these reasons if their selling price was reduced by a small amount, it is unlikely that a greater quantity of them would be sold and it is possible that the quantity demanded might fall. Many people are not in a position to distinguish differences in quality and often quality is considered to be synonymous with price. Let us imagine a man bringing his fiancee to the jewellers in order to purchase an engagement ring and he is thinking of spending approximately £500 on the ring. If the selection is narrowed down to two rings one of which costs £495 and the other £480, it is very possible that the £495 ring would be chosen. The difference in price between the two rings is not significant and price is associated with quality.

(c) *Goods the Purchase of which is Influenced by Expectations as to Future Prices.* If prospective purchasers think that prices are likely to be even higher in the future, the current level of demand may not diminish even if prices increase slightly. If a person is contemplating the purchase of a house or car the possibility that prices are likely to be even higher in the future will probably stimulate demand at current prices. Many salesmen are very well aware of this and constantly remind purchasers that future price rises are in the offing; you have probably heard the phrase "this good will never be cheaper".

Stocks and shares are another example of this type of phenomenon. If the price of stocks and shares is rising, investors are likely to think that prices will be even higher in the future and consequently they will buy now rather than at a higher price later. The opposite applies when prices of these are falling — people postpone purchasing in the expectation that prices will be even lower in the future.

QUESTIONS

Q1. What is meant by Effective Demand?

Q2. What is a demand schedule?

Q3. What is a demand curve?

Q4. In drawing a demand curve what does the vertical (or y) axis measure? What does the horizontal (or x) axis measure?

Q5. (a) What way does a demand curve normally slope?
(b) Which way does a perverse demand curve slope?

Q6. Write an explanatory note on Giffen Goods.

4 Supply

Definition

4.1. Supply refers to the quantity of a commodity which will be made available at a particular price or range of prices during a period of time.

Supply of a good has two meanings

4.2. The supply of a good can be analysed in a manner similar to that which was adopted in analysing demand. The term 'the supply of a commodity' is used to convey two different meanings. The term is used in reference to:—

(a) the quantity of the good which is currently being made available at the existing market price;

(b) the various quantities of the good which would be forthcoming at different price levels. It is on this latter meaning of the term that we will concentrate.

Supply must be related to price

4.3. As was mentioned in relation to demand, it is meaningless to discuss supply without mentioning price. If an item costs £1 to produce no supply will be forthcoming if the highest price at which people would be prepared to buy is 5p, but when the selling price exceeds the cost of production and provides a satisfactory level of profit, a supply of the good will come on the market. *The higher the selling price the greater the quantity of the good which will be supplied, other things being equal (or remaining unchanged).*

An increase in selling price results in an increase in the quantity supplied

4.4. Let us assume that the selling price of cigarettes increases while costs of production do not, i.e. other things remaining unchanged. The reaction of cigarette manufacturers to this development will be a desire to increase the quantity which they supply, since by so doing they will make more profit. They will utilise their existing machinery more intensively, existing staff will be employed on overtime work and possibly new staff will be recruited — all of which will culminate in a larger quantity being offered for sale in response to the price increase. Thus as a result of the increase in selling price the supply on offer is increased.

A time period is implied

4.5. It is clear that some sort of time period is implied when the supply of a good is being considered e.g. there is no economic significance in the observation that an increase in the price of Christmas trees will result in an increased quantity being made available — after Christmas. Similarly the supply of cigarettes at a particular price does not mean the quantities of cigarettes which the cigarette manufacturers have offered for sale at this price since they originally commenced production. If we say that the supply of cigarettes will be increased when their selling price increases, we are referring to that change in the quantity supplied which will occur in the immediate future or at least in the short run, unless there is a specific reference to a longer time horizon.

4.6. Supply at the Individual and Market Level

Just as we related individual and market demand curves in Sect 3.4 supply also may be expressed at the level of an individual economic agent (i.e. firm or person) or at the market level. Supply at the market level is often referred to as the total supply of the good.

Supply Schedule

Supply Schedules of Individual Firms

Price per container	Firm A	Firm B	Firm C	Other Firms	Market Supply
22	3000	2000	1200	1000	7200
23	4500	2500	1400	1080	9480
24	6000	3200	1580	1170	11950
25	7100	3800	1780	1260	13940
26	8300	4600	1980	1370	16250
27	10000	5500	2480	1480	19460
28	11300	6800	3200	1680	22980
29	12800	8200	4300	1810	27110
30	13900	9800	5050	2260	31010
31	15870	11000	6000	2590	35460
32	18000	12000	7000	3000	40000

Fig. 4.6.1. Supply Curve Firm A

Fig. 4.6.2. Supply Curve Firm B

Fig. 4.6.3. Supply Curve   Fig. 4.6.4. Market Supply
          Firm C

Supply and demand curves slope in opposite directions

4.7. It will be noted that a supply curve slopes upwards from left to right because the higher the price the greater the quantity which will be supplied, ceteris paribus, i.e., other factors remaining unchanged. When this supply curve is compared with the demand curve shown in Fig. 3.3, it will be seen that supply and demand curves normally slope in opposite directions.

While fig. 4.6.4. shows a typical supply curve which is upward sloping from left to right, signifying that if price increases, a larger supply will be forthcoming, there are also other forms of supply curves.

Perfectly inflexible Supply curve Supply Rigidity

4.8. A situation where there is a supply available and the quantity supplied will not fall even if there is a price reduction, is ilustrated in fig. 4.8. In this case a price reduction will not result in a reduction in the available supply — the quantity available is fixed irrespective of price. This type of supply situation is not usual but an example would possibly be the supply of fish available on a particular day — there is a fixed quantity which has been caught and they are sold for the best price which can be obtained. However, the price obtained would affect future supplies. If prices were very low there would possibly be less fishermen willing to go out fishing and a consequent reduction in the supplies available for sale in the future, while if prices were high, future supplies would probably increase. Thus the *long run* supply curve in this situation would be similar to the typical curve depicted in fig. 4.6.4.

Figure 4.8. Perfectly inelastic Supply Curve. Rigidity in quantity supplied.

Minimum acceptable Prices

4.9. Fig. 4.9 illustrates a supply situation where no supply will be made available below a certain price, but once this minimum price is being received, then a supply will be forthcoming and there will be no increase in price within a certain range of output.

However, if an even greater supply is required, then increased prices would be necessary. This sort of situation could apply to the supply of labour where there is a trade union which has negotiated a minimum wage. No labour will be forthcoming below the minimum wage, this minimum wage holds over a large range of supply and if additional quantities of labour are required, then it will be necessary for increased prices to be offered.

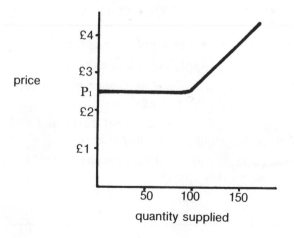

Fig. 4.9. A minimum price P_1, below which no supply will be forthcoming.

4.10. Fig 4.10 illustrates a situation where the initial part of the supply curve is upward-flowing as per the typical supply curve. In this case there is a maximum supply which can be made available and it is not possible to increase this quantity even if prices increase. This type of supply curve would apply where there is a capacity constraint, where the factory is incapable of providing an increased quantity despite the higher prices which are available.

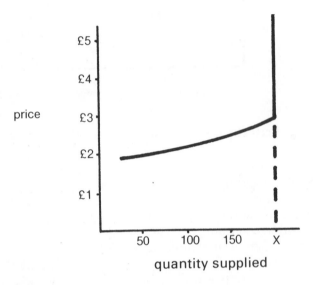

Fig. 4.10. Capacity constraint at quantity X — no further supply will be forthcoming even if price is increased.

QUESTIONS

Q1. What is meant by 'the supply of a commodity'?

Q2. Draw a typical supply curve and explain its shape.

Q3. Draw the supply curve of labour where the trade union has negotiated a minimum wage.

Q4. Draw a perfectly inelastic supply curve and state a circumstance where such a supply curve might apply.

Q5. Draw a supply curve with a capacity constraint. In what circumstance might this apply?

5 Market Equilibrium — Supply and Demand Combined

Excess demand results in price increase

In table 5.1 the market demand schedule of table 3.4. and the market supply schedule of table 4.6. are combined. At prices below 27p the quantity demanded is greater than the quantity being supplied — there is excess demand. When excess demand exists, suppliers are inclined to increase prices and those who are prepared to pay higher prices offer increased prices in order to ensure that they obtain the quantity of the good which they seek. Thus excess demand results in an upward pressure on the selling price — as shown in Fig. 5.1.

Excess supply leads to reduction in selling prices

5.2. At prices greater than 27p there is excess supply. At each of these prices the quantity supplied is greater than the quantity demanded e.g., at a price of 29p — 27110 units would be supplied but only 15290 units would be demanded or bought. There would be an excess supply of 11820 units.

Producers would then begin to accept lower prices for the goods and purchasers would offer lower prices as they see stocks building up due to suppliers not being able to sell all of their output. This situation would obtain at all prices in excess of 27p. Thus excess supply puts a downward pressure on selling price, as shown in Fig. 5.1. Similarly at prices lower than 27p the quantity demanded is greater than the quantity supplied — there is excess demand which puts upward pressure on prices.

Quantity Demanded	Price	Quantity Supplied
30335	22	7200
28767	23	9480
26835	24	11950
24800	25	13940
22077	26	16250
19460	27	19460
16970	28	22980
15290	29	27110
13170	30	31010
10820	31	35460
8800	32	40000

Table 5.1. Market Supply and Demand at Various Prices.

5.3. At a price of 27p the quantity demanded is equal to the quantity supplied. All of the output which is being produced is being sold — the market is clearing at this price which is known as the market equilibrium price.

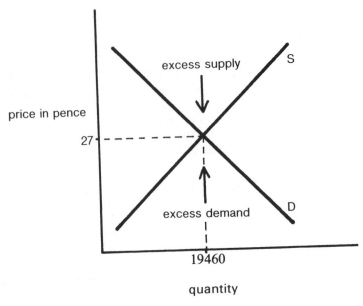

Fig. 5.1. Market equilibrium price for "Spotless" Washing-Up Liquid as per Table 5.1.

There is no tendency for the price of 27p to change under existing conditions of supply and demand. If, however, there should develop a change in any of these conditions then the equilibrium price would change. Examples of such changes are (a) change in costs of production (b) new firms entering, or existing firms leaving the industry (c) consumers in general becoming more wealthy (d) a change in the price of complementary or substitute goods (e) the good in question becoming more (or less) fashionable, — these factors are discussed in detail in chapters 6 and 7.

Two meanings of Equilibrium

5.4. The term "Equilibrium" in economics has two meanings which are closely associated.

(a) It refers to a situation where there is no pressure or tendency towards change. In table 5.1, 27p is the equilibrium price — there is no pressure for change once this price is arrived at. At this price producers are selling all of their output so there is no need for them to reduce selling price in order to sell all of their output. Similarly all of the people who are prepared to buy at that price can be accommodated by the supply which is forthcoming so that no consumer has to offer a higher price in order to acquire the good.

(b) Equilibrium may be considered also in terms of the attainment of objectives. In this sense, equilibrium is the situation or position in search of which there is constant movement in response to the pressure of economic forces. In table 5.1 there was a movement towards the equilibrium price of 27p, if in the period under analysis the equilibrium price of 27p had not emerged, the equilibrium would still have been the price towards which there was movement in response to the market forces of supply and demand.

QUESTIONS

Q1. Write an explanatory note on the concept of Equilibrium as the term is used in economics.

Q2. Distinguish between excess demand and excess supply.

Q3. When the quantity being supplied is greater than the quantity being demanded:—
(a) Does excess demand or excess supply exist?
(b) Is the present selling price too high or too low?
(c) Is employment in the industry likely to increase or decrease?

Q4. Set out some circumstances which might cause the equilibrium price to change.

6 Factors other than its own price which influence the quantity of a good demanded

6.1. The demand for a good or service is influenced by other factors in addition to its own price

In Chapter 3 the demand for a good has been analysed in relation to changes in its own price. It has been shown that apart from the unusual and exceptional cases which were discussed in Section 3.6, a larger quantity of a good will be demanded when its price is reduced and conversely a smaller quantity will be demanded when its price is increased, i.e., a downward sloping demand-curve for the good.

Ceteris paribus assumption

This analysis of the demand for the good was conducted as if a change in its own price was the only factor which affected demand for the good. This procedure was justified because in conducting our analysis we assumed that nothing had changed other than the price of the good. In such case then, the change in quantity demanded which is observed (i.e. the effect) must be due to the change in the price of the good (i.e. the cause) since this is the only factor which has changed. In this manner cause and effect are linked. This establishment of cause and effect through assuming that nothing else has changed is used often in economics and is known as the ceteris paribus assumption, i.e. other things being equal or everything else remaining unchanged.

It should be clearly understood that demand and supply curves are drawn, and movements along a demand and supply curve are discussed, on the assumption that other factors remain unchanged.

The next stage in the analysis of demand will be to analyse the other factors which affect the demand for a good. *The same technique will be employed in each analysis, i.e., it will be assumed that everything else remains unchanged so that attention can be focussed on the effect of the change which is being analysed.*

6.2. Demand for a commodity is affected by changes in the price of other goods

Goods which satisfy the same need or provide the same service are known as substitute or competitive goods. If there is little difference in the goods, e.g. different brands of tea, jam or soap powder, they are close substitutes and highly competitive. The keener the competiton is between goods, i.e. the closer their substitutability, the greater the effect a change in the price of one of the goods will have on the demand for the other.

Substitute or competitive Goods

If the price of Good B (a brand of strawberry jam) is increased, while the price of Good A (a different brand of strawberry jam) is unchanged, then Good A has become relatively cheaper and there will be an increase in the quantity demanded of Good A, due to consumers transferring from the purchasing of Good B which has become relatively dearer.

Effect of change in price of substitute Good B on quantity demanded of Good A

Price of Good A	Quantity Demanded of Good A before increase in price of substitute goods	Quantity Demanded of Good A after increase in price of substitute goods
25p	740	900
26p	680	810
27p	590	700
28p	500	590
29p	400	460

Table 6.2. Demand Schedule.

In fig. 6.2 below, the information contained in the Demand Schedule of Table 6.2. is expressed in the form of a demand curve. The demand curve which emerges as a result of a good becoming relatively cheaper lies to the right of the original curve at all prices, because more of the good will be bought at each price.

Fig. 6.2. Demand curve shifts to the right as good becomes relatively cheaper due to increase in price of substitute good.

6.3. The converse applies if the price of substitute goods are reduced while the good under analysis (Good A) does not change in price, i.e., the good under analysis (Good A) has become relatively dearer. The outcome of this would be that less of good A would be demanded at each

Economics

price, its demand curve would shift to the left, i.e. in towards the origin which is the opposite movement to that shown in fig. 6.2 (above).

6.4. The greater the substitutability of the goods the more highly competitive they will be, and therefore the greater the effect on one of a price alteration in the other — the more competitive the goods the greater the shift in the demand curve.

A wide definition of competitive goods

6.5. A wide or narrow meaning may be given to the term substitute or competitive good. The different brands of jam, tea or soap powder spring readily to mind as examples of close substitutes and therefore highly competitive goods. Using the term a little more widely, bicycles, motor bikes, motor cars and public transport may be considered as constituting competitive forms of transport within cities. Taking the term in its widest sense, if you are saving none of your income, an extra £1 spent on entertainment is £1 less available for spending on clothes or holidays. In this sense virtually all goods may be seen as competing for your expenditure, and thus the term competitive goods is probably a more significant economic term than substitute goods.

Complementary Goods

6.6. There are groups of goods which in no sense could be considered as competing with each other. These are goods which are used together and cannot be used separately, so that in the economics sense, they may be considered to represent a single good, e.g., a motor car is bought in order to provide transport but it cannot provide this without petrol — it is the combination of motor cars and petrol used jointly which provides the utility.

Other examples are pipes and tobacco, golf clubs and golf balls, pen and ink, electric machinery and electricity.

Joint demand

6.7. Goods of this nature complement each other and consequently are known as complementary goods. Since these goods must be used jointly in order to provide utility, they are said to be in joint demand.

Effect of price alteration on demand for complementary goods

6.8. In the case of complementary goods, if the price of one of them is increased, the demand for both of them will fall, e.g. if the price of petrol is increased there will be reduction in the demand for large cars and possibly for all cars. In fact in considering the effect on the sale of a good, a reduction in the price of a complementary good has a similar effect to a reduction in the price of the good itself i.e. a reduction in the price of the good itself, would lead to an increase in the quantity demanded of the complementary good, ceteris paribus. However in terms of demand curves there is an important difference in that a change in the price of the good itself (i.e. its own price) results in a movement along an existing demand curve whereas a change in the price of a complementary good results in a shift in the demand curve —inwards towards the origin if the complementary good is increased in price signifying a reduction in the level of demand for the good at all prices. This development should be contrasted with section 6.2. where the effect of a change in the price of a substitute good was analysed.

6.9. Changes in real income affect the demand for a commodity

Income effect

The general level of real income is another factor which has an effect on the demand for a good. This change in demand which comes about as a result of a change in income is known as the Income Effect. For most goods, if real income is increased, the demand for them increases and conversely, if real income is reduced, the demand for most goods falls. This latter aspect is clearly in evidence by looking at the smaller quantity of goods which people are able to purchase when their real income is reduced through illness or unemployment.

Normal good has Positive income effect

(a) Since the demand for most goods is reduced when real income is reduced and increased when real income is increased, the demand for most goods moves in the same direction as changes in real income. The expression for this is that the income effect is positive, and since this applies to most goods, goods to which it applies are known as **Normal Goods. The definition of a normal good is a good with a positive income effect.** Thus for a normal good an *increase* in the income of the consumers or potential consumers of the goods results in an outward shift, from the origin, of the demand curve as shown in fig. 6.9.

Fig. 6.9. An increase in income shifts outward the demand curve of a Normal Good.

Inferior good has negative income effect

(b) Goods which react in the opposite way to normal goods in response to a change in real income are known as **Inferior Goods**, i.e., the demand for them increases when real income falls and the demand for them falls when real income is increased, Inferior goods have a negative income effect in contrast to normal goods which have a positive income effect.

The definition of an inferior good is a good with a negative income effect.

The expression inferior good does not mean that the goods are in some way deficient but it is merely a term used to describe goods with a negative income effect. See also section 10.21 to 10.23 re inferior goods.

Money income and real income

(c)   It should be noted that the discussion in sections (a) and (b) refers to real income. Money income is income expressed in money terms, e.g., £65 per week. However, of much more importance to the recipient of the income is the purchasing power or value of the money income which he receives. When money income is related to its purchasing power we discover our real income, i.e., the real worth of our income.

6.10. Real income may be increased through:

Factors which result in an alteration in real income

(a)   An increase in money income in excess of any increase in the cost of living, so that our purchasing power is increased.

(b)   A reduction in the cost of living by a greater amount than any reduction in money income.

(c)   A reduction in the level of taxation in excess of any reduction in our money income.

Obviously the opposite to each of the above would result in a reduction in real income.

A movement in taste in favour of the good shifts its demand curve to the right

6.11. The demand for a commodity is affected by changes in taste or fashion.

When commodities come into fashion or into season there is an increase in the quantity demanded at each price, i.e. the demand curve for the commodity shifts to the right out from the origin.

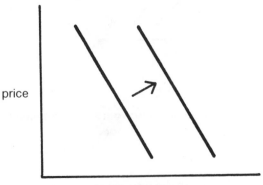

Fig. 6.11. Taste or fashion moves in favour of the good — increase in quantity demanded at each price.

*If the good
goes out
of fashion,
demand curve
moves to
the left*

6.12. Conversely if a good goes out of fashion or there is a movement in taste away from the good, then less of the good will be demanded at each price, i.e., the demand curve for the good moves to the left towards the origin.

Advertising

6.13. Advertising is one of the means by which producers attempt to influence taste in favour of their good. The more successful the advertising campaign the greater will be the shift to the right of the demand curve for the products.

*Market
research*

6.14. The market research which producers undertake before offering a good on the market is another example of the recognition by producers of the effect of taste or fashion on the level of demand. Through market research, producers gain information as to the taste of consumers, because it is much easier to sell to people what they want rather than to produce what you think the public wants or ought to want, and then convince them that they need it.

6.15. Expectation as to future prices or availability affects demand
If consumers in general consider that future prices are likely to be greater than they are at present, then there will be an increase in demand for the good at each price i.e. the demand curve will shift to the right. Conversely, if current prices are higher than expected future prices, then consumers will demand lower quantities at existing prices, i.e., the demand will shift left in towards the origin.

Similarly if the expectation is that supplies might be scarce in the future, the demand curve will shift outwards towards the right as consumers fearing a shortage will buy more.

Sales people are aware of this and in an effort to encourage people to buy immediately there is often vague reference as to price increases being due in the near future or that there is a doubt as to whether additional supplies will be available.

6.16. Summary of the factors which influence the demand for a good
(a)   If the various factors which have been discussed as influencing the demand for a good are gathered together the following functional relationship emerges:—

$$D_1 = f(P_1, P_2 \ldots n, Y t, E)$$

The demand for good one (D_1) is a function of (or depends upon):
P_1 ..... its own price
P_2 ..... n, the price of other goods, substitutes and complements
Y the level of income
t taste or fashion
E, Expectation as to future prices or availability of supplies.
(b)   When a demand curve is drawn, it is the graph of the relationship between the demand for the good (D_1) and changes in its own price

(P_1), on the assumption that the other factors which affect demand remain constant or unchanged i.e. ceteris paribus.

Under these circumstances, as the selling price of the good changes there is a movement along the demand curve.

(c)   If any of the factors other than the price of the good itself, change there is a shift in the demand curve. The shift is out to the right away from the origin, if more will be bought as a result of the change. Changes which would result in a shift on the demand curve to the right, out from the origin, are as follows:
● An increase in the price of substitute goods
● A reduction in the price of complementary goods
● For Normal Goods an increase in the income of purchasers (or possible purchasers) of the good.
● For Giffin Goods a reduction in the income of purchasers of the good.
● A change in taste or fashion in favour of the good
● Expectation of future price rises or scarcities

(d)   If the demand curve shifts to the right, from D_1 to D_2, e.g. as a result of any of the factors listed in section 6.16 (c) and if there is no change in the conditions of supply the market price will rise and a greater quantity will be sold as shown in Fig. 6.16. P_1/Q_1 were the original equilibrium price and quantity, the new equilibrium price/output are P_2/Q_2.

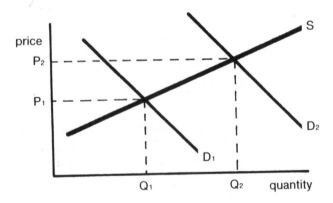

Fig. 6.16. Increase in equilibrium price/quantity when demand curve shifts to the right.

6.17. The other factors which affect the demand for a commodity are:—

(a)   The size of the population. It would be expected, other things, such as the degree of competition, being equal, that a firm supplying the

American market with clocks would sell more than a firm selling clocks on the Irish market. However, where a firm is supplying a particular market, e.g., the Irish market, changes in population usually occur only over reasonably long periods and therefore the size of the population is usually taken as given, i.e. being of a certain size not subject to change in the period under review. The technical term for this is that it is **exogenous** to the model.

These same remarks would apply to changes in the structure of the population, e.g. change in the proportion of the population over 65, or a change in the number of school-going children.

Distribution of income (b) The distribution of income. If the proportion of income going to certain groups alters, there could be an increase in the demand for the goods bought by such people and a reduction in goods bought by other groups, e.g. reduction in the level of income tax and old age pensions, so that young single employed people have more money to spend while the elderly have less. Consequently the demand for goods which young people buy would increase and the demand for goods which the elderly buy would be reduced. This change in the demand for goods would occur even if the general level of income was altered. However, it is usually assumed that the distribution of income is undisturbed and attention is forcussed on the general level of income as in sections 6.9. and 6.10.

QUESTIONS

Q1. What factors influence the demand for a good?

Q2. Distinguish between a movement along a demand curve and a shift in a demand curve.

Q3. Set out the factors which would result in a shift of the demand curve in to the left towards the origin.

Q4. Exogenous factors which affect the demand for a good are:—

Q5. Distinguish between complementary and competitive goods.

Q6. Distinguish between Normal and Inferior Goods.

7 Factors other than its own selling price which influence the quantity of the good supplied

7.1. The quantity of a good which is supplied is influenced by other factors in addition to its own price

Just as was mentioned in Section 6.1. in relation to the quantity of a good which is demanded, the quantity of a good which is supplied is influenced by other factors in addition to its own price.

When supply curves are drawn and movements along a supply curve are being analysed, it is assumed that the other factors which affect the quantity of a good which will be supplied remain unchanged. Section 6.1. discussed the identical position in relation to demand.

7.2. The quantity of a good which will be supplied is affected by the cost of producing the good

If there is an increase in costs of the factors of production which a manufacturer utilises in the production of his good, then it will be more costly for him to manufacture. He will not continue to supply the same quantity of the good at the old prices; there will be a reduction in the quantity supplied as per table 7.2.

£	Quantity Supplied before increase in costs	Quantity Supplied after increase in costs
1	142	100
2	197	148
3	264	205
4	351	267
5	460	330

Table 7.2. Reduction in quantity supplied due to an increase in costs.

The effect of the increase in costs may be shown by means of a supply curve which shifts to the left, in towards the origin, indicating that a smaller quantity will be supplied at each price due to an increase in costs.

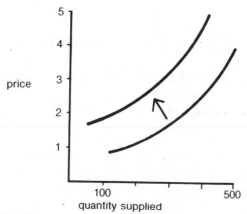

Increase in unit costs shifts supply curve to the left

price

5
4
3
2
1

100   500
quantity supplied

Fig. 7.2. Increase in unit costs shifts supply curve to the left.

Reductions in unit costs shifts supply curve to the right

7.3. The opposite would apply if costs of production were reduced, a greater quantity would be supplied at each price, i.e. the supply curve would shift to the right, out from the origin.

Taxation on raw materials

7.4. The cost of producing a commodity may also be affected by changes in taxation. If there is a tax levied on the raw materials which are used in the manufacture of a commodity, it represents an increase in the cost of production and the above analysis in respect of a cost increase would apply.

Subsidy on raw materials or labour

7.5. If a subsidy is granted on the raw materials, or on the labour employed by the firm, this has the effect of reducing the cost of production and the above analysis in respect of a cost reduction applies.

Improvements in technology reduce the cost of producing goods

7.6. Changes in the state of technology affect the supply of a good

As new machinery is invented, as labour becomes more specialised and efficient and as employers become more skilful in organising and combining the factors of production, it becomes possible to reduce the costs of production even though the price being paid to the factors of production remain unchanged. As has been discussed in section 7.2 if the costs of production are reduced a greater quantity will be supplied at each price — the supply curve moves outwards from the origin.

The reasoning in respect of changes in the state of technology or in production techniques is very similar to that adopted in Section 7.2. in respect of alterations to the costs of the factors of production (except that it would be unrealistic to discuss changes in production techniques which result in a commodity being produced at higher unit cost unless there had been an increase in the cost of factors of production.) To do this would be to imply that technology had taken a retrograde cost increasing step. However, since changes in the state of technology and changes in costs of factors of production are distinct (though close) concepts they are usually discussed and listed separately.

7.7. Changes in the selling price of other goods affect the quantity of a good which will be supplied

If there is an increase in the selling price of other goods which the manufacturer could produce through using his existing factors of production, he may switch from producing one commodity to producing another, e.g., if a manufacturer is producing wooden kitchen furniture and there is an increase in the price of dining room suites, ceteris paribus, he may switch from producing kitchen furniture to producing dining room suites. Similarly, if he has been producing both items he may now concentrate on producing the item which has increased in price and which for this reason has become more profitable for the manufacturers.

If the profitability of cattle increases, farmers will convert land used for tillage to pasture with a possible reduction in the supply of wheat.

7.8. Unplanned changes in quantity supplied

There may be changes in the quantity supplied which were never intended by the producer. The activity to which this has the most relevance is probably agriculture where due to inconsistencies in the weather, crops may vary from one season to another, or animals may be affected by diseases. In industry there may be shortages of raw materials, strikes or bottlenecks in the production process, which cause the quantity supplied to deviate from that quantity which it was intended to supply.

7.9. Summary of the factors which influence the quantity of a good which is supplied

If the various factors which influence the quantity of a good which will be supplied are drawn together the following functional relationship emerges.

$$S_1 = f(P_1, P_2 \ldots\ldots n, C, T, U).$$

The supply of good one (S_1) is a function of (or depends on):

P_1 its own price

$P_2 \ldots\ldots n$, the selling price of other goods to which the producer could switch his production

C, Costs of production

T, the state of technology

U, unplanned or unanticipated factors which result in the quantity actually supplied being different from the quantity which it was intended to supply.

7.10. When a supply curve is drawn it is the graph of the relationship between the quantity of a good which is supplied (S_1) and changes in its own price (P_1) on the assumption that the other factors which affect supply remain constant or unchanged, i.e., ceteris paribus. Under these circumstances, as the selling price of the good changes, there is a movement **along** the supply curve.

7.11. If any of the other factors which affect supply change there is a shift in the supply curve

The shift is out to the right away from the origin, if more will be supplied as a result of the change. Changes which would result in a shift to the right, out from the origin, of the supply curve of a good are:—

(a) A reduction in the selling price of other goods which are produced by the same factors of production so that the production of the original good is more profitable.

(b) A reduction in the costs of production.

(c) An improvement in the state of technology so that the costs of production are reduced.

(d) An unanticipated event such as favourable weather, which results in a bumper harvest and a consequent increase in the quantity supplied at existing prices.

QUESTIONS

Q1. If there is an increase in the cost of producing a good explain the effect(s) which this would have on the supply curve of the good.

Q2. Give 2 examples of the cost of producing a good being affected by an increase in taxation.

Q3. In what way would an improvement in technology affect the supply curve of a good?

Q4. Summarise the factors which influence the quantity of a good which is supplied.

Q5. Distinguish between a movement along a supply curve and a shift in a supply curve.

Q6. Set out four circumstances which would result in the supply curve of a commodity shifting to the right.

8 Effect of Changes in Demand and Supply on Price/Output Equilibrium

Generally demand reacts faster than supply to a price change

8.1. If there is a shift to the right on the demand curve facing the firm (see section 6.16. as to why this might occur), other things remaining constant or unchanged, the initial or impact effect will be that prices will rise from P_1 to P_2 — see Fig. 8.1. The explanation for this increase in price is that it will take supply a short time to adjust to the increased quantities which are demanded. Generally demand is more sensitive than supply to changes in price and responds more quickly. The reaction of demand to a change in price is usually considered to be instantaneous and thus the impact effect arises from the effect of change in demand with supply constant initially, and then supply responding after a short time lag to the changed conditions. The immediate effect is that the quantity available is fixed at Q_1 and by reference to demand curve D_2 in fig. 8.1. it can be seen that P_2 is the market clearing price for this quantity. When the firm has the opportunity to adjust its level of supply to this higher level of demand, equilibrium will be attained at P_3/Q_2. *Thus an increase (decrease) in demand results in an increase (decrease) in equilibrium price and quantity*.

To check your understanding of this, as an exercise you should trace the effects of a shift of the demand curve to the left:— Fig. 8.1 shows the effect of a shift to the right in the demand curve.

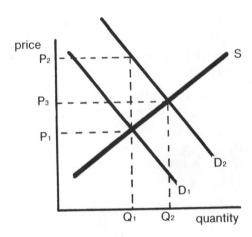

Fig. 8.1. Increase in quantity demanded raises price more in the short run.

8.2. If there is an increase in the quantity supplied at each price, (see section 7.9, as to why this might occur), the supply curve will shift to the right.

The effect of this development is that the equilibrium price is lowered from P_1 to P_2 and the equilibrium quantity is increased from Q_1 to Q_2; see Fig. 8.2. *Thus the effect of an increase (decrease) in supply is a reduction (increase) in price and an increase (reduction) in the quantity demanded.*

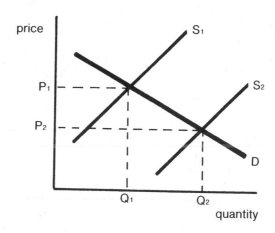

Fig. 8.2. Effect on price/output equilibrium of an increase in quantity supplied.

Movement of market to new equilibrium

8.3. The effects of Sections 8.1 and 8.2 can be combined in the following manner as shown in Fig. 8.3. At the initial equilibrium position the selling price was P_1 and the quantity supplied and demanded at this price was Q_1. There is a shift to the right in the demand curve due to a successful advertising campaign conducted by the firm (or any of the other circumstances set out in chapter 6 which would cause the demand curve of the firm to shift to the right). The new demand curve for the output of the firm is D_2. Initially price increases to P_2 since on demand curve D_2 this is the price which will be paid for quantity Q_1 which is the quantity being produced by the firm. When the firm adjusts its production level the equilibrium price/output is P_3, Q_3 as shown on Fig. 8.3. You will notice that on the supply side there is a movement along the existing supply curve S_1 because there has been no change in any of the factors which would cause a shift in the supply curve. All of this is identical with section 8.1 above.

The firm now discovers that this higher level of demand makes it economically viable for the firm to introduce larger and more modern machinery which lowers the cost of producing the good. This development shifts the supply curve to the right as explained in Chapter 7. Thus in the long run, when the full adjustment has taken place the market equilibrium situation is that a quantity of Q_4 is being supplied and demanded at a price of P_4 which clears the market.

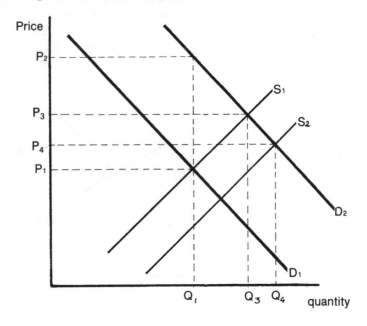

Fig. 8.3. Movement of market to a new Equilibrium.

QUESTIONS

Q1. Is supply or demand more responsive to a change in the factors determining the market?

Q2. Write a note setting out a possible sequence of developments in response to an increase in the demand for a commodity.

Q3. Draw a supply and a demand curve and show the equilibrium price and quantity.

Q4. Explain by means of a diagram the effect on price/output equilibrium as a result of a successful advertising campaign.

Q5. Repeat Q4 in respect of an increase in the level of taxation.

Q6. Repeat Q4 in respect of an increase in the general level of income.

9 Elasticity

Some measurement of change is required

9.1. In previous sections attention has been drawn to the effect which changes in selling price have on the quantity demanded and the quantity supplied. For some goods a price alteration will result in a significant alteration in the quantity supplied, while for other goods a price change of the same magnitude would result in an insignificant change in the level of demand. These references to a 'significant change in demand' and 'an insignificant change in demand' are far too vague and general, and convey little real information as to the actual changes. Similarly little light is thrown on the analysis by comments such as "less will be brought when price is increased".

Definition of price elasticity of demand

9.2. In order to permit decisions to be made regarding possible changes in price (or decisions on taxation by the government) it is necessary to know to what extent demand for a good will respond to a change in its own price, i.e., how sensitive, or responsive, is demand to a change in its own price or to a change in any of the other economic variables which influence the level of demand for the good. It is for this reason that the concept of elasticity of demand is introduced. *Elasticity of demand measures the sensitivity (or responsiveness) of demand to a change in an economic variable. Price elasticity of demand measures the responsiveness of demand to a change in its own price. When the expression Elasticity of Demand is used it refers to Price Elasticity of Demand.*

Absolute change in demand

9.3. However, it is not sufficient to say that demand increases by 25 units when price is reduced by 10p. This would raise the question of how important is a quantity of 25 units when related to the quantity sold. If 25 extra Rolls Royce cars were being sold per day, this would represent an astronomical increase in demand, whereas an increase of 25 boxes of matches in the number being sold per annum would constitute an insignificant alteration in the level of demand.

Absolute change in price

9.4. The same problem arises when one considers a change in selling price. An increase of 10p in selling price is astronomical if one is considering a 10p increase in the selling price of a box of matches, while a 10p increase in the selling price of a motor car is derisory.

*Relative
rather than
absolute
changes*

9.5. This problem is overcome by relating the alteration in the quantity demanded to the level of sales and the alteration in price to the actual selling price. Thus the formula is:—

$$\text{Price Elasticity of Demand} \atop \epsilon_d \qquad = \qquad \frac{\text{Proportionate Change in Quantity Demanded}}{\text{Proportionate Change in Price}}$$

Example 9.5.

Price	Change in price ΔP	Quantity demanded	Change in quantity demanded ΔQ
£50		1050	
£55	+£5	1000	−50

While the change in price is £5.00, this must be considered in relation to the original price, i.e., $\frac{5}{50}$ or to the new price $\frac{5}{55}$ and thus you could get two different answers describing the same situation. To avoid this source of ambiguity and to ensure consistency, it is conventional to relate the actual change to the mid-point of the two prices, i.e.,

$$\frac{5}{\frac{1}{2}(50+55)} = \frac{5}{52.5} = \frac{2}{21}$$

Proportionate change in quantity demanded now becomes

$$\frac{-50}{\frac{1}{2}(1050+1000)} = \frac{-50}{1025} = \frac{-1}{20.5} = \frac{-2}{41.}$$

9.6. In the light of this the formula for Price Elasticity of Demand becomes:—

$$\frac{\Delta Q}{\frac{1}{2}(Q_1 + Q_2)} \div \frac{\Delta P}{\frac{1}{2}(P_1 + P_2)}$$

where ΔQ = Change in Quantity Demanded
Q_1 = Original Quantity Demanded
Q_2 = Quantity demanded after the change in price
ΔP = Change in price
P_1 = Original price
P_2 = New price

using the figures from Example 9.5.

$$\text{Price Elasticity of Demand} = \frac{-2}{41} \div \frac{2}{21} = -0.512$$

*Arc
elasticity*

9.7. It will be noted that the formula provides the same numerical measurement of the price elasticity of demand whether the change is in respect of a price increase or a price reduction. What has been measured in this case is Arc Elasticity of demand. In Fig. 9.7 it is the elasticity between Point A and Point B.

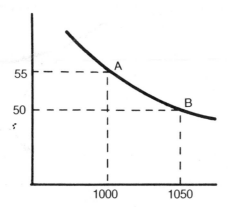

Fig. 9.7. Arc elasticity.

*Point
Elasticity
of Demand*

9.8. It is also possible to measure price elasticity of demand at a particular point on the demand curve. Because attention is being concentrated on a point, e.g., point A in Fig. 9.7, the problem of taking the mid-point between the original level of demand and the new level of demand does not arise, neither does the problem of the initial price and the new price. The formula for Price Elasticity of Demand at a particular point then becomes

$$\frac{dQ}{Q} \div \frac{dP}{P} \quad \text{or} \quad \frac{dQ}{dP} \cdot \frac{P}{Q}$$

where dQ and dP mean very small changes in quantity demanded and in price respectively.

*Point
Elasticity
of Demand
is different
at each
point on a
straight line
downward
sloping
demand curve*

9.9. From what has been said in section 9.8 regarding point elasticity of demand you will realise that elasticity is different at each point on a straight line (downward sloping) demand curve. Thus in measuring Arc Elasticity of demand in Sect 9.7 it should be realised that what is being measured is the *average elasticity* between the points A & B in fig 9.7.

Those who have studied mathematics will find this very easy when you look at the formula for Point Elasticity of Demand in section 9.8. The slope of a downward sloping straight line is a constant therefore $\frac{dQ}{dP}$ in the formula is a constant. $\frac{Q}{P}$ the ratio between quantity and price is different at each point on the straight line demand curve. Therefore $\frac{dQ}{dP} \cdot \frac{P}{Q}$ must be different at each point.

9.10. A downward sloping demand curve signifies that price and quantity demanded move in opposite directions. A price increase (P+) results in a reduction in the quantity demanded (Q-), while a reduction in price (P-) results in an increase in the quantity demanded (Q+). When related to the formula for Price Elasticity of Demand, this means that a price increase (+) divided into the change in quantity demanded which will be a reduction (-) will give a negative sign for the numerical measure of price elasticity of demand.

Similarly a price reduction (-) divided into the resultant increase in quantity demanded (+), will again result in a negative sign for the numerical measure for price elasticity of demand.

The numerical measure for Price Elasticity of Demand is usually negative

9.11. Giffen Goods do not obey the normal law of demand and in their case an increase in price (+) results in an increase in quantity demanded (+) and the numerical measure for price elasticity of demand will have a positive sign. Similarly a reduction in their price (-) results in a reduction in quantity demanded (-) again giving a positive sign (+) when division takes place in accordance with the formula for price elasticity of demand.

For Giffen Goods the numerical measure of Price Elasticity of Demand has a positive sign

9.12. Thus the numerical figure for price elasticity of demand is negative except for Giffen Goods, when it is positive. Because the sign is nearly always negative there is a convention of expressing price of elasticity of demand in absolute terms, i.e. without a sign. If price elasticity of demand is positive (i.e. a Giffen Good), the sign will always be shown. *However, for examination purposes be careful to remember that the sign is usually negative.*

Price Elasticity of Demand is usually expressed in absolute terms

9.13. In the following discussion on numerical measures of price elasticity of demand the numerical figure is expressed in absolute terms, i.e. ignoring sign. Thus -2 would be referred to as 2 and in the following analysis would be considered to be greater than 1, though often not clearly stated, this is the convention which is adopted in practically all text books.

9.14. When the application of the formula for price elasticity of demand results in a numerical figure greater than unity (in absolute terms) demand is said to be elastic in response to a change in its own price. An answer greater than 1 is possible only when the proportionate change in quantity demanded is greater than the proportionate change in price, i.e., what is above the line in the formula is greater than what is below the line.

Example 9.14. A 20% change in quantity demanded as a result of a 10% change in price would provide a numerical measure of 2, i.e., in absolute terms, in respect of price elasticity of demand. Demand in this case would be considered to be elastic.

$\epsilon_d > 1$
Elastic

9.15. When the numerical figure which results from the application of the formula for price elasticity of demand provides an answer of 1 (in absolute terms), price elasticity of demand is said to be of unit elasticity. Such a result is possible only when the proportionate change in the quantity demanded is equal to the proportionate change in the price, i.e., what is above the line in the formula is equal to what is below the line.

$\epsilon_d = 1$
unit elasticity

Example 9.15. A 5% alteration in quantity demanded as a result of a 5% price alteration would represent a situation of unit elasticity.

$\epsilon_d < 1$
inelastic

9.16. When the numerical figure which results from the application of the formula for price elasticity of demand is less than unity (in absolute terms), price elasticity of demand is said to be inelastic. This result is possible only when the proportionate change in the quantity demanded is less than the proportionate change in price, i.e., what is above the line in the formula is less than what is below the line.

Example 9.16. A 5% alteration in quantity demanded as a result of a 10% alteration in price would represent an inelastic situation.

Table 9.16. Summary Table of Price Elasticity of Demand.

Terms	Description	Measurement of price elasticity of demand in Absolute Terms	Diagrammatic representation (all diagrams drawn to the same scale)
perfectly inelastic	There is no change in the quantity demanded as result of a change in price	Zero	
Inelastic	The relative change in quantity demanded is less than the relative change in price	Greater than zero but less than one	
Unit Elasticity	The relative change in quantity demanded is exactly equal to the relative change in price	One or unity	
Elastic	The relative change in quantity demanded is greater than the relative change in price	Greater than one but less than infinity	
Perfectly or infinitely elastic	The producer can sell all his output at a particular price but if he increases his price his sales will fall to zero	Infinity	

*The slope of
the demand
curve is an
indication
of relative
elasticity
only when
the 2 demand
curves are
drawn on
the same
scale*

9.17. The slope of the demand curve is often taken as an indication of price elasticity of demand but great care should be taken when adopting this approach. In table 9.16. it is clearly stated that all the diagrams in the table are drawn to the same scale. Where this procedure is adopted the relative slopes of the demand curves do indicate relative elasticities.

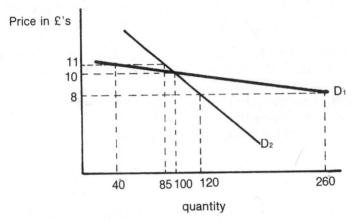

Fig. 9.17. Elasticity and slope.

In Fig. 9.17 at a price of £10.00 a quantity of 100 is bought of each of these goods, as is indicated by the intersection of the demand curves. When the price is reduced to £8.00 120 of item 2 is purchased and 260 of item 1. Thus the demand for item 1 is more elastic in response to the price reduction.

Similarly if price is increased to £11.00, the demand for item 1 reduces to 40 while the demand for item 2 reduces to 85. Again the demand for item 1 is more elastic. This greater elasticity of item 1 is shown by its demand curve being flatter, but as the following example shows this is dependent upon the diagrams being drawn to the same scale.

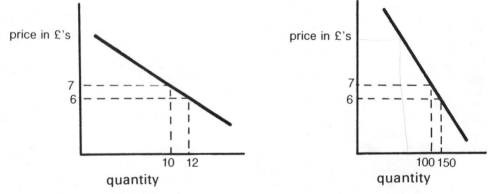

**Fig. 9.17.2 (a) and 9.17.2 (b). Flatter slope does not indicate greater
elasticity.**

The flatter demand curve does not represent greater price elasticity of demand in Figs. 9.17.2 (a) and 9.17.2 (b) because they are not drawn to the same scale. The demand curve in Fig. 9.17.2 (a) is flatter than the curve in Fig. 9.17.2 (b) but the response of demand to a price alteration from £7.00 to £6.00 is much greater in Fig. (b) i.e., 50 units which is a proportionate change of $\frac{50}{125}$ or 40% as against a change of 2 units which is a proportionate change of $\frac{2}{11}$ or 18% in Fig. 9.17.2 (a). Thus the curve in fig. 9.17.2 (b) represents the greater price elasticity of demand as compared to 9.17.2 (a) even though the demand curve in Fig. (a) is flatter. This is due entirely to differences in the scale to which the diagrams were drawn.

9.18. Relationship between price elasticity of demand and changes in total revenue

The total revenue which a firm receives through selling a commodity is Price per unit sold × Quantity sold. Thus, if the price of a commodity is **increased**, usually there will be a **decrease** in the quantity demanded. The effect which this development would have on total revenue depends upon the relationship between the increase in price which is received in respect of each unit sold and the reduction in demand as a result of the price increase.

Table 9.18. Relationship between price elasticity of demand and changes in total revenue.

Price P	Quantity demanded	Total revenue £	Price elasticity of demand
20	20 000	4 000 ⎫	−0.944
21	19 100	4 011 ⎬	
22	18 200	4 004 ⎭	−1.038

9.19. Table 9.18. illustrates a number of aspects of the relationship between price elasticity of demand and changes in total revenue.

When $\epsilon_d < 1$ price and total revenue move in the same direction

(a) When price is increased from 20p to 21p, quantity demand falls from 20 000 to 19 100. However, total revenue is increased from £4 000 to £4 011. Price elasticity of demand is inelastic (0.944) because the proportionate change in quantity demanded is less than the proportionate change in price.

(b) If the same situation is analysed with the alternative sequence, 21p being the initial price, when the selling price is reduced to 20p there is an increase in the quantity demanded from 19 100 to 20 000

Total revenue is reduced from £4 011 to £4 000 because the proportionate change in quantity demanded is less than the proportionate change in price. Price elasticity of demand remains unchanged at 0.944 and is inelastic.

(c) From (a) and (b) above it can be observed that *when price elasticity of demand is inelastic, i.e., less than unity in absolute terms, the direction of the price alteration and the direction of the alteration in total revenue are in the same direction.* In other words, when the price is increased (▲) total revenue increases (▲); when price is reduced (▼) total revenue is reduced (▼).   *inelastic*

9.20. If the price of 21p in table 9.18 is taken as the starting point,

When $\epsilon_{d'} > 1$ price and total revenue move in opposite directions

(a) it can be seen that if price is increased to 22p there will be a reduction in the quantity demanded from 19 100 to 18 200 and total revenue falls from £4 011 to £4 004. Price elasticity of demand is elastic (|1.038|) because the proportionate change in quantity demanded is greater than the proportionate change in price.

(b) If this development is analysed through reversing the sequence where 22p is taken as the initial price, the reduction in price to 21p causes an increase in quantity demanded from 18 200 to 19 100. As the proportionate change in quantity demanded is greater than the proportionate change in price, total revenue is increased. Price elasticity of demand remains unchanged at (|1.038|).

(c) From (a) and (b) above it will be noticed that *when price elasticity of demand is elastic, i.e., greater than unity in absolute terms, the direction of the alteration in price and the direction of the alteration in total revenue are opposite.* When price is increased (▲) total revenue falls (▼); when price is reduced (▼) total revenue increases (▲).   *elastic*

9.21. If the proportionate change in quantity demanded is exactly equal to other proportionate change in price, price elasticity of demand is unity (|1|) and total revenue does not change as a result of the price alteration.

Table 9.21.

If $\epsilon_d = 1$ total revenue is unchanged

Price £	Quantity demanded	Total revenue £	Price elasticity of demand
1	100	100	
2	50	100	−1 (Unity)

Marginal Revenue defined

9.22. Marginal Revenue is the term used to refer to the change in total revenue when sales/output increases by a small amount e.g. 1 unit. In table 9.18 when the price was increased from 20p to 21p marginal revenue was £11 i.e. the difference between the total revenue of £4011 when the price was 21p and the total revenue of £4000 when the price was 20p. When the price was further increased from 21p to 22p marginal revenue was negative at £7 as total revenue fell from £4011 to £4004.

9.23. An example of the relationship between changes in price and changes in total and marginal revenue is given in table 9.23 from which information fig 9.23 is drawn.

Price	Qty Demanded	Total Revenue Col 1 x Col 2	Marginal Revenue
16	6	96	
15	11	165	(+) 69
14	20	280	(+) 115
11	130	1430	—
8	200	1600	
7	226	1582	(—) 18
6	254	1524	(—) 58

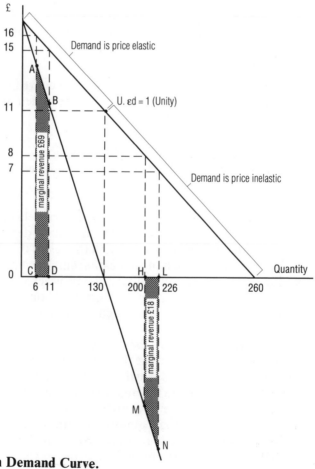

Fig. 9.23. Elasticity on Demand Curve.

9.24. From fig 9.23 which is drawn from the information contained in table 9.23 you will notice that at all price/quantity combinations represented by points on the demand curve to the left of point U, i.e. the upper half of the demand curve, marginal revenue is positive. Thus, in this area of the demand curve when price is reduced a higher quantity is sold and total revenue is increased since marginal revenue is positive. For example a price reduction from 16 to 15 results in an increase in quantity demanded from 6 to 11 so that total revenue increases from 96 to 165, thus marginal revenue is +69 as shown in table 9.23. In fig. 9.23 this increase in marginal revenue is represented by the rectangle abcd.

Conversely when price is increased the quantity demanded is lower and per the upper portion of the demand curve i.e. to the left of point U (positive) marginal revenue is lost so that total revenue is reduced. For example a price increase from 15 to 16 results in a reduction in the quantity demanded from 11 to 6, with a consequent fall in total revenue from 165 to 96, marginal revenue being negative at minus 69 as shown in table 9.24 and represented by rectangle abcd in fig 9.23.

Thus in this upper half of the demand curve price and total revenue move in opposite directions. You will remember that, in section **9.21** it was explained that this relationship between price and total revenue moving in opposite directions occurred when price elasticity of demand was greater than unity (i.e. elastic). It is now possible to make the following statements:

$\epsilon_d > 1$ in upper half of demand curve

1   In the upper position of the demand curve i.e. at all points to the left of point U in fig 9.23, price elasticity of demand is greater than unity i.e. demand is elastic.

$\epsilon_d > 1$ Price and Marginal Revenue move in opposite directions

2   If demand is elastic, when price is increased (+) marginal revenue is negative (-) and when price is reduced (-) marginal revenue is positive (+).

at point U $\epsilon_d = 1$ and marginal revenue is zero

9.25. It was shown in section 9.21 when price elasticity of demand is unity the proportionate change in the quantity demanded is equal to the proportionate change in price with the result that total revenue from the sale of the good is unchanged i.e. marginal revenue is zero. From fig 9.23 you will observe that marginal revenue is zero at a level of output to 130 and a price of 11 as represented by point U on the diagram. Thus at point U price elasticity of demand is equal to unity.

9.26. From fig. 9.23 it will be noted that at all price/output combinations represented by points to the right of point U marginal revenue is negative. In these circumstances it will be noted that, while a reduction in price results in an increase in the quantity demanded marginal revenue is lower (more negative) at the new higher level of demand so total revenue is smaller at the new price/quantity combination. This can be seen from table 9.23 when price is reduced from 8 to 7 even though the quantity demanded increases from 200 to 226 total revenue falls from 1600 to 1582 (marginal revenue is *minus* 18). This marginal revenue of minus 18 is represented by rectangle HLMN in fig 9.24. Conversely a price increase from 7 to 8 increases total revenue from 1582 to 1600 so that marginal revenue is *plus* 18 — again represented by rectangle HLMN in fig 9.24.

Thus in this lower half of the demand curve, i.e. at all points to the right of point U, a price reduction lowers total revenue and a price increase results in a higher level of total revenue. You will remember from section 9.19 that this relationship between price and total revenue moving in the same direction occurred when price elasticity of demand was less than unity (i.e. inelastic).

It is now possible to make the following statements.

In lower half of demand curve price and marginal revenue move in the same direction

1   In the lower half of the demand curve i.e. at all points to the right of point U, price elasticity of demand is less than unity (i.e. inelastic).

2   If demand is inelastic when price is reduced (-) marginal revenue falls (-) i.e. is more negative. Conversely when price is increased (+) marginal revenue is increased (+) i.e. is less negative.

Table 9.28. Summary of Relationship between Elasticity and changes in Revenue

Measurement of Price Elasticity of Demand	Price Increase	Price Reduction	Comment
$\epsilon > 1$	Total Revenue Reduced Marginal Revenue Negative	Total Revenue Increased Marginal Revenue Positive	Price & Total Revenue move in opposite directions Price & Marginal Revenue move in opposite directions
$\epsilon = 1$	Total Revenue Unchanged. Marginal Revenue zero	Total Revenue Unchanged. Marginal Revenue zero	Total Revenue constant. Marginal Revenue zero
$\epsilon < 1$	Total Revenue Increased. Marginal Revenue Positive	Total Revenue Reduced. Marginal Revenue Negative	Price & Total Revenue & Marginal all move in the same direction

*A profit
maximising
firm will
not be at
equilibrium
when
$\epsilon_d = 1$*

9.28. A profit maximising firm will not be at long run equilibrium when $\epsilon_d = 1$ because in this case if the firm increases its selling price, though it will sell a smaller quantity, it will earn the same revenue (because $\epsilon_d = 1$). However, since it is selling a smaller quantity its total costs of production will be lower, and this fact together with the earning of the same level of revenue means that a larger level of profits would be earned. Therefore, if the objective of the firm is to maximise profit it would not be at equilibrium but rather it would increase price if $\epsilon_d = 1$.

*A profit
maximising
will not be
at long term
equilibrium
when
$\epsilon_d < 1$*

9.29. Similarly a profit maximising firm will not be at long term equilibrium when $\epsilon_d < 1$ because by increasing price it can increase total revenue. However, when it increases its price, it will reduce the demand for its product and its total costs of production will be reduced. Thus when price is increased, total revenue is increased and total costs are reduced, therefore profit would be increased when price is increased. If the objective of firm is to maximise profits, price should be increased if $\epsilon_d < 1$.

When $\epsilon_d > 1$

9.30. It may seem feasible to extend the analysis in Section 9.24 to the other circumstance in Table 9.21, when total revenue is increased, viz, when $\epsilon_d > 1$ a reduction in price leads to an increase in revenue. However, if a reduction in price leads to a greater quantity being sold, total costs of production will be increased. Hence, when $\epsilon_d > 1$ the result of a price reduction is that both total revenue and total costs are increased. The effect which this would have on profits would therefore depend on the relative increase in costs and revenue. Consequently no general conclusion, similar to that in 9.22 and 9.23, is possible.

9.31. FACTORS WHICH AFFECT PRICE ELASTICITY OF DEMAND

(a) **The availability of close substitutes**

The availability of close substitutes at competitive prices is the greatest single influence on price elasticity of demand. Goods are purchased because they provide utility; if other goods at comparable prices provide more or less the same utility, consumers will switch to these substitute goods if the price of a good is increased and the price of the substitute goods are not. Thus, when substitute goods are available the demand for a good will be responsive i.e. elastic, if its price is increased. Similarly if the price of a good is reduced, consumers of substitute goods will switch to the good which has become relatively cheaper. The closer the substitutability between goods the more will consumers tend to switch their purchasing behaviour in response to a change in relative prices and thus the greater will be price elasticity of demand.

It is important in discussing the availability of close substitutes to advert to the price element. While the substitute good need not be identical in price, it is important that they be *in the same price range*. An increase in the price of public transport does not necessarily mean that there is likely to be a large increase in demand for Rolls Royce cars even though they both provide transport. Neither is an increase in the price of county council houses likely to affect the demand for large detached houses because they are not in the same price range. However, an increase in the price of one brand of tinned fruit is likely to result in at least some consumers transferring to other brands.

(b) **Complementary goods**

If the good in question is the cheaper of two goods which are in joint demand, then the demand for it is likely to be relatively inelastic in response to changes in its own price. If a person always uses mint sauce with lamb, his demand for mint sauce is likely to be affected more by changes in the price of lamb than by changes in its own price. Driving licences and motor cars are another example.

(c) **Whether the Commodity is a luxury or necessity**

The extent to which the item in question can be regarded as a luxury or necessity is often put forward as one of the factors which influence the price elasticity of demand for a product, the idea being that it is not vital that one should possess luxuries and consequently price elasticity of demand for them will be relatively elastic. Conversely, since necessities by definition are vital for life, then price elasticity for them will be relatively inelastic — people must continue to buy them even when their price is increased.

There is no flaw in this reasoning as far as it goes; the criticism is that it doesn't go far enough to be helpful. The classification of goods in this manner is too broadly based. It is far too general a comment and it contributes nothing to our understanding of price elasticity of demand for individual products.

Food is a necessity and the above comments would suggest that price elasticity of demand for food items will be relatively inelastic. If the analysis is taken down to individual food items the conclusions are less definite, e.g., if the price of potatoes is increased, people may replace them in their diet by other foods such as rice. Jam, white bread from commercial bakeries and breakfast cereals are other examples of items which come under the general classification of food and yet demand for them could be elastic in response to an increase in their price — people could switch to eating different foods.

(d) **The proportion of income which is spent on the commodity**

In general the greater the proportion of income which is spent on a commodity, the more elastic is demand for it likely to be in response to a change in its own price. This is true because the greater the proportion of income which is spent on the good, the more important is a change in its price. If an item on which I spend 10% of my weekly income is increased by 5% it will cost me an extra 0.5% of my weekly income if I continue to purchase the same quantity of the item. Whereas if I spend only 1% of my weekly income on this item it will cost me a smaller amount i.e. 0.05% of my weekly income if I continue to purchase the same quantity of the item.

Also, in so far as items which constitute a large element of my weekly income may be purchased on a repetitive basis there is greater scope for a reduction in the quantity purchased. For example, if I have lunch and dinner in a hotel each day, an increase in the price of meals may result in my reducing the number of meals which I eat away from home. On the other hand if I have dinner in a hotel three times a year, not only does this item of expense not bear heavily on my annual income but I have less opportunity to cut down my demand.

The usual example of the relationship between price elasticity of demand and income is the fact that a rise of even 50% in the price of a box of matches is unlikely to have a significant effect on the demand for them.

(e) **The durability of the commodity**

The more durable the commodity, the more elastic is the demand for it likely to be in response to changes in its own price. Thus if products such as motor cars, lawn mowers, bicycles, refrigerators are increased in price, it is likely that the public will extend the life of their existing model and postpone the purchase of a replacement.

(f) **Expectations as to future changes in price**

The expectations of consumers as to future trends in the price of the commodity will affect elasticity. If, in the face of a price reduction, the public considers that prices are likely to fall even further, they may wait for the further reduction in price, in which case demand may not be very elastic in response to the initial price reduction. However, developing this line of reasoning further it could be argued that when the further price reduction takes place (or it becomes obvious that expectations were wrong and that no further price reduction will in fact take place), then demand will respond in a manner based on the true price elasticity of demand for the product. Thus this expectation factor is merely introducing a time element in the analysis.

9.32. Income elasticity of demand

This concept measures the responsiveness, or sensitivity, of demand for a product in response to changes in income.

The appropriate Formula for income elasticity of demand is:—

$$\frac{\text{Proportionate Change in Quantity Demanded}}{\text{Proportionate Change in Income}} = \frac{\Delta Q}{\frac{1}{2}(Q_1 + Q_2)} \div \frac{\Delta Y}{\frac{1}{2}(Y_1 + Y_2)}$$

$$= \frac{\Delta Q}{\Delta Y} \cdot \frac{Y_1 + Y_2}{Q_1 + Q_2}$$

where
ΔQ = Change in Quantity Demanded
Q_1 = Initial Quantity Demanded
Q_2 = Quantity Demanded after the change in income

ΔY = Change in Income
Y_1 = Initial Income
Y_2 = Income after the alteration

Numerical measure of Income Elasticity of Demand is usually positive

The line of reasoning in respect of income elasticity of demand is analogous to that adopted in respect of price elasticity of demand. The numerical measure of income elasticity of demand provided by the application of the formula is usually positive because the demand for most goods increases as people's income increases, and falls with reductions in income. Since the direction of the change in demand will usually be the same as the direction of the change in income, the answer given by the application of the formula will usually be positive.

A normal good has Positive Income Elasticity of Demand

9.33. In fact the definition of a normal good is that it is a good with a positive income elasticity of demand, i.e., more of it is bought as income increases. The greater the alteration in demand as a result of an alteration in income, the greater will be the numerical measurement of income elasticity of demand.

Proportion of Income spent on a good

9.34. Another way of looking at the concept of income elasticity of demand would be by examining the proportion of income spent on the commodity and, if an increasing proportion of income is spent on the good as income increases, then there is certainly a high income elasticity of demand. However, care must be taken in this form of analysis, since a constant proportion of income spent on a good when income is increasing would also indicate positive elasticity of demand since more money is being spent on the good. Even when a smaller proportion of (an increased) income is being spent on a good it is possible that an extra sum of money is being spent in purchasing the good. In example 9.34 £10 which constitutes 25% of income is spent on the good when income is £40. When income increases to £60 though a smaller proportion of (the now increased) income, viz. 20%, was spent on the good an extra £2 was being spent on it. Notice that income elasticity of demand being positive captures this fact which was not obvious in basing our analysis in the proportion of income which is spent on the good.

Example 9.34.

Income	Qty Bought	Price	Amount of money spent on good	Proportion of Income spent on good
£		£	£	
40	10	1 each	10	25%
60	12	1 each	12	20%

$$\text{Income Elasticity of Demand} = \frac{2}{\frac{1}{2}(12+10)} \div \frac{20}{\frac{1}{2}(40+60)} = 0.45$$

Income elasticity of demand is greater than 1 for a luxury good

9.35. *As already stated, goods on which more money is spent as income increases have a positive income elasticity of demand and are known as* Normal Goods. However if an *increased* proportion of income is spent on a good when income increases such goods are known as *Luxuries*. If an increased proportion of income is spent on the goods as income increases this means that the proportionate change in quantity demand (i.e. the numerator in the formula) is greater than the proportionate change in income (i.e. the denominator in the formula), so that if the *calculation of Income Elasticity of Demand gives an answer greater than 1 then the good in question is a luxury good.*

High Income Elasticity of Demand

9.36. In many industrialised countries the demand for consumer durable goods has a high income elasticity of demand — the demand for washing machines, dishwashers, motor cars, transistors, tape-recorders etc. increase more rapidly as income increases, and it is the industries producing such goods which enjoy rapid economic growth when income is increasing or the standard of living is improving. In contrast the demand for food items does not increase very rapidly as income increases.

An Inferior good has negative Income Elasticity of Demand

9.37. There are goods less of which are bought as income rises, i.e., income elasticity of demand is negative. These are known as inferior goods. *The definition of an inferior good is a good with a negative income elasticity of demand.* The word inferior as used here does not mean that there is something "wrong" with the good. It simply refers to the fact that it has a negative income elasticity of demand.

Zero Income Elasticity of Demand

9.38. There may also be goods which have zero income elasticity of demand. These would be goods which people purchase when their income is low and they do not purchase any additional quantities of them when their income increases. The usual example taken is salt.

9.39. Fig. 9.39 shows the relationship between expenditure on a commodity and income. This could refer to bicycles where they are not bought at low levels of income because they are too dear. As income increases one is bought for each member of the family. Then follows a period of zero income elasticity as the family have the quantity which they require. If the family, as they become more wealthy replace their bicycles by motor cars, negative elasticity of demand would be explained.

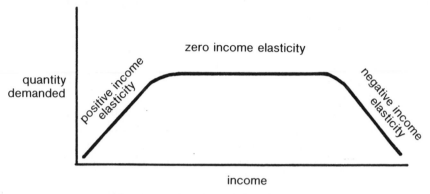

Fig. 9.39. Changing income elasticity of demand.

9.40. Cross elasticity of demand
Cross Elasticity of Demand measures the responsiveness of demand of a commodity (Good X) to a change in the price of another commodity (Good Y)

Formula for Cross Elasticity of Demand.

Proportionate Change in Quantity Demanded of Good X
──
Proportionate Change in Price of Good Y

$$= \frac{\Delta Qx}{\frac{1}{2}(Q_1 x + Q_2 x)} \div \frac{\Delta Py}{\frac{1}{2}(P_1 y + P_2 y)} = \frac{\Delta Qx}{\Delta Py} \cdot \frac{(P_1 y + P_2 y)}{(Q_1 x + Q_2 x)}$$

where ΔQx = Change in quantity demanded of Good X

   $Q_1 x$ = Initial quantity demanded of Good X

   $Q_2 x$ = Quantity demanded of Good X after the alteration in price of good Y

   ΔPy = Change in Price of Good Y

   $P_1 y$ = Initial Price of Good Y

   $P_2 y$ = Price of Good Y after the alteration in its price

9.41. The above formula refers to arc cross elasticity (see Sections 9.7 and 9.8. for distinction between arc elasticity and point elasticity)
   The formula for Point-Cross elasticity of demand is:—

$$\frac{dQx}{Qx} \div \frac{dPy}{Py} = \frac{dQx}{dPy} \cdot \frac{Py}{Qx}$$

Cross Elasticity of Demand for substitute goods is positive

9.42. If the 2 goods being analysed are substitutes for each other the numerical figure for cross elasticity of demand will have a positive sign. Let us take as an example 2 brands of jam which are close substitutes. If the price of Brand Y jam is increased (+) the demand for Brand Y jam will be reduced (-) as some consumers switch to Brand X jam (i.e. the substitute good), so that the demand for Brand X jam is increased (+). Reverting back to our formula there is a positive sign (+) in the numerator and a positive sign (+) in the denominator, so that the answer will be positive (+).

Conversely if price of Brand Y is reduced (-), the demand for Brand Y will increase (+) and the demand for Brand X (i.e. the substitute good) will reduce (-). A negative sign above the line and below the line in the formula again will give a positive sign (+) in the answer. *It is being assumed that there are no significant income effects arising from the price change.*

For close substitutes cross elasticity of demand will be a large positive number

9.43. *A definition for substitute goods is goods which have a high positive cross elasticity of demand.* The greater the substitutability, the higher will be the numerical measurement for cross elasticity of demand while the fact they they are substitute goods ensures the positive (+) answer.

9.44. If the two goods which are being measured by cross elasticity of demand are complements, then the application of the formula for cross elasticity of demand will result in a negative answer.

Cross Elasticity of demand for complementary goods is negative

The direction of the price alteration and the quantity demanded of the complement will always be in opposite directions. For example if the prices of cars are increased (+), the demand for cars is reduced (-) and the demand for petrol is reduced (-).

9.45. In Section 6.16 the factors which influence demand for a good were summarised. It was shown that:

$$D_1 = f(P_1, P_2........n, Y, t)$$

In Chapter 9 the elasticity of demand in respect to changes in the first three of these factors has been measured. Though the final factor in the relationship, taste (t), influences all the measurements of elasticity it is not used as a direct measurement of elasticity.

the relationship between D_1 and P_1 = Price Elasticity of Demand

the relationship between D_1 and $P_2........n$, = Cross Elasticity of Demand

the relationship between D_1 and Y = Income Elasticity of Demand

9.46. Elasticity of supply
All of the measurements of elasticity in this section have been in relation to demand. The concept of elasticity may be related to supply also. *Elasticity of supply measures the proportionate change in quantity supplied in response to a proportionate change in the price of the good.*

Formula for Price Elasticity of Supply

$$\frac{\Delta Q}{\frac{1}{2}(Q_1 + Q_2)} \div \frac{\Delta P}{\frac{1}{2}(P_1 + P_2)}$$

$$= \frac{\Delta Q}{\Delta P} \cdot \frac{\frac{1}{2}(P_1 + P_2)}{\frac{1}{2}(Q_1 + Q_2)} = \frac{\Delta Q}{\Delta P} \cdot \frac{(P_1 + P_2)}{(Q_1 + Q_2)}$$

This concept is identical with that of price elasticity of demand (Section 9.5.) except that now we are dealing with quantity supplied rather than quantity demanded.

Price Elasticity of supply will usually be positive

9.47. Price Elasticity of supply will usually be positive, since an increase in its own price (+) will normally lead to an increase in the quantity supplied (+). The more responsive is supply to a change in its own price, the greater will be the numerical measurement for price elasticity of supply.

Zero Elasticity of supply

9.48. Zero elasticity of supply would indicate that an increase in the selling price of the good does not result in any increase in supply. In terms of the formula the numerator is zero. The circumstances which might give rise to such a situation would be a catch of fish, which is being sold for the best price obtainable and the supply for that particular day cannot be increased even if higher prices are offered. (See section 4.8. also).

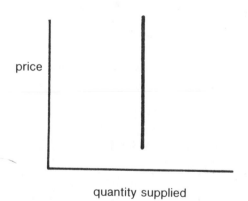

Fig. 9.42. Zero elasticity of supply.

Infinite Elasticity of Supply

9.49. Infinite Elasticity of Supply would apply where no supply is available below a certain price but large increases in the quantity supplied will not require an increase in price since an infinite quantity is available at the existing price. In terms of the formula for elasticity of supply the numerator approaches infinity in response to a change in the denominator (see also section 4.9).

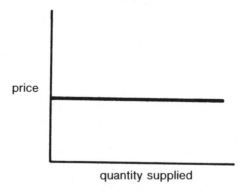

price

quantity supplied

Fig. 9.49. Infinite elasticity of supply.

9.50. *Any straight line supply curve which goes through the origin has unit elasticity of supply.* Both of the supply curves in Fig. 9.44 have unit elasticity of supply.

*Unit
Elasticity
of Supply*

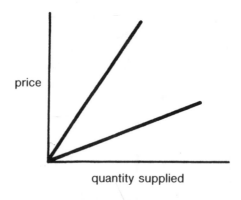

price

quantity supplied

Fig. 9.50. Unit elasticity of supply.

9.51. Summary of Factors which Influence Elasticity of Supply

(a) Cost Conditions

The main factor which affects elasticity of supply is the cost conditions under which the goods are being produced. If additional output can be supplied at a constant or reduced unit cost the supply will be responsive to an increase in the selling price of (demand for) for good.

However, if additional output could be supplied only at increased unit cost then supply would be less responsive to an increase in the selling price of, (or demand for) the good. For example if the increase in unit costs was greater than the increase in selling price then the supplier would be losing money on each additional unit supplied.

(b) Time Period

Supply less elastic in short term

The shorter the period involved the less elastic will supply be. The supply of fish on the market on a particular morning is fixed, if circumstances warranted it an increased supply could be made available in a relatively short period as all available boats could go out fishing while in the long run supply could be even more elastic as more and bigger boats are built and more fishermen are re-cruited/trained. The minimum period for an increase in the supply of trained labour is the training period involved.

Similarly the supply of vegetables in a particular season is confined to what was planted and harvested though an increased supply could be available from the next harvest by more planting now.

(c) Storage Costs

Supply is inelastic as storage costs are High

If the cost of storing goods is high then suppliers will be inclined to accept a lower price rather than involve themselves in the cost of storing the goods. Thus supply will be inelastic in the sense that even if there is a reduction in the price being offered more or less the same quantity will be supplied as suppliers seek to avoid the cost of storing unsold items.

On the other hand if goods are not stored because of high storage costs then there will be no stocks to draw upon if demand is buoyant so that an increase in price will not being about a significant increase in quantity supplied, i.e. supply would be inelastic.

(d) Perishability

Inelastic supply for Perishable goods

Perishability is just another aspect of storage costs. The more perishable the goods the greater the likelihood of goods deteriorating and thus the higher the storage costs which includes costs attribut-able to deterioration. Thus the more perishable the goods the more inelastic is supply.

(e) Products in Joint Supply

In joint supply, supply of less important good is inelastic

When the supply of a good necessarily entails the supply of another good then the goods are said to be in joint supply e.g. mutton & wool. If the demand for mutton is greater than the demand for wool, then sheep will be produced mainly to satisfy the demand for mutton and changes in the supply (production) of sheep, will be based primarily on the demand for mutton. Wool is also obtained from sheep so that the supply of wool will be determined primarily by the demand for mutton.

This point can be generalised into the statement that when a good is the less important of two goods which are in joint supply then supplies of this (less important) good will be relatively inelastic in response to changes in its own price.

QUESTIONS

Q1. "Price Elasticity of Demand is usually negative but Income Elasticity of Demand is usually positive". Explain.

Q2. Show the relationship between Price Elasticity of Demand and changes in total revenue.

Q3. Explain the factors which affect Price Elasticity of Demand.

Q4. Write an explanatory note on Inferior Goods.

Q5. In terms of Cross Elasticity of Demand distinguish between substitute and complementary goods.

10   Demand/Utility

10.1. Utility is the basis of demand

*Demand
inversely
related to
price*

In discussing market price in previous sections it has been taken for
granted that there exists a demand for the particular commodity and that
this demand is inversely related to price. The purpose of this section is to
analyse the basis of demand for commodities and to establish the
relationship between price and quantity demanded.

10.2. Utility is the satisfaction which we derive from goods

*Goods which
give the
greatest
utility will be
bought first*

Consumers seek goods because goods are capable of giving utility. It is
because goods are capable of satisfying a need or want that they are
sought after or desired. Naturally a consumer will give priority to the
purchase of those goods which give him the greatest satisfaction or utility
and, since most of us cannot afford to buy all of the goods which we
would like, we purchase that combination of goods which will give us the
greatest satisfaction.

*Utility of a
good is
subjective*

10.3. Utility is a subjective assessment — like beauty, it is in the mind of
the beholder. A good should not be seen as possessing inherent utility.
The same commodity may represent different levels of utility to different
people. If all goods at every point in time possessed the same degree of
utility for all people, they would never be bought or sold. For example, if
an article which I value at £1.00 is worth exactly this amount to the
person who owns it, there would be no price at which exchange would be
possible; at any price above £1.00, I would not buy, and at any price
which does not exceed £1.00 the owner would not sell and, since the item
is worth £1.00 to its present owner, he will not sell at that price either.

*Time is a
factor which
affects
utility*

10.4. Similarly time is important in the concept of utility. The same good
may represent different intensities of utility to the same person at
different points in time. After dining, additional food may possess little
utility, whereas before the meal food has considerable utility. On some
occasions we refuse extra portions of food even if there is no extra charge
involved, while on other occasions we are prepared to pay for exactly the
same portion of food. Also consider those items which interested you as a
young child and for which you have no use now.

*If a good is
bought then
it provides
utility*

10.5. A simple test of whether or not a good provides (or is capable of
providing) utility is whether or not we desire the good particularly when
acquiring it entails some cost in term of time, effort or money. The utility
which is derived from a good may stem from the need for food, shelter

and warmth, the desire for companionship or to keep up with the neighbours. That the utility attributable to a good may have diverse roots is obvious when you consider reasons why people might buy a good. These reasons include the following:

(a) **Functional Demand**
When the good possesses some intrinsic quality e.g. nutritional value, provides warmth etc.

(b) **Exclusivety**
Some goods are desired because of their exclusive nature e.g. fur coats, Rolls Royce cars etc.

(c) **Conspicious Consumption**
Though sometimes listed separately in reality this is similar to no. 2 above. This is known also as the Veblen Effect because Thorstern Veblen developed the Theory of Conspicius Consumption.

(d) **Expectations or Speculative Effect**
Expectations as to future price increases can stimulate the demand for any good about which such expectations are held. Moreover there are some goods where expectations as to future price changes may be the dominating factor influencing demand e.g. stocks and shares.

(e) **Bandwagon Effect**
The demand for a good may be stimulated because others are buying it. This bandwagon effect often is apparent in housing estates where an extension is added to a house or a porch is built and then a spate of such items appear.

(f) **Impulse Buying**
Some goods are bought on a sudden whim or desire. If this happens to any significant extent then it is likely that the good is relatively cheap. An example of this would be sweets/chocolate which is why they are located beside the check-out in many supermarkets. In terms of utility, impulse buying could be explained by reflecting that if the good is relatively cheap then the utility of the sum of money involved is rather low and consequently no major decisions are required as to whether to purchase or not.

10.6. Total utility

Some non-economic goods can provide utility

Since each good which we consume gives us utility or satisfaction we can consider total utility as being the sum of the utilities which we derive from all of the goods which we consume. Though not all of our utility comes from economic goods, non-economic goods, e.g., health, beauty etc. also provide considerable utility in the study of economics we concentrate on goods which are capable of being bought and sold, i.e. economic goods (see section 10.8 below).

10.7. Marginal Utility

Marginal Utility is the addition to total utility which we receive through consuming an additional unit of a good. From table 10.7 you will see that the marginal utility when I consume 3 apples is 28 utils. You will notice also that marginal utility from consuming the 3rd apple is the total utility from consuming 3 apples minus the total utility when I consume 2 apples, i.e. 103-75.

Table 10.7. Total and Marginal Utility.

Qty. of Apples Consumed	Total Utility	Marginal Utility
1	40	
2	75	35
3	103	28
4	122	19
5	132	10
6	132	Zero
7	129	-3

10.8. Characteristics of economic goods

In the study of economics we direct our attention only to goods and services which are capable of being bought and sold. (To avoid repeating the word "service" the word "good" will be used to embrace services also). However, if goods are to be traded they must have certain characteristics viz:—

(a) From what has been written above you will realise that if goods are to be sought after and desired they must possess *utility*. Thus all economic goods possess utility. It would be futile to attempt to sell something which is a nuisance or an irritant, e.g. weeds.

(b) The good must be *scarce* in relation to the demand for it. The word scarce as used in this context means that there is not enough of it to satisfy the demand of all those who want it. Thus in this country fresh air and water would not be economic goods because even though they provide utility they are not scarce in relation to demand for them.

(c) The good must be capable of being passed from one person to another, i.e., it must be *transferable.* People cannot sell what they cannot give and won't buy what they cannot receive or control. It is because they do not satisfy this criterion that good health, pleasant disposition, beauty and intelligence are not economic goods even though they satisfy the first two criteria of possessing utility and are scarce in relation to the demand for them in the sense that not everybody has them though all desire them

10.9. It is only when goods possess all of the foregoing three attributes that they are capable of being bought and sold and thus command a price. From which you will realise that the distinguishing feature of economic goods is the fact that they command a price.

10.10. Whether or not a good is an economic good is not fixed for all time. As societies develop and attitudes change, facilities which were free and not scarce become scarce and command a price. In the context of the problem of pollution, clean air and clean water become economic goods. Privacy and silence have become economic goods in modern urban societies.

10.11. We desire goods because we know that we will derive utility from them. When we say that we prefer one good to another good, we are stating that at that particular point in time the good which we prefer is capable of providing us with more utility than is the other good. While we are aware that utility is derived from goods, and through our preferences we rank goods in terms of the utility which they provide, nevertheless it is not possible to quantify or measure utility. It is possible to say that an apple is preferred to a bar of chocolate, because an apple gives more utility, but it is not possible to measure the difference in utility.

10.12. However, it is much easier to explain the concept of utility and to understand it if we assume that it is possible to measure utility. For this reason we will speak of deriving (say) 20 utils of satisfaction from the consumption of an apple at a particular point in time, utils being the units in which we will express the measurement of utility. It should be clearly understood that the conclusions are in no way dependent on utility being measurable. Through a technique known as Indifference Curve Analysis the same conclusions can be arrived at through stating preferences between goods rather than quantifying the measurement of utility.

10.13. Diminishing Marginal Utility

In section 10.3 it was explained that utility is not a quality inherent in a commodity. In addition it was shown in section 10.4 that the utility which is derived from commodities varies between people and even varies with the same person at different point in time. From this you will realise that marginal utility is not constant. If a person eats one apple he gets a certain amount of utility from doing so, if he eats a second apple though he enjoys an increase in (total) utility, the utility from the second apple is less than the utility from the first apple i.e. his marginal utility will be lower. Similarly the marginal utility from the third apple will be even lower. All of this is shown in Table 10.7.

10.14. Law of diminishing marginal utility

The Law of Diminishing Marginal Utility states that as a person acquires additional units of a commodity, marginal utility eventually diminishes. Note that the Law does not state that total utility will diminish, i.e. that marginal utility is negative. While this may happen eventually, consumers are unlikely to persist in consuming the commodity to that stage particularly if they must pay for it. In table 10.7 the sixth apple provides no additional utility (marginal utility is zero) consequently a person would not pay anything in order to acquire it. The seventh apple in this table is shown as having negative marginal utility i.e. marginal disutility, since total utility is reduced by consuming it. In that case not only would a person not buy it but they might even pay to avoid eating it. Because in real life things are unlikely to come to this the Law of Diminishing Marginal Utility merely confines itself to stating that total utility increases at a diminishing rate i.e. marginal utility declines. In terms of table 10.7 the demand for the good in terms of paying a price to acquire it would cease after five apples have been eaten.

10.15. Possible exceptions to the law of diminishing marginal utility

(a) The Law of Diminishing Marginal Utility begins to operate only after a certain point called the origin. The origin is the minimum quantity of the commodity which can be used effectively and until this stage has been reached marginal utility may not diminish. A person who uses one spoonful of sugar in his tea would find diminished utility from a second spoonful of sugar. We don't say the first grain of sugar, the second grain of sugar etc.; in fact, the utility of grains of sugar may increase up to a spoonful as the person gets the taste of sugar. Similarly we talk about a meal rather than minutely small portions of food.

    It is to include this concept of the origin that the word "eventually" is contained in the statement of the Law in Section 10.14.

(b) The Law of Diminishing Marginal Utility presumes that there has not elapsed a period of time sufficiently long to permit a change in taste, e.g. if a person eats a number of apples, each additional one consumed will give diminished marginal utility. However, if a person eats one apple on Monday, one apple on Tuesday and one apple on Wednesday, because of the time which has elapsed between the eating of each apple, there is no reason to suppose that the Wednesday apple will give less satisfaction than the Tuesday apple or the Monday apple. To make the same point from another aspect, how often have you desired something which you had rejected or refused on a previous occasion?

(c) With goods to which one becomes addicted the law will not apply. For this reason, up to the origin, such goods may be supplied free or cheap, the price being progressively increased as one becomes addicted.

(d) Medicine — the second dose may be just as important as the initial one. Perhaps the successive doses may be considered to be part of a single treatment, and the single treatment is the origin.

10.16. Observations from every day behaviour which confirm the existence of the Law of Diminishing Marginal Utility

(a) We don't spend all of our money on the same item of expenditure. If we spend our first £ on clothes it is because we prefer clothes to the other possible items of expenditure available to us. We don't persist in spending all our money on clothes, we eventually spend money on something else (say entertainment). This is because the marginal utility from further expenditure on clothes has diminished to such an extent that we gain extra utility by transferring expenditure to entertainment.

(b) Sellers often offer quantity discounts to consumers. While this may be because the seller can enjoy production economies at higher levels of output, it may also be a recognition of the Law of Diminishing Marginal Utility with the result that the additional quantities will not be bought unless the unit price on marginal items is reduced. Even if there are economies of scale why would the seller not sell at the original price and make a greater profit if the Law of Diminishing Marginal Utility did not apply?

This situation may be contrasted with 10.15.(c) above where marginal units are subject to a higher price.

(c) There is a limit to the amount which people consume, even of free goods.

(d) The fact that a consumer has a downward sloping demand curve for a commodity is often quoted as an illustration of diminishing marginal utility. This may be so but care should be taken with this example, because if a person buys just one type of commodity, and even if the marginal utility of the good was constant, according as the consumer spends money and therefore has less money, the marginal utility of the money remaining to him rises and he might cease buying the good (or purchase it only at a lower price) even if its marginal utility was not diminishing.

10.17. Consumers seek maximum satisfaction

In discussing most topics we make certain assumptions, e.g. if I am speaking to you I assume you are capable of understanding what I say; when I use terms like "television", I assume you know the meaning of the term. These assumptions which we are continually making are seldom specified — they are taken for granted. However, very often, when learning is of a formal type, assumptions are clearly specified. Students sometimes find this to be "off putting", since they would have taken the assumptions for granted had they not been specified. The following are the assumptions regarding the purchasing behaviour of consumers.

(a) Consumers must purchase the goods which they require, therefore their ability to acquire goods is related to their purchasing power.

(b) The consumer's income is not sufficiently large to permit him to purchase all of the goods which he requires — his resources are said to be limited. This introduces the element of having to choose between goods — the purchase of one good precludes the purchase of some other good.

Rational Consumer

(c)   A consumer will act rationally, given his preferences. this does not necessarily mean that a consumer acts in a manner which society considers sensible. Rational means that a consumer acts in a manner consistent with his preferences — if he prefers fruit to chocolate and they both cost the same, then a rational consumer will purchase fruit. An alcoholic who wears rags and is starving himself to death would, in the present use of the term, be acting rationally since, because of his disease, alcohol satisfies his desire better than anything else.

(d)   The Law of Diminishing Marginal Utility applies.

(e)   The consumer sets out to derive maximum utility (best value) from his resources. This means that the consumer spends his limited resources in the manner which, given his tastes and desires, provides him with the most satisfaction.

10.18. The Law of Equi-Marginal Returns

This law refers to the manner in which a consumer who is seeking maximum utility will spend his income: *The Law of Equi-Marginal Returns states that a consumer will enjoy maximum satisfaction when the ratio of marginal utility to price is the same for all of the different types of goods which he buys.*

i.e.
$$\frac{MU_1}{P_1} = \frac{MU_2}{P_2}$$

2 items the same price, the one with greater utility is purchased

Example (a). If there are two items which can be purchased for 20p, say an apple from which the consumer gets 17 units of satisfaction and a bar of chocolate from which the consumer gets 12 units of satisfaction, the consumer will purchase the apple because he gets more satisfaction from it and they both cost the same price.

Relative prices change and expenditure pattern changes

Example (b). Let us change the previous example slightly and imagine that the bar of chocolate costs 10p and the apple costs 20p and the levels of satisfaction are as in the previous example, viz., 17 units of satisfaction from the apple and 12 units of satisfaction from the bar of chocolate. The consumer will now buy the bar of chocolate rather than the apple, not because his preference between the two goods has changed but their relative prices have changed and the chocolate now is better value than the apple. The chocolate provides $12/10 = 1.2$ utils of satisfaction per 1p while the apple provides $17/20 = 0.85$ utils of satisfaction per 1p.

Example (c).

Quantity	Marginal Utility of Commodity A	Marginal Utility of Commodity B
1	110	97
2	103	87
3	94	75
4	74	60
5	51	40
6	26	18

When both commodities are the same price, highest marginal utility determines what is purchased

If the selling price of each of these commodities is £1.00, and a consumer had £1.00 to spend, he would buy one of commodity A since this provides him with the greater satisfaction. If he had £2.00 to spend he would buy 2 units of commodity A = 110 + 113 = 213 utils of satisfaction; if £3.00 was being spent, 2 units of commodity A and one unit of commodity B would provide the highest possible level of satisfaction for an expenditure of this amount and so on.

Relative prices change – ratio of marginal utility to price is determinant of purchasing behaviour

Example (d). Let us change slightly example no. 10.18 (c). Let us suppose that instead of both goods being the same price commodity A costs £1.00, but commodity B costs 80p. In these circumstances the expenditure pattern would change because the ratio of marginal utility to price has changed for these goods. 1 unit of commodity B would be chosen first since this provides 97/80 = 1.21 utils of satisfaction per 1p. Next 1 unit of commodity A would be bought since this provides 1.1 utils of satisfaction per 1p spent. If £6.00 was being spent, 3 of commodity A and 3 of commodity B would be bought and MU/P = 0.94 for each commodity.

$$\frac{MU_1}{P_1} = \frac{MU_2}{P_2}$$

is utility maximisation

10.19. The above examples show that, by concentrating on the ratio between marginal utility and price and adjusting his purchasing pattern accordingly, the consumer gets maximum satisfaction. When the ratio of marginal utility to price is the same for all of the different types of goods which he purchases, there is no way that the consumer can change his purchasing behaviour and increase his total utility. The consumer is said to be at equilibrium.

Savings can be included

10.20. The Law of Equi-Marginal Returns does not exclude savings. When a consumer saves, the savings may give him satisfaction through providing him with security in the present or through the anticipation of security in old age. If savings are being accumulated in order to enable a large purchase in the future i.e., house, motor car or holiday, the utility in the future is considered by the saver to provide greater utility than he could derive through spending all of his income in the present.

10.21. The price effect is a combination of an income effect and a substitution effect

It has been shown that when the price of a good changed, a consumer adjusted his spending pattern so that he bought more of the good which had been reduced in price. But can we be sure that this will always happen? That question can be answered only by analysing the effect of a price alteration (let us say a price reduction). When a good is reduced in price there are two effects; as is the usual practice in economics, we will isolate each of these elements in order to analyse the total or combined effect.

(a)   **Price falls but real income remains constant.**

It affects the real income of the consumer — his real income is increased as a result of the reduction in price — he is "better off". Normally when the price of a good falls our real income is increased but in this case let us assume that, when the price of the good falls, our money income is reduced by whatever benefit we enjoy from the price reduction, i.e. our real income remains unchanged. you may imagine a situation where as a result of a reduction in the price of some article we would be £1 per week better off but at the same time our income tax liability is increased by £1 per week so that our real income remains unchanged. Based on what has been said in relation to the Law of Equi-Marginal Returns, more would be bought of the good which has become cheaper relative to other goods because the ratio of its MU/P has risen and therefore this ratio (and consequently value for money) is greater in respect of this good. The consumer will have found his new equilibrium only when the diminished marginal utility, through increased purchases of this good, and the increased marginal utility, through buying less of the other good, result in MU/P being the same for all of the goods which are being bought by the consumer concerned. This is what happened in example 10.18 (c) and 10.18 (d). (Remember the Law of Diminishing Marginal Utility, 10.14 et seq.).

It will be noted that the consumer in his purchasing behaviour has substituted the good which has become cheaper for the goods which have become relatively dearer. *This is known as the substitution effect and is due to a change in relative prices.* You will notice in this example that the only thing that has changed is relative prices, real income was unchanged. *The substitution effect is always positive in favour of the relatively cheaper good (i.e. there will be a tendency to buy more of the good which has become relatively cheaper).*

(b)   **Real income is increased while relative prices remain unchanged.**

The good which has been reduced in price becomes cheaper relative to all other goods which have not been subject to any alteration in price. The easiest way to imagine this example is to consider that prices of all goods remain unchanged when money income is increased. The effect of this development on the quantity of each good purchased is not clearcut. For most goods, more of them will be bought when real income is increased as was discussed earlier — these goods are known as *Normal Goods.* However, as mentioned in section 9.37. there are goods known as *Inferior Goods* and there is a tendency to purchase a smaller quantity of these goods when real income is increased. So all we can say in this case is that for most goods, i.e., normal goods, a greater quantity of them will be bought when real income is increased but with some goods, i.e., inferior goods, a smaller quantity of them may be bought when real income is increased. *The change in the demand for a good as a result of an alteration in real income is known as the income effect; it is usually positive, i.e., demand and real income move in the same direction, so that an increase (decrease) in real income results in an increase (decrease) in the level of demand for the good.*

When there is a price change there is (a) an income effect because real income changes, and there is (b) a substitution effect because relative prices change. Thus the price effect is a combination of these two elements as set out below.

Table 10.21. Effect of a price reduction

	Substitution Effect (when relative price of a good changes)	Income Effect (When real income changes)	Price Effect (When price of good changes)	Type of Good
	Column 1	Column 2	Column 1 + 2	Column 4
A	A tendency to buy more (because the good is relatively cheaper) +	A tendency to buy more (positive income effect i.e. a normal good) +	More bought +	Normal Good
B	A tendency to buy more +	Tendency to buy less as real income increases (negative income effect i.e. an inferior good) —	More bought because positive substitution effect is greater than negative income effect +	Inferior Good but not a Giffen Good
C	A tendency to buy more +	Tendency to buy less as real income increases (negative income effect i.e. an inferior good —	Less bought because negative income effect outweighs positive substitution effect —	Inferior Good and Giffen Good

Giffen good

10.22. Where the negative income effect is stronger than the positive substitution effect we have Giffen Goods, as in case C in table 10.21 above. In case B in table 10.21, though we are dealing with an inferior good, it is not a Giffen good because the positive substitution effect outweighs the negative income effect and thus the good follows the normal law of demand in that more of it is bought when its price is reduced and less of it is bought when its price is increased. It could be said in regard to case B that an even greater quantity of the good would be bought when its price is reduced were it not for the fact that it is an inferior good.

All Giffen goods are inferior but not all inferior goods are Giffen goods

10.23. Table 10.21 illustrates the point that while all Giffen goods are inferior goods (case C above), not all inferior goods are Giffen goods (case B above). For a good to be a Giffen good not only must it be an inferior good but there must be a considerable negative income effect in order to outweigh the positive substitution effect. For this to happen a large amount of income must be spent on the good so that any change in its price has a considerable effect on the level of real income of consumers — see also sections 9.34 to 9.39.

10.24. *Consumer's surplus is the difference between what a person actually pays for a good and the maximum amount which he would have been prepared to pay rather than go without the good.*

Referring back to the table in Example 10.18 (c), in which we considered the case of a consumer who purchases 3 units of commodity A, which are being sold at £1.00 each. Since the consumer paid £1.00 for the third unit which gives him 94 utils of satisfaction, he must have felt that 94 utils of satisfaction were worth £1.00. However, the first item of Commodity A which he purchased gave 110 utils of satisfaction and thus he would have been prepared to pay a higher price for this unit. Since he got it for £1 he obtained this unit at a price lower than he would have been prepared to pay rather than go without the good, i.e. he enjoys a "consumer's surplus". This same concept of consumers' surplus may be illustrated by means of a demand schedule and a demand curve of a consumer.

Price P.	Quantity Demanded
120	1
110	2
100	3
90	4
80	5

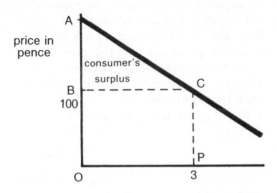

Fig. 10.24 Demand curve showing consumer's surplus.

If the selling price is 100p, the consumer purchases 3 units. However, by reference to the demand schedule it can be seen that the consumer was prepared to pay 120p for the first unit and 110p for the second unit, whereas each of the units which he purchased only cost him 100p — he enjoyed a consumer surplus in the sense that he would have been prepared to pay a higher price for the first 2 units of the good rather than go without them. This consumer surplus is depicted by triangle ABC in Fig. 10.24 i.e., that portion of the area under the demand curve which lies above the revenue rectangle. The revenue rectangle in Fig. 10.24 is OBCP, i.e. unit price multiplied by quantity.

10.25. Value

Value in use and value in Exchange

The value of a commodity is usually expressed in money terms and the price of a commodity is often considered to be its value in terms of money.

Earlier economists distinguished two concepts of value — "Value in use" and "Value in exchange". Value in use was based on the utility which could be derived from the good, e.g. utility is derived from food when we consume it. Value in exchange is a reference to the ratio in which goods exchange for each other — the relative prices of goods, e.g. if a pair of shoes costs £30.00 and a suit costs £60.00, then 2 pairs of shoes have the same value in exchange as one suit.

10.26. Adam Smith (1723—1790), an early economist, found it necessary

Smith's paradox of value

to draw this distinction between value in use and value in exchange in order to explain the fact that some trivial type goods which were not necessary in order to sustain life, e.g. jewellery, exchanged for large sums of money while at the same time essential goods such as water had a very low price.

This dilemma became known as *Smith's paradox of value*.

10.27. This paradox of value arose because a distinction was not drawn between marginal utility and total utility. In Section 10.18 the law of Equi-Marginal Returns showed that it is marginal utility which determines whether or not a consumer will buy an item. Thus it is marginal utility which determines the price which will be paid. Since water is in abundant supply its marginal utility is low; in contrast luxury items such as jewellery are scarce and therefore their marginal utility is high. Since it is marginal utility which determines price, the price of the luxury items will be high. It was on the basis of this solution that Adam Smith propounded the distinction between value in use and value in exchange.

Marginal utility influences price

10.28. Labour Theory of Value

David Ricardo (1772—1823), an English economist, also distinguished two types of value. He considered that there were certain goods which had a high exchange value because the supply of them was very limited, e.g., works of art. However, he put forward a labour theory of value; he stated that the vast majority of goods acquired value through the quantity of labour required to bring them into existence and that the exchange value of commodities will be in the ratio of the quantity of labour which was necessary to produce them, e.g. one pair of shoes was made by one man in one day and one table was made by a man in two days then one table would exchange for two pairs of shoes. Machinery was seen as being the stock of labour which was used to produce goods.

All value accrues to workers

10.29. Karl Marx (1818—1883) and his followers used this labour theory of value as a basis to declare that, since commodities gained value through the quantity of labour which they embody, all value accrued to the workers.

10.30. Criticisms of Labour Theory of Value

There is a difficulty in measuring the amount of labour which is necessary in order to bring a commodity into existence. The length of time which was required by workers in order to complete the commodity, which was the basis adopted by Adam Smith, was not a satisfactory unit of measurement because all workers are not equally efficient and thus they require varying periods of time in order to accomplish identical tasks. Karl Marx attempted to overcome this problem of inefficient or misdirected labour by using as a yardstick or unit of measurement the amount of "socially necessary labour" required.

In addition the labour theory of value ignores the influence of demand on the determination of price and value.

QUESTIONS

Q1.   Write an explanatory note on Utility.

Q2.   Explain some reasons why people might desire to obtain a good.

Q3.   Distinguish between Marginal Utility and Total Utility.

Q4.   What are the characteristics of economic goods?

Q5.   Explain the Law of Diminishing Marginal Utility.

Q6.   Set out possible exceptions to the Law of Diminishing Marginal Utility.

Q7.   Explain the Law of Equi-Marginal Returns.

Q8.   Show that a change in the selling price of a good causes income and substitution effects.

Q9.   Are all inferior goods Giffen goods?

Q10. Explain Consumer's Surplus.

Q11. Distinguish between value in use and value in exchange.

Q12. Write an explanatory note on the Labour Theory of Value.

11   Costs of Production

11.1. An analysis of costs

Just as utility constitutes the basis of demand, since it is because goods possess utility that they are demanded, costs of production form the basis of supply. For a given level of demand, it is the cost of producing the good which determines whether or not any supply will be forthcoming and/or the quantity which will be supplied.

11.2. Total costs of production vary with the level of output. If the level of output is increased, total costs of production are increased, conversely if the level of production is reduced total costs of production are reduced — this relationship is shown in Fig. 11.2.

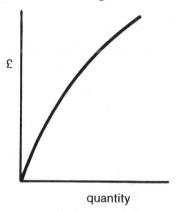

quantity

Fig. 11.2. Total cost of production is related to the level of output.

11.3. Total costs of production are composed of two elements. Fixed Costs and Variable Costs:—

Fixed costs do not vary within a wide range of output

(a)   There are certain resources used in production which are capable of supporting a higher level of output without any increase in cost, e.g. factory rent and rates. Once commitments of this nature are entered into, the charge must be met and the charge does not vary irrespective of whether the factory is on short time working or being operated to its fullest capacity. Because these costs do not vary within a wide range of output they are known as *Fixed costs*
It is important to note that fixed costs should not be considered to be fixed irrespective of the level of output, but rather that it is possible to accommodate relatively large variations in the level of output without any change in the level of fixed cost. In most cases the range of output which is under discussion is the range within which fixed costs do not vary, in which case fixed costs are as shown in Fig. 11.3.1.

Fixed costs
may
eventually
change

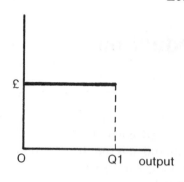

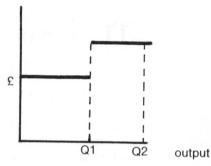

Fig. 11.3.1. Fixed costs does not change within the range of output.

Fig. 11.3.2. The level of fixed cost eventually changes.

In Fig. 11.3 1 costs are fixed for levels of output between zero and Q_1, but if a higher level of output is required the level of fixed costs increases as shown in Fig. 11.3.2. An example of this would be if premises are hired, the rent must be paid even if the premises are being used very little. The same rent will be paid irrespective of the level of use so that between zero and Q_1 in Fig. 11.3.1 the charge does not vary. However, if the firm wishes to increase its output to a level beyond the capacity of the premises, e.g. to Q_2, it will have to acquire an extension to its premises and thus the firm will have to pay a higher rent and its fixed costs are increased as shown in Fig. 11.3.2.

Fixed costs arise because of the indivisible nature of certain factors of production

(b) These fixed costs arise because of the indivisible nature of certain factors of production; it is not possible to buy or hire these factors in a sufficiently small size, so that the entrepreneur must hire or buy a size in excess of his immediate requirements. An entrepreneur may wish to commence business with one machine and the four people who are required to operate the machine. However, when he seeks a suitable premises he finds that the factories which are most suitable for him are big enough to accommodate 5 machines and the 20 people who are required to work them. If each machine working full capacity produces 100 items per day, the entrepreneur can increase his output up to 500 items per day (i.e., the output of the 5 machines and their crews which the premises can accommodate), without having any increased charge in respect of premises — the cost is fixed up to an output of 500 items, until such time as he wishes to increase his productive capacity or the lease expires.

Fixed costs and the short run period

(c) Fixed costs are very much a part of the concept of the short run period. *The short run period is defined as a period when the quantity supplied of at least one factor of production is fixed, consequently the costs appropriate to that factor of production will be fixed in the short run.*

11.3.2. Variable costs

Variable costs are costs which are directly related to the level of output. When the level of output increases variable costs increase and when the level of output is reduced variable costs reduce.

Average variable cost is total variable cost divided by the number of units produced.

Examples of variable costs

(a) Raw materials are the most obvious example of variable cost. The more items that are produced the greater the quantity of raw materials which are required. Electric power to propel machinery is another example.

Are wages a variable cost?

(b) Wages may, or may not, be a variable cost depending on circumstances. If workers are dismissed during slack periods and re-employed when the level of demand rises, then wages constitute a variable cost. However, because of the strength of trade unions, or the prohibitive cost of redundancy payments together with the cost of recruiting and training new workers when the recession ends, some employers may not dismiss workers immediately there is a reduction in the level of production. They may consider the downturn in the level of activity to be of a temporary nature. This is known as *Labour Hoarding*. If the fall in demand persists, then the firm will release the workers.

Existing slack caters for initial upturn in level of demand

Because of this hoarding of labour, when there is an increase in the level of demand as an economy emerges from a depression, usually there is not an immediate increase in the level of employment. The initial increase in demand is met through an increase in productivity from existing workers who had previously been underemployed. For these reasons wages are often considered to be a semi-variable cost.

Table 11.5. Cost structure of a firm

Col. 1	Col. 2	Col. 3	Col. 4	Col. 5	Col. 6	Col. 7	Col. 8
Units of Output	Fixed Cost	Variable Cost	Total Cost, i.e. Cols. 2 + 3	Fixed Cost per unit produced	Average Variable Cost i.e. Col 3 ÷ 1	Average Cost, i.e. Cols 4 ÷ 1	Marginal Cost (see Col. 4)
	£	£	£	£	£	£	£
100	2 500	5 830	8 330	25.00	58.30	83.30	–
101	2 500	5 900	8 400	24.75	58.42	83.17	70
102	2 500	5 975	8 475	24.51	58.58	83.09	75
103	2.500	6 052	8 552	24.27	58.76	83.03	77
104	2 500	6 132	8 632	24.04	58.96	83.00	80
105	2 500	6 215	8 715	23.81	59.19	83.00	83
106	2 500	6 302	8 802	23.58	59.45	83.04	87
107	2 500	6 394	8 894	23.36	59.76	83.12	92

11.4. *Average cost of production* which is known also as *unit cost of production* is obtained by dividing total cost of production by the number of units produced.

11.5. *Marginal cost of production* is the alteration in total cost of production when the level of output is altered by one unit.

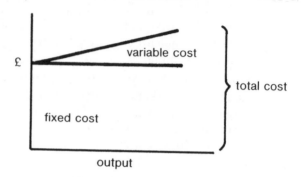

Fig. 11.5. Fixed costs plus variable equals total cost.

11.6. The costs incurred by a firm for which it has to pay a price are known as *Explicit Costs* e.g. if I pay a plumber £50 that is an explicit cost. An *Implicit Cost* is a cost which does not entail the paying out of money e.g. if I invest £1 000 in my own business I probably will not pay myself interest on this money. However, if I had invested this money elsewhere I would have received interest of (say) £100 so that there is an implicit cost of £100 involved in investing money in my own business. The same type of situation may occur through members of the family working in the family business if they are paid less than the appropriate rate of wages which a non-family member would receive.

Opportunity cost and explicit and implicit costs

11.7. *Opportunity cost is the cost of any thing in terms of alternatives foregone.* It is usually measured by explicit cost, i.e., the price which I pay for something represents the sacrifice which I must make in order to acquire it. For example if I pay £10 for a book, the sacrifice is all the other items which I could have purchased for £10 and which I must now do without. However, as explained in Section 11.6, in order to calculate true opportunity cost, any implicit costs which are appropriate must be included. The opportunity cost concept is still appropriate even when no money is involved e.g. the opportunity cost of watching a television programme is all of the other activities which you are precluded from undertaking as a result of watching the television programme.

Opportunity cost is never less than money cost (price)

11.8. Since opportunity cost is defined as the cost of anything in terms of alternative foregone the price which is paid for an item precludes the buying of other goods to this value. Thus these other goods are foregone and constitute opportunity cost. Very often this money cost (price) measures opportunity cost to an adequate degree of accuracy. However just to show that opportunity cost is never less than money cost it should be realised that buying an item also entails a time cost since travelling to where the good is to be purchased is another form of cost. Implicit costs may also be relevant if, for example, there is wear and tear on the motor car in travelling to buy the good.

11.9. Relationship between average cost and marginal cost

There is a precise mathematical relationship between average cost (or revenue) and marginal cost (or revenue). This relationship always applies. Though it is being explained in terms of average cost and marginal cost, it applies also to average revenue and marginal revenue.

(a) *If marginal cost is lower than average cost then average cost must be falling.*

In table 11.5. marginal cost is less than average cost for the production of the 100th, 101st, 102nd and 103rd item and average cost falls from £83.30 to £83.00. You will note that even though marginal cost is rising over this range of output, average cost is falling. It is not a case of whether marginal cost is rising or falling but merely a case of whether marginal cost is greater or less than average cost. If marginal cost is less than average cost then average cost will fall and vice versa.

(b) *If marginal cost is equal to average cost then average cost will remain unchanged.*

The marginal cost of producing the 105th item is £83.00. As this is the same as the average cost, this average cost remains unchanged at £83.00. Thus the same average cost applies when 104 items and 105 items are being produced.

(c) *If marginal cost is greater than average cost then average cost will rise*

For the production of the 106th and 107th item, marginal cost at £87.00 and £92.00 respectively is greater than average cost and thus average cost rises from £83.00 to £83.12.

(d) It may be noted in table 11.5 that marginal cost is equal to average cost when average cost is at a minimum.

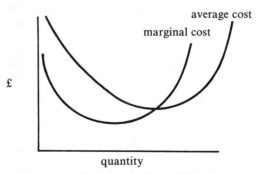

Fig. 11.9. Diagram showing relationship between marginal cost and average cost as derived from Table 11.5.

11.10. Unit (or average) cost in the short-run period

Short Run Average Cost refers to the effect on unit cost of production when there is an alteration in the level of production in the short run, i.e., while the supply of at least one factor of production cannot be altered. Short run average cost curves are usually depicted as being U shaped as shown in Fig. 11.9.

11.10.1. The downward section of the U curve is attributable to the following two reasons:—

Specialisation reduces unit costs

(a)   As the level of production increases there is sufficient work to justify the employment of specialists or to permit existing workers to concentrate on a narrow range of duties. As workers improve their dexterity through the constant repetition of a narrow range of operations, the time taken to produce each unit is reduced. The greater volume of output justifies also the introduction of cost reducing specialised machinery.

Fixed cost per unit produced is reduced as output expands

(b)   As a firm expands its level of production, its costs of production do not increase pro rata, e.g., fixed costs are defined as costs which do not vary over a certain range of output so that as the level of production increases the proportion of fixed cost which is included in unit cost is reduced. This is shown in Col. 5. of table 11.5. This spreading of the constant fixed charge over an increasing level of production reduces the fixed cost per unit produced, and thus contributes to a reduction in short run average cost.

11.11. (a) and (b) above explain the reduction in unit cost as shown in the downward section, $\bigvee$ of the cost curve. The question to be answered now is why should the curve eventually slope upwards, i.e., the $\bigvee$ portion. The increase in short run unit costs is explained by the *Law of Diminishing Marginal Returns*, which is known also as the *Law of Diminishing Returns*.

Law of diminishing marginal returns

11.11. *The Law of Diminishing Marginal Returns states that as increasing quantities of a variable factor of production are combined with a fixed factor of production, a stage will eventually be reached where marginal returns begin to decline:*
    This law is usually explained by taking two factors of production —land being the fixed factor (say one field) and labour being the variable factor.

In table 11.11 diminishing marginal returns begin to set in after the fourth man was employed. Notice that the factor of production, land, remained fixed in supply throughout the example and labour was the variable factor.

Table 11.11. Law of Diminishing Marginal Returns.

Land	No. of men employed	Total output	Marginal output
1	1	10	—
1	2	24	14
1	3	40	16
1	4	58	18
1	5	73	15
1	6	86	13
1	7	98	12

If law did not apply the whole population could be fed from a given piece of land

11.12. The common sense of this is easily seen by realising that if it did not apply, the whole population could be fed by devoting enough workers to the cultivation of a given piece of land. While it is possible that if the above example was taken far enough and ever increasing numbers of workers were employed in cultivating a single piece of land, then marginal output could eventually be negative, e.g., if so many workers were employed in the field that additional workers prevented existing workers from working as efficiently as they had been. However, it is not very realistic to take such an extreme point of view and the law does not go this far, it merely states that marginal returns will decline, i.e., total output will increase but at a diminishing rate.

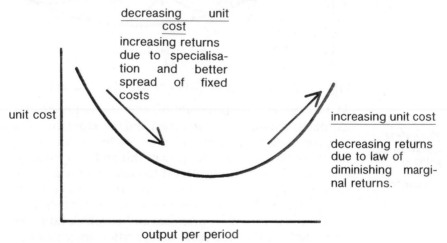

decreasing unit cost

increasing returns due to specialisation and better spread of fixed costs

unit cost

increasing unit cost

decreasing returns due to law of diminishing marginal returns.

output per period

Fig. 11.12. Short run average cost curve.

11.13. There are many ways in which factors of production can be combined by an entrepreneur in order to produce a given level of output. If an entrepreneur wishes to gain the maximum profit he will wish to keep his costs of production as low as possible. Of great assistance to the entrepreneur in keeping his costs of production as low as possible would be some information on the level of demand for his product; he does not know with certainty the quantity of his product which will be bought per day, per week, per year and what will happen in future years regarding the level of demand for his product. The manner in which he would set about producing 100 units per day would be different from the way in which he would organise his business in order to produce 10 units per week. In addition there arises the question of the level of demand in the future. The entrepreneur must decide if he should buy a machine which has a maximum output of 100 units per day and then buy a second machine when demand increases or buy a larger machine initially even though it will not be fully employed, in the beginning at least. Similar type decisions have to be made regarding the size of the factory and in respect of other factors of production.

These alternatives are set out in Fig. 11.13 where short run average cost curve (SRAC) no. 1 represents a smaller size operation than SRAC curve no. 2, while this in turn represents a smaller size operation than SRAC curve no. 3.

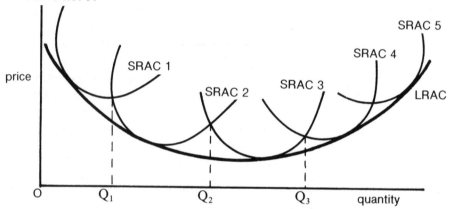

Fig. 11.13. The effect of different size plants on unit costs of production.

11.14. The greater the scale of operations the greater the amount of capital which the firm must invest and therefore the greater the risk which the firm undertakes, since it stands to lose more money in the event of failure of the business. Because of this and also since the demand for the good may increase only after it has been on the market for some time, a firm may decide to commence activities with a small scale of operation, e.g., as depicted by curve 1 in Fig. 11.13. As the level of demand increases the firm may extend its premises and purchase larger and/or additional machinery so that the scale of operation increases to that depicted by curve 2. Similarly, when warranted, there is further development to the scale of operations depicted by curve 3.

11.15. Up to the level of output Q_1 in Fig. 11.13 unit costs of production are cheapest when the scale of operation chosen by the firm is that represented by $SRAC_1$. If the firm is producing a level of output greater than Q_1 with the scale of operations shown by $SRAC_1$ then its unit costs are higher than necessary since by expanding its scale of operations to that shown by $SRAC_2$ the firm would have lower unit costs. In order to make the maximum amount of profit the firm, as quickly as it can, will change its scale of operation to that represented by $SRAC_2$. Similarly the scale of operations represented by $SRAC_3$ is more appropriate for levels of output between Q_2 and Q_3. The same type of analysis applies to $SRAC_4$ and $SRAC_5$.

By joining these sections of the curves as shown by the thick black line in Fig. 11.13 there is derived a curve of the lowest unit cost of production for each level of output. You can in fact imagine these SRAC curves to be so close together that there is a uniquely efficient SRAC for each individual level of output. The joining of the lowest point on these infinitely close SRAC curves results in the LRAC curve in Fig. 11.13.

11.16. Long run period

Definition of long run period

Thus the thick black line in Fig. 11.13 is the average cost curve which would emerge over time as the firm adjusts its scale of operations to the level of demand in order to produce its output at the lowest possible unit cost. Such a period is known as the *long run and this is defined as a period sufficiently long to permit an alteration in the quantity used of all of the factors of production.*

Long run period is not a calendar period and it varies from industry to industry

(a) The long run period does not refer to a calendar period. It is not three months, one year or five years, it all depends on the industry concerned. In the case of an electricity undertaking the long period may be a period in excess of seven years, if this is the length of time required in order to commission a generating station from the time the initial plans are drawn up. In contrast to this if a man can hire premises on a week-to-week basis and if he buys his other requirements on a daily basis, then in this case the long run period would not be greater than one week.

Is it true to say that in the long run all factors of production are variable?

(b) Because the long run period is a period sufficiently long to enable all of the factors of production to be varied, students often elaborate on this and state that in the long run all factors of production are variable, therefore there are no fixed factors of production and no fixed costs, in the long run. In the example in (a) above when the weekly hire of the premises had terminated, the entrepreneur had no fixed costs. However, in order to continue in business he must have a premises so he immediately renews the contract or signs a contract for a different premises, for a further period. At the moment when his control had expired and before he had signed his new contract all of his factors of production were variable, but immediately he signs the contract, he is once more subject to fixed costs and has entered a new short run period. Just as a week is made up of seven days and a year is made up of 12 months, similarly a long run period is made up of a number of short run periods; this coalescence of short run into long run is shown in Fig. 11.13.

Scale of operations and minimum costs of production

(c)   From what has already been written it should be realised that all of the production possibilities which are available to a firm in the short run are available to it in the long run also. The long run average cost curve is derived from the combination of those short run average cost curves at which unit costs of production are lowest. Thus if the price at which factors of production are purchased does not increase, then unit costs of production will never be greater in the long run period than they would in the short run period.

If the purchase price of factors of production does not increase, unit costs in long run will not exceed short run unit cost

11.17. Shape of long run average cost curve

(a)   The long run average cost (LRAC) curve is generally depicted as being U shaped. In the long run as the level of output increases, the scale of operations increases and certain economies, known as "Economies of Scale" accrue to these larger sized firms. These economies of scale which result in a reduction in average cost of production as the firm increases its scale of operations are reflected in the downward sloping section of LRAC curve in Fig. 11.17. *Increasing returns to scale* is another term used to signify economies of scale. Economies of scale occur when an increase in the factors of production used (inputs) results in a more than proportionate increase in the level of output e.g. when all inputs are doubled and output is more than doubled.

Downward sloping section of LRAC curve is attributable to economies of scale

(b)   The upward sloping section of the LRAC curve signifies that average cost is increasing, and this is attributed to *Diseconomies of Scale. Decreasing Returns to Scale* is another term which signifies diseconomies of scale. Diseconomies of Scale occur when an increase in the factors of production used (inputs) results in a less than proportionate increase in the level of output e.g. when all inputs are doubled the new level of output is less than twice the original level of output.

Upward sloping of LRAC curve is due to diseconomies of scale

(c)   It should not be thought that at certain levels of output economies of scale apply and at other ranges of output diseconomies of scale

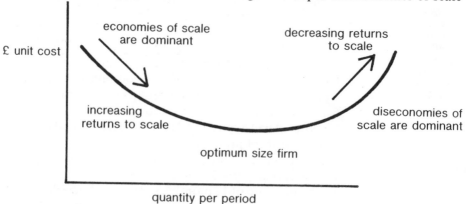

Fig. 11.17. Long run average cost curve.

Economies and diseconomies interact over ranges of output

apply. It is more realistic to envisage both economies and diseconomies of scale interacting at all ranges of output. When economies of scale are dominant, long run average cost will be reduced and the firm will enjoy increasing returns to scale. If diseconomies of scale are the more dominant, long run average cost will rise and decreasing returns to scale will apply.

Optimum size Firm

11.18. A firm is said to be of optimum size when the factors of production are combined in a manner which results in average cost being at a minimum.

11.19. Economies of Scale

Internal Economies of Scale are economies or benefits which accrue from the increase in the scale of output of an individual firm and they provide benefits to that firm alone. These are usually classified as:-

(a)   Technical Economies of Scale
(b)   Marketing Economies of Scale
(c)   Financial Economies of Scale

(a)   **Technical Economies of Scale**

(i)   Increased use of Machinery —
As the scale of operations increases larger machines which would not be economical in a smaller factory may be employed. Specialised machinery may be introduced.

(ii)   Labour Economies — a greater degree of specialisation by workers is possible. Economies in the use of non-productive workers are possible e.g., accountant, transport supervisor, wages clerk etc.

(iii)   Economies of Construction. The building costs of a 10 000 sq. ft. factory is not 10 times as great as a 1 000 sq. ft. factory. Also there may be economies in the use of land by building upwards if additional floor space is required.

(iv)   Linking of processes into a continuous sequence e.g., a large steel mill may be able to convert ore into pig-iron, iron into crude steel and crude steel into finished steel strips in a continuous process and thereby reduce costs of heating, reheating and transport costs.

(v)   Similarly glass making furnaces must be maintained at high temperatures because the cost of cooling and reheating is prohibitive. In these circumstances unit costs would be lower if the volume of throughput (production) is high.

(b)   **Marketing Economies of Scale**

(i)   Buying: A firm which buys in large quantities can negotiate larger discounts. Costs of ordering, handling, storing and recording do not increase pro rata with the quantities purchased.

(ii)   Selling: There are economies in distribution. If there is a complete van load of deliveries, it is more economical to have a delivery schedule where deliveries are made to specific districts on certain days rather than have the delivery van being driven to a number of districts each day. Similarly there are economies of scale in advertising — as explained in section 14.20.

(c)   **Financial Economies of Scale**

Generally large firms are considered to constitute a lower risk and thus they are likely to be able to borrow at lower rates of interest. In addition large firms may have access to sources of funds which are not available to the smaller firm, e.g., the Stock Exchange.

External Economies of Scale are benefits which accrue from the growth of an industry and thus they may be availed of by all firms in the industry.

External Economies of Scale

(i)   With the growth of an industry, specialised firms to which aspects of the work may be sub-contracted are established, e.g., marine engineering firms near ship building centres.

(ii)   Firms extending their range of production to satisfy the needs of an industry, e.g., the supply of specialised wrappers or containers to the egg industry.

(iii) Manufacturers of machinery will find a sufficiently large demand for specialised machinery to encourage them to concentrate on the production of this type of machinery, e.g., shoe making machinery.

(iv)   The local vocational school may institute classes in order to train workers in the skills required, e.g., glass making classes in Waterford, classes in mineral technology in Athlone.

(v)   The establishment of Marketing Boards and other specialised Agencies to assist the industry, e.g., National Dairy Council.

(vi)   The cost of Research may be shared between firms.

11.20. Diseconomies of Scale
This is the terms applied to the emergence of circumstances which increase unit costs of production as the scale of operations increases.

Internal Diseconomies of Scale

(a)   Management Problems: As a firm grows in size it becomes more difficult to manage and control its activities, so that inefficiencies develop which increase costs. The decision makers within the firm become more remote from the day-to-day working of the firm.

(b)   Accountability Problems: The difficulties associated with account-ability increase, so that it becomes more difficult to control stocks and to monitor efficiency.

(c)   Ratio of non-productive to productive workers increases. The number of administrators or non-productive workers within the firm increases.

(d) Staff Morale: Sometimes workers in larger firms consider themselves to be treated as factors of production "mere cogs in a wheel", rather than people. In these circumstances workers do not identify with the firm, loyalty to the firm is diminished, a "them and us" mentality prevails, the rate of staff turnover is high, costs of retraining increase — all of which increase costs of production.

(e) Firms become vulnerable. When the amount of capital invested in the business is large, it is costly if this is not being fully employed, so that the firm becomes vulnerable to demands make upon it by workers or other groups, e.g., if workers go on strike the expensive machinery will be left idle.

11.21. External diseconomies of scale

This term is applied to unit cost increasing developments, outside the direct control of the firm, which occur as the scale of operations increases. Because they affect all firms, they may be seen as Diseconomies of the Industry. Some examples are:–

(a) Scarcities develop. Firms seek to employ increasing quantities of factors of production as their scale of operation expands which leads to a shortage of the required factors of production and an increase in their price. Alternatively less efficient or less suitable factors have to be employed, which increase unit costs of production.

(b) Firms supplying components to the industry under review experience internal diseconomies of scale and these are further external diseconomies of scale to the industry under review.

(c) A general inability of the infrastructure to keep pace with the increasing demands of the firm, e.g., phone and telex services, houses for workers, adequate public transport, traffic congestion and bottlenecks etc.

Economies of Scale Advantages of Specialisation	Diseconomies of Scale Disadvantages of Specialisation
Work can be subdivided enabling workers to concentrate on a narrow range of activities	The narrower the range of duties in which a person is trained the less adaptable they are when flexibility is required
Through concentration on a narrow range of tasks workers become more skilled	Danger of workers becoming bored by constant repetition of a narrow range of duties
Because tasks are specific training schemes can be introduced	Boredom leads to absenteeism, reduction in output and shoddy workmanship
Greater output and/or improved quality of work	Morale of workforce may weaken leading to industrial unrest

11.22. Explanation of shape of LRAC curve and SRAC curve contrasted

Though both the SRAC curve and the LRAC curve are shown as being U shaped, the explanation differs in respect of the average cost curve for each of these periods. It is *not* correct to attribute the reduction in average unit cost in the short run to economies of scale because in the short run by definition one of the factors of production is fixed in supply. How then could there be a reference to an increase in the scale of operation in the short run? It is, of course, possible to have some alteration in the level of operation in the short run because firms can produce over a (narrow) range of output by using some factors of production more intensively, e.g., workers doing overtime even though the size of the premises or quantity of machinery available is limited in supply in the short run.

The possible variation in the range of output is much greater in the long run when all of the factors of production may be increased and thus the whole *scale* of operations may be increased.

11.23. The Very Long Run

Over the decades there evolve new methods of production — contrast the manner in which production was organised 30 years ago with the methods which are employed today. Gangs of men digging trenches with shovels are replaced by mechanical diggers, concrete is bought from manufacturers ready for use, large sections of buildings are delivered ready-made to sites and are merely assembled. New types of raw materials are developed, e.g., plastics, synthetic rubber etc., machines are invented to undertake tasks which previously had been performed by people. Workers are in better health, better fed, better housed, better educated and trained to carry out their duties. The experience gathered over the years can be communicated to workers by means of training courses, so that the workers of the present do not have to start with no knowledge of the tasks and learn from their own experiences alone, but rather they can build on the experience of others.

Production techniques improve. Engineers are able to combine factors of production in a more economical manner. Cheaper substitute factors of production are invented, e.g., plastic for rubber, machinery to undertake tasks previously performed by people. There are improvements in the quality of labour.

Changes of this nature are gradual and require lengthy periods to evolve and this period is known as the Very Long Run.

The Very Long Run is defined as a period sufficiently long for technology and the quality of factors of production to change. It affects the supply of commodities in the following ways.

(a) Products can be produced more cheaply, so that, if the costs of the factors of production which are required do not change, unit cost of production will be lower.

(b) The quality of goods can be improved.

(c) New commodities become available — motor cars, deep freezers, dishwashers, washing machines, televisions etc.

Inventions

11.24. These discoveries of new methods of production and new commodities are known as *Inventions*. Many firms have research and development departments which are continually experimenting in search of improved techniques. Development work of this nature is carried on in universities and institutes of higher education, though some of the more outstanding break-throughs have been the result of an intelligent inventor pursuing a hobby. The granting of patents is an effort by the government to stimulate research activity.

Innovations

11.25. While research is an ongoing process, it is given a thrust in a particular direction by economic stimuli, e.g., if labour becomes dearer considerable money will be expended to invent a machine to do the task; currently there is a search for alternative sources of energy. Just as inventional activity responds to economic stimuli, even if inventions are available they will not be introduced into the production process unless it is profitable to do so. The introduction of an invention into the productive process is known as *Innovation*.

Long run and very long run contrasted

11.26. When in economic analysis there is reference to the long run, the stae of production technique and quality of factors of production are taken as given. It is as if within the period of time to which the long run refers there has been no change in the state of production technique or the quality of factors of production.

11.27. Social Cost and Private Cost

The opportunity cost which was set out in section 11.7 was the opportunity cost to the individual and consequently is the private cost. There is also a social cost — the cost to society of certain actions; private cost and social cost need not necessarily be identical. Where there is a divergence between (i) social cost and private cost, and (ii) social benefit and private benefit, the divergence may be classified along the following lines:—

(a) *External economies of consumption* are said to occur when an action taken by a consumer results in a benefit to third parties for which the consumer taking the action is not recompensed, e.g., if a person maintains his house and garden in good condition, it benefits his neighbours; similarly if a person educates his children to be good citizens, there is a benefit to society. Thus in these circumstances there are social benefits.

(b) *External economies of production* are said to occur when an action taken by a producer results in a benefit to third parties for which the producer is not compensated. Examples of these benefits to society (i.e., social benefits) would be the manufacturer/producer who trains his staff even though some of them leave and work for others;

firms setting up in Ireland and creating jobs for Irish people; the increased output of one firm may permit those firms which supply it to enjoy economies of scale.

(c) *External diseconomies of consumption* occur when an action taken by a consumer imposes a cost on third parties for which they are not compensated. Examples of these arise when people in the course of gaining utility impose costs on others, e.g., radios played in a manner which causes a nuisance. There is a volume of opinion which states that one of the influences on a person's standard of living is how his standard compares with others; if this be true and if his friends purchase a new car, then he may feel somewhat deprived and badly off.

(d) *External diseconomies of production* occur when an action by a producer imposes a cost on third parties for which they are not compensated. Examples of these are the pollution of the air by smoke from factory chimneys or a firm disposing of its waste materials in a manner which creates a nuisance.

Externalities

11.28. You will notice that in each of the four classifications in the previous section there was reference to third parties, i.e. there were external effects. Hence you will not be surprised to learn that these social benefits and costs are usually referred to as *Externalities.*

11.29. The Equalisation of Social and Private Cost

If the social benefit arising from an action is greater than the private benefit, it is likely that the action will be undertaken less often than society would wish. Conversely, if social cost is greater than private cost then the action may be taken more often than society would wish. Consequently society would wish to equalise social cost (and benefit) and private cost (and benefit) i.e. the government would wish that third parties who suffer through externalities would be compensated by the party who perpetrates the externality and also that third parties who enjoy, or benefit from, externalities would pay those whose actions result in the benefit. The government can attempt to equalise the private and social aspect either by prohibiting the action or imposing a charge of some form until the two costs are equalised. The phrase *'there is an attempt to internalise the cost'* is often used when attempts are made to remove externalities.

(a) For external diseconomies of production the government may impose a tax or a levy, or the local authority may impose a high rateable valuation in order to provide funds which can be used to compensate those who suffer from the producer's action, e.g. the local authority may impose a charge on the firm so that the river which was being polluted by the factory can be cleaned up or the local authority may insist that the firm treat their effluent in some way which will remove its nuisance aspect. Alternatively the government may prohibit the production of the good or limit its production to certain areas by refusing planning permission.

(b) In respect of external diseconomies of consumption there is a tendency to introduce laws to prohibit those actions which constitute a nuisance e.g. a ban on smoking.

(c) The government attempts to encourage the establishment of firms in which there are external economies of production by grants for premises and training, by export tax relief and services of agencies such as Córas Tráchtála Teo, Bord Fáilte etc.

(d) Again the government attempts to encourage situations in which there are external economies of consumption, e.g., tidy towns competitions, free medical treatment for contagious diseases, talks on civics etc.

QUESTIONS

Q1. Distinguish between (a) Fixed Costs and Variable Costs.
(b) Explicit Costs and Implicit Costs.

Q2. State the Law of Diminishing Marginal Cost. Does it apply in the short run, the long run or both?

Q3. Is opportunity cost the same as money cost?

Q4. Explain the relationship between average cost and marginal cost. Illustrate the relationship.

Q5. Draw a short run and a long run average cost curve and justify the shape of each.

Q6. Write an explanatory note on Economies and Diseconomies of Scale.

Q7. Distinguish between Social and Private Cost. How might they be equalised?

12 Perfect Competition

12.1. Spectrum of market structures

There are several forms of market structure, extending from a monopoly where there is a single seller of a commodity, to perfect competition where there are many sellers each of whom has an insignificant share of the total market. Between the two extremes of monopoly and perfect competition there exist many different types of market structures to which the general term imperfect competition is applied. There may be imperfect competition which is very close to monopoly, or a form of imperfect competition which is close to perfect competition. Because of the wide range of market structures to which the term imperfect competition may be applied, specific terms are often included, e.g., Duopoly which means that the market consists of two sellers and Oligopoly which indicates that there are few sellers.

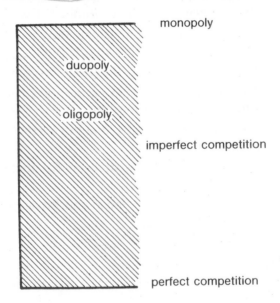

Fig. 12.1. Spectrum of market structures.

This section of economics is studied best by analysing the two extreme situations of perfect competition and monopoly initially and then analysing the intermediate situation of Imperfect Competition.

Table 12.1 Some Characteristics of Market Structures.

	Perfect Competition	Imperfect Competition	Oligopoly	Monopoly
No. of Sellers	Many small sellers	A large number	Few	One
Characteristics of Product	Homogeneous Product	Similar/Products are close substitutes	Identical or close substitutes	No close substitute
Barriers to entry	None	None	Some restrictions otherwise oligopoly situation would not continue in the long run	Some restrictions otherwise mon-opolyistic situation would not continue in the long run
Level of profit at long run equilibrium	Normal	Normal	Supernromal if firms are profit maximisers	Supernormal if firms are profit maximisers

12.2. Perfect competition

Assumptions of model must be understood

The model of perfect competition, or the perfectly competitive model, is a very well known economic model (see Section 1.6 re economic models). It should be realised that unless the assumptions on which the model is based are clearly understood, the analysis of the model and its conclusions make no contribution to our understanding of economics.

Concentrating on market in which the firm is selling

12.3. Each firm operates in at least two markets, (a) the market in which the firm purchases or hires the factors of production which it requires and (b) the market in which it sells its finished product. In this model of perfect competition we are concentrating on the market in which the firm is selling its product and we are assuming that perfect competition obtains in that market.

12.4. Assumptions underlying the Theory of Perfect Competition

Homogeneous goods

(a) Each firm is selling a homogeneous product, i.e., there is no distinguishable difference between the product produced by different firms. Potato production would be an example since in the marketing and purchase of potatoes we are unconcerned whether they are grown on farm A or farm B.

Individual firms cannot influence the selling price

(b) There are many competitive sellers in the market none of whom produces a sufficiently large quantity to influence, by his own actions, the price at which the good is sold, i.e., if a seller increases his level of production he will not have to sell at a lower price, conversely if the seller refrains from selling, the selling price of the good will not increase. Thus each firm is a Price Taker.

Buyers cannot influence price

(c) There is a large number of buyers so that no buyer is in a position to influence, by his own actions, the market price of the goods.

(d) There is no collusion between buyers of the good or sellers of the

No collusions

good. Thus buyers do not group together with other buyers, nor do sellers group together with other sellers in order to determine, influence or manipulate the price at which the good is traded.

Price, quality, profit are known to all

(e) Perfect knowledge. In the market everyone concerned has perfect knowledge as to prices, profit and quality.

Freedom of entry and exit

(f) Freedom of entry and exit. It is possible for firms to enter or leave the industry as they wish, i.e., it is not possible for firms already in the industry to prevent new firms from entering the industry.

Firms seek maximum profits

(g) The sole objective of each firm is considered to be the earning of maximum profits in the short run. It may be argued that since competition is so intense, this objective is nothing more than the expression of the fact that, in a market where the selling price of the product is outside the control of the individual firm and there is freedom of entry, a firm in such an industry must concentrate on working as efficiently as possible in order to survive. For this reason it is often said that firms are *cost minimisers*. However, in the present context where, for a given selling price, profits per item sold will be maximised when unit costs are minimised, either expression viz. profit maximiser or cost minimiser will suffice.

firm is a price taker

12.5. The price at which the product will be sold will, as usual, be determined by the total supply available on the market and the total demand. However, once the market price is determined, the price at which an individual producer can sell his product is given. Under the assumptions of the model, the individual producer cannot, by his own individual actions, affect this market price, i.e., the individual firm is a *price taker*. This is so because the individual firm is small and supplies an insignificant portion of the total supply. If *all* producers increase or decrease their supply it *would* affect market supply, but we are analysing the situation of an individual firm acting alone in accordance with the assumptions of the model. The effect of this in terms of the demand curve facing the firm and the demand curve facing the industry is depicted in Fig. 12.5.1 and Fig. 12.5.2.

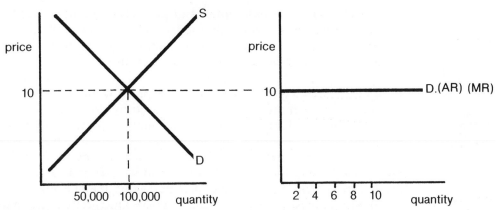

Fig. 12.5.1. Market price under perfect competition is determined by the interaction of aggregate (i.e. market) supply and aggregate (i.e. market) demand.

Fig. 12.5.2. Horizontal or perfectly elastic demand curve, which faces an individual firm under perfect competition.

Note especially difference in scale on quantity (or x) axis.

The market price is determined by aggregate supply and aggregate demand and is shown in Fig. 12.5.1. This market demand curve is downward sloping. If there is a significant increase in supply or a reduction in demand, then there will be a reduction in the market price. Once this market price is determined, an individual producer, because he represents such a small proportion of the total supply, can sell any quantity he wishes at this market price.

Individual firms supplies an insignificant quantity

12.6. If the total market supply of potatoes is 100 000 tonnes per annum, any alteration, within feasible limits, in the level of output by a farmer who is producing 10 tonnes per annum, will not have any effect on selling price, e.g., if the farmer increases his output by 100% he is still supplying only 20 tonnes out of a total supply of 100 000 tonnes.

In perfect competition average revenue curve of firm is also its marginal revenue curve

12.7. Another name for a demand curve is an average revenue curve; in the case of an individual firm selling its product under perfectly competitive conditions the average revenue of the individual firm does not change as its level of production changes, i.e., since the demand curve is horizontal, average revenue is constant. Referring back to Section 11.9, you will remember that if average revenue is not changing then marginal revenue must be the same as average revenue. Thus, in this case the marginal revenue curve of the firm is the same as its average revenue curve.

12.8. What quantity of goods will be produced by an individual firm which is selling in a perfectly competitive market?
The short answer to this question is the quantity which will give the firm the greatest total profit in keeping with the objectives of the firm as set

out in item (g) of the assumptions of perfect competition (see Section 12.4). However, this is too glib a reply and does not really answer the question. It is necessary to establish some criteria by which the actual quantity which will be supplied can be determined.

Output is expanded when MC is less than MR

12.9. A firm which is seeking to maximise profit would produce an extra unit of output if its total profit is increased by doing so. Total profit would be increased if the cost of producing the extra unit of output, i.e., marginal cost, is less than the additional revenue which is earned by selling it, i.e., marginal revenue. There is nothing involved or difficult about this. If you look at table 12.14 you will see that when the firm produces the *fifth* item the cost of producing this item (i.e. marginal cost) is £60. The increase in revenue as a result of selling this item (i.e. marginal revenue) is £100. Therefore if the firm wishes to earn the maximum level of profit it will produce this fifth item for by so doing it will increase its total profit by £40 (i.e. to £70 in table 12.14) because marginal revenue is greater than marginal cost.

Output is reduced when MC is greater than MR

12.10. Conversely, if marginal cost is greater than marginal revenue, the cost of producing the last unit is greater than the revenue which it earns. Thus, total profit would be increased if the level of output was reduced. This can be clearly seen by looking at the *eighth* item in table 12.14. The marginal cost of producing this eighth item is £120, the marginal revenue through selling it is £100. Thus there is a net loss of £20 on this item since marginal cost is £20 greater than marginal revenue at this level of output/sales. Thus net loss of £20 is shown in the profit column as the £80 profit falls to £60 when eight items are sold.

MC = MR is the first condition for profit maximisation

12.11. If output is expanded when MC is less than MR, and output is reduced when MC is greater than MR, then neither of these situations represents an equilibrium condition. In fact equilibrium is when MC is equal to MR, since when MC = MR, the firm is in its most profitable situation, given its cost structure and market price.

Equilibrium

12.12. *Equilibrium* is a condition from which there is no tendency to move unless the existing conditions change.

(a)   In the above discussion the firm had no incentive to change when MC = MR, therefore the firm is said to be at equilibrium at that price/output combination.

(b)   The term equilibrium is used also in reference to that situation in pursuit of which actions are geared. In the above example, if the firm had not arrived at the price/output combination where MC = MR, this equality of marginal cost and marginal revenue would still have been the equilibrium condition and the firm would have been continually adjusting in order to attain that equilibrium condition.

(c)   *Stable equilibrium* refers to a situation such that when equilibrium is

Stable equilibrium

disturbed market forces will bring about a return to the original equilibrium, e.g. there is a temporary shortage of bread and during the shortage the price of bread increases; as soon as the shortage passes, bread returns to its original selling price.

Unstable equilibrium

(d) *Unstable equilibrium* refers to a situation such that, when equilibrium is disturbed, there is not a return to the original equilibrium, e.g., there is a shortage of workers with a certain skill and employers pay higher wages in order to entice workers to work for them. Even when the shortage of such workers has passed, the trade unions concerned will not allow the wage rate to revert to its original lower level.

2nd profit maximising condition

12.13. For a profit maximising equilibrium to apply, not only must MC = MR but the situation must be such that at lower levels of output MC is less than MR, and at higher levels of output MC is greater than MR, i.e., *MC is increasing at a faster rate than is MR.*

12.14. In table 12.14, MC = MR at 2 levels of output — at an output of 2 units, and an output of 7 units. However, 7 units is the profit maximising level of output because the second profit maximising condition (i.e., MC is increasing faster than MR) is also fulfilled at an output of 7 units, but not at an output of 2 units. Note also that profit is minus £40 at the output of 2 units and plus £80 when output is 7 units.

Table 12.14. Costs, Revenues and Profit.

Selling Price £	Qty.	Total cost £	Marginal Cost £	Total Revenue £	Marginal Revenue £	Profit £
100	1	140	-	100	-	-40
100	2	240	100	200	100	-40
100	3	320	80	300	100	-20
100	4	370	50	400	100	+30
100	5	430	60	500	100	+70
100	6	520	90	600	100	+80
100	7	620	100	700	100	+80
100	8	740	120	800	100	+60

Marginal cost increasing at a faster rate than marginal revenue is the second profit maximising condition.

In terms of a diagram this second profit maximising condition means that MC curve must cut the MR curve from below (or from the left) See Fig. 12.14.

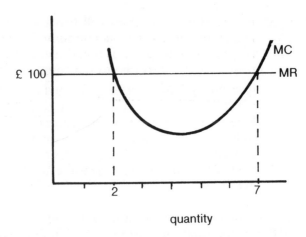

quantity

Fig. 12.14. Marginal cost curve must cut marginal curve from below (or from left). . . 2nd profit maximising condition.

12.15. This analysis of profit maximising equilibrium has been conducted on the basis of the output which the firm will supply when the objective of the firm is to maximise profits in the short run. It is possible that a firm might decide that it would be more advantageous to the firm if it withdrew from the industry; so a criterion must be established by which it can be ascertained whether or not the firm will produce and remain in business. This criterion is established by reference to *Variable Costs*.

Should a firm continue to produce in the short run?

12.16. In the short run a firm has fixed expenses which, by definition, must be paid in the short run, even if the firm ceased trading. The firm has signed a contract and undertaken to pay these costs. In addition to fixed expenses a firm has variable expenses which are directly related to the level of production and which would not exist if the firm ceased trading. *If the revenue of the firm exceeds its variable costs then the firm should continue to trade in the short run, though in the long run the firm must recoup all its costs and earn at least normal profits, i.e. the minimum amount of profit which is required in order to make it worthwhile for the firm to remain in business.*

A firm should produce in the short run if it covers its variable costs

Example 12.16

The output of a firm is 1 item per week; the firm's fixed costs are £85.00 and its variable costs are £270.00, thus the total costs of the firm are £355.00. If the firm can sell the item which it produces for an amount in excess of £355.00 which will provide an adequate profit, then the firm will continue to produce even in the long run. Let us suppose that the highest price at which the firm can sell is £310.00, what should the firm do? If the firm ceases to produce, it will lose £85.00 per week because its fixed costs must be paid in the short run. On the other hand if the firm continues to produce in the short run, its weekly loss will be £45.00 (i.e., total cost of £355.00 — revenue of £310.00). So *the firm should continue to produce in* the short run provided that revenue exceeds variable costs. The excess of revenue over variable costs makes a contribution towards the fixed costs which would have to be paid in the short run, even if the firm ceased trading. Of course in the long run unless the firm can recoup all of its costs and earn an adequate profit it will retire from the business, so that when the contracts which gave rise to the fixed costs expire, i.e., in the long run, the firm would not renew the contracts but would withdraw from the business.

Third profit maximising condition

12.17. *Thus the third short run profit maximising condition is that revenue must exceed variable costs since otherwise the firm would not engage in production even in the short run.*

12.18. The Short Run Supply Curve of a Perfectly Competitive Firm.
The supply curve of a firm is a graph or diagram which shows the quantity which will be supplied by a firm at each individual price.

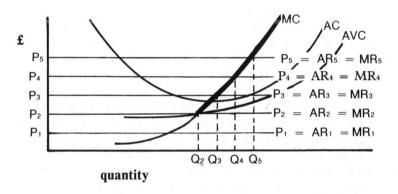

Fig. 12.18. Short Run Supply Curve of a Perfectly Competitive Firm.

A profit maximising firm will supply that output at which $MC = MR$ and MC is increasing faster than MR, (See Section 12.8. to 12.14.). Therefore if the price is P_2 quantity Q_2 will be supplied as shown in fig. 12.18. If the price is P_3, Q_3 will be the quantity supplied. P_4, Q_4, and P_5, Q_5 etc. However, if the price falls to P_1, the firm will not produce since it would not be recouping its variable costs (See Sections 12.15. to 12.17.). But provided the firm is recouping its variable costs, it will supply that level of output at which $MC = MR$ and MC is increasing faster than MR. Thus it can be seen that *the short run supply curve of a perfectly competitive firm is that portion of its marginal cost-curve which lies above average variable costs* — as shown by the thick black line in Fig. 12.18.

12.19. Normal profit is a cost of production
Costs of production are all those expenses which must be if production is to take place. If the revenue realised by the sale of the goods is insufficient

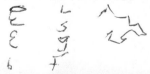

to pay the wages, rent and rates, raw material and all of the other expenses, then production would not continue.

Example 12.19.

Suppose your weekly costs of production were as follows:

		£
Labour	—	175.00
Raw Materials	—	220.00
Rent, rates, and all other expenses	—	200.00
Total costs of production		595.00

and you could sell the goods produced for £595.00, would you continue production? The answer is no because you are receiving no reward, so it would not be worth the risk and effort. Similarly you are unlikely to continue production if the selling price was increased to £595.01 or £595.02, because you would consider the 1p or 2p which you are receiving as being an inadequate return for the risk involved.

However, there is some price which will provide you with the minimum amount which you require in order to remain in production (say) £615.00 — thus £20.00 (£615.00 — £595.00) is the minimum amount of profit which you must receive if production is to take place. This £20.00 is a cost of production because it is a payment or cost which must be recouped if production is to take place. Production will not take place if this minimum amount of profit is not received. *This minimum amount of profit, which constitutes a cost of production, is known as* **Normal Profit.** *In economics it is to be understood that cost always includes normal profit.*

12.20. The Long Run Supply Curve of a Perfectly Competitive Firm

Again the profit maximising firm will supply that level of output at which MC = MR and where MC is increasing faster than MR. See Fig. 12.20.

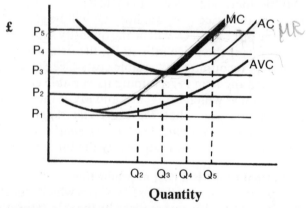

Fig. 12.20. Long Run Supply Curve of a Perfectly Competitive Firm.

If the selling price is P_3, the firm will produce Q_3 since this is the profit maximising level of output. Similarly, if price is P_4, Q_4 will be supplied, and at P_5, Q_5 will be supplied. However, if price is P_2, no quantity would be supplied in the long run, since in the long run all costs including normal profit must be recouped (See Sections 12.16 and 12.19). *Thus the long run supply curve of a perfectly competitive firm is that portion of its marginal cost curve which lies above average costs (Average cost includes normal profit) as shown by the thick black line in Fig. 12.20.* This should be contrasted with the short run supply curve of a perfectly competitive firm as developed in Section 12.18.

12.21. It has been established that a firm which wishes to earn maximum profit will be at *short run equilibrium,* when the following 3 conditions are fulfilled.

(a) Marginal Cost = Marginal Revenue
(explained in sections 12.9 to 12.11)
(b) Marginal Cost is increasing faster than Marginal Revenue
(explained in sections 12.13 and 12.14)
(c) When the firm is recouping all its variable costs
(explained in sections 12.15 to 12.17)

Long run profit maximisation

12.22. If a firm is to be in *Long Run Equilibrium,* normal profit at least must be earned. Since average cost includes normal profit this condition for long run equilibrium may be expressed as *at long run equilibrium average revenue must at least be equal to average cost.* If this condition is substituted for condition 12.21.(c) then we have the 3 conditions for long run profit maximisation. At long run equilibrium, average total cost (which is usually referred to as average cost and comprises average fixed cost plus average variable cost plus normal profit) must be at least equal to average revenue. Therefore if average revenue is equal to average cost a firm must, be definition, be recouping its variable cost and earning normal profit. Thus while a firm would, in the short run, continue to produce while average revenue is greater than average variable cost, in the long run, if a firm is to continue trading, average revenue must be at least equal to average fixed cost plus average variable cost plus normal profit, i.e., average total cost.

12.23. Guidelines/Conditions for a Profit Maximising Firm
A firm which seeks to earn the highest possible, i.e. maximum, level of profit (or at least to keep its losses at a minimum) will operate according to the following guidelines/conditions.

(a) The firm will produce the level of output at which marginal cost is equal to marginal revenue.

(b) At the level of output at which marginal cost is equal to marginal revenue, marginal cost should be rising faster than marginal revenue i.e. at higher levels of output marginal cost is greater than marginal revenue and at lower levels of output marginal cost is less than marginal revenue.

(c)   A firm if it is to continue to produce in the long run must at least earn Normal Profit.

(d)   If a firm is earning less than Normal Profit it may continue to produce in the short run providing its revenue is greater than its variable costs.

(e)   If a firm's revenue is less than its variable cost it will cease operation immediately i.e. a shut down situation.

N.B. These conditions/guidelines apply whether the market structure is Perfectly or Imperfectly Competitive, Oligopolistic or Monopolistic.

Does profit maximising equilibrium indicate that large profits are being earned?

12.24. To say that a firm is in a profit maximising situation merely indicates that the firm has struck the best balance possible in terms of maximising profits (or minimising losses) given its cost of production and the revenue which it can earn. There now arises the question of whether the firm, even when it is at a profit maximising equilibrium, is earning a large or small amount of profit.

(a)   If average revenue is greater than average cost at equilibrium then the firm is earning in excess of normal profit. This is known as *super normal profit. Supernormal profit is defined as profit in excess of normal profit.*

(b)   If average revenue is less than average cost then the firm is not earning even normal profit.

The relationship between average cost and average revenue indicates whether normal, supernormal or less than normal profit is being earned

(c)   If average revenue = average cost at equilibrium, then the firm is earning normal profit (remember that average cost includes normal profit) but is not earning supernormal profit.

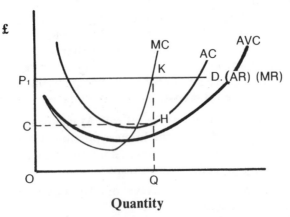

Quantity

Fig. 12.24. (a) Firm earning Supernormal Profit.

12.25. In Fig. 12.24 profit maximising equilibrium is at an output of OQ, since this is the level of output at which MC = MR, above Average Costs, and MC increasing faster than MR. If there is freedom of entry into the industry, other firms will enter the industry in pursuit of the supernormal profits of CP_1KH.

12.26. The effect of additional firms entering the industry is that there will be an increase in market supply from S_1 to S_2, as shown in Fig. 12.26.1 with a consequent reduction in market price from P_1 to P_2.

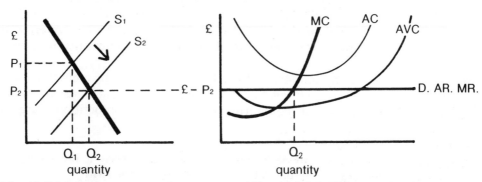

Fig. 12.26.1. Industry or market equilibrium.

Fig. 12.26.2. Firm earning less than normal profit.

When normal profit is not being earned, firms leave the industry

At the point of equilibrium in Fig. 12.26.2. the average cost is greater than average revenue, so that the firm is not earning normal profit. If normal profit is not being earned firms will leave the industry.

12.27. If firms leave the industry there will be a reduction in the quantity supplied from S_2 to S_1 and a consequent increase in market price from P_2 to P_3 as shown in Fig. 12.27.1.

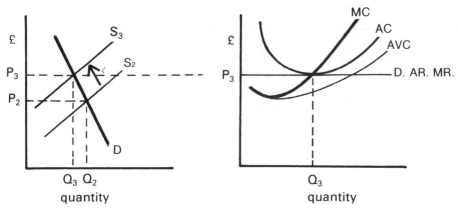

Fig. 12.27.1. Industry or market equilibrium.

Fig. 12.27.2. Long run equilibrium of the firm under perfect competition. $MC = MR = AC = AR$.

Fig. 12.27.2 shows long run equilibrium of the firm under perfect competition. The firm is at equilibrium because the three profit maximising conditions are being fulfilled, (see Sections 12.21 and 12.22). The industry is at equilibrium because normal profits are being earned since average cost equals average revenue at the point of equilibrium. Since normal profits are being earned, firms will not leave the industry and because only normal profits are being earned new firms will not seek entry into the industry. Average cost = Average Revenue, i.e., the earning of normal profits by firms in the industry is often referred to as the condition for equilibrium of the perfectly competitive *industry*.

12.28. Though MC = MR is the profit maximising condition, *in the case of perfect competition,* MR = AR. (Average revenue is just another name for price). Thus at equilibrium under perfect competition marginal cost = price.

12.29. The effects of the assumptions underlying the theory of perfect competition on the long run equilibrium of the firm
The assumption underlying the theory of perfect competition are set out in Section 12.4, while Fig. 12.27.2 shows the diagram representing long run equilibrium of the firm under perfect competition.

(a)   The firm faces a horizontal demand curve because (i) each seller is selling a homogeneous product (assumption 12.4(a)), (ii) consumers have perfect knowledge as to price and quality (assumption 12.4(e)), (iii) there are many competitive sellers, none of whom produces a sufficiently large quantity to influence, by his own action, the market price of the good — each firm is a price taker (assumption 12.4(b)).

(b)   The firm produces to the point where MC = MR, where marginal cost is increasing at a faster rate than is marginal revenue and at least normal profit is being earned, because profit maximisation is the objective of the firm (assumption 12.4.(g)).

(c)   At equilibrium only normal profit is being earned because there is freedom of entry and exit (assumption 12.4(f)). Other firms have perfect knowledge as to profits etc. (assumption 12.4(e)), so that if profits greater than normal profits were being earned firms would be entering the industry, while if less than normal profit was being earned firms would leave the industry.

QUESTIONS

Q1. What are the assumptions underlying the Theory of Perfect Competition?

Q2. Under what circumstances would a firm which seeks to maximise profits be at (a) short run, (b) long run, equilibrium.

Q3. The following are the costs incurred by an entrepreneur in producing his maximum output of one item per week.

	£
Rent (the lease has 6 months remaining and there is an option to renew it for a further 3 yeas at the existing rent).	50 per week
Wages	300 per week
Raw Materials	250 per week
Electricity Charges	80 per week

Normal Profits is £100 for unit produced.
What is the maximum price at which the item can be sold if production is to continue.
(a) in the long run?
(b) in the short run?

Q4. Show the effects of the assumptions underlying the Theory of Perfect Competition on the long run equilibrium of the firm.

Q5. Explain by means of diagrams the movement of a perfectly competitive firm towards a new equilibrium when costs of production have been subject to an increase.

Q6. Distinguish between Normal Profit and Supernormal Profit.

13   Monopoly

Dominant firms are more usual than absolute monopolists

13.1. In Section 12.1, perfect competition was shown as being an extreme in the spectrum of market structures; monopoly is the other extreme. Monopoly means a single seller in which case a single firm constitutes the entire supply of the good and there is no distinction between the firm and the industry because the firm is the industry. In practice *absolute monopolies* are less common than is usually imagined, particularly if you analyse the need which the firm is attempting to satisfy, e.g., C.I.E. has a monopoly in the supply of public transport but it is possible to walk, cycle or use private transport, while firms can use their own delivery vans. In economics we are concerned not with the fact of whether or not the firm satisfies the legal definition of a monopolist, i.e., is the sole supplier, but whether the firm dominates the industry to such an extent that it can act as if it were a monopolist. Hence the term *Dominant Firm* is often used to indicate a firm which dominates the industry and thus can act in a monopolistic manner. For the purpose of exposition, the remainder of this chapter will be based on the concept of a monopolist, as a single seller, with the understanding that the analysis can be applied to dominant firms.

Cross Elasticity of demand indicates monopoly power

13.2. The real indicator of the power of the monopolist is the degree of cross elasticity for his product. If cross elasticity of demand is high then one (or more) good is a close substitute for the good produced by the monopolist. Thus if the monopolist tries to take advantage of his monopoly power the consumer will purchase the substitute good. In fact in this example the firm is not really a monopolist in the market-power sense of the term.

13.3. The main features of Monopoly are:

(a)   Since the firm is the sole supplier there is no distinction between the firm and the industry.

(b)   The firm has control over **either** the price at which the commodity will be sold **or** the quantity which will be sold but the monopolist cannot control both. The monopolist may either set the price and then supply that quantity which the public is prepared to buy at that price or he may sell the quantity which he produces at the best price which he can get but he cannot make the public buy the quantity he (the monopolist) wishes at the price which he sets.

(c)   Since the earning of maximum profits is considered to be the objective of the monopolist he may earn supernormal profits.

(d)   If a monopolist is to continue to earn supernormal profits in the long run, there must be some restriction on entry into the industry. Thus if a monopolistic market structure is to persist in the long run, there cannot be freedom of entry into the industry. An analysis of these barriers to entry into industry is set out in the following section.

13.4. Examples of barriers to entry into an industry are:

(a) The government may grant to a company the sole right to supply a good or service so that there is a legal restriction on competition, e.g., E.S.B., C.I.E.. One of the main reasons for the government conferring such rights is to avoid the waste which would be inevitable if a number of independent companies were in competition with each other, e.g., the duplication of electricity generating capacity and the transmission network to bring electricity to the point of consumption. There are other reasons, which are not relevant at this stage, as to why the government might give sole rights of supply or production to a company.

(b) Patents and copyright laws confer monopolistic powers on those to whom patents and copyrights are granted, while the patent or copyright lasts. Patents are granted to inventors of original machines or processes in order to give them a "pay off period", during which they may enjoy commercial advantage from their invention. This practice is adopted in order to encourage firms and individuals to undertake research and development. If a firm was not permitted by law to have sole rights for a specified period to enjoy commercial advantage, firms would simply copy inventions and take advantage of whatever research other firms might, (foolishly, under the circumstances) undertake. In these circumstances there would be an obvious reduction in the commitment of firms to research development and a consequent slowing of the rate of technological development.

(c) Monopolies may arise due to a firm having sole rights to raw materials. The extractive industries would be examples — diamonds, gold, zinc, copper, etc.

(d) Monopolies may arise and persist due to economies of scale. If an industry requires a large investment in fixed capital, it will be important that a large volume of production be attained in order to reduce the fixed cost of production which must be borne by each unit produced (see Section 11.16). Since new firms would probably have to enter at a low level of production they might not be able to compete due to the high level of fixed cost which must be borne by each unit produced. For example if you were to manufacture a new motor car from scratch in your garage, the cost would be considerably greater than the price at which you could buy a motor car because of the economies of scale which apply in the motor car industry.

(e)   A monopoly may be perpetuated by a firm entering into trading agreements with other firms.

(f)   Many TV series and films have been devoted to monopolies based on fear, force or threats — mafia, industrial sabotage, price wars etc..

Average revenue and marginal revenue for monopolist

13.5. The monopolist faces a downward sloping demand curve for his product, as has already been stated; another name for a demand curve is an average revenue curve. If average revenue is falling, marginal revenue must be less than average revenue (see Section 11.9).

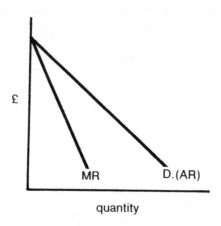

Fig. 13.5. Demand curve of a monopolist.

13.6. A profit maximising monopolist will produce that quantity at which MC = MR provided the other profit maximising conditions set out in section 12.23 are fulfilled also.

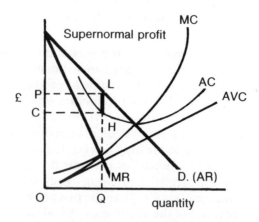

Fig. 13.6. Long run equilibrium of a monopolist.

Monopolist earns supernormal profits

As set out in Fig. 13.6 the profit maximising monopolist will produce a quantity of Q (where MC = MR) and by reference to the *Demand Curve* it can be seen that this quantity will sell at a price of P. By reference to the *Average Cost* curve it can be seen that the average cost of producing quantity Q is C. The monopolist is earning a supernormal profit of LH on each unit produced (supernormal profit because normal profit is included in average cost). The *Total* supernormal profit which the monopolist earns is the supernormal profit *Per Unit (LH)* multiplied by the quantity sold (which is O Q = CH in Fig. 13.6); the total supernormal profit is indicated by rectangle CPLH in Fig. 13.6.

Supernormal profits are earned at long run equilibrium

13.7. Even though the monopolist is earning supernormal profits, it is not possible for other firms to enter the industry because there exist barriers to entry (see Section 13.3.) so that the monopolist continues to earn supernormal profits in the long run.

If cost conditions are the same in the perfectly competitive and monopolistic industries, the monopolist will produce a smaller quantity and sell at a higher unit price

13.8. *If cost conditions are the same in the perfectly competitive and monopolistic industries,* the equilibrium level of output on the monopolistic industry will always be lower and the equilibrium selling price of the monopolist will always be higher than they would be in an industry in which the firms sell their products under conditions of perfect competition.

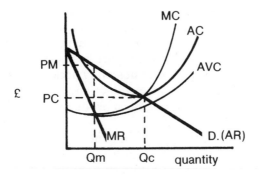

Fig. 13.8. Total output of the industry is lower and price is higher under profit maximising monopoly.

The profit maximising monopolistic firm will produce an output of Qm, which will be sold at a price of Pm. Because there is not freedom of entry, this situation will persist in the long run. Since the firm, being a monopolist, is also the industry, Qm is the total output of the industry. Under perfect competition each firm produces up to the point at which marginal cost = price; therefore the output of the perfectly competitive *industry* will be Qc which will be sold at a price of Pc.

13.9. Since the monopolist constitutes the entire industry, it is typically a larger firm than the small firm which represents the perfectly competitive firm. Thus it is possible that the monopolist may enjoy economies of scale, in which case the cost conditions would not be the same as under perfect competition.

*If cost
conditions are
not the same
under perfect
competition &
monopoly*
13.10. If cost conditions are not the same under perfect competition and monopoly, one can be less definite in stating that price will be higher and output lower under monopoly when compared with the perfectly competitive market situation.

Example 13.10

	Perfect Competition £	Monopoly £
Selling Price	2.00	1.90
Unit cost of production (including normal profit)	2.00	1.40
Profit (Supernormal)	NIL	0.50

In this example though supernormal profits are being earned by the monopolist, the selling price of the article is lower than under perfect competition because the monopolist enjoys economies of scale. It could be said that part of the advantages of the economies of scale are passed on to the consumer who can consequently buy at a lower price. The monopolist does not pass on part of his savings through economies of scale for altruistic reasons but simply because, having regard to elasticity of demand and cost of production, this price/output combination maximises his profits, i.e., he is producing where $MC = MR$.

*Distinction
between
supernormal
profits gained
through savings
in cost and
exploitation
of consumers*
13.11. Of course the public in general would wish that the monopolist would reduce his price even more and pass on all his supernormal profits by selling at a price of £1.40, i.e., quantity Qc in Fig. 13.8, but at least a distinction must be drawn between supernormal profits enjoyed through savings in the cost of production and supernormal profits gained through charging the consumer a price greater than he would pay under perfect competition. It is possible that though the unit costs of production of the monopolist might be lower than under perfect competition, the selling price of the item might be greater than the selling price which would prevail under perfect competition. In example 13.10, the unit cost of production (including normal profit) for the monopolist might remain at £1.40, i.e., lower than under perfect competition and the selling price might be £2.10, i.e., higher than under perfect competition. In case the unit profit in this example seems large, you may reflect on the fact that in 1946 the Reynolds International Pen Company were selling a ball-point pen at the very competitive price, compared with other models, of $12.50. The cost of the pen was estimated to be 60 cents — a profit of 1983%.

*If price is
lower under
monopoly then
quantity sold
would be
greater than
under perfect
competition*

13.12. If the selling price under monopoly was lower than the price under perfect competition, e.g., because the monopolist enjoys economies of scale, then the quantity sold would be greater under monopoly. Since both *Industries* face a downward sloping demand curve, if both industries experience the same demand conditions, a greater quantity would be sold at the lower price.

13.13. Because profit maximising monopolists tend to produce a smaller quantity and sell at a higher unit price than do perfectly competitive firms, governments and the general public usually monitor closely, by keeping under constant scrutiny, the trading policies of monopolists and dominant firms.

*A benign
monopolist*

13.14. The spirit of the charter of state sponsored monopolies is that they should produce the level of output which would be produced by the industry under Perfect Competition i.e. quantity Qc in Fig. 13.8 where Average Revenue = Average Cost and the firm is earning Normal Profits. By this requirement it is hoped to pass on to the consumer, through lower prices, the benefits of the economies of scale. Not only are prices lowered to original purchasers of the good but the lower prices enable a larger quantity of the good to be bought/sold.

*Cost control
in State
monopolies*

13.15. However since State Sponsored Trading Corporations tend not to be profit maximisers there is a danger that they may not be as efficient in controlling costs as would a private firm. Thus it may happen that costs escalate in the State Sponsored Monopolistic Trading Corporations so that while they are not earning supernormal profit the price which the consumer pays is not (significantly) lower than it would be under a monopolistic firm which is controlled by private interests which are more cost (and efficiency) conscious.

*Equilibrium
is not where
unit costs of
production are
at a minimum*

13.16. Another criticism which is often levelled at profit maximising monopolists is the fact that at equilibrium they have surplus capacity in the sense that they are not producing where average cost is lowest — they are said to be wasteful of resources. The monopolist is interested in getting maximum profits and consequently he is interested in the relationship between his costs of production and his revenue. When the monopolist is fulfilling the three profit maximising conditions he is not producing where his average costs of production are at a minimum. As already stated it is profit which concerns the firm and if the monopolist expanded his level of production to the point where average costs of production were at their lowest his selling price would have to be reduced in order to sell the extra production i.e. even though his average cost of production could be reduced his average revenue would be reduced by an even greater amount so that he would be losing on each unit produced beyond the profit maximising equilibrium level of output (see also Sections 14.11 and 14.12).

QUESTIONS

Q1. Explain the main features of Monopoly.

Q2. If a monopolist is seeking to maximise profits will he produce where his costs of production are lowest?

Q3. Are monopolies desirable from the community's point of view?

Q4. When the state sets up trading corporatives they tend to be monopolies why is this?

Q5. Explain, using a diagram, the long run equilibrium position of a monopolist who seeks maximum profits.

Q6. Give some examples of barriers to entry into an industry.

14 Price Discrimination/ Discriminating Monopolist

14.1. In previous sections it was shown that when the products of a firm are subject to a downward sloping demand curve additional units of the product can be sold, ceteris paribus, only by reducing price. Since the firm, because of market constraints must sell all of its output at a uniform price, this means that those units which had previously being selling at the higher price must now be reduced to the price at which the additional units are being sold.

Example 14.1.
Originally 10 units are sold at £10.00 each; in order to sell the additional unit the price must be reduced to £9.90 and all of the units will be sold at £9.90 because all the units must be sold at the same price.

Output	Unit Price	Total Return
10	£10.00	£100
11	£9.90	£108.90

Arising from this, consumers enjoy a consumers' surplus — see Chapter 10.

A discriminating monopolist may eliminate consumer surplus

If it was possible for the monopolist to sell to each consumer at the highest price which each consumer was prepared to pay, i.e., remove all consumers' surplus, then the monopolist would enjoy higher revenue and profit. Where a firm is in a position to eliminate consumers surplus in this way he is known as a DISCRIMINATING MONOPOLIST, i.e., he discriminates between consumers.

14.2. The most usual evidence of discrimination is where different consumers are charged different prices for the same article. In fact many people define price discrimination as the charging of different prices for similar goods or services. However, price discrimination goes deeper than that. It is possible for price discrimination to be operative even when the same price is being charged to different consumers, e.g., if I pay £2.00 for one hour's tuition and I am a member of a class of 20 and somebody else receives individual tuition for one hour in the same subject, at the same level, from the same person for £2.00, this would be a case of price discrimination. Conversely the same good may be sold at different prices and price discrimination may not exist, e.g., an orange may cost 1p more in Donegal compared with Dublin because the cost of transporting the oranges to Donegal must be recovered. **So it is really the relationship between cost and price in the different markets which is relevant in analysing whether or not price discrimination exists.**

Definition of price discrimination

THUS THE PRECISE DEFINITION OF PRICE DISCRIMINATION IS:— WHEN GOODS OR SERVICES ARE SOLD TO DIFFERENT CONSUMERS AT VARYING RATIOS BETWEEN MARGINAL COST AND PRICE, i.e., $\frac{P}{MC}$ IS NOT CONSTANT.

Of course if the marginal cost is the same in respect of a type of good supplied by a producer to different markets, then selling to consumers at different prices is evidence of price discrimination.

14.3. Necessary conditions for the implementation of Price Discrimination

(a) *Some monopoly power.*

A firm attempting to implement a policy of price discrimination must have some form of monopoly power. If there was freedom of entry into the industry, competitors would enter the market where the monopolist is charging the higher price and earning supernormal profit and this would continue until only normal profit was being earned.

(b) *It must be possible to separate the markets so that a good purchased in the low priced market cannot be offered for resale in the higher priced market.* If this was not so, goods would be bought in the low priced market and then resold in competition against the monopolist in his high priced market and this would continue while any difference in price existed. However, market separation is possible in international trade where there are customs officials to prevent the importation and sale of specified goods. Similarly market separation would be possible in the sale of a commodity which it is not possible to store and resell, e.g., electricity or transport. In the sale of services, market separation is possible because services provided tend to be on an individual basis and in addition there may be just enough variation in the service provided to confuse the consumers as to whether or not the service is different or identical, e.g., dentists, solicitors, tailors, hairdressers, doctors etc.

(c) *It must be possible to distinguish consumers with different elasticities of demand.*

There is often an assumption that students because of their lower income are not in a position to pay the full price for certain goods or services so that a much greater quantity would be bought if the price was reduced i.e., their elasticity of demand is great. Because of this they are offered the good or service at a lower price and it is possible for the seller to distinguish the student by insisting on the production of a student card. Similarly, old age pensioners and children are sometimes offered lower prices, spouses of people who are travelling on business trips by air are offered lower fares because it is considered by sellers that their price elasticity of demand is greater since the person travelling for business purposes must make the journey while the other person has more discretion in the matter and may or may not travel depending on the price.

14.4. Characteristics of consumers may make Price Discrimination possible

(a) If consumers are unable to distinguish the intrinsic qualities of the good and are of the opinion that in paying the higher price they are receiving a better good.

(b) If the difference between the higher price and the lower price is so small that consumers do not bother about it.

(c) If the consumers paying the higher price are not aware that the good is available elsewhere at a lower price.

14.5. First Degree Price Discrimination

With first degree price discrimination consumers' surplus is eliminated entirely

This is also known as perfect price discrimination and occurs when the seller is able to extract from each purchaser the highest price which the purchaser is prepared to pay rather than do without the good or service. In general it is not possible to implement price discrimination to this fine a degree. The more confidential the relationship between buyer and seller, the more possible it would be for the seller to estimate the elasticity of demand of the buyer, e.g., legal or medical service. If first degree price discrimination is being successfully implemented then consumers' surplus is entirely eliminated.

14.6. Second Degree Price Discrimination

Mainly in the form of price concessions which are not related to reduction in cost

Price discrimination of this nature is usually in the form of price concessions or quantity discounts, which are not related to reduction in the unit costs of production, e.g., when a consumer purchases a large quantity of the good or service the price of additional units may be reduced even though unit costs of production have not been reduced by an equivalent amount (if at all). Since the price concession is not related to cost factors it is a recognition by the seller that, due to the operation of the Law of Diminishing Marginal Utility, the consumer would be prepared to purchase the larger quantity only if the unit selling price is reduced.

14.7. Third Degree Price Discrimination

Most common form of price discrimination

This is the most common form of price discrimination. It divides consumers into classes based on estimates of their price elasticity of demand and each class of consumer is then charged a different price for the good or service. Examples of this form of price discrimination:—

(a) Business people who make short business trips of 2 or 3 days duration have an inelastic demand for air travel since time is very important to them, so they pay a higher price for a trip compared to someone who is away for 7 days or over a weekend. The person away for 7 days or over a weekend is considered by the airlines to be on some form of holiday and to have a more elastic demand for the service, i.e., time spent travelling is not so important to him so he might travel by boat or train.

(b) Students, old age pensioners and children charged lower prices for certain services.

(c) Spouses travelling with business people are carried at a lower rate.

(d) Lower admission charges for women to certain sporting events.

Price discrimination will never be implemented if goods are sold in perfectly competitive markets

14.8. A policy of price discrimination will *not* be implemented if perfect competition exists in all of the markets in which the commodity is sold. If perfect competition exists in all of the markets in which the producer can sell, the producer will supply all his output to the market where the price is highest. This is possible because under the assumption of perfect competition, the producer can sell all of his output at the existing selling price, i.e., he faces a horizontal demand curve for his output.

While it is possible that the producer may be selling in many markets we will confine our attention to two markets — e.g., the domestic market and the export market — the same principle applies irrespective of the number of markets involved.

Example 14.8.
If there is perfect competition in both the domestic and export markets the supplier of the goods will maximise revenue by selling only in the higher priced domestic market.

	Domestic Market				Export Market		
Qty.	Selling Price £	Total Revenue £	Marginal Revenue £	Qty	Selling Price £	Total Revenue £	Marginal Revenue £
1	10	10	—	1	8	8	—
2	10	20	10	2	8	16	8
3	10	30	10	3	8	24	8
4	10	40	10	4	8	32	8
5	10	50	10	5	8	40	8

Perfect competition in high-priced market

14.9. If the producer is a monopolist in the domestic market and sells under perfect competition in the export market, but if demand conditions are such that the selling price is higher in the perfectly competitive export market, then the supplier will maximise his revenue by selling only in the perfectly competitive market as shown in example 14.9.

Example 14.9.
Producer will maximise revenue by selling only in the export market which is the higher priced perfectly competitive market and ignoring the domestic market.

	Domestic Market				Export Market		
Qty.	Selling Price £	Total Revenue £	Marginal Revenue £	Qty.	Selling Price £	Total Revenue £	Marginal Revenue £
1	9.50	9.50	—	1	10	10	—
2	9.25	18.50	9	2	10	20	10
3	9.00	27.00	8.50	3	10	30	10
4	8.75	35.00	8.00	4	10	40	10
5	8.50	42.50	7.50	5	10	50	10

Monopolist in domestic market

14.10. If the demand conditions are such that the selling price in the domestic market in which the producer is a monopolist is higher, then the producer will supply only the higher priced domestic market while marginal revenue in that market exceeds marginal revenue in the export market.

(Remember that because the producer faces a downward sloping demand curve for his output, marginal revenue will fall as the level of output increases). At the stage when the marginal revenue in the domestic market falls below the marginal revenue which could be obtained in the export market, then he switches the sales of these marginal goods to the export market. **Total Revenue will be maximised when marginal revenue in the domestic market (MRd) = marginal revenue in the export market (MRe)** as shown in example 14.10 (a).

Example 14.10 (a)
The producer is a monopolist in the domestic market and perfect competition obtains in export market.

	Domestic Market				Export Market		
Qty.	Selling Price £	Total Revenue £	Marginal Revenue £	Qty.	Selling Price £	Total Revenue £	Marginal Revenue £
1	10	10	—	1	8.65	8.65	—
2	9.70	19.40	9.40	2	8.65	17.30	8.65
3	9.35	28.05	8.65	3	8.65	25.95	8.65
4	8.90	35.60	7.55	4	8.65	34.60	8.65
5	8.40	42.00	6.40	5	8.65	43.25	8.65

In this example if the supplier has an output of 1, 2, or 3 units he would supply only the domestic market because his marginal revenue is greater in the domestic market. If his output exceeds 3 units, e.g., 5 units, he will supply 3 units to the domestic market and 2 units to the export market — in this way he maximises his revenue.

The demand curves for the domestic market and the export market and the total or cumulative demand curve which faces the producer are as follows:—

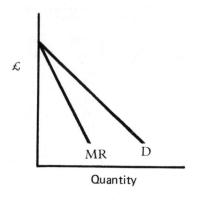

Fig. 14.10.1. Demand curve — domestic market.

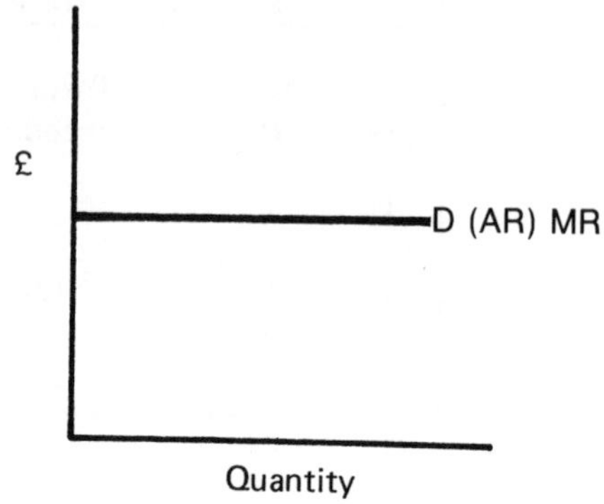

Fig. 14.10.2. Demand curve — export market.

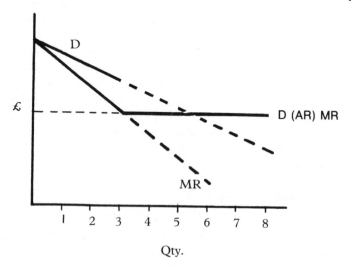

Fig. 14.10.3. Combined demand curve facing the firm: i.e., domestic market & export market.

The dotted lines above show that portion of the demand curves for the individual markets which the producer will *not* be prepared to supply because he would reduce his revenue by doing so as explained above.

Example 14.10 (b)
The producer is a monopolist in both markets.

	Domestic Market				Export Market		
Qty.	Selling Price £	Total Revenue £	Marginal Revenue £	Qty.	Selling Price £	Total Revenue £	Marginal Revenue £
1	10	10	—	1	9.35	9.35	—
2	9.70	19.40	9.40	2	9.00	18.00	8.65
3	9.40	28.20	8.80	3	8.85	26.55	8.55
4	8.90	35.60	7.40	4	8.50	34.00	7.45
5	8.40	42.00	6.40	5	8.00	40.00	6.00

If two items are produced the domestic market will be supplied with both units; if three items are produced two units will be supplied to the domestic market and one unit to the export market; if five units are produced three units will be supplied to the domestic market and two units to the export market. In this way the producer will maximise his revenue (and his profit since there are no costs).

Profit Maximisation under price discrimination MC = MRd = MRe

14.11. The analysis to this stage has been in terms of the manner in which the output would be divided between markets so that *revenue* would be maximised — the condition for *revenue* maximisation was marginal revenue in the domestic market (MRd) = marginal revenue in the export market (MRe). If attention is now directed to *profit* maximisation this means that some criterion must now be established for the quantity which should be produced. This is simply the criterion which has already been established for profit maximisation — that is, production continues until Marginal Cost is equal to Marginal Revenue together with the other profit maximising conditions which are set out in Section 12.8 to 12.23. Thus the profit maximising condition under Price Discrimination is

Marginal Cost = Marginal Revenue in Market D = Marginal Revenue in Market E

$$MC = MRd = MRe$$

plus the other profit maximising conditions which are explained in Chapter 12.

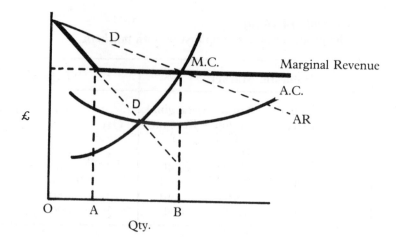

Fig. 14.11. Long run equilibrium under price discrimination.

In Fig. 14.11 those sections of the demand curves which are shown as dotted lines are not relevant as the firm would not supply to that section of the market. In table 14.10 (a) if the firm had 3 items to sell it would not be interested in the export market because it can earn more by selling the 3 items in the domestic market where it is a monopolist. Therefore in Fig. 14.11 up to a level of output of O.A. i.e. 3 units, the firm concentrates on the downward sloping curves which represent the domestic market and it is not interested in the perfectly competitive export market up to that level of output.

Similarly when the firm in table 14.10 (a) has supplied 3 items to the monopolistically domestic market the firm switches further sales to the perfectly competitive export market where it can earn more on these additional sales. Thus for levels of output greater than 3 units (O.A.) it is the perfectly competitive export demand curve which becomes relevant and the irrelevant portion of the monopolistic domestic demand curve is shown as a dotted line. Similarly with the marginal revenue curves. Equilibrium level of production is OB, OA is distributed to the domestic market and AB is distributed to the export market, ie., MC = MRd = MRe.

QUESTIONS

Q1. Define Price Discrimination.

Q2. What are the necessary conditions for the implementation of Price Discrimination.

Q3. Explain the various degrees of Price Discrimination

Q4. Show, by means of a diagram, long run equilibrium for a profit maximising firm which is able to engage in price discrimination between two markets in which it sells its product. In one market perfectly competitive conditions prevail while in the other market the firm is a monopolist.

Q5. If a discriminatory monopolist is selling in two markets, will the selling price (after allowing for transport costs) be the same in both markets. Explain your answers.

Q6. State 2 industries which you considered to be characterised by price discriminatory behaviour and comment on the basis of this behaviour.

15   Imperfect Competition

Imperfect competition lies between perfect competition and monopoly

15.1. In between the polar extremes of Perfect Competition and Monopoly there are the many forms of Imperfect Competition. There are forms of Imperfect Competition which are very close to Perfect Competition and forms close to Monopoly. Where the market forms are close to Monopoly, they are often given specific names, e.g., Duopoly means two sellers and Oligopoly meaning few sellers.

Goods are close but not perfect substitutes

15.2. Imperfect Competition is the form of market structure which is most common in every day living. It is characterised by many producers supplying close but not perfect subsitutes. Firms endeavour to establish in the mind of the public the fact that goods are not perfect substitutes by selling their goods under a brand name. In such case each supplier may be considered as a monopolist in the supply of his own branded good but he can take advantage of this monopoly position only as far as consumers do not consider the other brands to be close substitutes. Carrolls have a monopoly in the supply of Carrolls cigarettes but other brands of cigarettes are close substitutes, as evidenced by the fact that there is little, if any, difference in the price of competitive packages of cigarettes.

15.3. Assumptions underlying the Theory of Imperfect Competition

(a)   Product Differentiation exists. The goods which are supplied by different producers are not homogeneous but they are very close substitutes.

(b)   There is freedom of entry and exit. A firm has the right to supply a competitive product.

(c)   There is perfect knowledge as to the level of profits being earned by all firms in the industry.

(d)   There are many buyers and many sellers, each of whom acts independently of rivals.

(e)   The sole objective of producers is to maximise short run profits.

Each firm faces a downward sloping demand curve for its product

15.4. In view of the aforementioned assumptions each firm faces a downward sloping demand curve for his product. Because there are many goods which are close substitutes, if the producer increases his selling price, there will be a reduction in demand because some consumers will switch to the competitive goods which have become relatively cheaper. Not all consumers will switch to the competitive goods because consumers do not perceive the goods as being perfect substitutes (if they did it would be back to perfect competition). Similarly if the producer lowers his price he will increase his sales as some consumers of other substitute goods will switch to his good because it is relatively cheaper. Thus the level of demand is inversely related to price which means that there is a downward sloping demand curve facing each firm since if the firm increases the selling price of its good there will be a reduction in the quantity demanded.

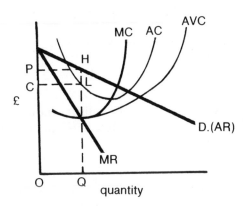

Fig. 15.4. Initial equilibrium of a firm in Imperfect Competition

The firm in Fig. 15.4. produces quantity Q where MC = MR and the other profit maximising conditions (see Section 12.23) are fulfilled. By reference to the demand curve it will be seen that this quantity will be sold at a unit price of P; by reference to average cost curve it will be seen that unit cost at this level of output is C. Supernormal profit per unit is PC (Average Cost includes Normal Profit) and total supernormal profit is indicated by rectangle CLHP, i.e., Supernormal profit per unit PC multiplied by quantity sold CL (= OQ).

New Firms entering the industry

15.5. The existence of supernormal profits results in other firms being attracted into the industry in pursuit of these supernormal profits. Remember that, according to the assumptions, there is perfect knowledge as to the profits being earned (assumption 14.3.c) and there is freedom of entry into the industry (assumption 14.3.b). When other firms enter the industry the firm which had been enjoying supernormal profits can now sell a lesser quantity at each price due to other firms entering into competition with it, i.e., its demand curve shifts in towards the origin as depicted in the diagram below.

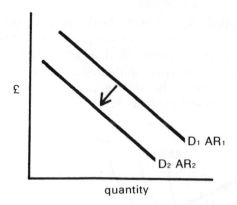

Fig. 15.5. As new firms enter the industry the demand curve of existing firms shifts to the left in towards the origin.

Firms leaving the industry

15.6. In Fig. 15.6, the firm in the short run would produce quantity Q, where MC = MR, above average variable costs and MC increasing at a faster rate than MR. However, at this level of output average cost C is greater than price P so the firm is not earning normal profit and, because of this, firms will leave the industry in the long run. As firms leave the industry the demand curve facing the remaining firms moves outwards from the origin because now the firm in question enjoys an increased demand at each price.

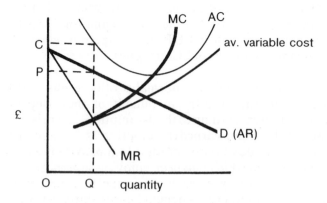

Fig. 15.6. Firm is not earning normal profit.

15.7. The Long Run Equilibrium of the Firm under Imperfect Competition

Long run equilibrium of the firm under Imperfect Competition

15.7. The Long Run Equilibrium of the Firm under Imperfect Competition is shown in Fig. 15.7. The firm produces quantity Q since this fulfills the long run profit maximising conditions (as set out in Section 12.21). At this level of output average cost is equal to average revenue so that only normal profit is being earned, i.e., C = P. Thus there is no incentive for firms to enter or leave the industry.

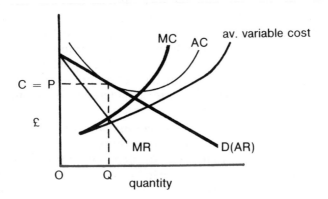

Fig. 15.7. Long run equilibrium of the firm under Imperfect Competition.

Long run equilibrium of the firm under imperfect competition has similarities to both perfect competition and monopoly

15.8. Long Run Equilibrium of the firm under Imperfect Conditions is said to be a combination of the long run equilibrium under Perfect Competition and under Monopoly. It is similar to the long run equilibrium under Perfect Competition in that only normal profit is being earned. Note however that in long run equilibrium under Perfect Competition MC = MR = AC = AR; under Imperfect Competition MC = MR and AC = AR, which is not the same as the Perfectly Competitive situation. It is similar to the long run equilibrium of the Monopolist in that they both face a downward sloping demand curve and in both cases long run equilibrium is not where average cost is at a minimum, so that there is excess, or unused, capacity.

Effect of product differentiation

15.9. The more successful producers are, in an Imperfectly Competitive market structure, in convincing consumers that their goods are different from and better than their competitors, the more will they move from an Imperfectly Competitive situation towards a Monopoly situation. (Conversely the more that consumers think the products of different producers to be perfect substitutes for each other, the closer you come to a Perfectly Competitive market structure).

15.10. Long run equilibrium under Imperfect Competition illustrates the source of the term "Wastes of Competition". Imperfect Competition is considered to be wasteful of resources for two reasons:

Wastes of competition

(a) Over-Capacity — At long run equilibrium the firm is not producing where average costs (unit costs of production) are at a minimum.

(b) Product Differentiation

Over-capacity

15.11. As shown in Fig. 15.7. the firm at long run equilibrium is not producing where average costs (unit costs of production) are at a minimum. If producing where unit costs of production are at a minimum is considered to be the optimum use of existing productive capacity, then the productive capacity of the Imperfectly Competitive firm at long run equilibrium is not being used at the optimum level of production. Putting this another way the firm has available greater productive capacity than it requires for the existing level of output — there is over-capacity — and consequently resources are considered to be wasted.

Forms of product differentiation

15.12. The existence of over-capacity together with an awareness that goods are close but not perfect substitutes for each other stimulates the efforts of firms to increase the demand for their product through product differentiation as mentioned in 15.9 above. Product differentiation is the establishment in the mind of the buying public that there is a difference in the products of different producers. Manufacturers attempt to establish product differentiation through:

(a) Product Development

(b) Advertising

Product development

15.13. Product development as its name suggests is the improvement of products through research and development. The manufacturer hopes, as a result of product development, to be able to increase his profits through increased level of sales and/or prices. The term product differentiation/product development is sometimes used in a derisory manner with reference to:

(a) Changes in the packaging and presentation of goods which are basically similar.

(b) Over-emphasis on minute and unimportant differences in goods, e.g., the colour and shape of breakfast cereals.

Cost of choice

15.14. It is often argued that the inefficiency of resource allocation under Imperfect Competition is the price that we pay for wanting a large range of choice rather than confining production to one or two types in each category even though this would lower costs and prices through economies of scale. The VW Beetle Motor Car was an example of this type of thinking.

*Two aspects
of advertising*

15.15. Attention is usually directed towards two different aspects of advertising.

(a) Informative advertising

(b) Competitive advertising

15.16. Informative advertising is directed towards increasing the knowledge of the buying public with regard to the product. It usually is a combination of making people aware of:

(a) The existence of the product

(b) Where it may be purchased

(c) Its uses and qualities

(d) Its price

It is universally accepted that this type of advertising is beneficial. It makes available to the general public information regarding the alternatives which are available and thus enables them to make a more informed choice. In addition it strengthens the forces of competition.

*Competitive
advertising*

15.17. Competitive advertising stresses the claims of one product against competing products. This is the type of advertising with which we are most familiar and it is usually the type of advertising to which people are referring when they refer in a general way to advertising. Competitive advertising usually stresses the brand name of the product or the name of the firm. The most common examples are the advertising by the manufacturers of different brands of toothpaste, different brands of detergent etc.

*Is advertising
beneficial to
the public?*

15.18. There is considerable disagreement as to whether or not advertising is beneficial. The critics of advertising argue that the considerable expenditure on advertising is unproductive and is wasteful of resources. Those in favour of advertising tend to concentrate on the benefits of informative advertising and to discuss the effects of advertising on demand and unit costs as shown in Fig. 15.19. Sometimes arguments in favour of advertising are based on the employment which is created directly by advertising. The employment increases the costs of the firm and for analytical purposes it is no different to the firm employing extra workers in any other branch of its activities. The real point at issue would be the unit cost of the firm per unit produced/sold at the post-advertising level of output/demand compared with what the unit cost would have been (at presumably a lower level of output) if advertising had not taken place.

Advertising by firms through Arts and Sports sponsorship has many of the features already outlined and the attitude towards these depends, to a large extent, on whether you see such expenditure as an allocation by such firms out of their profits or a means by which such firms may continue to enjoy supernormal profits.

15.19. Advertising, whether beneficial or otherwise certainly increases *total* costs as shown in Fig. 15.19.

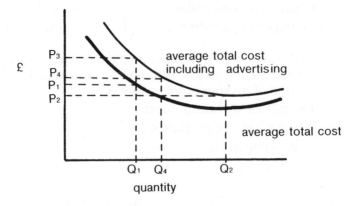

Fig. 15.19. Advertising.

In long run equilibrium under Imperfect Competition, the firm produces and sells where average total cost is equal to price. Prior to the introduction of advertising the firm is producing Q_1 and is selling at price of P_1. Those who stress the advantage of advertising would see demand being increased as a result of advertising so that cost reducing economies can be enjoyed in producing this larger level of output as a result of which the increased quantity of Q_2 is being sold at the lower price of P_2. The critics of advertising assert that the effects of advertising by competitors cancels out, so they would see no effect on demand from advertising, in which case the same quantity Q_1 would be sold at the higher price of P_3. Alternatively they might concede a slight enlargement of the total market through advertisements, a marginally higher quantity might be sold by each firm, say, Q_4 but the price would be higher than the original price, (say), P_4.

Economies of scale in advertising

15.20. There are economies of scale in advertising (you may have noticed the average total cost and advertising curve in Fig. 15.19 moving closer together as the level of output expands). If the advertising costs for a producer of 100 000 packets per week works out at 2p per packet this does not mean that a firm producing only 100 packets per week could conduct the same type of advertising for a cost of 2p per packet. There is need for some minimum level of expenditure before advertising becomes effective. This is known as a *threshold payment* and may be seen as a form of fixed cost for those who wish to advertise. From this point of view advertising may be used as a form of barrier to entry into an industry, particularly if it is a type of industry which by its nature does not enjoy economies of scale in production.

Where the nature of the industry is such that it does not lend itself to economies of scale in production, then small producers in the industry would not suffer any cost disadvantage through its production costs; for this reason, it is said that "technological barriers to entry into the industry are weak". This situation is depicted in Fig. 15.20 where at an output of Q_1 unit cost of production is P_1 and at the larger level of production Q_2 unit cost remains at P_1. However, with the introduction of advertising, unit cost at output Q_1 is P_4 which is higher than the unit cost of P_3 at output Q_2. Of course, it is implied in this analysis that it is necessary for the smaller firm to advertise in order to sell against the larger firm which advertises. Perhaps you might consider the example in relation to the sale of detergents where, according to submissions to the British Monopolies Commission, selling expenses represent approx. 30% of manufacturers' costs.

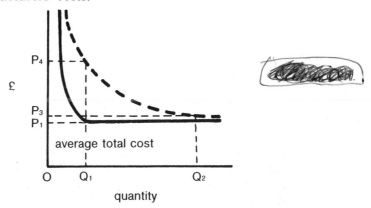

Fig. 15.20. Technological barriers to entry are weak.

15.21. *Only in Imperfect Competition will there be competitive advertising.* Under Perfect Competition the producers are supplying a homogeneous product so that it is not possible to distinguish between the products of different producers, e.g., there would be no point in John Murphy of Clonakilty conducting an advertising campaign in an effort to encourage people to eat his potatoes since it is not possible for purchasers to distinguish John Murphy's potatoes from the potatoes of other suppliers. In addition, each firm under Perfect Competition is considered to supply a very small portion of the market so that if, as a result of John Murphy's advertising campaign, more potatoes are eaten, John Murphy would benefit only to a very small extent.

Absence of competitive advertising under monopoly

15.22. Similarly since the Monopolist is by definition a single seller of the good there is no competition and consequently there is no need for him to engage in competitive advertising.

Public relations or industrial type advertising

15.23. Under perfect competition or monopoly there may be public relations or industrial type of advertising, e.g., "Eat more fresh fruit", "Look for the woolmark", "The E.S.B. looks after your needs 24 hours a day", "At your friendly bank your money is secure".

QUESTIONS

Q1. Set out the assumptions underlying the Theory of Imperfect Competition

Q2. Contrast the assumptions underlying Perfect Competition with those of Imperfect Competition.

Q3. Explain by means of a diagram long run equilibrium of the Imperfectly Competitive firm.

Q4. What is meant by the "wastes of competition."

Q5. Is advertising beneficial to the general public.?

16   Oligopoly

16.1. Oligopoly comes from the Greek and means few sellers. As shown in Fig. 16.1. Oligopoly is a form of Imperfect Competition — firms are producing goods or services which are close substitutes. Examples of oligopolistic markets are the markets for motor cars, television sets, washing machines, petrol, soaps, detergents etc. In chapter 15 the firm under Imperfect Competition is shown as pursuing a policy of profit maximisation without taking into account the possible reaction of its competitors. In contrast the essence of Oligopoly is that, since there are few sellers of a good, each seller is aware of, and can identify, his competitors so that he takes into account the possible reactions of competitors to any efforts he may make to increase his profits or market share, i.e., the **actions of firms are interdependent**. There is no general theory of Oligopoly, there are a number of models each based on different opinions by decision makers as to the reaction of competitors and the competitive interaction between firms.

16.2. Model of competitive interplay

Before proceeding to a discussion of some models of Oligopoly let us consider a simple model of market behaviour which captures the essence of competitive interplay. In this model there are two competitors producing identical products at zero cost, there is no limitation on supply, they are both individually capable of supplying any level of demand, they have perfect knowledge of the demand at each price, they both wish to obtain maximum profit.

Example 16.2

Stage 1

Price P	Qty. Demanded	Total Revenue (and Profit since there are no costs) £
1	980	9.80
2	840	16.80
3	700	21.00
4	630	25.20
5	570	28.50
6	480	28.80
7	380	26.60
8	310	24.80
9	200	18.00
10	85	8.50

Table 16.2.(a) Total Demand Curve

If A is first into the market and is of the opinion that B will not enter the market he will consider himself to be a monopolist in which circumstance he will sell 480 units at 6p each since this will give him the greatest profit.

Stage 2
B now enters the market and is aware that A is selling at a price of 6p per unit, since they are selling an identical product B is of the opinion that he cannot sell at a higher price. In addition B is of the opinion that A will continue to sell at the price of 6p even after B has commenced selling. Thus the demand which B perceives for his output is as shown in table 16.2 (b) i.e., the total demand curve as shown in table 16.2 (a) for prices of 6p and below, minus the 480 units which A is already supplying.

Table 16.2 (b) Demand curve facing B when A is supplying 480 units at a price of 6p each.

Price P	Qty. Demanded	Total Revenue (and Profit since there are not costs) £
1	500	5.00
2	360	7.20
3	220	6.60
4	150	6.00
5	90	4.50
6	0	0

In these circumstances B will supply 360 units at a price of 2p each since this gives him the largest profit.

Stage 3
When A learns that B is selling at a price of 2p he is of the opinion that if he tries to sell at a price in excess of 2p he will lose his customers so A now perceives the demand for his product to be the total demand as shown in table 16.2 (a) for prices of 2p and below, minus the 360 units which B is supplying at 2p each.

Table 16.2 (c) Demand curve facing A when B is supplying 360 units at 2p each.

Price P	Qty. Demanded	Total Revenue (and Profit since there are no costs) £
1	620	6.20
2	480	9.60

In this circumstance A supplies 480 units at 2p which gives him the largest profit. Since neither A nor B can increase their profit by a further reduction in their price in the absence of collusion (see section 16.4) the equilibrium price remains at 2p unless the firms change their strategies. Note that the total profit of £16.80 (which is divided between the two firms) is less than the initial monopolist profit of £28.80 being earned by A.

16.3. The Cournot model of Oligopoly

This model which is often taken as the starting point in the study of oligopoly was published by Augustin Cournot in 1838. However it did not attract much attention until the 1930's when the study of Imperfectly Competitive markets was a subject of considerable interest among economists.

Assumption of Cournot's model

(a) Two manufacturers are producing identical goods at identical and constant unit costs. (The classical example is of two firms selling spring water; each firm experiences zero cost of production).

(b) Both firms seek maximum profit.

(c) Both firms have full details of total demand and the demand curve is linear.

(d) Each firm observes the level of output of its rival and assumes that its rival will continue to supply that quantity.

(e) Both firms adjust their level of output (but not their prices) in pursuit of their goal of maximum profit.

With a linear demand curve and constant units costs, the profit maximising level of output for a monopolist is always half of the level of output if perfect competition prevailed★.

Footnote:

★Demand being linear P (average Revenue) = a+bq.
Total Revenue = P×Q = aq+bq².

Slope of demand (average Revenue) curve = b.

Marginal Revenue = $\frac{d}{dq}$ TR = a+2bq.

Slope of Marginal Revenue curve = 2b, i.e. the Marginal Revenue curve slopes (is falling) twice as fast as the Average Revenue curve.

With constant unit costs the Marginal Cost curve will be parallel to the horizontal axis. Under profit maximum monopoly the equilibrium is where MC = MR, whereas equilibrium for the perfectly competitive industry is at MC = AR.

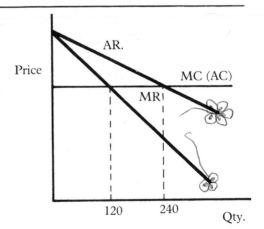

The output of the perfectly competitive industry would be 240 units and the output of the monopolistic industry would be **120 units.**

If the output under perfect competition would be 12,800 units, then when firm A enters the market first as a monopolist it will produce 6,400 units (i.e. ½ of the Perfectly Competitive output). When firm B enters it will supply ½ of the unsatisfied demand (i.e. ½ of 12,800—6,400) and so the development proceeds as shown in table 16.3.

Assume the perfectly competitive output to be 12,800 units.

Table 16.3. Equilibrium under the Cournot Model.

Stage	Firm A's Output	Firm B's Output	Explanation
1	6 400		½ of 12,800
2		3 200	½ of (12,000 — 6,400)
3	4 400		½ of (12,800 — 3,200)
4		4 000	½ of (12,800 — 4,800)
5	4 400		½ of (12,800 — 4,000)
6		4 200	½ of (12,800 — 4,400)
7	4 300		½ of (12,800 — 4,200)
8		4 250	½ of (12,800 — 4,300)
9	275		½ of (12,800 — 4,250)
10		4 262	½ of (12,800 — 4,275)
11	4 269		½ of (12,800 — 4,262)
Equilibrium	4 266	4 266	

If number of firms increase, the equilibrium level of output of industry increases

In this model of two sellers the market equilibrium level of output is 8,532 which is ⅔ of the competitive level of output of 12,800. If there were three sellers included in the example the market equilibrium level of output would be ¾ of the perfectly competitive level of output. If there where N sellers the market equilibrium level of output would be $N/N+1$ of the perfectly competitive level of output — as the number of competitive firms supplying the market increases (i.e., as N becomes large) the level of output approaches the Perfectly Competitive level of output, provided unit cost of production remains constant.

Note again that the total profits enjoyed by the firms in the industry is less than would be obtained by a monopolist.

16.4. Cartels/Collusion

Cartels can increase profits

It will be noticed that in both the above cases, as in many models of oligopoly, the level of output is greater and profitability is lower than would be possible under monopoly. In an attempt to obtain these extra profits firms often collude — they agree to act jointly on such matters as pricing, output and sales territories. When such an agreement is of a formal and explicit nature it is known as a cartel. Though the pursuit of extra profits encourages firms to enter into such agreements, the agreements are often short-lived because of the difficulties associated with ensuring that all firms act in accordance with the agreement. If there was complete agreement between firms in a profit maximising cartel they would agree to sell at the monopolistic profit maximising price/output combination. By so doing they would have the maximum profit available for the members of the cartel. In example 16.2 at equilibrium after competition has taken place A is earning £9.60 profit and B is earning £7.20 profit, in contrast to this when the industry was monopolistic the level of profit was £28.80. If the 2 firms A and B collude and act as a monopolist they could divide between them the monoplistic level of profit of £28.80 and thus they could be both better off with profits of (say) £14.40 each.

Price Rigidity

16.5. Studies of a number of oligopolistic industries suggested that prices tended to be fairly rigid in such industries. Price rigidity is the term used to describe a situation in which prices tend not to change even when there is a change in costs. Of course if there are major and fundamental changes in costs, prices will have to change since otherwise the firm would be suffering losses. Price rigidity must be distinguished from price constancy.

Price Constancy

16.6. It is not feasible for firms to reflect in their selling prices every small fluctuation in their costs. This is known as price constancy and is due to the following reasons:

(a)   There are administrative costs in changing prices — price lists must be changed, distributors of the product must be notified.

(b)   If the good is of a seasonal nature, it is inconvenient to change prices during a season, e.g., hotel charges for the Summer season, or a manufacturer of ladies' winter coats who is supplying them to a mail order firm which is conducting a campaign for the coats at a specified price, or high class shops who fear a loss of customers' goodwill if they change their selling prices during the season.

Attempt to explain price rigidity

16.7. "Kinked" Demand Curve Model of Oligopoly

This is one of the most popular models of Oligopoly because it suggested an explanation for the price rigidity which characterised some oligopolistic industries. Paul Sweezy introduced this model in 1939 which postulated a belief by decision makers that:

(a)   in the absence of cost increases competitors would not follow a price increase but would expand their market share and gain extra profit through selling an increased quantity at existing prices (or with a smaller price increase).

(b)   if they reduce their prices their competitors will match their price reduction and the enterprise will be less profitable.

In the light of these opinions firms would be reluctant to alter their prices in the absence of some fundamental change in costs, i.e., prices would tend to be rigid.

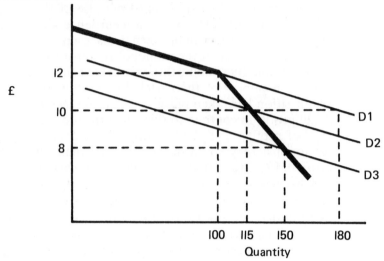

Fig. 16.7. Derivation of kinked demand curve.

Initially 100 units are being supplied at a price of £12 — the firm then reduced its price to £10 anticipating a demand of 180 units since on the original demand curve D_1 a demand of 180 units is forthcoming when the price is £10. However when the firm reduces its price to £10, its competitors reduce their price also. You will recall from section 6.2 to 6.4 that when competitive goods are reduced in price the demand curve shifts inwards — to D_2 in fig. 16.7 — so that when the firm reduces its price to £10 demand for its output is 115 units. Similarly if price is further reduced to £8 quantity demanded is 150 units. However if the firm increases its prices above £12 (in the absence of a cost increase) other firms will not follow suit so that the portion of demand curve D_1 above the existing price of £12 remains. Thus the demand curve is as shown by the heavy black line in fig. 16.7. This may be only a subjective demand curve, it may exist only in the mind of the decision maker, but pricing decisions will be based on this demand curve which has a "kink" at the existing price hence the name of the model.

Further justification for price rigidity

16.8. A further justification for price rigidity under the kinked demand curve model is shown in fig. 16.8. If there is a "kink" in the demand curve there is a discontinuity in the marginal revenue curve, there are, in fact, two marginal revenue curves, one for that portion of the demand curve above the kink which occurs at point K, and one for that portion below the kink. If orginally the firm is at equilibrium with a cost structure shown by marginal cost curve MC_1, and marginal costs increase to MC_2, the profit maximising level of output has not changed. (Average Cost curve has not been shown in diagram for the sake of simplicity).

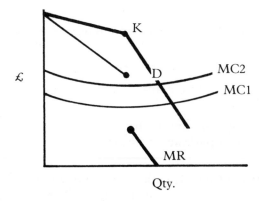

Fig. 16.8. Profit maximising equilibrium in kinked demand curve model

Pattern of price differentials

16.9. It should be noted that the price of the products of oligopolistic firms need not necessarily be identical but they are likely to be in line with each other — there is likely to be an established and accepted pattern of price differentials. In addition prices are likely to move in sympathy with each other so that price differentials are maintained e.g., Ford, Fiat and VW cars. If a particular model of Ford car is (say) £300 cheaper than a particular model of Fiat car and the price of the Ford car is reduced even further there will be a tendency for the price of the Fiat car to be reduced so that the price differential remains at (or close to) the original level of £300.

Dominant firm controls price

16.10. Price Leadership
Some oligopolistic industries are characterised by a form of price leadership. There may be a firm which dominates the industry through its lower costs, larger size, greater financial resources or some combination of these, while the smaller firms follow through fear, convenience or laziness. The dominant firm becomes the price leader, it acts as if it was a monopolist and choses the price/output combination which maximises its profits. The smaller firms consider the market price set by the leader as being a datum (or given) and they then choose the output which gives them the most profit — provided they do not interfere with the market share of the price leader, this dominant firm will leave them alone.

16.11. Non-Price Competition

Forms of competition other than price

Oligopolistic firms which do not wish to engage in price competition may adopt a competitive strategy in respect of the other factors which influence demand. This is known as non-price competition and may consist of competition in respect of:

(a) after sales service, or spare parts being available at competitive prices, e.g., in respect of electrical goods or motor cars.

(b) product differentiation or quality. Where the firms attempt to increase sales through the style or quality of their product, e.g., motor cars.

(c) advertising the product in an aggressive and highly competitive manner.

(d) promotional gifts or free coupons.

(e) demonstrations, free planning and advisory services, e.g., kitchen furniture.

(f) luxurious surroundings in shops, free car parks, late night shopping, credit terms, parking facilities etc.

16.12. Objectives of the firm other than short run profit maximisation

Reasons why firms may not seek to maximise short run profits

All of the models of the firm in this book have been based on the assumption of profit maximisation — the notion that firms set out to make as much profit as possible. Though it is necessary at this stage to consider some objectives other than profit maximisation which firms may pursue, the profit maximisation assumption should not be discarded lightly — how many businessmen are aware of different (and legal) courses of action which would increase their profits and not take such courses of action? However, there are situations when a firm does not set out to maximise short run profits. The following are some examples:

(a) Because firms are of the opinion that if they take advantage of their monopolistic position and earn large supernormal profits the government may intervene in the market and restrict the firm's activities in some way.

Limit Pricing

(b) Firms may not wish to encourage the entry of new firms by earning large supernormal profits. When prices are set at a level which is intended to discourage the entry of new firms the firm is said to be engaged in Limit Pricing. Since this limit pricing results in the firm earning less than the highest level of profit which it could earn the firm is sacrificing profits in the short term in order to enjoy benefits over a longer time horizon e.g. a firm earns £1000 each year for 3 years and other firms encouraged by the attraction of these profits enter the market and the profit of the original firm is £350 per year for the following 7 years so that over a 10 year period the firm earned £5450 ($1000 \times 3 + 350 \times 7$). In contrast the firm might have engaged in Limit Pricing so that its profits were £750 per year but due to this pricing policy other firms could not gain a foothold in the market so that the firm earned £750 per year for each of the 10 years i.e. £7500.

(c) Depending on the age, health, domestic responsibilities and other personal characteristics of the monopolist he may prefer a stable level of adequate profits rather than the constant striving for large supernormal profits, e.g., if his family is reared and not in the business he may not strive as hard as when his children were young and he was building up the business.

(d) If the managers of the firm are not the owners, they may tend to adopt a conservative approach, rather than dynamic profit maximising behaviour. This situation may be a problem in State sponsored trading corporations. The basic reason for this problem is related to the fact that the rewards to such people may not be sufficiently attractive to motivate (and compensate) them to seek out and undertake the risks which are an inherent element in a dynamic economy.

16.13. Baumol Model of Sales Maximisation subject to the earning of a target level of profit.

A well known model of non-profit maximising behaviour was introduced by William J. Baumol of Princeton University. In this model the management of the firm must earn a certain level of profits in order to permit the payment of an adequate dividend to shareholders, to provide funds for reinvestment in the firm and to satisfy banks and other such financial institutions as to the long term viability of the firm. In an ongoing situation this establishes a minimum level of profits which the firm must earn.

For various reasons the firm seeks to have a high level of sales e.g.

(a) When marginal cost is less than marginal revenue increased sales means increased profits.

(b) By increasing sales a breakthrough to economies of scale is possible.

(c) By ensuring that its goods are extensively available the firm makes it more difficult for other firms to enter the market.

(d) Production managers and Sales and Marketing executives may feel that their career prospects are improved if they increase the level of output/sales.

In this model we are really considering a level of sales beyond the profit maximising level so reasons (b), (c) and (d) above are more relevant than reason (a) for the present purpose. However while the firm is not seeking to earn the maximum level of profit, as already stated there is some minimum level of profit which the firm must earn. With these 2 purposes the objective of the firm may be stated as *"the maximisation of Sales Revenue with the requirement that some target (minimum) level of profit must be earned"*. Fig. 16.13 is the appropriate diagram. It should be noted that the objective of the firm is not merely to maximise sales revenue since this would be done by lowering prices to generate a large level of demand/sales. But if prices are lowered merely to generate demand without any regard to the cost of producing the goods the firm would be losing money on such sales. Thus it is unrealistic and naive to consider the objective of the firm to be the maximisation of Sales Revenue without also mentioning that the firm must earn at least some minimum (target) rate of return.

The point to note is that the target level of profits for this firm is less than the maximum profits which the firm could earn. The firm also wishes to

reach the highest possible level of sales consistent with the earning of the
target level of profits.

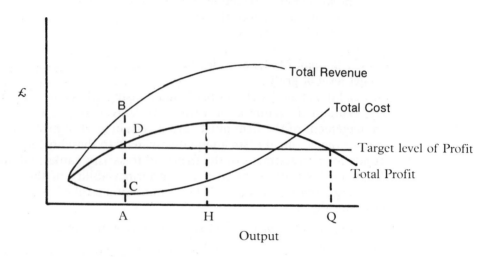

Fig. 16.13. Baumol's Model.

The total profit curve is the difference between the total revenue and
total cost curves at each level of output, e.g., at level of output A, total
revenue is B, and total cost is C and total profit is D (i.e. B—C). If the firm
was maximising profit it would produce quantity H — however the firm
produces Quantity Q — since at this level of output the firm is
maximising its level of sales consistent with the earning of the target level
of profit.

QUESTIONS

Q1. Is there any justification for studying Oligopoly separately from the
     general Theory of Imperfect Competition?

Q2. Explain why it is considered that prices under Oligopoly may not be
     very flexible.

Q3. Write an explanatory note on Non-Price Competition.

Q4. What is the objective of the firm in the Baumol Model. Show how
     the firm attains equilibrium in this model.

Q5. Distinguish between Price Rigidity and Price Constancy.

Q6. Refer to any oligopolistic industry with which you are familiar and
     explain how it conforms to the points discussed in this chapter.

17 Market Intervention by Government

17.1. Per unit taxes

If the government imposes a tax on goods such that the amount of the tax varies with the amount produced, this is known as a per unit tax. A tax of this nature increases the cost of production by the amount of the tax as shown in fig. 17.1.

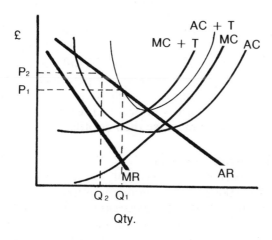

Fig. 17.1. Effect of a per unit tax

By the incidence of a tax we mean the people who actually pay the amount of the tax. It is possible that

(a) the selling price of the good may be increased by the amount of the tax;

(b) perhaps the selling price may be unchanged with the tax in effect being paid out of profits;

(c) alternatively the selling price of the good may be increased by an amount less than the amount of the tax so that part of the tax would be paid by the purchaser of the good and part of it would be paid out of profits by the supplier of the good.

The incidence of the tax depends on the relative elasticities of supply and demand. If demand is perfectly inelastic with respect to a price change then the same quantity of the good would be demanded (purchased) even if the selling price of the good is increased. In this case the price of the good would be increased by the amount of the tax — the full incidence of the tax would be on the purchasers. Conversely if the supply of the good is perfectly inelastic this means that the same quantity of the good would be supplied even if the supplier received a lower price. In this case the selling price of the good would remain the same and the incidence of the tax would fall entirely on the supplier of the good. If both the supply of, and demand for, the good are relatively elastic, part of the incidence of the tax will be on the supplier and part on the purchaser in a proportion dependent on their relative elasticities of supply and demand.

In Fig. 17.1 originally the equilibrium quantity was Q_1 which was sold at a price of P_1, *the per unit tax increased marginal costs to MC + T and this* increased marginal cost curve is equal to marginal revenue at an equilibrium level of output of Q_2 and the corresponding selling price is P_2.

If the Minister for Finance imposes the tax in order to increase revenue, he is likely to select goods with a relatively inelastic demand, e.g., petrol and alcohol. Because a per unit tax has the same impact on the unit costs of all producers of the good, it is likely to be passed on through increasing the selling price of the good by the full amount of the tax since all suppliers will be aware that all their competitors have been subject to the same increase. It is of course possible that some firms would, at least initially, not put up their prices in order to see if demand is sufficiently elastic for such a tactic to increase their profits.

17.2 A Social Loss from Taxation

Fig. 17.2 depicts a perfectly elastic supply curve and a downward sloping demand curve with the equilibrium price/output combination taken to be P_1/Q_1. *Consumers surplus is represented by the area covered by the triangle AP_1C.* A per unit tax is levied on the good as a result of which the supply curve moves upwards and price rises to P_2, the equilibrium level of output is Q_2 and consumers surplus is now AP_2K.

The revenue earned by the state is represented by rectangle P_2KMP_1 (i.e. tax per unit P_1P_2 multiplied by quantity sold P_1M).

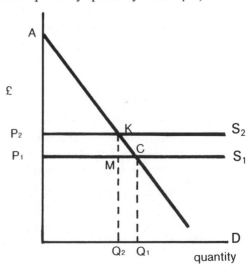

Fig. 17.2. Social loss from taxation

Consumers surplus lost is P_2KCP_1. Consumers surplus lost which the state obtained through tax revenue P_2KMP_1. *Social loss (i.e. consumers surplus which has been lost and which has not been obtained by the State) is KCM.*

17.3. Lump Sum Taxes

Will a lump sum tax affect the equilibrium price/quantity?

As their name implies, taxes of this nature are of a lump sum nature and the amount of the tax is not directly related to the quantity produced. It is not possible for the producer to escape a lump sum tax by altering the quantity which is produced. For this reason, a tax of this nature represents an addition to fixed costs. *However, this form of tax is not identical with fixed costs because it is possible to escape from this expense, even in the short run, by ceasing to trade.* A tax of this nature is often referred to as a form of licence tax.

17.4. Reaction of a firm to the Imposition of a Lump Sum

(a) If the amount of the lump sum tax is less than any supernormal profits which the firm is earning at equilibrium, then the firm will absorb the lump sum tax. This may be explained as follows: if the firm is a short run profit maximiser at equilibrium, then it has struck the combination of marginal cost and marginal revenue which maximises profits. This lump sum tax does not affect marginal cost therefore the profit maximising level of output, where $MC = MR$, remains unaltered.

(b) If the lump sum tax takes from the firm all of its supernormal profit but the firm stills obtains normal profit from the activity then neither the market price nor the market quantity will change for the reasons set out in (a) above.

(c) If, however, the lump sum tax is greater than any supernormal profits which the firm may be earning so that the firm could not earn even normal profit after the imposition of the tax, then the firm would in the long run withdraw from the industry (remember that the firm was at profit maximising equilibrium, therefore there is no way that it can alter its price/output equilibrium and increase its profits).

17.5. Subsidies

A subsidy exists when the government makes a contribution to the costs of production. The payment may be related to the number of units produced or it may be in the form of a lump sum. It is usually given to encourage the production of goods where such production is considered to be socially desirable, though it may not be economically viable, e.g., the subsidy which is given to C.I.E. Because the effects of a subsidy are the opposite to the effects of a tax, a subsidy is often referred to as a negative tax. A subsidy lowers the unit cost of production to the manufacturer and its precise effect in terms of increased quantity made available to, and purchased by, consumers depends upon price elasticity of supply and price elasticity of demand. Other things being equal, the effect of the subsidy on the quantity which producers would be prepared to supply would be greatest if the firm was to enjoy cost reducing economies at higher levels of output; whereas the effects would be lowest if unit cost increasing diseconomies occurred at higher levels of output.

Similarly the more elastic is demand in response to a change in price, the greater will be the increase in demand for any given reduction in price.

17.6. Price control

Price control exists when the government intervenes to cause price/output equilibrium to be different from what it would have been in the absence of such intervention. This intervention is usually of two forms:

(a) Maximum prices

This is usually done to prevent a producer exploiting his dominant market position and is often invoked in respect of goods the demand for which is inelastic in response to a price change.

(b) Guaranteed/intervention or minimum prices

This procedure is usually adopted in respect of agricultural products, the selling price of which could be subject to considerable variation. Usually the guaranteed price is the expected average price so that if there is a large supply in one year, the government buys the excess supply at the guaranteed price. In the subsequent year when there is excess demand (shortage of supply) the government sells at the guaranteed price the quantity which it had previously bought. This procedure is adopted because in the short term there is an inelastic supply of agricultural products which could result in the selling price being subject to wide fluctuations. If farmers had to sell in year one at a bad price, they might not produce an adequate supply in year two, so that there could be a cycle of gluts and shortages.

If the guaranteed price is set higher than the average price which would be determined by market forces, then the supply of the commodity will be greater than the market requires and considerable stores of surplus products will be created, e.g., butter mountain, wine lake etc.

The guaranteed price makes production of the good attractive because it removes or lessens uncertainty and places a floor to the possible losses of suppliers. Often, when there is in existence a system of intervention/guaranteed prices, it becomes necessary to place some restriction on the quantity which may be produced or the quantity in respect of which the intervention/guaranteed pricing system will apply.

17.7. Rationing

Rationing is the sharing out, on some predetermined basis, of a good for which there is excess demand. As has been stated previously, goods are usually shared out through market forces on the basis of price. On occasions, the government may intervene to share out the available supply on some basis of fairness or equity, rather than through price, so that rationing implies some form of limitation on price. A system of rationing is often introduced during wars or when there is some force of calamity or disaster in an area, e.g. earthquake, floods etc. In recent years petrol coupons were issued to motorists when it was thought that the availability of petrol might be restricted.

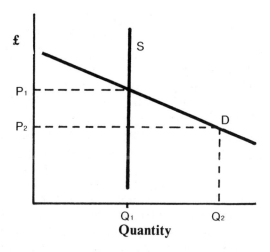

Fig. 17.7. With rationing and price control there is excess demand.

As shown in Fig. 17.7 the supply of the good is inelastic. Left to free market forces, price would settle at P_1. The government decides to restrict price to P_2 (at which price there is excess demand of $Q_1 Q_2$) and to allocate the available supply among those wishing to obtain the good. When rationing is in force:

(a)   Resources are required to administer the system

(b)   The basis of allocation must be decided and it is often difficult to obtain public acceptance for the method chosen.

(c)   The longer the period during which rationing has been in force the greater the likelihood that there is a difference between present conditions and the conditions which pertained when rationing was introduced.

(d)   Often a "black market" develops whereby supplies of the good are sold illicitly to the highest bidder.

17.8. Quotas
A quota is a limitation to the quantity of goods on sale. It is most usually heard of in relation to international trade, when there is a wish on the part

of the government to restrict the quantity of a good which may be imported. Quotas are introduced when there is an inelastic demand for the good in question and consequently the raising of the price of the good through rendering it subject to duties would not have a significant effect on the quantity which would be purchased. A limitation on the quantity of a good being imported may be considered desirable:

(a) In order to limit the quantity of foreign currency being used for the purchase of the good or for the goods of a particular country.

(b) In order to protect domestic industries which are producing competitive products.

When a quota is imposed, a licence is required in order to import the permitted quantity. Since this is a form of rationing there must be some basis for the allotment of the licences. In recent times the shoe industry was subject to this type of control. If the total annual sales of shoes were 100 000 pairs and the government wished to restrict imports to 10% of total demand, i.e., 10 000 pairs of shoes, they could grant a licence for the importation of 10 pairs of shoes to a person for every 100 pair of shoes which he purchased from Irish manufacturers.

Under free market conditions, if the supply of foreign shoes is restricted through the quota system, the price of such shoes will increase. In which case the sellers of such shoes will enjoy supernormal profits on each pair sold and may be inclined to devote more sales energy to the sale of such shoes. An increased price for these shoes may increase the cost of living so for this reason the government may place some form of price control on imports of this nature (though with the reduction in the quantity being imported the total profit of those relying solely on the sale of these goods will be reduced). Also there is a strong possibility that the quota licences may be sold, while constant vigilance is required in order to ensure that additional quantities of the good are not imported illegally.

QUESTIONS

Q1. What is meant by the incidence of a tax and what factors influence the incidence of a per unit tax?

Q2. Is there likely to be a social loss if a per unit tax is imposed on a good?

Q3. Will a lump sum tax affect the firm's price/output equilibrium?

Q4. Why should a government consider it to be desirable to impose a maximum price control on some goods?

Q5. Write an explanatory note on "Intervention Prices."

Q6. What affect(s) is likely in a market which is subject to rationing?

18   Factors of Production

18.1. All economic activities require the use of resources. While this point is very obvious when considering large factories, it is equally true in the case of the labour which is required in order to gather blackberries which grow wild throughout the country. These economic resources or inputs are usually referred to as Factors of Production. *Factors of Production are defined as those resources or inputs which contribute to economic activity.*

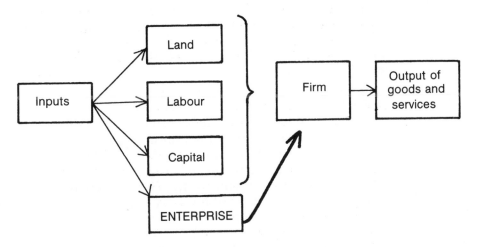

Fig. 18.1. Factors of Production.

Land, Labour, Capital and Enterprise

18.2. Factors of Production are usually classified into four categories — Land, Labour, Capital and Enterprise. Each of these terms has a precise meaning and they are defined in a manner which permits all factors of production to be placed into one of these categories. Thus these terms have a meaning which may be somewhat different from the meaning which you apply to them in everyday use.

Demands for factors of Production is a derived demand

18.3. Factors of production are sought after because of the contribution which they make to economic activity — builders purchase concrete blocks not because they consider them to be beautiful but only because they require them in order to build houses. Thus the demand for factors of production is a *Derived Demand* — the demand for them is derived from the demand for the goods which they help to produce. If there is a demand for houses there will be a demand for carpenters, bricklayers, window frames, concrete blocks etc. The price which will be paid in order to acquire the factor depends on the extra revenue which the firm earns through employing the factor.

Specific factors of production

18.4. *Specific factors of production* are factors of production of a specialised nature — they cannot be easily adapted to other uses. Not many factors of production are so specific that they cannot be transferred to other uses. Some examples of the more specific factors of production might be: mountain land which has no use other than for sheep grazing, a railway station, an intricate specialised piece of machinery, or bogland the only use of which is the production of turf. Scientific progress is constantly attacking this frontier and discovering alternative uses for factors of production, e.g., a use for bogland after it has given up its harvest of turf.

Non-specific factors of production

18.5. *Non-specific factors of production* are factors of production which can be relatively easily transferred to other uses: farmland can be transferred from the growing of different crops to use as pastureland. Unskilled labour can be transferred from one type of unskilled labour to another fairly easily, but it requires training before it can be used in more skilled occupations.

Occupational mobility

18.6. Closely allied to the concept of specificity is the idea of mobility of factors of production. Mobility of a factor of production refers to the ease with which a factor can be transferred from one use to another. *Occupational mobility* refers to the ease with which a factor of production can move from one occupation to another, e.g., how easily can workers move from one job to another — from labourers to doctors, from clerks to teachers etc., or how possible is it for workers to attain those positions for which they are qualified.

Geographical mobility

18.7. *Geographical mobility* refers to the ease with which factors of production can move from one area or country to another. As already stated, factors of production are required only because of the contribution which they are capable of making to production, i.e., there is a derived demand for them; consequently, the intensity of the demand for a factor of production and the price which will be paid for it depends upon the value of their contribution. The value of their contribution depends on their productivity which is reflected in the extra revenue which is earned when the factor is employed.

Marginal revenue productivity

18.8. *Marginal revenue productivity is defined as the extra revenue which is earned through employing an extra increment of a factor of production.* For example, if the revenue of the firm when 10 men are employed is £100.00 and £120.00 is the revenue of the firm when 11 men are employed and all other factors of production remain constant, then the marginal physical productivity through employing the 11th man is £20 i.e., (£120 — £100).

Marginal physical productivity

18.9. *Marginal physical productivity is defined as the extra output generated through the employment of an extra increment of a factor of production.* For example if output is 80 units when 10 men are employed and 95 units are produced when 11 men are employed and all other factors of production remain constant, then the marginal physical productivity through employing the 11th man is 15 units (95 — 80).

Meaning of Marginal Revenue Productivity Theory

18.10. Marginal revenue productivity theory does not state that each unit of each factor of production receives the value of its own contribution to production, but rather that each unit is paid the equivalent of the value that the **last unit** contributes when all other factors of production are held constant, e.g., each worker is paid a sum equal to the additional revenue which accrues through the employment of the last worker.

Difficulty in measuring Marginal Revenue Productivity

18.11. In all the above examples it has been assumed that it is possible to measure accurately and unambiguously the Marginal Physical Productivity and Marginal Revenue Productivity of a factor of production. In practice this may not be so as illustrated in the following cases.

(a)   If a combination of capital and labour is required to carry out an economic activity e.g. a truck and a truck driver, it is not possible to allocate a Marginal Revenue Productivity to either the truck alone or the truck driver alone. The best one could hope to do is to determine the Marginal Revenue Productivity of the economic unit i.e. the truck and the truck driver combined. This is often the source of industrial disputes, when new machinery with increased productivity is being introduced. The machinery in order to carry out the work generally requires a worker to operate the machinery, there then arises the question of how much of the increased productivity is due to the machinery and how much is attributable to the workers. Sometimes even when the duties of the worker is lightened in every way by the introduction of the machinery a wage increase for "increased responsibility" is given to the worker.

(b)   In many cases there is no definite end product to be sold at market prices e.g. teachers, gardai. In such cases there is an attempt to introduce some concept of Marginal Revenue Productivity by comparing the work done to other work of a similar nature which is subject to market forces e.g. Gardai and employees of security firms. Alternatively the value of the job may be established by relating the job to other jobs for which there is a measurable Marginal Revenue Productivity and where the standard of workers in terms of education, training and conditions of work are similar.

Transfer Earnings

18.12. The supply price of a factor of production is the minimum payment required in order to bring it into existence for a particular purpose and maintain it in its present use. The phrase "for a particular purpose" is important because a factor may have a physical existence but may not be available for a particular purpose. If I wish to employ a carpenter, I must pay a wage rate which will result in him agreeing to work for me. The supply price of this factor of production to me is what I must pay him in order that he may offer his services to me. Having got him to work for me I must pay him at a rate which will discourage him from going to a different employer. The wage he can get in the next best job available to him is known as his *transfer earnings*, e.g., if the best wages which my carpenter can get elsewhere is £180.00 per week, then his transfer earnings are £180.00 per week.

18.13. There is no reason to assume that there is any difference in amount between what I must pay in order to bring the factor of production into existence for a particular purpose and its transfer earnings, e.g., by offering my carpenter £180.00 per week, he enters my employment and stays with me.

18.14. Factors which influence transfer earnings include:-

(a)   The productivity of the factor of production in alternative uses, i.e., the adaptability of the factors.

(b)   The more narrowly alternative occupations are defined the greater will be their transfer earnings, e.g., if the occupation of a person is defined as "an electrician in Factory A", then his transfer earnings may be equal to his current earnings because he can earn the same wages as "an electrician in Factory B". However, if his occupation is defined as an electrician, his transfer earnings would be lower since the next best job available to him may be to work as a labourer.

(c)   The longer the time period under consideration, the greater will be the transfer earnings of a factor of production, since the adaptability of many factors may be improved over time and in addition there is better information on alternative uses.

Economic rent concept can apply to all of the factors of production

18.15. The supply price is the minimum payment which must be paid in order to acquire the services of a factor of production. Thus, by definition, any payment above the supply price of a factor is a surplus, in the sense that it is an excess over the actual sum which it was necessary to pay. This excess sum is known as *economic rent, which is defined as the amount by which a payment to a factor of production exceeds its supply price.* If I pay a carpenter £180.00 per week, and his supply price is £177.00, then £3.00 is an economic rent. Often "economic rent" is shortened to simply "rent", which word is used also to indicate a payment for the factor of production, land. It is likely that the payment for any factor of production includes some rent, particularly in the short run. (See also Section 19.10).

Quasi rent

18.16. To isolate rent payments which persist in the long run from those which are of a temporary nature, the term *economic rent is used for rent payments which continue in the long run and quasi rent is the term applied to rent payments of a temporary nature,* e.g., if there is a shortage of electricians, the demand for electricians will increase the earnings of existing electricians. These electricians will continue to earn a quasi-rent until such time as the supply of electricians is increased through an increase in those undertaking apprenticeship and eventually becoming qualified so that in the long run wages return to their normal level. If entry to the trade is restricted, then the rent will persist in the long run and it is an economic rent. Very often those who introduce new forms of entertainment, e.g., new type of bands or groups, enjoy a quasi-rent until such time as others copy. When additional bands enter the industry the wages of the bands which were originally in the industry will drop and the rent payment is removed.

Opportunity cost is zero for specific factors of production

18.17. Another approach to the analysis of economic rent is through the concept of opportunity cost. *Opportunity cost, you will remember from Section 11.7, is the cost of any item or course of action in terms of the alternatives foregone,* e.g., if I watch television, I cannot study. It is usually expressed in money terms, e.g., if I spend £30.00 on clothes, I have £30.00 less to spend on other things, and the concept of opportunity cost should include implicit cost in addition to explicit cost. There is no opportunity cost in the use of an use of an existing factor of production which is completely specific, i.e., it has no other use, not even a scrap value. If a payment is made for the use of a factor of production which is completely specific then the entire payment would constitute rent since the opportunity cost is zero. It should be noted that this applies to an existing specific factor. There will most likely be an opportunity cost in creating such a factor. The opportunity cost of a factor of production is its transfer earnings. If all possible uses of land constitute one form of employment, the payment for the use of the land would be an economic rent. For any given payment to a factor of production, the higher its transfer earnings, the lower its economic rent. If a worker is paid £100.00 per week and his transfer earnings are £20.00 his economic rent is £80.00. If his transfer earnings are £90.00 his economic rent is £10.00. Supernormal profit (see Section 22.10) is an economic rent for an entrepreneur.

18.18. Fig. 18.18 shows the supply curve facing a firm in respect of a factor of production. At a price of £10 one unit of the factor of production will be supplied which means that a payment of £10 is necessary if one unit of the fact of production is to be available to the firm — thus £10 may be thought of as the transfer earning of this factor of production. Similarly £14 is the transfer earning in respect of 2 units of the factor of production etc. If the equilibrium market price for the factor of production is £60 then there is an economic rent of £50 for the first unit of the factor of production, £46 when 2 units are supplied etc. All of this is shown in fig. 18.18. Area ABC represents economic rent and area BCD represents transfer earning.

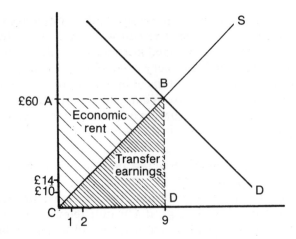

Fig. 18.18 A Factor of Production earning Economic Rent

18.19. When the supply curve relates to something other than a factor of production, e.g. the supply of a good, the same notion applies. Only in this case the difference between the price at which the good is sold (the market clearing or equilibrium price) and the supply curve is referred to as *Producer's Surplus. Producer's Surplus is defined as the difference between the price at which the item is sold and the price at which it would have been supplied – it is shown by area BCD in fig. 18.19.* This concept of Producer's Surplus is similar to the concept of Consumer's Surplus area ABC as shown in fig. 18.19.

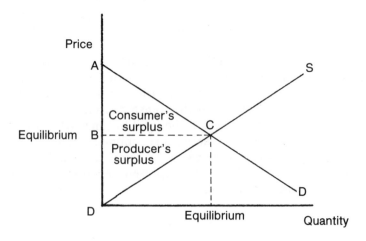

Fig. 18.19. Consumer's Surplus and Producer's Surplus.

Profit maximising condition expressed in terms of marginal revenue product and marginal cost of a variable factor of production

18.20. In discussing fixed costs in Section 11.3.(a) it was shown that it is not necessary to increase the quantity used of all factors of production in order to increase output (and thus revenue). Another way of saying that a profit maximising firm will produce the output at which MC = MR would be to say that the profit maximising level of output would be where the cost of the last unit of the variable factor of production employed is equal to the revenue which it earns, i.e., marginal cost of the variable factor = marginal revenue product of the factor.

Marginal physical productivity and law of Diminishing Marginal Returns

18.21. The Marginal Physical Product curve of a factor of production will eventually slope downwards because of the Law of Diminishing Marginal Returns. As we are analysing the effect on productivity through the employment of extra increments of one factor of production, it is assumed that the supply of other factors of production remained unchanged; therefore, the Law of Diminishing Marginal Returns applies, though marginal physical productivity may increase initially.

Table 18.21. Marginal Physical Productivity of Labour

No. of Men Employed	Total Output in Units	Marginal Physical Productivity (M.P.P.)	Selling Price per Unit	Total Revenue	Marginal Revenue Productivity (M.R.P.)
			£	£	£
10	110	-	1	110	-
11	124	14	1	124	14
12	140	16	1	140	16
13	155	15	1	155	15
14	166	11	1	166	11
15	175	9	1	175	9

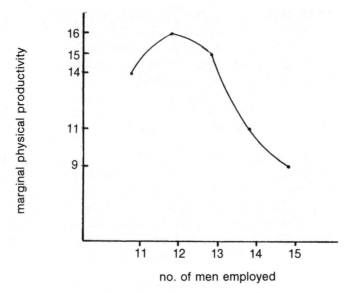

**Fig. 18.21.1 Marginal Physical Productivity
of labour based on data in Table 18.21.**

**Fig. 18.21.2 Marginal Revenue Productivity
of labour based on data in Table 18.21**

18.22. If the firm is selling its output under conditions of perfect competition and each unit sells at a price of £1 00, the marginal revenue productivity curve would be as shown in fig. 18.21.2.

You will notice that this marginal productivity curve of the firm is identical with the firm's marginal physical productivity curve and the slope of these curves will always be the same under Perfect Competition because the firm can sell its extra output at a constant selling price. *In Perfect Competition marginal revenue product of an individual firm is equal to marginal physical product multiplied by price, as shown in table 18.21.*

18.23. Under Monopoly or Imperfect Competition, as the firm employs extra increments of a factor of production its level of output is increased, but the firm faces a downward sloping demand curve in selling its product, so this extra output will have to be sold at a lower selling price.

No. of Men Employed	Total Output in Units	Marginal Physical Productivity (M.P.P.)	Selling Price per Unit	Total Revenue	Marginal Revenue Productivity (M.R.P.)
			£	£	£
10	100	-	10	1 000	-
11	130	30	9.50	1 235	235
12	155	25	9.00	1 395	160

The MPP of the 11th man is 30 units and even though each of these units is sold at £9.50, his MRP is *not* 30 × £9.50, because the original 100 units which were capable of being sold for £10.00 each must now be sold at the new price of £9.50 each. Therefore MRP is 30 × £9.50 — 100 × £0.50. which equals £235 (or 130 × £9.50 — 100 × £10). Similarly MPP for the 12th man is 25 units and MRP is £160.00 (£1 395 — £1 235) and *not* 25 × £9.00. From this example it can be clearly seen that where a firm faces a downward sloping demand curve for its finished product, MRP is *not* equal to MPP × Price. Even if MPP was constant MRP would still fall because of the downward sloping demand curve for the product of the firm.

18.24. Thus the marginal revenue productivity curve of a monopolist or an imperfectly competitive firm will slope downwards for two reasons:—

(a)   The Law of Diminishing Marginal Returns.

(b)   The firm faces a downward sloping demand curve for its finished product i.e. the selling price must be reduced in order to sell the additional quantity.

18.25. If Marginal Physical Productivity was identical in Perfect Competition and Imperfect Competition the Marginal Physical Productivity curve would be identical in each case and subject to the Law of Diminishing Marginal Returns. However the Marginal Revenue Productivity curve of the Imperfectly Competitive firm would slope downwards at a faster rate because, though the Perfectly Competitive firm can sell its additional output at the existing selling price, the Imperfectly Competitive firm must lower its selling price in order to sell the additional output. This contrast is illustrated in Fig. 18.25, and shown in table 18.28 in which table it will be seen that when 5 men are producing 580 units in the Perfectly Competitive market Marginal Revenue Productivity is £450 while when 5 men are producing the same number of units in the Monopolistic market Marginal Revenue Productivity is £395.

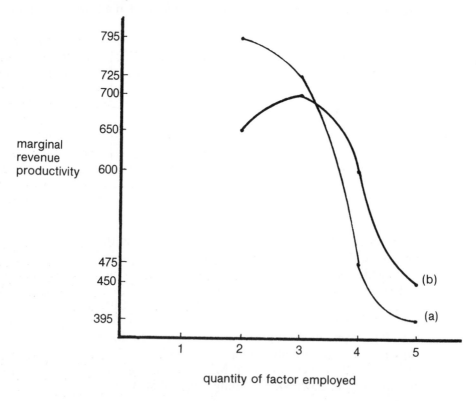

Fig. 18.25. When marginal physical production is the same, the marginal revenue curve of the imperfectly competitive firm (curve (a)), rises at a slower rate and falls at a faster rate than the MRP curve of a perfectly competitive firm (curve (B)).

18.26. The marginal revenue productivity determines the demand for a factor of production

Table 18.26 — Marginal Revenue Productivity.

No. of Men	Marginal Productivity £
10	35
11	34
12	33
13	32
14	31
15	30

mrp curve of a factor of production is also its demand curve

In the above table the Marginal Revenue Productivity of the 10th man is £35, therefore the highest price which an employer would be prepared to pay in wages to that man is £35; if he paid him an amount in excess of this he would lose money through employing him. Similarly, the maximum wages would be offered to the 11th man is £34, to the 12th man £33 etc. If the wage rate is £35 then 10 men will be employed; if it is £34 then 11 men will be employed and so on in accordance with the marginal revenue productivity of the workers as set out in Table 18.26. From this it can be seen *that the Marginal Revenue Productivity of a factor of production determines the maximum price which will be paid for the services of the factor and the Marginal Revenue Productivity curve of a factor of production is also its demand curve.*

Level of employment related to market structure

18.27. The MRP of a factor of production will always be lower, the greater is the downward slope of the demand curve for the firm's finished product as explained in Section 18.24. Therefore for a given Marginal Physical Productivity the level of employment by a firm will be greatest when a firm is selling its finished product under Perfectly Competitive conditions.

18.28. In 18.26 it was shown that for a given level of Marginal Physical Productivity the level of employment will be greater under Perfect Competition a point which is illustrated again in table 18.28 where it will be seen that if the wage rate is £450, 5 people would be employed in the Perfectly Competitive firm while only 4 people would be employed in the Monopolistic firm.

Economics

Table 18.28. Marginal Revenue Productivity under different forms of Market Structure

No. of men Employed	Total Output in Units	Marginal Physical Productivity	PERFECT COMPETITION			MONOPOLY/IMPERFECT COMPETITION		
			Selling Price £	Total Revenue £	Marginal Revenue Productivity £	Selling Price £	Total Revenue £	Marginal Revenue Productivity £
1	100		5	500		7	700	
2	230	130	5	1150	650	6.50	1495	795
3	370	140	5	1850	700	6.00	2220	725
4	490	120	5	2450	600	5.50	2695	475
5	580	190	5	2900	450	5.00	2900	395

18.29. Marginal Physical Productivity and Marginal Revenue Productivity curves are drawn on the assumption that other factors remain unchanged, i.e., ceteris paribus. If, while extra men were being employed, additional machinery to improve the productivity of the additional workers was installed, then the Marginal Physical Productivity curve for labour would shift to the right; conversely if competitors reduced their selling price, the Marginal Revenue Productivity curve would shift to the left.

18.30. While labour was the factor of production chosen to explain and illustrate the concepts of Marginal Physical Productivity and Marginal Revenue Productivity, it should be understood that everything written in these illustrations apply equally to each of the other factors of production.

QUESTIONS

Q1. What are Factors of Production?

Q2. Give 2 examples of specific Factors of Production.

Q3. Draw the Marginal Revenue Productivity Curve for a factor of production and explain why it slopes in the manner you have shown.

Q4. What factors affect the transfer earnings of a Factor of Production?

Q5. Name some factors of production which you consider to be earning economic rent and explain why this is so.

19   The Factor of Production
— Land

Definition

19.1. Land as a factor of production has a more embracing meaning than when the term is used in its everyday meaning. *Land as a factor of production refers to all the gifts of nature.* Thus it includes:—

(a)   Land
(b)   Seas, Rivers
(c)   Climatic Conditions
(d)   Mineral Wealth

The characteristics and location influence its productivity

19.2. The characteristics and location of land influence to a considerable degree its importance as a factor of production. Whether the land is fertile, marshland, mountainous or accessible, all influence the extent of its contribution to production. (See also Section 19.20 regarding factors which influence the location of industry).

Land as a factor of production includes seas

19.3. Despite the apparent paradox, seas and rivers are an element in the factor of production, land. These may contribute to economic activity through providing power, not only directly as in the past but also through the hydro generation of electricity. In recent years particularly, we have become conscious of the food harvest which seas and rivers are capable of providing. Fish farming is a commonly used term which stresses the similarity of these activities with agriculture and in fact the activity has certain characteristics in common with all extractive industries, e.g., mining.

Climatic conditions

19.4. Climatic conditions influence production in many ways. In addition to rendering possible or impossible the growing of certain crops, the climate may be of a type which encourages or discourages productive effort. In cold climates some people may intensify their work effort if for no other reason than merely to keep warm, while in warmer countries siesta periods are necessary. The availability of natural light may increase the possibility of economic activity and certainly lessen the cost to firms of lighting and heating. Climatic conditions are an important determinant of the profitability of tourism.

Mineral wealth

19.5. Little need be said regarding mineral wealth as being a gift of nature which assists (or makes possible) certain forms of economic activity.

19.6. Land as a factor of production is defined as a gift of nature and the fruits of land are in this sense a free gift of nature. However, it is possible to increase the yields from the gifts of nature by proper treatment, e.g.,

Yield from land is a combination of yield from the factor of production land and also from capital investment

the fertility of land may be improved by the application of fertilisers, land may be drained and its productivity increased. In such cases the yield from the land is a combination of two elements, the yield attributable to the qualities contributed by nature and the additional yield as a result of the manner in which the land was treated, e.g., the investment in fertilisers. It is possible also to reduce the natural fertility of land by misuse, e.g., overcropping. In practice it may be difficult, if not impossible, to state precisely what proportion of a given yield is attributable to the natural element and what proportion accrues from the manner of treatment. However, the yield may be conceived as comprising these two elements, with a proportion of the yield being attributable to capital investment in land and a portion attributable to the bounty of nature — the greater and more productive the natural element, the lower the unit cost of production for any given level of production.

Land has no cost of production

19.7. This point may be stated more categorically. Since the factor of production land is a gift of nature, it has *no cost of production*. In this way it differs from all of the other factors of production, the supply of each of the other factors entails some cost. Care should be exercised when considering this feature of land. It has no cost of production to society as a whole, it was provided by nature as is stated in its definition. However, it may have a cost of production to an individual who has to pay a purchase price or rental in order to enjoy its advantages. Payments of this nature are considered to be transfer payments between individuals.

Additional expenditure is required to avail of the productivity of land

19.8. Even when a rent has been paid for the use of land, additional expenditure is necessary before any economic benefit can be derived from it. Agricultural land must be worked, building land must be built upon, rivers and seas must be fished. Thus to be economically productive the factor of production, land, must be combined with other factors of production.

Land is fixed in supply

19.9. The second feature which distinguishes land from the other factors of production is the fact that it *is fixed in supply*. It is true that quantities of land may be reclaimed from the sea and soil erosion takes place but the effect of these features in relation to total supply is negligible. Since it is fixed in supply, an increase in the price being offered for it will not result in an increased supply — the supply curve of land is a vertical straight line as shown in Fig. 19.12.

Economic rent derived in relation to land

19.10. Land in relation to society has no cost of production and is fixed in supply. Developing this line of analysis, it can be said that its supply is independent of its price, since (a) it will remain in existence even if no rent is paid for it and it is unused and (b) irrespective of how high a price is paid for its use, its supply cannot be increased. Since land was considered to have no supply price the payment for its use — its rent — was considered to be a payment over and above its supply price. This gives rise to the term *Economic rent which is defined as a payment to any factor* *of production in excess of its supply price.* Though the concept of Economic Rent was derived in relation to land, the concept is applied to all of the factors of production. (See also Section 18.15).

Payment for land

19.11. Why will a person pay a rent in order to acquire a factor of production which has no cost of production? Simply because he cannot legally acquire it unless he pays. The actual amount which he will be prepared to pay depends upon the Marginal Revenue Productivity to him of the land. If a person by working for a farmer can earn £60.00 per week and if, by an equal effort, level of responsibility etc., the yield to him from working an acre of land would be £140.00 per week, then he would be prepared to pay up to £80.00 per week rent in order to acquire the use of the land.

Effect of fixity of supply on price when demand changes

19.12. If there is an increase in the Marginal Revenue Productivity of land, due for example to an increase in the selling price of agricultural products, the demand curve in Fig. 19.12 will move from D_1 to D_2 and the rent of land will increase. Because of fixity of supply of land the increase in rents in response to an increased demand will be greater than it would be if it was possible to increase the supply of land. The dotted supply curve S_2 in Fig. 12 illustrates the situation where an increased demand brings forth an increased supply and though the equilibrium price rises, the price increase is not as great as when the supply of the factor of production is fixed. Conversely the price reduction is greater in the face of a reduction in demand when supply is fixed. Thus fixity of supply results in price of land being sensitive to demand pressure.

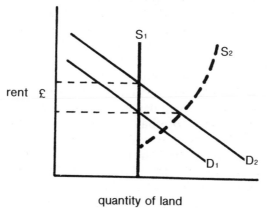

Fig. 19.12. In response to a given change in demand price fluctuations are greater when supply is fixed

Land is price determined rather than price determining

19.13. The demand for land as a factor of production is a derived demand. Since the supply of land is fixed, the determinant of the price paid for land is its Marginal Revenue Productivity. For a given Marginal Physical Productivity, changes in MRP will be related to changes in the selling price of the finished good. Thus the selling price of the finished good influences MRP (which determines demand for land) which in turn determines the rent which will be paid for land, particularly since land has no supply price, i.e., it has no cost of production and is fixed in supply. This phenomenon gives rise to the expression that *land prices or rent are price determined rather than price determining.* For example, a builder looks at a piece of land, calculating the number of houses he could build on it and their price. This gives him his income. He then looks at his labour costs, costs of raw materials and all other costs including the profit he requires. Then the residual provides him with the maximum price which he can afford to pay for the land. He does not pay a price for the land and then start his calculation.

19.14. *"High Rents are caused by High Prices"* is another expression which is commonly used to convey the idea that land is price determined rather than price determining. Higher rents will be offered for shops in the more popular or exclusive shopping centres because of the extra revenue which is generated through locating in such areas. This extra revenue results from a larger volume of business and economies of scale or from attracting a type of customer whose shopping decisions are not dominated by considerations of price.

High prices permit the payment of high rents

If similar high rents were paid by a shopkeeper in less popular or exclusive areas his profits would suffer because he could not increase his income pro rata.

Example 19.14.

If all other things are equal and the profitability of a shop in area A is £10.00 per sq. foot, which represents normal profit, while the profitability in area B which is more exclusive is £80.00 per sq. foot, then there can be a difference of up to £70.00 per sq. foot in the rental in these two areas. If a rent differential of less than £70.00 per sq. foot exists, then greater profits will be enjoyed from the more exclusive area, i.e., area B. Greater profits, in area B will increase the demand for shops in that area and this will continue until the extra demand pushes up rents to such an extent, i.e., £80.00 per square foot, that only normal profit is being earned.

19.15. The expressions "The price of land is price determined rather than price determining" and "High Rents are caused by High Prices" emphasise the concept of the fixity of supply. As has been mentioned several times, free market price is determined by the forces of supply and demand, price is the amount of money which is required to bring forth the quantity for which people are prepared to pay that price. If now there is no supply price, i.e. no price is necessary to bring forth the supply since the land is already there, while there is no means of increasing the supply even if the price is increased, then market price is perceived as being determined by demand considerations alone.

Similarly if land has no supply price, then the entire payment for the use of land is perceived as being *Economic Rent* which is defined as a payment to a factor of production in excess of its supply price: This concentration on land having no supply price is concerned with the totality of supply of land rather than with its supply in a particular use (see also section 19.17 and 19.18).

19.16. It is the very essence of the Law of Diminishing Marginal Returns that one factor of production is fixed in supply (See Sections 11.10. and 11.11). Because fixity of supply is one of the characteristics of land as a factor of production, this law was considered to have particular relevance to land. Because of the importance of land to food production, a knowledge of the Law of Diminishing Marginal Returns led some of the English economists, e.g., David Ricardo, and T.R. Malthus, to make gloomy predictions as to the inability of food production to match population growth — a prediction which still has popular currency — see also Section 40.39.

19.17. This concentration on fixity of supply of land is very much concerned with the totality of supply. The availability of land for **any particular use** is not subject to the same constraint of fixity of supply, e.g., if more building land is required it can be obtained by transferring land from alternative use. The mobility of land as between different uses is very great.

19.18. With this mobility of land as between different economic uses, its Marginal Revenue Productivity in different uses will determine the price offered and thus the manner in which land will be used. Central Dublin is mainly office blocks, shops and hotels. The return available from this intensive use of land permits high prices to be paid for land in this area. Luxury flats rather than houses are built where it is necessary to pay a high price for land in order to bid it away from other uses.

Gardens of houses are bigger as one moves from the centre towards the areas where land is less expensive. Similar mobility obtains as between pasturage and tillage and the allocation of land as between different crops. Those who make the most efficient use of the land can afford to pay the highest price and thus scarce land is bid into its most profitable use.

19.19. On occasions the government/corporation/local authority/planning authority intervenes in the free market of land and prevents the market bidding land into its most profitable use. It might be very profitable for a sports club to sell its land to a builder but the planning authority may refuse planning permission and they may insist that the land be used in a manner which is of the most benefit to society rather than most profitable to its owner.

19.20. What are the factors which would influence a firm in its decision where to locate its factory?

Location of industry

(a) *Weight losing industries,* which are industries in which the raw material used is more bulky than the finished article, will tend to locate close to the source of raw materials and, where raw materials come from different sources, a balance must be struck as between the cost of locating close to one source of raw material rather than another. Examples of this are where factories were built close to the coal fields which provided the raw material which was most bulky and therefore most costly to transport. Why transport coal hundreds of miles just to burn it when you can locate close to the coal field? Similarly, electricity stations which generate from turf will locate on the bogs, while those that generate from imported oil are located close to ports. Improvements in transport, insulated containers and new sources of power, e.g., electricity, have enabled firms to locate factories away from the source of power.

(b) The term *weight gaining industries* is applied to those industries where the finished article is more bulky, fragile or perishable than the raw material used in the manufacturing process, — e.g., ice cream, bakeries, glass manufacturers, furniture. Weight gaining industries will tend to locate close to their market.

(c) *Availability of suitable labour*
Obviously it is necessary that a pool of labour be available in the labour catchment area of the firm. If there are key workers with special skills it may be necessary to concentrate production where such workers are available. Not only will there be a greater quantity of labour available if the factory is located close to where the workers live but the wage which workers seek may be less if they can walk or cycle to work in minutes and get home for lunch rather than spend two hours a day travelling to and from work. In addition they may avoid the extra expense of eating their midday meal away from home. There are many examples of married women being available for morning shifts of 09.00 — 13.00 hrs and/or twilight shifts of 18.00 — 22.00 hrs., when factories are located in industrial estates close to their home.

(d) *Closeness to similar firms*
If a firm locates close to a similar firm it may enjoy external economies of scale, e.g., a local pool of trained labour, training schemes provided in local vocational schools, the availability of specialised firms to which work may be sub-contracted. There may also be a goodwill attaching to the geographical area, e.g., Waterford Glass, Donegal Tweed, Sheffield Steel etc..

(e) *Availability of infrastructure*
● Economic:— Good network of communication — telephone, roads, ports, railways etc.

● Social:— Unless a reasonable social life may be enjoyed by workers they may move to areas where there is more suitable provision for the social requirements of workers and their families.

(f)   *Government influence*
The government may exert a positive or negative influence on location of industry.
(i) *Positive influences*
The government may provide grants and subsidies, may institute training schemes for workers, grant taxation relief on profits, have advance factories built for and made available to firms, grant rates relief, subsidise housing for workers and generally provide an economic infrastructure which contributes to the viability of the firm.

(ii) *Negative influences*
The government may refuse planning permission for the building or operation of the factory or may impose stringent conditions which increase costs. The premises may be allocated a penal rateable valuation or the economic infrastructure may not be strengthened to ensure the efficient operation of the factory.

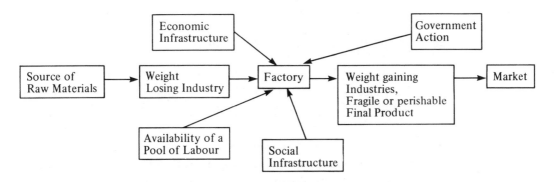

Fig. 19.20. Factors Influencing Location of a Factory

QUESTIONS

Q1. Define Land. (As a factor of production).

Q2. State two features which distinguish land from other factors of production.

Q3. Is it true to say that land has no cost of production?

Q4. "Land is price determined rather than price determining". Explain.

Q5. Comment on the factors which influence a firm in its decision where to locate.

Q6. Does the form of market structure affect the Marginal Revenue Productivity of a factor of production?

20   The Factor of Production — Labour

20.1. Labour is defined as all human activity used in the production of wealth

20.2. The total supply of labour in an economy is the total number of hours of work (man-hours) which the community is prepared to supply. Some factors which affect the total supply of the labour in an economy are:—

(a)   The size of the population; the greater the population, the greater the work force which is available — the work force of the U.S.A. is greater than the work force of Ireland.

(b)   The number of hours of work which constitutes a working week.

(c)   The extent to which members of the population seek employment, i.e., the Participation Rate.

20.3. The participation rate depends upon:—

(a)   Social conventions as to age of retirement and the period of compulsory schooling. The lower the age of retirement and the higher the school leaving age, the lower will be the participation rate.

(b)   Whether or not married women work outside their home.

(c)   Welfare provisions for the aged and sick. The better are the provisions of this nature, the less likely are people who qualify for such benefits to seek employment.

(d)   The state of the economy. When the economy is buoyant and employment is more easily obtained, people who otherwise might not have sought employment, e.g., older people or married women are encouraged to enter into employment.

20.4. As with most supply curves the supply of labour is considered to be upward sloping from left to right as shown in Fig. 20.4. This upward sloping supply curve reflects the fact that as the wage rate increases a greater supply of labour will be forthcoming.

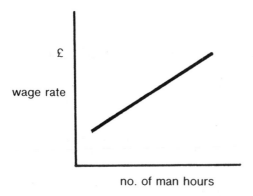

Fig. 20.4. Upward Sloping Labour Supply Curve.

20.5. It is possible that as people earn higher incomes, they may be anxious to enjoy life through a longer period of leisure rather than through earning higher income. If, for example, a worker who is earning £170.00 per week gets an increase to £190.00 per week, he may be less inclined to work overtime.

High marginal rates of income tax may encourage substitution of leisure for labour

20.6. A person who pays a high marginal rate of taxation may consider that after tax, the sum which he receives for working overtime is not worth the effort and inconvenience involved. A married woman, who works 10 hours per week at £4.00 per hour in order to augment the family income, may decide, if her hourly rate is increased to £6.00 per hour, to work less than 10 hours, say 7 hours, per week. At the new higher rates of pay her money income has been increased by £2.00 (from £40.00 to £42.00) and she has an additional 3 hours per week for other activities. Similarly for workers who have second jobs — they may give up the second job if their income in their main employment increases. In each of these cases there is said to be a *substitution effect* — workers substitute leisure for work, they take part of their increase in a non-monetary form.

20.7. Where this applies there is a backward bending labour supply curve as shown in Fig. 20.7.

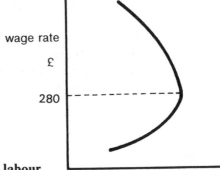

Fig. 20.7. Backward bending supply curve of labour.

Above the wage rate of £280 workers substituted leisure for work, e.g., the length of the average working week has been reducing in many countries including Ireland in recent decades. In this example £280 would be the optimum wage from the point of view of inducing the maximum supply of labour, because wage payments in excess of this wage rate would result in a reduction in the supply of labour. In this context leisure is a luxury good, since more of it is substituted for money income as income increases, i.e., more of it is bought as income increases. The price paid for the leisure is the money income sacrificed by not working.

20.8. The determination of wages by free market forces

In this initial example we are ignoring the existence of trade unions or government legislation regarding wages, hours worked and income tax. In these circumstances, the demand curve for labour will be the MRP of labour and will be downward sloping. The supply curve of labour will be upward sloping as depicted in fig. 20.4.

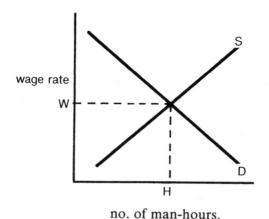

no. of man-hours.

Fig. 20.8. Determination of wage rate for the industry under free market forces.

The equilibrium wage rate is W and the level of employment is H man-hours. If the wage rate was above W, the excess supply of labour would force the wage rate downwards; if the wage rate was below W, the excess demand for labour would cause the wage rate to move upwards as employers competed with each other to secure workers.

*A small
individual
firm may
envisage a
horizontal
supply curve
of labour*

20.9. In a perfectly competitive market structure the individual firm would consider the supply curve of labour to be a horizontal line through the existing wage rate. This is so because the demand of the small individual firm for labour does not affect the wage rate.

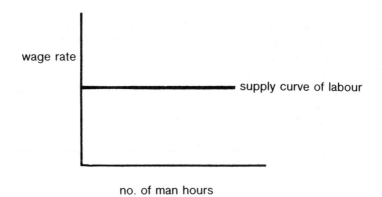

Fig. 20.9. Horizontal supply curve of labour faces a small individual firm.

The same situation would obtain for any firm whose demand for labour was not sufficiently large to cause a shift in the industry's demand curve for labour.

Money wages and real wages

20.10. A distinction must be drawn between *money wages and real wages.* Money wages refers to the wages received as expressed in money terms, e.g., £280 per week, and is often referred to as nominal wages. Real wages refers to the purchasing power of wages and as such it is a combination of nominal wages and the cost of living. When comparing alteration in wages over time, particularly during a period of inflation, real wages is the appropriate basis of comparison.

20.11. In times of inflation nominal wages are often linked to the Consumer Price Index by means of an "escalator clause", so that the value of wage in real terms is maintained. This is known as the indexation of wages. The usual objections to the system are:—

Escalator clause

(a)   The Consumer Price index as a measurement of the cost of living has its limitations.

(b)   It becomes difficult for trade unions to negotiate increases in the real incomes of their members unless the indexation of wages to the cost of living permits the negotiation of additional wage increases for other reasons, e.g., improvement in productivity.

(c)   Even if the level of real wages is maintained, income tax is based on nominal wages so that, after tax, pay in real terms is reduced.

(d)   Trade unions are loath to accept a reduction in nominal wage rates even if the cost of living is reduced.

(e)   An arrangement of this nature freezes wage differentials in real terms.

20.12. Similarly when comparing relative wages in different countries, an effort is made to compare real wages by relating the period which must be

*Real wages
is basis of
comparison
of wage levels
in different
countries*

worked at average wage rates in each country in order to earn the price of various goods and services. This may be seen in the following extract from one of the EEC publications.

"An Italian, for instance, has to work for more than one hour in order to earn enough money to go to the cinema (as against 18 minutes for a Luxembourger). A Londoner has to labour for 1 hour 29 minutes to afford to go to a soccer match (as against half an hour in Copenhagen). In Paris, a man's suit is equal to 61.5 hours of work, and in Copenhagen only 28.5 hours. 1 446 hours of toil in Rome will buy a new car but in Bonn, it will only cost 761 hours of sweat for the same car. A Belgian can buy a loaf of bread for 9 minutes work, an Italian needs 15 minutes. A Copenhagen hairdresser will demand payment equivalent to half an hour's work, and a Paris coiffeur will expect more than one and half hour's labour. A packet of cigarettes is worth 9 minutes work in Brussels, but 20 minutes work in London."

*The level of
wages affects
productivity –
poverty cycle*

20.13. In discussing Marginal Revenue Productivity in Sections 18.18 to 18.30 the importance of the productivity of labour in the determination of wage rates was stressed. However, the actual level of wages has an important influence on productivity; low wages may result in workers being incapable of sustained high levels of production due to lack of nutrition, inferior housing, lack of education and training, lack of commitment to the job; these factors may also increase the level of absenteeism resulting in a further deterioration in the level of productivity. This situation is sometimes referred to as the *poverty cycle* where not only is productivity low because of low wages but the children of such people seem condemned to be caught up in this system, e.g., due to overcrowding, bad housing, children are unable to do their school homework, their parents cannot afford to keep their children at school, there is no appreciation of the value and importance of education, employers are less inclined to employ people from these areas etc.

*Economy of
high wages*

20.14. Conversely when workers are well paid, the level of nutrition, housing, education, training and general health will be such as to enable workers to attain a high level of productivity, an attractive wage level encourages a high degree of commitment also. This concept is known as the *economy of high wages* and is manifest in the United States where workers are among the most highly paid and the most productive in the world.

20.15. Why are there differences in wage rates?

*A strong
union may
obtain for
their workers
their Marginal
Revenue
Productivity
but no more*

Differences in the wage earnings of different groups can be explained by variations in their Marginal Revenue Productivity and also differences in their negotiating strength and ability. A strong trade union can ensure that workers are paid up to their Marginal Revenue Productivity. However, a trade union, no matter how strong, cannot get for its workers payments above their Marginal Revenue Productivity, because to pay a worker above his Marginal Revenue Productivity means that you lose money through employing him, and the employer retains the right not to employ, even if such an attitude means that he must close down and withdraw from production.

20.16. The Marginal Revenue Productivity of a person's labour is not entirely under the control of the person concerned. It has already been shown that Marginal Revenue Productivity is a combination of Marginal Physical Productivity and price which is influenced by demand for the goods. The demand for the good is almost entirely outside the sphere of influence of the individual employee. Even a worker's Marginal Physical Productivity is not entirely within his own control. To take the extreme case, if the worker is not employed, his Marginal Physical Productivity is zero. Even if he is employed, his productivity depends upon the efficiency of the employer in organising production, the availability of complementary factors of production and the employer's ability to utilise to the fullest extent the ability of the workers.

20.17. Those factors influencing the Marginal Revenue Productivity of the worker (and thus the demand for his services), which are within his control, are his skill, application and commitment to the job. Skill is a combination of good health, natural ability, intelligence and training. Unless a person has been blessed with adequate health, he is unable to contribute whatever ability he may have. A person who possesses a high degree of natural ability and intelligence can undertake tasks which are not within the compass of less gifted people. Such people can be employed in those tasks which society values most highly and for which the remuneration will be highest.

20.18. Training assists trainees to acquire skills which improve their productivity. The rewards at the successful termination of the training period must be sufficiently attractive to compensate for the time and money involved in undergoing training; if there is a competitive examination at the termination of the training period this constitutes an additional risk for trainees since there is a possibility that he may not successfully complete the test. Strictly speaking, the higher reward in jobs, for which lengthy training periods are required, ought not to be considered as being the reward for undergoing training. Rather it is a reward for the increase in the Marginal Revenue Productivity of the person as a result of the training and the scarcity of people with the required skill.

20.19. There is also an element of tradition in the wage rates attaching to different occupations. This may be particularly important where Marginal Revenue Productivity is difficult to calculate. Certain wage relativities and differentials become accepted by the general public. The wages paid to various trades are related to each other, e.g., carpenters, electricians, plumbers. It is difficult to measure the marginal revenue productivity of workers when they provide a service rather than producing a tangible end product, particularly if the service is not sold in the market place. Gardai and teachers are examples of such occupations and their salary is based on pay in the Civil Service and the general public sector, which in turn is supposed to reflect the salaries which people of similar ability might earn in the private sector.

The nature and conditions of the job affect the wage rate

20.20. It may be necessary to pay a high wage because work may be dangerous, e.g., steeplejacks; unhealthy, e.g., miners; unpleasant, e.g, work connected with sewerage; or unsocial hours, e.g., night work or shift work. In addition, if work is of a temporary or seasonal nature, higher wages would have to be paid by way of compensation. A teacher or waiter on an hourly rate would probably receive a higher rate per hour worked than would the permanent employee. If you were seeking permanent employment and were offered two jobs which were identical in every except that one was seasonal and the other permanent you would take the permanent employment. Another way of saying this is that the seasonal job must offer better wages in order to be competitive with the permanent job.

Monetary benefits in addition to wages

20.21. There may be monetary benefits attached to the employment in addition to the wages received. There may be valuable pension rights, opportunities to travel, expense accounts, loans at preferential rates, subsidised housing, allowances for children etc.

Non-monetary benefits of the job

20.22. There are often non-monetary benefits related to employment. The work may be located in a pleasant area of the country; social working hours, e.g., 09.00 — 17.00 hrs; housing at reasonable rent may be available; lack of congestion; good schools for the family; theatres; museums; cinema; a social infrastructure which is conducive to the enjoyment of a full life.

Net advantages of the job

20.23. When one combines wages with other monetary and non-monetary aspects of a particular job, one arrives at the *net advantages* of a job. In comparing different jobs it is the net advantages of each job which should be compared rather than merely wages.

Non-competing groups

20.24. In a perfect world it would be seen that these net advantages would be equalised between different occupations. Extra workers would seek employment in those occupations where net advantages were more attractive and leave those occupations where net advantages were less attractive. The increased supply of labour to a particular occupation through extra workers seeking employment in the better occupations would cause a reduction of wages in those occupations. There would be a corresponding increase in wages in the less attractive occupations in order to attract and retain workers, until equilibrium was reached with the equalisation of net advantages. This does not happen. In fact often the occupations which are the most attractive in the non-monetary advantages and "perks" are also the most highly paid. The labour force to a considerable extent is composed of *"non-competing groups"* — there are restrictions on mobility which prevent the forces of competition equalising net advantages. Even accepting the situation of non-competing groups, there would still be a tendency towards the equalisation of net advantages if it was possible for school leavers to gain employment in those occupations of their choice, i.e., those occupations which enjoy the highest net advantages.

20.25. In acknowledging that a distinction should be drawn between the wages received by an employee and the net advantages of a job, from the employer's side the wages paid is not the total cost to the employer. Absenteeism, payments during holiday periods, canteen facilities etc. are all costs which are attributable to employing people. The impact of social security payments is shown in table 20.25.

Table 20.25. Average Labour Costs and Percentage Distribution thereof in 1974/75, 1978 and 1981

SECTOR	YEAR	ANNUAL COST PER EMPLOYEE	Percentage Distribution			All other Costs
			Wages and Salaries	Statutory	Other	
		£	%			
Industry	1975	3,067	86.9	5.2	4.2	3.8
	1978	4,876	86.9	5.9	4.0	3.1
	1981	8,176	85.0	7.0	4.5	3.5
Distribution	1974	2,076	88.6	5.3	3.5	2.5
	1978	4,399	86.0	6.7	4.2	3.1
	1981	7,020	85.1	7.3	4.7	2.9
Credit, Insurance	1974	3,335	73.8	3.6	14.2	8.4
	1978	7,103	74.8	3.8	13.5	7.9
	1981	11,069	72.8	6.3	13.2	7.6

Source: Labour Court's Survey 1981 in Industry, Distribution, Credit and Insurance. C.S.O. Pl 2387, May 1984.

Consumption wage and product wage

20.26. In considering the monetary benefits of a job an employee focuses on the after tax income in real terms (known as the *Consumption Wage*) which he receives. Due to increasing direct and indirect taxes the consumption wage of the average employee fell by 15% between 1979 and 1983. Labour costs including payroll taxes (e.g. P.R.S.I.) which a firm must pay is known as the *Product Wage*. The real product wage increased by 12% between 1979 and 1983.

Tax wedge

20.27. Any difference which exists between the after tax income which an employee receives i.e., the consumption wage and the wages, including payroll taxes, which it costs an employer i.e., the product wage, is due to taxation. Consequently the difference between the consumption wage and the product wage is known as *the tax wedge.* In the late 1980's it has been estimated that it costs an employer (on average) £2.50 in order to give an employee an increase in take-home pay of £1. The manner in which this tax wedge increased during the 1980's is shown in fig. 20.27.

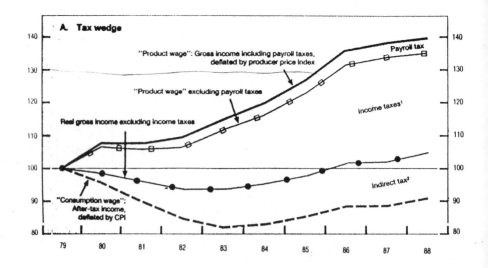

Fig. 20.27. Tax Wedge.

[1]   Includes net social security contributions.
[2]   Includes terms of trade effects.

Source: OECD.

Occupational immobility of labour

20.28. Occupational immobility, which is concerned with the inability of workers to change from one type of occupation or industry to another, is due to the specialisation of labour together with the activities of trade unions and professional associations. Restriction on entry of apprentices and trainees in terms of age and educational attainment, lengthy and expensive periods of training, competitive final examinations — all have the effect of lessening the supply of labour to specific occupations. In terms of supply curves this has the effect of moving the supply curve of labour to the left and resulting in a higher equilibrium wage, e.g., from W_1 to W_2 as shown in Fig. 20.28.

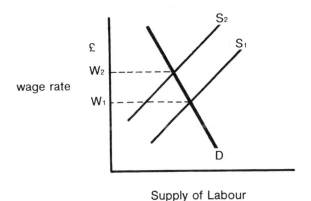

Fig. 20.28. Restriction on entry into an occupation raises the equilibrium level of wages

Geographical immobility of labour

20.29. Geographical immobility of labour is attributable to a number of factors. People develop social attachments in an area and are reluctant to start afresh in another area. The problems associated with moving house, the disruption of children's education through changing schools, reinforce the attachment to an area. In addition people are less aware of job opportunities in other areas.

Government efforts to improve mobility of labour

20.30. The government attempts to improve the occupational and geographical mobility of labour by:—

(a) Career advice in the first instance to direct labour into those occupations in which vacancies exist.

(b) The provision and formalisation of training programmes.

(c) The retraining of redundant workers.

(d) The setting up of employment exchanges where information on job opportunities is made available.

(e) Ensuring the availability of adequate housing and a social infrastructure in those areas where employment is available.

(f)   Discussions with trade unions and professional bodies to ensure that the manpower needs of industry are being satisfied.

Causes of
unemployment

20.31. The foregoing comments highlight the fact that the unemployment of labour may be attributable to one or more of a number of reasons. Efforts to isolate these reasons with a view to eliminating unemployment have resulted in the identification and classification of unemployment of labour as follows:—

(a)   *Frictional unemployment* which arises when there is a reduction in the demand for labour in a particular occupation, though jobs are available in other occupations and/or firms. Unemployment of this nature may be due to lack of knowledge of vacancies by those seeking employment, a degree of geographical immobility and possibly a mismatching between employment training programmes and the needs of industry.

(b)   *Seasonal unemployment* is due to seasonal variations in the level of demand, e.g., hotel industry during the winter period. Firms attempt to overcome this problem by offering a complementary range of products which provides an all the year round demand for their products, e.g., makers of summer sandals also make winter footwear.

(c)   *Structural unemployment* refers to unemployment which is the result of a change in the structure of an industry, brought about by technical progress, the forces of competition and/or relative factor prices, e.g., the computerisation of office work and the automation of factory work.

(d)   *Cyclical unemployment* brought about by swings in the pendulum of business activity.

(e)   *Institutional unemployment* which arises because of obstacles to the mobility of labour. The mobility of workers in pursuit of jobs may be hindered, e.g., by the non-availability of suitable housing in those areas where work is available. This can arise particularly in respect of people who are at present living in subsidised local authority housing and who are not prepared to move home unless similar type housing is available for them in the area in which the work is available. Closed shop practices by trade unions which limit entry to certain employments together with high social welfare payments which cushion the economic deprivations of unemployment also contribute to institutional unemployment.

(f)   If unemployment compensation is a high percentage of take-home pay there is said to be a high *income replacement ratio*. A high income replacement ratio lessens the money cost of being without a job, in addition since an unemployed person does not have to spend hours at the workplace additional utility may be derived from the extra hours of leisure available. In this way a *welfare trap* may *develop* as unemployment becomes more attractive than employment. High income replacement ratios increase the average duration of unemployment since people can afford to spend a longer period searching for a job which suits them. As shown in Fig. 20.31. the income replacement ratio increased significantly between 1979 and 1983 but since then it has declined substantially.

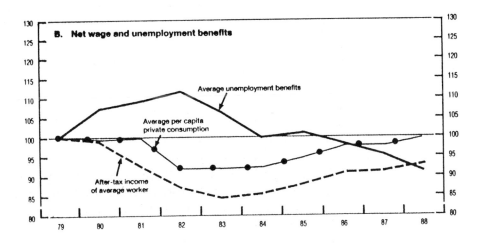

1. Includes net social security contributions.
2. Includes terms of trade effects.
Source: OECD; for details see technical notes.

Fig. 20.31. Net wage and Unemployment Benefits.

(g) *Residual unemployment* — all those unfortunate people who because of physical or mental disability are unable to gain employment.

Under-employment

20.32. Closely allied to unemployment is *underemployment*. Underemployment occurs when a factor of production, though not actually unemployed, is working below capacity. Labour hoarding where

*Disguised
unemployment*

employers retain workers during a downturn in the level of economic activity is an example of the underemployment of labour. Similarly when people are employed in the family business while they are waiting for a job elsewhere, they may be underemployed in the sense that the total volume of business is not increased through their employment. This is also referred to as *disguised unemployment.*

20.33. In considering causes of unemployment it would be remiss not to advert to the perennial reference that "too high a level of wages causes unemployment". It has already been shown that the maximum payment to any factor of production cannot exceed the Marginal Revenue Productivity of the factor if the firm seeks to maximise profits. One interpretation of the "wages being too high" phrase would be if workers were being paid or seeking to be paid wages in excess of their Marginal Revenue Productivity. It may be argued in such a case that wages are not excessive in the sense that workers are entitled to adequate standard of living and often similar work earns a higher real wage in other countries. Such an improvement could be achieved through increased productivity of the factor, i.e., an increase in Marginal Physical Productivity, or through an increase in the selling price of the finished good — though it is often implied in discussions of this nature that it is not possible to increase the selling price of the finished article.

*Factor prices
and the choice
of production
technique*

20.34. Another aspect of the "high wages causing unemployment" discussion is related to the substitution of the lower priced factors of production for higher priced ones in order to minimise costs of production and thus improve profitability. This approach which is taken in example 20.32 can be relevant even if an increase in the wage rate did not result in the labour force being paid in excess of its Marginal Revenue Productivity. For simplicity of exposition it is assumed that the machinery is rented on a fixed rental and that the wage includes all the expenses connected with the employment of an individual.

Table 20.34. Factor Prices influence the choice of production technique.

	Capital Input	Labour Input	Cost per unit of capital £	Wage Rate £	Total Cost of Producing 100 units £
before increase in cost of labour					
Technique A:	4	9	340	210	3250
Technique B:	6	6	340	210	3300
after increase in cost of labour					
Technique A:	4	9	340	260	3700
Technique B:	6	6	340	260	3600

In the first instance, from table 20.34 technique A would be used since this is the least cost method of producing the 100 items. However, after the wage rate has been increased technique B would be chosen because this is the cheaper method under the changed factor price ratio. Thus it will be seen that as a result of the wage increase 3 men have been replaced by 2 machines as capital was substituted for labour.

20.35. Factors Influencing the Elasticity of Demand for Labour

The factors which effect the elasticity of demand for labour are:—

(a) **The Elasticity of Factor Substitution**

The greater the extent to which production techniques facilitate the replacement of labour by capital when the price of labour increases relative to the price of capital the more elastic will be the demand for labour. Looking at it from another way if there is no machine capable of doing the work currently being performed by an individual then even if his wages increase he can't be replaced by a machine.

The introduction of machinery into the production process can take some time thus the elasticity of demand for labour will be greater in the long run. Also if there are significant increases in labour costs it stimulates research into the development of machinery, again increasing the elasticity of demand for labour in the long term.

(b) **The Elasticity of Demand for the Final Product**

If increases in the cost of labour can be passed on to the final consumer without affecting the level of demand then the less elastic will be the demand for labour.

(c) **The Ratio of Labour Costs to Total Costs**

If labour costs are a relatively small proportion of total costs then an increase in wages will not have a significant effect on the total costs (and profitability) of the firm. A firm which employs 2 maintenance electricians for its large factory is unlikely to be as perturbed by an increase in electricians' wage rate as would the owner of a large electrical contracting firm or the E.S.B.

(d) **The Elasticity of Supply of other Factors of Production**

If there is some limitation on the supply of factors of production which could be substituted for labour then this makes less elastic the demand for labour. However it is more likely to be a short run phenomenon and elasticity will be greater in the long run as set out in 20.35 (a).

20.36. Sources of statistics of the Irish labour force

Census of Population

● The most detailed and comprehensive analysis of the country's labour force is obtained from the *census of population*. In the census, individuals are classified on the basis of:-

(a) Their occupation, e.g., dentist, electrician, typist etc.

(b) On the basis of the industry in which they are employed, e.g., textile, agricultural etc.

The Census provides information on the whole labour force whereas most of the other sources of statistics refer to specific groups. The main disadvantage attached to reliance on this source is that there is a period of two to four years between the taking of a Census and the publication of the relevant figures.

Census of Production

● The annual *census of production* covers all establishments (with the exception of those with less than 3 persons engaged) in the transportable goods industries together with certain service industries, e.g, building and construction, gas and electricity. The results of the census are published in the Irish Statistical Bulletin and the Statistical Abstract.

Census of Distribution

● *The Census of Distribution* provides information on those engaged in the retail and wholesale trades.

Agricultural enumeration

● In intercensal years details of employment in the agricultural sector are obtained from the *agricultural enumeration.* The agricultural enumeration is conducted by the Garda Siochana each June. Up to 1953 a complete enumeration was conducted each year. With the exception of the years 1960 and 1965 when complete enumerations were carried out the present procedure is to base estimates on a sample of 60% and to take complete enumerations at five year intervals. The agricultural enumerations also provide data on livestock numbers and the areas under various types of crops. The details of the enumeration and published by the Central Statistics Office in the Irish Statistical Abstract.

Trends of employment and unemployment

● The most important single source of information on aspects of manpower during intercensal periods is the *"Trend of Employment and Unemployment"*. Information for this publication is compiled by the Central Statistics Office in conjunction with the Department of Industry, Commerce and Energy and the Department of Health and Social Welfare.

● Each issue of the Irish Statistical Bulletin contains a summary of employment in manufacturing and transportable goods industries together with estimated earnings and hours worked by all industrial workers. Unemployment statistics are published in the Live Register Section of each issue of the Bulletin.

20.37. Unemployment Statistics

"The Live Register"

Unemployment Statistics are usually based on the number of persons registered by Social Welfare. A person who registers as unemployed is considered to be willing and able to work but unable to gain suitable employment. In fact registering on the Live Register is undertaken only by (1) Claimants for Unemployment Benefit (2) Applicants for Unemployment Assistance and (3) Other Persons registering in order to be credited with Social Insurance Contributions. Since the Live Register is the means by which persons claim entitlement to payments from the State, there are some who though they are on the Live Register they are not available for employment. Also there is a (larger) number of people who though unemployed and seeking employment are not on the Live Register. While the Live Register may leave something to be desired when used as a measure of the numbers unemployed changes in the number on the Live Register is a good indication of the *trend* of unemployment.

20.38. A survey provides a much more comprehensive overview of the status of the labour force and in addition avoids many of the inaccuracies which are inherent in using the register of those signing on for unemployment benefits as a measurement of the numbers unemployed. Even though such surveys are costly they are undertaken from time to time in order to obtain a comprehensive assessment of the state of the labour force. Fig 20.38 contains a schematic representation of the type of information which would be sought from a survey of the labour force.

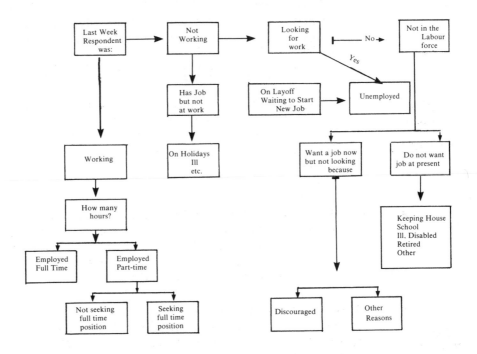

Fig. 20.38. Schematic Representation of Survey on Status of Labour Force

20.39. An analysis of short-term trends in employment and unemployment must take account of seasonal fluctuations in the demand for labour; annual figures are not affected by seasonal factors. Generally unemployment is highest in January/February and at its lowest in August/September.

Seasonally Adjusted Level of Unemployment

20.40. The trend in the level of unemployment may be derived by comparing the percentage of the workforce unemployed in the same month for different years. Alternatively a twelve month moving average series may be calculated. The Central Statistics Office calculates a "seasonally corrected" figure by applying to each monthly unemployment figure a seasonal adjustment. The seasonal adjustment is calculated by the estimated seasonal variation over previous years of the variable being analysed as set out in Example 20.40.

Example 20.40.

Annual average level of unemployment   = 100 000

If unemployment in August is generally 20% below average of year, average level of unemployment in August   = 80 00

Therefore 20 000 would be added to the recorded figure in August which can then be compared with the seasonally adjusted unemployment figures for other months in order to detect a trend. This is shown in Table 20.40.

It is important for the government to monitor the trend in the level of unemployment, i.e., whether it is increasing or decreasing, so that they may, when necessary, introduce new policies or change existing policies.

Table 20.40

SEASONALLY ADJUSTED LIVE REGISTER SERIES:
TOTAL PERSONS

Month	Unadjusted Series			Seasonally Adjusted Series★		
	Males	Females	Total	Males	Females	Total
1988 January	179,500	72,700	252,200	172,200	71,600	243,800
February	178,200	72,400	250,600	172,500	71,900	244,400
March	176,000	71,200	247,100	171,400	71,500	242,900
April	171,800	69,900	241,700	170,400	70,900	241,200
May	166,700	69,200	235,900	168,800	71,300	240,100
June	166,000	71,700	237,700	169,200	71,600	240,800
July	167,500	74,600	242,200	170,600	72,200	242,800
August	168,200	74,600	242,900	169,800	72,100	241,900
September	165,200	70,700	235,900	169,700	71,700	241,400
October	163,600	69,800	233,400	169,100	71,800	240,900
November	163,900	70,400	234,300	167,200	71,800	239,000
December	170,300	72,700	242,900	166,000	71,600	237,600
1989 January	171,700	73,700	245,400	164,400	72,600	237,000
February	168,900	72,600	241,500	163,100	72,200	235,300
March	168,000	72,700	240,700	163,400	73,100	236,400
April	162,600	70,500	233,100	161,200	71,400	232,600
May	158,900	69,700	228,600	161,100	71,800	232,800
June	157,600	72,700	230,300	160,800	72,600	233,500

Source: Statistical Bulletin. Sept 1989 (CSO)

20.41. The theory of Marginal Revenue Productivity is based on alterations in the supply of one factor while the quantities in use of other factors of production remain unchanged. If the quantities of the other factors of production are increased pro rata with an increase in the employment of labour, then economies of scale may be enjoyed. The ability to increase the supply of other factors pro rata with the incresed employment of labour depends, inter alia, on the availability of these other factors, i.e., the balance which exists between the size of the population and the availability of other factors of production such as capital.

Optimum Population

Thus there arises the concept of an *optimum population which is the level of population at which output per person is at a maximum.* If the level of population is such that there is increasing returns in the economy, so that GNP per person is rising, the economy is said to be underpopulated. Conversely, if the economy is experiencing decreasing returns, so that GNP per person is declining, the economy is considered to *overpopulated.* In many advanced countries emphasis would be focussed on the quality of life per person, rather than merely increasing or decreasing returns. They would feel that if increased production gives rise to pollution, deterioration in working conditions, lack of privacy etc., then the country is overpopulated. The underpopulation aspect is illustrated by certain countries, e.g., Australia, actively pursuing a policy of encouraging immigration. The fact that it is not merely a relationship between population numbers and an area of land but a relationship between the productivity of labour and the availability of the complementary factors of production is illustrated by the comparison in Table 20.38. For example in this table it can be seen that though the smaller area of the Netherlands supports a larger population than ours, GNP per head of population is greater in the Netherlands.

Table 20.41.

	POPULATION		UNEMPLOYMENT RATE as % of total labour force		GROSS DOMESTIC PRODUCT at market prices 1985 per capita at current prices in US$ using current ex-change rates
	Thousands	per sq. km	1984	1985	
Australia	15,540	2	(a) 8.9	(a) 8.2	11,178
Austria	7,552	90	(a) 3.8	. .	8,535 8,535
Belgium	9,852	323	(a) 14.0	(a) 13.2	7,697
Canada	25,150	3	(a) 11.2	(a) 10.4	13,285
Denmark	5,111	119	8.5		10,690
Finland	4,882	14	(a) 6.1		10.493
France	54,947	100	(a) 9.7	(a) 10.1	8,907
Germany	61,175	246	(a) 8.5	. .	10,025
Greece	9,900	75	8.1	. .	3,380
Iceland	240	2	1.7	. .	10.723
Ireland	3,540	50	15.5	. .	4,986
Italy	56,983	189	(a) 10.2	. .	6,114
Japan	120,018	322	(a) 2.7	. .	10,457
Luxembourg	366	141	1.9	. .	9,235
Netherlands	14,420	387	(a) 14.0	(a) 13.0	8,534
New Zealand	3,258	12	5.7	. .	7,159
Norway	4,141	13	(a) 3.0	(a) 2.5	13,215
Portugal	10,129	110	8.9	. .	1,905
Spain	38,387	76	(a) 20.1	. .	4,192
Sweden	8,337	19	(a) 3.1	(a) 2.8	11,369
Switzerland	6,507	158	(a) 1.1	(a) 1.0	14,002
Turkey	48,825	63	16.0	. .	1,018
United Kingdom	56,488	231	11.2	11.6	7,495
United States	236,681	25	(a) 7.4	. .	15,356

Source: OECD Observer No. 139,

20.42. In developing this discussion on a global basis, there is often reference to the rate at which world population is growing and doubt is often expressed as to the ability of world resources to sustain this rate of world population growth. This concern regarding population growth has been expressed over a number of centuries and is associated particularly with the English economist Thomas Robert Malthus (1766 — 1834).

Malthus and population growth

Malthus' views on this subject are expressed in his famous "Essay on the Principle of Population as it affects the future Improvement of Society", which was published in 1789. In his publication Malthus argued that population increased in a geometric progression (1,2,4,8,16), while the means of subsistence increased in an arithmethic progression (1,2,3,4,5), and concluded that famine and its consequent misery, in the absence of wars, could be avoided only by the moral restraints of late marriages and/or smaller families. Malthus did not foresee the opening up of new land and the increased productivity in the food industry, the growth of international trade and the fact that family size tended to diminish as material standards of living rose. Malthus' expressed opinions resulted in changes in the Poor Law system in Great Britain. In the 19th century relief under the Poor Law system was administered by local justices and was based on the price of bread and the family size of the recipient. Under the influence of Malthus' writing this policy seemed likely to result in overpopulation with the result that in 1834 the Poor Law was amended.

20.43. The writings of Malthus together with their influence on other economists of the period gave rise to the *Iron Law of Wages*. This theory salved the conscience of many employers during the industrial revolution and justified in their own eyes the payment of a mere pittance to workers.

Iron law of wages

The train of thought of the Iron Law of Wages is along the following lines. If workers are paid wages above the base level of subsistence, the workers will have larger families and when the wages above the subsistence level is spread over the larger size families there is no improvement in an individual's standard of living. In addition larger families will result in an increased supply of labour at future periods which will result in the wage rate dropping to the subsistence level. This latter aspect of an increased supply of labour gained attention from Karl Marx (1818 — 1883) who saw employers availing themselves of the "reserve army of the unemployed", who were unable to gain employment, and using them as a threat against workers who sought improvements in wages or working conditions. It is no surprise that there was a great increase in the number and membership of trade unions during this period and considerable legislative activity as evidenced by the Trade Union Acts of 1824 and 1825.

20.44. Trade unionism in Ireland

Trade Unions are associations of employees formed for the purpose of negotiating on behalf of their members on matters relating to wages and conditions of employment and the provision of other ancillary services, e.g. sickness benefits. Under the law, employers' associations which engage in negotiating conditions of employment are regarded as trade unions, e.g., Federation of Irish Employers (F.I.E.).

There are 88 trade unions in existence in the Irish Republic and they are often categorised as follows:—

(a) General Unions — which do not recruit members by occupation or industry — membership is open to all workers, e.g., The Irish Transport and General Workers Union of Ireland.

(b) White-Collar Unions — membership of which consists almost entirely of "white-collar" workers, i.e., distributive, office, professional and service workers. The Irish Union of Distributive Workers and Clerks and The Institute of Professional Civil Servants are examples of white-collar unions.

(c) Craft Unions — which limit their membership to workers possessing trade skills which are usually acquired through some form of apprenticeship. Their apprenticeship is supervised at least in part by the union concerned. The Union of Sheet Metal Workers of Ireland and the Irish Graphical Society are examples of such unions. Industrial Unions which cater for workers in a particular industry e.g. Irish Bank Officials Association (I.B.O.A.)

(d) Other Unions — refers to unions whose members do not readily fit into any of the other three categories.

High degree of unionisation in Ireland

20.45. Approximately 55% of Irish workers are members of trade unions and this is a high degree of unionisation by European standards. The three largest general unions account for almost half of the trade union membership, viz. The Irish Transport and General Workers Union (I.T.G.W.U.) with 152 000 members, Amalgamated Transport and General Workers Union (A.T.G.W.U.) and Workers Union of Ireland (W.U.I.) with 36 000 members. Half of the unions have membership of less than 1000.

Multiplicity of trade unions

20.46. There is general agreement that there are too many trade unions in Ireland and often more than one union represents the workers in a particular firm or industry. Industrial unionism, i.e., one union for all employees in the same industry irrespective of occupation, is common in most E.E.C. countries, in contrast to unions organised on an occupational basis as is the case in Ireland and Britain. In Germany, for example, there are 16 industrial unions catering for more than 7 million employees.

Methods to minimise the problems associated with the multiplicity of trade unions

20.47. Trade Unions, often with the encouragement, or under the auspices, of the Irish Congress of Trade Unions have attempted to find solutions to the problems attributable to the multiplicity of unions.

(a) There have been agreements between unions, especially those catering for the same type of worker, defining the areas within which they will operate. The prime purpose of such agreements is to avoid competition between unions.

(b) In large organisations, e.g., CIE, *group negotiation* was introduced whereby the unions which represent workers in the organisation come together for the purpose of conducting negotiations with employers.

(c) *Federation* has also been adopted. A federation is a permanent alliance of individual unions in whch each keeps its own separate identity, but forms with other unions a permanent point organisation for the purpose of presenting a common co-ordinated front to the employer(s) on issues which affect all the unions concerned. The Civil Service Alliance is an example of such a federation.

(d) *Amalgamation* is frequently suggested as a solution to the problem of the multiplicity of unions. This takes place when one (or more) independent union is absorbed into another union. Progress on amalgamations has been very slow among Irish unions and there are many obstacles to achieving such amalgamations, e.g., resistance to change and fear by smaller unions of losing their identity in the larger alliance. In an effort to overcome some of the obstacles associated with amalgamations the Trade Union Act 1975 was passed. This act facilitates amalgamations between trade unions.

A recent example of amalgamation was the formation in January 1990 of a new union entitled "Services, Industrial, Professional and Technical Union" (SIPTU). This new union was established through the amalgamation of the Irish Transport and General Workers Union (ITGWU) and the Federated Workers Union of Ireland (FWUI).

20.48. The Irish Congress of Trade Unions (I.C.T.U.)

The ICTU is the central co-ordinating body of the Irish Labour Movement and its sphere of activity covers the 32 counties. In the Republic, affiliated unions represent some 95% of total trade union membership. The ICTU is charged with representing the collective will of trade unions in industrial relations and in legislative and administrative matters. The individual affiliated unions guard their autonomy and retain complete freedom of action. Congress relies on the co-operation of its affiliated unions for the implementation of the resolutions passed by it. If such resolutions are approved and ratified by the affiliated unions, then they are binding on the unions, though they are not binding in any legal sense. Thus, if one or more unions do not comply with Congress resolutions, even if ratified by the said unions, the most that Congress can do is suspend or expel those unions which violate it regulations and policies. Congress provides a research and information service, a technical and advisory service and an educational service. There is provision for machinery for dealing with disputes between unions and demarcation problems (e.g., disputes as to what craft should do certain work). An Appeals Board, which hears appeals by individuals or groups of union members for alleged failure by their own union(s) to provide them with adequate service, is also provided by Congress. While Congress itself is not a trade union, it consults and is consulted by the Government on matters affecting industrial relations and trade unions. It has represented its affiliated unions in the Employer-Labour Conference which has provided the forum for the conclusion of the National Pay Agreements in recent years.

20.49. Employers' unions
The Federation of Irish Employers (F.I.E.) is by far the most important of the employers' unions and its activities are confined solely to industrial relations. The remaining 15 employer unions, which hold negotiating licences, deal not only with industrial relations but also with the trade interests affecting their members, e.g., The Irish Printing Federation.

The F.I.E. provides statistics and information to member companies and advises on industrial training matters. It also assists and advises companies setting up new industries or plants in Ireland.

Like the Irish Congress of Trade Unions (ICTU), the F.I.E. often consults and is consulted by the Government on matters of national concern in labour relations and social affairs. Unlike the ICTU however, the FUE is a trade union and actually participates, where necessary, in negotiations with trade unions of employees, on behalf of the employers it represents, on such matters as collective agreements, changes in terms and conditions of employment and the settlement of disputes.

There are 16 trade unions of employers in the Republic, and like their counterparts on the employee side, it has long since been thought that there are too many employer unions. In order to try and rationalise this multi-union problem on the employer side, the Irish Employers' Confederation (IEC) for Industrial Relations was formed some years ago, of which the F.I.E. was a founder-member. This body, which at present is made up of 12 employers' unions including the F.I.E., is the central co-ordinating organisation for employer associations concerned with Industrial Relations and related matters. The IEC represents the employer interests in the Employer-Labour Conference.

20.50. The Labour Court
Successive governments have considered that it is the job of employers and trade unions to regulate wages, salaries and conditions of employment, and to resolve disputes arising therefrom, through *free* collective bargaining between the parties concerned and without outside interference. Disputes, however, arise which are not solved through the process of collective bargaining. Such *trade disputes,* as they are known

can lead to strikes by the trade unions or lock-outs by the employers. In order to help the parties to help themselves in the case of such trade disputes, the Labour Court was established in 1946 under the Industrial Relations Act of that year, and Act which has been amended in certain respects by the Industrial Relations Act in 1969.

Apart from the settlement of trade disputes, the Labour court has a regulatory function in the following areas:—

(a)   Joint Industrial Councils

(b)   Joint Labour Committees

(c)   Registration of Employment Agreements

(a)   *Joint Industrial Councils*
      These are permanent joint negotiating bodies relating to a number of industries. They are voluntary bodies whose function is to agree on rates of wages and conditions of employment, but they may also deal with any matters between employers and employees or between different groups of employees, which are likely to lead to a dispute. Agreements when reached cannot be finalised until they are approved by the majority of workers and employers concerned. Such agreements are not legally binding and do not apply to parties not represented on the councils. Joint Industrial Councils consist of representatives in equal numbers of employers and employees with an agreed independent chairman. If a council fails to reach agreement, the services of the Labour Court are then available to it to help reach a settlement.

      There are at present 14 Joint Industrial Councils covering 114 000 employees. Examples of Joint Industrial Councils include those covering the Construction and Banking Industries.

(b)   *Joint Labour Committees*
      The Committees are composed of equal numbers of representatives from the employers and employees concerned, who are appointed by the Labour Court, together with independent members appointed by the Minister for Labour, who are chosen from people outside the trade or industry. The Chairman is always an independent member. The wages and conditions proposed by the Committees come before the Labour Court for confirmation and when confirmed, are the subject of Employment Regulation Orders. Thereafter the wages and conditions are legally enforceable minima.

      At present, there are 21 Joint Labour Committees covering 40 000 employees, including, for example, a Committee for Hotels, and a Committee for Law Clerks.

(c)   *Registration of Employment Agreements*
      Finally, on the regulatory side, a collective agreement may be

registered with the Labour Court and when registered, becomes legally binding not only on the parties to it but on every worker or employer "of the class, type or group to which it is expressed to apply". Before registration, several requirements must be satisfied by both parties including, for example, a provision that if a trade dispute occurs, a strike or lock-out will not take place until it has been submitted for settlement in the manner set out in the agreement.

Registration agreements may be varied or cancelled under certain specified conditions. Workers (and employers under the 1969 Act) may complain to the Labour Court if a registered agreement has been broken. The Labour Court can then proceed as it sees fit. If an offending party does not comply with the direction of the Labour Court, he is then liable to a fine in an ordinary Court of Law.

Since a collective agreement is not a contract, any action lies on the individual contract between an employer and an employee and not on the collective agreement.

At present 52 agreements are registered with the Labour Court, the most important of which is that relating to the Construction Industry.

The settlement of *trade disputes* is regarded as the most important of the Labour Court. At present, the Court consists of a Chairman, two deputy Chairmen, six ordinary members, i.e., three representatives of employers and three representatives of employees, all of whom are appointed by the Minister for Labour. The Court can be split into three divisions to expedite business.

How the Labour Court operates

The members of the Court are not civil servants and act independently of the Minister. Unlike an ordinary Court of law, the Labour Court does not enforce law; its recommendations are not legally binding and it cannot enforce penalties for failure to comply with them. It can, however, intervene, in certain trade disputes if it wishes and, like an ordinary Court of Law, it has power to summon witnesses, take evidence on oath and require the production of documents. The Labour Court provides a conciliation service in addition to the investigations of the Court proper. The Court may not investigate a trade dispute unless an industrial relations officer (before the Industrial Relations Act of 1969 known as a "conciliation officer") reports to the Court that the parties have failed to settle at conciliation and the parties themselves ask the Court to investigate the dispute. If, however, the Court thinks there are exceptional circumstances, it may, at its discretion, investigate the dispute irrespective of the foregoing provision.

The conciliation service is a very important part of the Labour Court's work. In the typical trade dispute, the Chairman of the Court may appoint an industrial relations officer, who is an experienced impartial third party to get the parties together to try and settle their differences at that level. If a permanent settlement is not reached at conciliation, the industrial relations officer tries to get a temporary settlement in order to avoid a stoppage of work pending the investigation of the dispute by the Court proper.

In line with the *voluntarism* which characterises the Irish Industrial relations system, the parties are free to accept or reject the Court's recommendations. The combined efforts of the conciliation service and the Court itself have succeeded in settling more than four out of every five cases that have been dealt with since the Labour Court was founded. In recent years there has been a very significant increase in the number of disputes dealt with by the Court itself. The Court issued 80 recommendations in 1970 compared with 403 in 1975. This increase in work, in each year since 1970, can be largely attrributed to the provisions of National Pay Agreements which commit the parties to refer to the Court for recommendations on those disputes which cannot be settled by direct negotiations.

In conclusion, it seems appropriate that reference should be made to the appointment of *Rights Commissioners*, made by the Minister for Labour under the Industrial Relations Act, 1969. A Commissioner must investigate, privately, a trade dispute which exists or is apprehended, when requested to do so by a party to the dispute, unless the other party objects, and must make a recommendation to the parties on the merits of the dispute. However, Rights Commissioners are precluded from investigating a dipute connected with rates of pay, hours of work or annual holidays of a body of workers. In practice they would be concerned with important matters like suspensions and dismissals of workers.

A Rights Commissioner may not investigate a dispute if the Labour Court has already made a recommendation in relation to the dispute. A party to a dispute on which a Rights Commissioner has made a recommendation may appeal to the Labour Court against the recommendation. If he does so, the Court must hear the appeal in private, and its decision will be binding on the parties. Finally, where a Rights Commissioner has made a recommendation on a dispute, the Labour Court cannot investigate that dispute except by way of appeal.

Rights Commissioners

A Rights Commissioner may not investigate a dispute if the Labour Court has already made a recommendation in relation to the dispute. A party to a dispute on which a Rights Commissioner has made a recommendation may appeal to the Labour Court against the recommendation. If he does so, the Court must hear the appeal in private, and its decision will be binding on the parties. Finally, where a Rights Commissioner has made a recommendation on a dispute, the Labour Court cannot investigate that dispute except by way of appeal.

The Rights Commissioners deal most with disputes affecting individual workers or small groups of workers. They travel extensively around the country in dealing with the relevant diputes, providing a speedy service and quick decisions. Their services are much in demand, e.g., in 1971 the two Commissioners at that time dealt with 146 cases, while in 1974, some 825 cases were dealt with by the one Commissioner.

For almost three years there had been only one Rights Commissioner. The Minister for Labour, in view of the increased work load, appointed a second Commissioner in January 1976.

20.51. Collective Bargaining and Collective Agreements

Collective bargaining is the process whereby negotiations take place on wages, salaries and conditions of employment between unionised workers on the one hand and employer(s), whether unionised or not, on the other with the purpose of reaching agreements. Such agreements, when reached, are known as collective agreements and are not legally binding on either side. The process of collective bargaining also extends to the settlement of disputes which may arise between the social partners.

Collective bargaining

Although there is no legal obligation on the parties to engage in collective bargaining, the State has pursued a policy of fostering *free* negotiations between voluntary organisations of employees and employers. To work effectively, collective bargaining pre-supposes a degree of unionisation among workers, mutual recognition by both parties of their respective positions and also an understanding that collective agreements must generally be observed.

The Government's role is a neutral one, adopting the attitude that the two parties should settle wages, salaries and conditions of employment between themselves, together with any differences arising therefrom, with Government intervention taking place only when necessary, e.g., when there is a conspicuous imbalance of power between the two sides.

The merits claimed for our system of collective bargaining are that it is *flexible* and free from the rigidity of law and secondly that *responsibility* rests on the shoulders of the parties themselves for the outcome of their deliberations, with little or no outside intervention taking place. Thus the parties, having freely negotiated agreements, should themselves feel responsible for their implementation.

Before 1970 criticisms levelled at collective agreements included assertions that these agreements were short and simple, loosely-worded and of indefinite duration. In turn, such characteristics were thought to lead to opportunism by one or both of the parties, who might take cover under the inadequate or ambiguous terminology of the agreements and thus break them.

Yet another criticism in regard to these collective agreements was that inadequate disputes procedures existed to handle problems arising out of agreements.

While the situation is still imperfect, significant changes have occurred, particularly since 1970, to help counter many of the criticisms and problems mentioned above in connection with collective agreements. The National Pay Agreements of 1970, 1972, 1974 and 1975 concluded under the auspices of the Employer-Labour Conference spell out, inter alia, the amount of pay increases and include escalator clauses tied to the cost of living. The exact duration of these agreements is fixed and procedures are set out for the resolving of disputes, the interpretation of the agreements and the removal of anomalies in pay between different groups of workers.

20.52. The effects of trade unions on the supply of labour

Wage Drift

When a trade union negotiates a wage rate for its members, this usually has the effect of ensuring that no supply of labour is available at wage rates below the standard wage rate, thus it acts as a monopolist in the supply of its members labour. Instead of the supply curve of labour being upward sloping it becomes horizontal at the union rate over a large range of levels of employment. If demand was to increase beyond the supply available at the negotiated rate, then in the short term there would develop "*wage drift*" which is an upward movement in wage rates above the negotiated rate and eventually the negotiation by the trade union of an increased rate of pay. This wage drift often manifests itself during a wage freeze when employers are prohibited from increasing negotiated and approved levels of wages. In these circumstances some employers may offer benefits like guaranteed overtime, longer holidays, and generally better and easier working conditions to retain workers with skills which are in short supply or to entice workers to enter their employment.

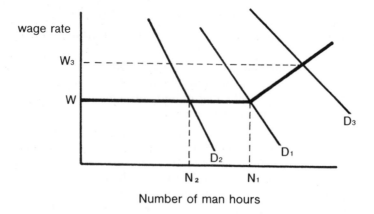

Fig. 20.52. Minimum wage rates for workers.

20.53. In Fig. 20.52 the union negotiated rate of wage is W with a level of demand represented by demand curve D_1. There is full employment at this wage. *Full employment is defined as a situation where all those prepared to work at the existing wage are employed.* Where the union negotiates a minimum wage the level of employment is determined by the demand for labour, i.e., its marginal revenue productivity. If D_2 represents the MRP of labour, the level of employment would be N_2 and some of those prepared to work at the union wage would not be employed. The union as a monopolistic seller of labour can decide the price at which labour is available but the market will then decide the quantity which it will demand at that price. As we know from experience, when there is unemployment within a union this does not lead to a reduction in the wage rate — wages tend to be rigid in a downward direction. Unions who have obtained certain standards for their members over several years of negotiation will not allow these to be eroded by what they (the unions) see as:—

- Temporary market conditions, or

- A tactic on the part of employers to reduce wages, or

- Circumstances which would not lead to a permanent increase in the level of employment even if wages rates were reduced.

20.54. This raises the obvious question of who speaks for the unemployed and this situation combined with a corresponding reluctance on the part of the employers to reduce prices when demand is not buoyant, results in a "Ratchet Economy". As you may know a ratchet screwdriver or a ratchet wheel engages when turned in one direction but does not engage when turned in the opposite direction. Similarly a *ratchet economy* indicates an economy where prices and wages increase when demand increases but prices and wages tend not to be reduced in the face of a reduction in demand. It is true, however, that trade unions may be less demanding when negotiating wage contracts in times of economic depression when there is a high level of unemployment. In keeping with the above comments on the ratchet economy, as shown in fig. 20.52 if demand increases to D_3 wages rise to W_3, though the wage rate is not reduced when the demand for labour is reduced from D_1 to D_2.

It is often said that in the face of a reduction in the level of demand for labour trade unions are inclined to allow all the adjustments to take place on the quantity side (i.e. level of employment) while leaving the price (i.e. wage rate) unaltered.

20.55. Systems of payments to workers
Time Rates refer to a system in which the employees are paid on the basis of an agreed sum per time period, e.g., per hour, per week, per month or per annum. The wage paid is not directly related to the work done,

though obviously there must be some concept of the work which can be expected from the worker, otherwise there might be a minimal amount of work completed which would result in the firm losing money.

Standardised Time Rates refers to a system in which all workers engaged in similar work are paid at the same rate and wage differentials are applied for agreed differences in the job. Standardised time rates are an essential feature of collective bargaining procedures.

Reasons for implementing a time rate system of payment

(a) Where each unit of work is not standardised, e.g., in repairing machinery, even if some notion may be calculated as to the average time required per unit of work, a payment related to work completed in each time period could result in considerable variation — to an unacceptable extent — in the money received by the worker. Hence payment related to work performed per time-period, could result in workers choosing only the easier type of repair or completing a quota of work at the expense of quality.

(b) If workers are using expensive and delicate machinery or raw materials, any attempt by workers to speed up their tempo of work could be costly.

(c) For certain types of work there is no end product which is capable of being measured as in service industries, e.g., policemen, teachers.

Disadvantges of time rates:–

(a) Workers are paid for some periods spent in virtual idleness.

(b) The lazy or incompetent worker (if he can avoid being sacked) receives as much as his competent, intelligent, colleagues who apply their talents for the benefit of the firm.

(c) There is lack of incentive for the better worker to attain and maintain peak performances.

(d) Expensive supervision of workers is necessary.

20.56. *Piece Rates:* Refers to a system of payment where remuneration is related to work actually completed. For such a system to be implemented it is necessary that the quantity of work performed by an individual or team of workers should be of a standard form and capable of being measured, e.g., repetitive type of work. The raw materials used must be standardised or any variations in raw materials should be capable of measurement so that an allowance can be made.

Advantages of piece rates

(a) Employer pays only for work done.

(b) Volume of output is likely to be close to maximum, so that fixed costs per unit produced are at a minimum.

(c) Absenteeism is minimised.

(d) A considerable degree of supervision of workers is eliminated though some form of quality control of work completed is vital.

Disadvantages of piece rates

(a) It may cause physical and mental strain in workers.

(b) The setting of rates of pay often causes friction.

(c) Employers may seek to impose more rigorous output quotas if workers are enjoying good income.

(d) Older workers may have difficulty in attaining an adequate weekly income.

(e) Sick workers may be at a considerable financial disadvantage.

20.57. *Profit sharing/commission*

These are systems of payment to workers which seek to provide a standardised time rate form of payment and an additional payment is made as an incentive to maximum commitment and effort. A commission system applies when the employee receives as a payment some percentage of sales or orders received. Profit sharing as the name implies entails the employee receiving some share of profit. The main advantage attributed to profit sharing schemes is that the "fixed cost" element of wages, i.e. the amount which the employer is committed to pay even if there is a (temporary) falling off in his level of sales is reduced when part of the employee's income is through profit sharing. This lower 'fixed' wage encourages the employer to recruit workers. A profit sharing scheme encourages employees to be more careful with the firms equipment, to minimise wastage and generally to identify more closely with the economic fortunes of the enterprise. Others state that the time lag is too great between the effort and the reward for the incentive to be really effective. In addition, if the level of profits fall the resultant reduction in the employees total remuneration can cause friction and bad labour relations.

QUESTIONS

Q1. What is meant by the "Participation Rate" and what facts influence it?

Q2. Distinguish between "The Poverty Cycle" and the "Economy of High Wages".

Q3. Discuss the factors which result in different categories of workers being paid at different wage rates.

Q4. Explain the effect on the labour market of each of the under-mentioned. Illustrate each answer with a separate diagram:
(i) A movement of taste in favour of the output of the firm
(ii) Trade Unions negotiate a contract whereby the firm agrees that the present wage is the minimum wage.
(iii) A shift in the preference of workers in favour of more leisure.

Q5. Explain some causes of unemployment.

Q6. Write an explanatory note on the elasticity of demand for labour.

21   The Factor of Production — Capital

21.1. *Capital as a factor of production is defined as man-made wealth which is used in the production of goods and services.* The man in the street generally considers a sum of money to be capital, but to the economist the sum of money merely permits the purchase of capital goods (it may in fact, be used for the purchase of consumption goods) and is not in itself capital in the factor of production sense. An increase of money in an economy will not increase the capital of an economy; unless the supply of goods and services is increased, prices will merely rise. Money is a store of wealth and can be exchanged for capital goods and to this extent only can money be interpreted as being capital as a factor of production.

Definition of Capital

21.2. *Income is defined as the flow of wealth which accrues to a person during a period.* It is usually expressed in money terms, e.g., £100.00 per week or £3 000 per annum. Income has been defined by Hicks as *the amount of wealth which the recipient may spend during a period without reducing the value of his capital stock.* Many textbooks describe income as being a flow and capital a stock.

Definition of income

21.3. Capital goods (also known as producer goods) are goods, e.g., factories, industrial plant and machinery, which are used for the production of other goods. They are sometimes referred to as intermediate goods in recognition of the fact that the end product of the industrial process is consumer goods.

Capital goods

21.4. Consumer goods (also known as final products) are the objectives of production. They are goods which consumers seek because they give utility, e.g., clothes, food etc.

Consumer Goods

21.5. Consumer Capital Goods (or Consumer Durables) is the term applied to consumer goods which have a fairly long life. A house is an example of a consumer capital good since it yields utility to its owner over a lengthy period; if a person pays £25 000 for a house and it has a 25 year life, the owner of the house may be considered to be receiving £1 000 worth of utility from the house each year. Similarly, a person buying a house is often referred to as making an investment of say, £25 000, and he will receive an income of £1 000 from the house each year over the 25 year life of the house, through the satisfaction which he derives from living in it. Similarly, people may make an investment in education, the return on which, apart from its contribution to a better quality of life, may be considered to be greater earning capacity over their lifetime. The division

Division into consumer goods and capital goods is sometimes arbitrary

of goods into consumer goods and producer goods is somewhat arbitrary, e.g., a camera purchased by a professional photographer is a capital good, an identical camera owned by a private person and used for his personal pleasure, is a consumer good; a motor car for private use is a consumer good; if used for business purposes it would be considered to be a capital good.

Capital goods improve productivity

21.6. The demand for capital arises because of the contribution which capital makes to production. Productivity is increased through the use of capital goods. If labour and material are used in producing a machine and the machine is then employed in the production of a consumer good, the cost of production of the consumer good is lower than it would have been if labour and material had been used in producing the consumer good directly (i.e., without first producing the machinery). As can be seen from this, capitalistic methods of production are more roundabout, the more capitalistic the production process, the greater the quanity of producer goods which are utilised and consequently the more roundabout the method of production.

Marginal efficiency of capital

21.7. The increase in profitability through the use of capital as a factor of production is known as the *efficiency of capital. The Marginal Efficiency of Capital (MEC)* is the increase in profitability due to (or the rate of return on) the last unit of capital employed. All the comments made in Chapter 18 regarding Marginal Physical Productivity, Marginal Revenue Productivity etc. apply to capital. *The Marginal Efficiency of Capital is the term applied to the Marginal Revenue Productivity of additional capital goods minus their cost.*

Robinson Crusoe Economy

21.8. That the supply of capital involves a cost is most easily seen by reverting back to a primitive existence— what some textbooks refer to as a *Robinson Crusoe Economy.* Let us assume that Robinson Crusoe is tilling the land with virtually his bare hands and he concludes that his work would be more productive if he had some form of plough. A plough would represent a capital good and could be acquired by him in any of the following three ways:—

(a)   At the end of his normal working day spending some time on the making of a plough, i.e., reducing his leisure period and thus lowering his present standard of living in the hope of an improvement in his future standard of living.

(b)   Building up a stock of goods which he needs for every day use and living off them while he is making the plough. Since his daily consumption of goods is thus lowered in the short run, his present standard of living has been reduced.

(c)   Working his usual hours each day but taking some time of from producing goods which he required for current consumption (and thus lowering his present standard of living) in order to make his capital good.

21.9. While the Robinson Crusoe example illustrates the fact that the production of capital entails an opportunity cost some readers may not see the applicability of this to a modern complex economy. In a modern economy, time, effort and materials are employed in the production of consumer goods and producer goods. Income is earned by those engaged in the production of both consumer and producer goods and this income may be used in the purchase of goods and services. Thus the pool of consumer goods is distributed among the producers of both consumer and capital goods in the ratio of their income.

The production of capital goods entails an opportunity cost

However, it is the pool of consumer goods and services which yield utility and it is these consumer goods and services which will be divided among those who have gained their income from the production of both consumer and capital goods. At any given point in time this available pool of consumer goods and services could be increased (and current standard of living improved) if all those employed were engaged in the production of consumer goods and services. Over the longer period this would be disastrous for, if an adequate supply of capital goods and services is not produced, then the future productivity of the community is jeopardised.

Lack of Capital Stock in lesser developed countries

21.10. This highlights the problems of the lesser developed countries. The availability of capital increases productivity and makes possible the enjoyment of a higher standard of living. In the lesser developed countries, the lack of a capital stock means that the level of productivity is low and all effort is directed towards satisfying current needs, i.e., survival. Because all effort is required for current needs, it is not possible to build up a capital stock.

Creation of a Capital Stock in U.S.S.R.

21.11. In recent times the introduction in the U.S.S.R. of the first Five Year Plan in 1928 directed economic activity towards the production of capital goods at the expense of the production of consumer goods. The non-availability of an adequate supply of consumer goods meant that the standard of living was low during the period of the building up of the capital stock. Eventually, when there was a stock of capital goods which was contributing to production, there was a greater availability of consumer goods and a standard of living higher than it would have been in the absence of such a policy.

21.12. The Production of Capital Goods is known as Investment

Investment

Often the term investment is used when people are placing money in a bank or buying stocks and shares. *Investment is the production of capital goods.* In so far as the purchase of stocks and shares results in the production of additional capital goods, then it is truly investment. However, if Mr. A, who owns shares in a company sells them to Mr. B, then the net effect of Mr. A's action is merely the transfer of the ownership of the shares and it does not constitute investment from the point of view of the economy. It may be argued that it is an investment in capital production by Mr. B which is matched by a corresponding disinvestment by Mr. A.

Gross investment, depreciation, net investment

21.13. *Gross investment* refers to the total production of capital goods. In the course of production, capital goods wear out and this consumption of capital goods in production is known as *Depreciation*. Net Investment is the excess of gross investment over depreciation. If gross investment is less than depreciation (i.e. there is negative net investment) there is said to be a *running down of the capital stock.*

Capital Widening

21.14. Gross Investment in the economy is usually in excess of depreciation which means that there is an increase in the capital stock in the economy. This increase in gross investment may mean that new firms are setting up production processes in this country. Alternatively, the increase in investment may be due to an increase in the capital stock of existing firms. A factory may increase its level of production by building an extension to its factory and installing new equipment and employing a number of workers to staff the new machinery, e.g., originally there were 80 machines and 320 workers, i.e., 4 workers per machine, now there are 105 machines and 420 workers still 4 workers per machine. The proportion in which the factors of production are employed has not changed so that the capital goods per worker employed has not altered. This is known as *capital widening,* i.e., an increase in the capital stock which leaves the capital/labour ratio unchanged.

Capital deepening

21.15. If the size of the capital stock increases at a faster rate than the employment of labour then the amount of capital per worker will increase — this development is known as *capital deepening* — and the production process is also referred to as becoming more capital intensive.

Captial formation

21.16. Because of the importance of the capital stock to the future productivity of the economy, the level of investment in the economy is closely monitored. Some details of this are shown in the following tables from National Income and Expenditure.

Savings

21.17. *Savings is defined as non-consumption* and this is represented by income (which is our command over goods and services, i.e., we have a right to acquire them with our money) minus consumption (which is the goods and services which we have purchased). As can be seen from this, savings is a claim over goods and services which we temporarily have not exercised. This abstinence from current consumption frees factors of production from the production of consumer goods for the production of capital goods; when saving and investment were carried out by the same person, their relationship was easily seen. When the act of saving is divorced from the act of investing, as it is in a modern economy, the relationship between savings and investment must be traced and analysed. When the act of saving is divorced from the act of investing, saving may be perceived as the act of abstinence, i.e., the freeing of resources, and investment may be seen as the activation of the resources thus freed in order to produce capital goods.

Rate of interest

21.18. People prefer current consumption to consumption at some future time. Thus it was considered that a payment was required in order to compensate the lender for the waiting involved. *This payment for the use of capital is termed the rate of interest.* It was considered that the higher the rate of interest the greater would be the level of savings. From the demand side the rate of interest was the payment by which the pool of loanable funds was allocated among those who had remunerative outlets for such funds. Those who had the most remunerative outlets for the funds, i.e., where the marginal efficiency of capital was highest, could afford to pay the highest price for the scarce funds and thus the available funds would be bid into their most remunerative uses. There was also an implication that the most remunerative uses were also the most socially desirable users, i.e., that social costs (benefits) and private costs (benefits) were equal.

Loanable Fund Theory

21.19. In the Loanable Fund Theory the supply curve of funds was perceived as being upward sloping indicating that the higher the rate of interest the greater would be the supply of funds. The demand for funds depended on the Marginal Efficiency of Capital and was downward sloping with respect to the rate of interest as shown in Fig. 21.19. The rate of interest fluctuated in order to equate the supply of, and demand for, loanable funds.

Table 21.16   SAVINGS AND CAPITAL FORMATION 1982-88

Description	1982	1983	1984	1985	1986	1987	1988[1]
Savings before adjustment for stock appreciation							
105. Personal	2,036.4	2,044.0	2,146.8	2,210.9	2,176.5	2,635	2,648
106. Companies	344.7	388.5	369.6296.6	469.8	593		
107. Public authorities	-1,188.0	-1,144.6	-1,055.5	-1,399.3	-1,484.6	-1,357	-757
108. Net national savings before adjustment for stock appreciation	1,193.1	1,287.9	1,461.0	1,108.2	1,161.7	1,871	1,891
109. Adjustment for stock appreciation	-257.8	-312.3	-187.9	90.4	49.7	-129	-55
110. Net National savings	935.3	975.6	1,273.1	1,198.6	1,211.4	1,742	1,836
111. Provision for depreciation	1,366.3	1,528.3	1,592.5	1,713.5	1,813.9	1,925	2,004
112(a) Net foreign capital transfers	99.0	91.5	7.1	50.4	30.8	-13	54
112(b) Net foreign disinvestment	1,315.7	925.2	945.4	650.1	509.4	-239	-437
113. Gross total available for investment in domestic physical capital formation	3,716	3,520.6	3,818.2	3,612.2	3,565.5	3,414	3,457
Capital formation							
114. Building and construction	1,947.7	1,772.1	1,779.5	1,675.6	1,699.0	1,617	1,581
115. Other home produced capital goods net of exports (including re-exports)	403.2	474.7	470.4	436.8	410.3	443	420
116. Imported capital goods	1,180.1	1,167.6	1,293.9	1,288.3	1,310.1	1,334	1,527
117. Value of physical changes in agricultural stocks	29.8	4.4	39.5	-23.9	-70.7	27	80
118. Increase in value of non-agricultural stocks and work in progress (incl. EC intervention stocks)	413.3	414.1	422.8	145.4	167.1	123	-96
119. Adjustment for stock appreciation	-257.8	-312.3	-187.9	90.4	49.7	-129	-55
120. Gross domestic physical capital formation	3,716.3	3,520.6	3,818.2	3,612.5	3,565.5	3,414	3,457

[1]Preliminary

In this table the total amount available for investment, (i.e. current savings, the provision for depreciation, net foreign capital transfers and net foreign disinvestment) is equated to gross domestic physical capital formation. The figures for capital formation are obtained by adding figures for imported and home produced capital goods ready for use to the value of the physical changes ins tocks, including the value of the changes in agricultural stocks. Since personal savings (item 105) is a residual figure it includes the effect of the changes in agricultural and certain other stocks. Personal savings accordingly includes a substantial non-monetary element.

Source: National Income and Expenditure 1982-1988 (C.S.O.)

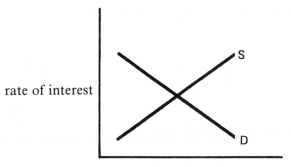

level of savings/level of investment

Fig. 21.19. Savings and investments brought into equilibrium through a fluctuating rate of interest.

This loanable fund theory is recognised now as being an over-simplification. It attributes too great an influence to the rate of interest in the determination of the level of saving and the level of investment.

Target saver, backward bending supply curve of loanable funds

21.20. If a person is a "target" type saver, i.e., saving in order to acquire a specific sum of money, then an increase in the rate of interest would mean that any given capital sum could be obtained by a lower level of saving (because of the higher rate of interest). In this instance a higher rate of interest would result in a lower level of saving, i.e., a backward bending supply curve of loanable funds.

21.21. In addition the Loanable Fund Theory implies that all savings are available for investment. This may not be so as will be recognised when attention is directed to the reasons why people save.

21.22. Reasons for saving

(a) Deferred spending. Income and expenditure are not perfectly synchronised. Income is received per week or per month, while expenditure is on a daily pattern or large items of expenditure take place at irregular intervals. In the same context, purchases such as foreign holidays, furniture, clothes, school expenses, cannot be met entirely from the normal flow of weekly income. Savings of the nature specified here are really deferred spending.

(b) As a precaution in order to provide for those items of expenditure which, on the law of averages, we know will occur but the timing of their occurrence is uncertain, e.g., medical expenses, breakdown of motor car or household appliance, house repairs etc.

(c) For Old Age. This was a particularly popular reason for saving in the past. With the advent of the Welfare State the pressure on people to engage in this form of saving has diminished through payments into superannuation funds. Certain forms of insurance policies may also be seen in this light.

(d)   Speculative Purpose. This type of saving is undertaken in order to permit savers to avail themselves of any investment opportunities which may arise. The rate of interest has a considerable influence on this form of saving, the level of which will be high when the rate of interest is high and low when the rate of interest is low.

(e)   Residual. Savings may be a residual. People spend that portion of their income which permits them to enjoy the standard of living which they desire and any income which remains is saved.

21.23. Saving is undertaken by:—

(a)   Individuals.

(b)   Business/Corporate Sector. When businesses do not distribute all of their profits, the undistributed profits constitute a form of saving — possibly to be used as internally generated investible funds.

(c)   State. If the government has a budget surplus, i.e. its revenue exceeds its expenditure.

Forced savings

21.24. *Forced savings* may arise in an inflationary situation when the quantity of goods and services which an individual on a fixed income can consume is reduced because of increases in the price of goods and services.

Compulsory savings

21.25. *Compulsory savings* is the term generally applied to compulsory deductions from a person's gross income, e.g., superannuation deductions, social welfare payment, income tax, etc.

Lending institutions

21.26. In addition to individual lenders of funds there are also institutionalised lenders who channel funds from those wishing to save to those wishing to borrow. Examples of these are Commercial Banks, Merchant Banks, Agricultural Credit Corporation, Industrial Credit Corporation, Insurance and Assurance Companies, Building Societies, etc.

Range of rates of interest

21.27. Reference has been made to the rate of interest, but as we all know there is not just one rate of interest at any given time but several. Thus it is obvious that the rate of interest must be affected by a number of factors, which result in differing rates of interest depending on circumstances.

21.28. Factors which influence the rate of interest

(a)   *The Bank Rate/Central Bank's Rediscount Rate/Minimum Lending Rate*
      This constitutes the basic rate and is the plateau from which all other rates are adjusted. The Bank Rate is set by government policy in response to current economic conditions; in many discussions on the rate of interest, the Bank Rate is taken as given.

(b) *"Pure" Rate of Interest.* A similar approach to that adopted in 21.28 (a) is through the concept of the "riskless" rate of interest or the "pure" rate of interest. This riskless rate of interest is the rate of interest on 2½% Consols which have no redemption date and therefore there is no complexity introduced through the date of redemption, and since they are a government stock there is no risk element. *Yield is the rate of return on the investment related to its purchase price.* The nominal scale of return on £100.00 Consols is £2.50, if the current rate of interest is 10% then the price which will be paid for £100.00 of Consols is $2.5 \times 100 = £25.00$ so that for an expenditure of £25.00, the income received is £2.50 which constitutes a return of 10%.

(c) *Degree of Lender's Risk.* The lender of funds has an expectation of two distinct but interrelated forms of monetary return from the borrower. The first is that the interest will be paid and secondly that the capital sum will be returned on the due date. The greater the risk involved, the higher the return which the lender will require if he is to be enticed to lend, e.g., if I borrowed funds from you and invested them in buying a lottery ticket, your interest payments and return of sum invested would be contingent on my winning money in the lottery. In these circumstances you would probably feel that no promised rate of return would constitute an adequate return for the risk which you are required to take. Where the risk is negligible it is said to be a "gilt edge" investment, e.g., investment in government loans. Similarly investment in companies where the risk is negligible, e.g., Guinness, Carroll Cigarettes are referred to as "Blue Chip" investments. Even when one chooses a company in which to invest it is possible to opt for different degrees of risk e.g., debentures which are loans at fixed rate of interest, preference shares which have a prior claim for payment, and ordinary shares. The rate of return will depend on the risk involved.

(d) *Degree of illiquidity. Liquidity refers to the ease with which an asset can be changed, if required, from one form into another without losing money.* Usually if we have an asset and we want to acquire a different type of asset, e.g., if you have a camera and require a guitar, it is necessary to go through the medium of money. Thus money is the most liquid form of asset. In order to entice an investor to hold his assets in a illiquid form, e.g., stocks and shares rather than cash, it is necessary to pay him a rate of interest.

This payment is necessary because in holding an asset other than cash there will be brokerage and stamp costs when the holder wishes to convert his asset back into money and there is also an inconvenience cost in so doing. Furthermore he has lost the ability to transfer quickly into some other asset at short notice, should he wish to do so.

The longer the period for which the loan is made, the greater the degree of illiquidity and the higher the rate of interest which must be paid. Conversely, the longer the period of notice which a saver undertakes to give before demanding repayment of his loan, the higher the rate of interest which he can obtain — you may confirm this at your local post office or bank. This reference to the period of the loan is often referred to as the *illiquidity of the loan.* (See also section 23.25 regarding liquidity.)

(e)   *The rate of inflation.* The rate of inflation affects the rate of interest both because of the affect which it has on the Bank Rate which forms the base interest rate, and because savers seek recompense for the erosion of their purchasing power in real terms. If £100 is loaned for 1 year at 10% interest and the rate of inflation during the period has been 14% then the saver is subject to a *negative interest rate of 4%* — the purchasing power of £110.00, i.e., his initial loan plus interest, is at the date of its repayment lower than the purchasing power of initial £100.00 on the day of the making of the loan.

Inflation will certainly affect the interest rate as between different types of loan. If a loan of £100.00 is returned in money form at the end of the loan period, this would not be as good as a share investment in a company with the £100.00 for, even if the company had neither made progress nor deteriorated but merely kept pace with the rate of inflation, the investor on selling his shares would receive the current purchasing power equivalent of his original £100.00, i.e., £150.00 for his initial investment of £100.00 if inflation was at the rate of 50% during the period for which the shares were held. As between these two alternatives if the degree of risk was the same, the person who was having his initial money investment returned at the end of the period would seek to be paid at a higher rate of interest. For this reason during periods of inflation the ordinary shares of blue chip companies which provide some protection against inflation may be more popular than government loans which repay the initial money sum at the end of the loan period. The opposite would apply if the general price level were falling.

(f)   The Demand for funds, i.e., by people who wish to invest. The greater the demand for funds (savings) the higher will be the rate of interest.

Marginal efficiency of capital schedule is downward sloping

21.29. Investment which is the purchase of capital goods is undertaken by producers. Because producers wish to maximise their profits they will, ceteris paribus, prefer those projects on which the rate of return, i.e., the Marginal Efficiency of Capital, is highest. The Marginal Efficiency of Capital schedule is shown as being downward sloping as in Fig. 21.29. indicating that the greater the level of investment per period the lower the rate of return, for the following 2 reasons:—

(a)   The greater the level of investment in a period, the greater the demand for new capital goods, which would tend to result in an increase in the price of these capital goods. An increase in the price of these capital goods means a reduction in the return on the investment. Suppose originally a machine was bought for £500.00 and the return on the investment was £125.00, i.e., 25%, if the price of the machine increases to £600.00 and the return on the investment remains at £125.00, then the rate of return on the investment has fallen to 20.83%, i.e., 125/600.

(b)   As the stock of capital increases through investment it would become subject to diminishing returns. This point is really part of a long run analysis and consequently is not relevant in the short run.

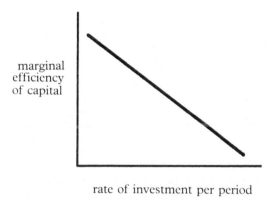

Fig. 21.29. Marginal efficiency of capital and rate of investment per period.

21.30. In Fig. 21.19. the equilibrium rate of interest was determined from the interaction of the supply of, and demand for, funds. In the present example let us suppose that the rate of interest is fixed as it may be for many small firms perhaps because the government has as a matter of monetary policy decided on a particular rate of interest. This situation is illustrated in Fig. 21.30, which illustrates the relationship between the marginal efficiency of capital, the level of investment and the rate of interest.

From this it can be seen that if the rate of interest reduces from 12% to 10% the level of investment would be greater — it increases from 850 to 1100.

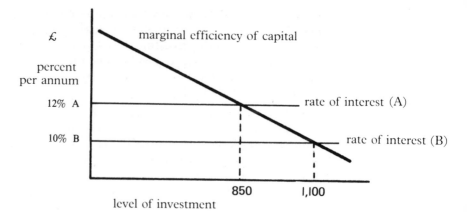

Fig. 21.30. Level of investment increases when rate of interest is reduced.

21.31. Factors which affect the level of investment:—

(a) *The rate of interest,* which has already been discussed.

(b) *The capital stock of the economy.* The greater the stock of capital goods, ceteris paribus, the lower will be the Marginal Efficiency of Capital and thus the lower the level of investment. As stated in Section 21.29 (b) this is a long-term analysis, in the short-term the capital stock may be taken as given.

(c) *Knowledge regarding production techniques.* As production techniques improve, the Marginal Efficiency of Capital increases i.e., the Marginal Efficiency of Capital schedule shifts to the right.

(d) *The cost of capital goods.* If the cost of capital goods increases there would be a reduction in the level of investment at each rate of return, i.e., the Marginal Efficiency of Capital schedule shifts to the left.

(e) *Business expectations.* Because production takes place in anticipation of a demand, the demand schedule which a businessman perceives for his goods is a demand at some time in the future, i.e., when the goods being produced are ready for sale. When a businessman is purchasing capital goods, he is purchasing these capital goods in order to produce consumer goods for which he perceives a demand when the goods are ready for sale.

However, he is projecting into the future and will be influenced by his expectations. If he becomes more optimistic about the future, e.g., election of government with plans to stimulate the economy, he would be willing to increase his level of investment, i.e., the Marginal Efficiency of Capital schedule will shift to the right. If he becomes *pessimistic,* e.g., international crises or recession, the MEC schedule shifts to the left. Keynes, among others, felt that this change in business expectation is the main reason for changes in the level of investment.

(f)   *Uncertainty.* This is closely related to the previous point about business expectations. Not only is it a case of business people having expectations as to future developments but also the certainty with which he holds his expectations. An increase in uncertainty may cause a postponement of investment plans, e.g., before an election, or while OPEC countries are holding meetings in order to decide the future price of oil.

21.32. In Fig. 21.30 was shown the relationship between the level of investment, the Marginal Efficiency of Capital and the rate of interest, ceteris paribus, i.e., other factors remaining unchanged. These other factors are set out as points (c) to (f) in section 21.31. A change in any of these factors causes a shift in the MEC schedule — to the right and therefore a higher level of investment for any given rate of interest if circumstances appear favourable for business and profitability, conversely a *shift* in the MEC schedule to the *left* if circumstances are perceived by potential investors as being unfavourable for business profitability.

QUESTIONS

Q1. Distinguish between Capital and Income.

Q2. Write an explanatory note on the opportunity cost of creating capital stock.

Q3. Explain the factors which influence the rate of interest.

Q4. Draw a curve depicting the Marginal Efficiency of Capital and justify its shape.

Q5. A financial institution has agreed in principle to grant a loan to an applicant. What factors will influence the rate of interest which will be charged?

Q6. State, giving reasons which of the following you would choose.
(a) £10,000 investment in a new government loan yielding 7% repayable in 25 years which is being issued at par

or

(b) £10,000 worth of shares in a company which has been paying a dividend of 7% in each of the past four years.

22 The Factor of Production — Entrepreneurship

Contribution of entrepreneur

22.1. Even if the three factors of production previously discussed viz. Land, Labour and Capital are available, production will not take place unless somebody sets about producing the goods for which a demand exists or can be created. There may be carpenters unemployed, wood available in the mills, machinery available from the machinery manufacturers and loans available from banks, but these resources will not be organised into a production unit unless somebody hires them and starts production.

If production is to take place, decisions must be made as to the type of commodity which will be produced, the factors of production to be employed, and payments must be made to the suppliers of the factors of production, all of which must be done before the goods are actually sold. Then the goods must be sold at a price which will recoup all the expenses which have been incurred and there will be the hope that there will be enough money remaining to provide sufficient recompense for the risks involved.

22.2. There are two forms of risk inherent in any form of business activity:

Insurable risks

(a) There are the risks such as fire, accidents to employees or third parties, water and storm damage etc. The essential feature of each of these types of hazards is the fact that insurance can be taken out against their occurrence. The payment of the necessary insurance premium is a legitimate expense of the business and the amount of the premium is included in the list of expenses of the business in the computation of selling price and the calculation of net profit.

Uninsurable risks

(b) In addition to the risks set out above there are other risks which are inherent in business in a dynamic economy and against which it is **not** possible to insure. For example, will the style of clothes or shoes which are at present being produced sell at the price and in the quantity required in order to earn sufficient profit? Will competitors produce a more fashionable or cheaper line which will adversely affect the demand for your product? Will it be a hot dry summer or a cold wet one and to what extent will this affect the sale of summer clothes and shoes? The person who bears risks of this nature, the risks against which no insurance is available, is known as the entrepreneur, i.e., he is the person with the enterprise. Profit is the term applied to the return which the entrepreneur receives for accepting these uninsurable risks — it is the payment for bearing the uncertainties inherent in business in a dynamic economy.

Insurable Risks	Non-Insurable Risks
Fire	Change in taste or fashion
Personal Accidents	Entry of new Firms
Burglary	Increase in costs of production
Dishonesty by Employees	Industrial Disputes
Non–Payment in foreign trade	Problems with deliveries from suppliers
	Trade agreements with other countries which increase competition.

Contribution of entrepreneur to production is unique

22.3. The contribution which the entrepreneur makes to production is unique and should not be confused with the factor of production labour — entrepreneurship should **not** be seen as some form of management function. To reinforce the idea in your mind you might consider the entrepreneur as employing somebody to organise and manage the firm, and paying salaries for the service. Similarly, let us assume that he borrows all his capital and pays interest on the funds borrowed (since finance houses would not be prepared to provide all the risk capital for a business, you may imagine that the entrepreneur has money elsewhere which acts a security for the money which he is borrowing). All other forms of labour employed by the firm receive wages and rent is paid for the land required. The entrepreneur must meet all these payments and, if the end product does not sell, he suffers a loss. If the revenue exceeds his cost, the size of the profit will depend upon the quantity which he sells, the selling price of each unit and his success in minimising his costs of production.

22.4. Thus the return to the entrepreneur is unique in the following three ways:

Return to entrepreneur is a residual

(a) His reward is a residual, it is what is left from the revenue when all expenses have been paid. This is different from the payment to all of the other factors of production since these other payments are contractual — workers agree to work for a specified wage, funds are loaned for a specific rate of interest and usually on specified repayment terms; similarly, the hiring of land is on agreed terms.

(b) Though the actions of the entrepreneur are motivated by the anticipation of profit, it is possible that he may suffer a loss, i.e., a negative rate of return.

Return to entrepreneur may be negative

This possibility does not arise with any other factor of production, workers will not pay their employers for the privilege of working for them (any payment to an employer by an employee for *training* is different), landowners will not pay people to use their land, while capital is not loaned out for negative nominal rates of interest, i.e., if you borrow £100.00 you will have to pay back not less than £100.00

(c)   The amount of profit tends to fluctuate more than does the return to the other factors of production. Since the return to the other factors of production is contractual and the return to the entrepreneur is a residual, any fluctuations in the difference between revenue and cost, at least in the short term, accrues to profit. If business is booming profits will increase. Though in the long run workers, conscious of the profitability of the enterprise, may seek some increase in wages. Similarly, if business is depressed, profit will be depressed and may in fact be negative, i.e., a loss.

Entrepreneur's return fluctuates more than does the return to the other factors

22.5. Who is the entrepreneur?

As stated in previous Sections, the entrepreneur is the individual who bears the uncertainty which is inherent in business in a dynamic economy. It is sometimes thought that directors, top management or decision makers in a firm are the entrepreneurs — this is not necessarily so. If these people are employed by the firm and receive a salary for their efforts on the firm's behalf, then they are merely an aspect of the factor of production labour.

Employees' profit-sharing schemes and any other system of payment to workers based on profit, could be considered as part of the entrepreneurial function only if workers had to pay money in the event of losses being sustained by the firm. In the absence of this, payments related to profits are merely an incentive form of wage payment.

With large State-sponsored bodies, i.e., CIE, ESB, the entrepreneurs are the general public, since it the general public who, through taxation, must bear any losses which these firms suffer.

In limited companies it is the ordinary shareholders who are the entrepreneurs since it is they who will be entitled to any profits which are made and who will suffer any losses if the firm's trading results in a deficit. It is quite possible that the directors of large companies are also shareholders; in this case the person concerned would be seen as providing two factors of production, labour and entrepreneurship, and consequently is entitled to receive a return for each.

22.6. In general terminology the word profit has different meanings so that it is necessary to contrast the concepts to which the word is applied.

Different meanings of profit

(a)   Profit is the term used to indicate the difference between revenue (received and due) on the one hand and expenditure (paid and owed) on the other. The concept of cost as being money paid and owed is something less than what an economist means by the term. An economist sees cost in terms of opportunity cost, i.e., the cost in terms of alternatives foregone. In relation to factors of production bought or hired by the entrepreneur, the cost which he pays for the use of goods and services measures their opportunity cost to the entrepreneur. The payment measures the opportunity cost to the entrepreneur because he foregoes the right to purchase other goods and services to the value of the money which he has paid out; it measures not less than the opportunity cost to the provider of the goods and services since otherwise he would sell them elsewhere or else not produce them. It is in assessing the opportunity cost of the entrepreneur that some misinterpretations may arise. It was shown in Section 22.5. that the entrepreneur may provide more than one factor of production and is entitled to a return for each factor of production which he supplies.

Example 22.6.

A manager of a supermarket who had been earning £13,000 per annum, won £50,000 which he decided to use to open his own shop. At the end of one year's trading his total revenue was £150,000 and he paid all his expenses to third parties which totalled £120,000. In economic terms it is **not** correct to say his profit is £30,000 (i.e., (£150,000 — £120,000). The economist would see the position in the following light.

	£
Revenue	150 000
Expenses i.e. payments to third parties	120 000
Excess of revenue over expenses	30 000
Implicit Cost	
Interest on investment of £50 000 at current rates (say 10%)	5 000
Salary for working in shop	13 000
True profit	12 000

These expenses, e.g., interest on £50 000 and salary for working in the shop are known as *implicit costs,* i.e., costs which would have had to be paid if the owner had not provided them himself, i.e., if the owner of the shop had not invested his own money the money would have had to be borrowed and interest paid on it; conversely the owner could have earned this interest by investing his money elsewhere. Similarly with wages if the owner has not worked in the shop these wages would have had to be paid to some one to do the job or the owner could have earned this sum of money by working elsewhere. *It is necessary to include these implicit costs in order to calculate the true opportunity cost and thus to ascertain the true profit.*

(b) *Normal Profit is a cost of production*
Normal Profit is the minimum amount of profit which an entrepreneur must receive if he is to continue to supply his services in the long run, i.e., it is the supply price of the factor of production — enterpreneurship. Unless Normal Profit is being received an entrepreneur will not remain in the particular line of business concerned

(c) *Supernormal Profit*
Supernormal Profit is any profit received by an entrepreneur in excess of Normal Profit. If the entrepreneur is earning £3.000 profit and Normal Profit to him is £1.200, then his Supernormal Profit would be £1.800, (£3.000 — £1.200). Supernormal Profit is an economic rent if it persists in the long run (e.g., under mononoply due to barriers to entry) and a quasi-rent if it is competed away in the long run (e.g., as in imperfect competition).

Profits are a necessary element in the free enterprise system

22.7. Profit is a term which is often used in an emotive context. It is often implied that profits are in some way immoral and those earning them are expected to be apologetic and on the defensive. Profits are a necessary element in the working of a free enterprise economy. Perhaps some of those who resent the earning of profits are of the opinion that the economy in question should be run on other than free enterprise lines. This is a valid point for discussion, but, given that an economy is operating on the basis of free enterprise, then profits are an essential element in such a system. Criticisms of the level of profits and the manner in which they are earned may be valid in particular cases.

22.8. The role of profits in a free enterprise economy.

(a) Normal Profit is the minimum price which must be paid in order to ensure the availability of the factor of production, entrepreneurship, in the long run. As such it is a necessary cost of production and unless such a payment is forthcoming production will not take place.

(b) Supernormal Profits are the rewards to enterpreneurs for successful innovation, for introducing new commodities for which the public is prepared to pay a price. Not only are Supernormal Profits of this nature accepted, but they are protected by the State through the granting of patents. Patents are granted to encourage a commitment by industry to research and development, which is a prerequisite for technological progress and development.

(c) Supernormal Profits act as a signalling system from consumers to producers to indicate those goods the supply of which might be increased. Conversely the absence of normal profits on certain lines of production indicates the non-acceptance by the public of such goods and results in their eventual withdrawal from production.

(d) The fact that Supernormal Profits are being enjoyed by a particular firm encourages the entry of new firms into the industry and thus an increase in the quantity of the good being supplied.

(e) Supernormal Profits provide the funds which enable the firm to expand and increase its level of production. While some money for expansion may be borrowed from outside the firm, it is necessary for the firm to provide a large share of such funds for expansion from its own resources. (These funds which the firm must provide from its own resources are usually referred to as internally generated investible funds).

(f) Where price competition takes place, the actions of competitors constrain the ability of a firm to increase its selling price. In these circumstances the firm earning the highest level of profit is the firm with the lowest costs of production. If factors of production are scarce, the most efficient firm can afford to pay the price necessary to bid factors of production from the less efficient firm. The Marginal Revenue Productivity of factors of production are higher when they are used by the more efficient firms. In this way production is concentrated in the hands of the most efficient firms.

22.9. Supply of entrepreneurs

Just as with any of the other factors of production, the supply curve of entrepreneurs may be shown as being upward sloping from left to right as set out in Fig. 22.9.

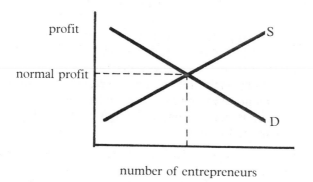

Fig. 22.9. Long run equilibrium of supply and demand for entrepreneurs is at normal profit.

The higher the level of profit in an industry, the more anxious will new entrepreneurs be to enter the industry. Since there is only one entrepreneur in a firm (though it is possible that the risk be divided among a number of people, but that would be interpreted as a number of people dividing the single risk) the supply of entrepreneurs must be related to the *industry*

22.10. Rent of Ability

Under market structures where there is freedom of entry and exit i.e. Perfect and Imperfect Competition, entrepreneurs are shown earning Normal Profit at long run equilibrium. However this does not mean that all entrepreneurs are earning the same amount of profit: Entrepreneurs do not constitute a homogeneous group, some are more gifted than others. Even if there is freedom of entry and exit into an industry and equilibrium is at Normal Profit, that is the earnings at long run equilibrium of entrepreneurs of average ability.

The more gifted entrepreneurs can still earn something in excess of Normal Profit due to his superior ability and it will not be competed away despite their being freedom of entry into the industry. These earnings in excess of Normal Profit are often referred to as a "Rent of Ability" and is an example of the concept of Economic Rent applied to the factor of production entrepreneurship.

22.11. In relation to Normal Profit being a cost of production and related to the transfer earnings of the entrepreneur it should be realised that, if the gifted entrepreneur under discussion has aptitudes which are particular to the industry in which he is earning in excess of Normal Profit then his higher earnings are definately a Rent of Ability. If however this gifted entrepreneur has entrepreneurial skills which could be used to earn high profits in other industries than the whole scene may be set in terms of the transfer earnings of this gifted entrepreneur being very high and his earnings are simply Normal Profit (though it is higher than the earnings of other entrepreneurs) since if he didn't earn this level of profit he would transfer to another industry and Normal Profit is defined as the supply price of entrepreneurship.

22.12. The activities of the I.D.A. may be seen as the importation of entrepreneurship and in relation to the foregoing the minimum amount which they must offer to foreign entrepreneurs varies from one entrepreneur to another.

QUESTIONS

Q1. Write an explanatory note on Entrepreneurship.

Q2. A man who worked alone for a twelve-month period in a shop which he owned sold for £60,000 stock which he had purchased for £35,000. Discuss the statement that his "profit" is £25,000.

Q3. Explain the role of profits in a free enterprise economy.

Q4. Under what circumstances will supernormal profits disappear in the long run?

Q5. In Perfectly Competitive market can an entrepreneur earn supernormal profit?

23 Money and Banking

23.1. *Barter* If each person is completely self-sufficient, providing entirely for his own needs and living entirely on what he himself provides, there is no need for exchange. As soon as people concentrate all their energies on the production of a narrow range of goods, through the division of labour or specialisation, it becomes necessary to exchange the surplus supply of one good for what is needed of other goods, e.g., one man devotes all his activity to hunting and then exchanges part of his catch for clothing, fish, shelter, etc. In earlier periods this exchange was on a direct basis of surplus goods in return for articles required — the direct exchange or swapping of goods is known as barter.

23.2. Disadvantages of a System of Exchange by means of Barter

(a) *Coincidence of wants* Exchange becomes dependent on a "double coincidence of wants". In a transaction of this nature each person is simultaneously a buyer and a seller. Not only must the boatmaker find someone who wants a boat but the person who wants the boat must have, and be willing to exchange for the boat, the good which the boatmaker requires. Barter is expensive in terms of time and effort, since time and effort are scarce resources barter is wasteful.

(b) *Rate of exchange* Even when the problem which the "double coincidence of wants" presents is solved, there remains the need to determine the rate at which the goods should exchange. This means that it would be necessary to negotiate a special rate of exchange for each transaction. You might contrast the ease with which something can be bought in a shop compared with buying something from a private person when a price for the good has to be agreed upon. Imagine how much more difficult it would be if the good you were offering was subject to the same degree of haggling in order to determine its value.

(c) *Non-standard goods* When goods are non-standard, i.e., similar though not identical, the variations in different units of the same good mean that exchange rates cannot be standardised, e.g., if one cow exchanged for one table there can be considerable variation in cows — fat, skinny, young, old, state of health, etc. There are as many possible variations of tables — in terms of type of wood, size, workmanship, etc. Thus there arises the problem as to what type of cow exchanges for what type of table.

Divisibility

(d)   If one party has a large item, e.g., a horse, and requires a small item, e.g., a dozen eggs, exchange becomes difficult if not impossible because it is not possible to divide the large item into small units for the purpose of exchange.

Transaction costs

(e)   There is considerable waste of time and resources in conducting exchange. In a transaction of this nature each person is simultaneously a buyer and a seller.

Box 23.2   Life without money

"Some years since, Mademoiselle Zelie, a singer ... gave a concert in the Society Islands ... in exchange for a third part of the receipts. When counted, here share was found to consist of three pigs, twenty-three turkeys, forty-four chickens, five thousand cocoa nuts, besides considerable quantities of bananas, lemons and oranges ... as Mademoiselle could not consume any considerable portion of the receipts herself, it became necessary in the meantime to feed the pigs and poultry with the fruit."

rubbish   W.S. Jevons
                              Money and the Mechanism of Exchange
                                              (Jevons 1898, p.1)

23.3. In order to overcome the hindrances to exchange caused by a system of barter, there developed a system of exchanging the good which you had available to trade for an item which was generally or universally acceptable. This universally acceptable item could then be used at the appropriate time in exchange for whatever good was required. The item which enjoyed universal acceptance and was selected for this purpose was in fact a medium of exchange, i.e., it was an intermediate good which facilitated the process of exchange. An item to be universally acceptable as a medium of exchange would require the following characteritics:

Medium of Exchange

(a)   It should be in common use.

(b)   It should be valuable in its own right.

(c)   It should be useful and/or ornamental.

23.4. Some examples of goods which were used as money are:— cattle in Ireland, fish in Newfoundland, beads in Africa, tobacco in USA, sugar in the West Indies, cigarettes and clothing during the 2nd World War, pieces of metal, coins, paper, bank notes in most of the world today.

Early forms of money

Items used as a medium of exchange were early forms of money. *Money is anything that is generally acceptable in payment for goods and services.*

23.5. QUALITIES REQUIRED FOR MONEY

Qualities of money

In order that it should fulfil adequately its prime function as a medium of exchange, the item chosen to be used as money should conform to the following:

(a) it must be *generally acceptable.*

(b) Its authenticity and quality must be *easily recognisable.*

(c) It must be *durable*, since it must retain its value over time.

(d) It must be *capable of being sub-divided* into small units to facilitate the purchase of inexpensive items.

(e) It should be *easy and cheap to store* with the additional requirement that it should not deteriorate during storage.

(f) It should be *easy to carry* about as required to make payment.

(g) It must be *relatively scarce* or otherwise it will lose its value, though it should not be too scarce or valuable as otherwise it might not be suitable for very small transactions.

23.6. THE VALUE OF MONEY IS THE RATE AT WHICH IT EXCHANGES FOR OTHER GOODS

Value of money

Just like any other good if the supply of money increases relative to the supply of other goods its value falls. Conversely if the supply of other goods increases faster than the supply of money then the value of each unit of money increases. The inflation which we have experienced in this country in recent years is an example of a change in the value of money. An even more dramatic example of this was the hyperinflation in Germany during the periods immediately after the first and second world wars when even a relatively cheap purchase involved the payment of large quantities of German bank notes. In situations of this nature people usually revert to some form of barter, or the substitution of some generally acceptable good for money, e.g., cigarettes, instead of bank notes and coin.

23.7. FUNCTIONS OF MONEY

Medium of Exchange

(a) **As a medium of exchange.** This function has already been referred to in Section 23.3 This is the most important funtion of money. Money as a medium of exchange constitutes half of virtually all transactions, e.g., workers exchange their labour services for money and then exchange the money for goods and services which they require.

Store of value

(b) **As a Store of Value.** It is quite possible that, although a person may not want to acquire any goods or services immediately, nevertheless it is in his best interest to exchange his own good without delay, e.g., because there is a very good demand for it at present, or because it is expensive to store or because it may deteriorate during storage. In these circumstances he can sell his good for money and then hold the money until he wishes to make his purchase. In this case money is acting as a store of value, i.e., it can be used to make purchase in the future. It is this quality of money which enables people to save for their old age or for future purchases. Inflation lessens the usefulness of money for this purpose.

Measure of Value/Unit of Account

(c) **As a measure of value/unit of account.** Money is the common denominator in which we measure and express value. It is the unit in which prices are quoted and accounts are kept. We refer to a house costing £60,000 or a car costing £15,000, etc.

Standard for Deferred Payment

(d) **As a standard for deferred payment.** This means that it is possible to express in money terms the price which must be paid at some future date. This feature of money makes possible credit trading and the drawing up of financial contracts.

23.8. THE DEVELOPMENT OF MONEY

Notes & Coin

Precious metals, e.g., gold and silver, fulfilled all the funtions of money and goods and services were traded for an agreed quantity of these metals. A further development from this was the introduction of coins which are nothing more than pieces of metal which were guaranteed in respect of fineness (quality) and weight to be equal to their face value.

This guarantee was conveyed by the imprint of its official stamp on the coin by the issuing authority (e.g., head of monarch). Eventually the issue of coins became the sole prerogative of the State.

There developed among unscrupulous citizens a system of clipping a thin sliver from the edge of the metal and passing off the coin at is original value. To prevent this practice of clipping coins, there was introduced the system of minting coins with a rough milled edge. In this way any attempt at clipping would be immediately obvious. This practice of producing coins with rough milled edges is still prevelant though clipping is no longer a problem because the value of coins is not now dependent on their metalic content.

Sweating of Coins

When the clipping of coins was no longer possible their ingenuity led the unscrupulous to devise a system of placing a number of coins in a bag and rotating the bag vigorously for long periods, so that the continual rubbing together of the coins created a dust of the precious metal. After sweating the coins in this manner the coins were passed off at their original value and the dust of precious metal was the profit from the activity.

Debasement of currency

Debasement of the currency was not confined to any one section of the community. Monarchs who were short of money were not adverse to reducing the weight and/or quality of the precious metal from which the coinage was manufactured. Between 1543 and 1551 the coinage was debased until the intrinsic value of the coinage was reduced to $\frac{1}{7}$ of its original value. Whenever the coinage was debased there was a fall in the value at which the coinage circulated, merchants were not prepared to accept the coins at their face value but would insist on weighing the coins in order to determine their true value. Thus there was a steep rise in prices, since traders would require more of the coins in exchange for goods.

Gresham's Law

This happened to such an extent during the reign of Henry VIII that Sir Thomas Gresham who was the Finance Minister of Elizabeth I was given the task of putting the coinage back on an acceptable standard. This gentleman became well known for his observation known as 'Gresham's Law' which states that "bad money drives good money out of circulation", i.e., that people pass around the worn coins and retain the full weight new ones. If you have a number of £1 notes and you are buying something for a pound, it is extremely likely that you will hand over the dirtiest note — how much more likely would this be if there was a danger that the dirty note might be worth less.

Gold standara Paper Currency

An important step in the evolution towards money, as we know it, was the introduction of paper money. Goldsmiths who worked with gold had secure rooms in which to store their precious metal. People who had large quantites of gold requested goldsmiths to hold their gold for safe keeping. When these depositors wished to make a purchase they took their gold from the goldsmiths and bought with it whatever they required — in many cases the person, who received the gold on selling his goods, redeposited it with the same goldsmith for safe keeping. In order to short circuit this procedure, the purchaser endorsed the receipt which he had received from the goldsmith in respect of his deposit of gold in favour of the person from whom he was buying the goods. The seller then either sought redemption of the receipt and took possession of the gold or else repeated the procedure of endorsing the receipt in favour of the person from whom he wished to buy goods. As this practice grew goldsmiths gave a number of receipts for smaller amounts instead of one receipt for the full value of the lodgement, e.g., if one hundred pounds' worth of gold was deposited (say) three receipts for ten pounds each, eight receipts for five pounds each and thirty receipts for one pound each were issued to the depositor.

When a purchase was being made a receipt for the appropriate amount could be passed to the seller. these receipts became paper money, they were *backed fully* by deposits of gold held in the vaults of the goldsmith and the notes could be CONVERTED into gold on request. *Because of this convertability feature the currency was said to be on the gold standard.*

Goldsmith's were the first bankers

23.9. As this business grew, goldsmiths began to charge for their service of holding, and issuing receipts for, valuables deposited with them for safekeeping. It should be noted that, at this initial stage in the evolution of banking, notes were backed 100% by gold reserves and the income which was earned by goldsmiths on this type of business was from fees which the goldsmith charged the depositors for keeping the gold in safe custody. With the development of this use of goldsmiths' services and the increase in profits therefrom, some goldsmiths concentrated on this type of transaction. Eventually these goldsmiths devoted all their attention to this aspect of their business, thus they became the first bankers and their receipts, i.e., goldsmiths' notes, became the original bank notes.

Bank Notes

23.10. That holders of such notes retained the right to convert their notes into gold was indicated by the written promise to this effect on bank notes, e.g., on a one pound note "I promise to pay the bearer on demand the sum of one pound", and this right persisted up to recent times. However, as these bank notes came to be used in payment for most transactions, they circulated as money with only a very small proportion of people exercising their right to conversion.

People were content to accept bank notes because they were confident that they could exchange them for gold if they wished. While people retained such confidence they did not seek to exercise their right of convertability.

Note Issue exceeded value of Gold Holding

23.11. Bankers realised that they could issue notes in excess of their holdings of gold provided they retained the confidence of holders of their bank notes. In order to retain this confidence they had to ensure that they had enough gold to pay out to the minority (approx ten percent) of bank note holders, who would seek to exercise their right of convertability. *It should be notes that at this stage in the evolution of banking, bank notes were not backed 100% by gold.*

Legal Tender

23.12. During the 1914-1918 world war most countries suspended the right to convert bank notes into gold. In England in 1925 bank notes again became convertible, but only in large amounts. Since 1931 bank notes have not been convertible. While, originally, people accepted the bank notes because of their convertability, at this stage people accepted the notes because they considered them to be valuable in themselves, an attitude which was encouraged by such notes being classified as legal tender.

A legal tender note is a note which the law of the country states must be accepted in payment of a debt.

If you bring to court someone who owes you money and win the case, he may offer legal tender notes in discharge of the debt. Obviously you may both agree to any other form of payment you wish, e.g., cheque, however if you wish you may refuse to accept a cheque but you cannot refuse legal tender.

23.13. The issue of bank notes, whether these notes were convertible or inconvertible, was regulated by the state. In England the Bank Charter

Fiat Money

Act of 1844 introduced a limit of fifteen million pounds on the value of notes which could be issued without being backed by gold. This issue of bank notes which was not backed by the bank holding precious metal, i.e., gold and silver, is known as the *Fiduciary Issue,* i.e., issued in faith. *Fiat Money* is the name given to such currency — it is money because the government declares it to be legal tender. In recent years the Central Banks have been the sole issuers of bank notes. You will notice that on recent bank notes there is no promise to pay the bearer on demand.

Token Money

23.14. Similarly the legal tender coins which circulate are *Token Money*, i.e., their face value, the value at which they exchange, is greater than the value of the metallic content. This means that if you melted down the coins, the metal which you would obtain by so doing would not be as valuable as the face value of the coin. Thus the value of "Token Money" is greater than its cost of production or its value in any use other than as money.

23.15. Other Forms of Money or Near Money
As already explained money is anything that is generally accepted in payment for goods and services. In addition to bank notes and currency there are other forms of payment which are generally acceptable and therefore they are considered as part of the money supply.

Cheques

(a) **Cheques.** A cheque is an instruction to a bank to pay to the person in whose favour the cheque is drawn the sum specified. The person in whose favour the cheque is drawn may obtain bank notes or have his bank account credited with the appropriate amount. Since cheques are not legal tender, it is only if the person to whom the cheque is offered is satisfied as to the creditworthiness of the drawer of the cheque and the bank on whom it is drawn that he will accept the cheque. However, since cheques are generally acceptable in payment for goods and services, they are considered to be part of the money supply. The various banks seek to increase the acceptability of cheques by issuing banker's cards to cheque book holders. These banker's cards declare to the person being offered the cheque that, irrespective of the creditworthiness of the drawer of the cheque, they (the banks) will guarantee the cheque up to a value of (at present) £100.★

Credit Cards/ Plastic Money

(b) **Charge and Credit Cards. "Plastic Money"**
In many transactions the seller of the goods will accept the use of credit cards in payment of a debt because it is the credit or charge card company — Access, Visa, American Express, Diners club etc. — which undertakes to pay the money. Admittedly the purchaser of the goods must pay the credit card company but as far as the seller of the good is concerned, the debt is owed to him by the credit (or charge) card company and he has no worry about non-payment of the bill provided that the credit (or charge) card was being used in a

★Footnote: of course the bank will only provide such banker's cards to those people whom the bank considers to be creditworthy and will withdraw the cards if necessary.

legitimate manner. Other attractive features of credit cards to sellers of goods is (i) that it encourages people to buy from such stores; (ii) the security risk is lessened since cash is not being handled. The reason why some sellers of goods will not accept credit cards is due to the fact that credit card companies charge a fee to, (or get a discount from), the seller. You will notice that in cases where particula.., low prices are being charged, the seller will insist "for cash purchasers only", i.e., he is not prepared to allow people to use credit cards since he is unwilling to concede the additional discount which sales of this nature would entail. With a charge card the account is due for payment by the holder of the charge card when a statement is issued, in the case of a credit card the account may be settled over a period, subject to interest charges.

*Deposit
Accounts*

(c) **Balances in Deposit Accounts**

Cheques are drawn on current accounts but balances in deposit accounts are also a liquid form of asset and can be converted readily into cash.

23.16. The Associated Banks

*Associated
Banks
deal with
most
transactions*

In the Central Bank Act, 1942, eight commercial banks were designated "Associated Banks" — the banks so designated were the banks which comprised the membership of the Dublin Bankers Clearing Committee together with the Chase and Bank of Ireland (International) Ltd. which was formerly the National City Bank Limited. With the amalgamation of various banks since then the banks which currently comprise the "Associated Banks" are listed in Table 23.16. For all practical purposes the term "Associated Banks" is equivalent to "clearing banks" and "commercial banks" as these terms are used in Britain. The major proportion of monetary transactions in Ireland are settled by cheques drawn on the Associated Banks. The non-Associated Banks tend to use the Central Bank's clearing exchange facilities.

*Irish
Financial
Sector*

23.17. The financial institutions in Ireland include banks, life insurance companies, pension funds, building societies, credit unions and finance companies. The aggregate balance sheet of the Irish financial services sector reached and estimated IR£25 billion (146% of GNP) at the end of 1986. In the ten-year period to 1986, the consolidated assets in the licensed bank sector has grown fourfold, though a substantial part of the business of the two largest bank groups is now generated outside the country. The share of the financial sector (financial institutions and insurance) in total value added in Ireland is slightly below 5% of GNP and remained stable between 1980 and 1985. There are strong hopes that this sector will experience considerable growth during the remainder of the century.

23.18. Ireland places few restrictions on foreign ownership of financial institutions and the penetration of the domestic market by foreign institutions has proceeded since the 1960s. Currently, there are 22 foreign owned banked licensed to operate in Ireland. Their major function is providing foreign currency loans to the Irish corporate sector at highly competitive international rates. They are regulated on the same basis as domestic licensed banks and their total financial assets in 1987 was approx. 21% of the total assets of the banking sector. There are 26 foreign insurance companies out of the total 67 operating in the domestic market and these foreign companies account for approx. 74% of the total net premiums paid during 1987.

23.19. The money supply refers not only to current but also other assets of a highly liquid nature.

The Principal Components of the Money Supply in Ireland are:

(1)   Notes and Coins, i.e., Currency Outstanding.

(2)   Money (Deposits) in Current Accounts — This also includes Bank loans as explained in 23.19 below.

(3)   Money (Deposits) in Bank Saving or Deposit Accounts.

(4)   Money (Deposits) in Post Office Savings Bank & Trustee Savings Banks.

(5)   Money (Deposits) in State Sponsored Financial Institutions.

(6)   Money (Deposits) in Building Societies.

(7)   Deposits in Government Savings Schemes.

Table 23.19. shows the relative magnitude of these components. One could not fail to be struck by the magnitude of the Associated Banks and their relative importance in the money supply.

Table 23.19. Money and Other Liquid Assets, Components and Selected Measures

£ million	1988	1989					
Bank-return dates	30 Dec.	31 Mar.	31 May	30 June	31 July	31 Aug.	29 Sept.
Licensed Banks							
1. Non-Government current accounts	1,395.4	1,334.78	1,408.2	1,419.0	1,483.5	1,465.8	1,581.4
1.1 Irish pound	1,328.7	1,287.4	1,348.8	1,358.8	1,425.8	1,396.1	1,500.7
1.2 Foreign currency	66.7	47.3	59.4	60.2	57.9	69.7	80.7
2. Non-Government deposit accounts	7,654.9	7,587.8	8,017.5	7,748.6	7,652.3	7,589.0	7,714.0
2.1 Irish pound	6,951.0	6,972.3	7,326.4	7,015.3	6,985.2	6,881.3	7,002.1
2.2 Foreign currency	703.8	615.5	691.1	733.2	667.1	707.7	711.9
3. Accrued interest payable on non-Government deposits	159.0	151.3	122.3	142.9	169.3	193.3	209.9
3.1 Irish pounds	149.3	139.9	108.7	128.7	155.8	174.5	195.7
3.2 Foreign currency	9.7	11.4	13.6	14.2	13.5	18.8	14.2
4. Holdings of Irish notes and coin	135.7	88.7	110.6	69.0	100.3	91.8	70.3
Central Bank							
5. Irish currency outstanding	1,347.4	1,246.6	1,256.0	1,256.4	1,317.2	1,297.9	1,277.5
Post Office Savings Bank and Trustee Savings Bank							
6. Deposits	1,131.7	1,127.2	1,121.1	1,121.9	1,117.3	1,128.2	1,132.5
State-Sponsored Financial Institutions							
7. Deposits	524.1	583.4	603.2	620.7	568.9	554.9	636.4
Building Societies							
8. Shares and deposits	3,283.1	3,313.0	3,331.4	3,361.5	3,361.6	3,350.8	3,391.5
Government Savings Schemes							
9. Amounts outstanding	1,566.6	1,654.0	1,694.8	1,712.1	1,730.5	1,752.9	1,772.9
Inter-Institutional Adjustment							
10. Inter-institutional deposits	488.8	478.8	490.7	403.5	389.9	397.4	420.7

Bank Return Date	Narrow Money Supply — M1 Components (Rows) 1 + 5 - 4		Wide Money Supply — M3 M1 + Components (Rows) 2 + 3		Money and other Liquid Assets M3 + Components (Rows) 6 + 7 + 8 + 9 - 10		
	Amount	Year-to-year change — %	Amount	Year-to-Year change — %	% change from previous end-year	Amount	Year-to-year change — %
29th September	2,788.6	+ 8.6		+ 4.2	+ 2.8	17,225.1	

Source: Central Bank Report Autumn 1989.

23.20. Measurements of Money Supply

*Narrow
Money
Supply
M.1*

M1   is a measure of the "narrow money supply". It consists of currency outstanding plus Current Account balances in the Associated Banks. This is shown in table 23.19.

*Broad
Money
Supply
M.3*

M3   is a measure of the "Broad (or wide) Money Supply". It consists of currency outstanding plus Balances in Current and Deposit Accounts in the Associated Banks plus Balances in the Non-Associated Banks. This also is shown in Table 23.19.

23.21. Supply of Money — Banks

*Commercial
Banks have
the Power
to create
Money*

It was shown in the previous section that, because cheques are generally acceptable in payment for goods and services, they are a form of money. If people have money on deposit in the bank (i.e., money to their credit) they have a claim on the bank to the value of their deposit and they can write cheques to the value of their deposit. If a bank gives a person a loan, it gives the borrower the right to draw cheques to the value of the loan, i.e., it has created a deposit in his account to the value of the loan. Thus every loan creates a deposit, a deposit is a liability to the bank in that the bank promises to honour cheques drawn for this amount and at the same time the bank has an equivalent asset since the bank is owed that amount by the person to whom it has given the loan. *This is very important because it means that bank deposits are money and that banks have the power to create money.*

If Mr. A deposits £5,000 in the bank, he can draw cheques to the value of £5,000; if Mr. B is granted a loan of £5,000, he too can draw cheques to the value of the sum which he borrowed, i.e., £5,000. It is a popular misconception that banks cannot create purchasing power, that they merely permit one person to use money which is deposited by another, i.e., that they merely transfer purchasing power and thus activate balances which otherwise would have been idle. It is often thought that when one person deposits £100 that this £100 can then be loaned to another customer, with the bank earning its profit through the difference between the interest which it charges for loans and any interest which the bank may have to pay to depositors (the bank pays no interest on balances in current accounts).

As stated above, the powers of the bank go beyond this. They do not merely transfer purchasing power, they create it.

23.22. Just as the goldsmiths, who were the early bankers, discovered that their depositors circulated the receipts from the goldsmiths and didn't withdraw their gold in order to pay for each transaction, similarly most of today's business is transacted by means of cheques. Banks are aware that only approx. 10% of deposits are normally required in cash form, therefore they are able to grant loans to the extent of approx. 10 times the cash which is lodged with them. The more successful the banks are in encouraging the general public to use cheques rather than cash, the lower the percentage of their assets which they need hold in cash form. It is for this reason that banks encourage all developments towards a "cashless society", e.g. cheques, plastic money etc. In addition the use of cash dispensing machines improves the accessibility of cash to its owners and thus lessens the demand for cash by removing the need to withdraw the relatively larger amounts of money which less frequent visits to the bank would make necessary. This is to the advantage of the banks because, instead of holding their assets in the form of cash which doesn't earn any interest, they can create interest earning loans or investments from their cash base. For the purpose of our example let us assume that there is only one bank in the economy and that only 10% of deposits need be met in cash form. Under these circumstances if £100 is lodged with the bank it can permit cheques to the value of £1,000 to be in circulation because only 10% of the value of the cheques in circulation will have to be met in cash form. Thus, £100 in cash which has been lodged with the bank can support £1,000 worth of cheques. This is so because the majority of people will lodge cheques to the credit of their account and then write cheques to the value of their lodgement without seeking cash. (There is no need to be worried about this situation and please read on before rushing down to the bank to withdraw the 5p which you have on deposit).

If the reserve ratio which the banks required was 20% then banks could create purchasing power (new deposits) to a multiple of 5 times any increase in its reserves, thus for an increase of IR£100 in cash lodgements with the bank, the bank could give loans up to the value of IR£500. This relationship between an increase in the bank's reserves and the additional purchasing power which may be created may be generalised as follows:

Increase in Purchasing Power (or money supply)

$$= \text{Increase in Bank's Reserves} \times \frac{1}{\text{Bank's Reserve Ratio}}$$

e.g. If £1,000 is lodged in a bank, its reserves are increased by £1,000. If it requires a reserve ratio of 20% (or ⅕th) then the increase in the money supply is £1,000 × ⅕ = £5,000.

It is assumed in the above example (1) that there is no leakage through a greater proportion of cash being kept on hand, and (2) that the banks have no *excess reserves*, i.e., if they must hold a reserve ratio of *at least* 20% that they hold this ratio exactly.

(a) Balance Sheet of Monopoly Bank when £100 is lodged and before any loans are made.

Assets		Liabilities	
Cash	£100	Mr. A	£100
(lodged by A)		(money lodged)	

(b) Balance Sheet of Monopoly Bank after loan was made.

Assets		Liabilities	
Cash	£100	Deposits	£1000
Advance(loan)	£900		
Total	£1000	Total	£1000

i.e., every loan creates an asset and a liability — an asset in that the person owes the bank the money which he has borrowed, and a liability in that the bank undertakes to honour cheques to the value of the loan.

Instead of there being just one monopoly bank let us suppose tht there are three banks: Bank A which has 50% of total banking business while Bank B has 30% and Bank C 20%. Again £100 is lodged in Bank A as shown in Example (1).

Bank A — Balance Sheet

(1)

Assets		Liabilities	
Cash	£100	Deposits	£100

Bank A wishes to earn income so it loans out some money. It knows that it requires to hold 10% of the total balances shown in depositors accounts in order to meet the demands on it for cash. This bank knows that it has 60% of total banking business so that when it gives loans to its customers and they spend it in various shops, garages, hotels etc. the owners of these businesses will either seek cash from them or lodge the cheque in their accounts in their own bank, this accounts for an outflow of £40 cash from bank A as shown below.

Balance Sheet of Bank A
(which has 60% of total banking business)

Assets		Liabilities	
	£		£
Cash	60	Deposits	600
Loans			
(Overdrafts)	540		
Total	600	Total	600

Note that there has been an outflow of £40 cash from the bank. The bank has an asset of £540 in respect of the money which it is owed by its customers to whom it has given loans.

Balance Sheet of Bank B
(which has 30% of banking business)

Assets		Liabilities	
	£		£
Cash	30	Deposits	300
Overdrafts/loans	270		
Total	300	Total	300

Balance Sheet of Bank C
(which has 10% of banking business)

Assets	£	Liabilities	£
Cash	10	Deposits	100
Overdrafts/loans	90		
Total	100	Total	100

Notice that the increase in the money supply (credit creation) is exactly the same whether there was only one bank (the monopoly bank) or whether there were three banks.

Transfer of Purchasing Power contrasted with Creation of Purchasing Power

23.23. The ability of the Commercial Banks to create money stems from the general acceptability of cheques in payment for goods and services. It is this feature which permits banks to create money and it distinguishes Commercial Banks from all other financial institutions in which people lodge money, e.g., Post Office Savings Bank. Because people who lodge money in the Post Office Savings Bank do not have the facility of writing cheques on their accounts, these institutions cannot create purchasing power as do commercial banks — these institutions merely transfer purchasing power e.g. they lend to Mr. B the £1,000 which Mr. A has deposited with them. If other thrift or savings institutions introduce accounts for customers on which they write cheques then they too can create purchasing power or money.

23.24. Limitations on the Power of Commercial Banks to Create Money

Restrictions on Power of Banks to create Money

(a)   Loans can be given only to those people who will be in a position to repay them at the appropriate time.

(b)   The Banks' ability to grant loans is dependent upon the Banks' ability to acquire cash lodgments.

(c)   The Bank must retain sufficient cash so as to be in a position to satisfy the demands of its customers for cash.

(d)   Closely allied to (c) above; the Commercial Banks must comply with the instructions of the Central Bank as discussed Chapter 24.

23.25. Structure of Bank Assets

Banks must be in a position to satisfy the needs of their customers for cash, i.e., they must maintain sufficient liquidity. They could fully meet this requirement by holding all their assets in the form of cash. However cash doesn't earn interest and banks also wish to be profitable. The more liquid the form in which assets are held the less profitable they are, on the other hand the more profitable the form in which the asset is held, the less liquid is the asset. *Banks must strike a balance between their twin objectives of liquidity and profitability.* The Banks have learned from their experience over the years that the best compromise is achieved in their pursuit of these objectives when they structure their holding of assets along the lines shown in fig. 23.24, i.e., they hold what is known as a portfolio of assets in which they earn maximum profits while maintaining the required degree of liquidity.

23.26. The liquidity of an asset is a term often used to refer to the ease (or cost) with which an asset can be converted into cash. There are a number of elements which combine to create liquidity viz:

(i) *Marketability.* This refers to the ease and speed with which the value of an asset can be realised.

(ii) *Capital Certainty* which refers to the extent to which it is possible to predict (or know) the value which will be received for an asset when it is sold at some future date.

(iii) *Reversibility* refers to any loss which may be suffered in reselling an article, if it is resold almost immediately after buying it.

(iv) *Divisibility* refers to the smallest unit of the asset which can be bought and sold.

23.27. If the above 4 criteria of liquidity are applied to a range of assets, it will be apparent that money is the most liquid of assets.

 Increases liquidity ⟶

Asset	Borrower	Period of Loan	Rate of Interest
Advances over-drafts and loans.	Industry and the General Public.	Overdrafts are payable on demand and term loans up to 5 or 7 years.	Greater than Bank Rate* (say) Bank Rate plus 3%
Investments Government and gilt-edged	Public Sector and Private industry.	Stocks and shares may be sold at any time on stock exchange but if they must be sold quickly there may be a capital loss.	Greater than Bank Rate (say) Bank Rate plus 1½%
Exchequer Bills and Bills of Exchange	Government and Private industry.	Max. 91 days but on a cyclical basis so that some would be continually becoming due for repayment.	Central Bank Rediscount Rate (i.e. Bank Rate).
Bills of Exchange.	Banks & Financial Institutions	1 - 14 days.	Less than Bank Rate (say) Bank Rate minus 1/8 %

Table 23.22. Details of Bank's lending programme.

 Increases profitability ⟵

* Footnote: Bank Rate is known also as Central Bank Rediscount Rate & in Great Britain it is known as the Minimum Lending Rate.

Fig. 23.24. Example of Structure of Bank's Assets

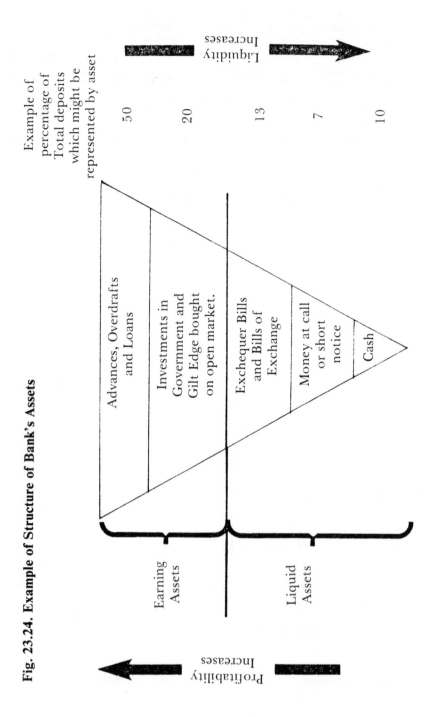

	Example of percentage of Total deposits which might be represented by asset
Advances, Overdrafts and Loans	50
Investments in Government and Gilt Edge bought on open market.	20
Exchequer Bills and Bills of Exchange	13
Money at call or short notice	7
Cash	10

Liquidity Increases

Profitability Increases

Earning Assets

Liquid Assets

QUESTIONS

Q1. What are the functions of money?

Q2. Explain: Fiduciary Issue. Token Money.

Q3. What are the principal components of the money supply in Ireland?

Q4. Explain how it is possible for commercial banks to create money.

Q5. Is there any limitation on the power of commercial banks to create money?

Q6. Show how banks attempt to reconcile profitability and liquidity.

24   The Central Bank

Central Bank Acts

24.1. The Irish Central Bank was established by the Central Bank Act 1942. Under this Act the Central Bank has as its first duty the safeguarding of the integrity of the currency and to ensure that, in what pertains to credit, the constant and predominant aim shall be the welfare of the people as a whole. The powers of the Central Bank were augmented by a number of Acts including the Central Bank Act of 1971 which is discussed in Section 24.8 below.

Central Bank implements Monetary Policy

24.2. The State owns the capital of the Central Bank and any profit which it may make is paid into the Exchequer. Unlike the Commercial Banks the Central Bank does not deal directly with the public, it controls and regulates the banking sector on behalf of the nation, i.e., it implements *monetary policy which is the term applied to actions which influence the money supply, interest rates or the availability of credit.*

The supply of money, the availability of credit and the level of interest rates have an influence on the level of employment and the price level, so it is important that monetary policy be consistent with fiscal policy and in keeping with the prevailing economic climate.

24.3. Monetary policy may be operated through

(a)   Control over the lending activities of banks and other financial institutions.

Operation of Monetary Policy

(b)   Control over international movements of capital.

(c)   Control over hire purchase and other forms of credit.

(d)   The influencing of rates of interest.

We will start by analysing the functions of a Classical Central Bank and then see how these functions apply to the Irish situation.

24.4. Functions of the Central Bank

Note issue

(a)   **It prints and issues Irish legal tender.**
Irish money (legal tender notes) is printed by the Irish Central Bank at its premises in Sandyford, Co. Dublin.

Exchequer Account

(b)   **It acts as banker to the Government.**
Just like any other economic agent the Government needs a bank. All taxes and any other Government revenues are lodged to its account and when the Government is making payments it writes cheques on its account.

(c) **It acts as the bankers' bank.**
It provides all of the banking services to the banking sector. These services are similar to those which the commercial banks provide for their own customers. The commercial banks may draw notes and coins from the Central Bank, they may use their balances with the Central Bank in settlement of interbank debts and they may get loans if necessary.

(d) **It represents the Government in International Monetary Institutions.**
The Central Bank represents the Government in its dealings with foreign Central Banks and participates in the work of international monetary institutions, e.g., World Bank, International Monetary Fund, etc.

(e) **It manages the Official External Reserves.**

Table 24.4. Official External Reserves.

£ millions End-month dates	Gold	SDRs	Reserve position in IMF	ECU	Foreign Exchange	Total
1989						
January	74.2	90.1	91.1	279.6	2,627.3	**3,162.3**
February	74.2	92.4	87.1	278.0	2,424.0	**2,955.7**
March	74.2	92.4	87.1	266.1	2,216.0	**2,735.8**
April	73.2	92.4	87.1	197.1	2,060.9	**2,510.6**
May	73.2	94.8	82.2	196.8	2,161.3	**2,608.3**
June	73.2	94.8	86.6	197.2	2,045.6	**2,497.5**
July	73.1	₊94.8	86.6	202.9	2,163.4	**2,620.8**
August	73.1	97.5	81.9	207.5	2,315.6	**2,775.5**
September	73.1	97.5	77.1	207.5	2,431.6	**2,886.7**
October	69.8	97.5	77.1	225.9	2,029.0	**2,499.3**

Notes:
1. These series can be significantly affected by occasional valuation adjustments which mainly take account of exchange-rate fluctuations.
2. With effect from 12 February 1981, the Bank's holdings of gold are revalued to reflect movements in the markket value of gold. The valuation price, updated each quarter, is the lower of:
   (1) 75 per cent. of the average daily price during the preceding two quarters, or
   (2) 75 per cent. of the price of the penultimate working day of the preceding quarter.

Source: Central Bank Report, Autumn 1989.

(1) In its capacity as manager of the Official External Reserves the Central Bank has the responsibility of ensuring that the Official External Reserves are at an adequate level for the purpose of facilitating international trade. It is this aspect of the Official External Reserves which are being emphasised when the size of the reserves are related to the amount of imports, e.g. "the level of the Official External Reserves is equal to the value of two months' imports".

(2) Ensuring that the value of the reserves does not decrease due to holding the assets in weak currencies. Sterling comprised 61% of our total external assets in December 1972 and 42% in December 1974. Following the termination on 31st December, 1974, of the guarantee arrangements for Sterling, the Central Bank diversified its sterling holding so that in January 1975 — one month later — sterling constituted only 27% of total external assets, while at December 1978 sterling constituted 12% of total external assets. The value of Official External Reserves expressed in Irish pounds can be significantly affected by occasional valuation adjustments which mainly take account of exchange rate fluctuations. In 1976 there was an increase of some £106 million which was attributable to a revaluation to reflect the appreciation against the Irish pound of the currencies in which the reserves were held. The Official External Reserves expressed in terms of Special Drawings Rights (SDR's) as shown in Table 24.4 give a more realistic view of the evolution of the Official External Reserves than a series expressed in Irish pounds since External Reserves are used to meet liabilities denominated in foreign currencies. The SDR which is a basket of the sixteen major currencies is a better measure of international purchasing power than any one currency.

(3) Earning, consistent with the foregoing, the optimum rate of interest which can be a significant gain to the economy considering the size of our reserves and current interest rates.

24.5. Traditional Approach to Implementing Monetary Policy

(a) **Open Market Operation**

The amount of money which the commercial banks can create is a multiple (approx. ten) of the amount of cash that they hold. If the Central Bank can regulate the amount of cash which the commercial banks hold, it can regulate the amount of money which they can create. If the Central Bank wishes to increase the amount of money in circulation, it can print bank notes (say £1,000) and then purchase government securities on the Stock Exchange. The people who receive the £1,000 cash for the government securities which they have sold will lodge most of this cash in their bank accounts. On the basis of this lodgement of £1,000 cash it is possible for the banks to create approx. £10,000 of money/purchasing power as explained in Sections 23.20 to 23.24.

Conversely if the Central Bank wishes to reduce the quantity of money in circulation it can sell government securities for cash. By reducing the cash base of the banks in this way the amount of money is reduced (approx. tenfold). This buying and selling of government securities by the Central Bank is known as "Open market Operations".

(b) **Bank Rate Policy**

Lender of Last Resort

If the cash reserves of the Commercial Banks have fallen below the minimum level which is necessary, e.g., by the Open Market Policy of the Central Bank, the commercial banks will call in some of the money which they have loaned. As it will take some (short) time for the banks to replenish their cash reserves to the required levels the Commercial Banks can borrow from the Central Bank to tide themselves over this period. The Commercial Banks give to the Central Bank as securities for these loans securities which they (the Commercial Banks) had received for loans to their customers. The securities which the Central Bank is willing to accept for these loans are (i) Exchequer Bills, which are certificates issued by the government in respect of loans made to it and (ii) Bills of Exchange, which are a form of postdated cheque issued by businessmen for loans made to them — the face value of the Bill of Exchange is greater than the amount of the loan the difference being the interest charge. There is no danger of non-payment in respect of the Exchequer Bills since they are issued by the government but the Central Bank will accept only First Class Bills of Exchange i.e. Bills of Exchange where there is no risk on non-payment. The Central bank will always meet demands for loans of this nature and in doing so they are acting in their capacity as "Lender of Last Resort". The rate of interest which the Central Bank charges on these loans is known as the *Central Bank Rediscount* Rate, (also called Bank Rate or Minimum Lending Rate). *It is defined as the rate at which the Central Bank will discount First Class Bills.*

Though the Bank Rate affects all other rates of interest in the economy as discussed below, it is not the rate of interest which is charged to the general public. The Bank Rate to be charged is decided each week by the Central Bank as being the rate appropriate to the economic conditions.

The Bank Rate (or Central Bank Rediscount Rate) is a penal rate of interest — it is higher than the rate of interest which the Commercial Banks charge on 'call loans' or loans for very short periods and the Commercial Banks are losing money when they are 'in the bank'. If the Bank Rate is increased, the Commercial Banks in order to remain profitable and maintain risks at an acceptable level will increase their interest charge on very short term loans. the whole structure of interest rates on other short term loans will be similarly affected and eventually the higher rates of interest will be reflected throughout the entire economy. Alterations in the Bank Rate are considered to have a considerable psychological influence as being an indication of a line of action which the government intends to pursue, e.g., an increase in the Central Bank's Rediscount Rate signifies a deflationary impulse.

(c) **Funding**

*Credit
Creation
based on
Liquid
Assets
rather than
Cash
Holdings
alone*

When banks based their credit creation on their holdings of cash the Central Bank, by selling Exchequer Bills to the banks through Open Market Operations, reduced the cash holding of commercial banks and thus the amount of money which they could loan. It was then noted that Banks were basing the amount of loans which they could make on their total liquid assets rather than on their cash holding alone. When the Central Bank was selling Exchequer Bills to the Commercial Banks in return for cash the Commercial Banks were merely exchanging one form of liquid asset for another and their credit creating ability was not being significantly affected. It became necessary for the Central Bank to sell to them medium or long term loans other than the 91 day Exchequer Bills.

The exchange of short term loans for long term loans is known as Funding.

(d) Because the rate of interest on long term loans is higher than that on short term loans, funding increases the cost of borrowing to the government. To overcome this problem, in 1958 the technique of Supplementary (Special) Deposits was conceived. Under this system the Central Bank may instruct that a specified sum be lodged by the Commercial Banks at the Central Bank. This sum earns for the Commercial Bank the Exchequer Bill rate of interest but it cannot be included as a liquid asset by the Banks in deciding on their policy of credit creation.

*Special or
Supplementary
Deposits*

(e) **Requests/Credit Guidelines**

*Private
Sector
Credit
Guidelines*

Since 1976 the Central Bank has established quantitative guidelines for the desired expansion in lending to the Private Sector (which is defined by the Central Bank in a manner which includes State Sponsored Bodies and Local Authorities). In the light of large fiscal deficits putting all the emphasis on the Private Sector was not a feasible way of controlling the expansion of credit. See also section on Domestic Credit Expansion — Chapter 33.

(f) **Liquidity Ratios**

The Central Bank may use Liquidity Ratios as a means of controlling the volume of credit. The Commercial Banks realise that liquid assets should be a certain percentage of total deposits. If the Central Bank directs the Commercial Banks to alter this ratio, this would have the effect of reducing the credit creating ability of the Commercial Banks.

(g) **Exchange Control**

On 28th Nov. 1978 the Exchange Control (Continuance & Amendment) Act 1978 was passed by the Oireachtas. Under this act dealings in foreign currencies and thus the raising of foreign loans by banks, are regulated. Any restriction on the importation of funds by Commercial Banks restricts their ability to expand domestic credit.

24.6. The Irish Situation Prior to the Central Bank Act 1971

Prior to the introduction of the Central Bank Act 1971 the control of the Irish Central Bank over the banking system was not very strong for the following reasons:

Marketability of Securities

(a) Because of the relatively small scale of operations on the Irish Stock Exchange, the possibility of the Central Bank engaging in open market operations was restricted. If the Central Bank issued or retired quantities of government stock, it could lead to considerable fluctuations in the price of such securities. Fluctuations of this nature would make such securities less marketable since the public would be wary about buying them and this would have a detrimental effect on the government effort to raise finance by the issue of these securities.

Movements of Funds

(b) Because of the free movement of money between Ireland and Great Britain, up to the breaking of the link with sterling, the effectiveness of Bank Rate Policy was constrained. If interest rates were higher here than in England, owners of funds would transfer them to Ireland in order to gain the higher interest rates. This could be on such a large scale that it would disrupt Irish money markets. Conversely, if the Irish Bank Rate was lower than the English Rate investors would invest in Great Britain and there would be a disruptive outflow of funds.

Central Bank took over Control of External Assets

(c) Because Irish Commercial Banks had External Assets in England, the effectiveness of credit control through the use of Special Deposits was limited. If the Irish Central Bank sought Special Deposits from the Commercial Banks, the Commercial Banks could repatriate some of their external assets rather than cut back on their level of credit creation in Ireland.

With the devaluations of Sterling during the 1960's there were large and continuing capital losses on the sterling holdings of the external assets of the Commercial Banks. In 1968 the Bank of England, in order to encourage the retention of sterling balances rather than have holders of sterling sell them for a stronger currency, undertook to indemnify foreign Central Banks against any losses of this nature. Since the indemnity extended to Central Banks only, the Irish Commercial Banks transferred their external assets into the control of the Irish Central Bank. This development eliminated the weakness in the control of the Irish Central Bank over the Irish Banking System which was discussed above. Special Deposits are more likely to be an effective form of control with the escape from the constraint through the repatriation of external assets by the Commercial Banks being no longer possible.

24.7. The Central Bank Act 1971 was a major innovation in banking legislation. The 1971 Act was introduced in order to give to the Central Bank additional powers which were considered desirable in order to enable it to control monetary policy in the Irish Economy.

24.8. Main Provisions of Central Bank Act 1971

(a) **Licences**

The issuing of banking licences, which authority previously had been vested in the Revenue Commissioners, was now transferred to the Central bank. In order to obtain a licence a bank must maintain, with the Central Bank, a deposit of between £20,000 and £500,000 in proportion to the size of the deposits held at the domestic offices of the licence holder.

(b) **Liquidity Ratios**

The Act empowers the Central Bank to use Liquidity Ratios as an instrument of credit control. The use of Liquidity Ratios as a form of credit control stimulates competition between banks for deposits, since the profitability of banks is related to their volume of loans and investments and these depend on the ability of a bank to attract deposits.

The *Primary Liquidity Ratio* is the ratio of the holdings of a bank of notes and coins, plus balances with the Central Bank, to its current and deposit account liabilities. In 1986 the required ratio was 10%.

The *Secondary Liquidity Ratio* is the ratio of the holdings of a bank of government paper (e.g., Exchequer Bills and government bonds) to its deposit liabilities. Currently the required (in 1986) minimum ratio which banks are required to maintain on a continuous basis is 25% for Associated Banks, 15% for certain Non-Associated Banks and 13% for the remaining Non-Associated Banks.

This Secondary Liquidity Ratio is a channelling of funds to the Government and it is not common in other countries within the EEC, only Italy and France operate controls of this nature and as they are 6.5% or 5% respectively they are much lower than in Ireland.

If banks do not conform to the directions of the Central Bank they may have their licences revoked. This obviously strengthens the control of the Central Bank over the Banking System.

24.9. Some Other Provisions of the Central Bank Act 1971

(a) It was considered desirable that the banking sector should remain predominantly in Irish hands. To this end
(i) A majority of the Board of Directors should be Irish.
(ii) In the case of a foreign owned corporation, what is deemed by the Central Bank to be an appreciable part of the share capital should be in beneficial Irish ownership.

Table 24.8. Regulation and taxation on financial institutions

	Principal super-vision agency	Principal requirements	Taxation
Licensed banks	Central Bank	Primary liquidity ratio of 10 per cent and secondary liquidity ratio of between 13-25 per cent. These ratios are based on hold-ings of cash and similar items and government securities. There is also a capital to assets ratio of 4 to 6.5 per cent and own funds to working assets of 7 to 15 per cent.	Corporation tax of 43 per cent. Bank levy as a stamp duty. DIRT[1]
Trustee savings banks	Department of Finance	80 per cent of deposits to be held with the Minister of Finance "prudent" level of primary liquidity	Corporation tax of 43 per cent (exempt from tax on income from deposit held with Minister of Finance). DIRT
Industrial Credit Corporation	Department of Finance	No ratio required	Corporation tax of 43 per cent. DIRT
Agricultural Credit Corporation	Department of Finance	No ratio required	Corporation tax of 43 per cent. DIRT
Post Office Savings Bank	Department of Finance	All deposits held with Minister of Finance	DIRT
Building societies[2]	Registrar of Building Societies	Minimum reserve rate of 4 per cent	Corporation tax of 43 per cent. DIRT
Credit unions	Registrar of Friendly Societies	10 per cent of surplus each year must be allocated to Statutory reserves. There are also restrictions on level of savings and terms of loan.	Exempt from corporation tax
Life insurance companies	Department of Industry and Commerce	EC life and non-life directives	Corporation tax of 35 per cent
Non-life insurance companies	Department of Industry and Commerce	EC life and non-life directives	Corporation tax of 35 per cent

1. **Deposit interest subject to Deposit Interest Retention Tax requiring deduction of 32 per cent from domestic depositors.**
2. **The Building Societies Bill 1988 provides for transfer of supervisory authority to the Central Bank.**

Source: Department of Finance

*Other
Provisions
of 1971
Act*

(b)   The Central Bank holds the government accounts, a function previously performed by the Bank of Ireland. (N.B. The Bank of Ireland is not the Irish Central Bank though the Bank of England is the English Central Bank).

(c)   The Central Bank acts as a clearing house for the Commercial Banks.

(d)   The Central Bank prints the Irish currency.

*Breaking of
direct link
between
Dublin &
London
Inter-Bank
Markets*

24.10. System for Implementing Monetary Policy in Ireland in the 1980's
When Ireland joined the European Monetary System (EMS) in March 1979 it entered at a value of the punt which maintained the one-to-one parity link with sterling, i.e., 1 punt = £1 sterling. Sterling began to appreciate in value shortly after the EMS was established and the Irish Authorities had to make a choice between seeking a realignment of the value of our currency within the EMS or breaking the one-to one parity link with sterling. A decision was made to maintain our position within the EMS, when the parity link with sterling was broken for the first time in 150 years a separate foreign exchange value was quoted for the Irish Punt. For the present discussion the important point to note is that this development broke the direct link between the Dublin and London Inter-Bank markets.

*Need for
Irish
Central
Bank to
provide
liquidity*

24.11. The Inter-Bank market is the means by which banks which have funds surplus to their immediate requirements, can lend, even for periods as short as one day, to banks which require liquidity. Prior to our entering the EMS Irish banks enjoyed virtually unrestricted access to the London Money Markets. However, with the U.K. remaining outside the EMS it was necessary for the Central Bank to become more actively involved in the domestic money market in order to smooth out temporary fluctuations in liquidity conditions and thus prevent or (minimise) volatility in interest rates.

*Dublin
Inter-Bank
Money
Market*

24.12. One of the outcomes of this turn of events has been the creation of a Dublin Inter-Bank Money Market. If there is an increase in credit creation it becomes necessary for banks to borrow money in order to maintain their Primary and Secondary Liquidity Ratios. If there is a general increase in credit creation the demand for money will exceed the supply and there will be upward pressure on interest rates. The Inter-Bank interest rate is very important as it effects all other interest rates in the economy — if Inter-Bank interest rates increase all other interest rates in the economy will increase also.

*Development
of Inter-Bank
Markets*

24.13. In 1969 approx. 70% of the liquidity requirements of the Non-Associated Banks were held abroad — mainly in England. As shown in Table 24.13 in the 1970's there was a considerable expansion in the Dublin Inter-Bank Market mainly from the activities of the Non-

Associated Banks. During the 1970's the Associated Banks were not very active in the Market, they satisfied their short-term liquidity requirements through rediscounting bills with the Central Bank.

Table 24.13. The Domestic Interbank Market (£ Million)

End Period	Non Associated★ Banks	Associated★ Banks	Total
1969	27.6	11.4	39.0
1971	72.3	7.4	79.7
1972	79.5	13.4	93.1
1973	135.0	7.9	142.9
1974	162.0	11.7	174.4
1975	182.3	42.8	225.1
1976	255.5	12.2	267.7
1977	307.5	30.9	338.4
1978	410.8	22.3	433.1
1979	654.3	91.8	746.1
1980	803.5	161.4	964.9
1981	1185.0	314.2	1499.2
1982	1178.2	505.5	1683.7

★ Balances of Non-Associated Banks with each other and with Associated Banks.

★★ Balances of Associated Banks with each other and with non-Associated Banks.

Source: The Control of Banking in the Republic of Ireland by Davy, Kelleher & McCarthy.

24.14. Short Term (Credit) Facility (STF)

Short Term (Credit) Facility (STF)

If banks cannot satisfy their demand for funds (at sufficiently attractive rates of interest) in the Inter-Bank Market, they may borrow from the Central Bank using approved securities as collateral — this is known as the Short Term (Credit) Facility (STF) of the Central Bank and the interest rate is set by the Central Bank. This system was introduced by the Central Bank in June 1979 and there is a quota (or limit) as to the amount of funds which a bank may borrow. A bank may draw against this quota four times per fortnight at the base STF rate of interest. If a fifth or sixth drawing is made within the fortnight the interest rate charged will be ½% higher than the base TSF rate and for any additional drawings within the fortnight the rate of interest charged will be a full 1% higher than the base rate. The actual base rate of interest under this short term facility is shown in Table B1 of the Central Bank Quarterly Report.

Alternatively, if banks have funds surplus to their immediate requirement for liquidity, they can lodge such funds with the Central Bank and earn a rate of interest on them. Though interest rates on the Inter-Bank Market are subject to fluctuations the interest rates would be even more volatile were it not for the stabilising influence of the Central Bank.

24.15. Secured Advances by the Central Bank

Banks can borrow funds from the Central Bank using their holdings of Government securities as collateral rather than having to sell their securities in order to gain funds.

24.16. Foreign Exchange Swaps

Bank customers require foreign currencies for the purpose of international trade and travel. In order to cater for this demand, under exchange control regulations, banks are permitted to hold the equivalent of IR£250m in foreign currencies. If a bank is short of liquidity (i.e., it needs cash), it may swap with the Central Bank some of its holdings of foreign currencies in exchange for Irish currency. Conversely when the Central Bank wishes to reduce liquidity in the banking sector it may swap (sell) foreign exchange for Irish currency. The importance of this facility is limited by the size of the foreign exchange requirements of the banks and the periods for which swaps can be effected.

24.17. Central Bank Bidding for Funds of Commercial Banks

If the banks have excess liquidity (i.e., more cash than they require for current business), the Central Bank can entice the banks to deposit these funds in the Central Bank by offering an attractive rate of interest. In this way the Central Bank can discourage the banks from holding excess primary liquidity (cash) though the Central Bank cannot inject liquidity into the banking system in this way.

24.18. Sale and Repurchase Agreements

This is a means by which the Central Bank can inject funds (liquidity) into the Banking Sector. Under this system the Central Bank offers to buy from the banks some of their holdings of Government securities and to sell them back to the banks at the end of a specified period. The difference between the price which the (Commercial) bank gets when selling and the price paid by the (Commercial) bank to the Central Bank for their repurchase is the interest charge. As this procedure is operated by banks making bids the interest charge is influenced by interest charges in other money markets.

24.19. Varying Liquidity Ratios

The Central Bank can also increase or decrease Liquidity in the economy through varying the Liquidity Ratios. A rise in the Primary Liquidity Ratio results in an increase in the demand for funds in the Inter-Bank Market and puts upward pressure on interest rates.

24.20. Exchequer Bills

Every two weeks the Minister for Finance invites tenders (bids) for Exchequer Bills, the usual amount on offer would be in the region of IR£25m. While the non-bank sector can purchase them they must be purchased through banks and the banks themselves purchase a high proportion of them. Exchequer Bills are repaid at their face value at the end of 91 days so the difference between the bid price (price offered) and the face value is the interest earned. These Exchequer Bills form part of the liquid assets of a bank because of the relatively short period before they are redeemed and because banks holding them can sell some of them to the Central Bank or to other banks before their maturity date. The price at which Exchequer Bills will be bought/sold before their maturity date depends on the period they have to run before being redeemed at their face value and the rates of interest pertaining at the time.

24.21. Is the Prime Purpose of Exchequer Bills related to Monetary or Fiscal Policy?

Exchequer Bills receive prominence when Monetary Policy is being discussed because (i) they form part of the liquid assets of the Banking System and (ii) the interest rate being earned on this form of Government paper is a benchmark/indicator of the other interest rates in the economy. Since Exchequer Bills are sold on a bid basis the rates of interest earned on them are market determined in the sense that rates of interest being sought by the bidders (banks) will reflect current rates of interest. Closely allied to this is the fact that the rate of interest on Exchequer Bills is a benchmark/indicator for other interest rates in the economy. While there is no denying the relevance of Exchequer Bills to Monetary Policy their prime purpose is to provide revenue for the Government on a short term loan basis. This fiscal aspect is apparent when you remember that they are issued for approximately the same amount regularly every fortnight — is it likely that Monetary Policy would require such consistent and predictable intervention? Though the Exchequer Bills have been issued through the agency of the Central Bank the initiating agency is the Department of Finance and since 1985 their issue has come more under the direct control of the Department of Finance.

24.22. On 25th May The Central Bank Bill 1988 was passed in the Dail. The Bill deals with the administration of the Bank and its functions and powers. It also strengthens the powers of the Central Bank in supervising licensed banks and extends the Central Bank's role into new areas such as moneybrokers, financial futures, options exchanges and companies operating within the International Financial Services Centre.

24.23. In May the Dail passed also the Building Societies Bill 1988. The main provisions of this Bill are:

(i)   To strengthen the competitive position of building societies by extending their powers so that they can provide a much wider range of services.

(ii) To transfer statutory responsibility for the regulation and super-vision of building societies from the Registrar of Building Societies to the Central Bank and to strengthen the powers available to the Bank as the supervisory authority.

(iii) To improve and update the statutory provisions relating to the running and management of societies, their accounts and audit.

(iv) To enable the provision of the deposit protection scheme as contained in the Central Bank Bill 1988 to be applied to building societies.

(v) To give building societies the option of investing directly in residential and other developments.

(vi) To help keep down the transaction costs associated with house purchase.

(vii) To allow societies to operate abroad.

(viii) To provide a statutory framework and mechanism whereby societies can, on certain conditions, convert from mutual status to become public limited companies.

24.24. Developments in the Financial Sector

1. The rapid growth of international trade and the expansion of multinational corporations has provided a strong stimulus for financial markets to operate a global basis.

2. There have been technological changes which have facilitated the introduction of financial instruments and stimulated competition.

3. With increasing uncertainty surrounding the economic environment there has been an increased demand for financial instruments which would be capable of providing some hedge against uncertainty.

4. There has been shift in the composition of savings as shown in fig. 24.24.

The technological development has brought about the following:

(i) Reduction of costs for traditional financial services.

(ii) Provision of new services e.g. new futures and options markets commenced operations in Dublin in May 1989.

(iii) A lowering of entrance barriers to the financial services industry from related industries, e.g. in the market for consumer credit.

(iv) Increased competition in financial markets. An indication of this can be seen at the retail end of the banking market with the growth in the number of Automatic Teller Machines (ATMS). In 1987 there were 77 ATMS per million people in Ireland compared to Germany (35), Italy (30), and the USA (250).

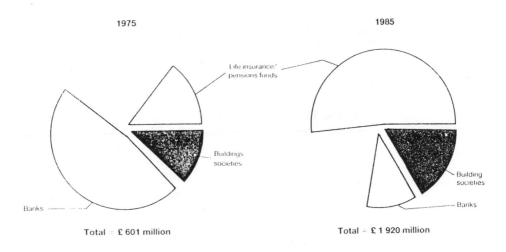

Source: T. O'Connell, "*The Flow of Funds 1960-1985*" Central Bank of Ireland Bulletin, (Summer 1986).

Fig. 24.24. Changing composition of Personal Saving

QUESTIONS

Q1. What are the functions of the Central Bank?

Q2. Explain the means by which the Central Bank may implement monetary policy.

Q3. Write an explanatory note on the traditional approach to implementing monetary policy.

Q4. Set out the system for implementing monetary policy in the 1980's.

Q5. Is the prime purpose of Exchequer Bills related to Monetary or Fiscal Policy?

Q6. "In recent years the powers of the Central Bank have been strengthened". Explain what is meant by this statement.

25 The Determination of Interest Rates

25.1. The Demand for Money

This term should be understood as the demand in the economy to *hold* money either in the form of notes and coins or as a balance in a current account rather than to invest it. The Classical Economists tended to see money as having a neutral role — people used it as a medium of exchange and if they wished not to spend it they lent it at the highest rate of interest, with due allowance being made for risk factors. Keynes put forward the notion that people desired to hold money balances rather than to invest — he introduced a *Liquidity Preference Theory*, i.e., thereby explaining a desire of people to hold their assets in the form of cash. In developing his Liquidity Preference Theory Keynes distinguished three reasons why people might desire to hold money balances: 1. a Transaction Motive; 2. a Precautionary Motive; 3. a Speculative Motive.

Three Reasons for holding Money

While the Transactions Motive is essentially money as a medium of exchange, the Speculative Motive suggested that funds could leak out of the Circular Flow of Income and that the rate of interest would not fulfill a market clearing function, i.e., at low rates of interest holders of funds would not lend them. This was in contrast to the approach of the Classical Economists who argued that lenders would prefer to receive a high rate of interest but they felt that these funds would continue to be lent even at low rates of interest on the basis that a low rate of interest was better than none.

(a) **The Transaction Motive:**

This is the term applied to the demand for money for day-to-day expenses. The actual quantity of money which is required for transaction purposes depends on *the level of expenditure*, the main determinant of our level of expenditure is our *level of income*. Generally speaking the higher our income the greater our daily expenditure. If you have a large income you are likely to hold a larger amount of money for day-to-day transaction purposes than would a person with a smaller income. Similarly a large business is likely to require larger sums for expenses, such as wages, in comparison with a smaller firm.

The rate of interest has virtually no effect on this transactions demand for money which is a function of the level of income (the price level is considered to be exogenous).

(b) **The Precautionary Motive:**

This is the term applied to the demand to hold money to meet those contingencies which arise in an irregular fashion, e.g., illness, house repairs, car breakdown, breakdowns or breakages in household

Determination of interest rates.

equipment. People are aware that expenses of this nature inevitably arise and it is necessary to have money available to meet them. The level of income will have an effect on the precautionary demand for money and so also will the rate of interest. If the rate of interest is high it will be more costly to hold money for this purpose and consequently people will be inclined to keep to a minimum the cash balances which they hold for precautionary purposes.

Thus the demand to hold money for precautionary purposes is a function of the level of income and the rate of interest.

(c) **The Speculative Motive:**
This is the element of the demand for money which is most likely to be subject to considerable fluctuations. This type of demand arises from people who wish to have money to take advantage of any profitable investment opportunity which might arise as it indicates a preference to hold money because the existing rates of return are considered inadequate. The rate of interest has a considerable influence on the speculative demand for money as is shown in Section 25.2 and 25.3.

Illustration of Speculative Demand

25.2. This illustration could be in terms of investment in capital goods or bonds but it is easier understood if we concentrate on government bonds. When a person buys a bond he lends money to the government. In return for this loan he receives a fixed rate of interest and the sum which he loaned is returned at some future date. It is also possible for the holder of the bond to sell it before its maturity, i.e., before the date on which the borrower has undertaken to return the sum borrowed. If a person buys £100 worth of 10% bonds he gets £10 interest each year and has £100 returned to him at the end of the period of the loan. If the person who purchased this bond wished to sell it at the end of the year and if at that time the rate of interest had increased to 15% no one would be prepared to give him £100 for his bond since a person could buy a bond from the latest issue for £100. With the rate of interest on the latest issue of bonds being 15% a bondholder could get £15 interest, i.e., an extra £5 interest for the investment of the same amount of money, viz., £100. Thus the holder of the 10% bond would have to sell his bond for a price lower than £100 — the price at which he would be able to sell it would be £66⅔ the purchaser receives a bond certificate which entitles him to receive £10 interest, thus he is receiving £10 return on his expenditure of   £66⅔ which is equal to a return of $\dfrac{10 \times 100}{66⅔} = 15\%$

return on investment★ or 15% yield.

★This ignores redemption aspect since the bondholder would have a capital gain of £33⅓ when, on maturity, he received £100 for the bond which he purchased for £66⅔.

9

25.3. However the original purchaser of the bond would have received £10 interest for the first year and then lost £33⅓ (£100-£66⅔) on the sale of the bond, i.e., he would have lost £23⅓ on the entire transaction —made up of a loss of £33⅓ when he sold the bond and £10 interest which he received. The realisation that the rate of interest is likely to rise (i.e., bond prices are likely to fall) means that people would prefer to hold their cash in liquid form than invest it, i.e., they would have a speculative demand to hold cash.

The main factor influencing the speculative demand for money is the rate of interest.

25.4. From the foregoing you will realise that whether or not people will prefer to hold their assets in the form of cash or invest it depends on whether they consider the present rate of interest to be too low. This implies that they are comparing the present rate of interest with their idea of the rate of interest that is appropriate to present conditions, i.e., the "normal" rate of interest. If the current rate of interest is lower than what a person considers to the "normal" rate, then such a person expects interest rates to rise. In these circumstances there will be a high speculative demand for money as people prefer to hold their assets in cash form — by so doing they are losing the interest payment they would have got by investing their money but they are avoiding the capital loss which they would have suffered when they attempted to sell their assets due to interest rates having risen. This capital loss would be greater than the interest they earned resulting in a net loss on the transaction.

25.5. There is no reason to suppose that everybody has the same idea as to which is the "normal" rate of interest — it is subjective. Whereas I might consider the current rate of interest to be too low, i.e., below the "normal" rate, and consequently hold my assets in a liquid/cash form, you might consider the "normal" rate to be lower than the current rate and consequently you would invest. Similarly a person's opinion as to what constitutes the "normal" rate may change, after a period of holding my assets in a cash form I might consider that the "normal" rate has fallen and is in fact lower than the current rate, in which circumstances I would start to invest.

25.6. Total Demand for Money
The total demand for money is the aggregate of the Transaction Demand, Precautionary Demand and Speculative Demand. The major influences on each of these types of demands are as shown in Fig. 25.6.

Type of Demand	Major Influence(s)
Transaction	Level of Income (y)
Precautionary	Level of Income (y) and Rate of Interest (i)
Speculative	Rate of Interest (i)

Table 25.6. Major Influence on each type of demand for money.

25.7. Thus if the level of income (GNP) is taken as given, the demand for money is a function of the rate of interest as shown in Fig. 25.7.

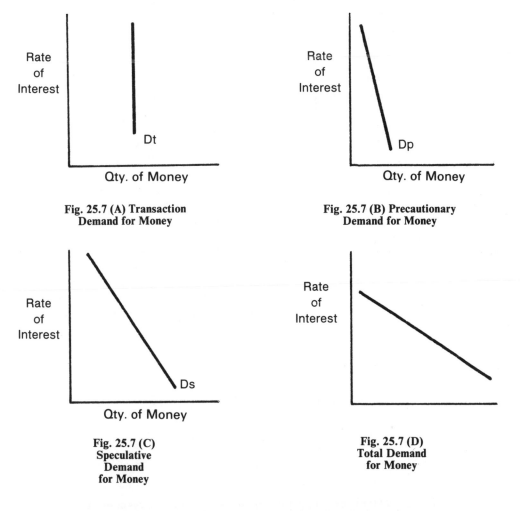

Fig. 25.7 (A) Transaction Demand for Money

Fig. 25.7 (B) Precautionary Demand for Money

Fig. 25.7 (C) Speculative Demand for Money

Fig. 25.7 (D) Total Demand for Money

Fig. 25.7. Demand for Money at a given level of Income (GNP).

25.8. Effect of a Change in Level of Income (GNP) on the Demand for Money

If there is an increase in the level of income (GNP) the curve showing the transaction demand for money will move to the right and the curve showing the precautionary demand for money will move to the right since both of these types of demand are affected by the level of GNP as shown in Table 25.6. These two effects will combine to shift to the right, from D_1 to D_2, the aggregate demand for money as shown in Fig. 25.9 (A) and (B).

25.9. Supply and Demand for Money

If there is an increased demand for money (say) from D_1 to D_2 while the supply of money does not increase (i.e., the supply of money remains at S_1) then the rate of interest will rise from R_1 to R_2 as shown in Fig. 25.9 (A).

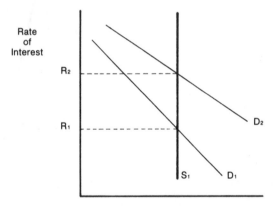

Fig. 25.9 (A) Increased Demand for money while supply remains unchanged raises interest rate.

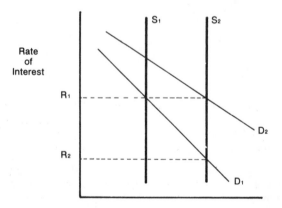

Fig. 25.9 (B) When supply of money is increased in response to an increased demand, the interest rate may be unchanged.

If the rate of interest rises this will constitute a disincentive to invest. If, in response to the increased demand for money, the supply of money was increased from S_1 to S_2 the rate of interest could remain unchanged at R_1 as shown in fig. 25.9 (B) and there would be no disincentive to invest because the interest rate would not have risen. The government by increasing the supply of money can peg or lower the rate of interest in an effort to encourage an increase in investment.★ If the money supply in Fig. 25.9 (B) had been increased from S_1 to S_2 without any increase in the demand for money then the rate of interest would have fallen from R_1 to R_3.

It is important that the money supply at least keep pace with the increase in the level of GNP since otherwise there would be a rise in interest rates which would be deflationary.

25.10. A low rate of interest tends to lead to an increase in the level of consumption/consumer demand and also in the level of investment. Consumption would be encouraged because the opportunity cost of spending money rather than saving it is the interest rate and thus this opportunity cost is low when interest rates are low, i.e., there is less incentive to save. On the investment side marginal investment projects which were not economically viable at high interest rates may become viable at lower rates of interest, e.g. if the (risk adjusted) rate of return from investing in a particular project is 15% this investment would not be economically viable if the rate of interest on borrowed funds was 16%. However, if the rate of interest fell to 14% investment in this project would be economically viable. This, then, raises the question of the desirability of the Central Bank increasing the money supply and thus reducing the interest rate until the level of activity is at the Full Employment level. There are various reasons as to why it might not be possible for the Central Bank to increase the supply of money but for the purpose of this section of the course let us see what might happen based on the Liquidity Preference theory.

If the rate of interest falls to a level which economic agents consider to be lower than the "normal" rate, then there is a general expectation that interest rates will rise in the near future. It has already been shown that if interest rates are rising capital losses are sustained when assets are sold. Therefore, in the circumstances envisaged if the rate of interest is below the "normal" rate an increase in the money supply will not encourage further investment and will not succeed in lowering the rate of interest — the demand for money becomes completely elastic as shown by the horizontal section in Fig. 25.10. Note that this perfectly elastic demand for money is at the "normal" rate of interest. This is known as a "Liquidity Trap" and is based on the Speculative Demand for Money as set out in Keynes Liquidity Preference Theory.

★Remember however that the rate of interest is not the only factor influencing the level of investment — for example, see Chapter 21. Also increasing the supply of money affects the economy in other ways.

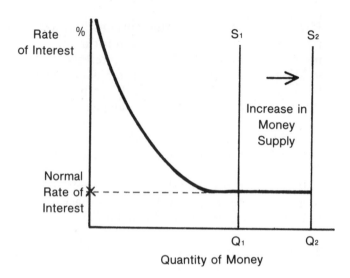

Fig. 25.10. Liquidity Trap.

If a Liquidity Trap existst then further increase in the money supply will not lower the rate of interest, but will spill over into current consumption leading to inflation and Balance of Payments problems.

It is not necessary that in the Liquidity Trap the demand for money be perfectly elastic (horizontal demand curve), if it is nearly so the same analysis applies.

Demand for
Money
determines
Interest
Rate

25.11. You will have noticed in Figs. 25.7 (A) and (B) that the money supply is represented by a vertical line indicating that the supply of money is independent of the rate of interest — the supply of money is a policy decision by the Central Bank. In which case since the supply of money does not change the rate of interest is determined by the demand for money (Liquidity Preference).

CLASSICAL THEORY OF INTEREST RATE DETERMINATION

Loanable
Fund Theory

25.12. This Keynesian theory of the determination of interest rates may be contrasted with the Classical theory. The Classical theory was a Loanable Fund Theory — the supply curve of funds was perceived as being upward sloping indicating that the higher the rate of interest the greater the supply of funds for investment purposes — the rate of interest was the price paid to holders of funds in order that they would postpone consumption. The demand for funds depended on the Marginal Efficiency of Capital and was downward sloping with respect to the rate of interest. while the rate of interest fluctuated to bring into equilibrium the supply of, and demand for, investment funds.

Criticism of Theory

25.13. This Loanable Fund Theory is similar to the manner in which the price of other factors of production are determined. However, it attributed far too great an influence to the rate of interest. The rate of interest is not the main determinant of the level of saving or the level of investment — Keynes suggested that expectation as to future profitability is the major determinant of the level of investment.

Empirical Testing of Theory

25.14. The most damning criticism of the Classical Loanable Fund Theory was that it didn't describe what happened in the economy. Under this theory the rate of interest would fluctuate to ensure that all funds were invested as no saver would hold idle cash while he could earn a rate of interest by investing it. All output constitutes income for sellers and this, in turn, is either spent or saved; under the Loanable Fund Theory the level of savings is brought into equilibrium with the level of investment by a fluctuating rate of interest so that all saving is invested (spent) by borrowers. Thus, the theory did not envisage a deficiency in demand through a leakage of this nature from the circular flow of income, though it did concede the possibility of temporary mismatchings of production and demand giving rise to the minor adjustments which would be necessary in a dynamic economy to match the type and quantity of goods produced with those required. In the light of the world depression in the 1930's, it was obvious that the classical theory did not conform to reality and Keynes Speculative Demand for money provided an explanation as to why the rate of interest might not fluctuate freely and might not perform a market clearing function.

QUESTIONS

Q1. State the three reasons which Keynes put forward for holding money.

Q2. Explain the major influence on each of these types of demand for money.

Q3. Explain the "Liquidity Trap."

Q4. Explain the Classical Theory of Interest Rate determination.

Q5. How do changes in the quantity of money affect the price level and the level of economic activity.

26   Value of Money/Price Level

26.1. The Value of Money is the Rate at which it Exchanges for Goods and Services

The Value of Money and the General Price Level are inversely related

Price is the relationship between a quantity of money and a quantity of goods. Thus the higher the price of a good, the lower the value of a unit of money in terms of that good. For example, if a table cost £10, £1 = one-tenth of a table; if the price of the table is increased to £15, £1 = one-fifteenth of table. This idea can be extended to any group of goods or the general price level. The value of money and the general price level are two ways of communicating the same idea — the lower the general price level the greater the value of a unit of money, the higher the general price level the lower the value of a unit of money. Inflation can be described as an increase in the general price level or a reduction in the value of a unit of money. Changes in the value of money can be seen in Table 26.1.

Table 26.1. Purchasing Power of the £
Taking value as equivalent to 100p in various years (read vertically)

Year	1922	1935	1945	1955	1965	1975	1981	1982	1983	1984	1985	1986	1987
1922	100												
1935	121	100											
1945	64	53	100										
1955	46	72	100										
1965	33	27	51	71	100								
1975	14	11	21	30	41	100							
1981	6	5	9	13	18	43	100						
1982	5	4	11	15	37	84	100						
1983	5	4	7	10	14	33	77	91	100				
1984	4	3	6	9	13	31	71	83	92	100			
1985	4	3	6	9	12	29	68	79	87	95	100		
1986	4	3	6	8	12	28	65	76	84	91	96	100	
1987	4	3	6	8	11	27	63	74	82	89	93	97	100
1988	4	3	6	8	11	27	62	72	80	87	91	95	98

Source: Central Bank

Thus in the remainder of this chapter we will use the term "the value of money" and "the general price level" to convey the same idea though it must be remembered that they are inversely related, i.e., an *increase* in the general price level is equivalent to a *reduction* in the value of a unit of money.

26.2. Measuring Changes in the Price Level

In order to measure changes in the price level we must first ascertain the price level. If we are analysing one item the matter is very simple, it is simply a matter of comparing the selling price of the item at different points in time.

Example 26.2 (a)

	1985	1986	1987
Selling price of Commodity A	£20	£28	£32

Index Number

It is desirable to use an index number so that the change in price may be compared more easily. An index number is allotted to the price of a good or group of goods in a base period, subsequent changes in price are reflected in changes in the index number. The index number for the base period is usually taken to be 100.

Example 26.2(b)

If £20 is the price in 1985 which is the base period then £20 is taken to be 100.

Index number in 1986 when price has risen to £28 becomes

$$\frac{28 \times 100}{20} = 140$$

Similarly the index number in 1987 when the price has risen to £32 is

$$\frac{32 \times 100}{20} = 160$$

26.3. If it is desired to measure changes in the price level of a group of three items, the above procedure would be adopted for each of the items and then an average would be taken.

Example 26.3

1988 (Base Year)			1989			1990		
Com-odity	Price £	Index No.	Comm-odity	Price £	Index No.	Comm-odity	Price £	Index No.
A	20	100	A	28	140	A	32	160
B	5	100	B	5.75	115	B	6.00	120
C	100	100	C	123	123	C	135	135
Total		300	Total		378	Total		415

Average

$$\frac{300}{3} = 100$$

Average

$$\frac{378}{3} = 126$$

Average

$$\frac{415}{3} = 138.33$$

Simple or Unweighted Index

26.4. Each of the items in Example 26.3 was considered to be of equal importance — they were all given the same weight. Consequently this form of index number *is known as a simple or unweighted index.*

Composite or Weighted Index

26.5. A *composite or weighted index* exists when each of the items is not considered to be of equal importance as some items are purchased more often and are therefore given a greater weight to reflect this fact. For example, if I purchase a bottle of lemonade once a week and if its price is increased from 90p to 95p, this has not as great an effect on my cost of living as an increase from 90p to 95p in the bus fares which I must pay four times a day.

Selection of Weights

26.6. Composite price indices are weighted on the basis of the proportion of income which is spent on each of the items. In the compilation of the Consumer Price Index, Household Budget Surveys are carried out in order to ascertain the proportion of income which is spent under various headings.

Example 26.6.

Let us assume that as a result of a Household Budget Survey it was ascertained that 70% of income is spent on Commodity A, 25% on Commodity B and 5% on Commodity C. Using this information, a weighted price index can be used by applying these weightings as shown in Example 26.6.

Example 26.6

1988 (Base Year)				1989			
Col. 1	Col. 2	Col. 3	Col. 4	Col. 1	Col. 2	Col. 3	Col. 4
Comm-odity	Index	Weight	(Col. 2 x Col. 3)	Comm-odity	Index	Weight	(Col. 2 x Col. 3)
A	100	70	7000	A	140	70	9800
B	100	25	2500	B	115	25	2875
C	100	5	500	C	123	5	615
Total		100	10,000	Total		100	13290

$$\frac{\text{Weighted}}{\text{Average}} = \frac{\text{Col. 4}}{\text{Col. 3}} = \frac{10,000}{100} = 100 \qquad \frac{\text{Weighted}}{\text{Average}} = \frac{\text{Col. 4}}{\text{Col. 3}} = \frac{13,290}{100} = 132.90$$

1990			
Comm-odity	Index	Weight	(Col. 2 x Col. 3)
A	160	70	11,200
B	120	25	3,000
C	135	5	675
Total		100	14,875

$$\frac{\text{Weighted}}{\text{Average}} = \frac{\text{Col. 4}}{\text{Col. 3}} = \frac{14,875}{100} = 148.75$$

Thus in the above example the Price Index in 1988 is 100, in 1989 it is 132.90 and in 1990 it is 148.75.

These composition Index Nos. may be compared with the simple Index Nos. in Example 26.3. Only in the base year are they the same and index numbers in base years will always be 100.

26.7. Stages in the Calculation of a Composite or Weighted Index

(a) Decide on the base period. It is desirable that the base period should be a representative or normal period so that subsequent changes can be related to some concept of normality.

(b) A decision must be made as to the goods which it is intended to include in the index.

(c) Ascertain the price of each article which is being included in the survey — if the article is sold in a number of shops at different prices then either an average price must be used or the article must always be priced in the same shop. This presupposes that the articles chosen for inclusion in the survey are in continuous supply during the periods being analysed.

(d) Calculate a simple index for each commodity.

(e) Ascertain the proportion of income which is spent on each commodity and use this proportion as the expenditure weighting for the commodity. As explained below in Section 26.10 this information for the Consumer Price Index is obtained by means of Household Budget Surveys.

(f) Multiply the index in respect of each commodity by its appropriate weight and calculate a weighted index.

26.8. Do price indices provide an accurate measure of changes in the price level?

Care should be exercised in the Application of Index Numbers

(a) Price indices are based on average patterns of expenditure. Care must be exercised when applying a general index to a particular group of people because the expenditure pattern of any group may differ from the average — for a non-smoker a change in the price of cigarettes will not affect his cost of living. The higher the standard of living of the community the more likely it is that there will be a considerable range in the pattern of expenditure and therefore the less representative is the average pattern of expenditure.

(b) The weighting of the various commodities in the index is derived from the expenditure pattern in the base year. If expenditure patterns change it is necessary to change the weightings.

(c) It is difficult to make provision for changes in the quality of goods. If there is an improvement in quality while prices remain static, this constitutes a price reduction in real terms. Alternatively, a price increase may be due to a corresponding improvement in quality, the net result being that the real cost of the good remains unchanged.

(d) The introduction of new commodities together with changes in taste and fashion alter the pattern of demand. An increase in the Consumer Price Index may overstate the actual increase in the cost of living as people may purchase cheaper substitute goods if there is a general price increase or if there is an increase confined to those goods which comprised the original bundle/shopping-basket of commodities.

26.9. Consumer Price Index (CPI)

CPI is a price index and not a cost of living index

This is probably the best known Irish Statistical Index. It is included here because of its importance in its own right and as a detailed example of how such indices are compiled. The Consumer Price Index (CPI) is compiled by the Central Statistics Office. The index is designed to measure changes in the general level of prices actually paid (inclusive of all indirect taxes) by private households for consumer goods and services. It is calculated on a quarterly basis in respect of the middle Tuesday of the months of February, May, August and November of each year. The index is released approximately five weeks after the date to which it relates. It is published subsequently in the monthly Economic Series and the quarterly Statistical Bulletin.

26.10. Summary of Considerations to be borne in mind when using the Consumer Price Index

(a) **It is a price index not a cost of living index**

It measures changes in the cost of buying a fixed basket of goods. It does not take into account the manner in which households may change their pattern of expenditure in response to changes in prices, income, composition of families or market conditions, e.g. switching from buying expensive cuts of meat to cheap cuts or vice versa. Furthermore, expenses such as income tax and PRSI which effect most household budgets are not included in the CPI. Neither does it include imputed rent of owner occupied dwellings nor the value of own garden or farm produce consumed by households. However, changes in the CPI give a reasonably good indication of changes in the cost of living since one of the most important factors determining changes in the cost of living is the extent to which consumer prices of goods and services vary and it is this particular aspect of the cost of living which is measured by the CPI.

(b) **The CPI refers to the "Average Person"**

The weights which are used to determine the relative importance of the various items in the CPI are averages based on surveys, consequently it may not be an accurate indicator of the pattern of expenditure of a particular person or a specific group of people. For example, expenditure on footwear might constitute 2.7% of the expenditure of the average or representative person, obviously many people spend considerably less of their income than this on that type of purchase. Similarly housing may have a weighting of 6.1 but people who own their own house don't spend 6.1% of their income on housing.

(c) **The CPI overstates changes in Cost/Expense arising from Price Changes**

Since the CPI is based on changes in the cost of purchasing a fixed basket of goods it fails to take into account the extent to which consumers may substitute (relatively) cheap goods for goods which have increased in price. The CPI merely shows how much more expensive it would be to purchase the original basket of goods.

(d) **The CPI does not reflect changes in quality**

It does not take into account changes which may have occurred in the quality of those goods which are included in the Index. If there is a price increase which is due to an improvement in the quality of the good (e.g. more fresh fruit in the jam) the CPI will record this merely as a price increase. Similarly the CPI would show no change if there was a "hidden price increase" due to the quality of the good being reduced while its price remained unchanged.

(e) **The Base Year must be Representative**

Quite distinct from the point regarding the CPI being based on an average pattern of expenditure is the question of the appropriateness of the base year chosen. The base year should be a representative year so a number of strikes or a time of catastrophically unreasonable weather would distort the purchasing behaviour of the majority of people and would not provide results which are representative even of the "average" consumer. The relevance of the entire Index is crucially dependent on the Household Budget Surveys which are undertaken for this purpose, which is why the index requires constant updating to ensure that it takes into account changes in purchasing behaviour as new goods and services appear on the market while other goods and services are no longer demanded.

(f) **The CPI measures price changes between periods and not absolute levels of expenditure**

From this it will be realised that excluding an item from the index does not necessarily result in the index being increased or decreased. The exclusion of an item is equivalent to including it in the index with its appropriate weighting and attributing to it the *overall* price change of all other items combined. Similarly the inclusion of an additional item will increase (or decrease) the index only if the percentage change in its price is greater (or less) than that of the rest of the index and then only in proportion to its weight in the fixed basket of goods.

26.11. Some uses of the Consumer Price Index

(a) **Wage negotiations.** A change in the Consumer Price Index is one of the indicators on which trade union negotiators base claims for cost of living increases for their members. Employers, if they concede this issue at all, would prefer to use changes in the Constant Tax Price Index as the basis for such negotiations. Changes in the

Constant Tax Price Index would be less than changes in the CPI because it (the CTPI) does not take into account that portion of price increases which are due to changes in Indirect Taxation. Employers would attempt to justify using the Constant Tax Price Index by arguing that if the CPI is being used instead then they are being asked to pay the indirect tax increase to which their employees are subject.

(b) **Fiscal Policy/Indexation**

Changes in the CPI affect Fiscal Policy. Governments usually try to maintain the real value of social welfare payments, i.e., to adjust them upwards in line with increases in CPI. Similarly, there are usually demands from income tax payers that income tax bands be adjusted to reflect increases in the CPI so that income tax bands be maintained in real terms. In the absence of the indexation of tax allowances a rising price level increases Government revenue even without tax *rates* being increased.

(c) **As a measure of inflation**

The rate of inflation is measured by changes in the CPI.

(d) **Indexation of Savings**

Some savings institutions provide index linked savings schemes under which the interest paid on deposits is related to changes in the CPI.

(e) **International Comparisons**

Changes in Consumer Price Indices in various countries are the basis on which rates of inflation in these countries are compared.

26.12. Base Years for Previous C.P.I's.

Development of Official Price Indices

(a) The first official index of consumer prices was compiled in respect of *March 1922* and was based on returns from 308 households.

(b) The second series commenced in *August 1947* and was known as the Interim Cost of Living Index. Because patterns of expenditure had not, at that time, stabilised after the war, the index included only changes in the retail prices of essential items, i.e., food, clothing, fuel, light, rent.

(c) The next series was introduced in *November 1953* when it was considered that expenditure patterns had stabilised after the war. In addition, the index was extended to cover the full range of consumer goods and services. The two earlier indices had each been called a Cost of Living Index even though they were designed to measure price changes only. This misleading title was changed to the present official title Consumer Price Index. The change was made to avoid the misunderstanding, then prevalent, that the index measured all factors causing changes in the cost of living.

Table 26.12 Consumer Price Index (All Items)

| Period | Consumer Price Index | | Annual Percentage Price Change |
	Current Base mid-November 1982 as 100	Former Base mid-November 1975 as 100	
1985 Year	122.0	334.2	+ 5.4
1986 Year	126.7	346.9	+ 3.9
1987 Year	130.7	357.8	+ 3.2
1988 Year	133.5	365.5	+ 2.1
1989 Mid-February	136.6	374.0	+ 3.3
Mid-May	138.0	377.8	+ 3.8

[1] Linked to current Consumer Price Index at mid-November 1982.

Source: Statistical Bulletin, September 1989 (C.S.O.)

(d)   This index series was introduced in *February 1969.* The number of separate articles priced was increased from 191 to 343.

(e)   The following series was introduced with *mid-November 1975* as the base period. Previous series had related only to urban households. The survey on which this series was based included rural households.

(f)   The present series was introduced in mid November 1982. The survey covered a national representative sample of 7,185 private households throughout the country. Fieldwork on the survey commenced in December 1979 and terminated in January 1981.

26.13. Constant-Tax Price Index

This is a new price index which has been added to Irish Statistical Tables in accordance with the January 1976 Budget Statement. It is *not* correct to see this price index as being a tax free consumers price index, it merely holds constant the indirect tax content (in absolute money terms) of goods at mid-November 1975 level. The *increase* in indirect tax on prices in future periods is removed for comparison purpose. For example, price in mid-November 1975 (including indirect taxes) £55 (£50 + £5 indirect tax); price in mid-November 1977 = £70 (£61 + £9 indirect tax). For the purpose of the Constant Tax Price Index the mid-November 1977 price would be taken as £66, i.e., the *increase* in indirect tax of £4 would be subtracted from the price. Thus, as can be seen, this index will not reflect the effect of changes in indirect taxes since mid-November 1975. No provision is made for the secondary effects of indirect taxation, i.e., where changes in taxation rates for one item influence the price of other items. In addition there may be a difficulty in estimating how much of a given price increase is due to indirect taxes. In those instances where the increase in indirect taxation is passed on to the consumer no problem exists. However, if demand is price elastic, part of the tax increase may be absorbed by the producer, in which case the rise in the constant-tax CPI would be *less* than it would have been in the absence of the increase in indirect taxation.

One of the main uses of this constant-tax CTPI will be in relation to wage negotiations. It will minimise the possibility of employees gaining wage increases to compensate for increases in taxation which the government has levied in order to fulfil its political mandate.

The Constant-Tax Price Index with a base of 100 in mid-November 1982 was 117.0 in mid-August 1985. The Constant Tax Price Index which derived from CPI data has also been rebased to mid-November 1982 as 100.

26.14. Other series of Price Indices which are currently used in Ireland are:

(a)   General Wholesale Prices

(b)   Manufacturing Output Prices

(c)   Agricultural Output Prices

(d)   Agricultural Input Prices

(e)   Export Unit Values and Import Unit Values from which our Terms of Trade are calculated, e.g.,

Export Unit Values: 276.6
Import Unit Values: 294.3

Terms of Trade: $\dfrac{276.6}{294.3} = 94.0$

Figure 26.14(a) Wholesale Price Index (base 1985 = 100)

—— Manufacturing Industry Output – Series 1.02
···· Building & Construction Materials – Series 1.03

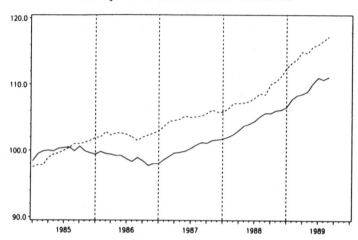

Figure 26.14(b) Consumer Price Index (base Mid-Nov 1982 = 100)

—— All Items – Series 1.13
···· Food Items – Series 1.14

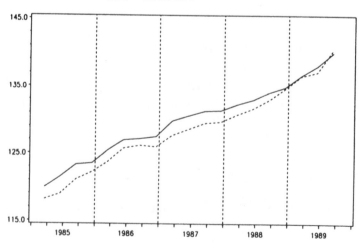

Figure 26.14(c) Agriculture Output Price Index (base 1985 = 100)

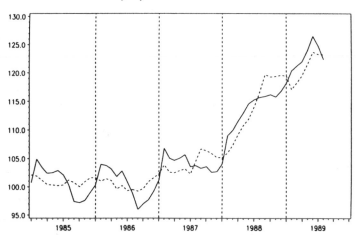

Figure 26.14(d) Agriculture Input Price Index (base 1985 = 100)

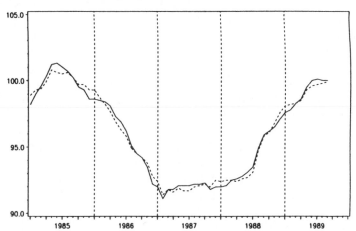

Fig. 26.14 Graphs of Selected Price Series

Source: Economic Series — October 1989 issue

*Use of
Consumer
Price Index
in
conjunction
with
Constant-
Tax Price
Index*

26.15. The Constant-Tax Price Index can be used in conjunction with the Consumer Price Index to separate price changes in a period between those caused by changes in indirect taxation and those caused by other factors. For this purpose changes expressed in index points to base mid-November 1982 as 100 must be used for both series. Thus, for the mid-May to mid-August 1985 quarter, of the total increase in the Consumer Price Index of 1.8 points (from 121.5 to 123.3) non-tax factors accounted for 1.6 points (i.e., the change from 115.4 to 117.0 in the Constant-Tax Price Index).

26.16. The value of money is the rate at which it exchanges for goods and therefore for a given volume of transactions the value of money will depend on the quantity of it which is available. The value of money, i.e., a unit of currency, depends on the supply of, and the demand for, it.

26.17. As discussed in Chapter 23 the money supply is made up of notes, coins and bank deposits. Notes and coins are printed by the government and the availability of bank credit is also under the direct control of the government through the Central Bank — see Chapter 24. Thus the money supply may be considered to be an exogenous variable determined by government decisions.

26.18. Changes in the Money Supply and the Value of Money

The value of money is the rate at which it exchanges for goods. An increase in the supply of money in excess of an increase in the supply of goods and services results in a rise in the general price level, i.e., a fall in the value of money. In recent years Ireland, in common with many other countries, has experienced this increase in the general price level, i.e., inflation. Inflation is the term used to describe a *continuing* rise in the general price level rather than a once and for all increase.

The term inflation is often reserved for those periods when prices are rising at a fast rate — but this begs the question as to what constitutes a fast rate of price increase. Deflation is the term used to describe the opposite situation to inflation.

26.19. Effect of Inflation on the Level of Economic Activity

Rising prices provide a stimulus to the level of economic activity. Profit is a residual, it is what is left over from revenue after expenses have been paid. At the outset of a period of inflation all costs will not increase immediately, thus when the selling prices of finished goods increase during this initial period of inflation, profits will be at a level higher than what was anticipated when production plans were being drawn up and implemented. This increased level of profit provides the resources for expansion while the possibility of higher selling prices in the future provides a further stimulus to the entrepreneur to invest and increase his level of production. The possibility of prices being even higher in the future assists in the maintenance of a buoyant level of demand through encouraging consumers to buy quickly before prices rise even further.

The opposite to the foregoing pertains when prices are falling viz.:— revenue and consequently the level of profit is lower than anticipated so that entrepreneurs not only lack the resources which they require in order to expand their level of output, but also they develop pessimistic expectations and are inclined to cut back on their level of production. A slowly rising price level probably strikes a balance between stimulating the economy and avoiding the undesirable consequences of inflation.

26.20. Redistributive Effects of Inflation

Profit

(a) Those whose income is non-contractual, e.g., profit earners, since profit is of a residual nature, are the first to experience an increase in income when prices begin to rise.

Suppliers of Factors of Production

(b) As entrepreneurs seek to increase their level of production in order to enjoy to the full the benefits accruing from an increase in their selling prices and revenue, they will increase their demand for factors of production. As a result of this increase in demand the price of factors of production may rise. You will notice in this development that the increased payments for the factors of production were a result of an increase in the selling price of the finished goods. Thus the increased payments to the suppliers of factors of production lag behind the rising selling prices and thus the real income of the suppliers of factors of production is reduced. However, since there is an increased demand for factors of production the level of employment is probably increased.

Lags in adjustment of income

(c) Because of the falling value of money those on fixed money incomes, e.g., those in receipt of pensions or social welfare payments, suffer an erosion of their purchasing power which is not fully compensated, even if they receive periodic adjustments in their money to reflect increases in the cost of living. The increases in the payments which they receive are implemented only because of increases in the cost of living and because there are lags in the adjustments of their payments to the price increases such people lose out through inflation. For example, if the money a person receives before inflation is £30 and the price level increases by 50% and after it has increased that person's income is increased to £45, the person in question has lost on the development because there was a period when the price level had increased and his income had not; the matter, of course, is much worse if the individual does not get an increase, or gets an increase smaller than the rate of inflation. When the inflationary process continues over a lengthy period the cumulative loss through these types of adjustment lags may be considerable.

Debtors and Creditors

(d) During a period of inflation debtors tend to gain at the expense of creditors. This situation pertains due to the fact that when borrowers pay back the sum of money which they borrowed, its purchasing power has diminished by the rate of inflation. For example, if an individual borrows £100 and pays interest at the rate of 18% per annum during a year when the rate of inflation was 20%, the £118 which the lender receives at the end of the year will not permit him to purchase as much as would the £100 at the beginning of the year. *In the case set out in this example real interest rates are said to be negative.*

Other Effects of Inflation

(e)   There is a transfer of resources to the State. Income tax allowances are stated in money terms so that with inflation the real value of these allowances are diminished and the average rate of tax payment is increased, e.g., if an individual has tax free allowances of £2,500 he is not liable for the payment of income tax on his income of £2,500 per annum. However if the rate of inflation is at the rate of 10% per annum and his salary is increased from £2,500 to £2,750, in order to compensate him for the 10% increase in his cost of living, he must pay tax on the £250 increase which he received because his tax free allowances remain unchanged in money terms. Thus, despite having received a salary increase to compensate him for the increase in the cost of living, his after-tax pay in real terms has been reduced. Similarly, as incomes are increased due to inflation individuals move into brackets of higher marginal taxation of income. In an analogous manner, as profits in money terms increase, the real burden of taxation on the business sector increases. All of this means that during a period of inflation there is a transfer of resources from the private sector to the State even if the *rates* of tax are not increased because tax free allowances are not adjusted to reflect the falling value of money. In addition, just as has been mentioned in 26.17 (d) above in respect of debtors gaining, the State is a major borrower and the burden of the National Debt is lessened by inflation.

26.21. Because the purchasing power of money is reduced there is said to be a negative yield on holding money during a period of inflation. In an effort to avoid losses of this nature people purchase assets such as land, houses, jewellery, antiques, etc. which, though they are a less liquid form of asset than money, yield an income or a capital gain. The transference of wealth into these forms of assets increases the demand for, and thus the price of, these goods. The purchase of land for investment purposes as a hedge against inflation has increased the price of land to such an extent that many farmers who wish to put the land into productive use are unable to pay the high price for the land which they require. In an effort to deal with this problem the government has promised to introduce a Land Act which would discriminate against the purchase of land as a hedge against inflation by non-farmers.

26.22. In an inflationary period it is difficult for firms to generate

Cash Flow

sufficient funds from current activities to enable them to cover the replacement costs of assets, in addition to which it is difficult for firms to know what the replacement cost of assets will be due to the rapidly changing price level. For example, a firm may set aside £1,000 each year for a five year period with a view to replacing at the end of its economic life an asset which originally cost £5,000. However, when the firm attempts to purchase the replacement asset its price has risen to (say) £7,000. If the firm has to borrow in order to obtain the extra £2,000 its cost will be further increased due to the interest which the firm must pay on the loan.

International Trade

26.23. If our rate of inflation is greater than the inflationary rate of our trading partners, it will be difficult for us to remain competitive in International Trade.

Perfectly Anticipated Inflation

26.24. If inflation was to continue at a steady rate which the public could anticipate it is possible that some of the evils of inflation could be avoided and the redistributive effects to which inflation gives rise could be minimised. *Perfectly anticipated inflation occurs when every transactor forecasts correctly future rates of inflation and is able to adjust to the anticipated conditions.* Thus it will be realised that there are two elements involved in perfectly anticipated inflation viz:—

(a) Perfect anticipation of future rates of inflation.

(b) The ability to adjust to the anticipated conditions, i.e., the prices of all goods and services would need to be perfectly flexible.

26.25. Factors which Contribute to Inflation

Higher Prices provide Increased Income

Once the inflationary process gets under way, it is a case of higher prices providing increased incomes which stimulate a level of demand which increases prices even further. It should be remembered that prices provide income to suppliers of factors of production and to the State through taxation. Thus when prices rise, these increases are channelled back as income to the suppliers of factors of production and to the State. As already noted this distribution is unlikely to be on an equitable basis across all sectors of the community because of the redistributive effects of inflation, i.e., those on fixed income or long term agreements suffer most while profit earners and flexible negotiators gain most.

26.26. Demand Pull Inflation

Level of demand

An increase in the level of demand without a corresponding increase in supply leaves an unsatisfied demand at existing prices. In these circumstances suppliers can increase their profits by raising their selling prices. Increased selling prices mean higher incomes and these higher money incomes stimulate an increase in the level of demand as a result of which prices rise further. There is evidence of excess demand being present in the Irish Economy in 1962, 1964-5, 1968-9 and 1973. Because of the openness of the Irish Economy, excess demand is likely to cause difficulties in our Balance of Payments — although it should be noted that a large portion of public expenditure may be on goods and services (including labour services) with a higher domestic content. However if the beneficiaries from public expenditure have a high marginal propensity to consumer imported goods the Balance of Payments will come under pressure as these people spend their increased income.

26.27. Cost Push Inflation

This is the term applied when the increase in selling prices results from increase in the price of factors of production for reasons other then excess demand. This may be illustrated through the example of wages. If workers are granted a wage increase, costs of production are increased and prices are likely to increase — not only because costs have increased but also because sellers are aware that workers have increased purchasing power which enables them to pay the increased prices. If prices are increased, the real income of workers is reduced and they seek to have their real income restored by further wage increases and the cycle commences again.

26.28. Imported Inflation

Suppose a country has a lower rate of inflation than that which is being experienced by its foreign trading partners. The theory here is as follows:

(i)   Because the inflation rate in country A is lower than than which pertains in its trading partners, its goods will be very competitive in foreign markets leading to a Balance of Payments surplus. The consequent inflow of money into country A will increase the level of demand in that country and that this will continue until such time as the price level is the same in each of the countries.

(ii) Also insofar as certain raw materials have to be imported, their costs will have risen relative to domestic costs which will cause an increase in the selling prices of the articles using these new materials. Both of these examples imply fixed exchange rates for foreign currencies and, in respect of example (i), that there are not unemployed resources which can be utilised to satisfy the increased demand by increasing supply rather than by increasing prices.

26.29. Expectations

Even after the initial causes of inflation have been removed, people's expectations may cause the inflationary process to continue. When people have become used to prices increasing, they build this sort of expectation into all contracts which are due for fulfilment at future dates, e.g., if workers are negotiating a real increase in wages of 5% and from past experience expect an inflationary rate of 10% during the period involved they will seek a money wage increase of 15.5% (i.e. a real increase of 5%, 10% to allow for inflation + 5% of expected price increase of 10%). Similarly potential purchasers may not be deterred by high prices because they may be of the opinion that prices will be even higher in the future.

The problems which this attitude imposes on attempts to eliminate inflation could be overcome by indexation (i.e., expressing prices in constant terms). By this strategy it may be possible to control inflation and also avoid the recession which might be necessary while expectations are slowly and painfully adjusted from inflation to normality.

26.30. Effect of Taxation of Inflation

The Constant-Tax Price Index

Taxation also contributes to the inflationary process. The effects of indirect taxation, e.g., V.A.T. on the price level is immediate and obvious. Direct taxation, e.g., income tax, will have an effect also if workers negotiate wage agreements on the basis of "take home pay in real terms". Surrounded by inflationary forces, workers are likely to be very conscious of the purchasing power of their earning and thus are likely to see their income in terms of take home pay in real terms, i.e. they are unlikely to suffer from money illusions. However the points made in Section 26.13 on the Constant-Tax Price Index are relevant here.

26.31. Mark-Up Inflation

Seeking a Constant Percentage Mark-up

If transactors, who determine prices by adding a certain percentage margin to costs in order to recoup general overheads and a satisfactory level of profits, seek during a period of rising prices to enjoy a constant percentage mark-up this will add to the inflationary process. Similarly if a tax was imposed on all inputs then a producer, who adds 25% to his costs in order to determine his selling price, would be earning a profit on the tax which he is paying.

26.32. Summary of Effects of Inflation

1. Consumption is stimulated.
2. Savings are affected — real rates of interest may be negative.
3. Redistribution of income from lenders to borrowers.
4. Those on fixed money incomes lose.
5. Burden of National Debt is lessened.
6. Tax Revenue increases if there is no indexation.
7. Movement out of Nominal Assets into Real Assets — Hedging.
8. Cash Flow Problems.
9. Implication for International Competitiveness.

QUESTIONS

Q1. Explain how the Consumer Price Index is compiled.

Q2. Are changes in the Consumer Price Index an accurate measure of alterations in the cost of living?

Q3. "Rising prices have no adverse effects because workers get wage increases to compensate them for the price increases." Give your views on this comment.

Q4. Write an explanatory note on the Constant-Tax Price Index.

Q5. State, giving reasons whether you consider the Consumer Price Index or the Constant-Tax Price Index to be the more appropriate index for use in wage negotiations.

Q6. Analyse some of the economic effects of inflation.

27 National Income

27.1. The manner in which payment to each of the factors of production is determined is analysed in micro economics. Putting it another way we can say that we analysed the manner in which the total income in the community, i.e., National Income, is divided among providers of factors of production. At this stage it is appropriate to consider National Income in a macro economic context and examine the interrelationship between the various elements in National Statistics.

27.2. Definition of some terms used in National Accounting

National income

(a) *National Income is defined as the income which accrues to the permanent residents of the country from current economic activity in the production of goods and services during a specified period which is usually one year.* It does not matter in what country the economic activity takes place provided that the income is received in Ireland.

Net National Product

(b) *Net National Product at Factor Cost is the total of all payments for productive services accruing to the permanent residents of a country. It is equivalent to National Income.*

Gross Domestic Product at Factor Cost

(c) *Gross Domestic Product at Factor Cost is the output produced by factors of production in the domestic economy irrespective of whether the factors of production are owned by Irish people or foreigners. It is equal to Net Domestic Product plus provision for depreciation. The relationship between Gross Domestic Product and Gross National Product is set out in sect. 27.4.*

(d) *Gross National Product at Factor Cost* is equal to *Net National Product* (National Income) plus provision for depreciation.

Gross National Product at Current Market Prices

(e) *Gross National Product at Current Market Prices* is equal to *Gross National Product* at *Factor Cost* plus taxes on expenditure less subsidies. It represents total expenditure on the output of goods and services of the national economy valued at the prices paid for the goods and services. *GNP at Current Market Prices is defined as the value, at current market prices, of the goods and services produced in the economy in a specified period – usually one year.*

27.3. Relationship Between National Accounting Terms

	1988 £ million
Net Domestic Product at Factor Cost (Net Domestic Income)	17026
Net Factor Income from rest of the world	-2542
Net National Product at Factor Cost (i.e. National Income)	14484
Plus Provision for Depreciation	2004
Gross National Product at Factor Cost	16488
Plus Taxes on Expenditure	3932
Minus Subsidies	-1636
	2296
Gross National Product at Current Market Prices	18784

27.4. Relationship Between "Domestic" And "National"

"Domestic" plus net income from abroad equals "National"

Most of the concepts mentioned in the previous section may be discussed in "Domestic" or "National" terms, e.g., Gross *Domestic* Product at Factor Cost and Gross *National* Product at Factor Cost. These two concepts are related through Net Factor Income from the rest of the world, e.g., GDP at Factor Cost + Net Factor Income from the rest of the world = GNP at Factor Cost.

A similar relationship holds between Net *Domestic* Product and Net *National* Product, etc.

GNP more commonly used

27.5. Students are sometimes surprised at the concentration on Gross National Product rather than Net National Product because they see the latter concept as being more meaningful in that it allows for capital depreciation, i.e., the capital which has been used up in creating wealth. However, it should be noted that the amount listed by most firms as depreciation is the amount allowed for income tax purposes. Since this depreciation may not accurately represent the actual wearing out of capital, the gross rather than net figure is considered to be more meaningful and accordingly is more commonly used.

27.6. The payments to each of the factors of production — rent, wages, interest and profit is the income which suppliers of factors of production receive. The following example shows that this income to factors of production also constitutes the *value of output*.

Example 27.6.

	£
Wages and Salaries	500,000
Rent	50,000
Interest Paid	150,000
Profit	100,000

Total Income Received by Factors of Production =
Total Output = Total Expenditure = £800,000

The expenditure in purchasing the firm's output constitutes income for the firm

The firm in this example did not have to purchase raw material. If a firm does have to purchase materials from other firms, in doing so it is providing income to the factors of production in the other firm and the same principle applies. Perhaps the output of the firm in Example 27.6 constitutes the raw materials for another firm, say Firm A — this merely complicates the example without changing any of the principles. The income which Firm A receives is distributed in a manner similar to that shown in the example.

The monetary value of output is the price paid for it

27.7. The value of the output of the firm (and thus the income paid to the factors of production) depends upon the price which purchasers are prepared to pay for it. In Example 27.6, if purchasers had been prepared to pay only £600,000, then then output of the firm would be £600,000. Conversely, if the purchasers had offered higher prices (perhaps because of a rumour of a likely scarcity), the output of the firm would have been equal to (say) one million pounds. Thus it will be realised that the monetary value of the output is what people pay for it.

In all of these circumstances, Value of firm's Output = Value of Expenditure of those buying the firm's output which in turn creates income for those factors of production which the firm employs.

Three methods of calculating National income

27.8. *Therefore National Income = National Expenditure = National Output*

27.9. The Central Statistics Office in calculating National Income uses each of the above approaches, viz.

(a) **Income method** — adding together all the income received in the economy.

(b) **Expenditure method** — the total expenditure in the economy, i.e. National Expenditure.

(c) **Output method** — the total value of goods produced, i.e., National Output.

In practice it is difficult to calculate accurately the value of National Income but, by using each of the above methods, cross checks are available and greater accuracy is achieved.

27.10. The Income Method of Calculation (National Income)

Source of information

This is the calculation of National Income by adding together the income received by all of the people in the economy for factors of production which they supplied during the year.

Information in respect of the non-agricultural sector is obtained from income tax returns. Information regarding income earned in the agricultural sector is obtained from the annual Agricultural Enumeration and the annual estimates of Agricultural Output which are published in the *Irish Statistical Bulletin* and the *Statistical Abstract*.

Table 27.10. Income Method of Calculating National Income.

Description	1982	1983	1984	1985	1986	1987	1988[1]
Income from agriculture, forestry, fishing	**1,122.8**	**1,285**	**1,513.7**	**1,397.5**	**1,326.9**	**1,597**	**1,870**
1. Income from self-employment and other trading income	1,018.0	1,170.8	1,389.3	1,261.3	1,185.2	1,447	1,710
Remuneration of employees:							
2. Wages and salaries	94.4	103.1	111.2	121.5	126.3	134	142
3. Employers' contribution to social insurance	10.4	11.7	13.2	14.7	15.4	16	17
Non-Agricultural income	**9,880.9**	**10,867.5**	**12,184**	**13,543.2**	**14,396.9**	**15,167**	**16,006**
Profits, professional earnings, interest, dividends and income from lands and buildings:							
4. Trading profits of companies (including corporate bodies) before tax[2]	1,520.8	1,820.6	2,360.0	2,764.2	3,040.7	3,412	4,799
5. Income of Post Office and Post Office Savings Bank	60.2	71.1					
6. Other trading profits, professional earnings etc.	896.2	902.9	872.9	936.7	964.3	984	
7. Adjustment for stock appreciation	-257.8	-312.3	-187.9	90.4	49.7	-129	-55
8. Rent of dwellings (actual and imputed)	208.8	240.1	267.6	333.1	347.7	323	331
9. Rent element in land annuities	5.9	6.2	6.3	6.2	6.1	6	6
Remuneration of employees.							
10. Wages, salaries, pensions	6,988.8	7,620.9	8,284.4	8,784.5	9,329.7	9,886	10,215
11. Employers' contribution to social insurance	458.0	518.0	581.6	628.1	658.7	685	710
Adjustment:							
12. Adjustment for financial services	-555.3	-675.4	-735.1	-807.0	-840.4	-853	-850
13. Net domestic product at factor cost	**10,448.4**	**11,477.7**	**12,963.4**	**14,133.7**	**14,883.4**	**15,911**	**17,026**
14. Net factor income from the rest of the world	-927.7	-1,183.9	-1,638.8	-1,965.7	-1,957.0	-1,957	-2,542
15. Net national product at factor cost = National income	9,520.7	10,293.8	11,324.6	12,168.0	12,926.4	13,954	14,484

[1] Preliminary
[2] The trading profits of An Post, Bord Telecom Eireann and the Post Office Savings Bank are included in item 4 from 1984.

Source: National Income and Expenditure 1988 (C.S.O.)

Some Notes on Table 27.10.

1. **Adjustment for Stock Appreciation**
   When the price level rises the value of stock increases and this results in extra profit being earned when the stock is sold. This extra profit does not arise from production and therefore it must be deducted from total profits which are listed as Items 1 and 4 in able 27.10 — remember we are calculating the income from current economic activity — see definitions in Section 27.1 if you are in doubt on this matter.

2. **Adjustment for Financial Services**
   This represents the excess of interest and dividends received by financial institutions over the interest payments which they made to those who deposited funds with them.

3. **Net Factor Income from the Rest of the World**
   Factor income means income earned by (paid to) factors of production. Some income is received in this country due to Irish factors of production working abroad. Some example of these types of earnings are:—

   (a) ESB personnel working overseas on a consultancy basis and the profit on the contract is sent back to/received in Ireland.
   (b) A foreign subsidiary of an Irish firm makes a profit which is returned to Ireland.
   (c) Aer Lingus planes are hired by foreign airlines.

   On the other hand foreign owned factors of production employed in Ireland earn income which is repatriated to the foreign country. Some examples of these are:

   (a) Profits earned by foreign companies on their Irish operation.
   (b) Interest payments on foreign loans.

Net Factor Income from the rest of the world is a net figure being the difference between earnings of Irish factors of production in other countries which are sent (brought) back to this country and income earned in Ireland by foreign factors of production and sent back to their own country. Up to the mid 1970's Net Factor Income from abroad invariably resulted in a net inflow into this country due mainly to interest earned on our foreign assets and emigrants' remittances while at the same time there were no significant outflows of funds. Net Factor Income from abroad has constituted a net outflow of funds in recent years (e.g. —£2542 million in 1988. The outflow of interest payments on our National Debt is one of the elements of this outflow of funds while the repatriation of profits by foreign firms amounted to 102% of GNP in 1988. (See Fig 27.10). *Thus National Income is lower than income earned through domestic production.*

Fig. 27.10 Profit Repatriation by Irish Based Foreign Owned Firms

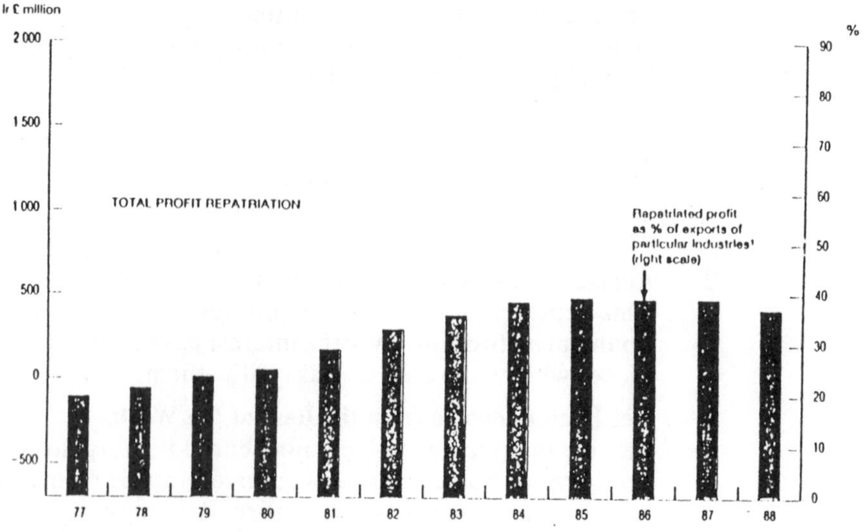

Ir £ million   %

TOTAL PROFIT REPATRIATION

Repatriated profit
as % of exports of
particular Industries[1]
(right scale)

1.   Exports of industries in which foreign firms account for the majority of production. See table 2 for the definition.
Note: See technical annex notes for a discussion of the underlying estimation equation.
Source: OECD.

27.11. Transfer Payments

(a)   Within the Private Sector

Transfer payments between individuals

In calculating national income allowances must be made in respect of income which people receive but for which they did not supply goods and services. I may make an allowance each week to an aged relative or to one of my children simply out of affection and not because they are providing me with goods or services. Transactions of this nature are gifts rather than payments for work done and are known as *transfer payments.* If my income is £1,000 per annum and I give my only son pocket money of £50 per annum the total income of our household remains at £1,000. If however my son works for me and I pay him £250, provided this payment is suitably recorded, it would be included in National Income because it is payment in return for work done.

(b)   From the State to the Private Sector

Transfer payments by the State

Similarly households may receive income from transfer payments made by the State. These are the various payments made by the State to individuals for reasons other than work done, e.g., student grants, children's allowances, non-contributory old age pensions, etc.

These payments are financed by tax payments of income earners and having regard to the definition of National Income, i.e., "income from current economic activity", such transfer payments must not be included in total income in the compilation of National Income.

Definition

27.12. The Expenditure Method of Calculation (National Expenditure)

DEFINITION:

National Expenditure is the total amount spent on consumer goods and services and on net additions to capital goods and stocks produced in the country in the course of a year.

Table 27.12. Expenditure Method of Calculating Gross National Product.

Description	1982	1983	1984	1985	1986	1987	1988[1]
55. Personal expenditure on consumers' goods and services	8,001.0	8,813.8	9,589.8	10,414.6	11,101.8	11,686	12,350
56. Net expenditure by public authorities on current goods and services	2,646.2	2,857.3	3,066.6	3,295.2	3,526.8	3,571	3,551
57. Gross domestic fixed capital formation	3,531.0	3,414.4	3,543.8	3,400.7	3,419.3	3,394	3,528
58. Value of physical changes in stocks	185.3	106.2	274.4	211.8	146.1	20	-71
59. Exports of goods and services[2]	6,433.3	7,751.6	9,770.0	10,738.4	10,351.5	11,785	13,533
60. less Imports of goods and services[2]	-7,414.5	-8,164.2	-9,815.1	-10,396.6	-9,860.4	-10,468	-11,565
61. Gross domestic product at market prices	13,382.3	14,779.2	16,429.6	17,664.1	18,685.1	19,989	21,326
62. Net factor income from the rest of the world	-927.7	-1,183.9	-1,638.8	-1,965.7	-1,957.0	-1,957	-2,542
63. Gross national product at current market prices	12,454.6	13,595.3	14,790.8	15,698.4	16,728.1	18,032	18,784

[1] Preliminary
[2] Excluding factor income flows

Source: National Income and Expenditure (1988) C.S.O.

EXPLANATION OF SOME CATEGORIES IN TABLE 27.12:

Item 1 – is more or less self explanatory in that it refers to normal consumption expenditure on goods and services, e.g., food, clothing and entertainment. It includes the purchase of durable goods such as private motor cars, furniture, washing machines etc. However, it does not include the purchase of capital goods, e.g., a dwelling house. Because a house lasts and provides its services over a considerable number of years it is considered to be an investment and a rent is imputed (see Section 27.15.4 (a)) to represent the payment for the current services derived from the house. The imputed value of the current services derived from the house is considered to be the expenditure on the services derived from the house in the year in question.

Item 2 – refers to payments by the State in respect of the salaries of teachers, gardaí and the civil service together with the purchase by the State of items such as stationery, electricity, etc.

Item 3 – includes expenditure on building and construction and other home produced capital goods.

Item 4 – this represents the estimated value of changes in the number of livestock on farms together with the physical increase in non-agricultural stock and work in progress during the year in question.

27.13. In calculating National Income through the expenditure method we include only those items of expenditure which create income within the economy. Therefore allowances must be made for the effects of international trade, taxation and subsidies.

Allowances required in the calculation of National Expenditure

(a) **The Effects of International Trade**

Exports create income in this country though they do not represent expenditure by people in our country. Conversely imports represent expenditure by people within the country which does not generate income within the country. Thus expenditure on imports must be deducted from, and expenditure by foreigners on our exports must be added to, National Expenditure in the calculation of National Income.

(b) **Taxation/Subsidies**

The price at which output is sold often includes indirect taxation such as value added tax. As indirect tax does not represent payment for a factor of production it is not part of National Income. Therefore indirect taxes must be deducted from National Expenditure in the calculation of National Income.

Subsidies, on the other hand, are the opposite to indirect taxes. They constitute a reduction of the selling price below its factor cost and therefore must be added to National Expenditure in the calculation of National Income.

(c) **Expenditure on the Purchase of Second-Hand Goods**
*The purchase of second-hand goods is not included in the calculation of
National Output.* If the good was produced in the year under review
it would have been included in National Output. The purchase of a
second-hand good is considered as the *exchange* of assets between
the purchaser and the seller rather than payment for wealth created
in the year in question — if its original purchase was in the same
year, then its value would have been included already.

27.14. *National Output is the total output of consumer (or final) goods and
services in a specified period which is usually one year.*
This is equal to the value added by each firm.

Table 27.14. Output Method of Calculating Gross National Product.

Description	1982	1983	1984	1985	1986	1987	1988[1]
			£ million				
16. Agriculture, forestry and fishing							
Remuneration of employees	104.8	114.7	124.4	136.2	141.7	150	159
Other	1,023.9	1,177.0	1,395.6	1,267.5	1,191.3	1,453	1,716
17. Industry							
Remuneration of employees	2,907.4	3,101.5	3,303.7	3,454.0	3,598.0	3,741	6,638
Other	1,278.4	1,554.2	1,832.8	2,100.6	2,130.0	2,479	
18. Distribution, transport and communication							
Remuneration of employees	1,272.6	1,398.1	1,526.4	1,612.5	1,713.0	1,802	2,940
Other	727.3	703.6	723.6	851.5	959.4	1,025	
19. Public administration and defence							
Remuneration of employees	848.9	908.4	1,005.2	1,079.7	1,168.9	1,190	1,221
20. Other domestic (including rent)							
Remuneration of employees	2,417.9	2,731.0	3,030.6	3,266.5	3,508.5	3,838	5,256
Other	680.3	776.9	944.1	1,081.9	1,263.3	1,215	
21. Adjustment for stock appreciation	-257.8	-312.3	-187.9	90.4	49.7	-129	-55
Industry	-148.5	-192.0	-110.4	103.0	116.5	-66	-104
Distribution	-109.3	-120.3	-77.5	-12.6	-66.8	-63	49
22. Adjustment for financial services	-555.3	-675.4	-735.1	-807.0	-840.4	-853	-850
23. Net domestic product at factor cost	**10,448.4**	**11,477.7**	**12,963.4**	**14,133.7**	**14,883.4**	15,911	**17,026**
24. plus Provision for depreciation	1,366.3	1,528.3	1,592.5	1,713.5	1,813.9	1,925	2,004
Agriculture, forestry and fishing	257.3	278.3	294.1	304.4	312.7	321	331
Industry	312.3	347.1	344.9	363.7	380.4	431	456
Distribution, transport and communication	233.4	256.4	274.9	314.4	357.4	395	416
Other domestic	563.3	646.5	678.6	731.0	763.4	777	801
25. Gross domestic product at factor cost	**11,814.7**	**13,006.0**	**14,556.0**	**15,847.1**	**16,697.2**	17,836	**19,030**
26. plus Taxes on expenditure	2,423.2	2,794.4	3,113.5	3,269.6	3,475.2	3,674	3,932
27. less Subsidies	-855.5	-1,021.2	-1,239.9	-1,452.7	-1,487.4	-1,520	-1,636
28. Gross domestic product at current market prices	**13,382.3**	**14,779.2**	**16,429.6**	17,664.1	**18,685.1**	19,989	21,326
29. Net factor income from the rest of the world	-927.7	-1,183.9	-1,638.8	-1,965.7	-1,957.0	-1,957	-2,542
30. Gross national product at current market prices	**12,454.16**	**13,595.3**	**14,790.8**	**15,698.4**	**16,728.1**	**18,032**	**18,784**

[1] Preliminary

Source: National Income and Expenditure 1988. (C. S. O).

27.15. *In calculating National Output care must be exercised with respect to the following:*

(a)   **To avoid Double Counting**

You will notice that the definition of National Expenditure refers to expenditure on consumer (or final) goods and services. Thus care must be taken to avoid the double counting which would occur if expenditure on intermediate goods was included in the calculation of National Expenditure. The price paid for a new car will be included but it would *not* be correct to include, in addition to the purchase price of the car, the price which the car manufacturer paid to the tyre manufacturer for the tyres which were on the car since the price which the purchaser of the car paid included the price of the tyres.

A simple solution is to adopt the value added method of calculation, i.e., the wages, profits and other factor payments generated at each stage of economic activity. If each link in the production process includes only its value added content, i.e., the value of its output minus the value of intermediate goods which were purchased by the firm, then the total of all of these added values will be equal to expenditure on final goods and services. The value added by each firm is the value of its output minus the value of bought-in goods and services.

	Supplier of wood £	Electric Company £	Furniture Manufacture £	Furniture Shop £
Total Sales	150	90	400	600
Purchase of Raw Materials or Services —		—	Wood 150 Electricity for heating and power 20 170	Furniture 400 Electricity 70 470
Values added by firm	£150	£90	£230	£130

Table 27.15. Value added by each Firm.

The total output may be seen as the sales of the final product, i.e., £600 or the total of the value added at each stage of production, i.e., £150 + £90 + £230 + £130 = £600.

(b)   **Non-Market Economic Activities**

In calculating national statistics only goods and services for which payment is made are included. As a result of this, as an economy becomes more market oriented with the development of specialisation and division of labour, National Income, National Output and National Expenditure will increase even if the volume of goods and services produced remains unchanged. If Mr. Jones paints his own house and services his own car and Mr. Lynch does the same with his property none of these items appear in National Statistics. However, if Mr. Jones paints Mr. Lynch's house and Mr. Lynch services Mr. Jones's car and each pays the other for the work done and these transactions are recorded, then National Statistics are increased even though the volume of production remains unchanged.

As married women remain in employment outside the home and purchase for their families the household services which previously they (the married women) had provided then National Income will be increased even if the output of goods and services remains unchanged.

In addition the increase in the practice of "nixers" whereby individuals take on jobs outside their normal working hours leads to an understatement of National Income because such jobs are not recorded in order to avoid the payment of more tax on the earnings.

(c) **Government Services**

The government provides services which are (or could be) provided by the private sector, e.g., education, health, housing, security. Services of this nature provided by the State are included in National Statistics at cost price (because there is no selling price). In contrast to this when similar services are provided by the private sector they are included in National Statistics at their selling price and, since a profit is made on them, this selling price will be greater than the cost price.

(d) **Imputed Values:**

(a) *Housing* – If Mr. Kelly rents the house which he occupies, the rent which he pays constitutes income to the landlord. (For the purpose of this example we will not advert to any expenses for the upkeep of the premises which the landlord may have to pay out of the rent which he receives). If Mr. Kelly owns his own house his income is increased by an amount which corresponds to the rent which he would have had to pay for use of the house if he did not own it himself, i.e., an imputed rent. It is very probable that the imputed rent is lower than the market rent, in which case the higher the proportion of the housing stock which its owner occupied the greater the understatement of expenditure on housing in National Statistics.

(b) *Agricultural Produce Consumed by Farm Households* – In assessing agricultural income an amount is included to represent that portion of their own agricultural produce which farm households consume. The quantity concerned is valued at cost or "farm gate" prices. This method understates the market price of the goods, and farm gate prices would need to be approximately doubled in order to represent the price which would be paid for such produce at the retail level.

27.16. Some Applications of National Income Statistics

(a) As an indicator of alterations in the standard of living (or welfare) in the economy

Many of the problems associated with the compilation of National Income cancel out when comparing the National Income statistics of different years. Nevertheless great care must be exercised when using changes in National Income as an indicator of changes in the standard of living. This is illustrated by the points which follow.

(i)   Since National Income is expressed in money terms some allowance must be made for changes in the value of money. If the price level increases each unit of output would be shown at a higher monetary value, thus the same output of goods and services would represent a higher monetary value. Thus if output remains unchanged and the price level increased, GNP in money terms would have increased. To overcome this problem GNP is expressed in constant money terms, i.e., at constant prices in order to compare changes in the level of production of goods and services. For this reason in addition to National Statistics being expressed at current market prices, they are also expressed at the constant prices on a base year as shown in Table 27.16. This table may be compared with Table 27.12 which expressed the same information at current market prices.

Table 27.16 Index Numbers of Gross National Product and its Expenditure Constituents at Constant Market Prices (base 1985 = 100)

Description	1982	1983	1984	1985	1986	1987	1988
Personal expenditure on consumers' goods and services	94.6	95.4	96.4	100.0	102.5	105.1	108.4
Net expenditure by public authorities on current goods and services	99.4	99.1	98.4	100.0	102.4	98.5	94.3
Gross domestic physical capital formation	119.8	107.0	110.0	100.0	96.7	90.7	86.1
Exports of goods and services	72.9	80.5	93.8	100.0	102.9	116.7	126.88
Imports of goods and services	84.2	88.2	96.9	100.0	105.6	110.9	115.2
Gross domestic product at constant market prices	93.9	93.6	97.7	100.0	99.7	104.5	108.4
Gross national product at constant market prices	98.5	96.9	99.2	100.0	98.9	104.4	105.7
Value of gross national product at constant market prices, allowing for changes in terms of trade[1]	97.1	97.3	98.9	100.0	101.9	107.3	108.2

[1] Various methods can be used to adjust gross national product for changes in the terms of trade. In the method used here, the adjustment was obtained as the difference between the figure obtained by deflating the current value of exports of goods and services by an index of import prices and the value of exports of goods and services at 1985 (export) prices. Where the terms of trade for goods and services are better than in the base year the adjustment is positive. In years in which there is an improvement in the terms of trade the adjustment is larger than that in the preceding year, so that the increase in the availability of goods and services to the community is larger than the change in gross national product at constant prices.

Source: National Income and Expenditure 1988 (C.S.O.)

(ii)   If the population is increasing, there is likely to be an increase in National Income. Whether or not this represents an improvement in welfare is not obvious from a comparison of the magnitude of the National Income figures alone. *National Income per head of population (or average National Income) is a better indicator of changes in the standard of living than changes in total GNP or National Income.*

(iii) *However, GNP per head of population, or average national income may conceal the considerable variations which may exist in the Distribution of National Income.* Even if the level of National Income and the size of population were the same in two countries there might be a wide disparity in the general standard of living in each of the countries. In country A there might be a small number of extremely rich people while the majority are very poor (e.g., in some of the oil rich countries). In contrast to this, country B may have a relatively even distribution of National Income, most people being of the middle class with few extremely rich and few dying from malnutrition (e.g., Ireland).

(iv) *Changes in Working Conditions*
An increase in National Income may be due to longer journeys to work as towns and cities expand. Alternatively there may be a change in working hours. If the same level of National Income is enjoyed with shorter working hours then the standard of living has improved though merely comparing the figures for National Income would not illustrate this type of development. Similarly, actual working conditions may change.

(v)   As the economy becomes more *market oriented* and people purchase goods and services which previously they provided for themselves, then National Income will increase. If a married woman returns to work and pays someone to do her housework, both of these incomes will be included in National Income, but the net addition to goods and services is only the teaching services which the married woman is providing.

(vi) While the amount of government expenditure may remain constant, its nature may change. If the government cuts back on money spent on the provision of parks and roads in order to finance extra expenditure on security against some new threat, the general well-being of the community has been lowered.

(vii) Services provided by the State are included at cost price whereas the same services when provided by the private sector are included at selling price, e.g., education and medical facilities. As the State provides services which previously had been provided by the private sector then National Income is understated.

(b) As a means of comparing the standard of living in different countries.
When using National Income Statistics for this purpose the following
points must be borne in mind.

(i)   Each country expresses its National Income in its own currency
      (naturally). Thus when comparing the National Income in different
      countries, *the figures must be expressed in some common denomina-
      tion.* This conversion is usually by means of foreign exchange rates,
      even though it is generally recognised that exchange rate conversion
      is a less than perfect method of measuring the comparative
      purchasing power of different currencies. At best exchange rates
      equal the price of internationally traded goods and services.
      Relative exchange rates may bear little relationship to the prices of
      goods and services which do not enter into international trade and it
      is these non-internationally traded goods and services which form
      the greater part of national product in most developing countries.
      Services and agricultural products are generally priced at a lower
      rate than industrial output in less developed countries in comparison
      with the price of services and agricultural products in industrialised
      countries. This problem is aggravated by the fact that agriculture is
      often the most important sector of the economy in less developed
      countries. In these circumstances an exchange rate conversion
      method tends to exaggerate the real income differences between less
      developed and more developed countries.

Fig. 27.16 illustrates Gross Domestic Product per head in terms of the
volume of goods and services produced. Using volume as a means of
expressing the magnitude, and changes in the level of Gross Domestic
Produce overcomes the problems which have been discussed above.

Fig. 27.16 Gross domestic produce per head, volume

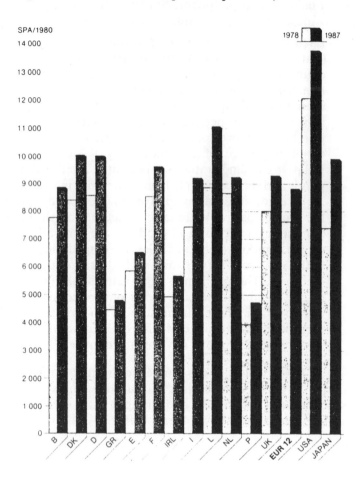

SPA/1980

1978 ☐ ■ 1987

Source: Eurostat.

(ii)   *Market Orientation*
The division of labour and specialisation may be practised more
extensively in some countries than in others. To the extent that
people provide services for themselves, National Income is understated. This may be particularly important in comparing the
National Income of less developed countries where market systems
may not be highly developed, with the National Income of countries
with strongly market-oriented economies. This caveat is important
in countries where there is a high degree of subsistence farming since
the output would be consumed by the producers without going
through the market system.

(iii) *The Nature of Government Expenditure*
The governments in country A and country B may spend the same amount of money. In country A the government may spend the money on parks, roads, libraries and various social amenities, whereas in country B the money may be spent on guards to combat vandalism which doesn't exist in country A.

(iv) *Different countries have different needs*
An Irish household will have to spend more on heating than a household in a warmer country. Similarly when the annual climate is subject to wide variations, housing and clothing will have to be geared towards both extremes.

(v) Where there is a high degree of owner occupied homes, because imputed rents tend to be lower than market rents, National Income will be understated.

(vi) Countries vary in the length of the working week, working conditions and the accuracy of National Statistics.

(vii) General living conditions such as road congestion, public transport system, etc., may vary between countries.

(c) To assist the government in formulating National Economic Policy
With the growth of Keynesian economics, the government has been exerting a greater influence on the development and growth of the economy. A prerequisite for effective planning is the availability of information about the economy such as is provided by accurate National Statistics.

(d) To assess macroeconomic changes in the economy and economic changes in the various sectors, and to provide a benchmark against which progress can be monitored.

QUESTIONS

Q1. Explain the relationship between Gross National Product at Factor Cost, National Income and Gross National Product at Market Prices.

Q2. Explain the main elements involved in measuring National Income by Income and Output methods.

Q3. Write short notes on the following terms as they are used in National Accounting
(a) Transfer Payments.
(b) Stock Appreciation.
(c) Adjustment for Financial Services.

Q4. Set out some application of National Income Statistics.

Q5. GNP at Current Market Prices in Country A = £100 million GNP at Current Market.
Prices in Country B = $180 million. On foreign exchange markets £1 = $1.8.
Do these figures prove that the citizens of each of these countries enjoy a similar standard of living? Explain your answer.

Q6. Which of the following would constitute part of National Income.
(a) Value Added Tax.
(b) Earnings of an Irish band on tour in Europe.
(c) Provision for depreciation.
(d) Pension payments to retired civil servants.

28   The Determination of National Income

28.1. FACTORS WHICH INFLUENCE THE LEVEL OF NATIONAL INCOME

(a) The Stock of Factors of Production

The greater the stock of factors of production which is available the greater will be the level of output which the economy is capable of producing — and consequently the greater the potential level of National Income. The U.S.A. has a greater stock of factors of production than are available in Ireland and consequently the National Income of U.S.A. is greater than our level of National Income. In considering the stock of factors of production we must also consider their suitability for production, e.g.,

- How fertile is the land?

- Are natural resources such as water available?

- Is the climate conducive to work effort or is it too hot?

- Is the labour force trained and motivated towards economic effort?

- Is there an adequate supply of risk capital?

- Does entrepreneurial flair exist in the economy?

(b) The State of Technology

The state of technology in an economy has a very important bearing on the level of National Income. The state of technical knowledge and ability is considered to be the most important determinant in the growth of an economy. One of the main reasons for the economic resurgence of Germany despite its defeat in the second world war was the level of technical knowledge, ability and application available within the economy.

28.2. The points already discussed refer to the level of output and National Income of which an economy may be capable, i.e. the *potential level* of National Income when all the available factors of production are fully employed. There still remains the question of what determines the *actual level of output or the actual level of National Income*. A very important determinant of the actual level of output or national income is the economic climate prevailing at the time. The economic environment within which Irish firms must operate is influenced by international as well as domestic forces.

(a) The International Economic Climate

If foreign purchasers of Irish merchandise and services are experiencing economic buoyancy in their domestic market, this will stimulate their demand for our exports. On the other hand, buoyant international economic activity will increase the competitiveness for factors of production which Irish manufacturers must import. Since the international economic climate is outside our sphere of influence it is an exogenous variable.

(b) The Domestic Economic Climate

Government Influence

Whether or not the domestic economy is buoyant depends, as already stated, to a large extent on international economic development particularly having regard to the openness of our economy. However we cannot overlook the influence of domestic factors such as the level of taxation on profits and income which influences the level of domestic economic activity. If these are too high they will act as a disincentive to economic effort. Conversely, expansionary economic activity by the government together with grants and industrial incentives will stimulate the level of economic activity. It is sometimes argued that a reasonable level of unemployment benefits and social assistance may discourage effort and raise the wages which must be offered in order to encourage people to accept jobs.

28.3. *The level of demand for the goods and services which the economy is capable of producing is considered to be the most important factor in determining the actual level of economic activity since in the absence of productive constraints firms will produce what consumers are prepared to buy at economic prices.*

Assumptions for Model

28.4. At this initial stage of our analysis of the factors which determine the level of economic activity in the country, i.e., the level of GNP, we will make some simplifying assumptions — each of these assumptions will be relaxed as the analysis is developed.

These simplifying assumptions are:

(a)   That no trade takes place with other countries, i.e., it is a closed economy.

(b)   That there is no government sector, therefore there are no taxes or government expenditure.

(c)   That there is no saving by firms or individuals — all income is spent.

This means that the entire income which firms receive is distributed to suppliers of factors of production (as rent, wages, interest and profit) and that all householders spend all their income in each period. This concept is usually explained by means of the diagram illustrated in Figure 28.5 which is known as the Circular Flow of Income. *The Circular Flow of Income is the flow of receipts and expenditure between firms and households.*

28.5. Households receive payments for the supply of factors of production; under the assumptions we have made households spend all of this income in purchasing the output of domestic firms. The firms will continue to hire the fctors of production provided that they can sell their output. Thus the circle remains unbroken and the level of economic activity continues at its existing level. If we put figures on it, the following could be the situation. Firms produce £1,000 worth of goods — they pay workers £600, owners of land £100, lenders of capital £120 and have a profit of £180. If all of these people spend their entire income they are buying £600 + £100 + £120 + £180 = £1,000 worth of goods from firms, who then produce a further £1,000 worth of goods and the cycle continues at the same level.

It is important to note that the income which households receive depends upon (and in this model is equal to) the level of the production of firms, i.e., their output. In turn the production of firms depends upon (and in their model is equal to) the expenditure of households. For example, if the output of firms if £1,000, this sum becomes income to others when it is used to pay for the factors of production which the firm employed. Since it is assumed that there are no savings, the £1,000 which is received as income is used to purchase the goods which the firms produce. THUS OUTPUT = INCOME = EXPENDITURE.

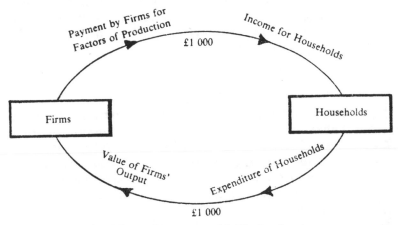

Fig. 28.5. Circular Flow of Income with No Leakages

28.6. The example may be enlarged by allowing for the possibility that people may save some of their income. Let us assume that people save 20% of their income, in which case when factors of production receive their payment of £1,000 as in the last example they spend only £800. In these circumstances there is no point in firms continuing to produce £1,000 worth of goods since their sales are limited to the £800 which people are prepared to spend. Thus firms gear their production to their sales and produce only £800 worth of goods. Now that the output of firms has been reduced to £800 the return to factors of production, and consequently the income of households, is reduced to £800. If firms continue to save 20% of their income, out of the income of £800 which they receive in one period they spend £640 in the following period.

This will cause a corresponding reduction in the output of firms (and income of households) to £640 and thus the level of activity continues to diminish.

Effect of Savings and Investment on the Circular Flow of Income

28.7. Is there any escape from this continually diminishing level of economic activity? Yes. If some people save it means that there are funds available for use by those who wish to spend, provided that they are willing and able to pay back the money they borrow together with the interest charge. Let us assume that people borrow the money saved and use it for investment purposes. The combined effect of savings and investment on the level of economic activity/circular flow of income is as follows:—

(a)   If the level of investment is equal to the level of savings then the level of economic activity will remain unchanged.

(b)   If the level of investment is less than the level of savings there will be a reduction in the level of economic activity.

(c)   If the level of investment is greater than the level of savings there will be an increase in the level of economic activity.

One of the means which makes it possible for the level of investment to be greater than the level of savings is the ability of banks to lend a multiple of the cash savings which are deposited with them as explained in Section 23.20.

Withdrawals and Injections

Since savings constitute a withdrawal from the Circular Flow of Income, they are often referred to as a *withdrawal or leakage. A leakage or withdrawal from the Circular Flow of Income occurs when some income is not spent on the purchase of domestic goods and services, i.e., is not passed on in the Circular Flow of Income.* Conversely, investment is often referred to as an *injection:* an injection is any addition to the Circular Flow of Income.

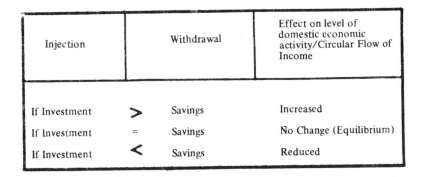

Injection	Withdrawal	Effect on level of domestic economic activity/Circular Flow of Income
If Investment > Savings		Increased
If Investment = Savings		No Change (Equilibrium)
If Investment < Savings		Reduced

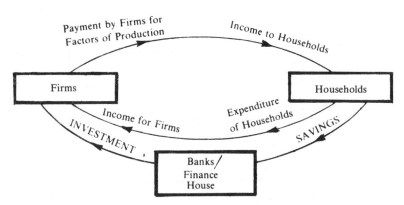

Fig. 28.7. Circular Flow of Income in a closed economy with savings and investment but no government sector.

28.8. EFFECT OF INTERNATIONAL TRADE ON CIRCULAR FLOW OF INCOME

Imports Reduce the Domestic Circular Flow of Income

We will now relax the assumption of a closed economy which has characterised our previous models of the circular flow of income though we will continue to assume that there is no government sector.

Money spent on purchasing imported goods constitutes a leakage from the Circular Flow of Income. When imports are purchased money is diverted away from domestic firms. For example, if £1,000 per week is paid by domestic firms to the households which supply the various factors of production and these households spend 30% of their income on imported goods, then domestic firms must reduce their level of output from the original figure of £1,000 to the level of production which they are capable of selling, i.e., £700 per week in this example. When the level of production by domestic firms is reduced to £700 per week the remuneration of factors of production will be reduced to £700. If households continue to spend 30% of their income on imported goods, out of their income of £700 their expenditure on domestic output will be £490. The output of firms as a consequence will be reduced to £490 in the subsequent week and so the diminution of domestic output and income continues.

28.9. It is due to this effect which the purchase of imported goods has on domestic income and employment that the government in the past introduced programmes to promote the sale of Irish goods, e.g., Guaranteed Irish campaign. (Such national campaigns are not allowed under EC rules.)If we don't support home industry by buying goods of Irish manufacture, there will be a deficiency in demandfor the output of Irish Industry with a consequent effect on employment opportunities. It makes good sense, where possible, to buy from your own customers because in that way you are ensuring that they will have sufficient income to enable them to continue to purchase the goods and services which you produce.

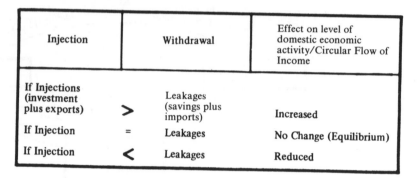

Injection	Withdrawal	Effect on level of domestic economic activity/Circular Flow of Income
If Injections (investment plus exports) >	Leakages (savings plus imports)	Increased
If Injection =	Leakages	No Change (Equilibrium)
If Injection <	Leakages	Reduced

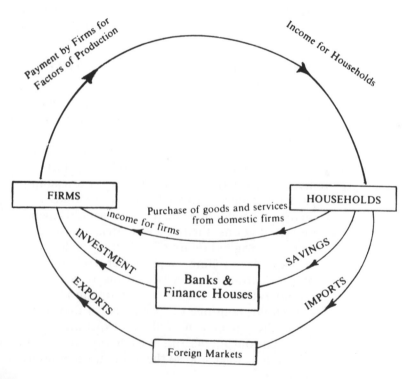

Fig. 28.9. Circular Flow of Income in an open economy with saving and investment and international trade but with no government sector.

28.10. Conversely, exports have the effect of increasing the level of demand for the products of Irish firms. Exports constitute a demand for domestic production. If there is an increase in exports there will be a consequent increase in demand for factors of production by Irish firms which will be reflected in an increased flow of income back to domestic households. There are certain industrial raw materials which must be imported since they cannot be produced by domestic firms, e.g., oil products. Exports may be seen as providing the foreign exchange which can be used for the purchase of essential imports of industrial raw materials.

Exports Stimulate the Domestic Economy

28.11. EFFECT OF GOVERNMENT ECONOMIC ACTIVITY ON THE CIRCULAR FLOW OF INCOME

The model discussed above may be made more realistic by introducing the effect of government economic activity into the circular flow of income. When the government imposes taxation it is reducing the disposable income of the general public which has the effect of reducing the disposable Circular Flow of Income of the private sector. Conversely, when the government spends money it is injecting purchasing power into, and consequently enlarging, the Circular Flow of Income.

Taxation and Government Expenditure

28.12. DISPOSABLE INCOME AND DISCRETIONARY INCOME

As the term implies *Disposable Income* is defined as the amount of money which a person has at his disposal. It is gross income minus compulsory deductions from income such as income tax and social welfare payments. *Discretionary Income* is another term which is often employed. Discretionary income tends to be used to indicate income against which there are no commitments and therefore may be spent according to whim. A single person and a married person may have the same amount of disposable income but the married person may have more commitments in terms of mortgage repayments, school fees for children, etc. In which case even though they both may have the same amount of disposable income, the single person would have a greater discretionary income. The highest ratio of discretionary income to disposable income is probably enjoyed by teenagers which is one reason why so much advertising is directed towards this age group.

High Ratio of Discretionary Income enjoyed by Teenagers

28.13. To return to the point made in Section 28.11, taxation, since it reduces the disposable income of households, reduces the amount which they can spend and thus constitutes a leakage from the Circular Flow of

Income. However, this taxation enables the government to purchase goods and services from domestic firms which is an injection into the Circular Flow of Income.Thus, whether or not government activity increases or decreases the Circular Flow of Income depends upon the relationship between government revenue and government expenditure. If government revenue is in excess of government expenditure there is a net leakage through government activity and the Circular Flow of Income is lower than it would have been in the absence of government economic activity.

Thus the aggregated model which includes government economic activity is as shown below.

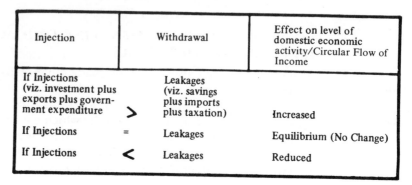

Injection	Withdrawal	Effect on level of domestic economic activity/Circular Flow of Income
If Injections (viz. investment plus exports plus government expenditure >	Leakages (viz. savings plus imports plus taxation)	Increased
If Injections =	Leakages	Equilibrium (No Change)
If Injections <	Leakages	Reduced

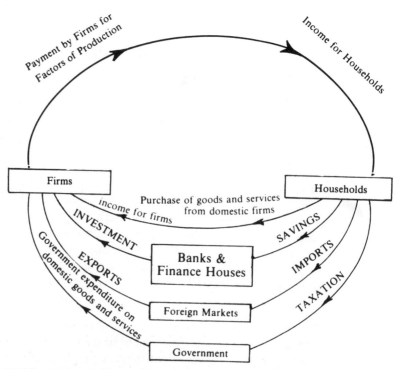

Fig. 28.13. Circular Flow of Income with foreign trade and government sector

*Marginal
Propensity
to Consume
and Marginal
Propensity
to Save*

28.14. Let us return to the simplest form of Circular Flow of Income in which there is no international trade and government sector — the only form of injection is investment and the only form of leakage is savings. This is illustrated in Fig. 28.7. Let us assume further that people spend 80%, i.e., 0.8 of each additional pound they receive, i.e., their Marginal Propensity to Consume is 0.8. The Marginal Propensity to Consume (MPC) is that proportion of each additional pound which is spent (or the proportion of the last pound of income which is spent). In this simple model all income received is either spent on domestic goods (or services) or it is saved. If the MPC is 0.8 then obviously the proportion of the last (additional) pound which is saved is 0.2, i.e., the Marginal Propensity to Save is 0.2 derived from 1 — MPC = MPS.

Example 28.14 (a)

		Income	Saving
		£	£
Stage 1	The £1 which is spent on investment in the domestic market provides an income to domestic suppliers of goods and services of	1,000,000	Zero
Stage 2	The people who receive the £1m have a Marginal Propensity to consume of 0.8 so that their spending in the domestic economy provides an income to others in the domestic economy of	800,000	
	The difference between income £1m and spending of 0.8m is savings		200,000
Stage 3	The people who receive the £800,000 have a MPC of 0.8 so their spending in the domestic economy provides income to others in the domestic economy of	640,000	
	Income of £800,000 — spending of £640,000 provides savings of		160,000
Stage 4	Next Stage	512,000	
	MPS of 0.2 out of income from previous stage of 640,000		128,000
Stage 5	Next Stage	409,600	102,400
	etc. etc.	— —	— —
At new equilibrium	Increase in Income	5,000,000	
	Increase on Savings		1,000,000

If you continue with this example through all of the stages you will find that there is an *increase* in the level of income of £5m. arising from the increased injection (investment) of £1m. Savings increased by £1m, which is equal to the increased injection (investment).

Example (b)

If you carry out a similar exercise with an injection of £1m and a MPC of 0.75 you will find that the total increase in income stemming from the original injection is £4m. While savings increase by £1m as before so that at equilibrium the increase in leakages (savings) is equal to the increase in injections (investment).

Example (c)

With an MPC of 0.5, the total effect of an increase in investment of £1m would be £2m. While savings once more increase by £1m as in the previous example, at equilibrium, so that the increase in leakages (savings) is again equal to the increase in injections (investment).

28.15. THE MULTIPLIER

Multiplier Formula

From the examples in the foregoing section it will be realised that the total income effect of an increase in investment (or any other form of injection) depends upon that proportion of their additional income which people spend, i.e., their marginal propensity to consume (MPC). In fact there exists a precise relationship between the initial injection and the eventual total increase in income resulting from the injection. This relationship which is known as THE MULTIPLIER is expressed as follows:—

$$\text{Multiplier Effect} = \frac{1}{1 - \text{MPC}} \times \text{Original Injection}$$

where MPC is the marginal propensity to consume.

In Example 28.14 (a) MPC = 0.8
Therefore the Multiplier Effect

$$= \frac{1}{1 - 0.8} \times \text{Original Injection}$$

$$= \frac{1}{0.2} \times £1 \text{ million}$$

$$= £5 \text{ million}$$

In Example 28.14 (b) MPC = 0.75
Therefore the Multiplier Effect

$$= \frac{1}{1 - 0.75} \times \text{Original Injection}$$

$$= \frac{1}{0.25} \times £1 \text{ million}$$

$$= £4 \text{ million}$$

In example 28.14 (c) MPC = 0.5

Therefore the Multiplier Effect

$$= \frac{1}{1 - 0.5} \times \text{Original Injection}$$

$$= \frac{1}{0.5} \times \text{£1 million}$$

$$= \text{£2 million}$$

At equilibrium leakage is equal to injection

28.16. It should be noted from the various examples in Section 28.14 that in each case at the new equilibrium level of income the leakage (amount of savings) was equal to the amount of the injection (investment). In these examples, investment was increased by £1m. and savings increased by £1m. In every case the *multiplier effect will continue until the leakage is equal to the amount of the original injection.*

Definition of Multiplier

28.17. The multiplier is a concept developed by the famous economist, John Maynard Keynes, to define the total increase (decrease) in national income which results from a given increase (decrease) in expenditure. In Example 28.14 (a) from an initial injection of purchasing power of IR£1 million the total increase in national income was IR£5 million, therefore the multiplier was 5. In Example (b) the multiplier was 4 and in Example (c) the multiplier was 2.

Multiplier and MPS

28.18. It has already been shown in section 28.15 that 1 — MPC = MPS. Thus the multiplier which has been expressed as $\frac{1}{1 - MPC}$

in section 28.15 can be written as $\frac{1}{MPS}$

28.19. While the MPC is that proportion of *additional* income which is spent, the Average Propensity to Consume (APC) is that proportion of *total* income which is spent. Analogously Average Propensity to Save (APS) is that proportion of *total* income which is saved. In Table 28.19 in Period 1:

the APC is $\frac{2800}{3000} = 0.933$

the APS is $\frac{200}{3000} = 0.067$

Again 1 — APC $= APS$

1 — 0.933 $= 0.067$

APC+APS $= 0.933 + 0.067 = 1$

With an increase in investment of £100 between period 1 & period 2, income went up by £500 so obviously the multiplier was 5. This is proven by the fact that out of the increase in income of £500 consumption increased by £400 so the MPC is 0.8 giving a multiplier of 5. The MPS is 1 — MPC = 0.2 so that out of the increase in income of £500; £100 (i.e., £500 × 0.2) was the increase in savings and at the new equilibrium, leakages (savings) were again equal to injections (investments).

At the new equilibrium in Period 2 the APC is $\dfrac{3200}{3500}$ = 0.914 and

$$APS = \dfrac{300}{3500} = 0.086.$$

As a further check 1 — 0.914 = 0.086 or 0.914 + 0.086 = 1.

Table 28.19.

	Income	Consumption	Savings	Investment
Period 1	£3,000	£2,800	£200	£200
There is an increase in investment of £100 so new equilibrium is				
Period 2	£3,500	£3,200	£300	£300

Multiplier may Magnify a Deflationary Impulse

28.20. It should be noted that the multiplier also works in a deflationary manner. *If investment is reduced* by (say) £1 million or *if savings are increased* by (say) IR£1 million, then if the MPC = 0.8, this withdrawal would be subject to a multiplier of 5 and consequently there would be a total *reduction in purchasing power in the economy of £5 million. Similarly at the new (lower) equilibrium level the change (reduction) in leakages (savings) would be equal to the change (reduction) in injections (investment).*

Effect of International Trade on the Multiplier

28.21. In Sections 28.8 to 28.10 the influence of international trade on the circular flow of income was discussed. An increase in exports constitutes an injection into the Circular Flow of Income and the total effect on income of this injection will be magnified by the multiplier to an extent which depends upon the MPC. However, being involved in international trade is not a case of exports alone — we import goods also, which means that not all of our earnings from exports is spent on domestically produced goods. Some of this money will be saved and some of it will be spent on imports. *That proportion of additional income which is spent on imported goods is known as the Marginal Propensity to Import (MPM).* In Ireland the Marginal Propensity to Import is approx. 0.3 which is very large.

Example 28.21

FOREIGN TRADE MULTIPLIER

Marginal Prospensity to Consume (MPC) = 0.8
Therefore Marginal Propensity to Save (MPS) = 0.2
Assume Marginal Propensity to Import (MPM) = 0.3

	Consumption/ Income (in the domestic economy) £	Imports £	Savings £
Stage 1: Initial injection (increase in exports) is income to those who produced the goods	1,000,000	Zero	Zero
Stage 2: This income of £1m is received by people who have a MPC 0.8 so they spend £800,000 and save £200,000. However their MPM = 0.3 so £300,000 is spent on Imports with the remainder of the £800,000 (i.e., £500,000) being spent (and providing income) in the domestic economy	500,000	300,000	200,000
Stage 3: The income of £500,000 in the domestic economy is subject to a MPC of 0.8 so £400,000 is spent and £100,000 is saved. Of the £400,000 which is spent £150,000 is spent on imports so £250,000 is spent, and provides income, in the domestic economy	250,000	150,000	100,000
Stage 4: Of the income of £250,000	125,000	75,000	50,000
etc.	—	—	—
etc.	—	—	—
at Equilibrium	2,000,000	600,000	400,000

28.22. The Multiplier in example 28.21 is often referred to as the Foreign Trade Multiplier, the formula for which is:

$$\frac{1}{MPS + MPM}$$

which in example 28.21 is equal to $\dfrac{1}{0.2 + 0.3} = \dfrac{1}{0.5} = 2$

Therefore the initial injection of £1m results in an increase in income of £2m which you can verify by working example 28.21 through to the end.

28.23. With the increase in income of £2m. in example 28.21 the

*At equilibrium
increase in
injection
equals increase
in leakages*

Increase in Savings   = MPS × Increase in Income

                          = 0.2 × £2m

                          = £0.4m as shown in example 28.21.

Increase in Imports   = MPM × Increase in Income

                          = 0.3 × £2m

                          = £0.6m as shown in example 28.21.

Note particularly that at the new equilibrium (i.e., when the effects of the change has worked its way through the system) the increase in injections (exports) at £1m. is equal to the increase in leakage, i.e., Savings of £0.4m plus Imports of £0.6m.

*Deflationary
Multiplier*

28.24. Again it should be noted that the foreign trade multiplier may work in a deflationary manner analogous to that already discussed. If *the level of demand for exports falls,* or if *the demand for imports rises* relative to the demand for exports, then there will be an increase in withdrawals relative to injections and this *reduction* in domestic demand will be magnified by the Multiplier. Again at the new (lower) equilibrium level the change (reduction) in leakages would be equal to the change (reduction) in investments.

28.25. In Sections 28.11 to 28.13 the model of the Circular Flow of Income was extended to include the effect of government intervention on the level of economic activity. By now you should realise that government expenditure is an injection which is subject to the Multiplier, while taxation is a withdrawal (or leakage) and affects the magnitude of the Multiplier.

Example 28.25.

Let us assume that 25% of all income is taken in tax then the Marginal Propensity to Pay (or levy) Tax (MPT) is equal to 0.25. Now if £100m is injected into the economy (say through increase in exports) and MPC = 0.8 and MPM = 0.3.

		Consumption of Domestically Produced Goods and Services	Savings	Imports	Tax
	£m	£m	£m	£m	
Stage 1:	The £100m which is earned by our exports provides income in the domestic economy to suppliers of goods and services	100	—	—	—
Stage 2:	Of the £100m. — MPT = 0.25; MPM = 0.3 & MPS = 0.2	25	20	30	25
Stage 3:	Of the £25m which is spent and provides income in the domestic economy	6.25	5.0	7.5	6.25
	etc. etc.	etc.	etc.	etc.	etc.
	TOTAL	133.33	26.67	40.00	33.33

28.26. The Multiplier in the above example is

$$\frac{1}{MPS + MPM + MPT}$$

$$= \frac{1}{0.2 + 0.3 + 0.25} = \frac{1}{0.75} = 1.33$$

The increase in savings = Increase in Income × MPS

= £133.33m × 0.2

= £26.67m.

Increase in Imports = Increase in Income × MPM

= 133.33m × 0.3

= 40.00m.

$$\text{Increase in Taxation} = \text{Increase in Income} \times \text{MPT}$$
$$= £133.33\text{m} \times 0.25$$
$$= 33.33\text{m}.$$

Notice that the total of the leakages, i.e., Savings + Imports + Taxation = £100m. which was the amount of the original injection.

28.27. Paradox of Thrift

Higher MPC out of a lower level of income

The Paradox of Thrift draws attention to the fact that an increase in the Marginal Propensity to Save (MPS) can result in a reduction in the level of income while bringing about no increase in the actual level (pool) of savings. Thus the Paradox of Thrift highlights the facts which underlie some debates as to the relative virtues of spending and saving.

You will have noticed in previous section that

(i)   it is the receipt of income which enables an individual (economic agent) to save;

(ii)   people in spending provide income for others;

(iii) savings which are a leakage from the Circular Flow of Income diminish income and thus the capacity of people to save;

(iv)   in this way people could end up saving a higher proportion of a smaller income as the level of economic activity declines.

Example 28.27. Illustration of Paradox of Thrift

1st Case — Injection £100. MPS = 0.2   Multiplier = 5

Increase in Income £500   Increase in Savings £500 × 0.2 = £100

2nd Case— Injection £100. MPS = 0.4   Multiplier = 2.5

Increase in Income = £250   Increase in Savings = 250 × 0.4
= £100

Notice that the increase in income is smaller in the second case, while the level of savings hasn't increased despite the increase in the Marginal Propensity to Save.

In this case as usual we are assuming ceteris paribus, i.e. that everything else remains unchanged. In section 28.28 we will consider possible developments if there is an increase in the MPS.

28.28. Some Relevant Points in Considering the Paradox of Thrift

(a) **Is Investment independent of Level of Savings?**

While savings are a withdrawal from the Circular Flow of Income is it correct to assume that an increase in the level of savings does not affect the level of investment? If, when there is the initial increase in the level of savings, savers deposit them in interest earning assets rather than simply holding increased money balances then the increased pool of investible funds will put downward pressure on interest rates and this development will help stimulate investment.

(b) **Induced Demand for Capital Goods**

As shown in the Accelerator Theory (Section 29.20). An increased demand for capital goods induces a demand for other capital goods, e.g. an increased demand for machinery to produce clothing implies an increase in the demand for the machinery which produces the cloth making machinery.

(c) **Switch in Demand towards Capital Goods**

An increase in the MPS would alter the ratio of demand for (and production of) capital goods relative to consumer goods.

(d) **Change in Expectations**

If the drop in consumption (through an increase in the MPS) continued for a lengthy period so that producers were suffering a loss in demand, and if they expected this to continue, then the demand curve for investment funds would shift to the left. This means that the level of investment might not increase even if there was a reduction in the rate of interest.

(e) **International Trade Aspect**

If the economy in question engages in international trade and the increases in the MPS is not taking place in all countries then the Balance of Payments of the country in question could be improved. An increase in the MPS would remove any upward pressure on prices in the domestic economy thus enabling firms to be more competitive in international trade. At the same time the increased MPS would ensure the availability of investment funds to enable firms to expand to meet the increased business arising from improved international competitiveness.

QUESTIONS

Q1. Set out the factors which influence the level of National Income.

Q2. Write a note explaining the Circular Flow of Income in an open economy with a government sector.

Q3. Show the effect of international trade on the magnitude of the multiplier.

Q4. What would be the effect of an injection of £100m on the levels of savings, imports and tax revenue if the MPS = 0.15, MPM = 0.25 and MPT = 0.2.

Q5. Explain the Paradox of Thrift.

29   The Keynesian Approach to the Determination of National Income

Output is demand determined

29.1. Prior to Keynes there was a belief among economists that price flexibility in all markets would ensure that the economy achieved equilibrium at full employment. In 1936 "The General Theory of Employment, Interest and Money" by Keynes challenged the theory of the Classical Economists. He suggested that the level of output depends upon the level of demand, i.e., that output is demand determined and equilibrium may be at a level which does not constitute full employment of the factors of production.

Income is prime determinant of spending

29.2. Keynes hypothesised that the level of income is the main determinant of the level of demand and the marginal propensity to consume is less than unity, this means that a person's expenditure increases with his income but not to the full extent of the income increase — he will save some of it.

Government intervention

29.3. Keynes' exposition argued that the level of output (i.e., GNP) is demand determined, that equilibrium may be at less than full employment and that the level of income is the main determinant of spending (i.e., demand). This theory opened the way for the government to intervene in the economy with a view to influencing the level of economic activity — macroeconomic policy was born.

This Keynesian approach to the determination of National Income is the subject of the remainder of this chapter.

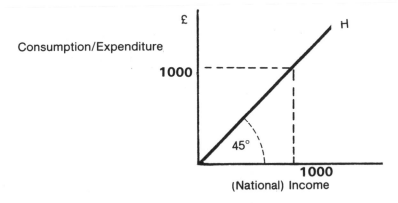

Fig. 29.4. Equilibrium Levels of Income — 45° Line.

*Equilibrium
level of
income*

29.4. Fig. 29.4 represents a closed economy. Consumption is shown on the vertical (or Y) axis and income is shown on the horizontal (or X) axis. The line H represents situations where all income is spent — if income is 2, expenditure is 2; if income is 3, expenditure is 3. Consequently the co-ordinates of this line H are 0, 0; 1, 1; 2, 2; 3, 3; etc. This line is known as the 45⁰ line, every point on this line represents an equilibrium level of National Income because if National Income/National Output is equal to consumption/expenditure, it means that all of output is being purchased, so that firms will continue to produce this existing level of output. This means that output is stabilised and therefore at equilibrium with all income being spent, and all output being consumed. This situation is identical to that depicted in Fig. 28.5 with reference to the Circular Flow of Income analysis where equilibrium is shown with all income being spent in the domestic economy.

45⁰ line /

*Circular flow
of income /*

Multiplier

29.5. It should be clearly understood that the 45⁰ diagrams which are used in this chapter are illustrating the same economic concepts as set out in the Circular Flow of Income diagrams in Chapter 28. Note also that the diagrams based on the 45⁰ line and consumption functions are a means of illustrating the Multiplier by means of diagrams.

29.6. The amount of money which a person spends depends on several factors, e.g. amount of saving/wealth, age, expectations etc. but generally speaking the most important factor affecting the level of consumption is the level of income — this does not mean that a person with no income is going to lie down and die, such a person may dip into past savings or take other action.

Marginal Propensity to Consume

$$(MPC) = \frac{\text{Change in Consumption}}{\text{Change in Income}}$$

Average Propensity to Consume

$$(APC) = \frac{\text{Total Consumption}}{\text{Total Income}}$$

Table 29.7. Income, Consumption & Savings

Income (Y) £m.	Consumption (C) £m.	Saving (S) (a minus indicates dissavings) £m.	Marginal Propensity to consume MPC	Average Propensity to consume APC
Zero	50	-50	-	-
100	130	-30	0.8	1.30
130	154	-24	0.8	1.18
200	210	-10	0.8	1.05
250	250	Zero	0.8	1.00
300	290	10	0.8	0.97
400	370	30	0.8	0.92
450	410	40	0.8	0.91
500	450	50	0.8	0.90
600	530	70	0.8	0.88

Some Points Illustrated by Table 29.7

1. £250 is the equilibrium level of income. When income is £250, all of this amount is consumed (spent), thus creating a demand for goods and services to the value of £250. In order to cater for this demand £250 of goods and services are produced which provides income of £250 to the suppliers of these goods and services. This income of £250 is spent and so the cycle repeats itself.

2. At equilibrium the APC = 1 as all increase is consumed (spent).

3. At levels of income lower than the equilibrium level (i.e., £250) consumption exceeds income, e.g. consumption of £130 out of income of £100. This consumption of £130 creates a demand for £130 of goods and services. Thus production is increased from the previous level of £100 to satisfy this demand for £130 of goods and services. Production of £130 of goods and services provides income of this amount to suppliers of factors of production and when income is £130 consumption is £154 so production expands to £154 and so the cycle continues with production expanding at levels of income below £250, i.e., if there is dissaving production expands.

4. At levels of income at which there is dissavings, APC is greater than 1 and the level of output expands.

5. When production is at the level of £500, income of this amount

accrues to the suppliers of factors of production. Out of this income of £500 consumption is £450 and thus the demand for goods and services is at £450. Production is set at this level in order to satisfy the demand (production beyond this amount wouldn't be sold) so that there is a reduction in the level of production from £500 to £450. Production of £450 provides income of this amount to suppliers of factors of production. Out of this income of £450 these people spend £410 as a result of which production is adjusted to this lower level of £410. So the cycle continues until production falls to the equilibrium level of £250.

6. When saving takes place APC is less than 1 and the level of output falls.

7. When MPC is less than APC then APC falls.

8. With an MPC of 0.8 — the multiplier is $\frac{1}{1-0.8} = 5$. Thus when consumption initially is 50 (an increase from zero in the previous period), the equilibrium level of income is £50 × 5 = £250.

9. The relationship between Income (Y) and consumption (C) which is shown in Table 29.7 is C = 50 + 0.8Y i.e., consumption of 50 when income is zero and an additional 0.8 is spent out of every increase in income.

29.8. All of Income has been either consumed (spent) (C) or saved (S). Therefore

$$Y = C + S$$

Consumption and savings functions

$$\text{or} \quad Y - C = S$$

In table 29.7. $\quad C = 50 + 0.8Y$

∴ in this case $\quad S = Y - (50 + 0.8Y)$

$$= -50 + 0.2Y$$

i.e., when there is no income there is dissavings of 50 and 0.2 is saved out of each £ received.

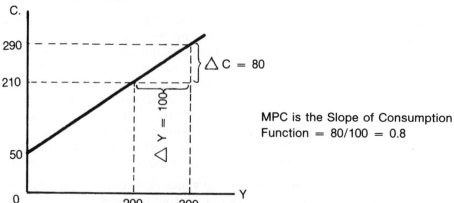

MPC is the Slope of Consumption Function = 80/100 = 0.8

Fig. 29.8 (A) Consumption Function drawn from data in Table 29.7.

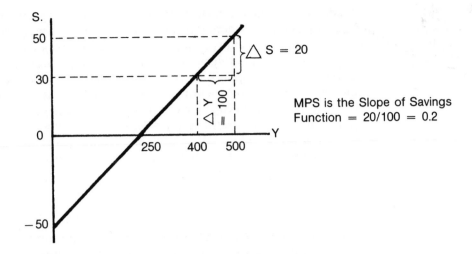

Fig. 29.8 (B) Savings Function drawn from data in Table 29.7.

*Equilibrium
level of
National
Income*

29.9. In Table 29.9 the Consumption Function based on the data in Table 29.7 is associated with the 45° line. At levels of income below £250 there is dissavings and at levels of income greater than £250 there are savings. The point at which the Consumption Function and the 45° line cross indicate the equilibrium level of income.

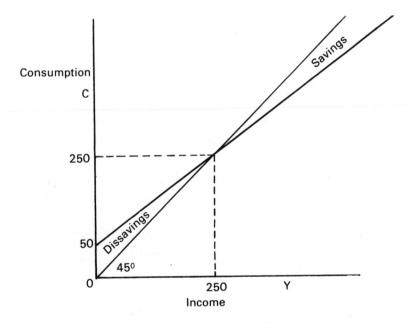

Fig. 29.9. Equilibrium Level of Income.

*Investment
increases
the
equilibrium
level of
(National)
Income*

29.10. As was shown in the previous chapter Investment constitutes an injection and consequently results in an increase in the level of (National) Income. If investment is equal to £15m then this results in production of capital goods and services to this value which provides that amount of income to the suppliers of the required factors of production. Thus income is created by spending on consumer goods and services (consumption) and spending on capital goods (investment). If Consumption (C) = £100m and Investment (I) = £15m then production to the value of £115m will take place to satisfy this demand, through the course of production income of this amount (£115m) is earned by the suppliers of factors of production, i.e.,

$$Y = C + I$$

This is shown by an upward shift of the Consumption Function to C + I as shown in Fig. 29.10. Notice that the equilibrium level of Income is greater as a result of the investment (from Y_1 to Y_2) and this development may be compared with section 28.7 where investment increased the Circular Flow of Income.

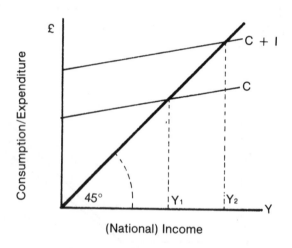

Fig. 29.10 Equilibrium level of (National) Income with inclusion of Investment

*Effect of
Government
economic
activity
on equilibrium
level of
income*

29.11. Similarly expenditure by the Government creates a demand for goods and services in the domestic economy and this provides income for the suppliers of the factors of production used in the production of these goods and services, i.e.,

$$Y = C + I + G.$$

Since the Government finances (some of) its expenditure through taxation whether or not the inclusion of Government economic activity results in an increase in the equilibrium level of National Income depends on whether Government expenditure is greater than its revenues (taxation)⋆. In the present context it is being assumed that Government expenditure is greater than its revenue (taxation) so that in fig. 29.10 C + I + G is shown corresponding to a higher equilibrium level of National Income (i.e. Y_3) than that corresponding to C + I (i.e., Y_2). This may be compared with the inclusion of Government economic activity in the Circular Flow of Income in Section 28.13.

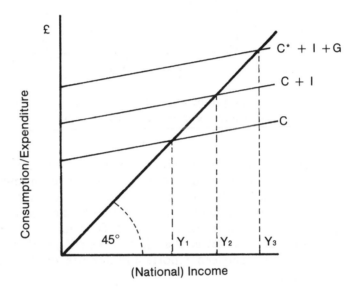

Fig. 29.11 Equilibrium Level of National Income with inclusion of Investment and government expenditure.

C⋆ — With the introduction of government a distinction must be drawn between the Marginal Propensity to Consume (MPC) gross income and after-tax income, e.g., if a person's gross income is £1,000 and he pays tax of £200 his after-tax income is £800. If he spends £600 his MPC out of gross income is 0.6 and his MPC out of net, or after-tax, income is 0.75.

Exports exceed imports

29.12. A demand for our goods and services in foreign lands (i.e., exports) provides income in the domestic economy for the suppliers of the factors of production which are used in producing the exports. Thus the demand for exports increases the equilibrium level of (National) Income. Conversely, our demand for imports constitutes money which does not provide income in the domestic economy and thus decreases the equilibrium level of (National) Income. Fig. 29.12 depicts a situation where exports exceed imports and thus the equilibrium level of (National) Income is increased to Y_4 as a result of International trade (M is the excess of exports over imports).

⋆More precisely it depends on the extent to which government expenditure is greater than what private expenditure would have been if tax payers had not had to pay taxes.

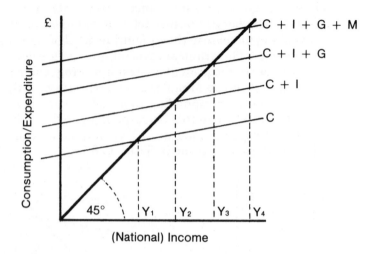

Fig. 29.12 Equilibrium Level of (National) Income with Investment, government expenditure and a surplus on International Trade.

Imports exceed exports

29.13. If imports exceed exports the net effect of international trade is that income flows out from the domestic economy and the demand for domestic goods and services is lower as a result of the trade. Thus the equilibrium level of (National) Income is reduced. This is shown in Fig. 29.13 where the equilibrium level of (National) Income with International trade at Y_4 is lower than it was (i.e., Y_3) without this trade. M is the difference between exports and imports and in this example would be negative.

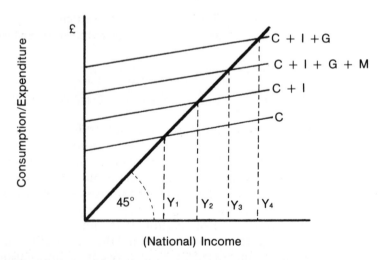

Fig. 29.13 Equilibrium Level of (National) Income with Investment, government expenditure and a deficit on International Trade. This may be compared with the effect of International Trade on the Circular Flow of Income in Section 28.9.

29.14. In example 29.7 the equilibrium level of output was £250 — it was self-sustaining in the sense that if (National) Income was at that level then under existing circumstances (MPC etc.) income would remain at that level. There has been no suggestion that this equilibrium is at a high or low level of economic activity, this is a point which we now address.

In Fig. 29.14 the equilibrium level of (National) Income is shown where the total level of Demand (C + I + G + M) crosses the 45⁰ line — let us say this corresponds to a (National) Income of £250m. The vertical line FE is the level of output which the economy is capable of producing at full employment, thus it is the Full Employment Level of (National) Income — let us say this is £260m. The extent by which aggregate demand would have to increase in order to bring about the full employment level of National Income is known as the deflationary gap. In our example if the multiplier is 2 then an injection of £5m would be required in order to increase output to the Full Employment level (i.e., from £250m to £260m.)⋆ Remember however that this injection would also have other effects on the economy — imports etc. as shown in example 28.21.

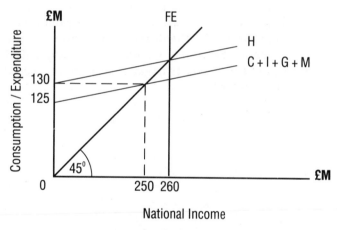

Fig. 29.14 Deflationary Gap

⋆This is shown in Fig. 29.14 by an increase of £5m in the vertical intercept which when subject to the multiplier results in an equilibrium level of (National) Income of £260m, i.e. the appropriate aggregate demand function after the injection of £5m is shown by line H in Fig. 29.14.

29.15. If the equilibrium level of (National) Income is greater than the full employment level then there exists an *Inflationary Gap* as shown in Fig. 29.15. This inflationary gap is the extent by which aggregate demand (C + I + G + M) would have to fall in order to bring about full employment without there being inflationary pressures in the economy. Remember that National Income shows the value of output in money terms (not output in terms of units produced) so that the value of National Output in this case would be increased as prices are pushed upwards when demand exceeds the ability to increase production.

In Fig. 29.15 the full employment level of National Income is £260m and the National Income at the current level of aggregate demand is £290m, thus there is an Inflationary Gap of £30m. In these circumstances where an Inflationary Gap exists domestic households, firms and government are seeking to consume more than the economy is capable of producing at full employment. This excess demand generates inflationary pressures in the economy. If in our example the multiplier is 2 then a reduction in injections of £15 would eliminate the Inflationary Gap and there would be equilibrium at the full employment level of National Income.

In an open economy where goods can be imported to satisfy demand there would be an alleviation of the inflationary pressures which over-full employment in the domestic economy would cause, i.e., the aggregate demand function C + I + G + M would shift downwards as M becomes smaller or becomes negative as imports exceed exports.

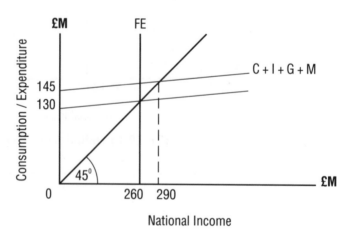

Fig. 29.15 Inflationary Gap

29.16. It should now be realised that

Y	=	C + I + G + M.
where Y	=	Equilibrium level of (National) Income.
C	=	Consumption.
I	=	Investment.
G	=	The difference between government revenue and expenditure. It may have a positive or negative effect on the level of economic activity. If government expenditure exceeds government revenue the difference is positive and constitutes an injection.
M	=	Difference between exports and imports. Again it may have a positive or negative effect on the level of economic activity. If exports exceed imports the difference is positive and constitutes an injection.
Y	=	C + I + G + M. This is usually referred to as the aggregate demand function.

Aggregate demand function

Terms for variations in level of GNP

29.17. The increases and decreases in the level of economic activity which hae been explained by means of a circular flow of income and graphs may be shown also in the manner depicted in Fig. 29.17.

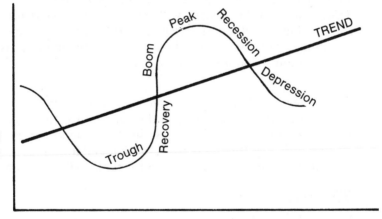

Time (in years)

Fig. 29.17 A series of Business Cycles around a rising trend.

Explanation of terms:

The *trend* is the general underlying movement during the period under review.

The *peak* is the upper turning point.

The *trough* is the lower turning point.

recovery is that part of the upswing below the trend.
boom is that part of the upswing above the trend.
recession is that part of the downswing above the trend.
depression is that part of the downswing below the trend.

29.18. Business Cycles

A number of economists noted that there seemed to be a regularity in the periodicity of the fluctuations, shown in Fig. 29.17, as a result of which the term *Business Cycles* was applied to the pattern. From 1795 to the outbreak of the second world war in 1939 there were seventeen cycles, the average duration of a cycle, i.e., from peak being $8\frac{1}{3}$ years. Considerable research has been devoted to analysing the factors which caused these cycles and there have been recurring references to the importance of investment in the determination of the level of economic activity.

Optimum capital stock

29.19. *Gross Investment* in capital goods consists of two elements (a) the replacement of depreciated capital assets and (b) net additions to the stock of capital goods which is known as *Net Investment.* The optimum or desired capital stock depends upon (a) the level of demand for goods which the capital stock produces, e.g., a demand for tables gives rise to a demand for table-making machinery, and (b) the capital/output ratio. When the capital stock is at the optimum level, net investment (i.e., additions to the capital stock as distinct from the replacement of depreciated capital assets) will be zero. Starting from a position of equilibrium in which the firm has the optimum capital stock, net investment will be undertaken only if consumption is growing. If consumption remains constant or falls, net investment will be zero.

Increase in demand is magnified

29.20. *The Acceleration Principle (or the Accelerator)* is based on the observation that an increase in the demand for final goods results in a more than proportional increase in the demand for capital goods. In Example 29.20 a 10% increase in the demand for tables in year 2 resulted in a 100% increase in the demand for table making machinery.

The Accelerator

EXAMPLE 29.20

Each machine is capable of producing 100 tables per year and the capital stock is at the desired level in year 1. Each machine has a 10 year life so that 1 machine is replaced each year.

Year	Total Demand for Tables	Total Number of Machines required	Gross Investment	Net Investment
1	1,000	10	1	0
2	1,000	10	1	0
3	1,100	11	2	1
4	1,100	11	1	0

QUESTIONS

Q1. Can the Average Propensity to Consume (APC) be greater than 1? Explain your answer.

Q2. If the consumption function is shown as C = 70 + 0.7y what does this mean?

Q3. Explain by means of the 45° line diagram the equilibrium level of income in an open economy.

Q4. What is meant by a "Deflationary Gap". Illustrate your answer.

Q5. Write an explanatory note on 'The Accelerator".

30 Government and the Economy

Policy of Laissez-faire

30.1. During the 19th century the State conformed to the economic wisdom of the period and adopted a policy of laissez-faire in economic matters. However, certain social ills forced governments to intervene in some aspects of economic activity, e.g., regulations were made pertaining to the employment of women and young children in factories. Though legislation was introduced to control monopolies and to establish public corporations which were introduced in order to operate certain essential public services e.g. water supply, sewerage, health services etc., the guiding philosophy of governments tended to remain one of laissez-faire. The State intervened only when absolutely necessary and then only to the minimum extent which was considered necessary.

Government intervention in Economy

30.2. The First World War in 1914 left governments with no option but to intervene in the management of the economy according as the exigencies of the war period dictated. The depression of the 1930's placed political, social and economic pressure on governments to involve themselves to a greater extent in the organisation and the running of the economic life of the State. The Second World War in 1939-1945 again required that the economies be organised on a war footing so that, on the conculsion of this war, the principle of State management of the economy had been firmly established.

Political commitment to full employment

30.3. In 1944 all political parties in Great Britain included as part of their policy a commitment towards full employment. There is a considerable *Demonstration Effect* between the Irish and English economies, consequently the introduction of a comprehensive social welfare service scheme in Great Britain in 1945, combined with that government's policy of nationalisation of major industries, increased the likelihood that policies of a similar nature would be introduced in this country and that their development would be accelerated.

Social policy and infrastructural development

30.4. It should be realised that it is not only the economic objectives which governments pursue that lead to State intervention in the economic system; social policy together with infrastructural provision and development also require a command over economic resources.

30.5. Policies, the pursuit of which entail considerable intervention by the government in the economic life of the country, tend to be classified along the following lines viz.:

- Social Policy.
- Infrastructural Development.
- The pursuit of Economic Objectives.

(N.S.)

Social policy refers to those objectives which the State pursues on the grounds of seeking equity between the citizens of the State or in order to provide those goods and services which assist in the enjoyment of a full life. Political parties place before the electorate at the time of elections a list of objectives which the political party in question considers to be in the best interests of the country and which they would attempt to implement if elected. Thus, the party which is elected to the majority of seats in the Dail feels that the policies which it pursues in accordance with the promises of its election campaign represent the wishes of the majority of the citizens of the state.

Social policy refers to the provision of income and/or services for those who for one reason or another would find it difficult to provide for themselves if exposed to the full rigours of a market economy, e.g., the elderly, young children, unemployed, physically or mentally handicapped, widows. In modern economics the term social policy refers also to the provision of education, housing and health facilities. Though proper standards of education, health and housing may improve the productivity of the labour force, these policies are often pursued by governments on humanitarian rather than on economic grounds. It is quite possible that these needs could be satisfied through the market system — in Ireland housing is supplied by private market forces and there are also private economic agents supplying education and health. However there is an acceptance in society that the needs satisfied by these goods are of a basic nature and consequently it is considered that some minimum quantity should be available to all. The fact that more than economic criteria are involved in these decisions is manifest in the term 'merit wants' which is applied to these basic requirements.

Merit wants

Social expenditure is a major item of expenditure and consequently has an important influence on the economy, because of its magnitude and nature and also because of the taxes which the government must extract from the economy in order to pay for it.

Infrastructural Provision and Development. This refers to the provision by the State of goods and services which assist the efficient and smooth functioning of the economy. Thus it includes systems of transport, roads, railways, harbours, postal and telecommunication services, energy requirements — electricity etc., sewerage facilities and also internal stability and security which ensure that there exists a climate in which economic activity may be stimulated and prosper and people may enjoy the fruits of their labour.

This latter point may be developed by widening the concept of infrastructure beyond the confines of economics and including under the heading such social amenities as parks, libraries, museums etc., which are often referred to as *public goods.*

*Public
Goods*

A public good is defined as a good the quantity of which that is available to one person is not affected by the quantity of it which is consumed (enjoyed) by another person. A simple additional example would be clean air.

*Private
Goods*

In contrast to public goods we also have the more usual classification viz. *private goods*. These are the opposite to public goods and are defined as goods which if consumed (enjoyed) by one person are not available to another person e.g. a chocolate bar. For any given stock of chocolate consumption by one person reduces the quantity available to others. Most goods are private goods.

The Pursuit of Economic Objectives

The economic objectives of national policy are set out in the programme for national recovery — see Sections 41.27 - 41.29. These objectives include the following:

(a) Fiscal Rectitude.

Our National Debt increased considerably between the mid 1970's and the mid 1980's. The servicing of this debt constituted a drain on our resources which was reaching crises proportions in the early years of the 1980's . There was a general acceptance of the magnitude of the problem together with a consensus on the need to give priority to policies directed towards the control of the problem. Thus the prime objective of national economic policy during the 1980's was the correction of the imbalances in the National Finances viz: fiscal rectitude.★

(b) To Achieve a High Level of Employment.

Full employment is defined as a situation in which employment is available for all those prepared to work at existing wage levels.

*Definition
of Full
Employment*

It is not conceivable that all of those available for work will in fact find employment as a consideration of the causes of unemployment will make clear, viz: frictional, seasonal, structural, cyclical and institutional reasons★. In addition pay related schemes for unemployment insurance and the PAYE means of collecting income tax mean that for a period after the termination of employment there is likely to be little reduction in the level of take home pay — this may have the effect of encouraging people to become voluntarily unemployed at regular intervals. Even though such people are not seeking employment they would appear as unemployed in National Statistics. Consequently, an employment rate of 96% of those shown in National Statistics are being available for work is considered to represent full employment of the work force.

*Greater
number
may seek
employment
as economy
improves*

The number of jobs which is stated as being required in order to bring about a situation of full employment often understates the actual position. As an economy approaches full employment, those who had been listed as employed in family businesses may in fact have been underemployed in such positions in that their Marginal Revenue Productivity was close to zero, i.e., the burden of producing a certain added value content was merely shared among a greater number of family

★ These policies are discussed in detail in Chapter 31. and in the Programme for National Recovery which is set out in Sections 41.27 - 41.29.

★★ See Section 20.31 for explanation of, and discussion, on these terms.

members rather than the level of output being increased through the employment of the individual in question. In addition, certain individuals who had not been seeking employment, e.g., married women or older people may seek employment, encouraged by the possibility of obtaining a job as the economy approaches full employment, whereas previously they hadn't even bothered looking for a job because they felt that they had little or no chance of obtaining employment.

The importance of jobs being available for those who seek them is self-evident, particularly to those students reading this book, so the desirability of the full employment objective need not be eulogised here. Because of the level of unemployment which has plagued this country for so long, we tend to state this objective as 'increasing the level of employment' rather than achieving full employment.

(c)   To assist economic growth and development.

There is an implicit assumption that economic growth is desirable — that its benefits of economic growth outweigh any costs to which it might give rise.

The Government attempts to achieve this objective by:

(i)   providing an economic infrastructure in which private industry can survive and flourish;

(ii)   adopting fiscal and monetary policies which stimulate private industry, e.g. low rate of taxation of corporation profits, low or subsidised rates of interest etc.;

(iii)   promoting other Government policies designed to encourage the private sector, e.g. grants, depreciation allowances, financing of training schemes from public funds, provision of advance factories, etc.;

(iv)   sponsoring State trading corporations, e.g. ESB, CIE, Bord na Mona, Bord Iascaigh Mhara, etc..

(d)   To achieve the optimum distribution of National Income.

Underlying this objective is some concept of fairness. It may be manifest in policies designed to achieve a more equitable distribution of the goods and services produced in the economy, e.g. the levying of taxes of a progressive nature in order to finance non-contributory old-age pensions, children's allowances etc..

It may also embrace concepts of "equality of opportunity" so that the economic system should contain no biases as a result of which one individual might have less chance than another to benefit from the system.

An optimum distribution of National Income between present and future consumption (i.e., consumption and investment) may also be included in this objective.

(e) **The Elimination of Inflation and the Achievement of a Steady Price Level.**

Government seeks to control inflation for the following reasons:

(i) A loss of competitiveness in international trade if our inflation rate is higher than that of our competitors as a result of which it would be difficult to sell our exports while at the same time imports would outsell domestic products on the home market.

(ii) A difficulty in encouraging foreign industrialists to invest in Ireland if our costs of production are high.

(iii) Continuing inflation tends to lead to a toleration of inefficiency.

Some problems caused by inflation

In the face of a buoyant demand, prices tend to be high and this may permit the survival of inefficient producers. The problem in some cases may be the availability of the goods rather than the actual price of them — think of the situation when a petrol shortage seems imminent. In addition, high prices are unlikely to act as a deterrent to customers who are encouraged to think that prices will be even higher in the future. In the face of a high level of demand, bottlenecks may develop in the supply of skilled labour, labour costs increase as absenteeism has to be tolerated in the face of labour shortages and inefficient working practices become endemic.

(iv) Inflation, particularly in its early stages before it can be anticipated with any resonable accuracy, results in an arbitrary redistribution of income. It is the economically weaker sections of the community which suffer most, e.g. pensioners, recipients of social welfare benefits etc.

(v) There emerges an 'inflation psychology' whereby the short term becomes the dominant time horizon and people spend as if there was no tomorrow or as if money was going out of fashion.

(f) **To Achieve Balance of Payments Equilibrium.**

Balance of payments constraint

The Irish economy is very open, for example in 1984 imports represented 59% and exports 60% of GNP. Thus it is very important that we maintain equilibrium on our Balance of Payments; it isn't necessary that in any one year our exports should equal our imports, but over a number of years our Balance of Payments should tend towards equilibrium. The Balance of Payments is discussed in detail in Chapter 34, but at this stage it should be noted that the need to remain competitive on world markets imposes a discipline on the management of the economy and the pursuit of the other national economic objectives — this is often referred to as '*The Balance of Payments Constraint*'.

(g) **To Achieve Balanced Regional Development.**

The Government attempts to discriminate positively, by giving more assistance in favour of those areas of the country which are not economically well endowed.

Fig. 30.5. Irish Macroeconomic Performance.

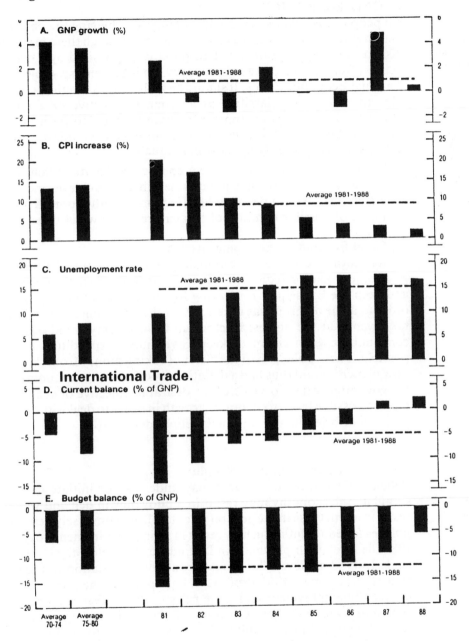

Source: OECD.

30.6. INTERACTION BETWEEN THE OBJECTIVES OF NATIONAL ECONOMIC POLICY

*Primary
and
Secondary
Objectives*

All people would agree on the desirability of achieving the objectives of national economic policies as set out above — though there may be some disagreement as to priorities. This point is emphasised by a distinction being often drawn between Primary and Secondary Objectives of National Economic Policy. It should be realised that whether a particular objective would be classified as a primary objective or a secondary objective could vary over time or between people. However, in Ireland the objective of increasing the level of employment would be given prime importance consistently by most individuals.

Unfortunately, there may well be a conflict in the attainment of these objectives in the sense that policies designed to achieve one of these objectives may have a detrimental effect on the other objectives. Some examples of possible conflicts of this nature are now discussed.

(a) Fiscal Rectitude v. Economic Growth

In attempting to redress the imbalances in the national finances the government had to reduce (if not eliminate) the current budget deficit and keep the Exchequer Borrowing Requirement as low as possible. In order to achieve this it was necessary for the government to maintain its tax revenue at the highest level which the economy could bear with a concomitant requirement to keep government expenditure as low as possible. These policies had the effect of taking money from the circular flow of income and thus had a deflationary effect on the economy so that the government had to sacrifice the desirable objective of achieving the highest possible level of economic growth in order to deal with the urgent problem of bringing the National Debt under control.

(b) Full Employment v. Price Stability.

Policies which the Government may undertake or initiate in order to stimulate the economy may result in a buoyancy in demand which will result in an increase in the general price level and conversely deflationary policies to reduce inflation may result in an increase in unemployment. In 1988 the level of employment in Ireland was 6% below the level in 1980 while Ireland achieved the largest reduction in inflation in the OECD area over the same period. Prof. A.W. Phillips researched the relationship between unemployment and wage rates in the British economy during 1862 and 1952 and showed a trade off between the objectives of full employment and price stability. His name is given to an illustration of this trade off which is known as the Phillips Curve and is shown below in Fig. 30.6 (a).

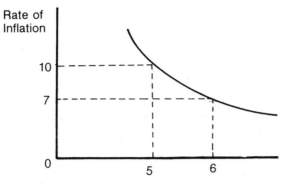

Level of Unemployment (Percentage)

Fig. 30.6 (a) Phillips Curve

During the 1970's many countries experienced "Stagflation", i.e., a combination of inflation and economic stagnation which was in contrast to the predictions of the Phillips curve that a rising price level would move the economy towards full employment.

In 1968, Milton Friedman & Edmund Phelps developed a new theory regarding unemployment and inflation. They argued that the Phillips Curve was only a short run phenomenon, it exists because people believe that the level of inflation in the future will be the same as it is in the present. Thus when an expansionary policy is implemented in order to reduce the level of unemployment, prices increase and there is an increased demand for labour services to produce the additional goods which are required to meet the increse in demand. Not being aware of the increase in inflation workers enter into labour contracts and work overtime in response to increases in money wages which they perceive to be an increase in real income. When they become aware of the increase in the rate of inflation they adjust their wage demands/expectations accordingly and the Phillips Curve moves to the right to correspond with the new (higher) rate of inflation. The process can then be continued as shown in Fig. 30.6 (b). Thus there is no long run trade off between unemployment and inflation, the long run Phillips Curve is vertical at the natural rate of unemployment. The Natural Rate of Unemployment is the rate at which labour markets are in equilibrium and in Fig. 30.6 (b) is taken to be 6%.

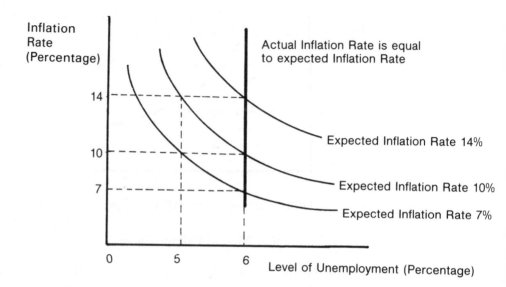

Fig. 30.6 (b) Long Run Phillips Curve

(b) Full Employment v. Balance of Payments

Stimulation of demand for imports

Policies designed to achieve an increase in the level of employment will increase the level of demand in the community which will create a demand, inter alia, for imported consumer goods, together with a demand for import substitutes if the price of domestic output increases. In addition to these developments an increase in the level of industrial activity will result in a demand for imported machinery and raw materials which in the short term, at least, may put the Balance of Payments under stress (though in the long term it may permit an increase in the level of exports and/or a reduction in imports). Thus policies to increase the level of employment may be constrained by Balance of Payments considerations, particularly in the short term.

(c) Economic Growth v. Redistribution of National Income

Disincentive effect

The redistribution of National Income in favour of the economically disadvantaged implies a transfer from those who are most economically productive. The taxation of business and individuals which this implies constitutes a disincentive to economic effort which may slow the pace of economic development.

(d) Balanced Regional Development v. Economic Growth

Costs of sub-optimal industrial location

Efforts by the Government to encourage industry to locate in areas which are economically sub-optimal either:

(i)   increase the cost of production of these firms which may result in the firm being uncompetitive as a result of the extra costs which the location of its plant imposes on the firm, or

(ii) require that the Government provides for these firms some form of financial concession or incentive by way of compensation. The Government may raise the resources which it transfers to these firms in a manner which constitutes a disincentive to industry in general.

30.7. Instruments of Macroeconomic Policy

The means by which the Government may attempt to achieve its economic objectives are known as the tools or instruments of macro-economic policy. These instruments are:—

(a) Fiscal Policy — which is discussed below in Chapter 31.

(b) Monetary Policy — refers to action which influences the quantity of money in circulation, rates of interest or the availability of credit. The Central Bank is the Government agency which implements national monetary policy as discussed in Chapter 24.

(c) Exchange Rate Policy — refers to government action which influences the external value of our currency and is discussed in detail in Chapter 34.

(d) Prices and Incomes Policy — as discussed in Section 32.9.

(e) State Trading Corporations/State Sponsored Bodies as discussed in Chapter 32.

(f) Economic Planning as discussed in Chapter 40.

QUESTIONS

Q1. What is meant by "Social Policy"?

Q2. Discuss the objectives of national economic policy.

Q3. State the means available to the government in its efforts to achieve these objectives.

Q4. Write an explanatory note on the Phillips Curve.

Q5. Discuss the effects which an increase in expenditure on social welfare schemes might have on other objectives of national economic policy.

Q6. To which objective of national economic policy would you give priority at present? How would you attempt to achieve this objective?

31 Fiscal Policy

31.1. *Fiscal policy is defined as any conscious action by the government which affects the magnitude, structure or timing of government revenue or expenditure.* Fiscal policy is enunciated and introduced in the annual budget. It is sometimes said that while practically all firms and individuals tailor their expenditure to their income and/or resources, the government is unique in that it first determines what it wishes to spend and then sets about deciding how it will raise the revenue it requires to finance its expenditure. While this is not strictly true, in that potential revenue is not infinite, even for governments, it justifies discussing first the expenditure aspect of government finance.

31.2. GOVERNMENT ESTIMATES OF EXPENDITURE

Towards the end of each year each government department sends an estimate of its expenditure for the following year to the Department of Finance. These estimates are scrutinised in the Department of Finance in order to ensure:

(a) that all of the items of expense are justified and in keeping with policy and

(b) that total allocation of funds which is being sought is not· prohibitively large.

Any points for discussion are taken up with the department concerned and when the estimates are agreed they are published in the form of a book which is appropriately titled the 'Book of Estimates'.

31.3. These estimates of expenditure are combined with estimates of the amounts which would be collected in the forthcoming tax year if the structure and level of taxation were not changed and are published under the title 'Estimates of Receipts and Expenditure'.

31.4. Expenditure is often classified as:—

(a) **Central Fund Services.** These are those items of expenditure which

constitute a prior charge on the revenue of the State and consequently are not open to debate. The largest items of expense under this heading include the interest and sinking fund charges in respect of the National Debt, the Road Fund and the salaries of the President, Comptroller & Auditor General and Judges, all of which positions are above politics.

(b) **Supply Services.** These services are administered by government departments. The main items of expense related to these services are the salaries of civil servants and the various expenses connected with the day to day running of the government departments.

The Minister for Finance in introducing the budget sets out the manner in which he intends, during the coming financial year, to raise the required revenue, together with details of any changes which he intends to make in respect of social welfare payments. In Table 31.4 items 1 and 2 in both Revenue and Expenditure show the financial position before the Minister introduces his budget proposals. This is usually referred to as the Opening (Current Budget) Deficit, it is the difference between estimated current expenditure for the forthcoming fiscal year and the estimated revenue which would be generated during the same period if there was no change in existing taxation regulations. In 1986 this Opening Current Budget Deficit was £1349.8m as can be seen from Table 31.4. The other items shown in this table, i.e. items 3, 4, 5 and 6 on the revenue side and items 3, 4, 5 and 6 on the expenditure side are the (expected) financial outcome of the Minister's proposals in respect of the budget for the current year.

The Budget

The Budget is debated in the Dail and at the conclusion of the debate the Dail passes two acts — *A Finance Act* — which authorises the imposition of the taxation proposals contains in the Budget and an –*Appropriation Act*— which authorises the spending, on the lines approved, of the revenues raised.

Table 31.4. Details of Current Budget, 1990

REVENUE

	£m	£m
1. Tax Revenue (including renewal of bank levy and PRSI allowance)		7,855.0
2. Non-Tax Revenue (incl. extra £5.5 million from BGE)		376.1
3. Income Tax Measures:		
Reduce 32% rate to 30%	−72.0	
Reduce 56% rate to 53%	−19.6	
Widening of standard rate band	−22.5	
Reduced life assurance relief	+7.9	−106.2
4. Indirect Tax Measures:		
Reduce 25% VAT rate to 23%	−76.0	
Miscellaneous excise reductions	−9.5	
Partial restoration of farmers' flat-rate rebate to 2.3%	−6.0	
Increase VAT on electricity to 10%	+11.0	
Impost 10% VAT rate on telecommunications	+3.0	−77.5
5. Miscellaneous (incl. stamp duty, residential property tax and other capital tax changes)		−1.7
6. Net effect on tax revenue of expenditure and tax changes		+91.0
7. Current Budget Deficit		261.1
		8,397.8

EXPENDITURE

	£m	£m
1. Central Fund Services (including £35 million saving on foot of new National Debt Office)		2,655.0
2. Supply Services (non-capital)	5,661.0	
Adjusted for:		
Net revisions to Estimates	−84.0	5,577.0
3. Welfare, Elderly and the Disadvantaged*		
— Social Welfare improvements	+78.6	
— Change in PRSI arrangements for lower paid	+8.0	
Health	+7.0	
— Disadvantaged Schools	+1.0	
— Adult literacy	+0.5	
— US Emigrants	+0.2	
— Increase in general and age tax exemption limits and in child addition	+13.1	
— Reduce marginal income tax relief rate	+1.1	+109.5
4. Environment Action Plan (including 5p reduction in unleaded petrol		+12.1
5. Employment initiatives		+11.0
6. Other Expenditure Measures		
— Special Pay Increases	+50.00	
— Other Education Measures	+3.65	
— Tourism Measures	+2.70	
— Trade Union Rationalisation	+1.27	
— Teagasc	+0.60	+58.2
7. Deduct: Estimated Departmental balances		−25.0
		8,397.8

Source: Budget 1990 (Stationery Office).

*Comptroller
and Auditor
General*

31.5 Towards the end of the financial year each government department forwards to the Comptroller & Auditor General details of the money which it received and the manner in which it was spent. The Comptroller checks to ensure that the sums were disbursed in the manner authorised. When the Comptroller completes his audit, he sends a report to a committee of the Dail, which examines the report and has it printed under the title 'Report of the Committee of Public Accounts'.

31.6. Current Section of the Budget

*"Above the
line"
revenue and
expenditure*

Current expenditure relates to the expenses incurred on the purchase of goods and services which are consumed (used up) during the year, e.g., salaries of civil servants, lighting and heating of government offices and public buildings, transfer payments, subsidies, etc. Similarly revenue is the income which accrues to the State from the day to day working of the economy, e.g., income tax, VAT, Corporation Profits Tax, government investment and trading income, etc., as set out in Table 31.6. Current revenue and expenditure are often referred to as 'above the line' revenue and expenditure.

Table 31.6 Current Government Expenditure and Revenue in 1988

Current Expenditure			Current Revenue		
Item	£m	% of gross expendi-ture	Item	£m	% of total
Service of Public Debt			**Budget Deficit** (financed by borrowing)	317	**4.0**
Central Fund Services (part)					
Interest	1,962	20.3			
Sinking Funds, etc.	179	1.9			
Total	**2,141**	**22.2**	**Tax Revenue**		
			Customs	108	1.3
			Excise Duties	1,481	18.5
Economic Services			Stamp Duties	198	2.5
Industry and Labour	229	2.4	Income Tax	3,055	38.1
Agriculture	403	4.1	Corporation Tax	334	4.2
Fisheries, Forestry	47	0.5	Value-Added Tax	1,805	22.5
Tourism	28	0.3	Motor Vehicle Duties	140	1.7
			Capital taxes	62	0.8
Total	**60**	**0.6**	Employment and Training Levy	126	1.6
			Agricultural Levies (EEC)	13	0.2
			Total	**7,322**	**91.4**
Social Services					
Health	1,173	12.2			
Education	1,163	12.1			
Social Welfare	2,644	27.4	**Non-Tax Revenue**		
Housing	33	0.3	Free Stamps	17	0.2
Subsidies	172	1.7	Interest and Dividends on Exchequer Advances	114	1.4
Total	**5,185**	**53.7**	Central Bank — Surplus Income (a)	157	2.0
			Proceeds of National Lottery Surplus	44	0.5
Security	**692**	**7.2**	Miscellaneous	36	0.5
Other	**864**	**9.0**	Total	**368**	**4.6**
Gross Expenditure	**9,649**	**100.0**			
Supply Service Receipts	1,642				
Net Expenditure	**8,007**		Total Revenue	**8,007**	**100.0**

(a) Includes £51,447 million for 1988 under the arrangements for advancing surplus income to finance the exceptional lump sum and related payments arising from the Public Service early retirement/voluntary redundancy schemes.

Source: Budget 1989 (Stationery Office)

31.7. Capital Section of the Budget

"Below the line" expenditure

Capital expenditure is expenditure on items which are not consumed (used up) during the year, e.g., expenditure on the laying of roads, telecommunications and the general infrastructure of the country. The revenue to finance capital expenditure is usually raised by borrowing and the loan raised is then paid back over the life time of the asset. Capital revenue and expenditure is often referred to as 'below the line' revenue and expenditure.

Table 31.7. Summary of Current and Capital Budgets 1989 and 1990.

	1989 Budget £m	1989 Outturn £m	1990 Post-Budget Estimate £m
CURRENT BUDGET			
Current Expenditure			
(i) Central Fund	2,555	2,453	2,655
(ii) Supply Services	5,595	5,566	5,722
Total	8,150	8,019	8,377
2. Current Revenue			
(i) Taxation	7,009	7,443	7,740
(ii) Non-tax	322	313	376
Total	7,331	7,756	8,116
3. Current Budget Deficit	819	263	261
(% of GNP)	(4.1)	(1.3)	(1.2)
4. Capital Budget			
Capital Expenditure			
(i) Public Capital Programme	1,392	1,414	1.666
(ii) Other (non-programme)	30	19	25
Total	1,422	1,433	1,691
5. Capital Resources			
(i) Exchequer	491	501	596
(ii) Non-Exchequer	695	716	907
Total	1,186	1,217	1,503
6. Exchequer Borrowing for Capital Purposes	236	216	188
7. Total Exchequer Borrowing Requirements (3 + 6)	1,055	479	449
(% of GNP)	(5.3)	(2.4)	(2.1)

Source: Budget 1990 (Stationery Office)

31.8. Budget Deficit

A Budget deficit stimulates the economy

When the current and capital sections of the budget are combined the revenue and expenditure of the government must balance — goods and services acquired must be paid for either from income or by borrowing. The term 'budget deficit' refers to the current section of the budget. If government expenditure on current items is greater than its current revenue than the government is said to have a 'budget deficit' because it is not collecting enough money in normal revenue to cover its day to day activities. The shortfall or deficit is made up by borrowing as shown in Table 31.7. When the government is running a budget deficit it is spending more money on its day-to-day activities than it is receiving in revenue. Since in this circumstance there is an injection of purchasing power into the economy, a budget deficit stimulates the economy (or it may be considered inflationary).

In all of the foregoing remarks it is assumed that the budget deficit follows a year in which there was no deficit or else that the budget deficit in the year is greater than it was in the previous year. However, if the budget deficit in the year in question is (say) £100m and the deficit in the previous year was (say) £1005m then the government is reduced to deficit and is in fact taking money (£5m) out of the economy compared with the previous year. Thus even though there is a budget deficit there would be a withdrawal/leakage from the circular flow of income compared with the position in the previous year.

31.9. Budget Surplus

Budget surplus is deflationary

Conversely, a budget surplus means that the government is taking more money from its day to day activities than it required to meet its current expenditure. Since in such a situation the government is taking money out of circulation a budget surplus constitutes a leakage from the circular flow of income and is deflationary. *Note however that a reduction in the budget surplus would constitute a withdrawal/leakage from the circular flow of income in the economy compared with the previous year.*

31.10. Neutral Budget

When a budget neither stimulates nor deflates the economy it is said to be a *'NEUTRAL BUDGET'*

National Debt

Amount of national debt

31.11. The cumulative total of outstanding government borrowing is known as the *National Debt*. This money has been borrowed by the government over the years in order to build schools, roads, houses, and generating stations; to finance land drainage schemes and afforestation, to purchase aeroplanes, etc.

The National Debt Outstanding at 31st December, 1988 was £2471 million. See table 31.11 for details of the composition and growth of this debt.

Table 31.11. Trend in National Debt.
1976 — 1988

Year	Foreign Debt Outstanding		Domestic Debt Outstanding		Total National Debt
	£m	% of Total	£m	% of Total	£m
1986	1,040	28.8	2,572	71.2	3,612
1977	1,039	24.6	3,190	75.4	4,229
1978	1,064	20.6	4,103	79.4	5,167
1979	1,542	23.6	4,998	76.4	6,540
1980	2,207	28.0	5,689	72.0	7,896
1981	3,794	37.2	6,401	62.8	10,195
1982	5,248	45.0	6,421	55.0	11,669
1983	6,899	47.9	7,493	52.1	14,392
1984	7,910	47.0	8,911	53.0	16,821
1985	8,114	43.8	10,388	56.2	18,502
1986	9,220	42.7	12,391	57.3	21,611
1987	9,690	40.9	14,001	59.1	23,691
1988*	9,495	38.6	15,115	61.4	24,610

*Provisional Outturn.

31.12. Often you will hear reference to the *'burden of the national debt'* but in considering whether or not (or to what degree) the national debt constitutes a burden the following points must be considered:—

Self-liquidating form of debt

(a) **The use which is made of the borrowed funds.** In some cases it may be a *'self-liquidating'* form of debt, in the sense that the investment may generate sufficient income (or benefits) to enable the borrowed funds to be repaid with interest.

Opportunity cost of borrowing

(b) **The opportunity cost of the funds which the government borrows.** If there are surplus savings and little demand from the private sector to borrow for investment purposes, then the opportunity cost to the community of the borrowed funds is zero (or negligible). On the other hand, if, as a result of the government borrowing, the private sector is starved of investment funds then there is an opportunity cost as the government borrows the funds in competition with the private sector.

Real cost of Government borrowing

(c) Income is generated when the government uses the borrowed funds in a manner which creates employment and this in turn lessens the amount of money which the government must allocate to unemployment assistance. Also as a result of this use of funds, government revenue from taxation increases and thus reduces further (but does not eliminate) the real cost of government borrowing.

Table 31.13 Trend in Service of Public Debt as % of Current Expenditure, as % of overall Taxation and as % of Income Taxation 1976-1988

Year	Service of Public Debt	As a % of Current Expenditure	As a % of Tax Revenue	As a % of Income Tax
1976	278	16.6	22.0	60.2
1977	334	17.1	22.5	64.0
1987	418	17.3	24.2	69.1
1979	514	17.7	25.6	70.2
1980	661	17.9	25.2	65.2
1981	885	18.5	26.7	71.2
1982	1,249	21.2	30.8	85.6
1983	1,456	21.8	31.1	87.5
1984	1,705	24.5	32.1	86.7
1985	1,967	25.8	35.2	93.5
1986	1,989	24.5	32.6	83.3
1987★	2,118	25.4	32.6	78.1
1988★★	2,173	26.6	32.7	80.3

★Provisional Outturn
★★Post-Budget Estimate

Source: Budget 1988. (Stationery Office).

31.13. Table 31.13 shows the percentage of current expenditure, tax revenue and income tax which is absorbed in servicing the Public Debt.

Deadweight Debt

31.14. Borrowing increases the National Debt and when the borrowings are used for purposes other than the purchase of real assets these borrowings are usually referred to as *"deadweight debt"*. This phase is used also when the borrowing is used for investment which is not self-liquidating. Thus borrowings which are necessary to finance deficits on the current account section of the budget would be of this 'deadweight' nature as would an increase in National Debt in order to finance a war — though perhaps in the latter case we are purchasing the most priceless asset of all, our freedom. A young growing economy, such as that of Ireland, probably has a relatively high borrowing requirement in order to finance economic development.

Exchequer borrowing as a percentage of GNP

31.15. The Current Budget Deficit as a percentage of GNP for each year since 1976 is shown in table 31.15. Exchequer Borrowing which comprises exchequer borrowing for current and capital purposes is shown also. Notice how the reduction in borrowing in 1982 was borne entirely by borrowing for Capital purposes — a policy which has been more or less maintained since. This also indicates the difficulty in reducing the Current Budget Deficit in circumstances where a large portion of current expenditure is on wages and salaries and it is difficult to reduce, in the short term the numbers employed in the public sector.

**Table 31.15. Trend in the Current Budget Deficit and the Exchequer
and Public Sector Borrowing Requirements
— (In Absolute terms and as % of GNP)
1976-1989.**

Year	Current Budget Deficit		Total Exchequer Borrowing		Public Sector Borrowing Requirements	
	£m	% of GNP	£m	% of GNP	£m	% of GNP
1976	291	4.4	506	11.0	595	12.9
1977	201	3.6	545	9.7	697	12.5
1978	397	6.1	810	12.4	973	14.9
1979	522	6.8	1,009	13.2	1,230	16.1
1980	547	6.1	1,218	13.5	1,559	17.3
1981	802	7.4	1,721	15.9	2,204	20.3
1982	988	7.9	1,945	15.6	2,466	19.8
1983	960	7.1	1,756	13.0	2,277	16.7
1984	1,039	7.0	1,825	12.3	2,375	16.0
1985	1,284	8.2	2,015	12.9	2,444	15.6
1986	1,394	8.4	2,145	12.9	2,506	15.1
1987	1,180	6.6	1,786	10.0	2,056	11.5
1988*[1]	317	1.7	619	3.3	751	4.1
1988*[2]	817	4.4	1,119	6.0	1,251	6.8
1989**	819	4.1	1,055	5.3	1,272	6.4

*Provisional Outturn
**Post-Budget Estimate.
[1] Inclusive of receipts under the Tax incentive scheme (amnesty)
[2] Exclusive of receipts under the Tax incentive scheme (amnesty)

Source: Budget 1988. (Stationery Office).

Economic Aspects of the Budget

31.16. *Period of budget.* Originally the budget was merely an accounting exercise concerned with the raising of the revenue required to meet proposed expenditure. The one year cycle of government budgets was probably chosen to coincide with the agricultural year and the payment of taxes by communities which were predominantly agricultural. In a modern economy the scope of the budget goes beyond the mere balancing of revenue and expenditure, it is the means by which the government regulates and controls the economy. The government in its budget strategy attempts to optimise its progress in pursuit of the objectives of government economic policy which are discussed in Section 30.5. Because of this use of the budget as an instrument of economic policy, there is a general feeling among economists that the annual budget adopts too short a time horizon. It has been suggested that there should be (say) a five year policy period with interim budgets to be introduced as required in order to keep the economy on the desired path. However, such a proposal might be difficult to implement and maintain due to the intrusion (!) of general elections.

Budget is an instrument of economic policy

31.17. The allocation and distribution of goods and services in the economy are affected by the manner in which the government raises and spends its revenue. The State redistributes income by the manner in which it imposes taxes and through the goods and services which it chooses to supply and make available other than through the market mechanism.

Redistributive aspect of Budget

31.18. The State makes available *collective goods* such as defence (armed forces) and internal security (the Garda Síochána) to the general public without a direct charge for the services. In addition the State provides for *merit wants* such as education, housing and health services without a direct charge based on the use of the services. These *'merit wants'* constitute goods and services which the government considers to be basic to life and development, and, consequently, they feel that some minimum quantity of such goods and services should be available to all, irrespective of income. The goods and services, which are considered to be *merit goods,* together with the standard and quality of them, change over time and reflect the feeling of society as to equity and social justice.

Merit Wants

Government Revenue

31.19. Though the government receives income from trading activities, the greatest portion of its revenue is raised by taxation in its many forms — income tax, corporation tax, VAT, customs and excise duties, etc. It is possible to classify taxes in many different ways , the most usual classification being into *Direct Taxes* and *Indirect Taxes.*

Taxation is main source of revenue

31.20. *Direct Taxes* are so named because the person makes payment direct to the Revenue Commissioners, e.g. income tax, corporation tax, etc., i.e. they are taxes which are levied on people or institutions rather than on goods and services. With the advent of PAYE it could be argued that an employer makes the payment to the Revenue Commissioners on behalf of the employee from whom he deducts the tax, rather than the taxpayer making the tax payment directly but this merely introduces an unnecessary complication into the analysis. Direct taxation is a tax on income and wealth as distinct from a tax on expenditure and consequently direct taxes are more difficult to avoid, since one cannot escape from them through a change in purchasing behaviour.

Taxes on income and wealth

31.21. *Indirect taxes* are taxes which are paid to the Revenue Commissioners through the intermediaries who collect them on behalf of the Commissioners, e.g. shopkeepers, manufacturers, importers, etc. They are often referred to as taxes on expenditure or sales taxes, since they are levied on goods and services rather than on people or firms. For this reason it may be possible to avoid paying a particular indirect tax through a change in purchasing behaviour, e.g., refrain from buying cigarettes. Indirect taxes may be

Taxes on expenditure

(a) *ad valorem*, i.e., a stated percentage of the value of the good, e.g. V.A.T., or

(b) *specific,* i.e., a fixed sum irrespective of the value of the good, e.g., tax on a gallon of petrol or on a bottle of whiskey. With ad valorem taxes, e.g., VAT, tax revenue increases when prices rise, whereas with specific taxes tax revenue increases only when there is an increase in the *level* of consumption of the good.

31.22. THE MAIN CATEGORIES OF INDIRECT TAXATION

(a) *Value Added Tax.* 'Added Value' is the difference between the amount which a firm receives from the sale of goods and services and the amount which it lays out on the purchase of goods and services from others. This difference consists of the firm's outlay on wages, salaries, interest, and profits. It is because the tax at each stage of production and distribution is based on the value added at that stage that the Value Added Tax is so called. In the operation of the system, tax is charged on the firm's full turnover but a credit or deduction is allowed for tax already borne on all bought-in goods and services.

Examples of indirect taxes

(b) *Excise Duties* which are duties or taxes on home produced goods and services, e.g., beer, Irish whiskey, cigarettes.

(c) *Customs Duties* which are duties on imported goods, e.g., motor cars, Scotch whisky, etc.

31.23. CANONS OF TAXATION

In his book "The Wealth of Nations", Adam Smith set out four canons of taxation viz.:—

*Adam Smith's
Canons of
Taxation*

(a) *The tax levied on each person should be related to the person's ability to pay* – 'from each according to his means'. This implies also that the system of taxation should be equitable in that persons in similar economic circumstances should pay the same amount of tax.

(b) *The amount of tax which a person must pay should be certain and clear.* Thus the tax liability of an individual should not be arbitrarily determined nor subject ot the whims of those officials charged with the implementation of the system. This criterion implies also that tax evasion should be difficult if not impossible.

(c) *The manner and timing of payment of taxes should have regard to the convenience of the taxpayer.* It is more convenient to have tax deducted at source from income as in PAYE, rather than to receive a bill for the total amount due in a single payment after the income has been spent. Similarly, VAT, is paid on goods and services at the time of purchase, thus the purchaser is aware of the total cost involved at the time of making the purchase and there is no carry-over of a tax liability. In this way bad debts through non-payment of taxes are avoided and the costs of tax collection are minimised.

(d) *The cost of collection should be small relative to the yield.* The raising of revenue is the prime purpose of taxation. Consequently the structure of taxation should be such that the revenue accruing to the exchequer should be, as nearly as possible, equal to the tax collected from the taxpayers, i.e., the cost of collection should be small relative to the yield. It is desirable that the Minister for Finance should be able to estimate with reasonable accuracy the gain to the Exchequer from the imposition of a tax in order to minimise the possibility of the yield accruing from taxation being significantly lower than anticipated. In addition it is preferable that there should be the minimum time lag between the imposition of a tax and the receipt by the Exchequer of the tax reveneues arising therefrom.

31.24. FURTHER CRITERIA OF TAXATION

With the growth in complexity of economies it is generally considered that the tax system should attempt to satisfy the following additional criteria:—

*Additional
Requirements
of a system
of taxation*

(a) **Should be variable.** Taxes should be capable of being varied upwards or downwards in accordance with government policy. Because of international trade agreements and competition from imports, customs and excise duties may not lend themselves to a wide degree of flexibility.

(b) **Should not constitute a disincentive to economic activity and growth.** This requirement is often quoted in relation to high marginal rates of income tax and is illustrated in economic theory by the backward bending supply curve of labour. It can also be instanced by people refusing to undergo training or accept promotion. This type of reaction implies, inter alia, that the workers concerned have some control over their work effort. If an individual's work contract specifies the period of attendance at the work place, e.g., 09.00-17.30 for five days a week, and the nature of the work is such that the intensity of the work effort is not capable of wide variation, e.g., working in pace with machinery, then high marginal rates of taxation may not inhibit net output except in so far as they may lead to absenteeism. In discussions on the possibility of high marginal rates of taxation constituting a disincentive to economic effort, opinions are often forthcoming to the effect that there are factors in addition to income which motivate workers. Other opinions, while concentrating on the relationship between income and effort, incline to the view that high marginal rates of income tax may stimulate work effort as employees seek to maintain the same real value of after-tax pay, and adduce as evidence of this worker reaction to inflation. Research on this matter has not provided conclusive evidence in support of either the incentive or disincentive effect of high marginal rates of taxation.

The relationship between high marginal rates of taxation and economic activity is likely to be much more sensitive in relation to investment decisions. Capital is a mobile factor of production and investment decisions affecting the Irish economy made in offices outside this country by individuals who are not Irish nationals may be influenced to a considerable extent by the level of taxation in the Irish economy. Thus taxation of profits, or of the factors of production, may act as a disincentive to investment, whereas 'negative taxation on investment', i.e., incentives to invest, such as grants, subsidies, accelerated depreciation allowances for tax purposes, etc., will stimulate investment.

(c) **Should be consistent with national economic objectives.** The structure of taxation should be such that if it cannot actively promote the objectives of national economic policy at least it should cause the minimum impediment to their achievement. Thus the Minister for Finance may:—

- attempt to provide concessions to PAYE taxpayers in order to gain from the trade union movement moderation in wage demands.

- differentiate for tax purposes between profits earned on export trading and profits earned in the home market.

- adjust personal tax allowances to encourage or discourage married women seeking employment outside their homes.

- distinguish, for the purpose of tax assessment, between profits reinvested and profits distributed.

- be reluctant to increase VAT because it would increase the price level and render more difficult the control of inflation.

- influence the use of agricultural land by a pattern of tax rates which distinguishes between different types of agricultural output.

- tax more heavily the incomes and profits earned in the more highly developed regions of the country, e.g., East Coast v West of the Shannon.

- provide tax allowances for those pursuing education and training with a view to stimulating economic growth and personal development, which is sometimes called investment in human capital.

- be reluctant to increase excise taxes less this will result in a fall off in demand for the products which are subject to the taxes and thus lead to a loss of employment in the industries concerned.

(d) **Should distribute the tax burden in an equitable manner.**
Progressive taxes take a higher *proportion* of income as the tax base increases, e.g., income tax. In contrast to this, *regressive taxes* take a higher *proportion* of income from a poorer person. Thus taxes which are levied on goods which are bought by rich and poor in quantities which don't vary significantly with changes in income are a regressive form of taxation e.g. VAT on necessities. Any tax, where everybody irrespective of income pays the same amount, is obviously a *regressive tax,* this would apply to the licence form of taxation e.g. T.V. licence and car tax. A tax which takes a fixed proportion of individuals' incomes is known as a *Proportional Tax.*

Example 31.24.

Mr. Jones   Mr. Smith

Income — £6,000   Income — £12,000

Both purchase an identical item at a price of £150 which includes VAT of £30

Tax paid	=	£30	Tax Paid	=	£30
Tax as a percentge of income	=	0.5%	Tax as a percentage of income	=	0.25%

Therefore even though they both pay the same amount of money the tax is regressive.

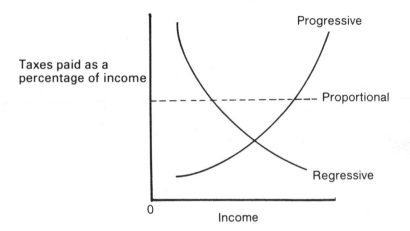

(e) **Should have a stabilising influence on the economy.**
    Stabilising as used in this context is not to be taken as meaning to
    avoid changes in the economy but rather that the economy would
    avoid wide fluctuations in the level of economic activity and
    continue on a steady path towards full employment without
    inflation, while avoiding crises in the Balance of Payments.
        Since taxes tend to be related to the level of economic activity in
    that they are levied either on income or expenditure, tax revenue
    tends to be high when the economy is buoyant and to fall when there
    is a reduction in the level of economic activity. For this reason
    government taxes are often referred to as *automatic stabilisers* in the
    sense that they take an increasing proportion of purchasing power
    away from the private sector when the level of economic activity is
    increasing and a decreasing proportion when there is a decline in the
    level of economic activity. Thus a system of taxation can prevent the
    level of economic activity rising as fast as it otherwise would when
    the economy is on an upturn, and can prevent the level of economic
    activity falling as fast as it otherwise would in a recession. This
    stabilising effect is accentuated when taxes are of a progressive
    nature. However, though these built-in (or automatic) stabilisers
    lessen the extent of fluctuations in the level of economic activity,
    they cannot eliminate them since the stabilising effect occurs, only
    in response to the initial fluctuation.

Table 31.24(a) Budget 1990: Changes in Take-Home Pay — Single Person

After Tax Gross Annual Income

Gross Annual Income	Private Sector			Public Sector		
£	89/90	90/91	change	89/90	90/91	change
8,000	5,824	5,921	+97	6,099	6,202	+103
10,000	6,907	7,100	+193	7,227	7,421	+194
12,500	8,000	8,206	+206	8,412	8,640	+228
15,000	8,906	9,199	+293	9,433	9,735	+302
17,500	9,875	10,202	+327	10,480	10,844	+364
20,000	10,951	11,352	+401	11,556	11,993	+437
25,000	13,101	13,652	+551	13,706	14,293	+587
30,000	15,251	15,952	+701	15,587	16,594	+737
40,000	19,551	20,552	+1,001	20,157	21,194	+1,037
60,000	28,151	29,752	+1,601	28,756	30,393	+1,637
75,000	34,601	36,652	+2,051	35,206	37,293	+2,087

Table 31.24(b) Progressive Nature of Irish Income Tax

Gross Income	After Tax Gross Income	Tax	Tax as a Percentage of Gross Income
10,000	7,100	2,900	29.00
20,000	11,352	8,648	43.24
30,000	15,952	14,048	46.83
40,000	20,552	19,448	48.62
60,000	29,752	30,248	50.41

Table 31.24(b) illustrates the progressive nature of the Irish income tax system, from table 31.24(a) you will notice that the higher income earners gained more from the budgetary changes thus the income tax structure has become somewhat less progressive as a result of the changes contained in the 1990 budget. An international comparison of the position after the 1990 budget is shown in table 31.24(c). Apart from the burden of taxation a comparison of the progressive nature of the taxation depends on factors including the magnitude of tax bands. However as an illustration, from this table it will be seen that at a gross income of £10,000 an Irish person retains 71.0% gross income after tax, a UK person 74.2% and a US taxpayer 78.4%. At a *gross income* of £20,000 the respective figures are 56.8%, 71.1% and 72.3%.

Table 31.24(c) International Comparison: Single Person's Tax

Pre-tax income	Irish After-tax income	UK after-tax income	US after-tax income	Australia after-tax income	France after-tax income	Germany after-tax income
£10,000	£7,100	£7,417	£7,842	£8,214	£7,672	£6,712
£15,000	£9,199	£10,717	£11,482	£11,229	£10,988	£9,520
£20,000	£11,352	£14,213	£14,469	£14,014	£14,107	£12,127
£40,000	£20,552	£26,927	£26,666	£24,214	£25,345	£23,048
£75,000	£36,652	£47,927	49,111	£41,976	£42,351	£39,654

All sums expressed in Irish pounds, using current exchange rates.
Compiled by Ernst and Young, Dublin, Melbourne, Munich and Paris.

In terms of Automatic Stabilisers notice that when there is an increase in the level of income in the economy an increasing amount is syphoned out of the Circular Flow of Income when the economy is in a rising phase. Thus a progressive form of taxation stops the economy rising as fast as it otherwise would in the absence of the tax — an increase in income of £20,000 from £40,000 to £60,000 gross income increased the individual's after tax gross income by £9,200. Conversely if an individual's gross income falls by £20,000 i.e., from £60,000 to £40,000 gross income the individuals after tax income falls not by £20,000 but by £9,200. In this way a progressive form of taxation dampens the fluctuations of the economy in an upward or downward direction, hence "Automatic Stabilisers". Automatic because no change in tax rates or other discretionary Government intervention was required.

Whether or not the money raised in taxation has a stabilising effect depends upon the relationship between government revenue and government expenditure. If the government spends all the money it raises through taxation then it has not lessened the level of economic activity. If the economy is headed towards an unacceptable level of inflation, the syphoning off of purchasing power through VAT and progressive rates of income tax may be considered desirable. However, suppose that the level of activity in the economy is increasing along a desired path, in which circumstances tax revenue, since it is related to the level of economic activity, will be increasing. Therefore taxation will be removing purchasing power from the private sector and slowing down the rate of growth in the economy unless government expenditure keeps pace with its increasing revenue. Since with unchanged *rates* of taxation tax *revenue* will increase automatically with the level of economic activity, if the rate of increase of economic activity is greater than anticipated, government revenue from taxation will be greater than anticipated. Government expenditure will have been based on the anticipated (lower) revenue and there may be a lag in the adjustment of government expenditure to the increase in revenue. This situation gives rise to the expression *Fiscal Drag which is the deflationary effect of fiscal policy when increased government revenue is not matched by increased government expenditure.*

31.25. DIRECT TAXATION — ADVANTAGES

(a) *Direct taxation is related to the person's ability to pay.* By a system of personal and other types of allowances it is possible to ensure that the payment of taxes does not bear unduly on people to an extent that they cannot provide for themselves the necessities of life. In addition the use of taxable bands ensures a progressive form of taxation with the greatest amount of tax being paid by the better off.

(b) *Amount of direct tax for which a person is liable is known.* Tax allowances and rates of tax are set out in legislation and the information is available to all, therefore the amount of tax for which a person is liable is not arbitrarily determined — it is not susceptible to the whims of the tax official with whom one is dealing. In addition it is possible for the Minister for Finance to calculate the likely revenue to the State from the taxes which he imposes.

(c) *There is regard for the convenience of the taxpayer.* In the PAYE system tax is deducted from salary which is probably the most convenient manner of paying the tax. The self-employed and other taxpayers who receive a demand for an annual amount can usually pay in instalments.

(d) *The cost of collection is low.* This is exemplified in the case of PAYE where employers act as tax collectors for the government.

(e) *Direct taxes stabilise the economy.* Because of the progressive nature of income tax an increasing amount of revenue is raised through taxation when the level of economic activity is increasing, and conversely the revenue from income tax is reduced as incomes decline in deflationary conditions.

31.26. DIRECT TAXATION — DISADVANTAGES

(a) *High marginal rates of direct taxation may act as a disincentive to effort.* This may apply particularly to entrepreneurs and the self employed who have discretion over their economic effort and earnings, in addition to which the activities of these individuals have a considerable influence on the level of job creation and thus the economic well being of others. Similarly, high marginal rates of taxation erode wages differentials and consequently may act as a disincentive to individuals undergoing education and training or incurring the inconvenience and cost of moving to new better paid positions. In this way the tax system may aggravate the problems associated with the immobility of labour.

(b) *High marginal rates of direct taxation lessen the financial penalties of inefficiency.* Inefficiency in firms increases costs and/or reduces profits. However, the financial penalties which firms suffer because of inefficiency are lessened when firms are subject to taxation on profits, e.g., if 40% of profits are paid out in taxes, then only 60% of increased costs, e.g., in respect of advertising, directors expenses, etc., fall on the after-tax profits of the firm. Similarly, you will hear of people purchasing expensive houses because the mortgage interest which they pay will be deducted from their income when calculating their liability for income tax.

(c) *High rates of direct taxation as a disincentive to investment.* Investors tend to perceive the return on investment in terms of what it is worth to them, i.e., the after-tax return. Thus investment may become more or less attractive with variations in the rate of taxation. Capital is very mobile between countries and, ceteris paribus, it will tend to be invested in those countries where rates of taxation are lowest. In addition high rates of taxation on profits reduce the capital available from which the firm may make further investment (the re-investment of profits within the firm is often referred to as the ploughing back of profits).

(d) *Direct taxes may reduce savings.* Direct taxes through reducing take-home pay reduce the resources available to individuals from which they can save.

(e) *High marginal rates of taxation encourage the growth of a tax-evading economy,* i.e., a "Black Economy", as people react in order to avoid paying high rates of taxation. In this way the tax revenue of the State is reduced and legitimate tax paying economic agents find it difficult to compete with those whose costs are lower by the amount of the taxes. Developments of this nature may have a pernicious effect on market activities if consumers find it difficult to obtain redress for (shoddy) workmanship as a consequence of those who are working in the Black Economy being difficult to contact when redress is being sought.

31.27. INDIRECT TAXATION — ADVANTAGES

(a) *Indirect taxes are productive of revenue.* If indirect taxation is imposed on goods which enjoy a relatively inelastic demand the Minister of Finance can calculate to a considerable degree of accuracy the increase in tax revenue which will accrue from such taxes. The cost of collecting indirect taxes is minimal since shopkeepers, publicans and petrol station cashiers do the collecting on behalf of the Exchequer.

(b) *Indirect taxes are equitable.* Direct taxes are levied on income while indirect taxes are levied on expenditure. It is often difficult to determine, for the purpose of levying tax, a person's income. However, a person's expenditure will be related to his income and thus a tax on expenditure may be more equitable than a system of taxation levied on the basis of estimates of income.

(c) *Payment is convenient for the taxpayer.* Payment is made at the time of purchase rather than paying the tax at some time subsequent to the purchase of the good. In addition most people when contemplating a purchase concentrate on the total cost of the item, including tax, and in fact they are often unaware of the apportionment of the total cost as between tax and price net of tax. In this way purchasers adjust their purchasing behaviour in a manner related to total cost, and in addition experience the minimum aversion to the payment of the tax.

(d) *Indirect taxes do not constitute a disincentive to work.* Since indirect taxes are based on expenditure rather than income, taxpayers may not perceive as direct a relationship between work effort and the payment of taxes as they do in the case of income tax. In addition, an individual may work harder in order to obtain the money required to purchase the same quantity of goods and services which he enjoyed prior to the imposition of, or increase in, indirect taxes on the goods and services concerned.

(e) *Indirect taxes may have a stabilising effect on the level of economic activity.* If the indirect tax is levied on goods which are subject to a high income elasticity of demand then the yield from the tax will increase as an increase in income is reflected in a higher level of demand. Conversely, the yield will fall when income falls. Thus indirect taxes levied on goods with a high income elasticity of demand would have a stabilising influence on the economy.

(f) *Indirect taxes are variable and specific.* Not only are indirect taxes capable of being varied upwards or downwards in conformity with government policy but through being capable of being levied in a discriminatory manner they constitute a very precise weapon of government policy. For example, a lower rate of taxation may be imposed on necessities, and/or on goods produced by domestic industry; alternatively the Balance of Payments may be strengthened by import duties on goods of foreign origin, while habits harmful to health, e.g., smoking, may be penalised by the imposition of indirect taxes.

31.28. INDIRECT TAXATION — DISADVANTAGES

(a) *Indirect tax may be regressive.* If indirect taxes are levied on goods which are bought in more or less the same quantities by rich and poor alike, e.g., necessities, then such taxes are regressive.

(b) *Indirect tax may be inflationary.* Taxes on good and services are included as an integral part of the price which must be paid for these goods and services, consequently indirect taxes increase the cost of living.

(c) *Indirect tax may lead to misallocation of resources.* Indirect taxes change the relative price of goods and services and thus result in consumers adjusting their expenditure from what it would have been in the absence of the imposition of the taxes concerned. This substitution effect lowers consumers' utility to a degree greater than that entailed in the paying of the same amount of income tax. As production is adjusted in response to the change in demand caused by the taxes there is said to be a misallocation of resources.

(d) *Indirect tax may affect employment and the viability of industries.* This depends on the elasticity of demand for the product on which the tax is levied. If a tax on cigarettes results in a reduction in the demand for cigarettes then employment in the cigarette industry may suffer, in fact, the very existence of the industry may be endangered.

(e) *Indirect tax discriminates between individuals of the same economic standing.* When a tax is imposed on specific goods, e.g., cigarettes, spirits, then individuals who purchase these goods are penalised whereas equally well off individuals who do not purchase these goods make a smaller contribution to the government's tax revenue. A non-smoking teetotaller who walks to work pays considerably less tax than his colleague of similar economic standing who smokes, drinks and drives a car.

31.29. INCIDENCE OF A TAX

Impact and effective incidence

The incidence of a tax refers to the manner in which the burden of the tax is borne. A distinction can be drawn between the *impact or formal incidence* of the tax which means the person or commodity on which the tax was imposed, and the *effective incidence* of the tax which means who actually pays the tax, e.g., a tax on farmers may result in an increase in food prices by the amount of the taxes, in which case, though the formal incidence of the tax would have been on farmers the effective incidence of the tax is on consumers of the products. It is possible for a tax to be shifted "forward" on to customers or "backwards" on to suppliers — depending on the relative elasticities of supply and demand.

With respect to direct taxes it is rather difficult to shift the incidence of the tax and thus the impact and formal incidence of the tax are likely to be the same, e.g., if I am paid £200 per week and I had been paying £40 income tax, and if my tax liability is increased to £48 per week, it is extremely unlikely that I will be able to negotiate a wage increase of £8 per week in order that I may maintain parity in my after-tax pay.

Effects of tax on quantity supplied

31.30. In contrast to this situation it may be possible to shift all, or some of, the incidence of an expenditure or excise tax, depending on the elasticities of supply and demand for the product on which the tax is levied. If the government levies a tax of 5p on a good it means that there is a difference of 5p between the price paid by the consumer and the price received by the supplier. If, prior to the introduction of the tax, the producer was willing to supply 1,000 units at a price of 75p; after the imposition of the tax if the producer is to continue supplying 1,000 units the selling price of the good would have to be increased to 80p in order that the producer would continue to receive 75p net of tax. If the selling price remained at 75p after the imposition of the tax then the quantity supplied would be 500.

Table 31.30. At each level of supply consumers pay a higher price after imposition of tax.

Quantity	Price paid by consumer and received by supplier prior to imposition of tax.	Price which consumer must pay after imposition of tax of 5p per unit in order that quantity supplied and price received by supplier may remain unchanged.
	p	p
500	70	75
600	71	76
700	72	77
800	73	78
900	74	79
1,000	75	80
1,100	76	81
1,200	77	82

31.31. DEMAND CONDITIONS AFFECT THE AFTER-TAX PRICE/OUTPUT EQUILIBRIUM

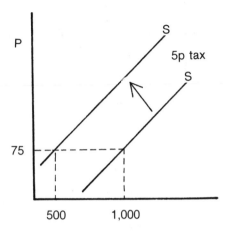

Fig. 31.31. Tax shifts supply curve upwards by the amount of tax — based on data in Table 31.30.

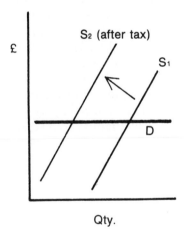

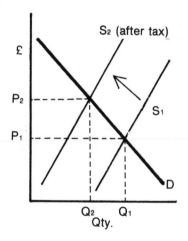

Fig. 31.31. (a) Perfectly Elastic Demand Curve. Equilibrium-quantity is reduced while equilibrium price remains unchanged. Incidence of tax is on sellers of good.

Fig. 31.31. (b) Moderately Elastic Demand Curve. Equilibrium-quantity is smaller while equilibrium price is higher. But price rises by less than the amount of the tax as the incidence of the tax is borne partly by sellers and partly by buyers.

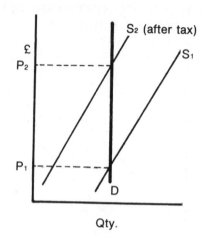

Fig. 31.31.(c) Perfectly Inelastic
Demand Curve. Equilibrium-
quantity is unchanged while equilibrium price is higher. Price rises
by the amount of the tax so that
the incidence of tax is on
purchasers.

*Incidence of
tax as between
producers and
consumers*

31.32. The incidence of the tax between producers and consumers depends upon the relationship between the elasticity of supply and the elasticity of demand, e.g., if demand is perfectly elastic the incidence of the tax will be borne entirely by suppliers as market price remains unchanged as shown in Fig. 31.31(a). In Fig. 31.31(c) demand is perfectly inelastic so the entire amount of the tax is passed on to the consumer as the selling price of the good rises by the amount of the tax. In Fig. 31.31 (b) price rises by less than the amount of the tax as the incidence of the tax is borne partly by suppliers and partly by purchasers on the basis of their relative elasticities. The quantity sold is reduced as a result of the increase in price.

QUESTIONS

Q1. State, and explain briefly, two headings which appear under "Receipts" and two headings which appear under "Expenditure" in each of the following.
(a) Account of Current Receipts and Expenditure of Central Government.
(b) Account of Capital Receipts and Expenditure of Central Government.

Q2. What factors have contributed to the increase in National Debt over the past few years? What have been the economic consequences of this development?

Q3. Explain what is meant by Value Added Tax. Do you consider it to be an efficient means of taxation? Explain your answer.

Q4. What is meant by a Current Budget Deficit? Trace the likely effect(s) on the economy if the Government incurs a Current Budget Deficit.

Q5. Distinguish between the Impact and Effective Incidence of a tax.

Q6. Write a note setting out the advantages and disadvantages of Direct Taxes.

32   Other Forms of Government Economic Intervention

32.1. Local Authorities

Sources of Finance

The various corporations, Urban and County Councils which are known collectively as Local Authorities have a large number of employees and their economic activities have a major influence on the level of activity in the economy as shown in Table 32.1. Local authorities are authorised to levy a form of local taxation known as '*rates*'. Each business premises if given a *rateable valuation* (say £40), the total of these rateable valuations constitutes the rateable base of the region (say £1 million). The local authorities in a manner similar to the government or central authority draw up estimates of expenditure for the coming year and then strike a rate which will raise the revenue required. The rate for the year may be £6 for £1 valuation, so that the premises with a £40 valuation would be liable for a charge of £240 in respect of its rates for the year. Rates were a regressive form of taxation and as a result of Local Government (Financial Provision) Act of 1978 rates on private dwellings were abolished. Each local authority now receives a subvention from Central Funds in lieu of income from rates on private dwellings. Because the government is the major source of finance for local authorities it has considerable control of the activities of these bodies.

32.2. State Sponsored Bodies

A Looser Form of Government Control

In addition to the control which the government exercises over the economy by means of Acts of the Oireachtas, budgetary policy and local government, the State has an additional means of controlling and influencing the economy through the many State sponsored bodies which exist. State sponsored bodies are organisations to which the government appoints directors and chief executives but whose staffs are not civil servants; though under the control of a minister the organisations and their staffs are not an integral part of his government department. These State sponsored bodies were given a degree of autonomy and independence from the civil service in the hope that, freed from bureaucratic control, they might exhibit a degree of flexibility and dynamism in keeping with the purpose for which they were established. President Roosevelt articulated their raison d'etre when he stated that 'public corporations are clothed with the power of government but possess the flexibility of private enterprise'.

Table 32.1 Receipts and Expenditure of Local Authorities 1982 to 1987

£ thousand

Description	1982	1983	1984	1985	1986	1987
Current receipts						
Rates	103,860	116,459	136,692	153,235	166,664	185,175
Gross rental income	93,980	117,950	141,080	170,860	167,680	172,340
Grants from central government	1,404,544	1,562,535	1,645,954	1,772,215	1,851,954	1,905,772
Repayments of loans under the Housing Acts — Interest	50,034	57,566	64,193	70,940	77,378	83,357
Miscellaneous receipts	141,320	181,706	218,433	245,824	295,874	314,991
Total receipts — current	1,793,738	2,036,216	2,206,352	2,413,074	2,559,550	2,661,635
Current receipts						
Grants from central government	120,860	149,514	157,139	181,476	208,035	211,342
Repayments of loans under the Housing Acts — Principal	5,823	6,400	6,980	7,669	8,364	9,052
Miscellaneous receipts	68,709	65,550	69,269	79,693	64,348	97,218
Loans received from central government	385,302	367,004	361,861	347,863	293,184	207,258
Other loans received and miscellaneous borrowing	17,270	4,109	20,806	52,350	127,045	80,232
Total receipts — capital	597,964	592,577	616,055	669,051	700,976	605,102
Total receipts — current and capital	2,391,702	2,628,793	2,822,407	3,082,125	3,260,526	3,266,737
Current expenditure						
Subsidies:						
Housing	15,006	19,837	8,342	13,836	19,219	6,572
Other	132	77	93	80	96	66
National debt interest:						
Central government	192,043	240,286	281,977	325,949	321,283	347,750
Other	19,970	25,541	19,872	22,170	27,247	54,595
Transfer payments	210,647	224,202	256,009	288,707	337,103	347,046
Transfers to central government	7,597	6,769	6,932	6,186	5,305	3,674
Expenditure on goods and services:						
Wages, salaries and pensions	710,833	779,085	849,963	903,972	966,170	977,454
Other	679,766	726,969	772,972	868,738	930,183	908,966
Total expenditure — current	1,835,994	2,022,766	2,196,160	2,429,638	2,606,606	2,646,123
Capital expenditure:						
Grants to enterprises	3,129	3,024	2,170	2,171	2,173	4,017
Other transfer payments	2,956	2,654	3,108	4,179	4,153	4,668
Loan repayments:						
Central government	19,189	22,211	25,796	29,808	35,819	33,914
Other	1,278	1,642	1,149	1,327	1,751	4,493
Loans to persons	102,793	81,000	73,000	71,937	85,130	146,540
Gross physical capital formation	426,363	495,496	521,024	543,065	524,894	426,982
Total expenditure — capital	555,708	606,027	626,247	652,487	653,920	620,614
Total expenditure — current and capital	2,391,702	2,628,793	2,822,407	3,082,125	3,260,526	3,266,737

Source: National Income and Expenditure (1988) (C.S.O.)

32.3. These State sponsored bodies are often classified along the following lines:—

Trading — CIE, ESB, Bord na Móna, etc.;

Promotional and Developmental – Bord Fáilte, Córas Tráchtála Teo., Shannon Free Airport Development Co., etc.

Research — Agricultural Institute, Dublin Institute for Advanced Studies, Institute for Industrial Research and Standards, An Foras Forbartha, etc.

Regulatory — Veterinary Council, Medical Registration Council, Dental Board, Opticians Board, Nursing Council, etc.

Financial — Central Bank, Industrial Credit Co., Agricultural Credit Corporation Ltd., Foir Teoranta, etc.

32.4. Reasons for the Establishment of State Sponsored Trading Corporations

(a) There are certain goods and services which constitute an important element in the production process of all firms so that any deficiency in the quality, availability or cost competitiveness of these goods and services, e.g., transport, electricity, communication, etc., would place an intolerable strain on many firms in the economy. These goods and services are often referred to as part of the infrastructure of the economy.

(b) A private monopolist of essential services might exploit his monopoly position, for example, by charging high prices.

(c) Where an industry requires a high capital investment in production or distributive facilities (i) competition would entail a wasteful duplication of facilities, e.g., railway lines, or (ii) the initial investment might not be forthcoming from the private sector, e.g., air transport.

(d) Organisations within the public sector (i) may have access to funds from international agencies, e.g., World Bank, which are denied to private companies which do not have government financial support, and (ii) may secure finance at more competitive rates than comparable organisations outside the public sector.

(e) It may be necessary for the State to assist industries which in the short term are unable to withstand economic onslaughts, though in the long term they may be viable. *Foir Teoranta* was established in 1972 in order to provide financial assistance to existing firms which, though economically viable in the long term, require capital which the commercial sector will not provide. *The Dairy Disposal Company Ltd.* was incorporated in 1927 to rationalise the creamery industry while *Irish Steel Holdings Ltd.* was the outcome of State intervention to assist the steel industry.

(f) The State sometimes undertook the entrepreneurial function in markets which the private sector was reluctant to enter, e.g., transport in rural areas *(CIE)*, credit for industrial development *(Industrial Credit Co. Ltd.)*, and air transport *(Aer Lingus)*.

32.5. Possible Impediments to the Economic Efficiency of State Sponsored Bodies

(a) The individuals whom the Minister responsible selects as directors and chief executives to control and guide State sponsored corporations may lack the necessary detailed knowledge of the industry or of business generally.

Table 32.4 Trading Results, Employment and Financial Position of Commercial semi-State Bodies — based on latest published accounts

	£m	£m	£m	£m	£m	£m	£m
(a) Trading Information:							
Combined Turnover	1,150	321	1,051	732	796	11	4,061
Combined Net Profit (Loss) before Tax and Financing Charges	235	9	81	—	128	1	454
Combined Financing Charges	208	32	43	—	415		
Combined Net Profit/(Loss) before Tax	27	(23)	38	4	(4)	1	43
Return on Shareholders' funds	5%	Negative	19%	6%	Negative	8%	4%
Return on Capital employed	12%	4%	14%	N/A	10%	7%	11%★
Net Profit/(Loss) as percentage of sales	2%	(7%)	4%	N/A	—	9%	1%★
(b) Employment Information:							
Number employed	17,223	3,383	22,514	2,377	27,001	258	72,756
(c) Financial Position							
Employment of Capital:							
Fixed and Intangible Assets	1,784	249	513	23	1,427	8	4,004
Long term Investments/Sinking Funds	61	18	115	—	—	—	194
Net Current Assets/(Liabilities)	143	(28)	(39)	316	(111)	6	287
Loans	—	—	—	3,260	—	—	3,260
Total (c)	1,988	239	589	3,599	1,316	14	7,745
(d) Financed by:							
Shareholders' Funds	514	27	199	66	268	13	1,087
Longterm Debt	1,474	187	361	—	1,046	1	3,069
Grants	—	6	5	—	—	—	11
Other	—	19	24	271	2	—	316
Policyholders' Funds	—	—	—	2,195	—	—	2,195
Deposits	—	—	—	1,067	—	—	1,067
Total (d)	1,988	239	589	3,599	1,316	14	7,745
(e) Longterm Debt/Shareholders' Funds	2.9:1	6.9:1	1.8:1	N/A	3.9:1	0.1:1	3.0:1★
Current Ratio	1.5:1	0.8:1	0.7:1	N/A	0.7:1	3.4:1	1.0:1★

★Excludes banking and insurance companies.

Notes:

Energy-Related Companies:	— INPC, ESB, BGE and BNM
Industrial Bodies:	— Irish Steel, NET and Siúicre Éireann
Transport Bodies:	— Aer Lingus/Aer Linte, B & I, CIE and Aer Rianta
Banking and Insurance	— ICC, ACC and Irish Life
Communications Bodies:	— BTE, An Post and RTE
Other Companies:	— Irish National Stud, OIE and Arranmara Teo.

Results are stated after extraordinary items and Government subventions.

Financing charges include interest, unrealised exchange movements and maortization charges when incorporated in the bodies' profit and loss account.

Source: Budget 88 (Stationery Office)

(b) Due to the requirement of public accountability, the boards of these corporations may adopt an unduly conservative approach to risk taking.

(c) Profits constitute both a target for firms and a measurement of their efficiency. While State sponsored trading corporations were not set up to maximise their profits, nevertheless the absence of the profit motive and criterion makes it more difficult to assess their efficiency. Any losses which these bodies sustain which are financed by the Exchequer add to the general burden of taxation.

(d) Because of their monopoly position these bodies may avoid losses through increasing their prices rather than through cost-reducing efficiencies.

(e) These corporations may undertake, without a mandate, uneconomic activities which they consider to be in the public good. However, the interpretation of the public goods should be left to elected representatives who can issue policy directions to these bodies on matters of this nature. In addition to this the board of each of these State sponsored bodies may have different opinions as to what constitutes the public good which may lead to a lack of consistency in overall public policy, e.g., transport to outlying rural areas may be considered uneconomical and not supplied by one board while electricity to the same areas may be subsidised by another board. While such bodies should have highly developed a social conscience as would be expected from the best firms in the private sector, they should not undertake activities which are not justified on economic grounds unless they receive a specific directive to do so from the Minister responsible.

(f) These boards may be subject to representations from pressure groups who wish the board to undertake non-economic activities or to push their level of production beyond that which is economic.

(g) The operation of these corporations may be made more difficult through government intervention in their day-to-day operations (as distinct from directives on general policy).

Privatisation

32.6. In the 1980's there has been a reversal of the policy of establishing firms under public control; there has developed (particularly in the UK) government policies directed towards the **privatisation** of industry. This privatisation consists of selling to the private sector enterprises which had hitherto been in public ownership. An emergence of a similar approach is detectable here also with:

(i) The transfer of the functions of Post & Telecommunications from government departments to the semi-state sector.

(ii) CIE hotels being transferred to CERT.

(iii) The winding up of Irish Shipping.

(iv) The reorganisation of B & I Lines.

(v)   The proposed restructuring of CIE into 3 separate companies.

32.7. The case for privatisation tends to be based on the following points:

(i)   Publicly owned firms which are sold to the private sector would be (more) subject to the rigours of the market place and private shareholders would exert pressure on the firm to be cost-efficient and profitable.

(ii)   Despite such firms passing into the private sector their pricing policies could still be subject to public control and regulation.

(iii) Prices changed by these firms while they were publicly owned would provide a benchmark for the evolution of future price increases so that the interests of the general public could be protected against inordinate price increases.

(iv)   There is a need for these firms to adopt the most efficient commercial practices since, often, they provide an essential service to the economy so that their efficiency and the prices which they charge are important elements in the efforts of domestic firms to retain international competitiveness.

(v)   By selling these firms to the private sector the state is serving notice on the employees of these firms that they are (now) subject to the full rigour of market forces. Often this is a prelude to some form of rationalisation of work practices and numbers employed.

32.8. Those against a policy of privatisation would cite the various points set out in section 32.4. The following points would also be adduced:

(i)   Only the successful public companies would be privatised since those with an unsatisfactory commercial record would not be purchased by the private sector. The ultimate outcome of this policy would be that the private sector would "cream off" the successful companies while the state would retain responsibility for unprofitable public companies.

(ii)   Some of these public companies are of national importance consequently it is undesirable that they come under the control of foreign controlled consortium who in the event of a commercial conflict might subordinate the interest of these firms to their own interests.

(iii) Decisions in the private sector are based on private costs and benefits, these might diverge from social costs and benefits.

32.9. Prices and Incomes Policy

As Ireland is an open economy, depending to a great extent on external trade, it is vital that we retain price competitiveness against foreign competitors. The economic and social disruption consequent on the inflation which persisted from the 1960's has focussed the attention of the government on the need to introduce policies designed to control payments to the factors of production with a view to relieving the upward pressure on prices. There is also the realisation that increased payments for factors of production provide the owners of these factors (including wage earners) with incomes which enable them to pay the higher prices. Thus the payments to factors of production and the prices of goods and services are so intertwined that neither aspect can be tackled in isolation — hence the need for a *prices and incomes policy* rather than either a prices policy or an incomes policy on its own.

Incomes Policy

32.10. It should be noted that an incomes policy will control inflation only when the inflation is being caused by an increase in money incomes. It may be that money incomes are lagging behind price increases and that incomes, e.g., wages, are being increased merely in response to price increases rather than causing them, i.e., the cause may flow from prices to wages rather than vice versa. If an incomes policy is to be successful it must enjoy the support of the various sectors in the economy. It is not possible to remove income differentials and redistribute income in favour of low income groups if the better-paid highly-organised sectors insist on maintaining differentials in real income and are prepared to take industrial action in support of their claims. Similarly, it is not possible to redistribute National Income between wages and profits if there is not at least tacit acceptance of the merits of such a policy. Otherwise, for example, whenever wages are increased there may be a price increase in order to give at least a pro rata increase to profits. The price increase in turn precipitates demands for further wage increases as labour attempts to maintain what it considers to be the optimal and proper distribution of National Income.

Difficulty in Controlling Profits

32.11. Very often an incomes policy is taken to mean a wages policy, but a proper incomes policy should embrace payments to each of the factors of production. Even if it was possible to control profits and dividends, entrepreneurs and investors may enjoy capital gains; in addition, where there is a restriction on the distribution of profits, the reinvesting of undistributed profits means that even higher profits and dividends may be enjoyed in the future when the restriction has been lifted. This postponement of the receipt of income, which is possible in the case of profits and dividends, is in sharp contrast to the fact that wages lost, through some control or standstill on wage increases, are unlikely ever to be regained by the workers concerned — though their children and future generations of Irish workers may benefit.

Rounds of Wage Increases

32.12. In Ireland since 1970 a series of well defined 'rounds' of wage increases have come from collective bargaining at national level by the *Irish Congress of Trade Unions* and the *Irish Employers' Confederation* with the government being represented merely as an employer. Each agreement specified the amount of, and the conditions attaching to, the pay increases. Employers and employees are expected to uphold the terms of the National Wage Agreement irrespective of whether or not they are represented at the negotiations which led to the agreement.

32.13. One consequence of these agreements has been a narrowing of wage differentials in real terms because:—

Narrowing of Wage Differentials in Real Terms

(a)   The percentage increases specified in the agreements tended to taper off at higher wage levels, e.g., 5% increase in the first £3,000 of annual wages, 2½% on the next £2,000 and 1% on the next £2,000

(b)   In some instances maximum increases were specified or implied as in the above example where the maximum increase would be £220 per annum in gross pay.

(c)   Lower paid workers received an increase which was specified in money terms and which exceeded the percentage increase which other workers received, e.g., if the percentage increase would have resulted in an increase of less than £300 per annum, an increase of £300 per annum was granted.

(d)   Due to the progressive nature of income tax, differentials in after-tax income in real terms were narrowed even more.

A narrowing of wage differentials in real terms has a disincentive effect on economic effort which can be manifest in:

(a)   high rates of absenteeism;

(b)   promotion being less sought after;

(c)   reluctance to work overtime;

(d)   difficulty in motivating workers particularly if there is a low level of satisfaction related to the actual work involved.

Effect on Promotional Grades

32.14. As lower paid workers are usually defined in terms of weekly wages, employees on the lower incremental scales in 'white collar' jobs receive increases of the same magnitude as lower paid manual workers with little opportunity for promotion. These increases in the lower incremental scales in 'white collar' jobs heighten the wage expectations of those entering these jobs and creates pressures for increases in the continuation and promotional incremental scales in order to maintain meaningful pay differentials. Let us suppose that the lower incremental scale was originally £7,500 per annum increasing by 10 annual increments of £150 to £9,000 per annum and as a result of a national wage agreement this was increased to £8,000 per annum increasing by 10 annual increments of £150 to £9,500 per annum. In order to avoid anomolies it became necessary to increase the commencing salary of the promotional grade from £9,000 to £9,500 per annum and so on throughout the system.

*Sheltered
Sector and
Exposed
Sector*

32.15. Because the sheltered sector of the economy, i.e., the industries which are not subject to foreign competition, e.g., state monopolies, civil service, service industries and building sector, have the largest representation at the negotiations on national wage agreements or national understandings, there was a danger that the settlement figures would tend to reflect what the sheltered sector could afford to pay — if necessary by increasing prices or taxes. The identical increase which the exposed or open sector of the economy was committed to pay placed this sector under considerable competitive pressure — and it is this exposed sector which is the source of our economic growth.

*Government
Guidelines
on
Magnitude
of Wage
Increases*

32.16. During the negotiations which determine the national wage agreements the government usually sets out guidelines as to the magnitude of the increase which the government considers to be appropriate and in the best interests of the economy. If the increase in GNP in real terms since the previous round of wages increases has been (say) 5% then this sets the average increases for the round in question, though account is taken also of changes which are likely to occur during the currency of the agreement. The word 'average' implies that there may be some increases above the norm of (say) 5%, in which case if the average of 5% is to be maintained there must be some settlements below 5%. If the lower paid are to receive percentage increases above the norm then the higher paid must be willing to accept increases below it if the average is to be maintained. What tends to happen in practice is the following:

(a) Those who have had no increase in productivity (particularly if they are not strongly unionised) settle for the norm of 5%.

(b) Those who can substantiate productivity claims in excess of 5% seek increases related to productivity.

(c) Others (particularly if they are strongly unionised) engage in spurious productivity agreements in an attempt to gain increases greater than the norm.

32.17. This setting of a "norm" for wage and salaries increase achieved its highest public profile in August 1981 when the then Minister for Finance, Mr. John Bruton set up a Committee on Costs and Competitiveness with the following terms of reference: "The Committee will make recommendations on the appropriate rate of domestic cost increases during a stipulated period consistent with sustaining the competitiveness of the economy at home and abroad.

The recommendations of the Committee which were published in Report of the Committee on Costs and Competitiveness (Pl. 154) Stationery Office, were to the effect that "domestic cost increases should be such that average 1982 costs should be not more than 11 per cent above the average level in 1981. A summary table setting out the basis for the recommendation is shown below — Table 32.17.

Table 32.17. Calculation of increases in Irish earnings in 1982 consistent with sustaining competitiveness at 1981 level

	USA	Japan	Germany	France	UK	Italy	Belgium	Denmark	Nether-lands	Weighted Average
Forecast increase in earnings in ecu 1982 (%)	15·6	9·5	4·4	13·4	7·7	18·6	9·1	9·9	4·0	
Normalised* productivity growth (%)	3·1	6·3	3·9	4·8	2·3	4·6	6·1	2·9	3·9	
Forecast increase in normalised unit wage costs (%)	12·1	3·0	0·5	8·2	5·3	13·4	2·8	6·8	0·1	6·1
Weights in Irish competitiveness γ	·1874	·0440	·1345	·0798	·4038	·0440	·0358	·0162	·0544	

WARRANTED INCREASE IN IRISH UNIT WAGE COSTS — 6·1%
INCREASE IN IRISH PRODUCTIVITY (NORMALISED) — 4·3%
WARRANTED INCREASE IN IRISH EARNINGS — 10·6%

Source: Report of the Committee on Costs and Competitiveness (P1154.) Stationery Office 1982.

★Normalised Productivity growth refers to the long term trend in productivity — there is a strong cyclical element in short term productivity movements. γWeights based on the proportion of our trade with the particular country.

Effect of Settlement in Excess of Guidelines

32.18. Where the national wage agreements did not conform to the guidelines which the government set out, the government did not take punitive action. Instead it adjusted fiscal and monetary policy in an attempt to maintain employment in the face of the higher pay levels. Though this policy has been facilitated in the past by the depreciation of the Irish currency in line with Sterling, it has resulted in large increases in our *National Debt* and an increase in employment in the public sector relative to the private sector.

National Understandings

32.19. In more recent times there has been a shift of emphasis from national agreements to social agreements or national understandings whereby trade unions state that they are prepared to 'trade' some element of wage increase for tax reliefs, job creation programmes and increased government social expenditure. The term for the current agreement is Programme for National Recovery.

Price Control

32.20. Since wage rates and prices of raw materials are often outside the control of individual firms, for these firms price control is effectively profit control. To the extent that it may be possible to confine prices to a level lower than they would be in the absence of official intervention, there is a relief in the upward pressure on the cost of living, and in this way claims are eliminated from wage earners and rentiers for compensatory increases as they seek to maintain the real value of their income. From 1965 price control was administered by the Department of Industry & Commerce. *In October 1971 was established the National Prices Commission which was charged with the responsibility to keep under review the prices of goods and services and to advise the Minister on these matters.* The Commission was a small, representative, part time, advisory body which met weekly. Its function was purely advisory though practically all of its recommendations were implemented. The Prices Commission submitted monthly reports to the Minister which were published as submitted. In these reports the Commission explained the background to its recommendations together with comments from interested parties.

National Prices Commission

The Commission in its recommendations recognised the link which exists between the costs of inputs, productivity, prices and profits. Increases in the costs of inputs which were not reflected in price increases resulted in lower profits or compensatory improvements in productivity. If profits are squeezed to such an extent that a firm is unable to maintain and/or replace capital equipment then such a firm will be unable to survive in the long run — even if it should wish to remain in the industry in the face of the lower profitability.

Interrelationship of Costs, Productivity and Prices

32.21. It is obvious from a perusal of the activities of the Commission that it considered competition to be the most efficacious method of controlling prices. Accordingly, the Commission tended to concentrate its attention on domestic firms which were dominant in the home market and not subject to serious competition from imports. A firm was considererd to be dominant if its sales in the Irish market exceed 30% of home consumption. Even such a firm would not be subject to detailed price control if it exported a minimum of 25% of its output and sold the balance of its output at an ex-factory price which were not greater than the average free-on-board export price. Less than 100 dominant firms were subject to detailed price control.

Competition Controls Prices

32.22. Firms, of which there are approximately 20, producing goods for which there were maximum retail price orders were subject to detailed price control. Examples of goods for which maximum retail price orders had been issued are bread, flour, butter, milk, turf briquettes, sugar, margarine and cooking fats. Believing competition to be the most efficient regulator of prices, the Commission paid particular attention to the '*sheltered sector*' of the economy, i.e., those firms which are not

Sheltered Sector and Exposed Sector

subject to external competition, in contrast to the '*exposed sector*' which is composed of agriculture and manufacturing industry and is subject to foreign competition. The sheltered sector for price control purposes may be classified along the following lines:— (a) retail prices; (b) profit margins of importers, wholesalers, and retailers; (c) professional fees; (d) prices charged by State monopolies, e.g., CIE, ESB.

Treatment of Cost Increases

32.23. If price increases were permitted by the Commission to allow firms to recoup fully any increase in costs, there would be less pressure on firms to seek greater efficiency or to economise on the use of inputs which have become more expensive. However, a policy which attempts to achieve some degree of absorption of the increase in costs by firms may be counterproductive if it reduces profitability and the attractiveness of investment to such an extent that the investment necessary for improved productivity and growth is not forthcoming. To add to this dilemma any lack of investment by domestic firms creates gaps in the supply to the home market which will be reflected in our Balance of International Trade as imports increase in volume in order to fill the vacuum.

Multinational Firms

32.24. Imports could increase and domestic employment opportunities suffer if Irish subsidiaries of international organisations are not allowed to increase their prices. In such a situation production of the company in Ireland could cease and the item be imported from a foreign subsidiary of the same company. Since these imports are not subject to our price control the price at which the good would eventually be sold on the Irish market might be even higher than that sought by the Irish subsidiary, in which circumstance we would lose on two fronts — employment and price level.

The Restrictive Practices Commission

Introduction of Legislation

32.25. This was another means by which the government regulated the market economy. The first Irish legislation dealing with the control of restrictive business practices was introduced in 1953. For some time prior to that date there had been a growing volume of public complaint regarding the development and extension of restrictive practices in the supply and distribution of various kinds of goods. This led to the enactment of the *Restrictive Trade Practices Act, 1953,* which was amended in some minor respects by the *Restrictive Trade Practices (Amendment) Act, 1959.*

Fair Trade Commission

32.26. The purpose of this legislation was to promote free but fair competition in the supply and distribution of goods. The Acts did not expressly declare any type of restrictive business practice to be illegal but provided a means of bringing all such practices under close public scrutiny in order to prevent abuses. Provision was made for the full investigation of any practice, whether operated by an individual or a group, by the *Fair Trade Commission*, an impartial body set up under the Act for the purpose of establishing whether or not a practice was unfair or contrary to the public interest. Provision was made for the elimination or prevention of unfair practices as outlined in the following paragraphs.

(a) The Fair Trade commission was empowered to hold public enquiries into the supply and distribution of any kind of goods (including ancillary services) or into one or more aspects of the supply and distribution of one or more kinds of goods. It reported its findings, with recommendations for remedial action to the Minister for Industry and Commerce who, at his discretion, could give effect to the recommendations by making an Order which became law if confirmed by an Act of the Legislature.

(b) The Commission was also empowered to make rules representing, in its opinion, fair trading conditions for the supply and distribution of any kind of goods (including ancillary services). These rules had not the force of law but, if they were not being observed, the Commission was obliged to report accordingly to the Minister, who might make an order giving legal effect to the rules, subject to confirmation by the legislature.

(c) The Commission was required to keep under review the general effect on the public interest of restrictive trade practices, as well as the operation of orders made under the Acts, and might submit a report on any such matters to the Minister, with recommendations for remedial measures.

Scope of Legislation

32.27. The Acts did not apply to arrangements between employers and employees concerning wages and conditions of work but the Commission was empowered to enquire into the refusal of employers and employees to use particular materials or methods for manufacturing or construction purposes. The Acts applied to activities of manufacturers and producers in the field of supply and distribution, and did not deal directly with monopolies as such.

Restrictive Practices Act

32.28. The *Restrictive Trade Practices Act, 1953* and *Restrictive Trade Practices (Amendment) Act, 1959* were repealed and replaced by the *Restrictive Practices Act, 1972*. This Act extended the scope of the legislation to cover investigation into the provision of services as well as into the supply and distribution of goods. Professional services are included within the scope of the Act but banking, insurance, electricity and transport services were excluded as were any services provided under a contract of employment.

Fair Practice Rules

32.29. Preliminary investigations into the supply and distribution of goods and the provision of services were carried out by the *Examiner of Restrictive Practices*, this new position having been created by the Act. The Examiner had powers of investigation relating to the inspection of premises and records and the obtaining of information by authorised officers, which had been vested in the Commission. Public enquiries were held by the Commission (now renamed the *Restrictive Practices Commission* although its constitution was unaltered) on the recommendation of the Examiner who was required to furnish a report of his investigations to the Minister for Industry, Commerce and Tourism★ through the Examiner. The Commission also held enquiries at the request of any person whose application for an enquiry has been refused by the Examiner. As before, the Commission's powers of enquiry included the power to summon and examine witnesses under oath and to require the production of documents in evidence. The Commission could, on the recommendation of the Examiner or at the request of an association representing persons engaged in the supply and distribution of goods or in the provision of services, prepare and publish *Fair Practice Rules* similar in scope to the Fair Trading Rules which could be made under the previous legislation.

Control of Mergers and Takeovers

32.30. As with the previous legislation, the Act did not apply to arrangements between employers and employees concerning wages and conditions of work, but the Commission was empowered to enquire into the refusal of employers and employees to use particular materials or methods for manufacturing or construction purposes. While the Act applied to activities of manufacturers and producers in the field of supply and distribution it did not apply directly to monopolies as such, the control of mergers and take-overs and criteria for action in the case of monopolies and oligopolies were the subject of additional legislation.

Scope of Commission

32.31. The Commission was empowered to carry out studies and analyses of relevant topics such as methods of competition, the structure of markets, types of restrictive practices and the operation of multi-national companies.

32.32. New Developments in Fair Trading & Consumer Affairs
On 17th January 1986 the Minister for Industry, Trade, Commerce & Tourism★ announced that he intended to introduce legislation which will give a new Fair Trade Commission (replacing the present Restrictive Practices Commission) greater power to enquire into anti-competitive and unfair trading practices. Banks, electricity and transport will be brought within the scope of trade legislation for the first time. The title of the new Office is to be Director of Consumer Affairs and Fair Trade and responsibility will include fair trade, consumer protection, prices and restrictive practices legislation generally.

The Fair Trade Commission will be empowered to make fair trading rules for particular trades or services on its own initiative where previously it could act only on the request of the Minister, the Examiner

★Title of Ministerial Portfolio has since been altered.

or certain other parties.

The Commission will investigate any proposed merger or takeover referred to it by the Minister under the Mergers, Takeovers and Monopolies (Control) Act 1978. Such investigations are at present carried out by the Examiner of Restrictive Practices. The Director of Fair Trade will take over the role of the Examiner of Restrictive Practices, the office of the Examiner will be abolished.

The Office of Director of Consumer Affairs was established under the Consumer Information Act 1978. The primary function of the Director is to keep under review practices in relation to advertising and the provision of information to the public in relation to goods and services. The Director also has the function under Section 55 of the Sale of Goods & Supply of Services Act 1980 of keeping under general review practices in relation to obligations imposed on persons under that Act.

In addition to his new responsibilities in relation to restrictive practices and competition, the Director will be given new powers to proceed against persons engaging in practices likely to be contrary to obligations imposed by the Sale of Goods and Supply of Services Act 1980 or the Sale of Goods Act, 1893. The Director will also have power to prosecute for offences under the Prices and Restrictive Practices Act, and under a number of other consumer related Acts and Regulations for overpricing, collusive practices etc.

The powers of the Minister to impose price controls, where restrictive practices result in excessive prices, will be continued as will current requirements in relation to the display of prices. The Fair Trade Commission will provide advice, where necessary, on matters affecting prices and will thus take over one of the main functions of the National Prices Commission.

The present requirements on some commercial operators to give prior notice of, or seek approval for, price increases are being allowed to expire. In some cases the cooperation necessary between operators to present such applications has led to concerted action diminishing competition and leading to higher prices than might otherwise have existed. This change will also remove an administrative burden which added to the costs of the businesses affected.

There has been a progressive decontrol of prices since 1975 when detailed control on most manufacturers, other than dominant firms, was removed. During the period of this gradual process of decontrol, prices were less volatile, inflation fell from 20.4% in 1981 to 4.9% in early 1986. The removal of price controls has done away with the use of official approvals as a means of validating price increases which might not otherwise have been possible to implement in the face of consumer resistance — the official approval was presented by sellers as a justification of the price increase and the "maximum" permitted increase often became the norm.

QUESTIONS

Q1. Explain two items under each of the following headings in respect of Local Authorities.
(i) Current Receipts
(ii) Current Expenditure
(iii) Capital Receipts
(iv) Capital Expenditure.

Q2. Give some reasons for the establishment of State Sponsored Trading Corporations.

Q3. Analyse the case in respect of the privatisation of public owned companies.

Q4. Comment on economic aspects of a Prices and Incomes Policy.

Q5. Detail the Irish experience in respect of Price Control.

Q6. Set out the new developments in relation to Fair Trading and Consumer Affairs.

33 Public Sector Borrowing Requirement and Domestic Credit Expansion

Exchequer Borrowing Requirement

33.1. The Exchequer Borrowing Requirement (EBR) is the amount of money which the State has to borrow in order to carry out the activities which are set out in the Budget. It includes any excess of current expenditure over current revenue, i.e., the Current Budget Deficit, in addition to any borrowing which must be undertaken in order to finance the Programme of Capital Expenditure. The 'Exchequer' refers to Central Government, as distinct from Local Government.

> Exchequer Borrowing Requirement (EBR) = Current Budget Deficit
> + Borrowing for Capital Purposes.

Public Sector Borrowing Requirement

33.2. The Public Sector does not consist of Central Government alone, there are also Corporations, County Councils, State Sponsored Commercial and Non-Commercial Organisations etc. Borrowing is undertaken also by the non-Central Government public sector. When the borrowing needs of these organisations are added to the Exchequer Borrowing Requirement we obtain the Public Sector Borrowing Requirement.

> Public Sector Borrowing Requirement (PSBR) = Exchequer Borrowing Requirement + Borrowings by State-Sponsored Bodies and Local Authorities

Non Monetary Financing of PSBR

33.3. There are various sources from which money can be obtained to meet the Public Sector Borrowing Requirement (PSBR). The State utilises "Small Savings" i.e., money which is being saved in institutions such as the Post Office Savings Bank. Also Government securities may be sold to the domestic non-bank public, e.g. Irish people investing in Government loans. In both of these cases the Government has obtained the money through non-consumption (saving) by people in the domestic economy. Thus there has been no increase in the money supply due to this borrowing, the Government can spend (consume) only to the extent that someone else in the economy saves (refrains from consumption). In recognition of the fact that transactions of this nature have caused no increase in the supply of money in the economy they are referred to as *Non-Monetary Financing of the Public Sector Borrowing Requirement.*

Table 33.3. Trend in the Current Budget Deficit and the Exchequer and Public Sector Borrowing Requirements — (In Absolute Terms and as % of GNP) 1976 — 1988

Year	Current Budget Deficit		Total Exchequer Borrowing		Public Sector Borrowing Requirements	
	£m	% of GNP	£m	% of GNP	£m	% of GNP
1976	201	4.4	506	11.0	595	12.9
1977	201	3.6	545	9.7	697	12.5
1978	397	6.1	810	12.4	973	14.9
1979	522	6.8	1,009	13.2	1,230	16.1
1980	547	6.1	1,218	13.5	1,559	17.3
1981	802	7.4	1,721	15.9	2,204	20.3
1982	988	7.9	1,945	15.6	2,466	19.8
1983	960	7.1	1,756	13.0	2,277	16.9
1984	1,039	7.1	1,825	12.4	2,375	16.2
1985	1,284	8.4	2,015	13.1	2,444	15.9
1986	1,395	8.6	2,145	13.2	2,506	15.5
1987*	1,180	6.8	1,786	10.3	2,056	11.8
1988**	1,125	6.3	1,457	8.2	1,675	9.4

* Provisional Outturn
** Post-Budget Estimate.

Source: Budget 1988. (Stationery Office).

Monetary Financing of PSBR

33.4. Money to meet the PSBR may also be raised by:

(a)   Government Borrowing from Domestic Banks

(b)   Government Borrowing Abroad (Foreign Borrowing)

(c)   Sale of Government Securities to non-Irish residents

(d)   It is also possible for the Private Sector to borrow abroad and invest in Government Securities. From the macro-economic point of view this is the same as the Government itself borrowing abroad.

Each of these methods of financing the activities of the Public Sector increases the domestic money supply and they are categorised as *Monetary Financing of the PSBR.*

Table 33.4 Financing the Exchequer Borrowing Requirement (IR£million), 1978-86

	Non-monetary sources	Monetary sources		Total EBR
		Bank lending to government	Government foreign borrowing	
1978	252	235	323	810
1979	283	267	459	1,009
1980	344	290	583	1,217
1981	285	187	1,250	1,722
1982	587	228	1,130	1,945
1983	733	194	829	1,756
1984	536	519	770	1,825
1985	1,051	75	889	2,015
1986	1,184	-30	991	2,145

Source: Central Bank of Ireland Quarterly Bulletin, various issues as printed in The Economy of Ireland. O'Hagan (Ed.) (IMI).
[1] These figures do not include borrowing by state-sponsored bodies.

*Domestic
Credit
Expansion*

33.5. As already stated the monetary financing of the PSBR increases the domestic money supply. The domestic money supply is increased also to the extent that banks increase the amount of their loans to the Private Sector. When these two sources of increase in the domestic money supply are aggregated they constitute Domestic Credit Expansion (DCE).

> Domestic Credit Expansion (DCE) = Monetary financing of the PSBR
> \+ Increase in bank lending to the private sector

*From DCE
to M3*

33.6. To the extent that there is a deficit on the Current Account of the Balance of Payments capital will flow out of the economy. Similarly there will be capital outflows (inflows) through foreign firms repatriating their profits (or investing in Ireland), and the payment of interest to foreign holders of Government loans. Also commercial banks will have some profits which they haven't distributed to their shareholders. These items will affect the amount of purchasing power in the Irish economy and must be subtracted from (or credited to) Domestic Credit Expansion (DCE) in order to arrive at the figure for the change in the broad money supply (M3).

	Domestic Credit Expansion (DCE)
$\pm$	Change in foreign liabilities of Central Bank & Government
$\pm$	Change in foreign liabilities of the Commercial Banks
—	Non Deposit Liabilities of the Banking system (mainly retained profits of the Commercial Banks)
=	Change in M3.

	Current Budget Deficit	1,200
Plus	Borrowing for Capital Purposes	+ 800
	= Exchequer Borrowing Requirement (EBR)	2,000
Plus	Borrowing by Local Authorities & State Sponsored Bodies	+ 100
	= Public Sector Borrowing Requirement	2,100
Minus	Non-Monetary Financing of PSBR	- 600
	= Monetary Financing of PSBR	1,500
Plus	Increase in bank lending to the Private Sector	+ 400
	= Domestic Credit Expansion (DCE)	1,900
	+ Change in foreign liabilities of Central Bank & Government	-450
	+ Change in foreign liabilities of the Commercial Banks	- 80
Minus	Non Deposit Liabilities of the Banking System (mainly retained profits of the Commercial Banks	- 70
	= Change in M3	1,300

Table 33.6. Outline of the interrelationship between Exchequer Borrowing Requirement Borrowing and change in Broad Money Supply
(figures are for illustrative purposes only)

Effect of Fiscal Policy on Monetary Policy

33.7. An increase in the money supply affects the price level and the rate of inflation. It can be seen from Table 33.7 that the major component in the increase of M3 is the monetary financing of the Public Sector Borrowing Requirement. Thus an expansionary Fiscal Policy increases the monetary financing of the PSBR and constrains the ability to conduct an independent monetary policy.

Table 33.7. Public Sector Borrowing, Domestic Credit Expansion and Money Supply 1978-83

Item		1978	1979	1980	1981	1982	1983
1	Exchequer Borrowing Requirement	810.0	1009.0	1217.0	1722.0	1945.0	1756.0
2	plus borrowing by State-sponsored bodies and Local Authorities	170.9	220.5	341.4	483.5	520.9	539.1
3	= Public Sector Borrowing Requirement (PSBR) = (items 1 + 2)	980.9	1229.5	1558.4	2205.5	2465.9	2295.5
4	less Non-monetary financing	252.0	535.0	371.0	280.0	587.0	721.0
5	= Monetary financing of PSBR (Items 3-4)	728.9	946.5	1187.4	1925.5	1878.9	1574.5
	of which						
	Foreign	325.7	577.3	871.6	1494.3	1379.2	1038.0
	Domestic Banking system	403.2	369.2	315.8	431.2	499.7	536.5
6	*plus* Changes in Government Deposits with the Central Bank	103.2	13.2	41.7	8.3	-56.4	-36.1
7	Changes in commercial bank lending to the private sector	649.0	773.1	647.4	758.7	406.7	497.6
8	= Domestic Credit Expansion (DCE) = (Items 5 + 6 + 7)	1481.0	1732.8	1876.5	2692.5	2229.2	2036.0
9	*less* Net non-deposit liabilities	99.9	-16.2	134.5	60.1	-40.8	19.1
10	*plus* Current Balance of Payments	-256.3	-843.7	-881.9	1399.0	1041.0	-340.0
11	Non-borrowed official capital flow	7.9	45.0	122.1	95.7	235.7	58.0
12	Private non-bank capital flows	-126.0	-123.9	-230.4	-222.4	670.1	1263.0
13	Statistical discrepancy	-15.2	-30.9	146.2	-83.3	-105.7	-66.4
14	= Change in Money Supply (M3) = (Items 8-9=10=11=12=13)	991.5	795.5	895.0	1033.4	900.3	405.5

Source: Proposals for Plan 1984-87. The National Planning Board, Dublin, 1984.

33.8. *"An Accommodating Monetary Policy"* is the term used when the money supply is increased in order to finance an expansionary fiscal policy.

Private Sector Credit has limited significance for DCE

33.9. Credit Guide lines which focus on the issue of credit to the private sector are an ineffective means of attempting to reduce the supply of purchasing power in the economy because the expansion of credit in the private sector is a small component of total changes in the money supply, e.g. from Table 33.7 it can be seen that in 1983 changes in Commercial Bank lending to the private sector was merely 24% of the total increase in Domestic Credit Expansion. A reduction of 50% in private sector lending that year would have been required to reduce DCE by 12% whereas the same reduction in DCE could have been achieved by a 11% reduction in the PSBR.

Domestic Financing of PSBR

33.10. To the extent that the PSBR is financed through non-monetary means it doesn't affect the money supply. However, if the Public Sector increases its demand on domestic sources of capital it will push up domestic interest rates and also make it difficult if not impossible for the private sector to raise capital — a "crowding out" situation.

Note also in Tables 33.4 and 33.7 that in 1983 Monetary Financing of the PSBR from foreign borrowing was £1038m.; the amount of government borrowing from the Domestic Banking System was £536.5m.; while non monetary financing was £721m and commercial bank lending to the private sector was £497.6 so there is no question of the Government being able to finance the PSBR entirely from domestic sources.

33.11. Table 33.11. shows the proportions of our National Debt which are of domestic and foreign natures. Though the proportion of our National Debt which is held outside the country is still large this proportion has been declining since 1983. Note also that the absolute amount of foreign debt declined in 1988.

Table 33.11 Trend in National Debt 1976-1988

Year	Foreign Debt Outstanding		Domestic Debt Outstanding		Total National Debt
	£m	% of Total	£m	% of Total	£m
1976	1,040	28.8	2,572	71.2	3,612
1977	1,039	24.6	3,190	75.4	4,229
1978	1,064	20.6	4,103	79.4	5,167
1979	1,542	23.6	4,998	76.4	6,540
1980	2,207	28.0	5,689	72.0	7,896
1981	3,794	37.2	6,401	62.8	10,195
1982	5,248	45.0	6,421	55.0	11,669
1983	6,899	47.9	7,493	52.1	14,392
1984	7,910	47.0	8,911	53.0	16,821
1985	8,114	43.8	10,388	56.2	18,502
1986	9,220	42.7	12,391	57.3	21,611
1987	9,690	40.9	14,001	59.1	23,691
1988*	9,495	38.6	15,115	61.4	24,610

*Provisional Outturn

33.12. An international comparison of the ratio of National Debt to GNP/GDP is set out in Table 33.12. This table shows also the proportion of national debt which is held by foreigners in respect of a number of countries.

Table 33.12 International Comparison — Per cent of GNP/GDP[1]

Total debt 1988	Government Debt	External debt (1987)	Net government external debt
Ireland	**132.8★**	**Ireland★**	**54.4★**
Ireland	123.3		
Belgium	126.0	Greece	23.0
Italy	95.0	Denmark	18.4
Netherlands	80.0	Portugal	16.5
Greece	71.5	Sweden	14.2
Canada	69.3	Finland	8.1
Japan	68.3★	New Zealand	6.9
Portugal	63.1	Australia	5.0
Sweden	59.0	Norway	3.4
Austria	58.6	Spain	1.4
Denmark	55.6		
United States	51.5★		
Spain	48.4		
Norway	46.7		
United Kingdom	45.3		
Germany	44.6★		
France	44.1		
Australia	20.3		
Finland	18.6		
Switzerland	17.5		

[1] OECD estimates
★ Indicates ratio of debt to GNP show ratios of debt to GDP.
Source: OECD, Department of Finance.

Economic Implications of Domestic Debt.

33.13. If the PSBR is financed domestically in Irish pounds this involves a redistribution of income within the country from general taxpayers to those who loaned money to the Public Sector. The cost to the Exchequer is reduced to the extent that those receiving these interest payments are liable to tax on such income.

QUESTIONS

Q1. What relationship exists between the Current Budget Deficit and the Public Sector Borrowing Requirement?

Q2. Explain monetary financing of the PSBR.

Q3. Show the relationship between DCE and M3.

Q4. Does an expansionary fiscal policy affect monetary policy?

Q5. Analyse the usefulness of credit guidelines for the private sector as a means of influencing credit creation.

Q6. To what extent has our PSBR been financed from foreign sources over the past decade?

34   International Trade

Reasons for Trading

34.1. Countries trade with each other so that their inhabitants can enjoy a higher standard of living. This trade in the case of Ireland may be based on the following facts:

(a)   Certain goods which we cannot produce here in Ireland are available elsewhere, e.g., petroleum products; or

(b)   Other countries can produce goods which would be difficult (if not impossible) to produce here because of the absence of certain factors of production, e.g., climatic conditions for the production of certain fruits; or

(c)   Other countries are more skilled in the production of certain goods, e.g., motor cars.

A Form of Specialisation

34.2. The decision to engage in international trade is similar to the decision of an individual to engage in the division of labour and to concentrate on a particular occupation. Just as an individual then trades in order to acquire those goods and services which he cannot produce himself or which he can acquire at a lower opportunity cost through trading, a country does likewise.

34.3. The examples used to develop the principles of international trade are based on two countries and two goods with labour being the only variable factor of production. However, it should be noted that the principle established in the examples hold even when there are many countries involved and when each country uses several factors of production in order to produce a range of goods. It simplifies the explanations and illustrations when we make the above assumptions.

Absolute Advantage

A country is said to have an absolute advantage in the production of a commodity when it can produce that commodity more cheaply than other countries.

Example 34.3.(a) *One country only can produce each good due to climatic or other reasons.*

Production per man per year	Irish butter	Petroleum
Ireland	1,000	—
Russia	—	40 (units)

In this case if Russia wants Irish butter and Ireland wants petroleum, each can acquire its requirements through exchange.

Example 34.3.(b) *Each country can produce one good more cheaply than the other country.*

Production per man per year	Butter	Machinery
Ireland	1,000 (units)	4 (units)
Russia	800 (units)	10 (units)
Total production of four men per year	1,800 (units)	14 (units)

In this case if each country concentrates on producing the item at which it is more efficient, the two men in Ireland would concentrate on the production of butter and the two men in Russia on the production of machinery, in which circumstance production would be as follows:—

Production per year	Butter	Machinery
Ireland	2,000 (units)	—
Russia	—	20 (units)
Total production of four men per year	2,000 (units)	20 (units)

Total production has been increased through specialisation; there has been a net gain of 200 units of butter and 6 units of machinery. Through trade the gains from specialisation can be distributed between the two countries as discussed below.

34.4. *It is possible that one of the countries may be able to produce both commodities more cheaply than the other.*

Example 34.4.

Production per man per year	Butter	Machinery
Ireland	1,000 (units)	5 (units)
Russia	1,250 (units)	10 (units)
Total production of four men per year	2,250 (units)	15 (units)

In this example Russia can produce both (all) of the goods more cheaply than Ireland, i.e., it has an *absolute advantage* in the production of *both* goods. The gains from specialisation and trade in this current example are not quite so obvious as in the two previous examples.

Will International Trade Develop if One Country is more efficient in the Production of all Goods?

In example 34.4 above one country is more efficient in the production of all (both) goods. Despite this international trade can still be beneficial to both countries.

Law of Comparative Advantage

This answer is based on the *Law of Comparative Advantage which states that a country should concentrate on the productioon of those goods in which it has the greater comparative advantage, i.e., in ths production of which it is relatively more efficient.* The Law of Comparative Advantage, which is known also as the *Law of Comparative Cost, shows the gains which are possible – in terms of increased output – if a country specialises in the production of those goods in which it is relatively more efficient and engages in trade.* Even though in Example 34.4 Russia was more efficient in the production of both (all) goods, total production could be increased if both countries specialise — Russia in the production of machinery and Ireland in the production of butter. This is so because Russia, though more efficient in the production of both goods, has a comparative advantage, i.e., is relatively more efficient, in the production of machinery. A man in Russia can produce 1,250 units of butter per annum while a man in Ireland produces 1,000 units per annum, the Russian is producing butter against the Irishman in the ratio of 1,250:1,000 or $1\frac{1}{4}$:1. However, in the production of machinery the ratio in favour of the Russian is greater being 10:5 or 2:1. This is analogous to the division of labour/specialisation in domestic trade whereby the dentist concentrates on his dentistry practice and pays the garage to service his car, even though the dentist is capable of servicing his own car. By concentrating on his dentistry practice during the time it would have taken him to service his own car, he can earn enough money to pay the garage and have something left over.

34.5. Increase in output through the application of the Law of Comparative Advantage.

The initial position is as shown in Example 34.4. When each country specialises the position becomes as shown in Example 34.5.

Example 34.5.

Production per annum	Butter	Machinery
Ireland (2 men)	2,000★ (units)	—
Russia (2 men)	—	20★(units)
Total production of four men per year	2,000 (units)	20 (units)

★These are constant returns to scale so 2 men produce twice what one man produced in table 34.4.

Analysis of Gains from Specialisation

When comparing total production in Examples 34.4 and 34.5 the increase in the production of machinery is obvious; however, the reader may be concerned by the fall in the production of butter from 2,250 to 2,000 units. We can still say that total production is increased because the increase in the production of machinery from 15 to 20 units is an increase of $33\frac{1}{3}\%$ whereas the reduction in the production of butter from 2,250 to 2,000 is reduction of $11\frac{1}{9}\%$. *In practice Ireland could devote extra resources to the production of butter in order to bring the level of production up to the initial level or the level required.*

Some Sources of Comparative Advantage

34.6. A country may enjoy a comparative cost advantage over its neighbours for a variety of reasons. The source of the advantage may be:—

(a)   Factor endowments, such as mineral deposits or climate.

(b)   The availability of machinery, or finance for investment, complemented by an appropriate economic infrastructure.

(c)   The availability of advanced technological knowledge in the economy, i.e., 'technological know-how'.

(d)   Where the social value system and culture attribute considerable importance to work, self-discipline and initiative, such countries enjoy an economic advantage over countries given to a more indolent way of life.

Opportunity Cost

34.7. This analysis of efficiency may be carried out through the medium of the concept of opportunity cost. You will remember that opportunity cost relates to the alternatives which must be foregone when one item or course of action is chosen rather than another. Thus in Example 34.4 the opportunity cost of the production of one machine in Russia is 125 units of butter — for every machine produced the production of 125 units of butter is foregone or sacrificed. In the example the opportunity cost in Ireland of producing one machine is 200 units of butter — for every machine which is produced in Ireland the production of 200 units of butter is foregone or sacrificed.

*Limits to
Rate of
Exchange*

34.8. If Russia produced an extra machine and exchanged it for (say) 160 units of butter both countries would be better off — Ireland because it has exchanged 160 units of butter for one machine, whereas the opportunity cost to Ireland if it had produced the machine itself would have been 200 units of butter; so by concentrating on the production of butter Ireland has a net gain of 40 units of butter. Similarly, Russia has received 160 units of butter in return for the machine but it could have produced only 125 extra units of butter for each machine which it sacrificed had it diverted resources from the production of machinery to the production of butter. Thus through this trade Russia has a net gain of 35 units of butter. The exchange rate for machinery in terms of butter could be anything between the 200 units of butter which it would cost Ireland and the 125 units of butter which it costs Russia. A rate of exchange within these limits would leave both countries better off through specialising in the production of the goods in which they enjoyed the comparative advantage, i.e., Ireland producing butter and Russia producing machinery. The precise rate at which exchange takes place depends upon the relative bargaining strengths of both sides which may be influenced by government intervention as discussed in Sections 34.11 and 34.12.

34.9. Assumptions Underlying the Theory of Comparative Advantage

*Transport
Costs do
not erode
benefits from
specialisation*

(a) **Transport costs.** These have not been included. It is possible that transport costs could eliminate the gains from specialisation. If in Examples 34.4 and 34.5 the cost of transporting machinery from Russia to Ireland was the equivalent of 76 units of butter, the cost of the machine in Ireland would be the equivalent of 201 units of butter — 76 units to cover transport costs plus the 125 units which the Russian must receive. If the Russian did not receive at least 125 units of butter in exchange for his machine he would be better off producing his own requirements of butter rather than concentrating all his resources on the production of machinery, bearing in mind that his opportunity cost (i.e., what he must sacrifice) for the production of each machine is 125 units of butter. But since the opportunity cost of producing one machine in Ireland is 200 units of butter, it would be too costly for us to pay the equivalent of 201 units of butter in order to import one machine when we could produce it in this country for 200 units of butter. Thus, in this example, the benefits of the Law of Comparative Advantage would be eroded by transport costs and trade would not take place. Would you pay £1 bus fare in order to travel to a shop in which the article you required was 10p cheaper?

(b) **Constant returns to scale.** There is a possibility that there may not be constant returns to scale. In the examples we have considered there were constant returns to scale — two men produced twice as much as one man. In practice, either increasing or decreasing returns to scale are just as likely to occur. It is possible that diminishing returns may set in if less efficient factors of production are employed as the scale of operations increases or as complementary factors of production become scarce. Thus it should be noted that the assumption of constant returns to scale is somewhat simplistic.

(c) **Availability of alternative employment.** It is assumed that when a country specialises in the production of a particular good, there is sufficient work available for the factors of production which are released through not producing the good in which there is a comparative disadvantage. For example, if 10 men are employed in the production of butter and 14 men are employed in the production of machinery, when the country concentrates on the production of butter will the 14 men who had been employed on the production of machinery find employment?

(d) **Mobility of factors.** While the theory assumes that there is mobility of factors of production within an economy it does not presume that factors of production, e.g., workers and capital, may move internationally. It should be noted that workers may not be perfectly mobile within the economy. In the Irish case in the past, labour and capital have been very mobile between Ireland and England, though the currency control restrictions affect the mobility of capital.

(e) **Distribution of benefits.** The Theory of Comparative Advantage illustrates the increase in total production, and thus the possible gains from trade. Whether or not there is an improvement in general welfare through international trade depends on how the gains are distributed, e.g., farming may become more profitable but the clothing industry may suffer — the benefits to the farming sector may exceed the losses in the clothing industry, but how are the benefits to be distributed throughout the economy? This point is very relevant to developments since Ireland joined the EEC.

34.10. Advantages Attributed to Free Trade

(a) Total Output in Increased

As shown by the Law of Comparative Advantage, there is an increase in total output if countries specialise in the production of those goods in which they are relatively more efficient and engage in trade. This is the basis for international trade and the other points adduced are very much subordinate to this.

(b) Increased Production of Goods

International trade extends the consumption possibilities of a country beyond the confines set by its own production frontier, e.g. Ireland consumes petrol and oil which it cannot produce itself;

similarly we enjoy fruits from warm climates, etc.

(c) Economies of Scale are Possible

Much production in which economies of scale are enjoyed e.g., aeroplanes, motor cars, etc., would be too expensive if production had to be confined to the level of demand within the national frontiers of the manufacturing firm.

(d) Encourages Efficiency

International trade intensifies competition and in this way lessens the likelihood of dominant firms emerging while also putting pressure on firms to be more efficient. Where there are restrictions on the entry of firms to a market, for example, because the good is not traded internationally, it is easier for firms to gain control of, and exploit, the domestic market.

(e) Fosters Links between Countries

International trade promotes closer links between countries and this has the effect of increasing co-operation and thus lessens the possibility of wars.

34.11. Arguments Against Free Trade

Having read the above section the reader might wonder why governments intervene and restrict international trade. Basically the reason is that governments think and act nationally rather than internationally. They consider that the losses which their own country may suffer are more important than the benefits which may accrue to other countries. The following are the more usual arguments against international trade.

(a) **To protect an 'infant industry'.**
When an industry is being established it may require, during its initial trading period, some protection against mature established foreign firms which are enjoying economies of scale or which have overcome the teething troubles which tend to beset new industries. This is a legitimate economic reason for providing protection to newly established industries, provided that the new firm is capable of competing with existing firms after this initial period of development. The danger in providing protection of this nature is that the protected firm becomes dependent on the protection and never develops sufficiently to compete successfully without such assistance. In addition, vested interests are created by such protection and it can become difficult to gain acceptance for the removal of these barriers to international trade.

(b) **To prevent dumping**
Dumping of goods is said to exist when goods are sold on foreign markets at an uneconomic price. Since people outside the firm in question usually do not have sufficient detailed information to determine what is an uneconomic price the usual criterion is that, if

goods are sold in foreign markets at a price lower than that of the domestic market, then dumping is considered to exist.

There may be economic advantages to a firm in pursuing a policy of dumping where one or more of the following conditions obtain—

(i)   If significant economies of scale are enjoyed through producing on a scale larger than the demand which exists on the domestic market. If a demand exists for 10,000 items for £6 each in country A and unit cost of production at this level of production is £4, the firm's profit on this operation is £20,000 (the difference between revenue of £60,000 and costs of £40,000).

If the level of production is increased to 15,000 units, the unit cost of production falls to £2. In this circumstance if the firm continues to sell 10,000 items for £6 each in country A while the additional 5,000 units may be sold (dumped) in country B for (say) £1.50 each the firm's profit is now £37,500 (revenue of £60,000 in country A and £7,500 in country B less total costs of £30,000) even though the additional output has been sold below cost in country B.

Country B may consider imports of this nature at this price as being available only in the short term and may fear that when the domestic manufacturers of competitive goods in country B are forced by the pressure of this competition to retire from business, the price of the dumped items may be increased.

(ii) If producers enjoy subsidies on goods exported, e.g., if a commodity is sold on the domestic market for £15 each and producers receive an export subsidy of £3 per unit then the good could be sold for £12 on foreign markets and be equally profitable to the producer — though the goods are being sold at a lower price on the export market than on the domestic market, this is not really dumping by the producer since he is getting the same price for goods sold in each market.

(iii) If a firm is allowed to charge high prices on its protected domestic market in order to subsidise its exports to highly competitive foreign markets.

(c)   **To stimulate the production of goods which are of strategic importance.** Most countries encourage the development of the agricultural sector because they do not wish to be dependent on other countries for their basic foodstuffs. In the event of war, if there was a crop failure a basic diet might not be available to food importing countries as supplies would be retained to satisfy domestic demand. A similar type of reasoning could apply to ship-building, armaments, etc.

(d)   **To maintain domestic employment during a recession.** If there is a deficiency of demand for domestic production then a country could place an embargo on 'import substitutes' so that the domestic market may be reserved for domestic production to prevent a decline in domestic employment. The danger is that the countries affected by such a policy may retaliate in a similar vein with a consequent contraction in the volume of international trade which impoverishes each of the countries. This sort of policy is often referred to as a *'beggar your neighbour'* policy.

(e) **To enable a domestic industry to decline gradually**.
The difference between this and the previous point in 34.11 (d) is that, whereas in the previous case the industries concerned have an economic future in the long term, in this case there is an acceptance that the industry has no long term future and it is being phased out rather than allowed to decline immediately. When an industry suffers a decline in demand, e.g., due to a loss of competitiveness or a movement of taste against the good, the government may decide to restrict imports of competitive/substitute goods so that the industry may decline gradually rather than collapse suddenly. By such a policy it is hoped that there would not be a sudden large increase in the numbers unemployed, but rather that in a phased development the existing work-force could be retrained over a period and/or the factories be converted to producing more economically viable goods.

(f) **To protect domestic industry from foreign cheap labour.**
(i) This type of argument usually has an emotional ring and it is often adopted without any real knowledge of the wage payments or working conditions in the exporting country at which the remarks are directed.

(ii) Even if wage costs are lower in the exporting country, it may be that the country concerned has a comparative advantage in the availability of labour and, according to the Law of Comparative Advantage which underlies the theory of international trade, each country should concentrate on producing those goods in which it has a relative advantage.

(iii) The concept under discussion in this section raises the question — at what point do lower wages become 'cheap wages'?

(iv) If wages in Ireland are lower than wages in England should England refuse to import goods from Ireland?

(v) A distinction must be drawn between low wages and low unit costs of production. It is possible for wages to be low and unit costs of production to be high because of inefficiencies or the lack of complementary factors of production, e.g., labour is available but there is a shortage of machinery. Should we refuse to import from countries simply because their unit costs of production are lower?

(vi) If the goods which are excluded in order to protect domestic industry are intermediate goods, i.e., goods which would be processed to a further stage in Ireland before sale to final consumers, this policy of exclusion will force the final goods industries to purchase the higher priced domestically produced intermediate good. In this way the Irish final goods industry will suffer a cost disadvantage vis-a-vis the foreign final good producer who can buy the cheaper intermediate good. The outcome of this situation may well be that the Irish final good producer, because his costs have been increased in this way, is unable to sell his output because it is too dear. So that we could end up with neither an intermediate good industry nor a final good industry.

(vii) To exclude cheap imports raises the cost of living in this country and this may stimulate claims for increased wages which would raise the costs of production for all firms in the economy.

(viii) To refuse to buy the produce of certain countries lessens the ability of such countries to buy our exports (even if they still so wished).

(g) To prevent a trade imbalance with a particular country.

There often arises the suggestion that we should refuse to trade with countries which do not purchase a sufficient quantity of goods and services from us. Obviously if no country purchases our goods we cannot (at least for any period of time) import goods and services because nobody will have any demand for our currency and consequently we would not be able to acquire foreign currency with which to pay for the purchases (in the absence of some form of foreign aid or borrowing). However, there is no need to have an equality of imports and exports with *each* country with which we trade, e.g., country A exports £100 worth of goods to country B while country B exports £100 worth of goods to country C, and country C exports £100 worth of goods to country a as set out in Fig. 34.11.

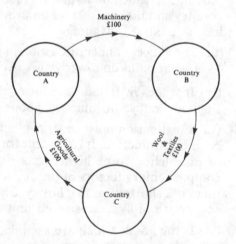

Fig. 34.11. Balanced Multi-national Trade.

In the last example each country has a balanced international trade, since the value of the exports of each country is equal to the value of their imports, even though none of the countries has an equality of imports and exports with each other. Notwithstanding this, many countries use a trade imbalance as a bargaining counter to encourage countries from which they import a lot of goods, to purchase a greater quantity of goods from them. Country A in the above example could do this, in an effort to encourage Country B to buy its (Country As) goods, by threatening to purchase from country C with whom they have a favourable balance of trade rather than from country B. Closely allied to this is the idea of entry into *Trade Agreements* with other countries. Ireland's external trade by areas is shown in Table 34.11 (a).

(h) For political purposes.
This reason is political rather than economic. Countries foster closer political ties through the development of international trade, e.g., the members of the EEC. Conversely, governments restrict trade with countries for political reasons, e.g., Britain and Rhodesia, USA and Cuba, and the anti-apartheid groups which seek to discourage trade with South Africa.

Table 34.11(a) External Trade by Areas

Area	Imports 1985	1986	1987	Exports 1985	1986	1987	Trade Surplus[1] 1985	1986	1987
					£ million				
European Community									
Great Britain	3,705.6	3,247.9	3,438.6	2,605.8	2,603.7	3,043.8	-1,099.8	-644	-394.8
Northern Ireland	320.5	339.9	377.4	605.3	597.6	618.8	284.8	257.8	257.5
Other Member States[2]	2,074.0	2,206.5	2,185.5	3,366.3	3,535.5	4,216.7	1,292.3	1,329.0	2,031.2
Other European Countries									
Members of EFTA[3]	437.8	374.0	381.9	545.7	547.0	625.4	107.9	173.0	243.5
State Trading Countries[4]	142.3	135.1	125.2	62.6	79.7	59.4	-79.7	-55.4	-65.8
Other	118.0	25.6	25.3	141.3	31.8	57.0	23.3	6.2	31.7
Other Countries									
U.S.A. and Canada including overseas forces	1,686.0	1,442.7	1,641.3	1,125.6	934.3	943.8	-560.4	-508.4	697.5
Other Industrialised Countries[5]	371.4	360.5	421.1	333.2	292.2	326.7	-38.2	-68.3	-94.4
Members of OPEC[6]	37.1	29.4	25.5	393.9	241.3	275.0	356.8	211.9	249.5
Other	476.5	411.4	478.3	455.1	421.2	462.1	-21.4	9.8	-16.2
Trade not classified by Country	59.0	48.5	55.2	108.1	90.1	94.7	49.1	41.6	39.5
Total	**9,428.2**	**8,621.3**	**9,155.2**	**9,743.0**	**9,374.3**	**10,723.5**	**314.8**	**753.0**	**1,568.3**
Of which members of OECD	*8,687.2*	*7,966.5*	*8,453.9*	*8,670.1*	*8,486.0*	*9,742.8*	*-17.1*	*519.5*	*1,288.9*

Percentage Distribution %

Area	Imports 1985	1986	1987	Exports 1985	1986	1987
European Community						
Great Britain	39.3	37.7	37.6	26.7	27.8	28.4
Northern Ireland	3.4	3.9	4.1	6.2	6.4	5.8
Other Member States[2]	22.0	25.6	23.9	34.6	37.7	39.3
Other European Countries						
Members of EFTA[3]	4.6	4.3	4.2	5.6	5.8	5.8
State Trading Countries[4]	1.5	1.6	1.4	0.6	0.8	0.6
Other	1.3	0.3	0.3	1.5	0.3	0.5
Other Countries						
U.S.A. and Canada (including overseas forces)	17.9	16.7	17.9	11.6	10.0	8.8
Other Industrialised Countries[5]	3.9	4.2	4.6	3.4	3.1	3.0
Members of OPEC[6]	0.4	0.3	0.3	4.0	2.6	2.6
Other	5.1	4.8	5.2	4.7	4.5	4.3
Trade not classified by Country	0.6	0.6	0.6	1.1	1.0	0.9
Total	**100.-**	**100.-**	**100.-**	**100.-**	**100.-**	**100.-**
Of which membvers of OECD	*92.1*	*92.4*	*92.3*	*89.0*	*90.5*	*90.9*

[1] A minus sign (-) denotes an excess of imports.
[2] France, Belgium and Luxembourg, Netherlands, Germany, F.R., Italy, Denmark, Greece; Spain and Portugal from 1986.
[3] Iceland, Norway, Sweden, Finland, Switzerland, Austria; Portugal up to and including 1985.
[4] U.S.S.R., East Germany, Poland, Czechoslovakia, Hungary, Romania, Bulgaria, Albania.
[5] Australia, Japan, New Zealand, South Africa and Namibia.
[6] Algeria, Libya, Nigeria, Gabon, Venezuela, Ecuador, Iraq, Iran, Saudi Arabia, Kuwait, Qatar, United Arab Emirates, Indonesia.

Source: Statistical Abstract 1988

Table 34.11.(b). Irish merchandise trade by area
Percentage

A. EXPORTS

	United Kingdom	EEC excluding United Kingdom	United States	Others
1960	74.8	7.4	7.5	10.3
1970	66.3	12.7	10.0	11.0
1980	43.2	32.1	5.3	19.4
1987	34.2	39.3	7.8	18.7
1988	35.4	38.6	7.7	18.3

B. IMPORTS

	United Kingdom	EEC excluding United Kingdom	United States	Others
1960	49.6	14.4	8.3	27.7
1970	53.5	18.8	7.0	20.7
1980	50.8	20.1	8.7	20.4
1987	41.7	23.9	17.0	17.4
1988	42.1	24.0	15.9	18.0

Source: Trade Statistics of Ireland.

The Means by which the Government can Intervene in International Trade

Ad Valorem
or Specific
Duties

34.12. Tariffs/Custom Duties are a form of tax/duty levied on imports. When the tax payable is levied as a proportion of the price of the good being imported it is said to be an '*ad valorem*' duty, e.g., a duty of 10% on the Free-on-Board value of the good. *Specific customs duties* are charged at a specific rate per physical unit imported, e.g., £10 duty on each unit imported.

Quotas

34.13. Quotas are a limitation on the quantity of a good which may be imported. The following points are relevant when considering quotas viz.:—

(a) Redistribution of Income from Consumers to Domestic Producers

Domestic producers of competing products are protected, and, since the quantity which may be imported is less than would be imported under free trade, domestic consumers may have to pay a higher price as a result of the restriction of imports. This development constitutes a redistribution of income from consumers to domestic producers.

(b) Redistribution of Income in Favour of Importers/Foreign Producers

Through the quota restriction the volume of the good imported is lower than it would be under free trade; therefore the importer can charge a higher price and still sell his (lower) level of imports. In this way the foreign producer or the importer, or both, may enjoy an increased profit on each unit imported. This is a redistribution of income from domestic consumers to importers/foreign producers. For example, at a price of £15 an importer of foreign shoes sells 1,000 pairs of a specific type of shoe. If the price was £24 per pair only 200 pairs could be sold. If the importation of these shoes is restricted to 200 pairs their price will be increased to £24 per pair because there is no point in holding the selling price to a figure less than this and stimulating a demand which it is not possible to satisfy.

(c) Quotas are Effective in Limiting Volume of Imports:

Quotas are effective in limiting the volume of imports to a specific quantity, tariffs on the other hand are less certain, as they are open-ended. If the importing country has an inelastic demand for the imported good, then the tariff will be paid and more or less the same quantity of the good will continue to be imported. Similarly, if the exporting country has an inelastic supply of the good it may be prepared to accept very low prices and continue to export the same quantity of the good. Thus a quota may be more effective than a tariff in circumstances where it is desired to reserve, or guarantee, some share of the market for domestic producers.

34.14. Some Disadvantages of Quotas

(a) Penalise New Entrants to Market

There has to be some basis on which quotas are to be granted to those seeking to import the goods, e.g., a licence may be granted to import 50 pairs of shoes for every 100 pairs of shoes purchased from Irish manufacturers, or alternatively, the government may allocate quotas on the basis of the average imports over the three years immediately prior to the introduction of quotas. This latter basis would favour an old established firm at the expense of a new expanding firm. Generally, with the passing of time the basis of the allocation of quotas becomes progressively more obsolete.

(b) Freeze Trade Routes

Since quotas are allocated on the basis of previous patterns of trading, they tend to 'freeze' trade routes, e.g., if Ireland allocated a quota for the importation of English furniture, English furniture manufacturers would expect this situation to continue. If (say) Swedish furniture manufacturers become more competitive and efforts are made to have their goods available on the Irish market, English furniture manufacturers would make representations to their government to introduce retaliatory measures if English furniture exports into Ireland were being cut back.

(c) Guarantees Market Share of Domestic firms

Because a quota imposes a quantitative restriction on imports it ensures a guaranteed share of the market for domestic producers. This could give rise to price increases by domestic producers since they are protected from competition from any additional imports. This possibility is less likely when a tariff rather than a quota system is employed since price increases by domestic producers would result in the tariff being less of an obstacle to the intrusion of foreign imports — foreign producers/importers could pay the tariff and pass it on in increased prices and still remain competitive against the high prices which domestic producers were charging.

A Complete Ban on Trade in Certain Goods

34.15. Embargo — Physical Control. The government may impose a complete ban on the importation of certain goods, e.g., if there are animal diseases in certain countries the government may place an embargo on the importation of animals from such countries, or when the accident occurs — as when the EEC banned imports of fresh food from Eastern European countries when there was a fear of radiation contamination as a result of the accident at the Chernobyl Nuclear Reactor Plant.

Exchange Control

34.16. This is a system whereby imports from a particular country (or currency area) are restricted to a certain monetary value, e.g., imports from the dollar currency area may be restricted to $100 million. Thus it can be considered as a system in which quotas are imposed but the quota is fixed in terms of a value of foreign currency.

A scheme of this nature is operated through the imposition of regulations whereby all earnings of foreign currency must be exchanged at the bank in return for local currency. Individuals who wish to import must seek an allocation of the required amount of foreign currency in order to pay for the foreign merchandise. All merchandise being imported would have to be supported by a licence to ensure that the importer had acquired legally the foreign currency which is required for payment. Through licensing the government could give priority to certain types of imports, e.g., capital goods rather than consumer goods. In addition, through restricting the value of imports to the quantity of foreign currency earned by exports the governments can ensure that the Balance of Trade (or Balance on Current Account) remains in balance, or within some acceptable limits.

34.17. Exchange Control may be introduced:—

(a)   To limit imports to a specific value of foreign currency.

(b)   To discriminate between the importation of essential and non-essential goods and services.

(c)   To discriminate between countries for trading purposes, e.g., a distinction may be drawn between countries with a 'hard' currency, (i.e., their currency is relatively scarce outside their own frontiers because they have a considerable surplus on international trade) and countries with a 'soft' currency.

(d)   For non-trading reasons e.g., to protect the currency against speculation.

34.18. Administrative Barriers

There may be a policy of making it difficult (and therefore costly in terms of money and time) to bring goods into the country. Not only may there be excessive (and therefore costly) delays in processing the documentation required to import the goods but detailed and unusual specifications which do not apply in other countries may be imposed in relation to goods being imported, e.g., additional safety equipment on imported motor cars. Because requirements of this nature would not be general to all countries, the production and assembly of these features would have to be separate from the mass production process and therefore increase costs. Similarly, veterinary regulations often constitute a barrier to the importation of agricultural produce (though there is no suggestion that there are not sound health reasons for the imposition of such regulations).

34.19. Subsidies

A subsidy, e.g., relief from, or a reduction in the rate of, tax on profits earned on exports, may be given to domestic producers to enable them to compete with foreign producers. The subsidy may be in the form of services supplied by the State at no charge to the exporter or at a rate lower than the going commercial rate. Preferential interest rates on money borrowed for export trading, subsidised insurance on export trading to cover not only possible damage to, or loss of, the goods but also the possibility of non-payment by the foreign purchaser, research and development carried out on behalf of exporters by government agencies without a direct charge to the exporter, government financed training schemes for employees, etc. are examples of such subsidies.

In addition a high level of national welfare benefits may have the effect of reducing the wage demands of workers. This type of thinking is manifest in the approach of the trade union movement to a round of wage negotiations, where acceptance of the specified wage increases is part of a 'social package' or 'national understanding' which includes, in addition to a wage increase, social welfare provisions and tax allowances. If these benefits, which have the effect of lowering the wage increases which trade unions will accept, are funded from general taxation they could constitute a subsidy to industry based on labour costs.

34.20. Some Effects Stemming from the Imposition of Tariffs

(a) **Protective Effect** in that there is a higher level of demand for the output of the domestic producer as a result of the duty.

(b) **Consumption Effect.** Because of the higher selling price of the good as a result of the levy the demand for, and consequently consumption of, the good will be lower than it would have been in the absence of the tariff.

(c) **Government Revenue Effect.** Government revenue is increased by the amount of the per-unit tariff multiplied by the quantity imported.

(d) **Redistributive Effect.**

(i) Income is transferred from purchasers of the good to the government and domestic suppliers of factors of production.

(ii) Depending on the price elasticity of demand for the product the duty may be borne by the foreign producer/importer/final consumer.

34.21. Terms of Trade

Definition of Terms of Trade

In Section 34.7 and 34.8 the opportunity cost of machines in terms of butter and the limits to the possible rate at which butter would exchange for machinery were discussed. However, in a modern economy barter does not normally occur — money is used as a medium of exchange. Thus exports are sold and the money obtained is used in order to pay for imports. *The ratio between the average price of exports and the average price of imports is known as the terms of trade.* It is the average price of exports expressed in terms of the average price of imports. Thus the terms of trade express the price of exports in terms of the price of imports.

34.22. Formula for Terms of Trade.

Terms of Trade =

$$\frac{\text{Index number showing the average price of exports}}{\text{Index number showing the average price of imports}}$$

*Terms of
Trade are
Determined
by Supply
and Demand*

34.23. As the terms of trade express the relationship between an index of the average price of exports and an index of the average price of imports, they are established by, and reflect changes in, the price of either exports or imports. Since the prices of exports and imports are determined by the forces of supply and demand, the terms of trade are determined by supply of, and demand for, a currency arising from the supply of, and demand for, imports and exports.

34.24. *Table of Ireland's Terms of Trade.*

1983	1984	1985	1986	1987	1988
105.1	103.8	104.2	108.7	108.8	109.5

Base Year 1980 = 100

★EST

Source: Central Statistics Office.

*Terms of
Trade and
Opportunity
Cost*

34.25. The terms of trade are a ratio between the price of exports and the price of imports. Thus the terms of trade show the opportunity cost of obtaining goods and services through international trade rather than producing them domestically.

*Favourable
Movement in
Terms of
Trade*

34.26. When the price of imports becomes cheaper relative to the prices of our exports, the index number for the terms of trade *increases* and the terms of trade are said to *"more in our favour"* or *"becomes more favourable"*, e.g., as can be seen from the above table in 1983 the terms of trade moved in our favour compared with the previous year. When the terms of trade move in our favour it means that we receive a greater volume of imports in return for a given volume of exports, i.e., imports have become cheaper relative to exports.

34.27. An increase in our terms of trade may be likened to an increase in our hourly rate of wages. It is fine if poeple continue to employ you for

Effects of Favourable Movement in Terms of Trade on Competitiveness

the same number of hours after the increase in your hourly rate of pay. However, there is little consolation in the hourly rate of pay of a singer being £1,000 if nobody is prepared to employ him at that price — he would be the highest priced (as distinct from paid) singer requiring unemployment assistance.

When the value of sterling began to rise in 1979 as Britain became an oil producing country, there was considerable anguish among her industrial exporters who were having difficulty in selling on foreign markets due to an increase in the value of sterling.

In March 1983 the Irish currency was devalued due to the first ever explicit devaluation decision taken by an Irish Government. The reason for the devaluation was because the value of our currency was rising relative to the value of sterling, this affected our ability to sell in U.K. markets so the devaluation was enacted in order to retain competitiveness in the market of our main trading partner.

In 1986, the value of the *Irish* currency relative to sterling had risen to an extent which rendered it difficult for Irish exporters to remain competitive on U.K. markets. The Irish currency was devalued in order to alleviate this loss of competitiveness.

Terms of Trade of Primary Producing Countries

34.28. Since the primary producing countries supply goods, e.g., food, for which there is a relatively inelastic demand and a relatively inelastic supply in any given year once the crop has been harvested, the price of these goods on international markets, and therefore the terms of trade of these countries are likely to be low. However, the terms of trade of such countries may be subject to considerable fluctuation in accordance with the bounty of nature.

Table 34.29 Change in export prices and terms of trade, 1965 to 1988
(average annual percentage change)

Country group	1965 -73	1973 -80	1980 -85	1986	1987[1]	1988[2]
Export Prices						
Low- and middle-income economies	6.1	14.8	-4.3	-8.3	11.5	4.8
Manufactures	6.4	8.2	-3.7	9.4	10.3	8.7
Food	5.9	8.6	-4.1	7.2	-7.4	16.1
Nonfood	4.6	10.2	-4.9	0.0	21.1	2.5
Metals and minerals	2.5	4.7	-4.5	-4.8	13.3	22.7
Fuels	8.0	26.2	-4.1	46.7	22.9	-17.4
High-income OECD members						
Total	4.8	10.3	-3.1	12.0	10.9	6.8
Manufactures	4.6	10.8	-2.8	19.6	13.4	8.4
Terms of trade						
Low- and middle-income economies	0.1	2.6	-2.0	-9.3	1.3	1.0
Low-income economies	-4.8	4.0	-1.1	-16.8	4.2	-1.6
Middle-income economies	1.7	2.1	-2.4	-6.7	0.3	1.7
Sub-Saharan Africa	-8.5	5.0	-2.3	-23.2	3.3	-5.3
East Asia	-0.6	1.2	-0.6	-7.0	1.4	1.8
South Asia	3.7	-3.4	1.7	2.8	-2.1	5.2
Europe, Middle East, and North Africa	..	..	..	..	..	..
Latin America and the Caribbean	3.9	2.4	-1.9	-14.0	-2.1	-0.4
17 highly indebted countries	1.4	3.5	-1.3	-13.7	-0.7	-0.8
High-income economies	-1.2	-2.0	-0.4	8.7	-0.1	0.2
OECD Members	-1.0	-3.3	-0.2	12.4	-0.2	0.7
Oil exporters	0.3	9.6	-2.2	-47.5	16.7	-17.3

[1] Estimated
[2] Projected

Source: World Development Report 1989.

34.29. In calculating terms of trade, it is the average price, derived from a country's entire range of internationally traded goods and services, that is utilised. However, many of the less developed countries are virtually "one crop economies" so that the price of this one crop has a dominant weighting in the determination of the average price of their exports. In the absence of a general world increase in the demand for their crop, the terms of trade of these countries are likely to move in their favour only when there is a below average crop — so that their increased price is obtained at the expense of low volume. Consequently these countries are unable to obtain the foreign exchange which they so vitally require in order to purchase the goods and services they need.

34.30. The foregoing may be contrasted with the Irish situation where our exports of primary products are supplemented by merchandise exports of greater value, while the *Common Agricultural Policy* of the EEC has ensured guaranteed prices for our agricultural exports.

34.31. Similarly, the oil producing countries enjoy an inelastic demand for their output, the market supply of which they are able to regulate. Their bargaining position is strengthened further through the OPEC cartel arrangement and thus their terms of trade remain favourable. In this way, in the past, they have been insulated from the problems which beset the primary producing countries of the less developed world. (See Table 34.31). The fluctuation in Oil Prices in 1986 is due to the difficulty of maintaining cartel agreements as explained in Section 16.4.

34.32. Summary of Effects of Changes in the Terms of Trade:

(a) There is an alteration in the quantity of imports received for a given volume of exports, e.g., if the terms of trade move in our favour we get a larger volume of imports in return for a given volume of exports and vice versa if our terms of trade become unfavourable.

(b) Because of terms of trade are determined by *total* demand for our exports and our *total* demand for imports even a favourable movement in our terms of trade may cause considerable internal economic disruption, e.g., if our terms of trade improve because of an increase demand/price for our agricultural produce this means that our industrial/manufactured goods increase in price to foreigners which may result in some of these industrial goods becoming uncompetitive against competing goods from third countries.

(c) If terms of trade move in our favour.

(i) Imported raw material becomes cheaper which results in a reduction in the cost of production of goods using these imported raw materials.

(ii) The general cost of living is reduced because imported consumer goods become relatively cheaper. This may lessen the demand for wage increases and thus make our goods more competitive.

(iii) Import substitutes become cheaper which will intensify competition for domestic producers of competitive goods.

(d) Since Terms of Trade are based on average levels of Prices/Demand the producers of some goods may find the currency to be overvalued in relation to the demand for their products and consequently find it difficult to retain competitiveness.

Table 34.31. Growth of merchandise trade.

	Merchandise trade (millions of dollars)		Average annual growth rate (percent)				Terms of trade (1980=100)	
			Exports		Imports			
	Exports 1987	Imports 1987	1965-80	1980-87	1965-80	1980-87	1985	1987
Low-income economies	95,802t	116,254t	5.6w	3.4w	4.5w	2.3w	92m	84m
China and India	52,090t	62,377t	4.8w	9.6w	4.5w	10.6w	104m	101m
Other low-income	43,712t	153,877t	5.9w	-0.1w	4.5w	-3.9w	91m	84m
1 Ethiopia	402	1,150	-0.5	-0.6	-0.9	7.6	99	84
2 Bhutan	25	88	..	..	..	..	..	..
3 Chad	..	..	..	..	..	..	..	..
4 Zaire	1,594	1,149	4.7	-3.4	-2.9	-0.4	82	74
5 Bangladesh	1,074	2,620	..	6.2	..	2.3	124	91
6 Malawi	264	281	4.1	3.4	3.3	-6.1	73	67
7 Nepal	151	569	-2.3	5.1	3.0	6.4	91	93
8 Lao PDR	30	70	..	..	..	..	..	..
9 Mozambique	89	486	..	..	..	..	..	..
10 Tanzania	348	1,165	-4.0	-7.4	1.6	-0.4	90	90
11 Burkina Faso	202	540	6.8	4.9	5.8	2.0	80	74
12 Madagascar	310	386	0.7	-3.1	-0.4	-2.9	104	105
13 Mali	216	447	11.0	6.6	6.2	3.4	82	86
14 Brundi	84	206	3.0	8.3	2.0	2.4	100	75
15 Zambia	869	745	1.7	-3.3	-5.5	-6.2	72	79
16 Niger	361	417	12.8	-4.8	6.6	-6.2	108	86
17 Uganda	320	477	-3.9	2.7	-5.3	3.0	96	67
18 China ★	39,542	43,392	5.5	11.7	7.9	14.2	95	87
19 Somalia	94	452	3.8	-7.7	5.8	-1.3	91	84
20 Togo	297	417	4.6	-3.0	8.6	-4.6	90	86
21 India	12,548	18,985	3.7	3.6	1.6	4.7	114	114
22 Rwanda	121	352	7.7	2.5	8.7	5.4	102	87
23 Sierra Leone	120	132	-3.8	-2.1	-2.7	-15.1	100	93
24 Benin	168	418	5.2	-0.1	6.7	0.4	90	88
25 Central African Rep.	130	186	-0.4	1.0	-1.1	-1.8	88	84
26 Kenya	961	1,755	0.3	-0.6	1.7	-3.0	92	80
27 Sudan	482	694	-0.3	4.2	2.3	-8.7	90	84
28 Pakistan	4,172	5,822	4.3	8.4	0.4	3.4	88	99
29 Haiti	261	378	7.0	-2.0	8.4	-2.5	97	109
30 Lesotho	..	..	..	..	..	..	..	..
31 Nigeria	7,365	7,816	11.4	-5.1	15.2	-14.0	90	54
32 Ghana	1,056	836	-1.8	-1.6	-1.4	-2.9	91	85
33 Sri Lanka	1,393	2,085	0.5	6.5	-1.2	3.2	99	96
34 Yemen, PDR	409	1,450	-13.7	1.7	-7.5	3.3	99	73
35 Mauritania	428	474	2.7	11.2	5.4	1.7	112	98
36 Indonesia	17,206	14,453	9.6	2.7	14.2	2.2	94	69
37 Liberia	385	208	4.5	-2.6	1.5	-10.2	91	93
38 *Afghanistan*	552	1,404	..	..	..	..	..	--

Table 34.31. Growth of merchandise trade.

	Merchandise trade (millions of dollars)		Average annual growth rate (percent)				Terms of tra (1980=100,	
			Exports		Imports			
	Exports 1987	Imports 1987	1965-80	1980-87	1965-80	1980-87	1985	1
39 *Burma*	219	628	-2.1	-4.7	-1.7	-8.7	70	
40 *Guinea*	..	..	..	..	..	..	..	
41 *Kampuchea, Dem.*	..	..	..	..	..	..	..	
42 *VietNam*	1,054	1,874	..	..	..	..	..	
Middle-income economies	**369,978***t*	**353,481***t*	**2.4***w*	**5.5***w*	**5.9***w*	**-0.5***w*	**92***m*	**7**
Lower-middle-income	**144,178***t*	**146,317***t*	**5.3***w*	**5.3***w*	**4.1***w*	**-1.7***w*	**92***m*	**7**
43 Senegal	645	1,174	2.4	6.7	4.1	2.7	100	
44 Bolivia	566	776	2.8	-0.8	5.0	-1.6	84	
45 Zimbabwe	1,358	1,055	3.4	0.9	-1.8	-6.8	84	
46 Philippines	5,649	7,144	4.7	-0.4	2.9	-4.0	92	
47 Yemen Arab Rep.	19	1,311	2.8	-4.0	23.3	-11.0	93	
48 Morocco	2,807	4,229	3.7	3.7	6.5	1.6	89	1
49 Egypt, Arab Rep.	4,040	8,453	2.7	8.4	6.0	2.8	84	
50 Papua New Guinea	1,172	1,222	12.8	4.9	1.3	0.3	95	
51 Dominican Rep.	711	1,783	1.7	-0.1	5.5	1.4	66	
52 Côte d'Ivoire	2,982	2,168	5.6	3.4	8.0	-3.1	96	
53 Honduras	827	895	3.1	3.1	2.5	-0.2	93	
54 Nicaragua	300	923	2.3	-5.2	1.3	0.8	85	
55 Thailand	11,659	12,955	8.5	10.2	4.1	3.4	74	
56 El Salvador	634	975	2.4	-4.6	2.7	-0.7	96	
57 Congo, People' Rep.	884	570	12.5	3.9	1.0	-0.7	94	
58 Jamaica	649	1,207	-0.3	-6.2	-1.9	-1.5	95	10
59 Guatemala	1,084	1,479	4.8	-1.6	4.6	-4.6	87	8
60 Cameroon	1,714	2,168	5.2	9.7	5.6	3.4	92	6
61 Paraguay	952	1,202	7.9	13.8	4.6	2.2	82	7
62 Ecuador	2,021	2,250	15.1	5.5	6.8	-1.4	94	6
63 Botswana	..	..	..	..	..	..	..	
64 Tunisia	2,152	3,022	10.8	2.2	10.4	-2.5	83	7
65 Turkey	10,190	14,163	5.5	17.1	7.7	11.1	91	1'
66 Colombia	5,024	4,230	1.4	7.5	5.3	-4.2	98	7
67 Chile	5,091	4,023	7.9	4.3	2.6	-8.3	79	7
68 Peru	2,605	4,060	2.3	-0.8	-0.2	-2.5	81	6
69 Mauritius	918	1,010	3.1	11.1	6.4	6.7	90	10
70 Jordan	930	2,691	13.7	5.9	9.7	0.6	93	10
71 Costa Rica	1,155	1,377	7.0	2.6	5.7	-1.5	95	8
72 Syrian Arab Rep.	1,357	2,546	11.4	-1.3	8.5	-5.3	95	7
73 Malaysia	17,865	12,506	4.4	9.7	2.9	-0.7	86	7
74 Mexico	20,887	12,731	7.6	6.6	5.7	-8.1	98	7
75 South Africa	20.066	14,629	6.1	-0.1	0.1	-8.8	75	7
76 Poland	12,205	10,844	..	4.3	..	1.2	106	11
77 *Lebanon*	591	1,880	..	..	..	..	..	
★Data for Taiwan, China are:	50,835	34,341	19.0	13.5	15.1	6.5	104	10

Table 34.31. Growth of merchandise trade.

	Merchandise trade (millions of dollars)		Average annual growth rate (percent)				Terms of trade (1980=100)	
			Exports		Imports			
	Exports 1987	Imports 1987	1965-80	1980-87	1965-80	1980-87	1985	1987
78 Brazil	26,225	16,581	9.3	5.6	8.2	-4.2	89	97
79 Uruguay	1,190	1,140	4.6	1.4	1.2	-6.5	87	97
80 Hungary	9,571	9,855	..	3.9	..	1.5	92	89
81 Panama	357	1,248	..	3.8	..	-3.3	94	71
82 Argentina	6,360	5,818	4.7	-0.3	1.8	-9.4	90	81
83 Yugoslavia	11,397	12,549	5.6	1.1	6.6	-2.0	111	116
84 Algeria	9,029	7,028	1.5	3.2	13.0	-4.6	97	56
85 Korea, Rep.	47,172	40,934	27.2	14.3	15.2	9.6	106	105
86 Gabon	1,285	836	8.1	-1.9	10.5	3.0	90	64
87 Portugal	9,167	13,438	3.4	12.2	3.7	3.8	85	99
88 Venezuela	10,567	8,725	-9.5	-0.4	8.7	-7.0	93	54
89 Greece	6,489	12,908	11.9	6.6	5.2	4.8	88	93
90 Trinidad and Tobago	1,462	1,219	-5.5	-7.1	-5.8	-15.1	96	61
91 Libya	6,061	4,877	3.3	-5.9	15.3	-15.3	92	47
92 Oman	3,941	1,882	..	..	..	..	..	..
93 *Iran, Islamic Rep.*	..	*10,359*	..	..	..	..	..	..
94 *Iraq*	*9,014*	*7,415*	..	..	..	..	..	..
95 *Romania*	*12,543*	*11,437*	..	..	..	..	..	..
Low- and middle-income	**465,780t**	**469,736t**	**3.1w**	**5.0w**	**5.5w**	**0.1w**	**92m**	**83m**
Sub-Saharan Africa	28,471t	32,516t	6.6w	-1.0w	5.0w	-5.8w	91m	84m
East Asia	193,993t	170,740t	9.7w	10.1w	8.6w	6.1w	94m	84m
South Asia	19,616t	30,871t	1.7w	4.8w	0.6w	3.7w	95m	94m
Europe, M.East, & N. Africa	113,691t	146,301t	..	..	..	0.4w	92m	93m
Latin America & Caribbean	89,943t	74,679t	-2.1w	3.0w	4.4w	-5.6w	90m	76m
highly indebted	**112,628t**	**95,193t**	**0.4w**	**2.1w**	**6.3w**	**-6.0w**	**92m**	**84m**
High-income economies	**1,924,470t**	**2,007,404t**	**7.0w**	**3.3w**	**4.4w**	**4.8w**	**94m**	**97m**
OECD members	1,784,793t	1,871,384t	7.2w	4.2w	4.2w	5.2w	94m	98m
Other	139,677t	136,020t	6.0w	-4.2w	10.6w	0.4w	95m	54m
96 Spain	34,099	49,009	12.4	6.9	4.4	5.6	90	111
97 Ireland	15,970	13,614	9.8	8.1	4.8	2.6	107	107
98 *Saudi Arabia	23,138	20,465	8.8	-16.3	25.9	-9.3	95	54
99 *Israel	*8,475	14,300	8.9	7.3	6.3	3.8	94	89
100 New Zealand	7,179	7,255	4.2	4.5	1.1	4.2	97	98
101 *Singapore	28,592	32.480	4.7	6.1	7.0	3.7	101	102
102 *Hong Kong	48,475	48,462	9.5	11.4	8.3	9.1	103	106
103 Italy	116,582	122,211	7.7	3.8	3.5	4.3	95	114
104 United Kingdom	131,128	154,388	4.8	3.0	1.4	4.8	96	99
105 Australia	25,283	29,318	5.5	6.0	0.9	2.9	89	72

Table 34.31. Growth of merchandise trade.

	Merchandise trade (millions of dollars)		Average annual growth rate (percent)				Terms of trade (1980=100)	
			Exports		Imports			
	Exports 1987	Imports 1987	1965-80	1980-87	1965-80	1980-87	1985	1987
106 Belgium	82,951	82,598	7.8	4.5	5.2	3.2	87	98
107 Netherlands	92,882	91,317	8.0	4.6	4.4	3.0	91	93
108 Austria	27,163	32,638	8.2	5.3	6.1	4.7	90	108
109 France	143,077	157,524	8.5	3.5	4.3	2.2	94	104
110 Germany, Fed. Rep.	293,790	227,334	7.2	4.7	5.3	4.6	88	120
111 Finland	20.039	19,860	5.9	3.8	3.1	3.5	96	109
112 ★Kuwait	8,355	5,297	-1.9	-3.2	11.8	-5.5	92	54
113 Denmark	24,697	25,534	5.4	5.7	1.7	5.7	96	106
114 Canada	92,886	92,594	5.4	6.3	2.6	7.3	122	101
115 Sweden	44,313	40,621	4.9	5.7	1.8	2.8	88	96
116 Japan	229,055	146,048	11.4	5.8	4.9	3.6	112	153
117 ★United Arab Emirates	12,000	7,226	10.9	0.1	20.5	-7.1	91	54
118 Norway	21,449	22,578	8.2	6.2	3.0	3.5	97	72
119 United States	252,567	422,407	6.4	-0.5	5.5	9.7	114	116
120 Switzerland	45,357	50,557	6.2	4.6	4.5	5.3	88	113
Total reporting economies	**2,390,197t**	**2,477,661t**	**6.1w**	**3.4w**	**4.6w**	**3.9w**	**93m**	**84m**
Oil exporters	**168,325t**	**153,727t**	**3.0w**	**-3.7w**	**9.3w**	**-5.7w**	**94m**	**61m**
Nonreporting nonmembers	..	..	..	..	..	..	..	..

Note: For data comparability and coverage, see the technical notes. Figures in italics are for years other than those specified. a. See the technical notes. b. Figures are for the South african Customs Union comprising South Africa, Namibia, Lesotho, Botswana, and Swaziland; trade between component territories is excluded. c. Includes Luxembourg.

Source: World Development Report 1989

QUESTIONS

Q1. Explain the Law of Comparative Advantage and the assumptions underlying it.

Q2. Analyse the arguments for and against Free Trade.

Q3. By what means might the government intervene in International Trade.

Q4. Write an explanatory note on Terms of Trade.

Q5.

	Food	Machinery
Country A	10 tonnes	2 units
Country B	15 tonnes	8 units

(a) In the above situation would international trade be justified?
(b) What other factors might determine whether or not international trade takes place.
(c) In the event of international trade taking place, comment on the possible Terms of Trade.

35 Balance of Payments

*Current
Section and
Capital
Section*
35.1. International trade inevitably gives rise to indebtedness between people in different countries. The record of economic transactions with the rest of the world is conventionally known as the *Balance of Payments*, though this might be more correctly titled the *Balance of International Payments*. The balance of Payments is composed of two main divisions viz.: (1) *The Current Account* and (2) *The Capital Account*.

*Balance
of Trade*
35.2. The Current Account section relates to transactions arising from the purchase or sale of goods and services, i.e., it may be considered as a record of income, as distinct from capital transactions. That portion of the current account which is confined to the import and export of merchandise (goods) is known as the *Balance of Trade which is an account of the value of merchandise imported and exported during a given period, usually one year.* A monitoring of the annual figures takes place by making available quarterly figures.

*Favourable/
Unfavourable
Balance of
Trade*
35.3. It is extremely unlikely that the value of merchandise imported would be exactly equal to the value of merchandise exported in which case there will be either a deficit on the Balance of Trade (if the value of merchandise imported exceeds the value of merchandise exported), or a surplus (if the value of merchandise imported is less than the value of merchandise exported). *When there is a surplus there is said to be a 'favourable' Balance of Trade, whereas when there is a deficit there is said to be an 'unfavourable' Balance of Trade.*

35.4. These terms 'favourable' and 'unfavourable' originated in the 16th and 17th centuries with a group of thinkers who developed the first systematic body of economic thought. These people considered that economic activities ought to ·be directed towards the objectives of sufficiency and national power. They became known as *'Mercantilists'* because their theories perceived the attainment of these objectives through domestic production and foreign trade. The Mercantilists★ considered the economy of a nation to be strengthened when it exported more than it imported and weakened when the opposite occurred. In modern times it is realised that an excess value of goods exported over goods imported is neither favourable nor unfavourable 'per se', rather it is necessary that an analysis be carried out to determine the source of, and reason for, the imbalance.

35.5. When Irish *services* are bought by foreigners, e.g., foreigners

★ See Section 40.10.

Invisible Exports

staying in Irish hotels, nothing of a tangible nature leaves the country in return for the money which is received, hence the term *'invisibles'* is often applied to the purchase by foreigners of Irish services. Other examples of 'invisible exports' are emigrants' remittances, income earned on capital invested abroad, transportation charges paid to Irish carriers by non-residents of this country, tourism receipts, etc. The terms 'invisibles' and 'invisible exports' are contrasted with the export of merchandise when a tangible commodity is exported for the payment which is received. For this reason the export of merchandise is sometimes referred to as *'visible'* exports.

Balance on Current Account

35.6. Just as has been stated with regard to the Balance of Trade, it would be surprising also if there was a balance on our international trade of 'invisible' items. Since the combination of trade in merchandise and trade in invisible items constitutes the *Balance on Current Account* it is extremely unlikely that there will be an equality of imports and exports (i.e., a balance) on the current account — it is likely to be either in surplus or deficit.

Capital Account

35.7. The Balance of Payments is completed when the Capital Account section is associated with the Current Account section. *The Capital Account section of the Balance of Payments is an account of a country's inflow and outflow of capital which gives rise to a consequent net increase or decrease in the external reserves of the country.* When money comes into the country our holding of foreign currency and consequently our external assets increase.

Financing of Deficit on Current Account Section

35.8. Money may be transferred into the country, i.e. the Capital Account section could be in surplus as a result of any of the following transactions:
(a)   Reduction in External Reserves.
(b)   Foreign Borrowing.
(c)   Receiving grants or aid from foreign sources.
(d)   Investment by foreigners in Irish industry or agriculture.
(e)   The Irish government or Irish residents selling assets which they own in other countries.
(f)   The receipt by Irish residents of dividends on foreign investments.
(g)   The receipt by Irish residents of interest on foreign loans.
   One, or a combination, of these developments would take place if the Current Account section of the Balance of Payments was in deficit while the opposite would apply in the event of there being a surplus in the Current Account section of the Balance of International Payments.

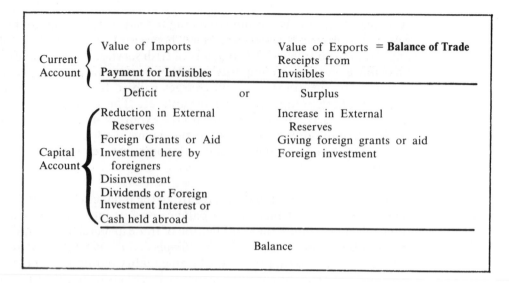

Fig. 35.8. The Balance of Payments in Outline.

*Balance of
Payments
must Balance*

35.9. In contrast to the probability of an imbalance on the Current Account section, the Balance of Payments as a whole must balance. Any imbalance of the Current Account section must be made good by a compensating adjustment in the Capital Account section, e.g., a deficit on the Current Account Section must be compensated by a corresponding surplus on the Capital Account section. Sometimes the Balance of Payments is said to be in *deficit* when the combined effect of current and capital transactions causes our *external reserves to fall* and in *surplus* when our *external reserves rise* — see Table 35.10.

*Necessary to
Analyse the
Underlying
Trends*

35.10. Since the Balance of Payments is a financial statement of a country's financial affairs arising from international transactions, it is a book-keeping exercise and consequently it must balance in the accounting sense that total credits must equal total debits. When reference is made as to deficits or surpluses in the Balance of Payments it is usually a reference to a deficit or surplus on the Current Account section of the Balance of Payments. Like all financial statements, e.g., the balance sheet of a company, it is a snapshop of the financial position at a particular moment in time. Accordingly, it is much more important to analyse the underlying trend rather than to form conclusions based on a deficit or surplus at a particular point in time.

Table 35.10 Balance of International Payments: Current account £ million

Item		1982	1983	1984	1985	1986	1987	1988
1. Merchandise[1]	Cr	5,591.9	6,812.7	8,696.0	9,526.8	9,180.7	10,447	12,073
2. International freight	Cr	86.0	86.7	98.0	104.2	88.8	93	81
3. Other transportation								
3.1 Passenger fare receipt	Cr	120.8	130.3	149.0	167.0	156.9	167	187
3.2 Other	Cr	167.8	205.0	242.0	257.7	270.1	303	304
	Db	-194.9	-246.0	-271.0	-267.0	.271.3	-279	-262
4. Tourism and travel[2]	Cr	355.0	390.0	442.0	518.0	492.2	564	655
	Db	-346.9	-363.0	-378.0	-401.7	-511.1	-556	-630
5. Other services	Cr	111.8	127.0	143.0	164.7	162.8	211	232
	Db	-160.4	-221.0	-273.5	-337.7	-332.6	-496	-625
6. Remuneration of employees	Cr	10.6	12.4	12.0	13.4	16.0	16	16
7. Trading and investment income	Cr	584.6	549.1	692.1	793.8	732.1	766	920
	Db	-1,522.9	-1,745.4	-2,342.9	-2,772.9	-2,705.1	-2,740	-3,478
Components of debit item: Profits, dividends, royalties, etc.[3]		-498.7	-658.6	-982.7	-1,320.6	-1,319.6	-1,307	-1,908
National debt interest		-525.7	-597.3	-719.7	-761.1	-804	-894	
Other[4]		-498.5	-489.5	-640.5	-657.1	-624.4	-629	-676
8. International transfers	Cr	765.9	901.8	1,071.3	1,319.3	1,365.9	1,322	1,408
	Db	-172.7	-230.6	-332.8	-345.5	-409.3	-443	-397
9. Net balance on current account		1,314.7	-925.2	-945.4	-650.1	-509.4	239	437
10. Private capital		285.3	87.2	-137.6	-108.0	-723	-826	
10.1 Semi-state companies		282.4	183.7	90.8	19.3	31.5	-43	-116
10.2 Direct investment		170.0	134.6	110.0	150.0	-30.0	-680	-710
10.3		-167.1	-231.1	-338.4	-277.3	-408.3		
11. Official capital		1,220.7	712.7	854.3	1,028.9	1,198.3	1,231	523
11.1 Exchequer foreign borrowing		1,114.8	749.1	594.2	854.5	899.1	405	-282
11.2 Irish government securities		-18.0	34.7	121.0	83.4	239.7	460	867
11.3 Other		123.9	-71.1	139.1	91.0	59.5	366	-62
12. Banking transactions		132.2	605.6	368.2	285.7	553.8	-79	365
12.1 Associated banks		166.4	442.6	221.8	221.6	-216.5	-178	306
12.2 Other banks		54.8	286.7	209.4	-97.3	676.6	-66	44
12.3 Other financial institutions		-3.0	4.8	0.0	0.3	22.0	75	110
12.4 Counterpart to valuation changes		-86.0	-128.5	-63.0	161.1	71.7	90	-95

Economics

Table 35.10 (Continued). Balance of International Payments: Current account

£ million

Item	1982	1983	1984	1985	1986	1987	1988
13. Official external reserves[5]	-90.7	-227.1	32.7	-195.7	72.3	-606	-352
13.1 Reserve position in the IMF	0.0	-36.1	-8.1	3.8	-8.6	0	-3
13.2 Gold	5.4	-24.9	5.0	11.9	1.1	-8	8
13.3 SDR holdings	-4.2	8.4	-23.9	9.3	-11.2	-12	-7
13.4 Other external assets	-122.1	-368.3	-59.3	-195.8	85.5	-597	-337
13.5 Counterpart to valuation changes	30.2	193.8	119.0	-24.9	5.5	11	-13
13.6 Counterpart to allocation of SDRs	0.0	0.0	0.0	0.0	0.0	0	0
14. Net balance on capital account	1,547.5	1,178.4	1,117.6	1,010.9	1,417.6	-176	-290
Net residual[6]	-231.8	-253.2	-172.2	-360.8	-908.2	-63	-147

[1] Adjusted for balance of payments purposes
[2] Excluding passenger fare receipts
[3] Including associated interest flows
[4] Including semi-state and bank interest flows
[5] Computed on a transactions basis i.e. change in total reserves less valuation changes and allocations of SDRs; N.B. minus equals net increase in reserves
[6] Balance of current and capital accounts

Source: National Income and Expenditure 1988 (C.S.O.)

35.11. In the Irish Balance of Payments there is usually a deficit on our Balance of Trade and a surplus on invisible transactions to mainly to tourism, the net result being a deficit on the Current section of the Balance of Payments, though in recent times our balance of trade has been moving towards a surplus as shown in table 35.11. A deficit on the Current Account section must be compensated for by a surplus on our Capital Account, e.g. through foreign investors setting up business in Ireland or foreign borrowing by the government. The net effect is often an increase in our external reserves despite the deficit on the Current Account section as shown in Table 35.10. However, the Current Account is the most accurate barometer of our international competitiveness.

Irish Balance of Payments

Table 35.11 External Trade[1] — Balance of Trade

Year	Value of trade at current prices (£000)			Annual index of the volume of trade (base: year 1975 = 100)	
	Imports	Exports	Trade Surplus[2]	Imports	Exports
1980	5,420,705	4,082,496	-1,338,209	162.6	157.1
81	6,578,406	4,777,571	-1,800,836	16.0	158.3
82	6,816,155	5,691,442	-1,124,713	160.3	169.8
83	7,366,775	6,943,836	-422,939	165.3	190.2
84	8,912,170	8,897,525	-14,646	182.6	225.2
85	9,428,198	9,743,038	314,840	188.7	239.9
86	8,621,291	9,374,310	753,019	194.4	249.5
87	9,155,207	10,723,498	1,568,291	206.4	284.9

[1] A new system of estimating trade consigned by parcel post was introduced in 1955. Data from 1964 and subsequent years include the external trade of Shannon Free Airport. In each case figures compiled according to the old and new system are shown for comparative purposes.
[2] A minus sign (-) denotes an excess of imports.

Source: Statistical Abstract 1988 (CSO)

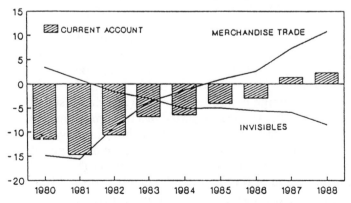

Fig. 35.11 Balance of Payments as percentage of GNP
Source: Economic Review and Outlook 1989 (Ph.6764) (Stationery Office)

35.12 Because the Balance of Payments is set out in book-keeping or accountancy terms and must balance, for the purpose of economic analysis an attempt is made to examine the interrelationships of the component parts of the Balance of Payments, i.e., to examine the manner in which the balance was achieved. For this purpose there is extracted a *Balance of Autonomous Transactions* which consist of the balance on the Current Account section plus inflows of long term capital (this inflow of long term capital is recorded in the Capital Account section of the Balance of Payments). For example, a deficit of £70 million on the current account section together with long term capital inflows of £110 million would result in a surplus of £40 million on the Balance of Autonomous Transactions.

35.13 Having referred to Autonomous Transactions the other types of transactions which appear in the Capital A/c. Section of the Balance of Payments are known as Accommodating items. These transactions are accommodating in the sense that they react passively to the Balance on Autonomous Transactions, these accommodating transactions draw the Balance of Payments into balance in the accounting sense. If there was a deficit of £100m on our Balance of Autonomous Transactions then our Official External Reserves would fall by this amount or foreign borrowing of £100 would be necessary or some combination of these two types of development to the value of £100 would ensue.

There are certain ambiguities in some of the transactions on the Capital A/c. Section as a result of which it is difficult to unambiguously classify each item as being either autonomous or accommodating. *However, any official transaction in the Capital A/c. Section the purpose of which is to maintain the exchange rate between the domestic currency and a foreign currency (or currencies) at some desired level may be unambiguously classified as an Accommodating Item.* Thus though the Balance of Payments always balances in the book-keeping or accounting sense, the expression "the Balance of Payments always balances" is devoid of economic significance — it is necessary to examine the manner in which the balance was achieved.

35.14. Often there is an interrelationship between transactions which appear on the Balance of Trade and Autonomous Capital Transfers, e.g., a transfer of funds by a multinational company to its Irish subsidiary (long term capital inflow) in order to enable the Irish subsidiary to purchase foreign capital equipment (merchandise import). In a similar fashion a loan may be negotiated in a foreign country in order that capital equipment may be imported from that country. In each of these two examples it was the inflow of capital which made possible the purchase of the merchandise. Though the foregoing type of analysis assists in the interpretation of the Balance Payments it should be noted that because of the difficulties which exist in practice in distinguishing transactions of an Accommodating nature from Autonomous Transfers the concept of the

Balance of Autonomous Transactions has not got the same level of popular acceptance as the Balance on Current Account. Notwithstanding this, you will notice rerferences to Autonomous Transfers and Accommodating Items in articles analysing the Balance of Payments.

Analysis of Deficit

35.15 A deficit on the Balance of Trade or on the Current Account section of the Balance of Payments would *not* give rise to concern under the following circumstances: —

(a) The deficit from the current years trading may be the using up of surpluses which had accrued in previous periods. A deficit or surplus should not be seen in isolation but in the context of the pattern of previous periods.

(b) The deficit may be covered by, or arise, from autonomous capital transfers as discussed in Sections 35.11 to 35.14.

(c) The deficit may be due to the importation of foreign capital goods which will enable the productive base of the economy to be expanded — see table 35.15. In this way exports may be increased at some future period and/or domestic produced goods may replace goods which are currently being imported. A deficit of this nature is often referred to as a *'growth deficit'*.

(d) Similarly a government may tolerate a deficit on international trading where the corrective action required would be deflationary and result in unemployment. This situation is sometimes referred to as *'a full employment deficit'*.

(e) There may be exceptional circumstances in this particular year's trading, e.g., the purchase of planes by Aer Lingus, or the building up of an industrial stock of imported raw materials.

Table 35.15 Distribution of Imports according to Main Use

Use Category	1982	1983	1984	1985	1986	1987
	£ million					
Producers' capital goods ready for use	943.6	937.9	1,084.2	1,253.2	1,192.3	1,338.6
Consumption goods ready for use:	1,786.9	1,875.7	2,097.8	2,317.4	2,331.6	2,413.7
Food, drink and tobacco	462.5	506.4	585.4	631.1	641.0	676.1
Other	1,324.5	1,369.3	1,512.4	1,686.3	1,690.6	1,737.6
Materials for further production	4,072.2	4,540.7	5,719.5	5,827.6	5,080.3	5,360.2
Agriculture	327.7	379.7	425.4	455.2	432.0	413.2
Other	3,744.5	4,161.0	5,294.1	5,372.4	4,648.2	4,947.0
Unclassified	13.4	12.5	10.7	29.9	17.1	42.7
Total Imports	**6,816.2**	**7,366.8**	**8,912.2**	**9,428.2**	**8,621.3**	**9,15.2**
	Percentage Distribution %					
Producers' capital goods ready for use	13.8	12.7	12.2	13.3	13.8	14.6
Consumption goods ready for use	26.2	25.5	23.5	24.6	27.0	26.4
Food, drink and tobaco	6.8	6.9	6.6	6.7	7.4	7.4
Other	19.4	18.6	17.0	17.9	19.6	19.0
Materials for further production	59.7	61.6	64.2	61.8	58.9	58.5
Agriculture	4.8	5.2	4.8	4.8	5.0	4.5
Other	54.9	56.5	59.4	57.0	53.9	54.0
Unclassified	0.2	0.2	0.1	0.3	0.2	0.5
Total	**100.-**	**100.-**	**100.-**	**100.-**	**100.-**	**100.-**

Source: Statistical Abstract 1988 (C.S.O.)

Means by which a Deficit on the Balance of Payments may be corrected

A Continuing Deficit Requires Attention

35.16 As already stated the Balance of Payments when taken in its entirety must balance — this point is emphasised by looking at the note regarding item 15 — Net Residual in Table 35.10. If merchandise and service exports are less than corresponding imports, either (a) external reserves must be used in payment, (b) foreign disinvestment by Irish nationals must take place or (c) foreign borrowing is necessary, in order to bring the Balance of Payments into balance. When there is a deficit on the Current Account section of the Balance of Payments it is often said that there is a deficit on the Balance of Payments and it is in this sense that the expression is used here. Section 35.15 sets out circumstances in which a deficit on Current Account would not give rise to too much concern and might be tolerated. However, if year after year a country continually runs such a deficit and there is no likelihood of being able to reverse the trend under normal trading conditions, it will be necessary for the government to adopt policies to rectify the fundamental disequilibrium of international trading.

35.17 PROCEDURES FOR CORRECTING A BALANCE OF PAYMENTS DEFICIT

The policies adopted may be any one, or a combination, of the following:

(a) Imports may be restricted as discussed previously.

(b) Exports may be stimulated along the lines set out in an earlier section.

(c) A deflationary government policy, e.g., cuts in government spending or increases in taxation, would restrict the level of aggregate demand and thus the demand for imports. Allied to this, in the face of declining domestic demand, producers would be stimulated to seek an export market for goods which they had been supplying to the domestic market prior to the onset of deflation.

(d) An incomes policy might be introduced. This would have an effect similar to that set out above as demand for imports would be lessened. In addition, since a successful incomes policy would probably result in unit costs of production being lower than they would otherwise be, our exports would become more competitive in terms of price.

(e) Enter into trade agreements with other countries whereby in return for our buying from them they agree to buy from us.

(f) Alter the international value of our currency and, consequently, the price of our goods and services in terms of foreign currencies.

35.18 EXCHANGE RATES

There is no international money, there is no currency which is legal tender across national frontiers — the American deals in US dollars, the

Frenchman in Francs, the Englishman in Sterling and the Irishman in Puint. Thus when an Irishman receives US$'s he goes to the bank and receives Irish money in return, or he may have the Irish money equivalent of the dollars credited to his account. Thus the banks in Ireland and U.S.A. exchange $'s for IR£'s at a rate or price determined by the supply of and demand for the currencies concerned. The international value of our currency is its exchange rate, since the exchange rate is the price at which purchases and sales of foreign currencies are transacted it is the price of one currency in terms of another, e.g., an exchange rate of IR£1 = $1.20 means that $1.20 may be purchased (or exchanged) for IR£1.

An Example of a Foreign Exchange Transaction

35.19 If an American tourist is coming to Ireland, he can purchase Irish pounds in his American bank by paying in the appropriate quantity of dollars — if the exchange rate ruling at the time of the transaction is $1.20 = IR£1, then by paying in $1,200 he receives IR£1,000. Thus, whether the American pays in Irish currency which he purchased with his dollars before he left America or pays American dollars in Irish hotels and shops, the net effect is the same — $1,200 is debited to (comes out of) his account and IR£1,000 is credited to (goes into) the accounts of Irish business people. In the international sense there was a supply of $1,200 seeking Irish currency.

35.20 FLEXIBLE EXCHANGE RATES

Changes in Exchange Rates

If American goods and services become more price competitive vis-a-vis Irish goods and services, Irish people will seek to purchase more from the USA than Americans are prepared to buy from us. In this situation there would be an excess supply of Irish currency (or a shortage of $). The exchange rate is the price of a currency in terms of a foreign currency and like all prices it is determined by the forces of supply and demand. Thus the scarcity of dollars will drive their price up until an equilibrium is attained at a price (exchange rate) at which supply and demand are equal. The development being discussed would lower the value/price of our currency in foreign exchange markets. A lowering of the value of our currency would lower the price of our goods to foreigners. Thus, an American who wished to buy an article costing IR£1,000 would have to pay in terms of his own currency $1,200 if the exchange rate is IR£1 = $1.20 but he would have to pay only $1,100 if the exchange rate was IR£1 = $1,10. This reduction in the price of our goods to foreigners would stimulate demand for our exports to an extent which depends on their price elasticity of demand. At the same time the price of imports from America will have risen in terms of Irish currency, and thus the demand for these will decrease to an extent which depends on their price elasticity of demand. In this manner under floating exchange rates the Balance of Payments is brought into equilibrium by changes in the external value of our currency. When rates of exchange are free to fluctuate in this manner in response to the market forces of supply and demand, there is said to be a *'a free float'* or *'floating exchange rates'*.

*Illustration
of
Purchasing
Power
Parity
Theory
in terms
of one good*

35.21. *The Purchasing Power Parity Theory* which was propounded by the Swedish economist Gustav Cassel in 1916 came to the fore in discussions on how to determine the appropriate equilibrium exchange rates at which countries should rejoin the Gold Standard after the First World War. Purchasing Power Parity asserts that, in the absence of non-price barriers to international trade, after allowing for costs of transportation, the price of a commodity will be the same in each country.

Example 35.21
An American exporter sells a refrigerator which he sells at $120 in America to an Irish importer for IR£100, and sells an identical refrigerator to a French importer for 930 French Francs (transport costs are being ignored). The American exporter then uses the £IR100 and 930 French Francs to buy whatever goods and services he wishes. If he could buy more goods and services with his $120 than he could for his IR£100 he would sell to the American market rather than the Irish market or he would require a higher price from the Irish importer. A similar analysis applies with respect to the French price of 930 French Francs so

IR£100 = US$120. = 930 French Francs or
IR£1   = US$1.20 = 9.30 French Francs.

Should the general price level rise in Ireland (say double) while prices in all other countries remain unchanged, then the American exporter would seek IR£200 for his refrigerator because after the doubling of prices in Ireland IR£200 would buy only the same amount of goods and services as US$120 or 930 French Francs. Thus IR200 = US$120 = 930 French Francs or IR£1 = US$0.60 or 465 French Francs, i.e., the foreign exchange value of our currency halved when our price level doubled. With this development our **real exchange rate** remained unchanged.

The situation depicted in the above example could also be explained by considering that a doubling of Irish prices implies an increase in the money supply in Ireland. This increase in the money supply results in increased demand for imports and consequently an increased supply of **Irish money on foreign exchange markets. If exchange rates are free to** fluctuate the increased supply of Irish money on foreign exchange markets will result in a reduction in the value of each unit of our currency.

35.22. All of the foregoing illustrations have been related to one commodity, i.e., a refrigerator. In more general terms Purchasing Power

Parity Theory states that the equilibrium exchange rate equalises the
general purchasing power of a given income in terms of domestic and
foreign prices. You will realise that this implies that changes in inflation
rates in different countries will result in changes in the exchange value of
currencies on foreign exchange markets — as shown in example 35.21 —
so that real exchange rates remain unaltered.

35.23. Problems associated with Applying Purchasing Power Parity Theory

1.   The problem of selecting the appropriate price index for calculating
     Purchasing Power Parity rates.

2.   In choosing a base year it is necessary to identify a year in which
     exchange rates were in equilibrium.

3.   Changes in the rate of growth of real income, tastes or technology in
     different countries may cause shifts in the real exchange rate or
     Terms of Trade. The appropriate equilibrium exchange rate will
     then be different from PPP rates calculated on the basis of relative
     inflation rates.

*Factors other
than trade
influence
Rates*
35.24. However, exchange rates are determined by the total supply of,
and demand for, currencies. A considerable proportion of this supply
and demand arises from trade but this is not the only factor. Capital
Flows, Speculation, Borrowing etc, all are elements in the supply of, and
demand for, currencies so that the Purchasing Power Parity Theory is
only a partial explanation of the determination of exchange rates.
Notwithstanding the foregoing most analyses of movements in foreign
exchange rates includes a comparison of what the rate would have been
under Purchasing Power Parity.

Fixed Exchange Rates

35.25. The period between the despatch of goods by the seller and his
receipt of payment for them is longer in international than in domestic
trade. In addition to this the absence of an international currency and the
possibility of fluctuations in exchange rates increase the possibility of the
real value of the price received for the goods being different from that
*Some
Advantages
of Fixed
Exchange
Rates*
intended when the selling price of the goods was fixed. Rather than
permit exchange rates to continually fluctuate to reflect momentary
conditions of supply and demand, a country may adopt a policy of
maintaining the parity of its exchange rate, or at least confining
fluctuations in the exchange rate to a narrow band. Stable exchange rates
assist in the development of international trade through lessening
instability and enabling future commitments to be entered into with a
greater degree of confidence. The Irish government has tended as a
matter of policy to maintain fixed rates of exchange against other
currencies and, since accepting membership of the *European Monetary*

System (EMS), has undertaken to confine fluctuations in the external value of our currency within a band of $\pm 2\frac{1}{4}\%$.

*Fixed
Exchange
Rates and
Balance of
Payments
disequilibrium*

35.26. Fixed exchange rates prevent the automatic correction of a Balance of Payments disequilibrium on the lines set out in Section 35.20. If the prices of imports/exports are not free to alter and to bring about equality on the Current Account, and if the government does not intervene by exercising control over the volume of international trade as discussed in Section 35.16 , then the ensuing deficits must be met by a compensating alteration of the Capital Account of the Balance of Payments as set out in Section 35.9. However, it should be noted that the financing of deficits on the Current Account through stimulating inflows of capital cannot continue indefinitely (a policy of this nature has been compared to a household borrowing in order to purchase normal groceries). Deficits which continue over several periods are due to some fundamental economic disequilibrium which must be corrected.

*Government
Intervention
on Foreign
Exchange
Markets*

35.27. It is because exchange rates are determined by the *total* demand for and *total* supply of a currency, rather than merely the supply of, and demand for, the currency to which the purchase and sale of goods and services gives rise, that the government can utilise additional weapons in its attempts to control exchange rates viz.:—

(a) **Monetary Policy**
Interest rates in Ireland may be increased to stimulate inflows of foreign capital. If rates of interest in Ireland are higher than the corresponding rates in other countries, then capital will be transferred into this country to take advantage of the extra interest to be earned. However, these inflows — known as *"hot money"* — can leave the country just as easily.

(b) **Central Bank Intervention in Foreign Exchange Dealings**
Since exchange rates are determined by the forces of supply and demand, the government can maintain exchange rates at a specified par value by releasing from its reserve holding of foreign currencies the required supply of any foreign currency. This procedure is often implemented through an *Exchange Equalisation Account*. When there is an excess of supply of Irish puint seeking a foreign currency, the Irish Central Bank can sell the quantity of the foreign currency required in order to maintain the existing par value of our currency on foreign exchange markets, e.g., if at a particular moment Irish people wished to import IR£10,000 worth of German goods while Germans wished to import 29,000DM worth of Irish goods, there would be an excess supply of Irish puint (or a deficiency of DMs) at the required par value of (say) £1 = 3.03DM. The Central Bank could sell from the reserves of foreign currencies in its exchange equalisation account say 1,300DM for Irish puint. There would then be available IR£10,000 and 30,300DM and in this way the existing par value of IR£1 = 3.03DM would be maintained. If the

following day there are excess DMs the Central Bank could buy back the DMs by selling Irish puint for DMs. In this manner the par value of the currency is insulated from the daily swings in the conditions of supply and demand, and the par value of the currency will change only in response to fundamental changes in the value of the currency.

If there is an over-valuation of the Irish currency vis-a-vis the Deutsch Mark, there will be a continual over-supply of Irish puint. Despite a demand for German goods by Irish people there will not be a corresponding demand for Irish goods in Germany. Though the reserves of foreign currency which the Central Bank holds are large they are not infinite and it would not be possible to sustain a continuing drain on the holdings of foreign currencies. Thus, in the absence of some cost reducing efficiencies by Irish industry or a restriction on international trade, a devaluation of the Irish currency would be inevitable.

Arbitrage Operations

35.28. In order to buy from other countries you need their currency or some other currency which they require. If no foreigners wished to engage in economic activities with any person or firm in Ireland then there would be no demand for Irish currency and we could not acquire any foreign currency to pay for imports. Obviously one way of acquiring a country's currency is to engage in economic transactions with that country. However, it is possible also to acquire the currency of a country through dealings with other (third) countries, e.g., Ireland could sell to France and use the French Francs which are earned in order to purchase the Deutschmarks which enable us to buy from Germany. Due to this multinational aspect of international trade and foreign exchange transactions, relativities must be maintained between exchange rate parities, e.g., if IR£1 = 3.03DM & IR£1 = 9.33 French Francs, then 3.03DM must equal 9.33 French Francs.

Example 35.28.

Let us suppose that:
            IR£1 = 3.03DM & IR£1 = 9.33 French Francs
            but 3.00DM = 9.33 French Francs

Now if an Irish importer bought goods to the value of 9330 French Francs, the importer could buy this amount of French Francs for £1000. (IR£1 = 9.33 French Francs). However instead of doing that the Irish importer could buy 3030DM for his IR£1000 (IR£1 = 3.03DM). With the 3030DM he could buy 9423.3 French Francs (3.00DM = 933 French Francs). With the 9423.3 French Francs the French exporter could be paid his 9330 French Francs and the importer would have 93.3 French Francs left.

While the exchange rates remain out of alignment transactions of this nature would be profitable. Sales and purchases of this nature are known as Arbitrage Operations. Arbitrage Operations are profitable if exchange rates are not properly adjusted, i.e., if exchange rates are disorderly. Arbitrage operations have the effect of driving exchange rates to mutually consistent parities, i.e., in the above example mutually consistent parities are   IR£1 = 3.03 Dm = 9.33 French Francs.

35.29. Crawling Peg

Advantages of Crawling Peg System

This system is known also as a *'sliding peg'*. Rather than permit, on the one hand, exchange rates to be perfectly flexible and continually adjusting in order to reflect momentary conditions of supply and demand, or on the other hand, Central Bank attempts to maintain a rate of exchange which doesn't reflect underlying market conditions, the government may adopt a crawling peg system of exchange rates. Under this system, which was first adopted in1944, exchange rates are allowed to fluctuate within a relatively wide band about the par value, e.g., if the par value was £1 = 3.03 Dm, the pound might be allowed to fluctuate within a band of $\pm 2\frac{1}{4}\%$, i.e., the exchange rate of the pound may vary from 2.962 Dm to 3.098 Dm before there is any official intervention by the Central Bank. If necessary, the par value of the currency is allowed to "crawl" to a new parity.

In this way it is hoped:

(a)   to avoid the uncertainty and speculation to which completely flexible exchange rates give rise and which impede international trade and

(b)   to obviate attempts to maintain a fixed rate of exchange which doesn't reflect market conditions and eventually requires a devaluation or upward revaluation of the currency which will be even greater and more traumatic because it was delayed.

35.30. Effects of devaluation on the Irish Balance of Trade

A country which has a persistent deficit on international trade may have to devalue its currency, i.e., lower the rate at which its currency exchanges for the currency of other countries. This means that more of the devalued currency would have to be given for a unit of the foreign currency.

(a)   Our exports become cheaper as a result of the devaluation of our currency. The benefits of this to our earnings of foreign currency depend upon the price elasticity of demand for our exports. The elasticity of demand for our agricultural exports is likely to be low so that a reduction in their price would probably not lead to a significant increase in the demand for them. We could end up exporting more or less the same quantity of agricultural produce but receiving a lower sum of money for it — unless there was an adjustment in the value of our "Green" currency as discussed in Chapter 37.

(b) Industrial exports would be more competitive and this would probably be reflected in an increase in the demand for them.

(c) Imports would be dearer but industrial machinery which cannot be obtained from domestic sources would have to be imported even at the higher price, while the demand for imported consumer durables such as motor cars, dishwashers etc., might not be very susceptible to change in their selling price. Import substitutes which can be produced locally might well enjoy a competitive advantage..

(d) The effect of a devaluation on our Balance of Trade depends on the elasticities of demand for our exports and imports. *The Marshall-Lerner Condition* states that a currency depreciation will improve the Balance of Trade (and a currency appreciation worsen it), if the sum of the elasticity of demand for a country's exports and its elasticity of demand for imports is greater than unity in absolute terms.

10% devaluation of our currency in each example

Pre-devaluation: Imports = 1000 units at £10 each = £10,000
                     Exports = 1000 units at £10 each = £10,000

Example A:

Price Elasticity of Demand
    for Exports   = 2 with devaluation of 10% demand
                             for our exports increased by 20%

Price Elasticity of Demand
    for Imports   = 1.5 with devaluation of our
                             demand for imports reduced by
                                     15%

		Unit Price £	Qty.	Value £	Pre-devaluation Value £	Change in Value £
Post Devaluations	Imports	11	850	9350	10,000	-650
	Exports	9	1200	10800	10,000	+800

Net Change   = Improvement of £1450
Sum of Elasticities = 2 + 1.5 = 3.5 which is greater than unity (in absolute terms)
                       And Balance of Trade is improved by devaluation.

Example B:

		Price Elasticity of Demand for Imports	= 0.4	with devaluation of 10% demand for imports decreased by 4%

Price Elasticity of Demand
for Imports $\qquad$ = 0.4 with devaluation of 10% demand
for imports decreased by 4%

Price Elasticity of Demand
for Exports $\qquad$ =0.1 with devaluation of 10% demand
for exports increased by 1%

		Unit Price £	Qty.	Value £	Pre-devaluation Value £	Change in Value £
Post-Devaluation	Imports	11	960	10560	10,000	+560
	Exports	9	1010	9090	10,000	-910

Net Change = Deterioration of £350

Sum of Elasticities = 0.4 + 0.1 = 0.5 which is less than unity (in absolute terms) so Balance of Trade deteriorates as a result of the Devaluation.

35.31. Developments Arising from Devaluation

The competitive benefits of devaluation depend to a considerable extent on the reaction of the general public to a reduction in their standard of living consequent on the devaluation of their currency. The devaluation of a currency will set in train the following sequence of events in the devaluing country:—

(i) Increases in the local currency prices of imported consumption goods, e.g., the local cost of an article costing £10 sterling was IR£10, when the rate of exchange was IR£1 = £1 sterling. If our currency is devalued to IR£1.10 = £1 sterling, the local cost of the same articles would rise to IR£11.

(ii) Increases in the prices of domestically produced goods which use imported raw materials due to increases in the prices of these imported raw materials.

(iii) Even domestically produced goods which don't use any imported raw materials but which sell on domestic and foreign markets would be likely to be increased in price. This situation arises because some of these goods may continue to be sold on export markets at the predevaluation price, i.e., a good which sold in England for £5 may continue to sell in England for £5 despite a devaluation of our currency relative to sterling. However, the £5 sterling which prior to devaluation was worth IR£5, is now worth IR£5.50 after a 10% devaluation of our currency. In this case if the item had been selling on local markets for IR£5 prior to devaluation it will now sell for IR£5.50, since otherwise it would be more profitable to ignore the domestic market and sell the entire output in England. Thus, in order to retain a supply of these goods in the domestic market the domestic price may have to rise, since in the absence of such a price increase the goods might be diverted towards the export market which would be more profitable at the post-devaluation rate of exchange.

(iv) Even the prices of goods and services which do not enter into international trade may be affected. In the face of an increased demand for exports there will be an increase in the demand for those factors of production which are used in their manufacture. Thus higher prices may have to be offered to factors of production to retain them in the production of those goods and services which are required for the domestic market. This rise in costs will lead to increased prices particularly since there would be a buoyant demand due to the high level of economic activity.

(v) Increased prices will erode the purchasing power of wages which may stimulate demands for wage increases which would put further pressure on costs and prices.

35.32. The effects of a 10% devaluation on the Irish economy could develop along the following lines — the figures are being used merely to indicate the idea of time lags and to suggest possible orders of magnitude.

(a) Since some element of our prices are due to indirect taxes and some costs are of a non-traded nature, the CPI would rise less than the full amount of the devaluation.

(b) The time lag between the increase in the Consumer Price Index and the increase in wage depends on the timing of the devaluation relative to the negotiating of a new round of wage increases.

(c) When discussing profits in Chapter 22 attention was drawn to the fact that profits being non-contractual tend to bear the initial impact of changes in prices of the factors of production i.e. profits increase first when conditions are buoyant and fall first when demand is depressed. Thus in example 35.32 the major impact gain accrues to profits.

Example 35.32. Illustration of the Possible Effects of a 10% Devaluation

	Period 1	Period 2	Period 3	Total Effect
Consumer Price Index	+3.5%	+1.5%	+1.0%	+6.0
Wages	+1.5%	+3.0%	+1.5%	+6.0
Profit Margins of those engaged in traded Sector	+8.5%	-3.0%	-1.5%	+4.0

35.33. Those who had invested outside the state and who had the return on their investment paid or denominated in the foreign currency would gain from the devaluation since each unit of foreign currency would purchase a greater quantity of domestically produced goods and services. On the other hand, those who had invested their money locally, e.g., in Irish farms, or in Irish building societies, Agricultural Credit Corporation, Commercial Banks, Post Office Savings Bank etc., would be relatively worse off, in that sense they would have been better off had they invested their money abroad.

Devaluation and our National Debt

35.34. A devaluation of our currency would also increase both the outstanding value of that portion of our National Debt which is denominated in foreign currencies and also its servicing.

Currency Appreciation and Competitiveness

35.35. An increase in the foreign exchange value of our currency — usually referred to as a revaluation — can be analysed along similar lines as has been applied to a devaluation. However, it should be noted that in the event of an increase in the foreign exchange value of our currency we may suffer a loss in competitiveness. In 1983 and 1986 the value of our currency appreciated relative to sterling to an extent which made it difficult for our exporters to sell in UK markets and to remain competitive against UK competitors in third countries. In order to regain competitiveness our currency was devalued by the Central Bank. See section 37.48.

QUESTIONS

Q1. Distinguish between the Balance of Trade and the Balance of Payments. Much each of these always balance?

Q2. In what circumstances might a deficit in the Balance of Trade in a particular year
   (a) give cause for economic concern
   (b) be considered tolerable

Q3. Set out the arguments for and against Floating Exchange Rates.

Q4. Explain Purchasing Power Parity Theory.

Q5. Would you expect a devaluation to improve our Balance of Payments?

36 International Finance

36.1. The present system of financing international trade developed from the gold standard, so that a knowledge of the gold standard is necessary in order to understand that system. The gold standard was not conceived and introduced as the basis of international financing but rather it emerged and developed through usage and refinement just as did the price system. Up to the outbreak of the First World War in 1914 the currency of most countries was freely convertible into gold at a fixed rate (you will see an undertaking to this effect on old legal tender notes). Each country specified its basic monetary unit to be the equivalent in value of a specified quantity of gold. By doing this each country in fact determined the value of its currency relative to the value of all other currencies, e.g., one pound sterling was convertible into 0.257 standard ounces of gold, while one US dollar was convertible into 0.053 standard ounces of gold. Thus one pound sterling had a value equivalent to

$$\frac{0.257}{0.053} = 4.85 \text{ US dollars}$$

This ratio between the values of different currencies was known as *The Mint Par Value of Exchange*, and on the basis of this valuation international trade took place.

36.2. If trade between Ireland and America was such that Irish people wished to import more goods from America than Americans wished to buy from us, there would be a shortage of dollars (i.e., an excess supply of Irish pounds). However, instead of this excess supply of Irish pounds forcing up the value of the US dollar, Irish purchasers of the American goods converted their Irish currency into gold and shipped the gold to America in payment for the goods since it was cheaper to do this rather than pay a higher price for dollars.

Example 36.2

Suppose Irish people wished to import £100,000 worth of goods from America while they wished to buy only $339,500 worth of goods from us. At the mint par value of exchange £1 = $4.85.

$$\$339,500 = £70,000$$
$$\$145,500 = £30,000$$

At the mint par value of exchange there would be a shortage of $145,500 for Irish people who wished to import from America. This amount of dollars could be bought in America using an amount of gold to the value of $145,500 (i.e., £30,000). Thus a country with a surplus on international trade would receive gold while a country with a deficit on international trade would lose gold.

Gold Points

36.3. Because of the cost of transporting the gold and insuring it while it was in transit, the official rate of exchange could vary within narrow limits before it became more economical to transfer gold. The upper limit and lower limit were known as the *Gold Import Point* and *Gold Export Point* or simply the *Gold Points*.

Self regulating Mechanism of the Gold Standard

36.4. The quantity of money in each country was tied to the quantity of gold which was held by the banking authorities for the purpose of supporting the note issue. The *Bank Charter Act of 1844* in Great Britain allowed a small fiduciary issue of legal tender but the remainder, that is the greater proportion, of the issue of legal tender notes had to be backed by gold. In example 36.2 with Ireland losing gold, the quantity of money in Ireland would be reduced while America, having a surplus on international trade, would gain gold as a result of which its money supply would be increased. According to the quantity theory of money the price level is related to the money supply. Thus the reduction in the money supply in Ireland consequent on the shipment of gold out of the country in settlement of foreign debts reduced the general level of prices in the deficit country (Ireland) and increased the general level of prices in the surplus country (America). The fall in the general level of prices in the deficit trading country would make its goods more competitive in international trading while the price rise in the surplus trading country would lessen the competitiveness of that country's products on international markets. In this way the changing price level would adjust the flow of trade to an equilibrium position. In addition to this development the rise in interest rates consequent on the reduction of the money supply

Fig. 36.4 Balance of Payments Adjustment under the Gold Standard System.

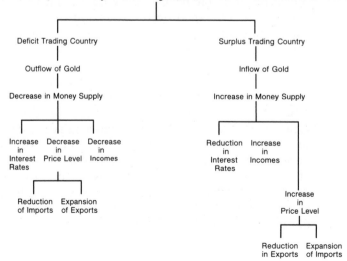

would attract an inflow of gold which would provide a short term respite to the deficit nation. Advocates of the gold system considered that in this fashion, which is summarised in Fig. 36.4, a deficit or surplus in international trade was 'automatically' adjusted through a self-regulating mechanism when countries were on the gold standard.

The Gold Standard

Position up to 1914

36.5. Up to the outbreak of the First World War in 1914, as trade had been increasing between countries without any crises being experienced on Balance of Payments, the gold standard seemed to be living up to the claims of its advocates. However, on the outbreak of war in 1914 countries were forced to abandon the gold system. Subsequent research withholds from the gold standard the credit for the expansion in world trade prior to 1914 but suggests that as the price levels in the various trading countries were close to their equilibrium levels, no major trading country had to inflate or deflate as the transmission mechanism of the gold standard system requires.

36.6. 1916-1925 A Period of Floating Exchange Rates

Movement from Pegged Rates of Exchange

At the termination of the First World War the rates of exchange between the currencies of the various countries were allowed to float in order to reflect the market conditions of supply and demand. This development was in contrast with the pegged rates of exchange which the exigencies of the war had dictated.

36.7. 1925-1931 a Return to the Gold Standard

The chaos in the monetary systems of many countries in the years immediately preceding the termination of the First World War was in sad contrast with the stability which had characterised the pre-war years. Since countries had been on the gold standard during the pre-war period, when there was an orderly expansion of world trade, while the gold standard was not in operation during the chaotic period of fluctuating exchange rates in the post-war period, a return to the gold standard was prescribed as a panacea for the economic ills which were prevalent in the post-war period. The example of Austria in returning to the gold standard in 1922 was followed by many countries with Great Britain returning to the gold standard in 1925. However, Great Britain did not return to the full gold standard which had operated in that country prior to the 1914-18 war, in that there was not a restoration of gold coinage. Paper money could be exchanged for 400oz. gold bars which were valued

Gold Bullion Standard

at approximately £1,560 each. Consequently this system became known as the *Gold Bullion Standard.* This gold bullion standard had the advantage over the full convertibility of the gold standard in that it was not necessary to:—

(a)   incur the expense of replacing worn coins or

(b)   set aside a gold reserve for the legal tender issue, although a gold reserve was still required for international transactions.

Gold Exchange Standard

36.8. Rather than holding a gold stock themselves many countries adopted a *Gold Exchange Standard* under which they maintained their reserves in the currency of a country which had a currency that was convertible into gold, e.g., sterling. The advantage of the gold exchange standard to a country adopting this policy was that it could hold its reserves in the form of treasury bills issued by the Bank of England. These treasury bills were convertible into sterling which in turn was convertible into gold bullion standard. In this way the reserves of the country were convertible into gold but instead of incurring the expense of holding and guaranteeing sterile non-interest-bearing gold bars, interest could be earned on the holding of the Treasury Bills. It was an additional advantage that London was one of the major financial centres of the world and a centre for international payments. There was a disadvantage in that, if the currency in which their reserves were held went off the gold standard or was devalued, there would be a loss on the investments. The problems of this nature which devaluations of sterling caused in this country illustrate this point.

There was a disadvantage also to the country in whose currency the reserves were held. In the event of Great Britain suffering an unfavourable Balance of Payments, the problem could be aggravated by capital outflows due to loss of confidence in the ability of Great Britain to maintain the exchange value of its currency.

The Collapse of the Gold Standard

Non-Implementation of the "Rules of Gold Standard"

Attitude to deflation

36.9. It is shown in Fig. 36.4 that the correcting mechanism of the gold standard required that deficit/gold-losing countries should deflate, while surplus/gold-receiving countries should inflate. During the 1920's countries were not inclined to follow these dictates of the system. Deflation was politically unpopular and difficult to implement in the face of strong trade union pressure for the maintenance of money wages, and this was combined with a downward inflexibility of administered prices.

Attitude to inflation

36.10. Similarly gold-receiving countries were unwilling to inflate lest it would introduce an element of inflation into their domestic economy and affect the competitiveness of their exports. During the 1920's the USA and France which were surplus trading countries did not allow their money supply to increase despite the inflow of gold. This attitude placed the entire burden of correcting the Balance of Payments disequilibrium on the deficit country and intensified its deflationary requirement.

*Trade
imbalance in
1920's were
greater than
hitherto*

36.11. It should be noted that the adjustments required due to trade imbalances in the 1920's were greater than in any previous period. There are economists who suggest that the gold standard system worked well in the period prior to 1914 because it was not required to rectify any major disequilibrium and when called upon to do so in the 1920's, the system was inadequate.

36.12. Capital Inflows

Hot Money

Prior to 1914 capital inflows were of a long term nature and related to investment requirements. After the 1914-1918 was there was in existence a considerable amount of 'refugee capital' which was moved to those countries which seemed to offer the greatest security for this 'hot money'. Security, rather than the interest which could be earned, was the prime consideration in the placing of these funds, so that if an increase in the Bank Rate was implemented in order to attract foreign capital inflows it could be considered as indicative of a basic weakness in the economy and result in the withdrawal of the 'hot money'. Movements of capital related to reparation payments and the repayment of war debts added further to what proved to be the intolerable strain placed on the workings of the gold standard during this period.

36.13. Exchange Rates

*Overvaluation
of Sterling*

Great Britain, on returning to the gold standard in 1925, choose for sterling the same exchange rate which had existed at the outbreak of the First World War in 1914. Sterling at that time was the major international currency and this rate was adopted in order to consolidate London as the major financial centre of the world. At the rate of exchange which was chosen sterling was overvalued. This overvaluation was manifest in the lack of price competitiveness of British exports while imports to that country were at a price which British manufacturers were unable to match. The degree of deflation required to rectify the Balance of Payments disequilibrium which resulted from this overvaluation was too great and could not be attained. As deflation increased the level of unemployment became intolerable culminating in The Great Strike of 1926. Great Britain was enmeshed in a trade recession some time before the world recession of the 1930's.

The 1930's ended with the commencement of the Second World War in 1939 and hostilities continued until 1945. The post-Second World War attitude to the problems associated with the financing of international trade and the structures to which they gave rise form the subject of the next chapter.

QUESTIONS

Q1. Explain "Mint Par Value of Exchange".

Q2. Explain the "Gold Exchange Standard".

Q3. Analyse the Balance of Payments adjustment mechanisation under the gold standard.

Q4. Trace the circumstances which led to the collapse of the gold standard.

Q5. Explain the "Gold Bullion Standard".

37 International Economic Institutions and Structures

International Monetary Fund (IMF)

IMF set up to Assist International Trade

37.1. Being conscious of the problems to which economic affairs had been subject both in the period immediately prior to the first world war and in the 1930's, most of the major trading countries of the world attended a series of conferences which were held at Bretton Woods, New Hampshire, in 1944 for the purpose of achieving a system of exchange rates which would permit and stimulate world trade. One of the major achievements of this conference was the establishment of the *International Monetary Fund (IMF)*. This institution commenced operations in 1947 with the purpose of minimising the interruptions to world trade which short term trade imbalances might occasion.

37.2. These objectives are set out in the articles of agreement of the International Monetary Fund which state that the purpose of the fund is:—

Objectives of Fund

(i) To promote international monetary co-operation through a permanent institution which provides the machinery for consultation and collaboration on international monetary problems.

(ii) To facilitate the expansion and balanced growth of international trade and to contribute thereby to the promotion and maintenance of high levels of employment and real income and to the development of the productive resources of all members as primary objectives of economic policy.

(iii) To promote exchange stability, to maintain orderly exchange arrangements among members and to avoid competitive exchange depreciation.

(iv) To assist in the establishment of a multilateral system of payments in respect of current transactions between members and in the elimination of foreign exchange restrictions which hamper the growth of world trade.

(v) To give confidence to members by making the general resources of the fund temporarily available to them, under adequate safeguards, thus providing them with an opportunity to correct maladjustments in their Balances of Payments without resorting to measures destructive of national or international prosperity.

(vi) In accordance with the above, to shorten the duration and lessen the degree of disequilibrium in the international Balances of Payments of members.

37.3. Exchange rate parities were seen as being of particular importance and the members of the fund agreed that prior to a specified date each country had to declare the par value of its currency and then undertook to maintain this par value on foreign exchange markets. In order to avoid the restrictions which inflexible par values might impose in changing economic conditions, each country was permitted changes of up to 10% in the par value of its currency, i.e., changes of up to 5% on either side of the par value. Any change in excess of these limits was considered to be a major change and was to be contemplated only in the face of continuing disequilibria on the Balance of payments and introduced only after consultation with the IMF.

Exchange Rate Parities

37.4. The IMF was in fact operating an *Adjustable Peg System,* i.e., though the exchange rate was fixed or pegged, its parity could be adjusted in the event of a persistent imbalance. The requirement to notify the IMF in advance of any changes in the par value has not proved feasible and since 1950 countries have unilaterally declared changes in the foreign exchange value of their currencies.

Adjustable Peg System

37.5. In order to assist in the stabilisation of exchange rates, each member country of the IMF was allocated a quota of currency which it must contribute to a pool which constituted a form of foreign exchange equalisation account. 75% of each members's quota was to be contributed in its own currency and the balance in some combination of gold and US dollars. Members could borrow from this fund in order to maintain the par value of their currency in the face of temporary deficits on their Balance of Payments or speculation against their currency.

A Fund to Assist the Maintenance of Par Value

37.6. Should there be a persistent demand from members for a particular currency, the IMF could declare such a currency to be scarce and ration it amongst the applicant countries. Alternatively the IMF could purchase some of the currency for which there was a heavy demand in exchange for some of its stock of gold or else raise a loan in the 'hard currency' country. The IMF has been instrumental in enabling a number of countries to survive temporary disequilibria on their Balances of Payments without having to resort to the devaluations which would have been inevitable in the absence of assistance from the fund.

"Hard Currencies"

The International Bank of Reconstruction and Development (IBRD). This is known also as The World Bank.

37.7. This was another major financial institution which was established as a result of the *Bretton Woods* conference in 1944. Whereas the IMF deals with short term loans the IBRED was set up to facilitate the movements of long term capital. The member nation subscribed to the capital stock of the World Bank in a ratio related to their GNP's. The bank makes loans only to governments, though governments can borrow

IBRD Concentrates on Long Term Capital

and then pass the funds over to institutions in their own country for specific projects, e.g., ESB, CIE, thus in effect once the loan is guaranteed by national governments, the resources of the IBRD may be sought. Technical and economic experts are employed by the World Bank to examine all applications for loans and in so doing they bring a fund of knowledge and expertise to the benefit of the applicant country. The operation of the IBRD has been very successful, though at times its lending policy has been criticised as being too conservative, with an overemphasis on the self liquidating type of project.

Agencies of World Bank

37.8. The IBRD has acquired further capital through bond issues and has used the proceeds of these bond issues to fund loan applications which it found acceptable. In addition to these activities it has engaged in the underwriting of loans being raised by other institutions. Because of the economic standing of the World Bank, loans underwritten by it are usually fully subscribed at competitive rates of interest. The transactions of the IBRD are conducted at going market rates and its loans are not a form of subsidisation. The World Bank set up two agencies:

(a)   *The International Development Agency* (IDA) which makes 'soft loans' to underdeveloped countries for the construction of roads, hospitals, schools, etc.

(b)   *The International Finance Corporation* (IFC) through which funds are channelled to private investment projects.

The Bank for International Settlements (BIS)

A Grouping of Central Bankers

37.9. This bank is a grouping of Central Bankers and was established in 1930 in order to tackle the financial problems besetting the world economy at that time. Its headquarters are in Basle, Switzerland, and its meetings of representatives of the various central banks are held each month in order to decide on the courses of action to be pursued in the light of the economic conditions being experienced. This institution is banker to the Organisation for Economic Cooperation & Development (OECD), and the European Coal & Steel Community (ECSC).

The General Agreement on Tariffs and Trade (GATT)

To Assist the Free Flow of International Trade

37.10. At the conclusion of the Second World War there was a general desire among nations that there should not be a return to the protectionism of the 1930's. With this object, an agreement on tariff reductions to assist the free flow of international trade was introduced in 1948. The signatories to the agreement represent over 80% of world trade and they meet in Geneva, Switzerland, twice a year for the purpose of monitoring the operation of existing agreements and negotiating further tariff reductions.

37.11. The passing in America of the Kennedy Trade Act in 1962 which was directed towards the achievement of multilateral tariff reductions motivated GATT negotiations which began in November 1964 and were completed in May 1967. These negotiations culminated in the single most spectacular GATT agreement (known as the Kennedy Round of Tariff Reductions) by which agreement, over a five year period from 1967-1972, the tariffs on world trade were reduced by approximately 30%.

Kennedy Round of Tariff Reduction

37.12. One of the features of GATT regulations is the 'most favoured nation' clause whereby any agreement between member states on tariff reductions must be extended to all member states, so that no discrimination is permitted in the application of tariffs between member states. While tariffs are undoubtedly lower than they would have been in the absence of such an agreement, some advocates of free international trade have been disappointed that tariff reductions have not been greater. These advocates point also to the growth of non-tariff trade barriers.

"Most Favoured Nation" Clause

The European Economic Community (EEC)

37.13. In 1945 in an attempt to return to normality after the ravages of the Second World War, nations began to re-establish their social and business life. Assistance was given to these efforts by the implementation of the American Aid Programme known as THE MARSHALL PLAN. This aid programme tended to perceive Europe as a single unit and thus stimulated thoughts towards communal action by European states. By communal action it was hoped to minimise the development of rivalry between nations and the possibility of future conflicts and wars.

Marshall Plan

37.14. Initial economic co-operation in Europe was manifest when in 1947 Belgium, the Netherlands and Luxembourg established between themselves a customs union known as *Benelux. A customs union is an agreement among countries to eliminate customs duties and other restrictions on trade between them and to impose a common system of tariffs and taxes on goods being imported into the customs union.* A customs union is a closer economic alignment than a free trade area because a free trade area imposes no commitment in respect of members imposing a common tariff wall on goods being imported from countries which are not a party to the free trade agreement, i.e., a free trade area refers only to the free movement of goods within the area.

Customs Union

37.15. In 1952 economic co-operation was extended further when West Germany, France and Italy joined with the Benelux countries to establish the *European Coal and Steel Community.* The success of this grouping led to these six countries signing the *Treaty of Rome* which established the *European Economic Community (EEC).* Commencing with a 10% tariff reduction in January 1959, tariffs continued to be reduced until 10 years later there existed a *Common Market* between members. *A Common*

Common Market

Market is an agreement between countries whereby they agree to eliminate customs duties and other restrictions on trade between them, to impose a common system of tariffs and taxes on goods being imported from outside the area and in addition to permit the free movement of capital and labour within the Common Market area. Thus, because of this free movement of factors of production, a common market is a more complete economic alignment than is a customs union. In January 1973 the EEC grouping of six countries was enlarged to nine with the accession of England, Denmark and Ireland. In 1981 Greece joined the Community and the European Community was increased to 12 member countries when Treaties of Accession to admit Spain and Portugal to membership from 1st January 1986 were signed in Madrid and Lisbon on June 12th 1985. These 12 member countries have more than 321 million citizens.

Relationship between Free Trade Area, Customs Union and Common Market

37.16. The relationship between a free trade area, a customs union and a common market may be perceived in the following manner:

Free Trade Area= Free movement of goods within an area.

Customs Union = Free trade area plus a common system of tariffs and taxes on goods being imported from outside the area.

Common Market= Customs union plus the free movement of capital and labour within the Common Market area.

37.17. Common Agricultural Policy (CAP).

In Europe, generally, agriculture is an important industry, both in its own right and for its contribution to other sectors of the economy. An agricultural policy to be effective must guarantee regular and adequate supplies of good quality produce at reasonable price to consumers and to the food processing industry. Though an increase in the standard of living tends to lower the percentage of income which is spent on food, e.g. in developed countries from 30% of total expenditure in the 1960's to 20% in the 1980's, nevertheless a considerable portion of expenditure is on food.

Purpose of Intervention in Agriculture

Throughout the world public authorities consider it necessary to intervene in agriculture in order to regulate markets, guide production and improve farm facilities, balancing the social and economic needs of farmers with the interests of consumers. The advent of the EEC implied an opening up of frontiers and a balancing of trade flows and economic benefits between Member States, some of these states are more agricultural and some are more industrial so that the development of a common market for industrial goods would have been untenable without a concomitant development of a common market for agricultural produces. The preservation of conflicting national agricultural policies would have made free trade in agricultural goods impossible. thus there was instituted in 1974 a Common Agricultural Policy (CAP), the objectives of which are:—

*Objectives
of Common
Agricultural
Policy*

(a) To raise the standard of living of the agricultural sector to a level comparable with that enjoyed by the industrial sector.

(b) Guaranteed access to community markets and free competition between the member states in respect of agricultural products. This implies that farmers in one country should not suffer any disadvantage in competing with farmers from any other country which is a member of the EEC, e.g. Irish farmers should not suffer any disadvantage when competing with French farmers on the French market.

(c) Through removing cyclical fluctuations in the prices of agricultural products, the long term survival and development of the agricultural industry would be enhanced.

37.18. The EEC set about achieving these objectives by a policy of
(a) guaranteed prices for agricultural produce, and
(b) a system of common prices for agricultural produce throughout the community.

*Guaranteed
Prices*

These guaranteed prices placed a support or minimum to the price of agricultural produce by means of EEC using some of its funds to buy whatever volume of output could not be sold to the general public at prices at or above the guaranteed price. If the intervention price was above the market clearing price then the overproduction would be put into intervention stock — hence the reference to butter mountains and wine lakes.

*European
Unit of
Account*

37.19. In order to ensure that common agricultural prices applied throughout the community, for administrative and accounting purposes, the prices of agricultural products were expressed in terms of a European Unit of Account — which became known as the "green currency".

Example 37.19.

Let us suppose that IR£1 = 2.0 units of account, ⋆ and 1DM = 0.5 units of account and that the rate of exchange on foreign exchange markets is IR£1 = 4DM. In this case, if the support price for a particular commodity is 4 units of account and trading takes place at this support price, then the price of the item would be IR£2 in Ireland and 8 DM in Germany. Thus there would be no incentive for an Irish farmer to sell the item in Germany rather than in Ireland because if he sold it in Germany he would get 8 DM which at the official rate of exchange would be worth IR£2; which is the price at which he could have sold the item in Ireland.

*Alteration in
Exchange
Rates*

37.20. This procedure was fine during a period of fixed exchange rates between the currencies of the member states but the position became somewhat complicated when the parity of exchange rates began to alter due to the devaluations of the late '60's and the floating exchange rates of the '70's as shown in Example 37.20.

⋆ The unit of account is the numeraire used by the EEC and has a value related to the currencies of member states.

Example 37.20

Suppose that the Irish currency had fallen in value from IR£1 = 4 DM to IR£ =3DM, while the green exchange rate remained unaltered at £1 = 2.0 units of account and 1 DM = 0.5 units of account. If the item which was discussed in Example 37.19 would still sell in each country at the support price of 4 units of account, then the price in Ireland would be IR£2 and in Germany 8 DM. But at the official rate of exchange after the dealuation of the Irish currency 8 DM = IR£2.67, therefore it would be more profitable for the Irish farmer to sell in Germany at a price of (say) 7 DM which at the exchange rate is equal to £2.33 and is better than the £2 which is obtainable on the domestic market. This would raise the possibility of the Irish farmers dominating the German market through undercutting the prices of the German farmers. There could also be a diversion of output from the Irish market to the German market.

Monetary
Compensatory
Amounts
(MCA's)

37.21. In order to avoid this type of development and to maintain the parity of prices for consumers, a system of *Monetary Compensatory Amounts* (often referred to as border taxes) was introduced. These are used to counterbalance deviations between green and official rates of foreign exchange.

Calculation
of MCA's

37.22. Monetary Compensatory Amounts (MCA's) are calculated by the difference between the green and foreign market exchange rates. In Example 37.20 the official green exchange rate was IR£1 = 2.0 units of account; after devaluation the market exchange rate was IR£1 = 1.5 units of account. Therefore the MCA would be

$\dfrac{2.0-1.5}{1.5}$ = 33⅓% of the support price of 4 units of account which is equal

to 1⅓ units of account. Since the Irish green exchange rate was IR£1 = 2.0 units of account, the MCA of 1⅓ units of account would be £0.67 in Irish currency. When the Irish farmer pays this levy on the IR£2.67 which he received for the item in Example 37.20 he ends up with the equivalent of the £2 which he could have received for the item on the Irish market.

Devaluation
of Green
Currency

37.23. The Irish government has on occasion devalued its green currency, by so doing we have avoided the necessity to pay higher MCA's and raised farm incomes by the amount saved. However, this results in a raising of food prices on the domestic market as shown in Example 37.23.

Example 37.23

Let us suppose that initially IR£1 = 2.0 units of account; 1 DM = 0.5 units of account and IR£1 = 4 DM on foreign exchange markets. After devaluation the foreign exchange value of currency is IR£1 = 3 DM and the Irish green currency is altered from IR£1 = 2.0 units of account to IR£1 = 1.5 units of account. An Irish farmer can now sell for IR£2.67 in Ireland (= 4 units of account) or 8 DM in Germany (= 4 units of account). The price in Ireland has increased from £2 to £2.67 as a result of the devaluation of the Irish green currency. The price in Germany remains unchanged and the Irish farmer is relieved of the payment of the M.C.A. which would have applied in Example 37.20.

MCA's do not apply to imported agricultural machinery

37.24. It is because of the advantages to Irish farmers as shown in Example 37.20 that Ireland, as a net exporter of agricultural produce, has on occasions devalued its green exchange rate despite the higher food prices on the domestic market to which such actions give rise. As a net exporter of agricultural produce, this country is not a net beneficiary from the subsidy aspect of M.C.A.'s since the subsidy does not apply to imported agricultural inputs such as agricultural machinery.

Britain's Green Currency

37.25. In contrast with this situation Great Britain is a net importer of food and thus it has suited that country to permit a wide gap to develop between the foreign exchange rate for sterling and the green exchange value of the currency.

Increase in Irish Food Prices

37.26. When Ireland joined the EEC there was a transitional period during which the level of support prices in Ireland was brought up to the level pertaining throughout the community. During the first five years of Irish membership the prices received by Irish farmers for their produce increased by 163%, and this has increased food costs in Ireland. Apart from the fact that there was a need to remove the disparity between incomes in the agricultural and industrial sectors, it should be noted that the Irish economy is a net beneficiary from these higher food prices. For every £3 in gross receipts gained by Irish farmers through these increased prices, Irish consumers other than farmers pay £1 and foreign consumers pay £2. However, it has given rise to a redistribution of income in favour of the agricultural sector.

Increases in Agricultural Production

37.27. The EEC has achieved complete security of supply in agricultural produce.

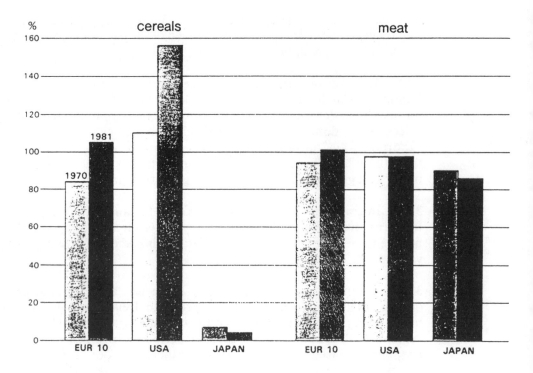

Fig. 37.27. Degree of self-sufficiency of cereals and meat.

Source Eurostat.

Agricultural productivity has grown more rapidly than has industrial productivity due to mechanisation and the rationalisation of the size of farm holdings. This development, however, resulted in a 60% reduction in agricultural employment since 1960. In recent years there has been a slowing down in the rate of labour shedding in the agricultural sector. In Ireland, the agricultural labour force fell from 390,000 in 1960 to 215,000 in 1980.

Market Supports

37.28. There are four principal types of market organisation which between them account for 94% of all European farm produce.

(a) **Support Prices** About 70% of products (including soft wheat, barley, rye, sugar, dairy products, beef, sheepmeat, port, some fruits and vegetables and table wines) which carry either a permanent or conditional guarantee of price and sale. When market prices fell below a certain level and other conditions are fulfilled, the intervention authorities buy up the produce offered to them and stock it or sell it according to Community rules. But note also the reduction in support prices when production quotas are exceeded as set out in section 37.29.

(b) **Protection from Low-Price Imports** About 21% of produce (other cereals, other wines, other fruits and vegetables, eggs and poultry) are protected from low price imports.

(c) **Direct Subsidies** These apply to only 2.5% of production (hard wheat, olive oil, certain other oils and tobacco). This system is used for products imported by the Community. It guarantees a minimum return for the producer while keeping prices low for the consumer.

(d) **Flat-Rate Aid** which is related to hectares planted or quantity produced covers only 0.5% of production (cotton seed, flax, hemp, hops, silkworms, seeds and dehydrated fodder).

Table 37.28. State and EC Expenditure (IR£ millions)

	State expenditure in relation to agriculture	EC (FEOGA) expenditure in relation to Irish agriculture	
1976	129.4	2.5	102.0
1978	155.1	9.3	366.0
1980	199.3	26.4	380.4
1982	292.9	57.5	341.3
1983	305.8	76.5	436.7
1984	309.2	48.8	644.6
1985	295.2	57.2	836.6
1986[2]	320.0	46.0	884.0

Sources: Department of Finance, *Budget Booklet,* various years; and Commission of the European Communities, *Development in the European Communities,* varius issues.

[1] State expenditure in relation to agriculture does not include general administration and overhead costs.

[2] Estimates.

Expenditure in relation to the Guidance Section (FEOGA) is in respect of measures for the structural reform of agriculture, e.g. farm investment aids, costs associated with retirement pensions for farmers, aid to improve marketing and food processing. The Guarantee fund relates to price support payments in respect of minimum price guarantees to farmers. Note also in Table 37.28 that considerable financial support for agriculture comes directly from the National Exchequer.

Reactions to Supply Surpluses

37.29. In response to the growth of permanent surpluses and the expenditure they generate, the Community has decided to pursue a policy of extremely prudent pricing and no longer to guarantee prices or subsidies for unlimited quantities of produce. Restrictive measures have been introduced to try to restore market balance; obligatory distillation in the wine sector; financial co-responsibility of producers, who pay part of the cost of storage or disposal through a tax or levy in the milk sector; production quotas, again in the milk sector; guarantee thresholds, which bring a reduction in guaranteed prices when a certain volume of production is exceeded (for cereals, colza, sunflower seeds, processed fruit and raisins); similar mechanisms have been introduced for sugar and cotton. In the mid 1980's persistent surpluses in many products were costing the Community a considerable sum of money and the Community's farmers were in danger of losing hard-won world markets. Faced with sharp and uninterrupted increases in agricultural expenditure as a result of this surplus production, the Summit of Heads of Government in July 1987 confirmed the need to trim supplies of agricultural produce by actions which would stabilise markets. The current position is that whenever output exceeds the set production limit, financial support for that product is automatically reduced. Between 1985 and 1989 support prices for agricultural produce were eased downwards by an average of 10% in real terms.

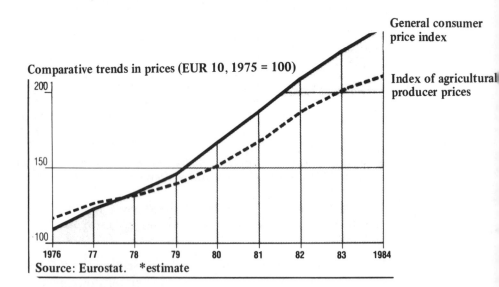

Comparative trends in prices (EUR 10, 1975 = 100)

General consumer price index

Index of agricultural producer prices

Source: Eurostat. *estimate

37.30. Agriculture and The Irish Economy

Agriculture is relatively more important in Ireland than in any other EEC country with the exception of Greece as shown by the gross value added per country in the EEC in Fig. 37.30. In 1983 the agricultural sector accounted for 10% of Irish GNP and 17% of total employment compared with averages of 4% and 8% respectively for all EEC Member States.

The relative value of outputs and inputs in the agricultural sector—comparison between Member States

Inputs and income expressed as a % of final output
in each Member State and EUR 11 (1985) (¹)
(current price)

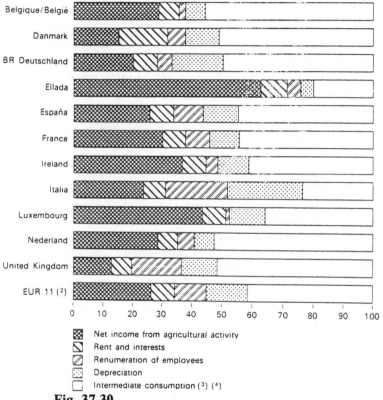

Net income from agricultural activity
Rent and interests
Renumeration of employees
Depreciation
Intermediate consumption (³) (⁴)

Fig. 37.30.

Source: Eurostat — Economic accounts for agriculture.

(¹) Average of 1984-86.

    (²) No results are available for Portugal.

    (³) Including adjustments for taxes and subsidies.

    (⁴) See footnote 1, p. 47.

Changing Pattern of Agricultural Exports

37.31. Sixty per cent of the increase in agricultural output between 1972 and 1981 was exported while 86% of agricultural exports originate in the cattle and milk sectors. One of the main attractions to the Irish agricultural sector of EEC membership was the opportunity to diversify its agricultural exports away from the relatively low price UK market. Between 1972 and 1982 the proportion of Irish food, drink and tobacco exports going to the UK has fallen from 74% to 43%, the proportion going to other EC countries rose from 15% to 24% and exports to non EC countries increased from 11% to 33%.

*Agricultural
Prices &
Profitability*

37.32. As shown in Table 37.32 the selling (output) prices of farm produce increased faster then the rate of inflation between '70 and '78 due to —

(a)   the increase in Irish agricultural prices to the European level;

(b)   increases in the level of EC prices;

(c)   increases as a result of Irish "Green Pound" devaluation.

Part of this increase was eroded by higher costs of inputs from 1974 particularly as a result of increases in oil based products such as fertilisers and machinery consequent on the oil price increase. This coincided with a glut in the cattle market which depressed cattle prices, so that profitability was lower in 1974 and 1975 than it was prior to entry into the EEC. During the subsequent years up to full transition to EC membership in 1978 there was a recovery and the output/input price ratio — which is a measure of profitability — reached its highest level in 1978. Between 1971 and 1978 there was a redistribution of income in favour of farmers as income per family worker in farming increased at a rate of 7.8% per annum in real terms compared to an increase of 4.9% per annum in average real industrial earnings. The cost of inputs rose at a faster rate than did output prices in subsequent years as price increases under the CAP have been kept relatively low in recent years while the inflation rate (and the cost of domestic inputs) has risen faster in Ireland than in other EC countries. Allied to this the stability of the Irish pound within the EMS precluded devaluations of the "Green Pound".

Table 37.32(a) Development in Certain Indices in Irish Agriculture, 1970 to 1986 (average, 1969-71 = 100)

	'71	'72	'73	'74	'75	'78	'80	'81	'82	'83	'84	'85	'86
Real output prices	97	109	126	108	118	142	107	14	97	93	88	81	79
Real input costs	98	94	105	122	122	124	116	110	103	101	100	96	88
Output/input prices	99	116	121	88	97	115	92	96	94	92	88	85	90
Volume — gross output	105	111	111	113	120	134	133	133	141	146	158	155	150
Volume — net output	104	110	109	115	128	129	125	119	133	135	156	151	136
Real per capita income	104	140	163	126	157	205	129	132	144	152	173	161	148

Source: NESC, *Farm Income: Analysis and Policy* (Report no. 65), Stationery Office, Dublin 1982; and Department of Agriculture. *Annual Review of the Situation in Agriculture* 1986.

Table 37.32 (b). The 'cost-price' squeeze'(^{1}): the ratio of producer prices to input prices

(1980 = 100)

	1982	1983	1984	1985	1986	1987
1	2	3	4	5	6	7
EUR 12	98,0	95.7	93,4	93,7	96,7	96,8
Belgique/België	96,7	99,0	94,0	94,6	94,9	97,4
Danmark	95,8	94,1	91,3	92,0	96,3	95,1
BR Deutschland	97,1	92,7	91,8	92,6	94,0	94,0
Ellada	105,8	100,6	104,8	105,6	100,1	104,1
Espana	98,0	92,1	90,0	87,5	93,3	90,8
France	98,1	96,1	90,9	90,6	93,3	92,3
Ireland	99,4	100,8	96,2	92,1	97,9	106,5
Italia	94,2	93,6	91,5	94,6	98,7	99,1
Luxembourg	101,1	98,4	94,5	102,7	104,0	112,0
Nederland	99,4	97,2	97,1	99,8	101,2	104,5
Portugal	:	:	:	:	:	:
United Kingdom	100,1	98,2	95,7	93,5	97,4	97,9
EUR 10	98,0	96,1	93,8	94,5	97,1	97,6

Source: Eurostat and EC Commission. Dir.-Gen. Agriculture

(1) The "cost-price squeeze" is calculated by dividing changes in the deflated index prices of the value of final agricultural production by changes in the deflated index prices of the value of inputs.

EEC Regional Fund

Disparities between Regions

37.33. There exists also a *Regional Fund* to which the EEC allocates funds to be used as a form of assistance in the poorer areas of the community. Regional differences in levels of economic development exist within all the community's member states. But when one compares regions throughout the community as a whole, the disparities are obviously much greater. The poorer regions are in the south of Italy and the west of Ireland, where income per head can be as low as a quarter of that in the most prosperous regions — Hamburg, Paris, etc.

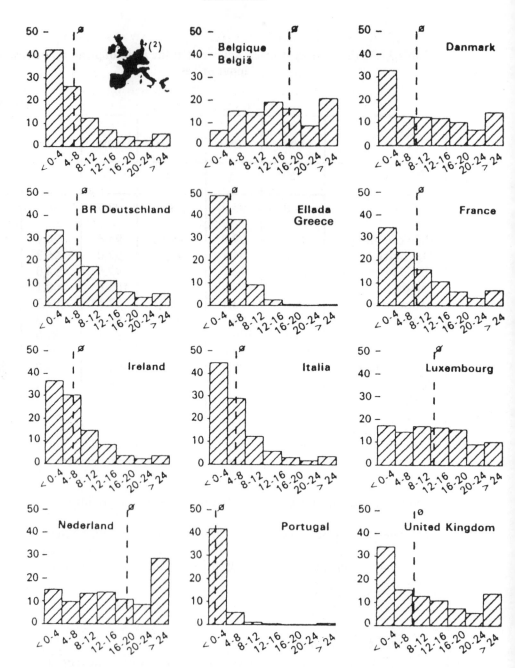

Revenue Categories (in 1000 ECU's)

Source:FADN, 1985-86 results.
[1] The measure is family farm income per unit unpaid labour on commercial holdings.
[2] EUR 12 excluding Spain.

Fig. 37.33. Distribution of farm incomes per person([1]).

37.34. The main problem regions fall into two categories:

Problem
Regions

(a) The underdeveloped rural areas, largely dependent on agriculture and characterized by low levels of income, high levels of unemployment, underemployment, outward migration, and an inadequate public infrastructure. Typically such areas are in the Italian Mezzogiorno, Ireland and parts of France.

(b) The once rich regions based on industries now in decline, like coal, steel, shipbuilding and textile. Such areas are found in the older industrial regions of the United Kingdom in particular, but in parts of France, Belgium and elsewhere too. They are characterized by an outdated industrial structure and high levels of unemployment.

Many of the regions concerned are located at the periphery of both their national and Community territories, a fact which aggravates the problems.

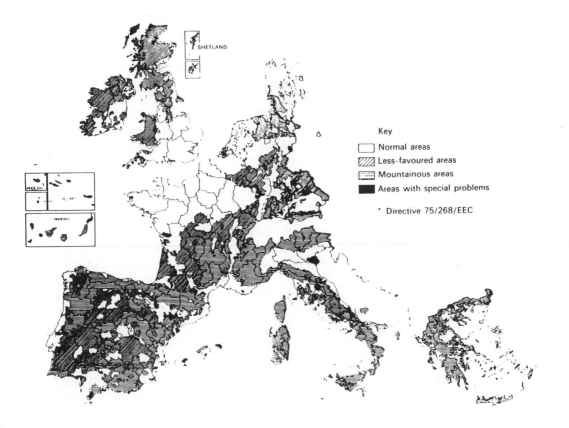

Fig. 37.34. Map of the agriculturally less-favoured areas of the Community.
(Situation end 1986)

Source: The Agricultural Outlook. (EC Publication).

37.35. National governments have for many years operated their own regional development policies, aimed at stimulating economic development in the regions faced with the sort of problems outlined in Section 37.34. This involved in the main two types of measure:

(1)   financial and other incentives (grants, loans, tax concessions, etc.) to encourage industrial and other firms to set up in these regions, so as to create more jobs;

(2)   development of the public infrastructure which is necessary both to improve living conditions generally and to help attract outside investors. This involves, typically, the improvement of the transport and telecommunications networks and of water and electricity supply, the development of industrial estates, and so on.

37.36. In order to develop beyond the Customs Union stage and towards a real economic union, the EEC has accepted responsibility with the national and regional authorities of the member states, for helping to narrow the gaps between its regions. The main reasons for this are as follows.

(a)   National regional policies aim to reduce the differences in levels of economic development within one country. But the gaps are even bigger when seen at Community level. The economic growth of the 1950s and 1960s — which the Community helped to generate — although it brought benefits to all regions, rich *and* poor, did not reduce the gaps. The community is now attempting to reduce these regional disparities. This is not only in the interest of the less favoured regions but also of the others: the former will gain the opportunity of more rapid development, the latter an expanding market for their goods.

(b)   Excessive differences in levels of economic performance, and in particular in levels of productivity, increase inflationary tendencies. This is because of the inevitable political and other pressures to ensure that wage levels and social welfare provisions in the poorer regions keep up with those in the richer ones even though productivity in the poorer regions remains lower. This has long been true within the national context, and will become so at European level as the Community moves towards more closely integrated economic unity. An increased Community effort is needed to help reduce these inflationary pressures, to the benefit of all.

(c)   Undertaken in isolation, at national level, rival regional policies are both more costly and less effective. For public infrastructure like roads and canals, co-ordination is obviously necessary between regions on either side of the community's internal frontiers. But it is also necessary to co-ordinate state aids to investors; otherwise there can develop a sort of aid auction in which investments go to the regions where most help is available, which forces governments to compete by increasing their aid levels. Common rules make it possible to avoid this waste of funds and to ensure that incentives are greatest in the areas of greatest need, rather than in those able to pay most.

(d) As more policy decisions in fields such as external trade, agriculture, industry and so on, come to be taken collectively at European level rather than unilaterally by individual governments, they will clearly have their consequences, good or bad, for the regions. This imposes on the Community a responsibility to seek a balanced regional development.

(e) The persistence of huge regional differences imposes major economic and financial burdens on the governments least able to bear them, and increases the pressures on these governments to reject the constraints which further integration inevitably implies. Thus for example, the Irish and Italian governments felt able to agree to join the European Monetary system — which will limit their freedom to adjust their exchange rates — only if the Community agreed to make available to them additional assistance to help develop their poorer areas.

(f) Last but not least, one of the fundamental aims of the Rome Treaty is to help the economic development of the less favoured regions. Indeed, tne Community will never gain the active sympathy and support of its citizens unless it can demonstrate its will and its ability to help those who have to live and work in its less prosperous parts.

37.37. Community Regional Policy has two main aims:

(1) the reduction of the existing regional imbalances found in both the traditionally less-developed regions and those in the process of industrial or agricultural redevelopment;

(2) the prevention of new regional imbalances likely to occur as a result of the trends in world economic development or of policy measures adopted by the Community. These aims must be achieved within the framework of an active employment policy. In the present economic situation the creation of new jobs in the regions suffering from the greatest structural unemployment is a major priority.

Some Examples of Community Regional Aid

37.38. From its inception the EEC has acknowledged the existence of its regional problems and regional disparities. The Treaty of Rome permits various exceptions to normal Community rules in order to protect the less-favoured regions. And the Community has always had various financial instruments which make available loans and grants to help solve the problems of these regions.

(a) The European Coal and Steel Community (ECSC) has made loans totalling over 5,500 million EUA to help modernize the coal and steel industries or to attract new job-creating industries in coal and steel regions.

(b)   The European Investment Bank (EIB) has made available over 10,500 million EUA in loans, the bulk of it for regional development purposes.

(c)   The European Social Fund (ESF) and the European Coal and Steel (ECSC) have together made grants totalling more than 1,600 million EUA for training and retraining workers otherwise unable to obtain jobs.

(d)   The Guidance Section of the European Agricultural Fund (FEOGA) has to date spent over 1,700 million EUA in the form of grants to help modernize the structure of agricultural production and distribution.

(e)   The European Regional Development Fund has made available over 1,500 million EUA since its creation in 1975 to help encourage new industrial investment and improve public infrastructures in the Community's problem regions.

Countries with Greatest Regional Problems

37.39. The Regional Fund is the only financial instrument whose purpose is exclusively the development of the less favoured regions. Until the end of 1978 its resources were spent exclusively according to a system of national quotas which aim to ensure that the money goes to help the countries with the most serious regional problems. Thus approximately ⅔ of the assistance has been channelled to the three countries faced with the greatest regional difficulties: Italy, Ireland and the United Kingdom.

Establishing Priorities for Future Action

37.40. What is a poor area by the standards of a more prosperous country may clearly be fairly rich in the context of another country. In the European Commission's view, Community-wide criteria are necessary if Community money is to be concentrated on helping the areas of greatest need and with real development potential, rather than being spread fairly widely as in the past.

Effect of other Community Policies on Regional Development

37.41. Community activity in many other fields — agricultural policy, policy on the different industrial sectors, external trade agreements, etc. — has its consequences for the less prosperous regions. A regional element should be built into all of them, so that their regional consequences are beneficial and not the opposite. This has already been achieved to some extent, for example in certain aspects of how the Agricultural and Social Funds operate. But much more needs to be done. The European Commission would like, for instance, to see regional differences taken account of in the Community's farm price policy. However, Community decisions clearly cannot be dictated just by the interests of the less favoured areas. In some cases decisions are bound to have adverse effects on certain regions, and here the Community has a clear and direct responsibility to find other ways of giving help to offset whatever difficulties may arise.

*Co-ordination
of National
Regional
Policies*

37.42. There is no intention of trying to impose a uniform pattern of regional development on all member states of the Community. However, both the European Commission and the Council of Ministers consider that some co-ordination of national regional policies is essential, especially of member states' regional development aids. This is necessary in order to ensure that resources are used where they are most needed, so that a more even balance of economic activity and prosperity can be gradually achieved. Member states have to draw up regional development programmes as a guide to where European Regional fund money should be spent. These programmes also provide the best means of comparing and co-ordinating national regional development policies.

*Future of
the
European
Regional
Fund*

37.43. New rules for the European Regional Fund came into force in February 1979, making it a more flexible instrument, better able to help solve the very different problems which different regions face. The main part of the Fund will continue to offer support for national regional development measures as before. It can help finance two types of investment in member states' aided areas:

(1) industrial or service-sector investments which create new jobs or guarantee existing ones. Rates of grant can go up to 20% of investment cost;

(2) public infrastructure works which contribute to the development of the region concerned (roads, ports, industrial estates, tourist facilities, etc.); rates of grant can go up to 40% of investment cost

*Grants are
paid to
National
Governments*

37.44. Grants are paid to the national governments which, in accordance with the Fund rules, can either pass the money on to the investor or treat it as part reimbursement of national aid. In all member states grants to industrial investments are retained by the national authorities; for infrastructural investments the grants are in most cases passed on to the local authority involved, though practice varies from country to country.

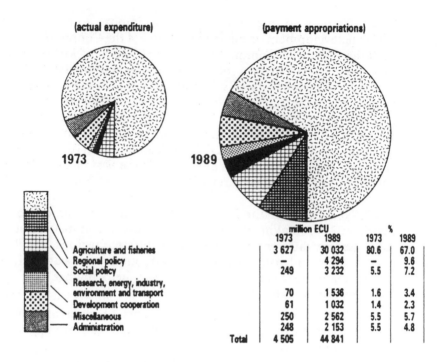

	million ECU		%	
	1973	1989	1973	1989
Agriculture and fisheries	3 627	30 032	80.6	67.0
Regional policy	–	4 294	–	9.6
Social policy	249	3 232	5.5	7.2
Research, energy, industry, environment and transport	70	1 536	1.6	3.4
Development cooperation	61	1 032	1.4	2.3
Miscellaneous	250	2 562	5.5	5.7
Administration	248	2 153	5.5	4.8
Total	4 505	44 841		

Fig. 37.44. Development of the general Community budget, 1973-89.

Source: Community Revenue and Expenditure Account.

European Monetary System (EMS)

Pegged Exchange Rate Policy

37.45. In January 1979 the EEC introduced the *European Monetary System* (EMS). The EMS is an attempt to establish monetary union within the EEC whereby member states maintain parity of their currencies vis-a-vis each other and conform to a common monetary system. The system is based on the currencies of the member states — Belgium-Luxembourg have a common currency while the UK is not a party to the system. Under the system each of the participating countries has set a value for its currency in terms of each of the other participating currencies and they undertake to maintain the exchange rates within a band of ±2¹/₄%, Italy originally opted for a wider band of ±6%, but since 8th January 1990 Italy has joined the narrow (±2¹/%) regime, the EMS is essentially a crawling peg exchange rate mechanism.

Support for Currency

37.46. If the market rate of a currency diverges from the agreed band the Central Bank of the country in question should intervene in the foreign exchange market — selling its own currency if there has been an excessive upward movement in its value, and buying its own currency if there has been downward pressure. Should the foreign exchange reserves of the Central Bank concerned be inadequate to support its currency, it may have recourse to very short term, short term, or medium term support as detailed below. In this manner movements in foreign exchange values of currencies may be smoothed, in addition to which the availability of considerable resources to support a currency will discourage speculation and thus avoid unnecessary uncertainty and monetary instability. While it should be noted that a sound exchange rate policy will assist the development of an economy, no amount of ingenuity in respect of foreign exchange management will compensate for fundamental economic problems, e.g., lack of investment or productive effort.

Financial Support:

(a) *Very Short-Term Financing (VSTF)* which is an intra-Central Bank financing facility which makes funds available to banks which have to borrow foreign currencies. Settlement of debt must be made in ECU's within 45 days of the end of the month in which the intervention took place.

(b) *Short Term Monetary Support (STMS)* automatically makes available to us a quota of IR£66m. There is also a further extension of "rallonge" which is a fund of IR£5,800m from which any country can draw provided that it does not draw more than half of the total fund.

(c) *Medium Term Financial Assistance (MTFA)* entails loans of from 2 to 5 years duration to support a country's Balance of Payments. Ireland could be called upon to provide a quota of 180m ECU's (approx. IR£120m) but each country has a borrowing limit of 50% of its quota.

37.47. Ireland and the EMS

Increased transactions costs in Anglo-Irish trade

When Ireland joined the EMS in March 1979, the United Kingdom Government did not. By the end of March 1979 the strength of Sterling relative to the EMS currencies forced the Irish Government into making a choice between seeking a realignment of the value of our currency within the EMS or breaking the one-to-one link with Sterling. It was decided to break the link with Sterling and for the first time in over 150 years a separate exchange rate was quoted for the Irish currency. One of the effects of this development was to increase the transactions costs of trading with the UK, all Anglo-Irish trade now involved foreign exchange transactions.

Foreign Exchange Value of our Currency

37.48. The first six realignments of EMS currencies involved Ireland only indirectly. On none of these occasions was there a change in the value of the Irish currency in terms of ECU's, the value of our currency relative to other EMS currencies changed only to the extent that these other currencies revalued or devalued. The realignment in the value of the Irish currency in March 1983 was the first explicit devaluation decision taken by an Irish Government. Though this devaluation of our currency occurred within the EMS its purpose was to reduce the value of the Irish currency relative to Sterling, the high value of the Irish pound relative to Sterling was affecting our competitiveness in Anglo-Irish trade which is still our most important trading relationship.

A similar position developed on 2nd August 1986 when the Irish currency was devalued by 8%. Again though the devaluation was expressed in terms of changing the value of our currency within the EMS, the real purpose of the devaluation was to reduce the value of our currency relative to sterling. Sterling had fallen in value and prior to the devaluation it was trading at 95p sterling = IR£1, this rate of exchange was making it difficult for our industrialists who were selling goods in competition with British goods. Because Britain is still our main trading partner our trade is very vulnerable to changes in the value of sterling. This exposure is far greater than that experienced by any of the other member countries of the EMS so that the devaluation of 2nd August 1986 was unilateral.

Real Exchange Rate

37.49. Though our (nominal) exchange rate within the EMS has remained relatively stable there has been a considerable appreciation in our *Real (Foreign) Exchange Rate.* The Real Exchange Rate is the nominal exchange rate adjusted for changes in prices in the relevant countries, e.g. if the nominal exchange rate between the Irish Pound and the Deutschmark (DM) remains unchanged while prices increase by 10% more in Ireland than Germany, then there is a 10% appreciation in our real exchange rate against the DM. This raises the question as to how this is possible, since, if prices rise relative to prices in other countries (say German) then the demand for our exports to Germany (and consequently the demand for Irish Pounds) will decrease while demand for imports from Germany (and consequently the demand for DM) will increase.

These changes in demand for the two currencies would result in an over-supply of our currency, arising from trade, and consequently a downward pressure on the foreign exchange value of our currency. However, the Irish Government engaged in a considerable amount of foreign borrowing which made available sufficient foreign currency to maintain a (relatively) unchanged nominal foreign exchange value of our currency.

Some Developments in International Finance

Gold is Ultimate Reserve Asset

37.50. In order to maintain fixed parities on rates of exchange it is necessary for governments to intervene in foreign exchange dealings in their currency. For the purpose of buying its own currency when it was in excess supply, it was necessary for each country to have reserves of currencies which enjoyed general international acceptance, e.g., US dollars. Sterling was freely convertible into dollars while the Federal

Reserve system (which is the Central Bank of America) undertook to convert freely dollars into gold at $35 per ounce. Thus gold was the ultimate reserve asset in the sytem.

Fall in Stock of Monetary Gold

37.51. However, the world's monetary supply of gold did not expand at a sufficiently fast rate to permit the expansion of monetary reserves which expanding world trade required. Though world trade was growing at a rate of 10% per annum, the stock of monetary gold actually fell during the 1960's — gold which had represented 66% of total monetary reserves in 1959 had declined to 30% in 1972, the monetary vacuum being filled by an increased reserve holding of dollars and sterling.

Speculation

37.52. The inadequacy of the total monetary supply of gold, which was aggravated by the outflow of gold from the US, consequent on that country's Balance of Payments deficits in the 1960's, raised doubts about the ability of the US to maintain the then prevailing rate of convertibility of dollars into gold, so that an increase in the price of gold seemed imminent. Speculators moved into the market and speculated against the dollar, encouraged by the thought that if the price of gold increased they would show a profit on the gold which they had bought before its price increased, whereas if the existing parity between dollars and gold was maintained they could at worst resell their stock of gold at the price of $35 per ounce which was the guaranteed price at which the monetary system had undertaken to purchase gold.

Two Tier System

37.53. All these pressures against the dollar culminated in the suspension of free convertibility in 1968 and the introduction of a *Two Tier Gold System.* In the *Official Tier* Central Bankers undertook to buy from, and sell to, each other at the official IMF parity rate. Those excluded from this group could buy and sell gold at prices dictated by the free market forces of supply and demand. This was known as the *Free Market Tier* and the protection of minimum gold prices which the IMF parity rate provided was denied to this free market.

Revaluation of Gold

37.54. Despite initial fears that gold might leak from the official tier to the free market tier when prices in the free market were greater than the fixed price of the official tier, the arrangement has been effective and has resulted in the retention of a fixed quantity of gold within the world monetary system. However, this limited quantity of gold could not fulfill its function as a financial basis for an expanding volume of world trade without a considerable upward revaluation in the price of gold. There has been a reluctance to revalue gold for a number of reasons, e.g., (a) It would confer a considerable benefit on the gold producing countries of South Africa and Russia and confer a windfall gain on those countries which in the past had hoarded gold, often to the detriment of world monetary stability. (b) At some future time a similar revaluation would be necessary and the knowledge of this eventually could influence actions during the intervening period. (c) Many financiers regard gold as an anachronism. They question the practice of digging gold out of the ground in South Africa just to ship it across the world and bury it in vaults in Fort Knox in America. They point to the fact that just as domestic currencies have been freed from the gold standard a similar freedom should be possible in respect of international trade. However, despite this, the price of gold has moved upwards in a spectacular manner.

*Special
Drawing
Rights*

37.55. Considerations such as these have led to the introduction of *'paper gold'*. This concept was introduced in 1969 with the institution of *Special Drawing Rights (SDR's)*. The SDR, which was defined in terms of gold and was equal to the US dollar, could be used in exchange for the currencies of other countries and to supplement existing reserve assets.

QUESTIONS

Q1. Write an explanatory note on the International Monetary Fund.

Q2. Distinguish between a Free Trade area, a Customs Union and a Common Market.

Q3. By what means does the CAP attempt to achieve its objectives.

Q4. Write a note on Irish agriculture.

Q5. Write an explanatory note on the EMS.

Q6. Write a short account of the performance of the Irish currency within the EMS.

38 Economic Growth and Development

38.1. The benefits of economic growth can be seen in the spectacular improvement in the standard of living of the average citizens of many countries as they enjoy a high standard of housing, together with motor *Improves the* cars, central heating, washing machines, colour television sets, foreign *general* travel, etc. Total world production has doubled in the past 15 years and, *standard of* despite a considerable increase in world population during this period, *living* output per person for the world as a whole was twice as high in 1975 as it was in 1950. However, it should be realised that economic growth of this nature is a fairly recent phenomenon. Studies have shown that the real income of groups of British workers did not significantly improve between the 13th and 18th centuries. In addition the benefits of economic growth have been spread very unevenly over national frontiers. Growth has been concentrated in the developed countries in which a mere 20% of the world's population live, while the standard of living in the Less Developed Countries (LDCs) has not changed significantly over the past 1,000 years.

38.2. Rostow★ noted a similarity in the pattern of economic development and growth in the USA and in a number of western European countries. He stated that the process consisted of five stages viz:

Stage 1 – The Traditional Society. This term characterises a society which operates within the constraint of limited production possibilities. Without the benefits of modern science and technology, the opportunities to increase output are limited to ad hoc innovation, e.g., irrigation and the introduction of new crops. A high proportion of the resources of such communities is devoted to agriculture and rooted in the agricultural system is a hierarchical social structure based on clans and families with power residing in the hands of those who control the land. There tends to be a long run fatalism which, though it perceives the possibility of working hard and improving one's lot, considers that basically the opportunities and options open to an individual are related to the status of his parents.

Stage 2 – The Pre-Conditions For Take-Off. At this stage of economic development it is necessary for a country,

(a) to be aware of the potentialities of modern science for improvements in agriculture and industry,

★Footnote: The Stages of Economic Growth by W. Rostow (Cambridge University Press) 1960.

(b) to be in a position to break away from the poverty cycle of subsistence farming so that an industrial base may be developed.

The intrusion by more economically advanced societies into less developed countries encourages ideas and the sentiment that economic progress is possible and desirable. Thus there emerges a social climate which not merely condones, but actively encourages the pursuit of economic objectives. To this end there is a development of the banking sector; the pace of investment increases — particularly in an economic infrastructure such as transport and communications; the scope of commerce is enlarged and manufacturing enterprises using modern methods are founded. In many instances this development of the economy is initiated and developed, to some limited extent at least, by a colonial power and may exist side by side with the traditional native sector, i.e., dualism exists within the economy.

Stage 3 – The Take-Off. This third stage is probably the most critical in that it determines whether or not the economy will make the breakthrough from being a traditional hierarchical society which produces primary products to become a modern market-oriented industrial society. At this stage the forces of economic growth dominate society and the economy enjoys a period during which the level of output grows at a compound rate. The rate of investment may rise from (say) 5% of GNP to 10% or more. New industries are established, there arises a demand for industrial workers and the services to support them, the population changes from being predominantly rural to being predominantly urbanised. There are revolutionary changes in agriculture as it develops to feed the increasing proportion of the population which is engaged in industrial production. Economic growth becomes self-sustaining.

This take-off period occurred in Britain during 1780-1800, in France and USA during 1880-1900, in Russia and Canada during 1890-1914.

Stage 4 – The Drive to Maturity. After the take-off stage there follows a long interval of sustained economic progress. An annual investment of 10% to 20% of GNP permits an increase in GNP per head of population. Older industries diminish in relative importance as new industries develop. Goods formerly imported are produced domestically and the pattern of imports changes. Approximately 60 years after the commencement of the take off period, economic maturity is achieved and the economy which based its take off on a relatively narrow range of products, e.g., the USA originally developed by specialising in the production of agricultural goods, has at this mature stage extended its range of industry and technology into more refined and complex areas.

Stage 5 – The Age of High Mass Consumption. As societies attain economic maturity there is an increase in real income per head of population and the community enjoys a standard of living which transcends the basic needs of food, shelter and clothing. The pattern of demand shifts towards durable consumer goods and services. There is an urbanisation of the population as the greater proportion of the population gains employment in offices or as skilled industrial workers. At this stage societies cease to consider technological progress as being of overriding concern and devote increased resources to social welfare and security.

Post-Industrial Society

38.3. This leads to a stage which is often described as *The Past Industrial Society* where the emphasis shifts from the acquisition of consumer durable goods to the quality of life. Technical progress and automation permit the enjoyment of more leisure time and real income per head of population tends to increase at a slower rate than the increase in productive capacity as the working week is shortened, holiday periods are increased, the period spent in full time education is extended and retirement is introduced.

38.4. Many economists consider that the pattern set out by Rostow is merely a description of the development which took place in a number of countries. They stress that this pattern of development is not to be seen as a model to be applied to less developed countries and state that development programmes should be more 'person centred'. This 'person centred' approach is directed towards improving the life of individuals in their existing environment rather than the adoption of development programmes which stimulate mass movements of the population into urban industrial areas. Rapid urbanisation of this nature may lead to the emergence of industrial slums. In addition, they point out that whatever benefits may accrue from rapid urbanisation and industrialisation may take a long time to 'trickle-down' to the average worker.

38.5. A DISTINCTION BETWEEN ECONOMIC DEVELOPMENT AND ECONOMIC GROWTH

Benefits of economic growth have been spread unevenly

Though the process of economic growth may be analysed in evolutionary stages on the lines discussed by Rostow, a distinction is sometimes drawn between the related concepts of economic development and economic growth. Though both terms are concerned with changes in the level of GNP and productive capacity, *the term economic development is often used to define the situation in which an increase in the level of income in the economy involves a change in the structure of society, whereas economic growth is used to describe a situation in which an increase in the level of GNP is attained without an alteration in the structure of society.* Thus the first two stages in the Rostow pattern, i.e., the traditional society and the pre-conditions for take-off together with the beginning of the take-off stage could be considered as economic development as the structure of agriculture changes and there is a movement of the population from rural to urban areas to coincide with the movement of the workforce out of the production of primary products into the secondary sectors of manufacturing and construction.

38.6. BASIS OF ECONOMIC DEVELOPMENT AND GROWTH.

(a) Social and cultural environment.

(b) Availability of economic resources/factors of production.

(c) An aequate level of demand.

(A) Social and Cultural environment.

Entails a change in the structure of society

38.7. Attention has already been drawn to the fact that economic development entails a change in the structure of society. For such a change to take place it must be considered desirable and the community must have the knowledge and means by which such change may be effected. As already described in Section 38.2, in traditional hierarchical societies the religious and cultural values do not accord high esteem to economic development, economic and social mobility is sluggish, positions of importance are obtained through blood relationships rather than merit and just as it is difficult for people of ability but no property to proceed to positions of power, the incompetence of the influential is not reflected in downward mobility.

38.8. As Samuelson⋆ has noted $HAPPINESS = \dfrac{Consumption}{Desire}$ so that

Demonstration effect

happiness can be achieved, or increased, by increasing consumption (the numerator) or suppressing desire (the denominator). In the past, in traditional societies the denominator (desire) may have been suppressed through the members of the community being isolated from other communities and, consequently, being ignorant of the standards of living to which they might aspire. With the sophisticated means of communication and the opportunities for travel which are at present available there is a considerable "*demonstration effect*" which raises the expectations of people and increases their reluctance to accept poverty as if it was divinely ordained.

38.9. Economic development will be stimulated also in the following circumstances:

(a) if the culture and value system of the community holds in esteem those who are successful in industrial and commercial activities,

Stimulants for economic development

(b) if those who enjoy economic success can enjoy the benefits of their efforts through the taxation system not being so punitive as to act as a disincentive, complemented by freedom of choice in the spending of income,

(c) if there is sufficient confidence in the future so that people are prepared to invest and adopt a long term time horizon.

⋆Economics by P.A. Samuelson (McGraw-Hill).

The prospect of a continuing period of political stability is vitally important in encouraging people to adopt a long term policy — uncertainty shortens the time horizon which people are prepared to adopt.

(B) Availability of Economic Resources/Factors of Production.

Self sustaining rather than 'once off' improvement is sought

38.10. A discussion on economic development and growth implies that there exists within the economy an adequate supply of economic resources/ factors of production. In the short term the productivity of existing resources may be improved through their being used in a more intensive manner, e.g., shift working, overtime working, division of labour, economies of scale and optimum forms of industrial organisation. However, if economic growth is to be self-sustaining rather than a 'once off' improvement, there must be the possibility of increasing the availability, and improving the quality, of factors of production within the economy.

Important to improve productivity of workers

38.11. An increase in the work force may be realised through an increase in the population of working age and/or an increase in the 'participation rate', i.e., the proportion of the population which is gainfully employed. At present with the shortening of the working week, an increase in holiday entitlements, extended periods of full time schooling and earlier retirements, the participation rate is unlikely to increase despite a tendency in recent years for married women to seek employment outside the home. In these circumstances it is particularly important to improve the productivity of the work force through education, training and capital deepening.

Sources of investment

38.12. Investment is vital if an economy is to develop from the stage of a rural based population producing primary products to an urban based industrial society. If the pre-conditions for growth are satisfied, retained profits and/or borrowed funds will constitute a source of funds for entrepreneurs who wish to expand their productive capacity — profitable business activity provides the source of, and incentive for, additional investment. Where necessary the flow of funds for investment can be augmented by an inflow of capital from abroad. When foreign firms invest in Ireland, they make available foreign currency for investment purposes. In addition they have the technological knowledge, marketing expertise and distributive network which ensure markets for their output.

Foreign owned firms

38.13. In the event of such firms being unsuccessful the loss is not borne by the Irish economy in contrast with the position which pertains when the government undertakes investment, when any losses must be met from the general exchequer. The ideal would be to have successful firms based in Ireland with profits accruing to Irish entrepreneurs or to the

Irish exchequer. However, it is preferable to have Irishmen and Irishwomen working in Ireland, even for foreign entrepreneurs, than have them doing similar work abroad.

Capital widening and capital deepening

38.14. A distinction must be drawn between "capital widening" and "capital deepening". Capital widening is an investment in additional units of existing type machinery so that an increase in the numbers employed may be accommodated without reducing the capital/labour ratio. For example, 20 men are employed in the operation of 5 machines. If an additional 4 men are employed another machine is required if the existing capital/labour ratio is to be maintained. In contrast to this, "capital deepening" occurs when the capital/labour ratio is increased, i.e., a greater amount of capital is available to each worker — the operation has become more capital intensive.

Inventions and innovations

38.15. Over time, research and development result in inventions which culminate in the introduction of new and improved methods of production which increase the productive possibilities of the economy.
   Thus when investment takes place it is unlikely that the new machinery introduced into a firm will be an exact duplication of the machinery which the firm had been using — the new machinery will embody the latest technological developments which will improve productivity.

Technological development assists economic growth

38.16. This technological development will assist economic growth and prevent the diminishing returns which otherwise might have occurred as the capital stock in the economy is increased, i.e., as a result of technological development the marginal efficiency of capital curve moves outward to the right.

(C) Adequate Level of Demand

Export led growth

38.17. Entrepreneurs undertake investment in order to make a profit, so that unless there is a demand for goods and services investment will not be forthcoming. One way in which the level of aggregate demand may be increased is through an increase in our exports. This would constitute an injection into our Circular Flow of Income and would have a multiplier effect on the economy as demand spills over into other sectors of the economy. When the injection which results in an increase in the level of aggregate demand comes from exports the subsequent growth is usually referred to as *Export Led Growth*.

Necessity for demand to grow with capacity

38.18. It should be noted that when investment takes place the productive capacity of the economy is increased and unless there is an increase in demand sufficient to utilise fully the existing productive capacity and justify further investment then that rate of investment will not continue. If investment does not take place, or is reduced, then those employed in the production of capital goods will become unemployed, as a result of which their demand for consumer goods will diminish leading to a further reduction in the level of economic activity.

Example 38.18.

If the capital/output ratio is 4 this means that an investment in capital equipment of IR£4 is required if output is to be increased by IR£1. Thus if GNP is to grow by 5%, an investment of 20% (i.e., 4 × 5) of GNP is required in addition to an investment of (say) 6% of GNP in respect of depreciation, resulting in a total investment requirement of 26% of GNP.

Period	Investment	Capital Stock	Capacity Output (Capital/Output Rate is 4)	Demand
0	100	1000	250	250
1	105	1100	275	275
2	110.25	1205	301.25	301.25
3	115.7625	1315.25	328.8125	328.8125

Demand grows in a manner which fully utilises increased capacity

38.19. In the above table the capital/output ratio is 4. The capital stock (column 3) divided by the capital/output ratio gives the capacity output. The marginal propensity to consume is 0.8 so that the multiplier is 5. Thus in this example when investment increased from 100 to 105 demand increased by 25, i.e., the increase in investment of 5 constitutes an injection and this injection is subject to a multiplier of 5, so that there is increased demand of 25 units which means that there is a demand for the additional 25 units by which capacity output is increased since the investment increases the capital stock in the following period. In this way the (increased) available capacity is fully utilised. A similar type of analysis may be applied to periods 2 and 3.

"Balanced Growth path"

38.20. The growth path shown in Example 38.18 is said to be a "balanced growth path" since capacity and demand grow in harmony with each other. This growth is often said to be finely balanced on a 'razor's edge' between excess capacity on the one hand and insufficient demand on the other. If demand exceeded capacity inflation could develop while if there was a deficiency in demand there would be excess capacity in which case additional investment would not take place and this could lead to a contraction in the level of economic activity.

Benefits of Economic Growth.

38.21. The principal reason for pursuing economic growth is that it improves the general standard of living in the economy. An economy in which the GNP is growing at a rate of 4% per annum will double its GNP in approximately 18 years.★ A comparison of the average standard of living in Ireland now and 25 years ago is indicative of the benefits which our country has enjoyed as a result of the economic growth during this period.

Assists investment

38.22. When an economy is enjoying a period of economic growth it becomes possible to undertake investment in the sources of further economic growth, viz., investment in capital goods, human resources and research and development, without lowering current standards of living. Also, when the economy is growing there is sufficient buoyancy in government revenue to finance the necessary investment in social overhead capital, viz., housing, roads, schools, telecommunications, etc. Thus the benefits of economic growth are compounded.

Redistribution of income

38.23. Through economic growth it is possible to alleviate poverty, but it should be realised that the benefits of economic growth are not distributed equally throughout the community. It may not be possible for many of the economically disadvantaged, e.g., the aged and the incapacitated, to partake in economic activity. Thus they are precluded from enjoying the benefits of economic growth through their own efforts and activities. However, it is easier to gain acceptance for policies designed to redistribute income towards the economically disadvantaged when standards of living are rising since the redistribution need not result in the lowering of the standard of living of those being taxed but merely a slowing of their rate of improvement.

Growth of public expenditure and growth in GNP

38.24. A large proportion of current government expenditure is devoted to the payment of staff in the public sector and to public benefits. It is difficult for the government to significantly reduce this type of expenditure in the short term. Consequently in the absence of economic growth, it is difficult to significantly reduce public expenditure as a percentage of GNP. A significant reduction in public expenditure as a percentage of GNP would be possible if, through economic growth (which was not dependent on increasing government expenditure), there were economies of scale in public administration, together with savings through a reduction in the numbers seeking unemployment assistance and other benefits from the public purse.

★Footnote: The "rule of 72" is the method by which one can gain an approximation of the number of years required in order to double GNP. Divide the average annual growth rate into 72 and the answer is the approximate number of years which must elapse before GNP is doubled, e.g., at a growth rate of 4% per annum GNP would be doubled in

$$\frac{72}{4} = 18 \text{ years.}$$

Costs of Economic Growth.

Costless growth

38.25. Like many other things economic growth is a mixed blessing and thus we must advert to the costs of economic growth. When an economy is operating at a level below its productive capacity, it is possible to increase the level of GNP by utilising the capacity which is not being used. Increases in GNP attained in this manner are universally acclaimed as being desirable and beneficial and it is usually referred to as being 'costless' because there are relatively no disadvantages to counterbalance the considerable benefits which accrue to the community.

Opportunity cost of growth

38.26. However, when an economy is operating at the full employment level, further growth becomes possible only through expanding the productive capacity of the economy through investment in capital goods and human resources, e.g., education, training and health. This investment is possible only by accepting inthe short term a standard of living lower than it would have been in the absence of investment.★ This lowering of the current standard of living is the opportunity cost of growth.

Some costs of economic growth

38.27. Just as the benefits of economic growth are not evenly distributed the costs of economic growth may fall more heavily on certain sectors of the community. Economic growth may cause a redistribution of income from the middle aged workers to young workers. Growth implies change so that during a period of economic growth, industry in the process of changing creates a demand for new jobs and new skills. New entrants to the work force are more likely to be equipped with these required skills and in allocating places on retraining programmes preference is likely to be given to young workers because they are more adaptable and more tractable. Also the pay-off period from the training is greater in the case of young workers because their post-training working life is longer. One outcome of this could be that older workers would be forced to accept early retirement. Developments of this nature have implications also for authority and the way of life, if the economic and social base of parents and older people is eroded. In addition the uncertainty, which is the companion of growth and change, is a source of worry and concern to many people.

"The good old days"

38.28. The pollution of the environment which may be a consequence of industrialisation is a well known cost of economic growth. It is proper that in pursuing improvements in our standard of living attention should be devoted to the retention of all that is best in our environment with the objective of improving the quality of life rather than concentrating solely

★Footnote: See Section 21.9.

on the acquisition of consumer durables. However, there is a danger of adopting an unbalanced attitude in that, while enjoying the benefits of economic growth, we seek the illusory idyllic way of life based on nostalgia for 'good old days' which never existed. You might consider what would have been your standard of living if you had been born 200 years earlier.

Economic Growth and Less Developed (or Newly Industrialised) Countries

Lack of investment

38.29. Because of their poverty and a lack of effective domestic demand, less developed countries (LDC's) see international trade as providing their main source of growth. Many of these LDC's are producers of primary products, e.g., cotton, linen, tea, coffee, cocoa, live animals, raw ores, etc. These products are usually exported in an unprocessed state. Thus, through a lack of investment and deficiences in techology the value of their exports is relatively low with a consequent depressing effect on their level of employment and national income. In many instances the export sector of the less developed countries is run very efficiently by non-nationals, but the profits are repatriated to the motherland of the non-nationals with a consequent lessening of the investment capital available within the producing (LDC) country.

Table 38.29. Sectoral Distribution of Gross Domestic Product related to wealth of the economy 1987.

	Agriculture %	Industry %	Services %
Low Income Economies	31	37	32
Middle Income Economies	20	34	46
High Income Economies	5	41	55

Source: World Bank, World Development Report 1989.

Terms of trade of LDC's

38.30. Often the comparative advantage which a less developed country enjoys is confined to a single primary product and the low elasticities of supply and demand, together with the price fluctuations and expense of storage which are inherent characteristics of primary products place LDC's in a weak bargaining position in their efforts to increase their revenue. Most of the trade of LDC's is with developed countries rather than between themselves. The need which the LDC's have for the products of these developed countries, e.g., capital equipment, together with their own weak trading position is manifest in the pressure on their Terms of Trade and Balance of Payments.

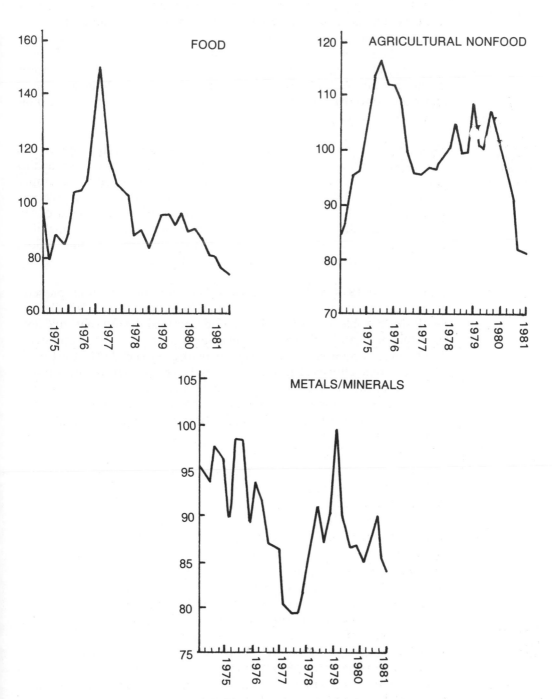

Weighted Indices of Commodity Prices
(constant US dollars (1974/76 = 100))

Fig. 38.30. Commodity Price Fluctuations

Industrial Development within LDC's.

38.31. The low level of national income which constrains domestic demand for consumer durables and industrial goods combined with their lack of technological skills results in the LDC's initial steps on the path towards industrialisation being concentrated on the manufacture of simply produced import substitutes (i.e., the domestic production of goods which previously had been imported) e.g., agricultural tools, footwear, clothing, etc. Moreover, in the absence of aid, the capital equipment and technology of the industrially advanced nations can be purchased only by obtaining the currencies of these countries through international trade.

38.32. The selection of the technology which is most appropriate for LDC's is a matter of considerable importance and can have far reaching consequences. The technology of the most industrially developed countries, e.g., USA, Japan, Germany, is very capital intensive and requires a highly skilled work force whereas the endowments of the LDC's are usually the opposite to this with their typically large unskilled workforce and a shortage of capital for investment. Thus labour intensive industries may be more suited to the LDC's.

38.33. In May 1974 the General Assembly of the United Nations passed a resolution called for a New International Economic Order (NIEO). The resolution emphasised the need for co-operation at the international level to reduce the gap between the developing and the developed countries. The Brandt Commission which was a private group headed by the former German Chancellor W. Brandt, conducted an enquiry into the economic problems of the low income countries and made recommendations as to how existing unequalities might be lessened — see *North – South: A Programme for Survival.* Report of the Brandt Commission 1980.

Fig. 38.33 Basic Indicators.

| | Population (millions) mid-1987 | Area (thousands of square kilometers) | GNP per capita | | Average annual rate of inflation (percent) | | Life expectancy at birth (years) 1987 |
			Dollars 1987	Average annual growth rate (percent) 1965-87	1965-80	1980-87	
Low-income economies	**2,822.9t**	**37,015t**	**290w**	**3.1w**	**8.9w**	**8.6w**	**61w**
China and India	**1,866.1t**	**12,849t**	**300w**	**3.9w**	**2.9w**	**5.5w**	**65w**
Other low-income	**956.9t**	**24,166t**	**280w**	**1.5w**	**18.2w**	**13.3w**	**54w**
1 Ethiopia	44.8	1,222	130	0.1	3.4	2.6	47
2 Bhutan	1.3	47	150	..	..	..	48
3 Chad	5.3	1,284	150	-2.0	6.3	5.3	46
4 Zaire	32.6	2,345	150	-2.4	24.7	53.5	52
5 Bangladesh	106.1	144	160	0.3	14.9	11.1	51
6 Malawi	7.9	118	160	1.4	7.0	12.4	46
7 Nepal	17.6	141	160	0.5	7.8	8.8	51
8 Lao PDR	3.8	237	170	..	..	46.5	48
Mozambique	14.6	802	170	..	..	26.9	48
10 Tanzania	23.9	945	180	-0.4	9.9	24.9	53
11 Burkina Faso	8.3	274	190	1.6	6.2	4.4	47
12 Madagascar	10.9	587	210	-1.8	7.9	17.4	54
13 Mali	7.8	1,240	210	..	..	4.2	47
14 Burundi	5.0	28	250	1.6	8.5	7.5	49
15 Zambia	7.2	753	250	-2.1	6.4	28.7	53
16 Niger	6.8	1,267	260	-2.2	7.5	4.1	45
17 Uganda	15.7	236	260	-2.7	21.2	95.2	48
18 China	1,068.5	9,561	290	5.2	0.0	4.2	69
19 Somalia	5.7	638	290	0.3	10.5	37.8	47
20 Togo	3.2	57	290	0.0	6.9	6.6	53
21 India	797.5	3,288	300	7.6	7.7	58	
22 Rwanda	6.4	26	300	1.6	12.4	4.5	49
23 Sierra Leone	3.8	72	300	0.2	8.0	50.0	41
24 Benin	4.3	113	310	0.2	7.4	8.2	50
25 Central African Rep.	2.7	623	330	-0.3	8.5	7.9	50
26 Kenya	22.1	583	330	1.9	7.3	10.3	58
27 Sudan	23.1	2,506	330	-0.5	11.5	31.7	50
28 Pakistan	102.5	796	350	2.5	10.3	7.3	55
29 Haiti	6.1	28	360	0.5	7.3	7.9	55
30 Lesotho	1.6	30	370	4.7	8.0	12.3	56
31 Nigeria	106.6	924	370	1.1	13.7	10.1	51
32 Ghana	13.6	239	390	-1.6	22.8	48.3	54
33 Sri Lanka	16.4	66	400	3.0	9.4	11.8	70
34 Yemen, PDR	2.3	333	420	..	..	5.0	51
35 Mauritania	1.9	1,031	440	-0.4	7.7	9.8	46

Fig. 38.33 Basic Indicators.

	Population (millions) mid-1987	Area (thousands of square kilometers)	GNP per capita Dollars 1987	GNP per capita Average annual growth rate (percent) 1965-87	Average annual rate of inflation (percent) 1965-80	Average annual rate of inflation (percent) 1980-87	Life expectanc at birth (years) 1987
36 Indonesia	171.4	1,905	450	4.5	34.2	8.5	60
37 Liberia	2.3	111	450	-1.6	6.3	1.5	54
38 *Afghanistan*	..	648	..	..	4.9	..	..
39 *Burma*	39.3	677	..	..	..	..	60
40 *Guinea*	6.5	246	..	..	2.9	..	42
41 *Kampuchea, Dem.*	..	181	..	..	..	..	..
42 *Viet Nam*	65.0	330	..	..	..	..	66
Middle-income economies	**1,038.5***t*	**36,118***t*	**1,810***w*	**2.5***w*	**20.4***w*	**62.3***w*	**65***w*
Lower-middle-income	**609.6***t*	**16,781***t*	**1,200***w*	**2.2***w*	**16.9***w*	**36.7***w*	**64***w*
43 Senegal	7.0	196	520	-0.6	6.5	9.1	48
44 Bolivia	6.7	1,099	580	-0.5	15.7	601.8	53
45 Zimbabwe	9.0	391	580	0.9	6.4	12.4	58
46 Philippines	58.4	300	590	1.7	11.7	16.7	63
47 Yemen Arab Rep.	8.5	195	590	..	..	11.4	51
48 Morocco	23.3	447	610	1.8	6.1	7.3	61
49 Egypt, Arab Rep.	50.1	1,002	680	3.5	7.3	9.2	61
50 Papua New Guinea	3.7	462	700	0.8	7.5	4.4	54
51 Dominican Rep.	6.7	49	730	2.3	6.8	16.3	66
52 Côte d'Ivoire	11.1	322	740	1.0	9.5	4.4	52
53 Honduras	4.7	112	810	0.7	5.6	4.9	64
54 Nicaragua	3.5	130	830	-2.5	8.9	86.6	63
55 Thailand	53.6	514	850	3.9	6.3	2.8	64
56 El Salvador	4.9	21	860	-0.4	7.0	16.5	62
57 Congo, People's Rep.	2.0	342	87	4.2	6.6	1.8	59
58 Jamaica	2.4	11	940	-1.5	12.8	19.4	74
59 Guatemala	8.4	109	950	1.2	7.1	12.7	62
60 Cameroon	10.9	475	970	3.8	8.9	8.1	56
61 Paraguay	3.9	407	990	3.4	9.4	21.0	67
62 Ecuador	9.9	284	1,040	3.2	10.9	29.5	65
63 Botswana	1.1	582	1,050	8.9	8.1	8.4	59
64 Tunisia	7.6	164	1,180	3.6	6.7	8.2	65
65 Turkey	52.6	781	1,210	2.6	20.7	37.4	64
66 Colombia	29.5	1,139	1,240	2.7	17.4	23.7	66
67 Chile	12.5	757	1,310	0.2	129.9	20.6	72
68 Peru	20.2	1,285	1,470	0.2	20.5	101.5	61
69 Mauritius	1.0	2	1,490	3.2	11.4	8.1	67
70 Jordan	3.8	98	1,560	..	..	2.8	66
71 Costa Rica	2.6	51	1,610	1.5	11.3	28.6	74
72 Syrian Arab Rep.	11.2	185	1,640	3.3	8.3	11.0	65

Fig. 38.33 Basic Indicators.

	Population (millions) mid-1987	Area (thousands of square kilometers)	GNP per capita		Average annual rate of inflation (percent)		Life expectancy at birth (years) 1987
			Dollars 1987	Average annual growth rate (percent) 1965-87	1965-80	1980-87	
73 Malaysia	16.5	330	1,810	4.1	4.9	1.1	70
74 Mexico	81.9	1,973	1,830	2.5	13.0	68.9	69
75 South Africa	33.1	1,221	1,890	0.6	10.0	13.8	60
76 Poland	37.7	313	1,930	..	..	29.2	71
77 *Lebanon*	..	10	..	..	9.3	..	..
Upper-middle-income	**432.5t**	**20,272t**	**2,710w**	**2.9w**	**23.2w**	**86.8w**	**67w**
78 Brazil	141.4	8,512	2,020	4.1	31.3	166.3	65
79 Uruguay	3.0	176	2,190	1.4	57.8	54.5	71
80 Hungary	10.6	93	2,240	3.8	2.6	5.7	70
81 Panama	2.3	77	2,240	2.4	5.4	3.3	72
82 Argentina	31.1	2,767	2,390	0.1	78.2	298.7	71
82 Yugoslavia	23.4	256	2,480	3.7	15.3	57.2	71
83 Algeria	23.1	2,382	2,680	3.2	9.8	5.6	63
84 Korea, Rep.	42.1	98	2,690	6.4	18.8	5.0	69
85 Gabon	1.1	268	2,700	1.1	12.7	2.6	52
86 Portugal	10.2	92	2,830	3.2	11.5	20.8	73
87 Venezuela	18.3	912	3,230	-0.9	10.4	11.4	70
88 Greece	10.0	132	4,020	3.1	10.5	19.7	76
89 Trinidad and Tobago	1.2	5	4,210	1.3	14.0	6.2	70
90 Libya	4.1	1,760	5,460	-2.3	15.4	0.1	61
92 Oman	1.3	212	5,810	8.0	17.6	-6.5	55
93 *Iran, Islamic Rep.*	47.0	1,648	..	..	15.6	..	63
94 *Iraq*	17.1	435	..	..	..	..	64
95 *Romania*	22.9	238	..	..	..	..	70
Low- and middle-income	**3,861.4t**	**73,133t**	**700w**	**2.7w**	**16.5w**	**43.9w**	**62w**
Sub-Saharan Africa	441.7t	20,999t	330w	0.6w	12.3w	15.2w	51w
East Asia	1,512.7t	14,019t	470w	5.1w	8.8w	5.4w	68w
South Asia	1,080.9t	5,158t	290w	1.8w	8.4w	7.8w	57w
Europe, M.East, & N. Africa	389.6t	11,430t	1,940w	2.5w	13.1w	23.7w	64w
Latin America & Caribbean	403.5w	20,306t	1,790w	2.1w	29.3w	109.1w	66w
highly indebted	**582.5t**	**21,213t**	**1,430w**	**2.0w**	**26.0w**	**91.2w**	**63w**
High-income economies	**777.2t**	**33,757t**	**14,430w**	**2.3w**	**7.9w**	**5.2w**	**76w**
OECD members	746.6t	31,085t	14,670w	2.3w	7.6w	5.0w	76w
★Other	30.6t	2,673t	7,880w	3.5w	15.9w	13.3w	70w
96 Spain	38.8	505	6,010	2.3	12.3	10.7	77
97 Ireland	3.6	70	6,120	2.0	12.0	10.2	74
98 ★Saudi Arabia	12.6	2,150	6,200	4.0	17.2	-2.8	63
99 ★Israel	4.4	21	6,800	2.5	25.2	159.0	75
00 New Zealand	3.3	269	7,750	0.9	10.2	11.5	75

Fig. 38.33 Basic Indicators.

	Population (millions) mid-1987	Area (thousands of square kilometers)	GNP per capita Dollars 1987	Average annual growth rate (percent) 1965-87	Average annual rate of inflation (percent) 1965-80	Average annual rate of inflation (percent) 1980-87	Life expectanc at birth (years) 1987
101 ★Singapore	2.6	1	7,940	7.2	4.9	1.3	73
102 ★Hong Kong	5.6	1	8,070	6.2	8.1	6.7	76
103 Italy	57.4	301	10,350	2.7	11.2	11.5	77
104 United Kingdom	56.9	245	10,420	1.7	11.2	5.7	75
105 Australia	16.2	7,687	11,100	1.8	9.2	7.8	76
106 Belgium	9.9	31	11,480	2.6	6.7	5.1	75
107 Netherlands .	14.7	37	11,860	2.1	7.3	2.3	77
108 Austria	7.6	84	11,980	3.1æ5.8	4.3		74
109 France	55.6	547	12,790	2.7	8.0	7.7	77
110 Germany, Fed. Rep.	61.2	249	14,400	2.5	5.2	2.9	75
111 Finland	4.9	337	14,470	3.2	10.5	7.2	76
112 ★Kuwait	1.9	18	14,610	-4.0	16.3	-4.6	73
113 Denmark	5.1	43	14,930	1.9	9.3	6.8	75
114 Canada	25.9	9,976	15,160	2.7	7.1	5.0	77
115 Sweden	8.4	450	15,550	1.8	8.0	7.9	77
116 Japan	122.1	378	15,760	4.2	7.8	1.4	78
117 ★United Arab Emirates	1.5	84	15,830	..	..	-0.3	71
118 Norway	4.2	324	17,190	3.5	7.7	6.1	77
119 United States	243.8	9,373	18,530	1.5	6.5	4.3	75
120 Switzerland	6.5	41	21,330	1.4	5.3	3.9	77
Total reporting economies	4,638.6*t*	106,890*t*	3,010*w*	1.5*w*	9.8*w*	13.7*w*	64*w*
Oil exporters	578.4*t*	17,303*t*	1,520*w*	2.1*w*	15.0*w*	20.1*w*	61*w*
Nonreporting nonmembers	371.5*t*	26,645*t*	..	..	..	..	69*w*

Note: For data comparability and coverage, see the technical notes. Figures in italics are for years other than those specified. For countries with populations of less than 1 million, see Box A.1. ★Economies classified by the United Nations or otherwise regarded by their authorities as developing. a. See the technical notes. b. GNP data refer to GDP.

Source: World Development Report 1989.

QUESTIONS

Q1. Explain Rostow's analysis of the process of economic growth and development.

Q2. Distinguish between Economic Growth and Economic Development.

Q3. Set out, and explain, the conditions which are necessary to enable a country to embark on a programme of economic development.

Q4. Give an example of a "Balanced Growth Path."

Q5. Write a short note setting out the benefits of Economic Growth.

Q6. Discuss some of the problems encountered by less-developed countries as they seek to achieve a period of economic growth.

39   Economic Aspects of Population

Demographic patterns of lesser developed countries

39.1. GNP per head of population will increase when national output increases faster than the growth of population. One means by which this increase in income may come about is through external aid which increases the level of output. Some of these foreign aid programmes may be directed at improving the general health of the population. But anything which increases GNP per head of population usually has the secondary effect of improving the general health of the nation, particularly when it is a poor country. Thus improvements in the wealth of poor countries are reflected in the rate of growth of the population through the effects of the increased wealth on the birth and death rates. The demographic patterns of Less Developed Countries (LDC's) tends to be characterised by high birth rates and high death rates.

Improved standard of living reduces death rate

39.2. As the standard of living in these countries improves it becomes possible for the inhabitants to avoid the diseases which are attributable to inadequate diets, and this combined with improvements in standards of housing and clothing minimises the health hazards to which deficiencies of this nature give rise. Further development of the economy provides resources for improvements in public health and sanitation, e.g., drainage, sewerage, supply of clean water, hospitals, preventive medicine, etc. In Puerto Rico improvements of this nature were reflected in a reduction in the death rate by approx. 50% during a 10 year period.

Malthusian Thesis

39.3. The improvement in health which rising standards of living make possible affect also the other end of the demographic scale, i.e., the birth rate. Improved accessibility to medical facilities not only increases the number of live births but also decreases the rate of infant mortality. It is the combination of a decrease in infant mortality and an increase in life expectancy which has given rise to the world population explosion and has resulted in a re-emergence of the Malthusian Thesis which states that the population will outstrip the food production capabilities of the world.

"Green Revolution"

39.4. In the 1960's the introduction of new high yield varieties of wheat and rice caused an increase in food production, which was so dramatic that it became known as 'The Green Revolution', and ensured that the dire predictions of Ehrlich[*] and others did not come to pass. However, the

---

[*]Paul R. Ehrlich 'The Population Bomb', Ballantine Books (New York) 1968. Ehrlich predicted that "in the 1970's the world would undergo famines — hundreds of millions of people are going to starve to death, in spite of any crash programmes embarked upon now."

present state of debate on the matter is finely balanced between (a) those who pessimistically contend that much of the increased food production has been due to costly subsidy programmes and that the problems of irrigation and plant disease cast doubts over the future, and (b) the optimists who have trust in the ingenuity of men (and divine providence) to introduce the technology to feed a growing world population.

"Poverty Trap"

39.5. Table 39.5 shows the relationship between the rate of population growth and average GNP per capita. Those countries with the higher rate of population growth tend to have a lower per capita GNP. An examination of this situation illustrates 'The Population Poverty Trap' in which poorer countries with increasing populations can become enmeshed.

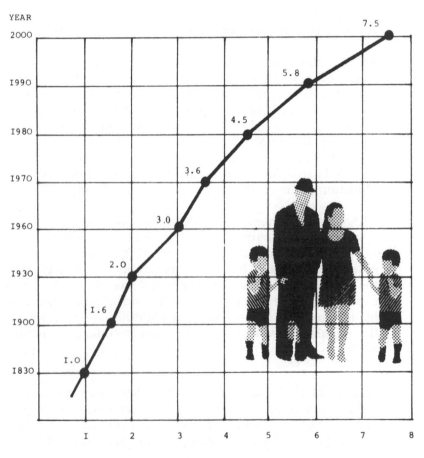

SCALE (BILLIONS OF PERSONS)

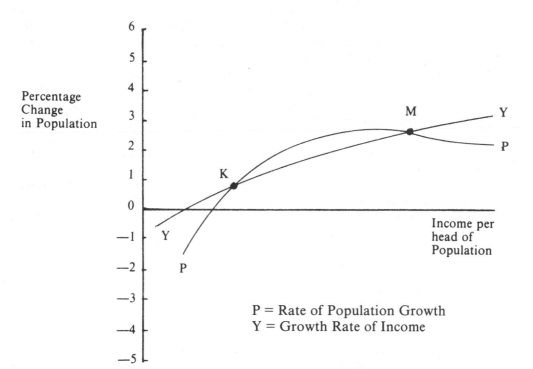

Fig. 39.5. The Poverty Trap.

39.6. Fig. 39.5 illustrates the relationship which exists between the rate of population growth and the level of income per head. At low levels of income the standards of health and nutrition are such that the high death rate exceeds the high birth rate, while those inhabitants who survive are confined to a subsistence level of existence. Higher per capita incomes are characterised by falling birth rates, as illustrated by a reduction in the rate of population growth at points beyond M in the diagram.

Curve Y illustrates the growth rate of income. Income in the economy depends upon the level of investment and the capital/output ratio; in the absence of external aid the level of investment will be related to the level of savings. The proportion of income which people save increases with income and this, combined with a fixed capital ratio, i.e., constant returns to scale, results in an increasing rate of growth — the rich get richer.

Point K in fig 39.5 is an equilibrium point. An increase in savings at this point will stimulate economic growth, but the attendant decline in the death rate will increase the rate of population growth even more, so that the per capita income is driven towards point K, where income and population grow at the same rate. Similarly a reduction of per capita income below point K results in population decreasing at a faster rate than income, so that per capita income increases back towards point K. At points to the right of Point M, self sustaining growth occurs as the growth of incomes exceeds the growth of population.

Wealthy countries and population change

39.7. This example illustrates the dilemma of developing countries as they seek to raise the general standard of living in their communities. In contrast, in the more wealthy countries, increasing wealth is reflected in a reduction in the birth rate. In Fig. 39.7 it will be noted that the projected population of Germany, the U.K., Belgium and Luxembourg will be lower in the year 2020 and the population of the European Community Member States as a proportion of total world population will decline from 6.8% to 4.2%.

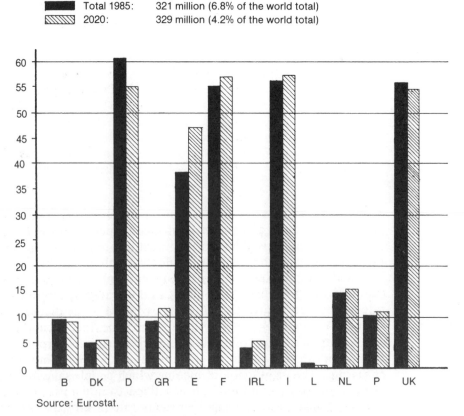

Source: Eurostat.

Fig. 39.7. Europe and its citizens; the population of the European Community Member States (1985 and forecast for 2020 in millions).

39.8 Many reasons have been adduced to explain this lower rate of population growth in wealthy countries, viz.:—

(a) In wealthy countries a high priority may be allotted to economic status and material wealth so that the energy of individuals is devoted to career development rather than early marriage and the raising of a family.

(b) The rearing and education of children may be expensive, consequently married people may feel that they can afford only a small number of children.

(c) As societies become urbanised the cost of rearing families increases — in agricultural communities there is a relatively abundant supply of food, housing is cheaper and children can help in the work of the farm.

(d) Increasing numbers of married women wish to continue with a job outside their home.

(e) With the availability of jobs outside the home for married women the opportunity cost of rearing children increases.

(f) Social norms as to the size of family can vary over time.

(g) Greater knowledge regarding the control of conception.

Over-population

39.9. The relationship between the standard of living and population size gives rise to the economic concepts of over- and under populated areas. Whether or not an area is overpopulated is not only a question of the size of the population, but also of the size of the population relative to the available economic resources and the efficiency of their use, i.e., the size of the population which the area is capable of supporting at some specified (or acceptable) standard of living. The Netherlands which has a land area approx. half that of Ireland supports a population almost 4 times greater than ours at a GNP per capita which is approx. twice as large as ours — see table 39.9. *An area is considered to be overpopulated in the economic sense when the economic resources of the area are insufficient to support an increase in population without a lowering in the average standard of living. There are diminishing returns to labour in such an area.*

Under-population

39.10. Conversely, there are countries, such as Australia, which have the economic resources to sustain a larger population than lives there at present. In an underpopulated country an increase in the population, in addition to augmenting the labour force, would constitute an increase in the level of domestic demand which would facilitate a growth in the scale of operations of domestic firms catering for the home market and as a result of which economies of scale could ensue. Countries which actively pursue an immigration policy recognise that they are underpopulated in the economic sense. A *country is said to be economically underpopulated when an increase in the population would raise the general standard of living, i.e., when there are increasing returns to labour.*

Table 39.9 Some Statistics of Selected Countries

Country	Area 1,000 sq.km 1983	Agri-cultural area 1,000 sq.km 1983	Tillage 1,000 sq.km 1983	Population thousand	Population per sq.km	Gross Domestic Product at market prices per capita at current prices in US$ using current exchange rates
Australia	7,686.8	4,916	465.7	15,540	2	11,178
Austria	83.9	35	15.2	7,552	90	8,535
Belgium	30.5	14	7.7	9,852	323	7,697
Canada	9,976.1	702	462.8	25,150	3	13,285
Denmark	43.1	29	26.4	5,111	119	10,690
Finland	337.0	25	23.6	4,882	14	10,493
France	547.0	313	187.2	54,947	100	8,907
Germany	248.6	121	74.5	61,175	246	10,025
Greece	132.0	92	39.7	9,900	75	3,380
Iceland	103.0	23	0.1	240	2	10,723
Ireland	70.3	58	9.7	3,540	50	4,986
Italy	301.2	173	122.2	56,983	189	6,114
Japan	372.3	54	48.1	120,018	322	10.457
Luxembourg	2.6	1	0 6	366	141	9,235
Netherlands	37.3	20	ى.6	14,420	387	8,534
New Zealand	268.7	146	4.7	3,258	12	7,159
Norway	324.2	9	8.5	4,141	13	13,215
Portugal	92.1	41	35.5	10,129	110	1,905
Spain	504.8	312	205.1	38,387	76	4,192
Sweden	450.0	37	30.0	8,337	19	11,369
Switzerland	41.3	20	4.1	6,507	158	14,002
Turkey	780.6	356	263.9	48,825	63	1,018
United Kingdom	24.8	187	69.8	56,488	231	7,495
United States	9,372.6	4,314	1,899.1	236,681	25	15,356

Source: OECD

Optimum size population

39.11. A country is said to have an optimum size population when there are constant returns to labour there.

Changes over time

39.12. Obviously under- or overpopulation is not a constant over time. Countries which were underpopulated may, over time, have such a growth in their population that they become overpopulated — you will be aware of difficulties at present in emigrating to countries which in the past had been actively encouraging a policy of immigration. Similarly, you may have overpopulation in some parts of a country and under-population in other parts of the same country.

The Population of Ireland

High birth rate

39.13. The improvements in standards of living and in medical knowledge are reflected in the falling death rate. However, Ireland has been somewhat unique among the developed countries in that our birth rate has not declined during the period shown. The effect on the size of the population of the national haemorrhage of emigration is reflected in the decline of our population for most of this century despite the excess of the birth rate over the death rate as shown in Table 39.13.

Table 39.13 Annual changes in total population, natural increase and net migration over the period 1951 to 1986

1951[1]	2,961	-14	27	-41
1961[1]	2,818	+16	30	-14
1971	2,978	+46	35	+11
1972	3,024	+49	35	+13
1973	3,073	+51	35	+16
1974	3,124	å3⁴53	34	+20
1975	3,177	+51	35	+16
1976	3,228	+44	34	+10
1977	3,272	+42	35	+7
1978	3,314	+54	38	+16
1979	3,368	+33	41	-8
1980	3,401	+42	40	+2
1981	3,443	+37	38	-1
1982	3,480	+24	38	-14
1983	3,504	+25	34	-9
1984	3,529	+11	31	-20
1985	3,540	-3	18	-31
1986	3,537			

¡ **The changes shown for 1951 and 1961 are annual averages for the periods 1951/61 and 1961/71, respectively.**
Source: CSO (1986), Report on Vital Statistics, 1983.

*"Push"
factors in
emigration*

39.14. *'Push and Pull Factors'* contribute to emigration. The push factors are those domestic circumstances which lead people to look beyond their own shores for a satisfactory standard of living, e.g.,

(a) lack of job opportunities at wage levels which enable an individual to settle down and enjoy a place in the community.

(b) a decline in the numbers employed in the agricultural sector without a corresponding increase in industrial employment to absorb those made redundant,

(c) lack of suitable housing at reasonable prices or rents,

(d) lack of social amenities, etc.

*"Pull"
factors in
emigration*

39.15. The *pull factors* are those conditions in other countries (or reports of conditions in these countries) which lead individuals to believe that they could enjoy a fuller and more rewarding life outside of this country. The examples would be the opposite to the push factors listed above with the inclusion of immigration regulations, i.e., whether or not foreigners are allowed to work and settle in these countries.

39.16 ECONOMIC EFFECTS OF EMIGRATION

(a) Emigration tends to be concentrated in the '18 plus' age group and, since this reduces our working population, it increases the dependency ratio for those who work in Ireland.

(b) There is no return to the State for the money spent on the education and training of the people who emigrated (through emigrants' remittances may be interpreted as a return of this nature).

(c) The more highly skilled workers enjoy the greatest mobility in the geographical sense. Their training and skills are such that they are welcome immigrants in many countries. In contrast to this workers without skills may find it difficult to gain immigration to other countries. Consequently highly skilled workers may constitute a large proportion of those who emigrate.

(d) Wages in Ireland cannot be significantly lower than those on offer in areas to which individuals might emigrate, e.g., England, without increasing the possibility of highly skilled workers emigrating.

(e) A declining domestic market creates problems for firms which set up in order to cater for domestic demand.

(f) National enterprises, e.g., transport, are under-utilised and this raises unit costs.

(g) Depression and fatalism prevail so that enterprise and investment are stifled.

(h) An under-utilised economic and social infrastructure remains in areas with declining populations.

39.17. Irish Demographic Pattern

Increase in population

The Irish population which had been in decline since the beginning of the century began to increase from 1961, and over the 1961-'81 period the population incresed by 18%, in contrast to falling levels of population in many of the western industrialised countries. This increase in the Irish level of population was the outcome of (i) the opposing forces of an increasing number of the population getting married and a decline in the average number of births per marriage, and (ii) a reduction in the level of emigration.

Dependent sectors

39.18. With an increasing level of population it is to be expected that a large proportion of our population would be in the younger age group, this point is emphasised by table 39.18. Those below the age of 15 and above the age of 65 are considered to be economically inactive — even though some people over 65 may still be in full time employment. Table 39.18 shows that the proportion of the Irish population in the dependent age groups (44%) is considerably higher in Ireland than the European Community average (35.1%). The high proportion of the population in the economically inactive age groups imposes demands on the economically active, for example, in terms of resources required for the education of the young and health care for the young and old.

Table 39.18. Population by age group of selected countries (1985, as %)

21% AGED UNDER 15 IN EUROPE, 45% IN AFRICA

	0-14	15-64	>64	Total population (in millions)
IRL				3.6
P				10.3
E				38.5
GR				9.6
NL				14.6
F				54.8
I				57.0
UK				56.3
B				9.8
DK				5.1
L				0.4
D				61.1
Africa				533.2
Asia				2 824.0
World				4 842.0
JAP				120.7
USA				240.0
EUR12				321.1

39.19. Not all of those within the economically active age groups (i.e., between 15-65) are actually employed. Some of this age group are not seeking employment while others though anxious to obtain employment have not been able to do so. Those who are in employment or seeking employment are referred to as *the labour force.* The proportion of the population which is in the labour force is known as the *Participation Rate.* In Table 39.19 which sets out participation rates it will be noticed that in respect of Ireland relative to other countries there is —

(a)   a low participation rate among females above the age of 24;

(b)   a high participation rate for males in the 14-24 age group;

(c)   a high participation rate for males over 60.

Table 39.19. Labour Force Percentage Participation Rates by Sex and Age, EC[1] and US, 1981

Age Group	Bel.	Den.	Fr.	Ger.	Gr.	Irl.	It.	Neth.	UK	EC	US
Males											
14-24	47.0	55.2	51.9	53.5	42.1	61.5	43.8	42.6	59.6	51.5	71.5[2]
25-59	90.7	93.9	93.6	93.7	93.3	94.8	88.9	91.4	94.3	92.6	92.3
60+	11.9	24.7	12.8	14.4	32.8	41.4	15.2	16.1	25.4	17.9	30.2
Total	65.7	70.9	70.0	69.9	70.9	75.7	64.7	66.9	71.8	69.0	77.0
Females											
14-24	43.1	49.0	44.7	48.6	27.8	47.8	33.1	40.8	46.6	42.9	61.7[2]
25-59	47.0	76.0	59.8	50.5	37.5	27.9	34.3	33.5	57.5	48.8	63.3
60+	2.5	9.4	6.0	3.8	9.0	7.7	3.1	2.0	7.3	5.1	14.0
Total	35.0	53.3	43.5	37.2	29.0	29.0	26.9	26.8	41.4	36.4	52.1

Sources: *Labour Force Sample Survey 1981,* Eurostat, Luxembourg 1983, and *Yearbook of Labour Statistics 1982,* International Labour Organization, Geneva 1982. Kennedy & McHugh *op. cit.*
[1]No survey data available for Luxembourg for 1981. [2]16-24 years.

39.20. As shown in Table 39.19 the participation rate for females of the 25-59 age group in the Irish labour force is low by international standards, e.g. it is 37%, 47%, 48%, 44%, of the Danish, French, U.K. and U.S. rates respectively. This is due to the low participation rate among married women which was 17% in 1981. If there is a continuing decline in marital fertility this percentage is likely to increase in future years.

39.21. The participation rate in Ireland among the younger age groups has traditionally been high by international standards due to the tendency in Ireland to leave full time education at an earlier age than that which obtained in other countries. With the introduction of free secondary education in 1967, the number of persons in full time secondary education increased from 78,000 in 1961 to nearly 200,000 in 1981.

*Participation
rate of
older people*

39.22. The high participation rate among the older age group is attributable to the large numbers engaged in farming in a self-employed capacity. The lack of adequate pension systems together with the self-determining decision as to when to retire, contributed to a high percentage continuing in employment.

*Employment
by sectors*

39.23. The change in the structure of employment in Ireland between the years 1961-84 is shown in Table 39.23. The increase in employment during the 1960's and 1970's is remarkable given the considerable decline in the numbers employed in agriculture, in 1984 the numbers employed in agriculture is half of the 1961 level. The effect of the depression in the 1980's is shown in the decline in the numbers engaged in industry.

Table 39.23 Level and Structure of Employment in Ireland, Selected Years, 1961-86

	1961	1971	1981	1986
	'000			
Agriculture	360	272	196	161
Industry	253	320	363	296
of which Manufacturing	175	211	236	n.a.
Building	58	84	101	n.a.
Mining and Utilities	20	24	27	n.a.
Services	405	457	587	600
of which Public	118	150	237	n.a.
Private	288	304	350	n.a.
Total Employment	1018	1049	1146	1057
	%			
Sector Shares				
Agriculture	34.5	25.9	17.1	15.2
Industry	24.9	30.5	31.7	28.0
Services	39.8	43.6	51.2	56.8
Total Sector Shares	100.0	100.0	100.0	100.0

Sources: Manpower Policy in Ireland (Report No. 82), Stationery Office, Dublin 1985 and ESRI Quarterly Economic Commentary.

Sector
employment
growth rates

39.24. In Table 39.24 is shown the average annual growth rates in total employment by sectors. A decline in employment in agriculture is shown for all countries, though the significance of this is greater in Ireland given the large proportion of our economic activity which is attributable to agriculture. Industrial employment also declined in many of the countries of the European Community.

Table 39.24 Average Annual Percentage Growth Rates of Total Employment by Sector, EC and US, 1973-85

	Bel.	Den.	Fr.	Ger.	Gr.	Irl.	It.	Lux.	Neth.	UK	EC10	US
Agriculture	-2.5	-1.8	-3.1	-2.7	-1.0	-3.3	-3.4	-4.5	-0.8	-1.3	-2.6	-0.€
Industry	-3.0	-1.3	-1.7	-1.7	0.9	-0.8	-0.7	-1.8	-1.3	-2.5	-1.6	0.5
Services	1.2	1.8	1.7	0.9	2.6	1.9	2.7	2.7	2.0	1.2	1.6	2.7
Total	-0.4	0.6	0.0	-0.4	1.0	0.1	0.6	0.1	0.8	-0.2	0.0	2.€

Source: Eurostat, *Employment and Unemployment,* Luxembourg 1986; Irish figures as for Table 8.7; US figures from OECD, *Labour Force Statistics 1964-84,* Paris 1986

Youth
unemployment

39.25. Unemployment is not spread evenly over all age groups. Young persons tend to experience a higher level of unemployment due to lack of the skills and/or experience which some employers seek; also in the early years of working life people often go through a settling down period in which some periods of unemployment are experienced before they discover a job which they consider suitable. Unemployment related to age is shown in Table 39.25.

Table 39.25. Unemployment by age: levels and rates for 1971, 1979 and 1981

	1971		1979		1981	
Age	'000	Rate%	'000	Rate%	'000	Rate%
15—24*	14.2	4.8	20.2	5.8	33.9	9.7
	(25.4)	(8.4)	(34.2)	(9.5)	(52.0)	(14.1)
25—44	16.1	4.2	33.3	6.6	51.3	9.5
45—64	17.6	5.2	19.4	6.1	26.4	8.2
65+	1.7	2.6	1.1	2.2	1.3	2.5
Total*	49.5	4.6	74.0	6.1	112.9	8.9
	(60.7)	(5.6)	(88.0)	(7.1)	(131.0)	(10.2)

Sources: *Labour Force Survey 1979.* Sexton (1981). *Census of Population 1981.*

* The figures in parentheses include first job seekers. Contained in Kennedy & Conniffe (editors) *Employment and Unemployment Policy for Ireland,* ESRI, Dublin 1984.

Some Economic Implications of Ireland's Demographic Pattern

39.26. Less than 1 in 3 of the population 'at work', as shown in Table 39.20, underlines the high dependency ratio. Under present concepts of social justice this high dependency rate means that the level of State transfer payments, e.g., old age pensions and children's allowances will be high, necessitating a high level of taxation.

39.27. The high proportion of the population which is in the young and student category ensures a continuing high demand for child and youth oriented services, viz., education, health and job creation programmes.

39.28. The continuing increase in the population will place additional demands on the housing sector, though the nature of this demand may change if the average number of children per family falls, and if a developing tendency for both parents to be employed outside the home persists.

39.29. The increasing population will place increased demand on the social infrastructure in certain areas, with schools, building land and the transport network being subject to particular pressure. In addition, the shift of population from inner city to outer suburbs, if it continues, will mean that schools and teaching staffs will need to be relocated to the areas of need, thus saving transport costs and lessening the traffic congestion of inner city areas.

39.30. In the absence of government intervention, it is likely that land values close to major centres of population will increase at a rate in excess of the general price level. Those owning such land will enjoy large capital gains.

39.31. An increased domestic demand for goods and services will enable domestic firms to expand and enjoy economies of scale, which may act as a springboard to enable these firms to compete in export markets.

QUESTIONS

Q1. Distinguish between Overpopulation and Underpopulation.

Q2. Explain the "Population Poverty Trap."

Q3. Set out some of the "push" and "pull" factors which lead to emigration.

Q4. Explain some of the reasons which are usually put forward to explain the lower rate of population growth in wealthy countries.

Q5. Comment on some economic implication of Ireland's demographic pattern.

Q6. Analyse the economic effects of emigration.

40 The Development of Economic Thought

40.1. Greece and Rome

Studies in the Context of Ethical Inquiry

The earliest references to economics have been found in the writings of ancient Greece. Economics was studied in the context of ethical inquiry rather than as a subject worthy of study in its own right. These states of old were based on a system of slavery, work was the business of slaves and the study of such matters was not considered to be worthy of intellectual analysis and investigation. Members of the ruling class, since they were to be protectors of the State would be educated in philosophy and the acts of war. These 'philosopher kings' would be free from the degrading pursuit of wealth and able to devote themselves to the affairs of state.

Plato

40.2. *Plato (427 – 347 BC)* in his masterpiece *The Republic* addressed himself to economic matters in analysing the origins of the State which he considered to be rooted in economic considerations arising out of the needs of man and the lack of individual self-sufficiency. Given the different classes which Plato perceived as existing in an ideal state, viz., peasants, warriors, and philosophers/rulers, he recognised that a division of labour was necessary. Production in such a system necessitated exchange or trade as a result of which a merchant class developed, similarly the exchange of production which was surplus to the requirements of the State created a need for sailors and foreign traders.

Aristotle

40.3. *Aristotle (384 – 322 BC)* was a pupil of Plato's and probably the greatest scholar of antiquity. Though he left no specific economic treatises, he discussed economic matters in considerable detail in his own writings. In his *Ethics* he dealt with the functions of money. In his *Politics* he distinguished between value in use and value in exchange; he wrote that when exchange is just it rests upon equality of wants and not upon costs in a labour-cost sense. He opposed retail trade which he considered to facilitate the gaining of wealth unnaturally.

Roman Empire

40.4. Given the conquests of the Roman Empire (27 BC to the 5th Century AD) and the extensive areas of the world which were subject to Roman rule it is not surprising that there was considerable economic activity during this epoch. Roman roads aided exchange in addition to which seaborne commerce and banking activities were extensive, the tax structure though predictably very efficient, is also recorded as being very fair. The "true price" of a commodity was related to a crude cost of production which included a profit. However, from available records no original thinking on economic matters can be attributed to the Romans.

40.5. The Middle Ages

Feudalism

Scholars disagree on the precise dates which this term covers but it is generally accepted as covering approximately a one thousand year period from the fall of the Roman Empire 476 AD. to about 1500. By the 8th century western Europe had reverted to being predominantly an agricultural economy, land was the chief form of wealth. Soldiers came from the serfs and rulers from the landowners. Authority rested with landowners and not with a sovereign who headed a State, kings were unable to control landholders and these people became virtual independent rulers.

Birth of Modern Capitalism

40.6. Towns and cities grew throughout Europe, usually they were enclosed by walls for protection. These towns became trading centres, with goods being produced by craftsmen who formed themselves into guilds. There was a division of labour in the production and trading of goods, money and other credit instruments were used and crude book-keeping systems developed. Modern capitalism had its beginning in this period as a money and price economy replaced a barter economy, the ownership of factors of production became divorced from their use, and a wage system emerged.

Trading Practices

40.7. Fair wages were considered to be an amount sufficient to maintain the worker in his own social class and it was felt that goods should sell at a price which would cover their costs of production. Freedom of competition was not considered to be an efficient regulator of markets and regulations were in existence to impede monopolistic practices. Regulations were drawn up also in respect of weights and measures, trade practices, methods of payments and debts.

Scholasticism

40.8. The Church and Christianity were powerful unifying influences during the Middle Ages. In the 12th Century there began *Scholasticism* which reconciled faith and reason and organised all knowledge under theology — the supreme authority. In the economics sphere, the scholastics codified temporal laws and rules which for many centuries were guides for men in their trading relations.

St Thomas Aquinas

40.9. *St. Thomas Aquinas (1225 - 1274)* is regarded as the greatest of the Scholastics, his *Summa Theologica* attempts to reconcile theological dogma with actual conditions in economic life. The principles which were set down by Aquinas were interpreted and developed by his successors, a lot of the writings were concerned with what is "just" or "right". e.g. a "just price", a "fair wage", interest and usury etc. Two kinds of justice were identified: (a) distributive justice which dealt with the distribution of wealth and income according to a person's place in society; (b) commutative justice which related to the exchange of goods and services between indviduals.

Mercantilism

Emergence of Mercantilism

40.10. By the end of the Middle Ages strong states had emerged, there was a growth of nationalism which led to the development of new concepts of economic organisation. The development of the modern study of economics is grounded in these 16th and 17th centuries, with the emergence of the first systematic body of economic thought — *Mercantilism.*

Mercantilists – General Principles

40.11. Towards the end of the 15th Century states had been gaining in power, colonies were being sought and in order to exploit such conquests the development of commerce and trade was necessary. A money economy with banking and credit institutions developed; competition and the profit motive was the spur towards the expansion of commerce. It was a period of intense nationalistic rivalry and competitiveness. This approach is captured in the following tenets which guided economic policy:

(1) Precious metals were the most desirable form of national wealth.
(2) If a nation did not possess natural sources of such metals, they could be gained by trade.
(3) The gaining of precious metals implied that a country's imports exceed its exports.
(4) Colonies could be the source of raw materials and a market for exports.
(5) The mother country should have a monopoly of trade with a colony — colonies must not be allowed process their own raw materials lest they interfere with the trading pattern of the mother country.

Bullionists

40.12. *"Bullionists"* is the term applied to a group of writers of the early 17th century who introduced the early elements of what became the mercantilist approach. These objectives were to increase the stock of bullion and in order to achieve this end they recommended a restriction on the import of luxury goods, a control of dealings in foreign exchange and a prohibition on the export of bullion.

Mercantilism One of the Nation Shaping Forces

40.13. Mercantilism should be seen as a phase in the development of the States of Europe, it is an integral element in the combination of the forces — political, religious, social and economic — of the era. Many of the wars during the 16th and 17th centuries were caused by commercial rivalries. England, particularly during the reign of Elizabeth (1558 — 1603) presents the best case study of Mercantilism and English writers were most prolific on the theme.

English Mercantilists

Thomas Mun

40.14. *Thomas Mun (1571 – 1641)* in his publication *England's Treasure by Forraign Trade or the Balance of Our Forraign Trade is the Rule of Our Treasure* set out the mercantilist doctrine in a systematic way. Like most Mercantilists he identified wealth with money, his exhortations were for the accumulation of treasure and he considered a favourable balance on foreign trade as the means of achieving it. Mun advocated prices based on "what the traffic will bear" for export sales but saw the necessity of keeping prices low in the domestic market.

John Locke

40.15. *John Locke (1632 – 1704),* though primarily a philosopher, in his writings on economic matters: (a) Adopted a subjective value of money rather than accepting that money had an absolute and unchanging value; (b) Showed an appreciation of the importance of the relationship between the quantity of money and its velocity of circulation; (c) Considered that an unfavourable balance on foreign trade would lead to national ruin.

Sir William Petty

40.16. *Sir William Petty (1623 – 1687)* had a more liberal approach to the principles of Mercantilism, he regarded prohibitions on the export of bullion as being futile and unwise though he stopped short of advocating free trade. He saw the wealth creating functions of both capital and labour, was an advocate for the division of labour, and considered a subsistence theory of wages arguing that if wages were too high it would affect the supply of labour. His insight into aspects of taxation are interesting: (a) Reasons for high taxes are the unwillingness of some to pay their taxes and the extravagance of the ruler; (b) If the government supports a large list of supernumeraries some of them would at times be idle.

David Hume

40.17. It has been said of the Scottish Philosopher *David Hume (1711 – 1776)* that he would have been ranked as a great economist were he not an even greater philosopher. Hume's theory of international trade is substantially the doctrine of Ricardo and J.S. Mill. He argued that the trade balance of any country could not be either favourable or unfavourable for extended periods because the inflow of money when trade was favourable would increase the domestic money supply and thus domestic prices so that price competitiveness ebbed and flowed.

Colbertism

40.18. The form of Mercantilism which was current in France is sometimes referred to as Colbertism after *Jean Baptiste Colbert* who was Louis XIV's Minister for Finance. In many respects Colbert's version was narrower than the British form, he advocated state control over all economic activity. Colbert is remembered as one of the foremost practitioners of the doctrine rather than for his writings on the subject.

Richard Cantillon

40.19. *Richard Cantillon (1680 – 1734)* who carried on a banking practice in Paris is considered to be an important writer on economic matters. His Essay on the Nature of Commerce in General was one of the first comprehensive works on Political Economy. He wrote on domestic and foreign trade, national wealth, money and prices. he adopted a supply and demand analysis of price etc., He placed great emphasis on the importance of agriculture — a point on which Quesnay subsequently dwelt.

Cameralism

40.20. The Mercantilists in Germany and Austria were known as *Cameralists.* During the period of Cameralism the emphasis was on the strengthening of the power of the state. *Philip Wilhelm Von Hornick (1638 – 1712)* is one of the best known, in his book *Austria Over All, If Only She Will* he set out the principles of the doctrine. Just like Mercantilism, Cameralism was devised to enable the states to recover from recurring wars and to develop their self-sufficiency.

Nationalism and Self-Sufficiency

40.21. The strength of the nation was fundamental in the various forms of Mercantilism. Commerce and trade were perceived as the means of increasing national wealth and to that end policies of nationalism and self-sufficiency were advocated. Thus it will be realised that it was the Mercantilist's philosophy to encourage manufacturing within the country by every possible means including subsidies and patents. Foreign trade was stimulated by colonial conquests and assisted by tariffs and trade restrictions, while the agricultural sector also was protected and encouraged.

Demand for Laissez Faire

40.22. While this policy suited the large merchants, smaller traders and farmers reacted against the taxation which these policies entailed. They also opposed the monopolistic privileges which were conferred on large traders. This discontent was manifest in a demand for 'laissez faire' or free trade.

THE PHYSIOCRATS

A belief in a Natural Order

40.23. The first scientific school of economics developed in France in the middle of the 18th century, it emerged as a reaction to the intolerable political and economic condition which many years of war and extravagance had created. Followers of this school advocated the maximising of individual freedom and the minimising of state control. They believed that there was a natural order which prevailed over human activities, the problem, as they saw it, was to discover the natural order and then to conform to it. From this idea they have been given the name *Physiocrats* which means the "rule of nature".

Francois Quesnay

40.24. The leading member of this school of thought was *Francois Quesnay (1694 – 17774),* court physician to Louis XV, who emerged as an economist at the age of sixty two. Quesnay took issue with the mercantilist doctrine that wealth originated in industry and trade. He argued that only agriculture, by virtue of the life-giving qualities of nature coud produce a surplus in excess of the resources devoted to it. He argued that manufacturing could change only the form of wealth derived from nature while commerce could change only its location and ownership.

40.25. In 1758 Quesnay set out his famour Economic Table which attempted to explain how the surplus produced in the agricultural sector spread through the entire economy. As befits a physician he likened the flow of resources throughout the economy to the circulation of blood in the human body and in this way he emphasised the interrelationship of the various sectors within the economy. Quesnay was a firm believer in the natural law and felt that all wealth was derived from the divine life-giving process. He also argued strongly in favour of economic freedom.

Agriculture as the Source of Wealth

40.26. Another well known member of the Physiocratic school was *Ann Robert Jacques Turgot (1727 – 1781)* who during his very short period as Comptroller General (1774 — 1776) attempted to introduce anti-mercantilist policies in France. Though he had the support of the king for his policies, the opposition of the noblemen whose interests he threatened resulted in his removal from office.

Ann Robert Jacques Turgot

40.27. The Physiocrats showed the interdependence of all groups within an economy; using the analogy of blood within the money they showed that net outflows of money and wealth from an economy impoverished it. The era of the Physiocrats was a mere 20 years — 1756 to 1758 and their main importance is due to the influence which they had on subsequent economists.

An Indirect Influence

Economic Liberalism.

40.28. This school of thought which had its beginnings in the late seventeenth and early eighteenth centuries was in the mainstream of the economic philosophy of the nineteenth century and is the essence of the present capitalist ideology. The economic liberals sought the removal of tariffs and restrictions on trade. They argued that people in pursuit of their own ends would contribute to the general good and that government intervention should be confined to the maintenance of justice and national defence — a philosophy expressed in 'The Fable of the Bees' by *Bernard de Mandeville* which was published in 1704.

Sought the Removal of Trade Restrictions

40.29. *Dudley North (1641 – 1691)* whose work 'Discourse Upon Trade' was published posthumously in the year of his death, argued strongly the case for free trade against the mercantilist hypothesis of the desirability of a favourable Balance of Trade. He stressed the advantage of specialisation and the mutual benefits of trade, and emphasised that restrictions on trade reduced the general welfare.

Specialisation

40.30. *David Hume (1711 - 1776),* the philosopher and historian, developed this free trade theme and pointed out that movements of gold caused by deficits or surpluses on international trade would affect the money supply, prices and trade flows. From this he argued that the mercantilist goal of continuous trade surpluses and inflows of gold and silver was not possible.

40.31. The Economic Liberals of the eighteenth century considered human labour to be the source of wealth, i.e. a labour theory of value, and stressed that without human effort very few natural products could satisfy human wants. Thus the greater the human effort the greater would be the level of production and the higher the standard of living. These ideas were developed by *John Locke (1632 – 1704)* who drew attention to the importance of private wealth in this scheme of things. He showed that human effort produced wealth and conferred property rights and that it was only by protecting property rights that human effort would be encouraged. Accordingly, he perceived the role of the State to be the protection of the property rights, the maintenance of justice and national defence.

40.32. *Adam Smith (1723-1790)* who was born in Kirkaldy, Scotland, in 1723, a few months after his father's death, is universally acclaimed as the greatest of the Economic Liberals and the founder of economic science. He entered the University of Glasgow at the age of fourteen and won a scholarship to Oxford where he remained for six years. He was very disappointed with academic standards at Oxford and in 1751 he took a position as lecturer at the University of Edinburgh. In the following year he was appointed Professor of Logic at Glasgow University, and one year later he was appointed professor in his favourite subject Moral Philosophy.

Adam Smith (1723-1790)

40.33. At the age of forty Smith was offered and accepted the position of tutor to the young Duke of Buccleuch at a lifetime pension of £300 per annum. Much of his time while in that position was spent in France where he had an opportunity to discuss with Quesnay and Turgot the Physiocratic doctrines and he began writing a book on economics. He returned to Scotland where he completed *'An Inquiry into the Nature and Causes of the Wealth of Nations'* which was published in 1776. On publication the book enjoyed only moderate success. It was the next generation of writers who, some twenty years after Smith's death in 1790, bestowed acclaim on the book and established Smith as the founder of economic science. It has been said that before Adam Smith there had been much economic discussion, but with him it reached the stage of discussing economics.

"An Inquiry into the Nature & Causes of the Wealth of Nations"

40.34. In the eighteenth century economic problems were examined by reference to the means by which wealth was created. The Mercantilists considered the source of wealth to be grounded in a favourable Balance of Trade, the Physiocrats considered agriculture to be the source of wealth, while Adam Smith considered labour to be the source of wealth and that increases in wealth would be related to the skill, dexterity and judgement with which labour is applied — the Labour Theory of Value with labour as the measure of the exchange value of a commodity. This led Smith to advocate the division of labour. This was not a new idea but Smith laid particular stress on it as a way of increasing wealth. The accumulation of wealth to which this development would give rise could be encouraged by State protection for property rights, while the accumulation of wealth would provide the resources for further expansion and growth. The division of labour/specialisation implies exchange which led Smith to study value and money.

Labour Theory of Value

40.35. Smith was in the Liberal Economic tradition and considered that "the invisible hand of competition" and a self-adjusting market mechanism were the means by which economic progress was to be achieved. Whereas the Mercantilists had advocated government regulation on the assumption that the selfish attitudes and desires of individuals would lead to less being available for others, Smith showed that individuals in pursuing their own selfish interests could benefit society, since if they wished to sell they must produce what others required at a price that they were prepared to pay. Competition among sellers as they strove to increase their profits would ensure that production fulfilled the requirements of the buying public. Similarly, with freedom of entry into markets, profits would be no greater than the minimum necessary to motivate entrepreneurs and ensure continuity of supply while inefficiency would be penalised — the theory of Perfect Competition. Smith reasoned that goods had a 'natural price' which in primitive societies was based on the cost of production, and that market equilibrium would occur at this 'natural (or normal)' price.

Perfect Competition

40.36. The foregoing is the familiar model of the perfectly competitive market structure. In an era when the establishment of a business did not require large amounts of capital, Smith was of the opinion that a private monopoly could not persist for a lengthy period and that competition would erode supernormal profit. In these circumstances he saw no justification for government intervention and considered the duty of government to be confined to national defence, the maintenance of justice and the erection and maintenance of certain public works and, where possible, these public works should be paid for by charges for use rather than by general taxation.

No Justification for Government Intervention

40.37. In an era when the medieval social system of status and obligation was being superseded by the growth of large cities, Smith's perception of the market economy showed it to be compatible with social order and national wealth. In addition Smith laid the analytical framework for the science of economics, which resulted in his being universally acclaimed as the founder of what became known as 'The Classical School'.

Founder of Classical School

The Classical Economists

40.38. This school of economists was particularly strong in England and for almost a century their theories dominated the subject in Europe and the United States. The Classical School represents the orthodox approach to economic problems and accepted the spirit of Economic Liberalism viz.: freedom of action for business, the minimum of government intervention, free trade and free movement of capital. The equilibrium of supply and demand in competitive markets as set out by Smith formed the basis of their analytical structure. The structure of the Classical School which was laid by Smith was developed and refined by Thomas Robert Malthus and David Ricardo, which resulted in economics becoming the first of the social sciences.

Economics was the First of the Social Sciences

Thomas Robert Malthus

Population Grows at a Faster Rate than Food Supply

40.39. *Thomas Robert Malthus (1766-1834)* Malthus is remembered for his famous 'Essay on the Principle of Population as it affects the Future Improvement of Society' which was published in 1798. In this essay Malthus stated that population increased in a geometric progression (1, 2, 4, 8, 16) while he supposed that, at best, the food supply would be doubled in a 25 year period with an equal increase in each subsequent 25 year period so that the food supply would increase in an arithmetic progression (1, 2, 3, 4, 5.).

Malthusian theory must be set in the context of the period — the wars and revolutions of the late eighteenth and early nineteenth centuries, the wartime increases in the price of food, the enclosure of common land which left many farmers with no land, and the Industrial Revolution. All these happenings stimulated the movement of the population from rural to urban areas, and gave rise to a population influx which resulted in the creation of slums with attendant water and sewage problems. In the light of these developments Malthus's comments on the effect of population growth on society attracted attention. He stressed that population would outgrow the means of subsistence so that, in the absence of moral restraint, the outcome would be vice and misery, viz., famine and disease.

Iron Law of Wages

40.40. This line of thought led to the idea of a subsistence level of wages — *The Iron Law of Wages* — which stated that payment to workers in excess of the subsistence level would lead to an increase in the size of the workers' families until the larger family size dragged the workers down once more to a subsistence level of existence. This analysis suited many employers since it removed any pangs of conscience to which they may have been subject and they felt justified in paying low wages. It was pointed out also that a larger population would force up food prices which would transfer wealth from the productive manufacturing sector to the non-productive land owners. This transfer of wealth was perceived as slowing the rate of economic growth.

Was Malthusian Analysis Accurate?

40.41. This dismal analysis of Malthus remained the basis of wage theories for over a century and constituted a major element in classical economic theory. Malthus's theories have not been realised in many parts of the world because of the opening up of new lands, increased productivity in the food industry, the growth of international trade and the fact that family size tended to diminish rather than increase as material standards of living rose. In contrast, one is aware of the plight of many overpopulated areas of the world where the Malthusian doctrine has relevance, as population growth depresses wages and creates unemployment resulting in extreme poverty.

David Ricardo

Became MP

40.42. *David Ricardo (1772-1823)* Ricardo was born in London of Jewish parents. When at the age of 21 he married a Quaker girl, it caused a rift between him and his stockbroker father as a result of which he was disinherited. Friends came to his aid and set him up on the stock exchange where over a five year period he amassed a large fortune, partially by helping to raise finance for the British government during the Napoleonic War. In 1819 he became a member of parliament for an Irish borough and concentrated on economic and public affairs for the remainder of his life.

Theory of Rent

40.43. At the end of the Napoleonic war in 1815 the Corn Laws were the subject of parliamentary debate in England. The Corn Laws introduced a system whereby, through the application of a sliding scale of tariffs on imported wheat, it was hoped to protect English farmers from cheap wheat imports and place an upper limit on food prices. Ricardo opposed the increases in tariffs arguing that increases in food prices would raise the subsistence wage level and render British industry uncompetitive. He argued also that landowners, not farmers, would be the main beneficiaries of increased food prices and in support of this argument he introduced a theory of rent which he set out on the following lines — if food prices rise there will be an increase in the production of food, so that land which previously it had been uneconomical to cultivate would be profitable at the higher food prices and would be brought into use. Fertile land would now be more profitable and the rent payable for its use would increase. Additional labour would be required to work on the land in order to satisfy the increased demand for food and this, in turn, would result in an increase in wage rates. In keeping with the wisdom of the period, increased income was expected to lead to an increase in population which would increase further the demand for, and the price of, food.

40.44. Not only would increased food costs lead to increased wage rates and place industry under competitive pressure, but due to increased rent charges as outlined above there would be a transfer of wealth from

Transfer of Wealth to Landowners

industrialists to the landowning sector. Since landowners were perceived as spending their money in a non-productive manner on larger houses and a greater number of servants while the industrialists would find it more difficult to accumulate capital which was the source of economic expansion and growth, the whole economy would suffer in the process.

Law of Comparative Costs

40.45. Ricardo, whose principal work was 'Principles of Political Economy and Taxation', developed also the *Law of Comparative Costs* which forms the basis of international trade.

Say's Law

40.46. *Jean Baptise Say (1767-1832).* Say, who was a Frenchman, published in 1803 'A Treatise on Political Economy' which was based on the analytical framework of Adam Smith. In this publication he set out a principle which became known as *'Say's Law of Markets',* in which he explained that, people produced goods either for their own use or to exchange for what they required, in the very act of production these originated a demand for other goods and services, i.e., *'production creates its own demand'.* While Say conceded that there might be some temporary mismatching of production and needs in that some people might produce goods for which there was not a sufficient demand, the price of such goods would be reduced until a buyer was found and the resources thus released by the sale of the goods would then be channelled into the production of goods for which there was an adequate demand as indicated by the relatively high prices which they were fetching. Say's Law, together with Henry Thornton's 'The Paper Credit of Great Britain' which was published in 1802 and argued that a fluctuating rate of interest would bring savings and investment into equilibrium, provided a logical model in which full employment was assured in a free enterprise economy. A theory of this nature prevailed until the world depression of the 1930's resulted in an alternative theory being obviously necessary and such a theory was forthcoming.

Other Classical Economists

40.47. The Classical School of economic thought was refined further by many others including *William Senior* who wrote on the scope and method of Political Economy and the function of capital in production. The main contribution of another well known economist *John Stuart Mill (1806 – 1873),* was his restatement and presentation of the economic

John Stuart Mill

doctrine of the period in his 'Principles of Political Economy' which was published in 1848 and which is still arguably the best general survey of classical economics.

The Economics of Marx

Utopian Associationists

40.48. *Karl Marx (1818-1883).* Some people suggest that socialism begins with Plato by virtue of his advocacy of communism, whole others take More's Utopia with its denunciation of private property as its starting point. For those who consider that it has its real beginnings in the revolutionary socialism on Marx, the scene was set for its introduction by the group who have been labelled the *'Utopian Associationists'*. These envisaged the introduction of socialism through the coming together of groups to live according to socialistic principles. While the Industrial Revolution resulted in a considerable improvement in the living standards of the wealthy and middle classes it also imposed long hours of work and harsh conditions for meagre wages on workers. This situation resulted in a number of idealistic people seeking to improve the lot of the working classes, mainly through some form of cooperative movement, and this constituted the form of socialism prior to the advent of Marx. The best known of this group is an Englishman, *Robert Owen (1771 – 1858).*

Friedrich Engels

40.49. This then is the setting for the introduction of Karl Marx who was born in the German Rhineland in 1818. He was a brilliant student who studied law at the Universities of Bonn and Berlin but his opposition to the government precluded him from the governmental career which he had intended to pursue. Presumably because he had become an atheist, his philosophical studies for which he was awarded his doctorate failed to result in the university professorship which he sought. It was this route that led Marx to become the editor of a Cologne newspaper in 1842, and, when the government suppressed the newspaper because of its liberal views, Marx went to Paris. While in Paris Marx met the son of a wealthy German textile manufacturer named *Friedrich Engels* and the two men worked together in the furtherance and propagation of socialistic ideals for the remainder of Marx's life.

Karl Marx (1818-1883)

40.50. At the request of the Prussian government Marx was expelled from France for writing articles which were critical of the Prussian government. He then went to London where together with his wife and five children he spent over 30 years. He was supported by Engels and this enabled him to devote most of his time to his magnum opus *'Das Kapital'* (Capital). The first volume of this work appeared in 1867 and this was the only part completed by Marx before he died in 1883. Volume 2 which was edited by Engels was published in 1885, with volume 3 following in 1894.

"Das Kapital"

40.51. Marx in collaboration with Engels produced the *Communist Manifesto* which was published in 1848. The manifesto denounced the capitalist system which they considered to contain the seeds of its own destruction. Marx adopted a materialistic conception of history — he considered economics to be the dominating influence and traced history in terms of a series of class struggles, as workers merely changed their oppressors. Marx considered that society passes from slavery to feudalism, to capitalism, to socialism and communism through conflict between opposing economic groups.

Communist Manifesto

40.52. He adopted a *Labour Theory of Value*, and perceived the value of a good as being the cost of the number of hours of necessary labour which is required to produce it. (The term necessary labour is us used to distinguish productive labour hours from non-productive labour hours). He argued that the wage rate paid to the worker is at a subsistence level and that the employer works the employee as hard as possible, so that output is at a maximum and certainly greater than the wages which are paid to the worker. This excess of value of output over wages paid is the *'surplus value'* of production and this is appropriated by the capitalist class through profits. Thus in Marxian theory the worker is exploited by the capitalist.

Surplus Value of Production

40.53. Marx perceived the profits of the capitalist as providing the incentive and resources for the introduction of capital intensive production processes which displace workers and cause unemployment, while those who are still employed find that their work has been 'deskilled' so that instead of being skilled workers they are mere machine minders. This, he argued, leads to alienation while the army of unemployed which the process has created weakens the bargaining power of the workers who are thus precluded from any real improvement in their conditions. As a result of this development there would be a diminution in purchasing power which would be manifest in reductions in the levels of demand, production, profits and employment. At this stage the larger, wealthier capitalists are able to buy up smaller firms and there is a centralisation of control and power. The depression is relieved only when the overproduction has been eventually disposed of and the upward section of the cycle is set in motion again. However, according to Marx, this process cannot continue indefinitely and growing numbers of the proletariat who are being exploited and alienated will eventually rise up

Centralisation of Control and Power

and take control from the small number of capitalists under whose control the economy has fallen.

Criticism of Marxists

40.54. There are those who, in support of their refutation of Marx, point to the growth of labour unions, the development of social legislation, the economic and political power which is enjoyed by workers, together with the improvements in the standard of living which the working classes have achieved relative to changes which have taken place in the life style of other social classes. Marxists answer that exploitation has been transferred from the domestic working class to the people of the less developed countries of the third world and also draw attention to the unequal distribution of national income which results in extreme poverty even in wealthy nations. Many writers have addressed themselves to assessing Marx's role in history and in the process his economic theories have been adversely criticised. However, all agree that Marxism constantly awakens the conscience of the world to inequalities in living standards both within and between countries, and indicates some consequences to which such inequalities can give rise.

After Marx

Defence of Existing System

40.55. The demands of Marx for social justice and the development of socialistic theories made it incumbent on the supporters of existing policies to develop theories which could be adduced to support the capitalist system and refute Marxism. Their efforts contributed to the continuance of the laissez faire system up to the outbreak of the First World War in 1914. Most economists of the period did not advocate a completely unfettered private enterprise system but rather, while conceding that there could be circumstances in which social benefits could accrue from government intervention, they felt that the general interest was best served by a policy of individualism.

Concept of Marginal Utility

40.56. In the 1870's the concept of marginal utility which concentrated on the demand side of the price equation was introduced to replace the labour theory of value which had concentrated on the supply side of the equation. The development of this *marginal utility concept* which stated that the price of a good will be related to the utility of the last unit purchased is attributed to three people — an Englishman *William Stanley Jevons (1835-1882)*, a Frenchman *Leon Walras (1837-1910)* and an Australian *Karl Menger (1840-1921)*.

Alfred Marshall

40.57. The great English economist, *Alfred Marshal (1842-1924)*, reconciled the supply and demand aspects in the establishment of price by the analogy of a piece of cloth being cut by both blades of a scissors in the same way as price is determined by the twin forces of supply and demand. The concept of marginal utility was extended to embrace income distribution and it was shown that at long run equilibrium under Perfect

Alfred Marshall (1842-1924)

Competition the return to each factor of production would be based on the Marginal Revenue Productivity of the factor, which implied some form of economic justice.

Neoclassical Economists

40.58. The term, *Neoclassical Economists* is applied to those economists who wrote after 1870 in the Adam Smith mould of a private enterprise economy with production responding to free self-adjusting markets, while they considered that economic growth would be achieved through capital accumulation and investment. Their studies were conducted within an analytical framework which showed full employment to be the equilibrium situation. These economists had grafted on to the Adam Smith model the concept of marginal utility to replace the Labour Theory of Value and had built their studies in an analytically rigorous framework. In addition they subjected their hypotheses to empirical testing.

The Fabian Society

40.59. Parallel with these developments there was the debate on the relative merits of socialism and capitalism. *Pope Leo XIII (1810-1903)* in a famous encyclical *'Rerum Novarum'* which was issued in 1891 sought common ground between labour and capital on the basis of social justice. In 1883 there was formed in England a group known as *'The Fabian Society'* (which included George Bernard Shaw). This group sought to reorganise society in accordance with the highest moral principles in order to bring about the greatest happiness for the greatest number. The writings of these *Fabian Socialists* and other like minded individuals contributed to the introduction of legislation

(a) to permit increased powers for trade unions (1890-1900),

(b) to provide factory safety regulations (1891),

(c) to impose a restriction on working hours for women and children (1895),

(d) to prevent industrial accidents (1906),

(e) to introduce old age pensions (1908).

Developments of a similar nature in the USA by a number of people including *Thorstein Veblen (1857-1929)* prepared the ground for the *New Deal Administration* of Franklin D. Rossevelt in the 1930's.

The Keynesian Revolution

John Maynard Keynes

40.60. Economics in the present century has been dominated by *John Maynard Keynes (1883-1946)* who vies with Adam Smith for the mantle of the greatest ever economist. Keynes who was son of the prominent economist John Neville Keynes was born in Cambridge, England, in 1883. He was educated at Eton and Cambridge where he studied economics under Alfred Marshall. His area of specialisation was monetary economics and in addition to lecturing at Cambridge he was employed at the Treasury so that in 1919 he represented the Treasury at the Versailles peace conference. At that conference Keynes argued the importance of economic considerations in the peace settlement. However, his advice was ignored and the peace treaty imposed huge repatriation payments on the German nation. As a result of this Keynes resigned and analysed the peace settlement in his publication *'The Economic Consequences of the Peace'* in which he forecast the economic turmoil which subsequently ensued. This publication caused an estrangement in his

John Maynard Keynes (1883 - 1946)

relationship with the government which lasted for a decade. Meanwhile he returned to lecturing at Cambridge and gained a fortune through stock exchange transactions. Though he lost his fortune in the stock market collapse of 1929 he borrowed some funds and made another fortune in the 1930's.

Return to Gold Standard

40.61. In the 1920's Keynes recorded his preference for a managed system of foreign exchange and criticised Britain's decision to return to the gold standard. His advice was rejected and his prognostications of economic disaster were confirmed by subsequent events. Keynes acted as advisor to the British Treasury during the Second World War (1939-1945) and was the British representative at the Bretton Woods agreement. He was rewarded with a knighthood and died in 1946 at the age of sixty two.

"The General Theory of Employment Interest and Money"

40.62. It would be difficult to overestimate the contribution of Keynes to the development of economics. His most famous work was *'The General Theory of Employment Interest and Money'* which was published in 1936. In this book he presented in a more developed and refined manner the theories which he first introduced in his *'Treatise on Money'* which was published in 1930. The great depression of the 1930's caused people to realise the weaknesses of the conventional economic theories of the period and created a climate of opinion which ensured a receptive ear for the theories introduced by Keynes.

Less than Full Employment Equilibrium

40.63. Keynes showed that employment depended upon total spending, the level of investment which is one of the components in total spending depended upon the profitability of new investment. He analysed the reasons why people save and invest and suggested that there may be no positive rate of interest at which the injection of investment would be as great as the leakage of savings, in which circumstances there would be a deficiency in aggregate demand. He also stated, inter alia, that prices and wages might not be sufficiently flexible in any feasible time period to ensure market clearance and full employment. Thus, in contrast to the Classical Economicsts who considered that interest rates, wages and prices would fluctuate to clear markets and so ensure full employment equilibrium, Keynes suggested that there could be equilibrium at less than full employment. In the light of a deficiency in demand Keynes emphasised that an active fiscal policy, e.g., by increasing expenditure on public works programmes, could increase total spending and bring economic activity to the full employment level. Thus he justified government management of the economy.

New Terminology

40.64. In developing his theories Keynes introduced a new terminology, e.g., marginal propensity to consume, the multiplier, liquidity preference, etc.

Macro-Economics – Current Areas of Debate

*Classical
v.
Keynesian*

40.65. A market is said to clear and be at equilibrium when the quantity sellers wish to supply is equal to the quantity which buyers demand. This implies that prices change when there is a change in the conditions affecting supply and/or demand, *but an important issue is how fast do prices change in order to clear markets.* In the classical school of economics, prices were considered to be very flexible in all markets, so that all markets cleared and were in equilibrium. In contrast to this the Keynesian analysis considered that prices were not sufficiently flexible and that rather than prices coming down when required, quantities fell to create an equilibrium at less than full employment.

Expectations

40.66. Whether or not prices are flexible depends a lot on people's perception and expectations. What we see as likely to happen in the future has an influence on what we do today — if you think inflation is likely to be higher next year it will affect your decision as to whether or not to buy now or whether to accept the wage increase being offered. This can be seen at present as people's expectations are adjusting to lower rates of inflation. The quicker (and more correctly) that people's expectations adjust the more flexible market prices will be.

Neo-Classical/The New Classical Economists/Extreme Monetarists

*Prices
Instantly
Flexible*

40.67. *The New Classical Economists* are termed classical because they are in the tradition of the Classical Economists who assumed that wage and price flexibility would always ensure the full employment of factors of production. Their approach is new because it assumed that prices are instantaneously flexible whereas the Classical Economics were vague about the time period required for prices to adjust. This neo-classical approach was propounded originally in the USA by *Professor Thomas Sergent* and *Professor Robert Lucas,* in the UK. The most prominent advocate in the UK is *Professor Patrick Minford* of Liverpool University.

*Process
of
Adjustment*

40.68. The New Classical approach would be along the following lines: Since both management and workers are interested in real wages, wage contracts are negotiated on the basis of expectations as to the likely rate of inflation during the period of the wage contract. If inflation during the period of the contract is higher than it was expected to be then profits increase and real wages are lower than expected. However, when wage contracts are renegotiated by Unions they take into account the higher rate of inflation and seek higher money wages. If during the period of the new wage agreements inflation is lower than expected then real wages gain at the expense of profits and this will influence future wage contracts. Under this analysis contracts will be negotiated at the market clearing level which will equate to full employment.

40.69. Following this line of analysis, if the government injects demand into the economy, then prices will rise, as demand was previously at the full employment level. This price rise will lower the real wages of workers who will seek compensation for the price increase when wage contracts are due for renewal. *In this analysis fiscal or monetary policies increase the price level but do not increase the level of real output.*

Fiscal and/ or Monetary effect prices only

40.70. Economists of this school would seek *supply-side policies* from the government. *Supply side policies are policies designed to increase the level of output by enabling markets to operate efficiently through the unfettered operation of factors affecting the supply of factors of production, goods and services.* Examples of such policies would be —

Supply Side Policies

(a) cuts in income tax or the provision of retraining grants so as to ensure the maximum availability of labour skills at each level of real wages;

(b) reducing inflation could be a supply side policy if inflation retards the supply of factors of production.

Monetarists/Gradualist Monetarists

40.71. This is the policy with which the name of *Milton Friedman (1912-)* is associated. Milton Friedman is Professor of Economics at the University of Chicago and people who espouse his theories are often referred to as *'The Chicago School'. Professor David Laidler* of the University of Western Ontario in Canada and *Professor Sir Terry Burns,* Chief Economic Adviser to the British Treasury, are also identified with this school of thought.

The Chicago School

40.72. The term *"Monetarist"* is applied to those economists who argue, along the line of the Classical Economists, that increases in the money supply result in an increase in prices rather than an increase in the level of output. While this is the essential feature, their analysis of the transmission process leads on to (a) a belief in the inherent stability of the private sector; (b) a disapproval of government economic intervention; (c) a greater priority for the removal of inflation rather than unemployment; (d) a preference for monetary over fiscal policy.

Monetarists

40.73. Milton Friedman was born in New Jersey in 1912. During World War II he held a position in the US Treasury and in 1946 he was appointed Professor of Economics at the University of Chicago and he still holds this position. In 1951 he was awarded the John Bates Clark Medal by the American Economic Association and in 1976 he received the Nobel Prize in Economics. His major works include:

Milton Friedman

> *Essays in Positive Economics (1953)*
> *A Theory of the Consumption Function (1957)*
> *Inflation – Causes and Consequences (1962)*
> *A Monetary History of the United States 1867-1960. (1963)*
>   *written with Anna Schwartz.*

40.74. The New Classical Economists considered that markets adjust

Monetarists'
Policies

almost instantaneously with departures from full employment being attributable to unanticipated shocks or disturbances which cannot be nullified by wage adjustments. In contrast to this the Gradualist Monetarists, as their title implies, consider that the restoration of full employment may take a little longer — maybe a few years — but that price adjustments will ensure a return to a full employment equilibrium. Given that a full employment equilibrium will be reestablished, it is not necessary for the government to intervene and if they do so they will increase the price level (inflation) rather than the level of output. Also by the time that the government has diagnosed a reduction in the level of aggregate demand and implemented the necessary policies, the problem which was diagnosed could have disappeared, e.g. in a recession the government introduces an expansionary policy, but by the time the policy becomes effective the economy might have pulled out of the recession. Again economists of this school see the elimination of inflation and supply side policies as being the most effective contribution which the government can make. Thus Milton Friedman has recommended that Governments adopt a low but fixed rate of growth of the money supply — through being low it controls inflation and by being constant it ensures adequate financing for long term growth in the economy.

Neo-Keynesian/Eclectic Keynesians

40.75. The word eclectic comes from the name of an ancient philosopher

Espouse
Elements of
both
Keynesianism
& Monetarism

who combined doctrines which he considered worthy from different schools of thought, hence the use of the word in relation to this group of economists who tend to espouse Keynesianism for short run policy and Monetarism in relation to the long run. They accept the conclusion that the economy will eventually return to full employment but because they perceive wages and prices as adjusting slowly the reattainment of full employment equilibrium could be a lengthy process, thus there could be significant short run deviations from the full employment level of aggregate demand. Consequently they perceive a need for demand management, i.e., the manipulation of aggregate demand, in the short run, to stabilise the economy.

Long-Run
Considerations

40.76. They believe that the economy will *eventually* return to full employment and accept that rapid monetary growth when the economy is at full employment causes inflation. They acknowledge that supply side policies are important in the long run and are the means by which the full employment level of output may be increased.

Exponents
of Theory

40.77. *Professors Sir John Hicks and James Meade* from the UK and *Professor James Tobin* of Yale University all of whom are Nobel Prize winners in economics would be exponents of the Neo-Keynesian school of macro-economics.

Extreme Keynesians

40.78. Two of the best known advocates of this approach are *Professors Nicholas Kaldor and Wynne Godley* of Cambridge University. The extreme form of Keynesians would argue that not only do markets not clear in the short run but they may not clear in the long run either, so that there will be equilibrium at a level of aggregate demand which fails to achieve full employment, unless the government intervenes to boost aggregate demand through demand management policies. Thus it is only the new Classical Economists who maintain that wages and prices will be quick to adjust, Gradualist Monetarists believe that full employment will be restored in a year or two, Eclectic Keynesians think it would be 5 or 6 years before full employment is restored while Extreme Keynesians think that it would be even longer.

Equilibrium at less than Full Employment

40.79. To develop the position of the Extreme Keynesian School it is necessary to assume (a) that real wages will not fall when there is involuntary unemployment. A fall in real wages would decrease the labour supply and increase the demand for labour bringing the labour market into equilibrium and removing involuntary unemployment. (b) That there is no automatic mechanism by which a full employment level of aggregate demand can be achieved. The mainstream view would be that reductions in nominal (money) wages would lead to price reductions which (i) increase the real money supply, (ii) lower interest rates and (iii) stimulate both investment and consumption expenditure. Furthermore in an open economy this process improves competitiveness which stimulates the domestic economy.

Real Wages Inflexible Downwards

40.80. Extreme Keynesians argue that workers will not accept the wage reductions which initiate this process. Workers may accept lower money wages when prices fall but prices won't fall if workers don't accept a reduction in wage levels. They also argue that even if workers accept lower wages so that the real money supply increases then it is likely that as the demand for money falls, its supply will be reduced by the banks so that existing interest rates will be maintained rather than allowing the price of money (i.e., the interest rate) to fall. They argue further that it is the expectation of profits rather than the interest rate to be paid on borrowed funds which is the main factor affecting investment so that when prices are falling investment will be seen as less profitable (more risky) and will not be undertaken even at lower rates of interest. It is more difficult to argue the Extreme Keynesian case in respect of an open economy when a reduction in the level of domestic costs and prices would improve international price competitiveness if the nominal exchange rate remains unaltered.

Price Inflexibility

40.81. Because this group of economists consider that there can be considerable deviations for lengthy periods from the full employment level of output they stress the importance of demand management

Demand Management Required

policies which they see as being more important than supply side policies even though supply side policies will increase the full employment level of output.

QUESTIONS

Q1. Write a note explaining Mercantilism.

Q2. What were the principal ideas put forward by the Physiocrats? Name some of the leading Physiocrats.

Q3. Discuss the place of Adam Smith in the development of economic thought.

Q4. Who were the Classical Economists?

Q5. Write an explanatory note on the Economics of Marx.

Q6. Explain the Keynesian Revolution.

41 Economic Systems

41.1. Since the acceptance by government of responsibility for the level of economic activity within their national frontiers is a recent phenomenon, the development of the earlier industrialised countries, e.g., USA and England, which commenced prior to this era of government intervention was an evolution based on responses to market forces. Though government planning of the economy has been adopted with varying degrees of commitment by many countries, the introduction of the concept in its modern form is credited to the USSR which introduced its first five year plan for economic development in the 1920's in an effort to build an industrial base. In recognition of this approach to economic development the USSR was considered to have a *'centrally planned economy'*.

41.2. Economic planning in most countries has the following characteristics:—

(a) An inventory is taken of the existing economic resources in the country, e.g., availability of labour with specific skills, adequacy of energy requirements, etc.

(b) Policies are set out which permit the maximum growth in individual sectors consistent with the total requirements of the economy.

(c) Quantified targets or goals are set for the period of the plan.

Centrally Planned Economies

41.3. On *V.I. Lenin* (1870-1924), who had successfully led the Bolshevik Revolution, devolved the task of developing the USSR semi-feudal agricultural society into a socialist economy. To this end he envisaged an alliance between workers which would facilitate the growth of the urban industrialised economy which he considered to be the path along which the economy should develop. The death of Lenin created a debate as to the precise procedures to be adopted. When *Joseph Stalin* (1875-1953) seized power he adopted a form of authoritarian economic planning in pursuit of ambitious economic targets and, though the current administration is less authoritarian, the USSR economy is subject to a greater degree of central planning than most others.

41.4. In the USSR economic plans are formulated by the State Planning Commission which is known as *Gosplan*. This commission draws up plans for a five year period which are passed for comment and approval to various economic ministries, constituent republics and firms. In the light of these comments specific targets are set on the annual basis for 200

Gosplan

to 300 key industries. The pursuit of these targets in turn imposes specific production targets on the individual firms in the economy on the basis of an input/output method of analysis, e.g., a production target of 100 million tonnes of steel requires that the steel industry have available to it all of the intermediate products which this level of steel production entails. A problem with this form of central planning is that it does not facilitate the development of the economy in response to the wishes of consumers as manifest by their actions in a free market economy. For example, central planning does not facilitate the development of markets for factors of production which would facilitate efficient resource allocation, while the absence of free enterprise commodity markets eliminates the price signalling mechanisms by which producers can respond to the preference of consumers — though as a form of national welfare maximisation, the latter comment raises questions as to the equity of existing income and wealth distribution.

Preference given to production of capital goods

41.5. The USSR concentrated on the development of the economy through the production of capital goods at the expense of consumer goods. Thus there was a lowering of present standards of living in order that the standard of living might be higher in the future. Also workers were transferred out of agriculture into industry in the hope that fewer agricultural workers could through increased productivity provide more or less the same quantity of food. In 1956 there was a significant change in that policy when workers instead of being assigned to jobs were allowed freedom of choice.

Russia's economic growth

41.6. In 1955 Russia's GNP was approx. 40% of the US's and in the early 1980's it was almost 60%. However in recent years there has been a slowing down in the rate of growth of the Soviet GNP. Some observers believe that the Command Economy was effective when the economy was less developed but that at the present stage of development, it fails to provide the necessary incentives for further growth and that it may not be flexible enough to enable the economy to innovate. A testimony to the accuracy of these observations is the statements on Russian Economic Policy in 1986 which refer to the role of profit in economic development and the importance of an appropriate economic reward system.

CHINA

First Five-Year Plan

41.7. After over a decade of war, in 1949 the Communists under Mao Tse-tung gained control over the whole of mainland China. At that time GNP per capita was in the region of £60. The thrust of their first 5 year economic plan was similar to Russia's in emphasing the importance of investment in heavy industry. Farms were placed under collective control and during that period output grew at a rate of 13% per annum while agricultural output grew at a rate of 5% per annum.

41.8. *The great leap forward*

Chairman Mao then introduced a policy to accelerate economic development which was known as *"The Great Leap Forward"*. There was a concentration on Labour intensive small-scale industry which was symbolised by the back-yard steel furnace. Agriculture was to be organised on the basis of communes of up to 50,000 people. The collectivisation of agriculture had been a failure due to bad weather and the lack of incentives for the previously self-employed peasant farmers; meanwhile, on the industrial development front the back-yard furnaces were inefficient. In 1960 GNP was 14% below its 1957 level. In 1961 there was a return to a more orthodox approach and in 1965 GNP was 60% above the level in 1961.

41.9. *Cultural Revolution*

In the late 1960's with China apparently on the road to prosperity the leaders of the country decided that complacency was setting in and a form of re-assessment was promoted. Thus was born *The Cultural Revolution*. Schools and Universities were closed and young people, the Red Guard, were encouraged to question critically the existing structures of society while intellectuals and bureaucrats were assigned to undertake manual labour. The level of GNP fell and it was only in 1969 when the Cultural Revolution was over that GNP attained its 1966 level.

41.10. *Opening of economy*

During the 1970's the annual rate of GNP growth was close to 7%, and the Chinese development which had been attained on the notion of a closed economy with an ideological commitment to equality and the common good is now beginning to trade extensively with the rest of the world.

41.11. *Future targets*

The Chinese have declared their objective of building a modern socialist economy by the turn of the century. Their targets are annual growth rates of 4% for agriculture and 10% for industry.

EASTERN EUROPEAN ECONOMIES

41.12. *COMECON*

China and the USSR are the largest centrally directed economies and in the past they have been among the least market oriented. Other Eastern European countries have allowed market forces to play a larger role. In 1968 Hungary introduced a *New Economic Mechanism* as a result of which the market mechanism replaced the administrative allocation of goods. Most Eastern European countries are a member of COMECON which is a Council of Mutual Economic Assistance designed to integrate the Eastern European economies into a single interdependent trading bloc.

41.13. Yugoslavia is not a member of COMECON and trades freely with Eastern economies, 65% of Yugoslavia's trade is with non-Communist bloc countries. In that country there are many worker-owned co-operatives and a workers' council determines production and pricing policies and investment plans. Bank finance, based on normal commercial criteria, is available to these firms.

Mixed Economies

41.14. Most of the private enterprise economies, e.g., West European and USA, in pursuit of their economic objectives have introduced economic planning in some degree. In the mixed economies of Western Europe participation in economic planning tends to be voluntary — hence the description '*indicative planning*'. This type of planning, which is associated with France and the Scandavian countries, may be contrasted with the practice in socialist countries where the planning tends to be centralised and, in some instances at least, imposed by the central governing authority. In indicative planning, representatives of various industries and sectors of the economy form committees with members of the government. The government sets out its growth aspirations for the economy to which representatives of the private sector respond by explaining the implications of these growth aspirations for production levels in their industries. As necessary, the aspirations of government in terms of economic growth are modified until they are consistent with the interrelationships which exist between the production possibilities and the input requirements of the various industries and sectors of the economy. This exercise is facilitated by an input/output form of analysis. For example, a growth in the production level of particular industry or firm may entail:—

(a)   an appropriate increase in the output of firms which are supplying the industry with intermediate products,

(b)   a manpower policy to ensure the availability of workers with the required skills,

(c)   energy availability,

(d)   an economic infrastructure which will facilitate the survival and growth of industries.

   In this way any barriers or impediments to economic progress can be identified and appropriate policies devised to overcome them, so that the highest possible rate of economic growth can be achieved. When the details of the plan are mutually consistent and agreed upon as being feasible, businessmen can proceed with their production plans secure in the knowledge of the path on which the economy has been set for the period of the plan. France is generally considered to be the country which has enjoyed the most spectacular growth under this form of indicative planning which was introduced into that country in the 1950's.

41.15. The benefits of indicative planning are:—

(a)   It harmonises the intentions of producers and consumers. In a modern economy production takes place in anticipation of demand with the price system operating as a market clearing and allocation mechanism. However, this procedure can be wasteful of economic resources and it is more efficient if the production of industries could be co-ordinated so that the twin evils of bottlenecks and overproduction can be avoided. A development of this nature is facilitated when the various interests are involved in the planning of the economy.

(b) In circumstances where economic growth entails an increase in imports, the government may, e.g., by restricting the importation of non-essential consumption goods, ensure that there is no Balance of Payments constraint on the importation of capital goods which could impede the growth of the economy.

(c) The government may adjust its own expenditure pattern in order to give priority to those items of expenditure which will best facilitate the development of the economy along the lines set out in the national plan.

(d) Regular meetings and discussions between the representatives of the business sector and the government minimise uncertainty and improve the confidence with which the business sector can undertake its investment and production plans.

Economic Planning in Ireland

first Programme for Economic Expansion

41.16. A form of economic planning was introduced in Ireland in 1958 with the publication of the *First Programme for Economic Expansion* which covered the period 1959-1963. This programme was mainly the adoption by the government of a report entitled *'Economic Development'* by Dr. T. K. Whitaker who was at that time Secretary to the Department of Finance. In this first programme long term economic objectives were set out, while short term targets which were consistent with these long term objectives were specified. The plans set out the role of the government in the achievement of these objectives, a major policy implication being the switching of government expenditure from *'social investment'*, e.g., the building of hospitals and schools, to *'productive investment'*, e.g., the financing of industrial development and an economic infrastructure.

Quantified Sectoral Targets not set

41.17. The First Programme did not set quantitative targets for the various sectors of the economy because of

(a) The political commitment to a market economy and decentralised decision making.

(b) The openness of the Irish economy which was considered to complicate detailed economic planning.

(c) The belief that, having regard to the virtual economic stagnation of the 1950's, a modest development programme in general terms was more likely to inspire confidence and support than a detailed

quantitative programme. The plan forecast a rate of growth of 2%
per annum. When economic progress over the period 1959-1963
averaged 4½% per annum, economic planning was hailed as a
panacea and the introduction of a second programme was assured.

41.18. The *Second Programme* which was drawn up for the period 1964-
1970 was a much more specific and comprehensive document. It set
quantitative targets for individual sectors of the economy. The programme assumed that by 1970, which was the terminal year of the second
programme, Ireland would be a member of the EEC (we did not in fact
enter until January 1973). In keeping with the development towards free
trade, the programme emphasised the need for increased investment in
industry and agriculture and envisaged export led growth of 50% over the
period of the programme, i.e., an average growth rate in excess of 4% per
annum. By 1967 it was obvious that the target growth figures were not
attainable and the programme was abandoned though the policy
measures were continued.

41.19. In 1969 a *Third Programme* was introduced to cover the period
1969-1972. a comparison of the targets and out-turn of this programme is
set out in Table 41.19.

**Table 41.19. Comparison of Targets of Third Programme with growth rate
during the period of the programme.**

Expenditure on Gross National Product at 1968 prices.

	1968		1969-72	
		Third Programme projected annual growth rate	Estimated annual growth rate	Percentage of total shortfall
	£m	%	%	
Personal expenditure on consumers' goods and services	907	3.3	3.6	— 38
Net expenditure by public authorities on current goods and services	165	3.7	6.5	— 79
Gross domestic physical capital formation	274	6.8	7.6	— 39
Net factor income from abroad	63	2.5	—5.6	73
Export of goods and services	486	8.8	4.3	395
Less Imports of goods and services	565	8.7	6.6	—212
Expenditure on GNP	1,330	3.8	3.3	100

**Source: Review of 1972 and Outlook for 1973. Government Publications prepared by Dept.
of Finance.**

41.20. In 1973 our entry into the EEC and the oil crisis combined to produce a climate which the new government considered was not conducive to the introduction of a *Fourth Economic Programme* at that time. In November 1974 a White Paper entitled *'A National Partnership'* was laid by the government before each House of the Oireachtas. This document which was addressed to the social partners — employees and employers — was intended to focus public discussion on economic issues, particularly inflation and economic growth.

"A National Partnership"

41.21. In January 1978 the Fianna Fáil party, as the new government, introduced an economic *White Paper* which basically set out the economic programme which had been contained in their election manifesto. This document has been followed by a *Green Paper* on the economy in June 1978 and a *White Paper* in January 1979.

Recent Government Papers

41.22. The National Planning Board was established on 18th March 1983 with the objective of:

National Planning Board

(a)   reporting to the Government through the Task Force of Ministers on how to maximise output and employment in competitive conditions, and

(b)   examining, at the request of the Task Force, specific issues within these terms of reference.

In particular the National Planning Board was requested to:

(a)   review the potentialities and weaknesses of the productive sectors; assess their likely future contributions to output and employment on the basis of present policies, and recommend what policy changes may be needed in order to maximise this contribution;

(b)   examine and recommend the means by which public works, essential to the provision of an infrastructure for productive development, might be undertaken and financed at minimum net cost to the Exchequer as compared with the cost of unemployment compensation;

and

(c)   to examine measures by which the needs of social equity and of securing the efficient use of public resources can best be reconciled.

41.23. Responding to this brief the National Planning Board in April 1984 published "Proposals for Plan", in which, inter alia, it identified unemployment as the most serious economic problem, recommended that an objective of fiscal policy should be to balance the budget over the full economic cycle in order to even out fluctuations in economic activity.

Proposals for Plan

41.24. In July 1984, the Government published its *White Paper on Industrial Policy,* which according to the Minister for Industry, Trade & Commerce will "change the face of Irish industry over the next 10 years".

The objectives set out in the White Paper are:

(a)   to create an maintain the maximum number of sustainable jobs, as many as possible of them high-skilled, in manufacturing and international and international service industries;

(b)   to maximise value-added by these sectors and to capture the wealth thus created for further investment and employment creation in the Irish economy;

(c)   to develop a strong and internationally competitive industrial sector in Ireland made up of both Irish and foreign-owned industry;

(d)   to promote the more rapid development of our natural resource-based industries, particularly food and timber;

(e)   to promote the integration of foreign industry into the Irish economy through greater linkage with Irish industry and educational institutions.

41.25. The main changes of emphasis in the Industrial Policy set out in the White Paper are:

(a)   increased importance of development through indigenous industry;

(b)   in respect of foreign firms, a preference for "stand-alone" projects which (i) can survive without significant reliance on the parent company, (ii) provide employment of a high-skilled nature, (iii) can create trade linkages within the Irish economy;

(c)   the identification of promising firms which with support can become strong, this is usually known as "picking winners";

(d)   instead of offering high grants to firms locating in certain areas, i.e., "Designated Areas" there will be a more flexible approach.

41.26. In September 1984, the Government introduced a programme entitled *Building a Reality 1984-87*. This programme provided the outline for the national Budgets of 1985 and 1986. It emphasised the need for reducing the Current Budget Deficit and the Public Sector Borrowing Requirement as proportion of GNP. It contains plans for providing social employment of a part time nature for long term unemployed and stresses the need for the improvement of the road infrastructure.

PROGRAMME FOR NATIONAL RECOVERY

41.27. In October 1987 was published the *Programme for National Recovery*. The preamble to the programme commences as follows "The Government, the ICTU, the FUE, the CII, the IFA, Macra na Feirme and the ICOS, conscious of the grave state of our economic and social life, have agreed on this Programme to seek to regenerate our economy and improve the social equity of our society through their combined efforts. The principles that should govern such efforts were set out in the National Economic and Social Council study '*A Strategy for Development 1986-1990*'.

The Programme which is to cover the period to end-1990 envisages progress being made in that period in four broad areas:

Target Areas

(i)   creation of a fiscal, exchange rate and monetary climate conducive to economic growth;
(ii) movement towards greater equity and fairness in the tax system;
(iii) diminishing or removing social inequities in our society; and
(iv) intensification of practical measures to generate increased job opportunities on a sectoral basis.

MACROECONOMIC POLICIES OF PROGRAMME

41.28. Section 2 of the Programme which deals with macroeconomic policies declares:

(i)   A fiscal policy which faces the financial realities is the key to putting the economy back on the path to long-term sustained economic growth.

(ii) The National Debt/Gross National Product ratio will be stabilised in the course of the Programme. This will involve reducing the Exchequer Borrowing Requirement to between 5% and 7% of GNP, depending on developments in economic growth and interest rates. Reduced Exchequer borrowing will have a beneficial effect on interest rates and help to stimulate new investment and economic growth.

(iii) The exchange rate will be firmly linked to the EMS in order to bring about greater cohesion of our interest rates with the EMS average. In this way it is intended to promote investor confidence and inhibit movements of capital.

(iv) Monetary policy will be determined by the need to bring about the lowest possible interest rates consistent with international developments and exchange rate policy. A low inflation rate is essential for increased competitiveness and economic viability during the Programme and all interests are concerned to ensure this.

(v)   An appropriate pattern of pay developments has an essential part to play in the success of this Programme. Lower income taxation and a low level of inflation can help to bring about more moderate pay expectations. Against this background it was agreed that pay increases were to be at a level not exceeding 2.5% during each of the years 1988, 1989 and 1990.

SECTORAL OBJECTIVES OF PROGRAMME

41.29. The Programme specifies objectives under the following headings:
(i)   Tax Reform
(ii)   Greater Social Equity. This section sets out the main objectives of Government policies in the areas of Social Welfare, Health, Education and Housing.
(iii)   Employment
(iv)   Labour Legislation. This section covers such topics as conditions of employment, employment equality, worker participation and industrial relations.
(v)   Proposals in respect of State-Sponsored Bodies.

QUESTIONS

Q1. Explain "Centrally Planned Economy".

Q2. Trace in general terms the economic strategy adopted by the USSR over the past 50 years.

Q3. Write an explanatory note on Indicative Planning.

Q4. Comment on the Irish Economic Planning experience.

Q5. Write a short note on the National Planning Board.

Q6. What are the objectives of the White Paper on Industrial Policy which was published in July 1984.

42 1992 — Completing the Internal Market*

42.1. In the early 1970's world economic activity was at a low ebb following the break-up of the international system of monetary management and the deflationary consequences of the first oil crisis of 1973. The American and Japanese economies proved to be more resilient and adaptable than were European economies so that economic performance in Europe during the 1970's and early 1980's was significantly worse than it had been in the US and Japan.

Non-Europe

42.2. Studies analysing these trends identified "non-Europe" as one of the principal contributory factors to this state of affairs. "Non-Europe" is a term which was coined to refer to the low level of co-operation between the Member States of the Community and the weaknesses of the common policies which were being pursued. The Member States of the European Community had responded to the slow growth and high inflation of the 1970's by adopting a nationalistic rather than a Community approach, this can be seen from the national protectionist policies, viz, non-tariff barriers, to trade, which were adopted. Even though these non-tariff barriers did not contravene Community rules nevertheless they were outside the spirit of them.

Single European Act

42.3. Against this economic background the European Parliament set up a Committee on Institutional Affairs in July 1981 in order to draw up amendments to the existing Treaties. This Committee under the chairmanship of S. Spinelli instituted proposals which were adapted by the European Parliament in Feb. 1984 as a draft Treaty on European Union. In 1985 the incoming Commission adopted a programme which had the completion of the internal market as its central theme. In June 1985 the Commission presented to the European Council a White Paper entitled *Completing the Internal Market.* This draft Treaty, laid great emphasis on the resumption of progress in removing tariff and non-tariff barriers to the movement of goods, people, services, and capital; this process has become known as the *Completion of the Internal Market.* The draft Treaty advocated also the creation of Monetary Union including the establishment of an European Central Bank. The Single European Act 1986 which revised the Treaty of Rome was based on this draft Treaty. The date set by the Act for the completion of the internal market was 31st December 1992.

*This chapter is based on *Ireland in the European Commuity; Performance, Prospects & Strategy* NESC Report No 88 Aug 1989.

42.4. The following have been recognised as the elements in completing the internal market:

(i) joining the individual markets of the Member States into one single market of 320 million people.

(ii) ensuring that the single market is also an expanding market.

(iii) ensuring that the market is flexible so that economic resources — people, material, capital and investment — are free to move in a manner which optimises economic benefits.

The 300 measures which were considered necessary to complete the internal market were classified as the removal of

                              (i) physical barriers;

                              (ii) technical barriers;

                              (iii) fiscal barriers.

42.5. Removal of Physical Barriers.

Peter D. Sutherland a former European Commissioner records★ that an American truck driver can take a load from New York to Los Angeles without needing any more documentation than a motorist. In contrast to this in Europe a driver shifting foods from Copenhagen to Naples requires no fewer than 37 separate pieces of administrative documenta-

tion. The cost of these intra-Community controls has been estimated at 7.5 billion pounds per year. In order to facilitate the freer movement of goods within the Community it is intended to abolish frontier and customs controls. In order for these measures to have the desired effect it is necessary that individual Member States can no longer pursue any independent commercial policy such as import quotas.

42.6. Removal of Technical Barriers.

The free movement of goods has been inhibited by the existence of different national technical standards. A new approach towards achieving technical harmonisation has been suggested, this involves the mutual recognition of national technical standards rather than engaging in lengthy negotiations in an attempt to agree on some new Community

standard. Thus if an item produced by a UK company satisfies the technical standards for that item in the UK market then its sale could not be prevented in Ireland even if we have a different technical standard. This "new approach" applies to financial services as well as to manufactured goods.

It is intended to increase competition in the tendering for public contracts by improving existing Community directives and extending their coverage to energy, transport, water, telecommunications and public service. There is to be free movement of labour and the professions within the Community. The movement of labour within the Community is considered to be (desirable) migration rather than (undesirable) emigration.

★ Completing the Internal market pp 8-13 *The Irish Banking Review* winter 1986.

Completion of the internal market will open up markets for services —banking, insurance, information technology etc. — trade in these sectors has not developed to the same extent as intra Community trade in commodities.

In keeping with the improved mobility of other factors of production the movement of capital between Member States will be facilitated under the new proposals.

42.7. Removal of Fiscal Barriers

Harmonisation of Tax Rates

This refers to the harmonisation of tax rates which is an integral part of the movement towards a closer degree of economic integration. These proposals have implications for the Irish economy in which marginal rates of direct taxation are higher than in most other member states and also our standard rate of VAT is higher than that which obtains in the economy of our nearest trading partner. The implications of these proposals for fiscal harmonisation are set out in section 42.16.

Little change can be expected in financial markets which are already international in nature e.g. wholesale banking. Increased competition is likely in retail banking and price reductions are expected. Given that the scale of operations is not a critical factor in such markets then Irish financial institutions should not be at a disadvantage as a result of our small domestic market. Since the Irish financial market has not been as protected as the financial sectors of other European countries some opportunities are likely to exist for Irish banks to compete abroad in markets which will become easier to enter under the new trading regime.

42.8. Some Economic Effects Arising from the Completion of the Internal Market.

There will be direct effects which will affect costs and indirect effects which will come from probable changes in the structure of markets as steps are taken towards more complete economic integration. A structure for analysing these effects is set out in Fig. 42.8.

Direct Effects.

(i) **Removal of Non-Tariff Barriers.** Customs costs, national packaging and labelling requirements, and national technical standards are examples of non-tariff barriers which will be removed as a result of the implementation of the legislation. These non-tariff barriers impose costs on industry and therefore their removal will lower costs. These cost reductions should, in turn, permit price reductions which will increase the levels of demand, output and employment. The importance of this development obviously depends on the height of existing non-tariff barriers and this varies across countries and between industries.

(ii) **Increased Competition.** The extent of the price reductions which will follow from an increase in competition depends on the degree to which present market concentration will be eroded consequent on the removal of non-tariff barriers.

Indirect Effects.

(i) **Market Size.** As already noted one of the direct effects of the removal of non-tariff barriers will be to reduce costs and consequently put downward pressure on prices. This will cause an increase in demand to an extend which depends on price elasticity of demand for the item in question. As firms expand supply in order to meet this increase in demand they may find costs of production falling further because of economies of scale (EOS). This further reduction in costs will stimulate additional price reductions and growth in output. In the process of exploiting economies of scale large scale producers may, through an intensification of competition, eliminate smaller higher-cost firms and a restructuring of the industry may develop. Firms which find themselves threatened by the lower cost of the larger firms may well attempt to create for themselves market niches through strategies such as product differentiation and innovation. Developments such as these will bring about an expansion in the variety of goods and services on offer.

With regard to economies of scale the result of some recent studies suggest that (i) in many industries economies of scale in production are obtainable; (ii) there are considerable economies of scale obtainable in the distribution process; (iii) the innovation process is not characteristised by economies of scale.

(ii) **Competition.** The effect of competition on the profitability of firms will put pressure on these firms to improve their efficiency and in this manner maintain (or improve) their profitability. In addition to attempting to match the lower market prices which are likely to follow from the intensification of competition, firms may seek to protect their market through market segmentation/product differentiation i.e. attempting to establish in the mind of the public the notion that their product is different from (and superior to) the substitutes being offered by their competitors.

Fig. 42.8. Direct and Indirect Effects of Market Completion.

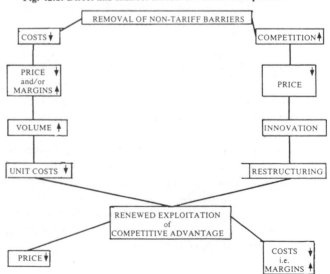

Source: *Ireland in the European Community* NESC Report No. 88
August '89.

42.9. SOME POSSIBLE EFFECTS ON THE IRISH ECONOMY AS A RESULT OF COMPLETING THE MARKET.

The Manufacturing Sector. Since the Irish manufacturing sector comprises a large diversity of firms it is meaningless to consider this sector as if it was a homogeneous grouping of firms. However, having regard to the experience of this sector during the 1970's and 1980's consequent on our joining the Community, the following classification may be used as a basis for analysing the possible effects on our manufacturing sector as the internal Community market is completed in 1992.

(i) Foreign Owned, Granted Aided, Export Oriented Firms.
(ii) Naturally Protected Large Scale Firms.
(iii) Firms in Naturally Protected Fragmented Markets.
(iv) Relatively Large Scale Firms which engage in International Trade.
(v) Food Processing Firms.

The effects of completing the market will not be confined to the manufacturing sector, the Services Sector also will be affected and this is discussed in section 42.15.

42.10. Foreign owned, Grant Aided, Export Oriented Firms.

Whatever reduction in costs follows from the removal of non-tariff barriers is likely to be favourable to foreign owned firms in Ireland. This is because barriers of this nature do not provide any protection for such firms but their export efforts are hampered to the extent that such barriers exist in other countries. For this reason the attractiveness of Ireland would increase as a location for new foreign firms of this nature. However, any increase in the number of competitive firms may have a detrimental affect on those firms which are in highly concentrated industries since increased competition would be likely to bring about price competition which would reduce their profitability.

Obviously the affect on a particular market and the response of a firm will vary in individual cases, some of these firms are in industries such as office machinery, telecommunications or chemicals in which economies of scale in production are important. Such firms may engage in merger or take-over activity at the EC level. For those firms which are currently servicing specialised markets e.g. medical and surgical equipment or microprocessors, further product differentiation may be their competitive response as they attempt to protect their markets and profits.

42.11. Naturally Protected Large Scale Firms.

Firms of this nature are in the food drink and tobacco, paper and printing, and wood and furniture sectors. There will be a reduction in costs for such firms due to a reduction in transport costs, access to cheaper inputs, removal of customs barriers and a more competitive insurance industry. Cost reductions of this nature may be greater in Ireland than in other countries. There will also be an increase in competition as foreign competitors enter the Irish market, this will put downward pressure on the prices which dominant Irish firms are currently charging. Firms in these industries in other EC countries will be experiencing developments of a similar nature so that the net effect on the Irish economy depends on the extent to which we can increase our exports to the markets of other Member States relative to the extent to which increased imports from these sectors penetrate our markets.

42.12. Naturally Protected Fragmented Markets.
Industries such as metal articles, mechanical engineering and carpentry workshops are included in this classification. These industries have been growing in relative importance since we acceded to the European Community. Non-tariff barriers are not an important consideration for such firms since they are mainly geared towards satisfying domestic demand. In so far as the developments contained in the completion of the internal market stimulate a faster rate of growth in domestic demand these firms will be operating in a favourable economic climate which should result in an increase in the level of output and employment in these industries.

42.13. Relatively Large Scale Firms Which Engage in International Trade.
Industries in this category which have been in long run decline e.g. clothing, footwear and textiles, have had little protection since tariff barriers were removed in accordance with our Treaty of Rome obligations. In these circumstances the further liberalisation of trade through the removal of non-tariff barriers will not seriously affect them. Some of the competitors of these firms which are located in Member States do receive protection from non-tariff barriers, to this extent these Irish industries will receive some boost from the removal of such barriers.

42.14. Food Processing Firms.
There has been an increase of concentration in the food processing industry in Ireland in recent years. This development which has placed our production efficiency on a par with the best in Europe has, unfortunately, been achieved through labour shedding rather than through an increase in output. Any new threat which these Irish firms experience from the completion of the internal market may come about through the emergence of economies of scale in the distributive process.